THE GUITAR AND MANDOLIN

THE GUITAR AND MANDOLIN

Biographies of Celebrated Players and Composers

BY

PHILIP J. BONE

LONDON:
SCHOTT & CO. LTD.

First Edition, 1914

Second Edition, enlarged, 1954

Reprint of Second Edition with new Preface, 1972

1972 SBN 901938 02 5

Printed by Caligraving Limited
Thetford, Norfolk, England

THIS book was the outcome of a lifetime of research by my father. He travelled the Continent, visited museums and libraries, corresponded extensively, and continuously sought further information to the time of his death, in his 92nd year, in 1964.

The first edition of this book was published in 1914 at a time when interest in the subject was at a low ebb in this country. The enlarged second edition was published in 1954, and both editions have long since become collectors' items. With the ever increasing interest in the guitar and mandolin in recent years, copies have been much sought after, and both the publishers and I have received numerous enquiries about the book. We have, therefore, decided to issue this reprint.

No attempt has been made to revise or add to the book. It is my wish that it remain as the author left it, a pioneer work for the instruments he loved.

IRENE BONE

Luton,

November, 1970.

"It is almost impossible to write well for the guitar without being a player on the instrument."

HECTOR BERLIOZ.

Modern Instrumentation and Orchestration

AUTHOR'S NOTE TO THE FIRST EDITION

IT is customary for a certain section of the English musical public to deride and disparage the guitar and mandolin, speaking with loud authority as to their novelty and lack of musical qualities. To such power is ofttimes regarded as perfection in the musical art and the delicate nuances and charms of the still, small voices therefore possess no attraction, no beauty. It may be that these persons are unacquainted with the true capabilities and character of the instruments ; for it is admitted that the guitar and mandolin are seldom studied seriously, or even heard to advantage in this country.

These biographies, undertaken at the earnest suggestion of the late Dr. John Farmer, M.A., Baliol College, Oxford, were commenced to ascertain to what extent the greatest musicians had employed the guitar and mandolin. The research once begun, a revelation of the early and honourable position of these instruments dawned, unfolding facts hitherto undreamed of, and culminating in the present volume.

That Mozart, Handel, Beethoven and other of the immortal masters, should esteem the guitar and mandolin worthy of expressing their noblest inspirations, is sufficient proof of the musical value of these instruments.

Several of the first of these biographies appeared in a musical periodical, and such numerous requests for the complete compilation were received from readers in various parts of the globe that it was decided to issue thus. This volume, the research of one person, cannot record all the celebrated composers and players of these instruments ; but being the first work devoted to this subject, it is hoped others more able will continue the research, and thus bring honour to the instruments.

No living composers or players are recorded, to discriminate would be too difficult a task ; time alone must judge of these. Nor are the well-known particulars of the lives of the immortal masters reiterated, or their portraits reproduced ; but only those interesting facts concerning their association with the guitar and mandolin, which patient research has brought to light, and which have not been published heretofore, being unknown, omitted or ignored by modern musical dictionaries.

To my esteemed friend and pupil, Mr. A. J. Maskell I gratefully acknowledge my indebtedness for generous and enthusiastic assistance in the actual production of this volume ; and if the work should be the means of attracting strangers to the subtle charms of the guitar and mandolin, should encourage or stimluate present devotees, then my years of pleasant labour will not have been in vain.

PHILIP J. BONE.

New Bedford Road, Luton.

September, 1914.

Forty years have passed since the first edition . . . Fortune has favoured me, for again I express gratitude to my esteemed friend, Mr. A. J. Maskell, for assistance in the practical production of this edition and also to Mr. E. J. Tyrell for loan of programmes, etc.

P.J.B.

Bedford House, Luton.

January, 1954.

PORTRAITS AND ILLUSTRATIONS

MUSIC

Extracts from original compositions for Mandolin and Guitar

ABBREVIATIONS.

A.M.Z. Allgemeine Musikalische Zeitung, Leipzig.

I.G.V. Internationalen Gitarristiche Verband, Munich.

THE OLD GUITAR

Sweet eyes were hers, who bent and sang
Demurely to the old guitar.
Through musky walls and alleys rang
Her voice ; and dear as blossoms are
To poets in the happy spring
Were the blithe songs I heard her sing.

Sweet eyes were hers, sweet eyes that smiled
As fast her fingers thrummed.
How many wits that smile beguiled,
I think the bees more loudly hummed
Amid the scarlet phlox, to hear
A voice so exquisitely clear.

But that was long ago, you say,
And where is she who thrills this rhyme?
Where are the withered blooms of May?
Ask of the arch destroyer, Time.
The old guitar hangs on the wall
And fancy pictures her—that's all.

* * *

Neglected now is the old guitar
And mouldering into decay ;
Fretted with many a rift and scar
That the dull dust hides away,
While the spider spins a silver star
In its silent lips today.

The keys hold only nerveless strings
The sinews of brave old airs
Are pulseless now ; and the scarf that clings
So closely here, declares
A sad regret in its ravellings
And the faded hue it wears.

But the old guitar, with a lenient grace
Has cherished a smile for me ;
And its features hint of a fairer face
That comes with the memory
Of a flower and perfume haunted place
And a moonlit balcony.

Music sweeter than words confess,
Or the minstrel's powers invent.
Thrilled here once at the light caress
Of the fairy hands, that lent
This excuse, for the kiss I press
On the dear old instrument.

JAMES WHITCOMB RILEY.

THE

GUITAR AND MANDOLIN

Celebrated Players and Composers

ABREU, Don Antonio, a Portuguese musician and guitarist living during the latter half of the eighteenth century, a professor of the guitar in Salamanca and Madrid and the author of a method for the instrument issued in Salamanca in 1799 entitled: *Method for playing perfectly the guitar of five or six strings by the well-known Portuguese, Snr A. Abreu.* At this time an innovation was introduced in the stringing of the guitar by the addition of a sixth string, the lowest bass; until this time the guitar was strung with five single or six doubles tuned in pairs. A copy of this rare method was displayed in the Vienna Music Exhibition of 1892.

Abt, Valentine, was born at Alleghany, Penn., U.S.A., and died 1923. At an early age his fondness for music was a ruling passion. It was his mother's wish that he should enter the priesthood, and with this intent, he was placed, when fourteen years of age, in the Pittsburg Catholic College. Here he contrived to save sufficient from his allowance to buy a violin, which he studied for five years, and later a mandolin, on which he was entirely self taught and this claimed his whole attention. Progress was phenomenal and his playing soon became a source of income. After leaving the Seminary he joined a music firm in Pittsburg where he remained three years, meanwhile studying harmony and composition in Utica and becoming more fond of his fascinating little instrument. It was at this period that his professional career commenced by accepting a position in the Utica School of Music as mandolin teacher. Meeting with popular appreciation as teacher, he transferred his services to the more important sphere of Pittsburg where he organised large concerts of mandolinists—having on one occasion more than one hundred and fifty performers under his direction. He also gave attention to the harp on which he was an able performer but neglected this to specialise as a mandolin virtuoso. He removed from Pittsburg to New York, with a studio in Carnegie Hall, was in constant demand as teacher and virtuoso and undertook annual extended concert tours through the States as mandolin virtuoso, receiving the praise of the musical public and the press. In 1908 he founded the first American classic quartet for mandolins, mandola and mandoloncello and was chosen to direct the eighth annual convention of the American Guild at the Waldorf

Astoria, New York. While eminently successful as a teacher, it was as concert mandolinist and composer that he was best known. In 1902 Abt gave harp recitals and his reputation as harpist was scarcely less than that of a mandolinist: but his artistic career terminated when a patient of a mental hospital where he lingered until released by death. He was a popular composer for the mandolin and the first American to introduce the duo style of playing. It was in 1897 that he composed *Impromptu* for mandolin solo, revealing the novel effects of left hand pizzicato, tremolo combined with staccato accompaniment, etc. Nothing like it had been published previously in America and the country was soon flooded with this style of mandolin composition. His compositions are many, all published in U.S.A.; the most widely known are *Impromptu* and *Fantasia,* issued by Jacobs, Boston, and Meyer, Philadelphia.

Adame, Rafael, born Jalisco, Mexico, September 11, 1906, a professor of the guitar in the National Conservatoire, Mexico, was the composer of competently academic music. His early studies were on the guitar and 'cello. Adame is the first Latin American musician to write a concerto for the guitar with orchestra. Its first performance was given in Mexico City with the composer as guitar soloist. He made concert tours through Central America and the West Indies and has written concertos for 'cello with orchestra and *Concertino on popular Mexican airs for guitar and orchestra* which are in the Fleisher Collection of the city library of Philadelphia, U.S.A.

Aguado, Dionisio, one of the most celebrated guitarists, was born at Madrid, April 8, 1784, and died there December 20, 1849. He was son of a notary of the ecclesiastic vicar of Madrid, and while very young displayed a strong predilection for music. His first musical education was acquired at a college in Madrid where, Basilio, a monk, taught him the elements of music and the guitar, but, like his countryman, the guitarist Huerta, it was to Manuel Garcia, the renowned singer, that he was indebted for a thorough knowledge of the resources of the instrument, at which time Garcia was unknown beyond Spain. On the death of his father in 1803, Aguado inherited a small estate in the village of Fuenlabrada, near Aranjuez, where he retired with his mother during the invasion of the French Army. Here he devoted himself exclusively to the further study of the guitar and developed the system of fingering and harmonic effects which were afterwards given to the public in his Method, published in Madrid in 1824. He had already published several volumes of studies for the guitar, and after peace was proclaimed he returned with his mother to Madrid; but in 1824 she died and the next year he visited Paris, where his compositions had made him famous. It was during his first residence in Paris that a second Spanish edition of his Method, revised and enlarged, was issued, which was translated into French by F. de Fossa, and published by Richault, Paris, in 1872. A third edition of this valuable work appeared in Madrid in 1843 published by D. Berito Campo. He resided in Paris again from 1835 to 1838 where, by his charming personality and talents, made many friends, associating with the most eminent intellectuals. It was in Paris that he met the Spanish guitar virtuoso, Ferdinando Sor, and for whom he formed a lasting friendship. Towards the end of 1838 Aguado had a strong desire to return to his native land, so quitted Paris that year for Madrid, where he remained until his death in 1849, at the age of sixty-five. His Method for the guitar is an excellent one: it is progressive, and shows great care and appreciation of the difficulties to be encountered by the pupil; it is concluded by a short treatise on harmony as applied to the guitar. Aguado and Sor, although of the same nationality and period, represent totally different schools of guitar playing and their styles of execution are very dissimilar. Aguado had been taught to make note after note, and scale after scale, with extraordinary velocity. His first teacher played with his nails and shone at a period when rapid passages alone were required of the instrument, when the primary object was to dazzle and astonish. Aguado, however, was an inborn musician, and from the time he began to act without any other guide than his own exquisite taste and understanding he inclined as much as he could toward a style as musical as that of any of the most renowned guitarists. Strange to relate, he performed with his nails, and so far as is known he was the only artist who ever used this style of playing, producing a soft clear thin tone. He did not, however, strike the strings with the back of his nails, although that was then, and still is, the customary Flamenco or Spanish style. After meeting Sor and hearing him play and produce the full, round and powerful tone for which he was so celebrated, Aguado said that he had a new study to commence, and confessed in his later years to Sor that he much regretted ever having used his nails. He also added that he was beyond the time of life in which he could overcome the inflexibility of the fingers of his right hand; but that were he allowed to commence again, he should certainly adopt Sor's method.

Aguado was an intimate friend and great admirer of Sor, and in his Method mentions him many times in terms of praise and friendship. They resided in the same house in Paris and were so intimate that Sor composed a duet for two guitars—for Aguado and himself—and entitled it *Les deux amis.* Sor, writing of this composition says: "My duo in A major, *Les deux amis* is extremely easy in comparison with the works of other professors who have the reputation of writing easy music. The part of M. Aguado only has a very rapid variation but it is in single notes and in the style most known. My part is the least complicated of what I have hitherto done. My object was to produce the best effect at smallest expense." Speaking of Aguado, Sor says: "It is necessary that the performance of M. Aguado should have so many excellent qualities as it possesses, to excuse his employment of the nails. He himself would have condemned the use of them if he had not attained such a degree of agility, nor found himself beyond the time of life in which we are able to contend against the bend of the fingers acquired by a long habitude. His master played with the nails and shone at a period when rapid passages alone were required of the guitar, when the only object in view was to dazzle and astonish. A guitarist was then a stranger to all other music besides that for the guitar. He called the quartet—church music—and it was from such a master that M. Aguado received all the principles which have directed the mechanism of his play. But he felt good music himself, and from the time when he began to act without any other guide than his own exquisite taste and his own understanding, he inclined, as much as he could towards a more musical style than that of other guitarists. M. Aguado had justice done him—he acquired a certain celebrity, which his excessive modesty induced him to think of very little importance. It was at that time that I became acquainted with him. He no sooner heard some of my pieces than he studied them and even asked my opinion of his playing; but too young myself to think of openly blaming the way of teaching a master of his reputation, I but slightly pointed out the inconvenience of the nails, especially as my music was then far less removed from the fingering of guitarists in general than it is at present, and by taking a little more pains he succeeded in playing all the notes very distinctly, and if the nails did not allow him to give the same expression as I did, he gave one peculiar to himself, which injured nothing. It was only after many years that we met again and he then confessed to me that if he were to begin again he would play without using the nails. I cannot do better than refer any guitarist who wishes to play detached notes with rapidity and in difficult passages to M. Aguado's method, who, excelling in this kind of execution, is prepared to establish the best rules respecting it."

Aguado was the inventor of the tripod or tripodion, a three-legged stand with a wooden flap attached, after the manner of a table. While playing, he sat or stood and rested his guitar upon this table. It was claimed by this invention that the volume of tone of the guitar was greatly increased and that the performer could give all his power to execution by relieving him of the necessity of holding the guitar. Sor evidently had good opinions of the usefulness of this article, for he advises its use in his Method. Sor also composed *Fantasie Elegiaque Op. 59*—a work of great merit and difficulty—which was written to be played on the guitar held in position by the tripodion. Of this fantasie Sor says: "Without the excellent invention of my friend, Denis Aguado, I would never have dared to impose on the guitar so great a task as that of making it produce the effects required by the nature of this new piece. I would never have imagined that the guitar could produce at the same time the different qualities of tone—of the trebie—of the bass, and harmonical complement required in a piece of this character, and without great difficulty, being within the scope of the instrument."

In the execution of this composition great clearness, taste, and the power of singing on the instrument are required. The portrait of

Aguado playing his guitar on the tripodion is reproduced. Aguado was not a voluminous composer but his published works proclaim his genius ; his three *Rondos brilliants*—really sonatas—are gems of beauty. Op. 1, 3, 4, 7, 8, 9, 11, 12, 13, 14, are *Minuets, Waltzes,* etc. *for guitar solo,* published by D. Berito Campo, Madrid ; *Le menuet afandangado,* Op. 15 ; *Le fandango,* Spanish dance, Op. 16, the same publisher ; *Three rondos brilliants,* Op. 2 ; *Collection of six studies for guitar,* published in 1820, Madrid ; *Grand Method for the Guitar,* Op. 5, published 1825, and *New Method for Guitar,* with an appendix, published in 1843 by D. Berito Campo, Madrid. Several of Aguado's compositions are issued by Schott, London.

Aibl, Joseph, a guitar virtuoso and teacher of the instrument who lived in Vienna and Munich during the commencement of the nineteenth century. He published many of his own compositions for the guitar and also those of his contemporary Diabelli, and thus founded, in 1824, the renowned music publishing firm of Jos. Aibl, Munich. The following are the most popular of his works ; Op. 1, *Rondo in C ;* Op. 2, *Twelve landler ;* Op. 3, *Rondo in G ;* and *Airs de ballet,* all for guitar solo.

Aichelburg, a mandolin virtuoso and composer who lived at the beginning of the nineteenth century in Vienna and there wrote Op. 1, *Potpourri for mandolin (or violin) and guitar.* Op. 2, *Variations for mandolin and guitar ;* Op. 3 *Nocturne concertantes for mandolin and guitar* and Op. 4 *Variations concertantes for mandolin and guitar.* These compositions were published in Vienna by Haslinger and also by Steiner and Co.

Aimon, Pamphile Leopold Francois, born October 14, 1779, at L'Isle Vaucluse, and died in Paris, February 2, 1866, was a French musician, a skilful guitarist, violinist, and dramatic composer. His father, Esprit Aimon who was 'cellist in the service of Count de Rantzau, minister of Denmark, gave his son early musical instruction. At a very tender age he displayed exceptional musical ability and while a lad distinguished himself by masterly performances upon both violin and guitar. At the age of seventeen he was orchestral conductor of a Marseilles theatre during which he wrote numerous quartets for stringed instruments, and also duos for violin and guitar and violin and 'cello which were published in Marseilles and also by Janet, Paris. His employment at the theatre gave him the opportunity of studying the dramatic art and in 1817 he was living in Paris as a dramatic composer. His opera, *Jeux Floraux*, in three acts, script by Bouilly, was performed at the Royal Conservatoire of Music, early in 1818, and other representations were accorded it in November of the same year. Encouraged by this success he produced many other works for the French theatres. Several were popular and by 1821 he had attained an enviable reputation among contemporary musicians for his original and musicianly compositions. The most noteworthy are *Velleda,* a grand opera in five acts ; *Abugar,* in three acts ; *Alcide and Omphale ; Les Cherusques ; Les Sybarites* and *Les deux Figaros,* the latter written for the Opera Comique, Paris. Aimon was an industrious composer and his works were highly esteemed during the commencement of the nineteenth century. His numerous quintets, quartets and trios are characterized by a peculiarly happy vein of melody. He left numerous solos and duos for 'cellos, and also duos for violin and guitar, three books of which, Op. 15, were published by Gaveaux, Paris.

In 1821 he was conductor of the orchestra of the Gymnase Dramatique, Paris, and on the retirement of Baudron in the following year he succeeded him as conductor at the Theatre Francaise, where his opera *Michel et Christine* met with immense success. Aimon was the author of several theoretical volumes appertaining to the science of harmony and the elements and theory of music, the *Connaissances preliminaries de L' Harmonie*, was the most popular.

Aksenoff, Simon Nicolas, born 1773 and died in the village of Loschki, Russia, May 30, 1853. He was a favourite pupil of the celebrated Russian guitarist Sychra who dedicated compositions to him. Aksenoff composed about twenty works for guitar solo which are not known beyond his native land. Op. 1, consisted of fantasias on Russian folk songs and he transcribed the six string guitar method of Ignaz, von Held for the seven string Russian guitar. His biography with portrait edited by Dr. Sajaitzki was published in Moscow.

Albaneze, born in the village of Albano in Apulia, southern Italy in 1729 and died in Paris, 1800. He received his musical education in the Naples Conservatoire and at the age of eighteen commenced to tour as guitarist. He arrived in Paris the same year and was employed as musician in the Royal Chapel. Albaneze was the author, among other works, of three volumes of songs with guitar and violin accompaniments which were published in Paris.

Albert, Heinrich, born July 16, 1870, at Wurzburg and died March 12, 1950, after a protracted and painful illness at Gauting near Munich. From 1882-8 he studied the violin, piano and horn in the local conservatoire and during 1888-1892 was orchestral musician in Sweden, Russia and Switzerland. In 1894 he commenced the study of the guitar under Silvo Negri ; his progress was phenomenal and the year following appeared in his native land as guitar soloist. He was guitarist of the Kgl. Theatre, Munich, and in 1909 was appointed guitar virtuoso to the Royal Court. He published many compositions for the guitar, for violin and piano in Trieste in 1895 ; mandolin quartets in Milan, in 1897, and various songs with guitar issued by Hofmeister, Leipzig, and he compiled a *Method for the Guitar,* in four books which was published simultaneously by Lienau, Berlin, and Haslinger, Vienna. Zimmerman, Leipzig, issued many of his compositions and transcriptions in 1918, in volumes, under the title of *Modern Guitar.* Albert made transcriptions of the classic works of the ancient lutenists for the guitar, and also arrangements for two, three, and four guitars which were issued by the same publishers. He also edited a most important series entitled: *Die Gitarre in der Haus and Kammermusik vor 100 Jahren,* comprising twenty-two volumes, new editions of original works in which the guitar is requisitioned, the quintets of Boccherini and J. Schnabel are included. Albert was playing in public as guitarist of the Molino Trio in his seventieth year and also broadcasting. His daughter Betti was a vocalist of renown, who accompanied her songs with the guitar.

Albrechtsberger, born February 3, 1736, at Klosternburg, near Vienna, and died in Vienna, March 7, 1809. His fame to posterity is principally due to the fact that he was the teacher of Beethoven. He was an organist, composer and teacher of church music who commenced his musical career as chorister in his native town and continued it in Melk. In the latter town his singing attracted the notice of the Emperor Joseph, then crown prince, and on a later occasion, when Emperor, and passing through Melk, renewed the acquaintance and invited him to apply for the post of Court organist of St. Stephen's, Vienna, when vacant. Meantime Albrechtsberger continued his musical studies and after serving locally as organist, was in 1772 appointed Court Organist of St. Stephen's, Vienna. He then commenced teaching and among his numerous pupils were several whose reputation became world-wide, the most celebrated were Beethoven, Hummel and Seigfried. The last was the author of a biography of his teacher, in which he enumerates a catalogue of his two hundred and sixty-one compositions, of which only twenty-seven were published. The majority of the manuscripts were in the library of Prince Esterhazy Galantha. His most important work was a treatise on harmony, composition and thorough-bass published in Leipzig in 1790. His *Te Deum,* which was not performed until after his death, is regarded his noblest work. In the list of his compositions, as recorded in his biography by Seigfried, there is *Concerto for the Mandola,* Op. 27.

Alday, a family of French musicians of repute. The father, born in 1737, at Perpignan, France, was a mandolin player of rare ability. The elder of his two sons, born 1763, was also a mandolinist. He received his early instruction from his father and appeared at the Concerts Spirituels, Paris, as mandolin virtuoso and was highly praised by musicians and critics. He was compelled, however, to turn his ability to the violin, there being little demand for a mandolin virtuoso ; he performed at the Concerts Spirituels a second time, as violin soloist. His compositions for the most part, for mandolin and violin, remain in manuscript ; but his method for the violin, which was published by Ricordi, Milan passed many editions.

Alfonso, Francisco, Antonio, born October 15, 1908 in the district of Alicante, Spain, and died in 1939. At a very early age his parents removed to Barcelona and he commenced to play the guitar in his sixth year. He manifested such precocious talent that his father, acting on the advice of Pujol, changed his Flamenco style of playing for that of Tarrega. The lad made a first public appearance when eleven and later in conjunction with the concert pianist, Julio Pons, gave a series of concerts in Barcelona. Their joint programmes were divided into three sections—guitar solos, piano solos, and duos for guitar and piano. When seventeen, Alfonso undertook a tour of Western Europe and in Paris, Leipzig, Brussels and other important musical centres, received great praise and acclaimed a brilliant exponent of the musical art. In 1928 he was in Buenos Aires as a professor of the guitar in various institutions and from this city he made extended concert tours through the Latin states after which he returned to Europe and was a frequent broadcaster from Scandinavia. He gave recitals in Oslo during 1935 and then toured Finland and Russia. Alfonso was one of the most representative exponents of the traditional school, founded by Sor and Tarrega; his playing was characterised by beauty and resonance of tone, and austerity and freedom from spectacular effects. A brilliant career was terminated by premature death at the age of thirty-one. He edited a series of classical publications for the guitar and the Pathe Co., Paris, issued gramophone records of his interpretations.

Alfonso, Nicolas, born Santander, Spain, received his primary musical instruction in his native town and continued it in Madrid. His first public appearance as guitar soloist was in 1944 at the Palace of Music, Barcelona, and then followed many successful concerts with ever growing success throughout his native land. His concert tours were extended in 1948 and he appeared in recitals in the Brussels Conservatoire. The press said: " M. Alfonso possesses a great ease in playing, a beautiful tone, exact style and a maturely developed talent. It is the first time he has performed outside his native land and he upholds a worthy position with our great contemporary artists." He visited England and gave a recital in London, April 19, 1950, which unfortunately was sparsely attended.

Allix, a French musician, inventor and mechanic, who during the middle of the seventeenth century at Aix, Provence, France, constructed an automatic model, which, when set in motion, imitated the tone of the guitar. Bonnet in his History of Music, gives the tragic death of this artist. Allix put in the hands of his model, a guitar which was tuned in unison with one that he held himself. The fingers of the model were placed in position on the fingerboard, the windows opened, and Allix seated in a corner of the room played a passage on his guitar, which the model echoed. There is reason to believe that the guitar held by the figure was set in vibration by the air, in the manner of the aeolian harp, and that the mechanism which caused the fingers to move had no connection whatever with the production of sound. This caused the superstitious people of Aix to accuse him of witchcraft and committed him to trial as a wizard. He could not convince the Chamber of the Tournelle that his work was a machine, and was condemned to be hanged and burned in a public place with his model, the accomplice of his sorceries. The sentence was executed in 1664 to the satisfaction of the people of Aix.

Ambrosche, Joseph Charles, a celebrated vocalist, guitarist and composer, was born at Crumau, Bohemia, May 6, 1759, and died in Berlin, September 8, 1822. He received his musical education in Prague under Kozeluch and then removed to Berlin where for a period he was leading tenor in the National Theatre. He was a skilful guitarist and among his published compositions are Op. 5, *Romance des Pagen aus Figaros Hochzeit,* for voice with guitar and numerous other songs with guitar which appeared between the years 1800-1817.

Amelia, Anna, Duchess of Saxony, born 1739, died 1807, displayed great interest in the guitar and was a clever performer and enthusiastic admirer of it. Through her influence the guitar was introduced and established in Germany in 1788 and she composed several pieces for guitar solo. At this time the guitar had but five strings, and Jacob Otto, musical instrument maker to the Court, and the author of the celebrated treatise on the construction of the violin, was commissioned by Naumann, first musician to the Court of Saxony, to add an extra bass string, and from this time guitars were made with six strings. Otto also substituted a covered fourth in place of the then very thick gut string. For the first ten years after its introduction into Germany, Otto and his sons were the only guitar makers, before this they had been imported from Italy and Spain. Otto, the leading German guitar maker in his treatise wrote: "The guitar very quickly won general favour, since for anyone who loves singing, and can sing, it provides the pleasantest and easiest accompaniment, and moreover it is easily carried about. Everywhere one saw guitars in the hands of the most respected ladies and gentlemen."

Amon, Johann Andreas, born at Bamberg, Bavaria in 1763 and died at Wallerstein, Bavaria, March 29, 1825, was a skilful guitarist and composer of good repute. While a child he was placed with Mlle. Fracasini for singing and was a chorister in his native town. During the latter part of this period he also studied the guitar and violin under Bauerle, a local musician and when his voice broke his parents placed him with Giovanni Punto to study the horn. Punto was the most celebrated master of this instrument and under his tuition Amon obtained extraordinary skill. Before 1781 he had visited England as a horn player and in that year, when eighteen, he toured with his teacher Punto, and they performed together in Paris. He lived in Paris studying under Sacchini for two years after which he again associated with Punto and they travelled through France as horn duetists, with success, arriving in Strasburg in 1784. He accepted an engagement in the city, remaining for some time, and then undertook a more extended tour, which included all the most important cities of eastern Europe. Amon's excellent playing, both of the horn and the guitar brought him to the notice of Haydn, Mozart, and other eminent musicians and his appearance with them in public enhanced his reputation. In 1789 his health compelled him to relinquish playing the horn and he taught the guitar and piano, the same year officiating as musical director in Heilbronn. Amon was appointed Kapellmeister to the Prince of Oettingen Wallerstein in 1817 remaining as such until his death. As a teacher of the guitar and piano he was very successful and the number of his pupils who attained eminence, was considerable. Just previous to his death he had completed a requiem and mass ; the first was performed by the members of the Royal Chapel at his funeral obsequies. He was a prolific composer, his published works embrace all classes of music and one of his operas, *The Sultan Wampou,* staged in 1791, obtained marked success. His various symphonies, quartets, concertos, guitar and piano solos and songs with guitar were popular in their day and on his early compositions he styles himself " pupil of Punto." Op. 26, 32, 36, 38, 41, 43, 51, 53, 54, 62, 64 and 89 are albums of six songs with accompaniment of guitar and flute obbligato which were published by Gombart, Augsburg ; Andre, Offenbach ; Simrock, Bonn, and Schott, Mayence. Op. 46, *Divertimento for guitar, violin, alto and 'cello in C* published by Andre, Offenbach ; Op. 69, *Three sonatas for guitar and piano ;* Op. 52, *Six waltzes for guitar and piano,* published in 1810 ; Op. 65, *Six waltzes for guitar and piano ;* Op. 123, *Three serenades for guitar and piano* and many books of useful guitar studies and other duos for guitar and piano. His biography was published in the A. M. Zeitung.

Anelli, Joseph, an Italian guitarist, vocalist and composer born in Turin at the commencement of the nineteenth century. He was a very successful teacher and performer, was guitarist to Her Royal Highness Princess Paoline Borgese and as guitar virtuoso was in request at the fashionable and brilliant concerts and serenades of Turin. He came to England, lived for a time in London, but eventually settled in Clifton and Bath where he was popular as guitarist and a teacher of singing. His concerts in the west of England were patronised by persons of the highest rank and musicians of renown. Anelli was a prolific composer, both vocal and instrumental, and his publications include a guitar solo entitled: *The triumph of the guitar* based on a theme from Bellini's opera *Norma.* This, a favourite solo of the author, was performed by him, November 27, 1837, in the Royal Gloucester Rooms, Clifton, when he was accorded an ovation. At the same recital, Anelli, in order as he stated, to prove the guitar capable of great wealth of harmony, and an instrument admirably adapted to accompany the voice with regularity and particular delicate and touching effects, belonging to no other instrument whatever, played the overture and the first and second acts, with the recitatives of Rossini's opera *The Barber of Seville.* This was arranged by Anelli as a comic cantata for three voices with full accompaniment for the Spanish guitar, as directed by Rossini in his original score, comparatively producing the effect of an orchestra; it elicited general admiration for the arrangement, performance, and accompaniment of the guitar as a leading instrument. The musical journals of the time speak in praise of Anelli's guitar playing and he is eulogised in The Hermit in Italy and The Musical World. Anelli was the author of eight treatises and studies on singing, a *New Method for the Guitar,* and a *History of the Guitar,* published by Somerton, Bristol, also many articles on the guitar and its music, contributed to music journals. He published nearly three hundred songs with the guitar, about twenty quartets and terzets with guitar; Two *Concertos for guitar and orchestra,* the first *in A,* the second *in G;* Two *Overtures for guitar solo; Sonatas for flute and guitar;* Two *Duos for guitars* and about thirty solos for guitar, chiefly variations.

Anido, Maria Luisa, contemporary, born 1907 at Moron near Buenos Aires, Argentina. Her father Juan Carlos published in July 1923 a magazine, La Guitarra in the interest of the guitar, which contained music and portraits of guitarists, etc. It was an artistic publication continued for several years, one illustration was a sketch of Maria Luisa by her teacher Miguel Llobet who was also an excellent portrait artist. She had previously studied under Prat, the compiler of a Dictionary of Guitarists. In June 1925 she gave important concerts in Buenos Aires with her teacher Llobet when they played guitar duos. The popular newspaper, La Prensa, said " a dignified partnership to the great Spanish Guitarist" and praised the brilliance and beauty of her technique. She has made many recordings and broadcasts and is a professor of the guitar in the National Conservatoire of Music. She gave a recital in London, March 1, 1952; her transcriptions and arrangements of Argentine folk songs are published by Antigua Casa Nunez, Buenos Aires.

Araciel, Don Diego, a Spaniard living during the eighteenth century in the province of Estremadura. He studied the guitar and violin without a teacher, when a youth, and, displaying great determination and ability, his parents placed him under a local teacher from whom he had instruction also in harmony and counterpoint. Among his published compositions the most widely known are Op. 48, *Valses for violin with guitar* and *Three Trios for violin, viola and guitar,* also vocal studies, all published by Ricordi, Milan.

Arcas, Julian, born 25 October, 1832 at Almeria, Spain, and died 16 February, 1882 at Antequera, Malaga. He was a distinguished Flamenco guitarist and composer of national dances which are mentioned in the musical histories of Saldoni, Fargas, Soler and others. He was at the height of his fame, as virtuoso during 1860-70. After touring his native land and central Europe he made a visit to England in 1862. In October of that year he performed at Brighton Pavilion before members of the Royal family and a distinguished audience. The Brighton Guardian of October 29, 1862, gives a lengthy and eulogistic account of his marvellous playing, stating that in his hands the guitar is a miniature orchestra and that his execution was incredible. He was accorded an ovation and the personal congratulations of their Royal Highnesses. In 1864 he was living in Barcelona and later with a young pianist, Patanas, they toured Spain. Becoming tired of this roving life, the minstrel—described as a Professor of the Royal Conservatoire and Knight of the Royal Order of Carlos III, returned to the city of his birth and established a business in the Calle Granada. Arcas became acquainted with the guitar maker Torres, of Seville and influenced him in the construction of the instrument, particularly of the table. After about ten years of business life in Almeria, he retired to Antequera, Malaga, where he died shortly after his arrival. He was a renowned composer of national melodies and dances for the guitar. Vidal and Roger of Barcelona published thirty of his Valses, Variations, Preludes and dances and another fifty were issued by the Union Musical Espanola, Madrid.

Armanini or **Arminini,** Pietro, an Italian mandolin virtuoso born in 1844 and died September 8, 1895, at Bordeaux, France. A famous exponent of the Milanese mandolin, a professor at La Scala, Milan, and the first to bring his instrument seriously to the notice of the British. He made extended continental music tours, appearing with phenomenal success and then visited England. His final appearance in London was in 1895 ; but he did not realize his ambition of making his type of mandolin popular in this country. The journals wrote : " His cadenzas and improvisations were little short of marvellous and he is undoubtedly a maestro of the very highest order."—" an artist without an equal ; as an executant, he had no rival, and probably will have no successor, his scale passages, part-playing, pizzicato, double stopping, of the left hand, and marvellous rapidity, proclaim him the Paganini of the mandolin." In 1895 he retired from public life and was living in Bordeaux, where, the same year he was stricken by an illness from which he died. He was the author of an excellent treatise on the Milanese mandolin and his sons and daughters were also talented performers ; one son was a professor of the mandolin at the Academie International de Musique, Paris. His portrait is from a photograph kindly loaned by the late Richard Harrison, Esq., of Brighton.

Arne, Michael, born in London 1741 and died there about 1806. He was the son of Dr. Arne, educated by his aunt, Mrs. Cibber, and became a prolific composer of dramatic works. He was musical director of Dublin Theatre in 1779 and from 1784 director of various London theatres. Among his many dramatic works, the most successful was the music for Garrick's dramatic romance *Cymon,* composed in 1767.

In conjunction with Battishill, he wrote in 1764, the music for the opera *Almena* in which he employs the mandolin to accompany a charming aria.

Arnold, Johann Gottfried, a German composer and renowned performer on the 'cello and guitar, was born February 15, 1773, at Neidernhall, near Oehringen, in Wurtemburg (a town near Forchtenburg, where the 'cellist Willmann was born). He died of tuberculosis July 26, 1806, at the premature age of thirty-three while first 'cellist at the opera Frankfort. Arnold was son of a schoolmaster and received his first musical instruction from his father during his earliest childhood. When but six, he displayed a remarkable passion and aptitude for music, so when he was twelve, his father articled him to the musical director of the neighbouring town of Kunzelsau, where he studied for five years. The guitar had been his favourite instrument but now he adopted the 'cello in addition. During his apprenticeship he practised these assiduously but all he accomplished was due to his powers of observation and the enforced severity of his self-imposed task. In 1789 the term of apprenticeship was completed and in March of the following year he obtained his first regular engagement with his uncle Friedrich Adam Arnold, musical director at Wertheim-on-the-Lauber. He still continued the study of his instruments and also harmony with an organist named Frankenstein. In April, 1795, he began a series of concert tours, visiting Switzerland and Germany, but his efforts in this direction were futile. After this failure, he travelled to Ratisbon to renew his 'cello study under Willmann. His progress was rapid and decided, but after several months Willmann was called to the position of solo 'cellist in the Royal Opera, Vienna. This was the first really legitimate instruction that he had received and when his teacher departed, Arnold visited Berlin and Hamburg where in the last city he had the good fortune to hear Bernard Romberg, whose pupil he became. He derived great benefit by studying this virtuoso's method and style and in 1797, through the recommendation of Romberg, Arnold became first 'cellist of the Frankfurt Opera. It was while in Frankfurt that he published his first compositions. As a recognised virtuoso on both instruments he enjoyed a great reputation both as executant and teacher. Arnold published in addition to numerous other compositions and transcriptions, five concertos for 'cello with orchestra and several concertos for flute, one of which is of classical distinction. He is the author of innumerable short and easy pieces for the guitar and many volumes of original songs with guitar. Four of these books, each containing six songs are published by Schott, London. The principal compositions for the guitar are: *Twenty-four pieces for guitar solo; Marches and Dances for guitar; Six duos for guitar and flute,* in three books; *Nine Waltzes for flute and guitar; Six Serenades for guitar, flute and alto; Three volumes of waltzes for guitar and flute*—six in each volume—and *Favourite airs for two guitars.* All these were published by Schott, London, and Bohme, Hamburg.

Two other musicians of the name of Arnold have published compositions for the guitar. The first of these: —

Arnold, Friedrich Wilhelm, a doctor of philosophy, was born at Southeim near Heilbronn, March 10, 1810, and died February 13, 1864, at Elberfeld. He studied music as a pastime under his father whose intention was for him to become a theologian and for this career he entered a seminary in Heilbronn. Continuing his education in the University of Tubingen for a time he later graduated at the Fribourg University when his passion for music fully asserted itself and he accepted a position in Drury Lane Theatre, London. He relinquished this occupation and returned to his native land, where in Elberfeld he founded a music and musical instrument business and gave his leisure to composing for the guitar and piano. F. W. Arnold has published *Twelve operatic arrangements for guitar and flute (or violin)* by Andre, Offenbach; *Two potpourris for guitar and flute* by Hofmeister, Leipzig; *Two books of melodies for flute or violin and guitar; Trio for flute, violin and guitar,* Op. 7; *Potpourris for flute or violin and guitar,* Op. 13 and 14; *Six duets for two guitars,* Op. 15; *Cadenzas for guitar solo* Op. 16; *Twelve brilliant and progressive waltzes for guitar,* Op. 17; and *Twelve waltzes for guitar,* Op. 18, published by Eck & Co., Cologne, and Hofmeister, Leipzig.

Arnold, Charles, born 1820 at St. Petersburg, was a son of the pianist of that name (1794-1873). Little is recorded of his life beyond the fact that he was for a period 'cellist in the Royal Chapel, Stockholm. He composed a number of light pieces for the guitar. Four albums of favourite airs entitled *The guitar melodist* were published by Robert Cocks, London.

Arrevalo, Miguel S, a guitarist of Spanish descent who spent the greater part of his life in California, principally in Los Angeles and San Francisco and died in the former city in 1899 or 1900. Arrevalo who was the teacher of Romero, was an excellent performer and capable teacher. His published compositions are few, not more than about a dozen being issued.

Asioli, Bonifacio, born August 30, 1769, at Correggio, Italy, died May 26, 1832 in his native town. He commenced the study of music at the age of five and before he was eight had written several masses, twenty-four other works for church and theatre, and many instrumental pieces. In 1787 he removed to Turin, residing there until 1796 when he accompanied, as private musician, the Duchess Gherardini to Venice, remaining until 1799. Asioli acted in a similar capacity to the Empress Marie Louise in Versailles until the fall of the Empire when he returned home. He was the author of several theoretical treatises on music, which were published by Ricordi, Milan, and also *Trio for mandolin, violin and bass; Duo for voices with guitar* published by

Ricordi, Milan, and two methods for the guitar; a *Short method,* also published by Ricordi, and a more comprehensive work published by B. Girard & Co., Naples, which included a diagram of the instrument and airs arranged for the guitar. His life was published by Ricordi, Milan in 1834.

Auber, Daniel Francois Esprit, born January 29, 1782, at Caen, France, while his parents were on a visit and died May 12, 1871, at Paris. His father, an amateur musician, intended his son for a business career and although the child evinced musical talent at an early age—when eleven he composed a number of ballads and romances in vogue at the time—he was sent to London as a commercial clerk where his vocal compositions were also successful. At the breach of the Treaty of Amiens in 1804, he had to leave England so returned to Paris and after Cherubini had superintended his musical studies, in 1813, he gave the whole of his time to music. He commenced a series of comic romantic operas which with the exception of two grand operas, followed in quick succession to a total of fifty. This illustrious French composer uses the mandolin in the score of his three act opera, *Fra Diavolo,* composed in 1830. In the first act the Marquis takes the mandolin which Zerlina had left on the table and sings to a delightful accompaniment the air, *The gondolier, fond passion's slave.* Auber was the recipient of many marks of distinction, from his and foreign sovereigns and societies. He was described by the novelist, Charles Dickens as " a stolid little elderly man, rather petulant in manner."

Aubert, Pierre F. O., born at Amiens, France in 1763, was for twenty-five years violoncellist of the Opera Comique, Paris. He was the author of instruction books for the violoncello and the guitar, the last under the title of *New Method for the Guitar.* He published solos for the guitar, duos for violin and guitar, and included the guitar in string quartets. His Op. 34, consists of *Duos for two guitars.*

BAILLON, Pierre Joseph, a French musician living in Paris towards the end of the eighteenth century. He was musician, guitarist and composer, in the service of the Duke of Aiguillon and the author of a method for his instrument, entitled: *New method for the guitar, on the systems of the better authors, containing the clearest and the easiest method for learning to accompany the voice, and to succeed in playing everything that is suitable for the instrument.* This book, in quarto size, published in Paris, did not attain popularity. Baillon was editor and director of the music journal La Muse Lyrique, from 1772-1784, which contained numerous compositions and arrangements by him, principally songs with guitar accompaniment.

Baillot, Pierre Maria Francois de Sales, born Passy, October 1, 1771, and died September 15, 1842. He was a very renowned French violin virtuoso whose playing was distinguished by power, grace, elegant bowing and grandeur of tone. He studied the violin under the Italian, Polidori, and afterwards in Rome under a pupil of Nardini. Baillot spent many years in Corsica and Italy. For a period he was private secretary to a nobleman in the south of France and in 1791 was appointed a professor in the newly organised Conservatoire. Grove says he was the last representative of the great classical Paris school of violin playing, as after him the influence of Paganini's style became paramount in France. He was the author of several violin concertos, airs with variations, duos, etc., and there are also published at least two of his original compositions with guitar. Op. 33, *Air tantis,* for violin with accompaniment of violin trio, or with guitar accompaniment, published by Andre, Offenbach ; and *La Romanesca,* a sixteenth century melody composed originally for viole d'amour with accompaniment of guitar and string quartet which Baillot transcribed for violin with guitar and string quartet, published by Richault, Paris.

Barbieri, Francisco Asenjo, born August 3, 1823, at Madrid, died there February 19, 1894. Being born in very humble circumstances he was compelled to depend, at a very early age, on his own resources. His musical instincts were awakened when listening to opera in the theatre of which his grandfather was caretaker, and as a lad was forced to obtain a precarious living by playing various musical instruments—clarinet, guitar and bandurria (Spanish mandolin)—with street musicians and in third-rate theatres. He then organised a troupe of musicians who travelled the country, received no financial support and were compelled to return home on foot ; but wherever he went and in whatever circumstances he was placed, his skill in playing the mandolin, his singing, and his jovial spirit of camaraderie made him welcome. In after years he was universally acknowledged a natural musician, renowned musicologist, and a dramatic composer who established the true type of Spanish music and one of the originators of the Spanish national idiom, carried on by Pedrell and his followers. He most decidedly influenced the future of Spanish music, and his compositions were the principal factors in stimulating those of Albanez and Manuel de Falla. In his comic operas he made frequent use of mandolins and guitars, and the *Plaza de toros* with its celebrated chorus and march, accompanied on the stage by mandolins and guitars, is replete with genuine and popular zest. He was elected a member of the Spanish Academy of Arts in 1873.

Barco, Va., an Italian guitarist living in Vienna during the eighteenth century, whose solos and duos for the guitar were published there. He toured as guitar virtuoso, residing for some time in Paris and after in Rheims where he issued other compositions, several of which are of merit. Op. 1, *Rondo for two guitars,* published by Artaria, Vienna, and also by Richault, Paris ; Op. 2, *Brilliant Caprice for two guitars,* Weigl, Vienna ; Op. 3, *Twelve Exercises for two guitars,* Bermann, Vienna ; Op. 4, *Twelve Dances for two guitars,* Diabelli, Vienna. On

Dionisio Aguado

Valentine Abt

Valentine Abt

Pietro Armanini

Francisco A. Alfonso

Julian Arcas

Heinrich Albert

this last publication Barco is described as, " Capitaine de Cavallerie au service de sa Majest. Imp. Roy. Apost."

Barrios, Angel, born Granada, Spain, 1862. He was taught theory of music, the violin and the guitar by his father after which he studied composition under C. del Campo in Madrid, continuing in Paris up to 1926 with Gedalge. During his early career he was an orchestral violinist but neglected this instrument to specialise on the guitar, to which he concentrated all his energy and became one of the most remarkable players in the Flamenco style. In 1900 he formed the celebrated Trio Iberia, comprising a bandurria (Spanish mandolin), lute (bass mandolin) and guitar. He and his father, also a talented guitarist and vocalist, are considered the authorities on Flamenco music, of which the guitar is an integral part. Trend in " Manuel de Falla and Spanish music " refers to two of the members of this trio. It was shortly after Trend's first meeting with Falla in 1919 that he experienced the thrilling effect of a trio of two Spanish mandolins and a guitar. On page 38 he says: " I was able to make closer acquaintance with the guitar in a house just outside the Alhambra (this house, the casa di Apolonio is a little tavern in the precincts of the Alhambra whose upper floor was tenanted by Barrios). The player, whose father's house it was, Don Angel Barrios, is a composer of distinction and one of the best guitarists in Spain. On hot summer nights Falla and he would sit on the patio, where by means of a towel the fountain had been muffled, but not altogether silenced, and the guitar . . ." and " when Falla was confined to his bedroom with a cold, Barrios would come every evening with his guitar." Barrios has composed serious and comic operas (zarzeulas) symphonic poems and many works for the guitar, several of which are in the repertoire of Segovia. Barrios was profoundly influenced in his music by the folklore of his native city, Granada. He has done much to popularise ensemble music for bandurria (Spanish mandolin) laud (modern lute) and guitar. Dr. W. Starkie in " Don Gypsy " describes his visit to the guitarist Angel Barrios and Falla in Granada.

Bathioli or **Barthioli,** Francois, an Italian guitarist living during the commencement of the nineteenth century in Vienna, where many of his compositions were published. He had removed to Venice previous to 1830, for he died there that year. His compositions for the guitar and his romances with guitar accompaniment were very popular in his day. He was the author of an excellent Method for the guitar, which also includes introductory instructions in singing and songs with guitar accompaniment. This volume was issued originally in German and a French edition, translated by the guitarist, Joseph Fahrbach was published by Cranz in Leipzig and Hamburg. An Italian edition by the author was issued simultaneously with the German edition. Later, Bathioli augmented his method by a series of twenty-four studies, also published by Cranz, and Diabelli issued two volumes of his theoretical works and a Method for flageolet. The following are his best known compositions; Op. 3, *Concerto for guitar with string quartet;* Op. 4, *Twelve Waltzes and coda for one or two guitars;* Op. 5 *Grand Variations on the German melody, 'An Alexis send ich dich' for flute and guitar;* Op. 6. *Potpourri for flute, alto and guitar;* Op. 7, *Hunting Rondo, guitar solo;* Op. 8, *Grand Variations in A, guitar solo;* Op. 9, *Potpourri for two guitars,* all of which were published by Diabelli, Vienna.

Baumbach, Frederick August, a guitarist, mandolinist, and orchestral conductor, born at Leipzig in 1753 and died there November 30, 1813. His musical education was thorough and his progress most rapid, for in 1778, at the age of twenty-five, he was conductor of the Hamburg opera orchestra and in 1782 was appointed musical director of the theatre, Riga. He occupied this position for seven years, until 1789, when he resigned and settled in Leipzig as musical composer, author and critic. Mendel states that Baumbach excelled as a player on the piano, guitar and mandolin; but he is known more by his compositions and writings than his performances. His published compositions, which include sonatas for the pianoforte, instrumental trios, concertos, violin duos, songs with piano and guitar, studies and solos for the guitar, are all characterised by their noble and profound nature. His first publications appeared in 1790 and his later years were occupied almost solely, editing musical articles and criticisms. He is the author of those interesting articles in the Kurz gefasstes Handworterbuch über die schönen Künste, which appeared in 1794. The following are his best known guitar compositions; *Sixteen studies as preludes in all the major and minor keys; Twenty-four progressive pieces; Two airs and two romances, guitar solo; Russian air with variations;* and *Rondo for guitar solo.* These were all published in Leipzig by Peters, Hofmeister, and the Musical Industrial Agency. The musical compositions, writings and criticisms of Baumbach are characteristic of a man of scholarly and refined taste and great literary attainment.

Bayer, Anton, born 1785 in Bohemia, a dramatic composer, skilful guitarist, flautist and vocalist, who has written much for the flute and guitar. Although destined by his parents for a legal profession, he displayed such exceptional interest and love of music in his childhood that they placed him under the best available local teachers. His musical ability soon asserted itself and he continued his music studies in Vienna with the celebrated Abbe Vogler (1802-5), maintaining himself meanwhile by giving tuition on the guitar and in singing. His most celebrated pupil was the famous Henriette Sontag. Bayer was her first music teacher and gave her instruction until she was fifteen. In 1815, he was the first flute in Prague Opera, under the direction of C. M. Von Weber, and with whom he was most intimate, both having studied under the same master. Whether Bayer was a member of that merry musical company of the Abbe's pupils of which Weber and Gansbacher were the leading spirits, is not known. He was of the same age and he too was another of the Abbe's pupils who played, composed, and sang to his own guitar. In April, 1827, Bayer's quartet took part in important concerts in Vienna, in the company of Schubert, when Baron Ransonnet played mandolin solos. The most successful of Bayer's operas were *Der Tausendsassa* and *Frau Ahndl.* His compositions for the guitar, and his songs with guitar, were popular in their day and include transcriptions and arrangements, principally of a light character, and under his name are many duos for flute and guitar, and violin and guitar, *Three Romances for voice and guitar,* published by Schott, London. *Twelve waltzes for flutes and guitar* Op. 8, and many arrangements for guitar, were issued by Hofmann, Prague.

Bayer, Johann Gottfried Edward, born March 20, 1822, at Augsburg, Bavaria, died March 23, 1908, Hamburg. He was a well-known German guitar and zither virtuoso, the son of a magistrate's clerk who died when his son was six. Musical ability manifested itself very early and endowed with a fine soprano voice he was in frequent requisition as soloist in the church. He was also a most accurate and fluent music reader and during his teens commenced to play the guitar. At the age of fifteen he was apprenticed draughtsman and engraver to a prominent firm in the city. For six years he was employed in this occupation, his leisure being given to the further study of music and the guitar. As proof of his musical ability and esteem with which he was regarded by those acquainted with him, the manager of the works, where he was employed, requested Bayer to give him instruction on the guitar and he became an enthusiastic and keen guitarist. Bayer's ambition was to become really proficient on his instrument and he spared nothing to accomplish his purpose. Such persistent determination and ability could not long pass unnoticed, and a certain municipal official in Augsburg, named Schmözl, an eminent performer on the guitar, recognised in the youth the possibilities of a rare artist, so generously undertook to direct and encourage him in his studies. The Methods of Sor, Giuliani, Legnani, and Mertz, he placed at his disposal and were all studied thoroughly, till the young musician appeared as guitar soloist in Augsburg. The reception he received was most encouraging, and his spare time not being sufficient to meet the demands of his pupils, he quitted the workshop for the more congenial occupation of teaching the guitar. Bayer stated that he was now perfectly happy, engrossed in his unhindered study of music and imparting knowledge to earnest students. In 1848 with a talented pupil named Loe, he undertook his first concert tour. Both were young and inexperienced; but youth and enthusiasm saw no failure, and gave them courage. Without recommendations, introductions, or experience, they travelled and receiving no encouragement were on the point of returning when their fortune suddenly changed. Passing through Darmstadt on their way home, they were unexpectedly commanded to perform before the court. They were accorded the genuine and hearty applause of the Hereditary Grand Duke and Duchess, the latter a daughter of King Ludwig of Bavaria. Provided now with weighty recommendations, success was assured. One court after another commanded their appearance and musicians of renown, Lachner, Franz Abt, Reissiger and others paid homage to their genius and provided them with eulogistic testimonals. Having been absent from home for some time, he returned ; but was soon travelling again. He went alone, through Holland and Belgium, performing in all the important cities on his route. The most celebrated musicians welcomed him and took part in his concerts. In Dresden he played in the Royal Court Theatre, in Leipzig in the Music Society's Hall, Euterpe, receiving unstinted applause. His experiences were varied, for when he arrived at the concert hall in Wilbad, he found to his consternation that his guitar had been seriously damaged during the coach journey ; on another occasion, when an aristocratic audience was awaiting his performance, the bridge of his guitar and all the strings flew off suddenly. The damp atmosphere had affected it : so in future he was particular to have his instrument inside the coach, and his trunk, containing his clothes and possessions outside. On arrival at his destination he found that his trunk had been cut away and he had lost all, with the exception of his recommendations, which were found by the police on the roadside, saturated with rain. A concert given the same day at Pyrmont, made good the loss. Bayer's tour had extended for a period of about two years when he arrived in Hamburg. Here he met the lady who became his wife, and being offered the position of musical adviser to the publishing firm Niemeyer, settled in Hamburg for life. On the advice of his firm he made a special study of the zither on which he was an acknowledged expert, but he never neglected the guitar. His first compositions for the zither brought him communications and friendship with the most celebrated players and composers for this instrument, and also with the music publisher, P. Hoenes, of Trier, who then issued all his works. One of his most renowned guitar pupils was Otto Hammerer, who when attaining manhood, did much for the guitar and was one of the founders of the International League of Guitarists, Munich, the library of which contains an original manuscript guitar solo by Bayer. Bayer is held in the highest esteem as a composer in Germany ; but is practically unknown elsewhere, and he also published under the name of A. Caroli. Op. 1, *Collection of pieces for guitar solo ;* Op. 23, *Souvenir d'Ems, for two guitars,* both published by Niemeyer, Hamburg ; Op. 19, *Operatic arrangements for guitar solo ;* Op. 20, *Petite Fantasia for guitar,* published by Schuberth, Leipzig ; Op. 37, *Six landler for two guitars,* Andre, Offenbach ; Several collections of songs with guitar ; a *Method for guitar,* Boehm, Augsburg ; *Guitar school* published by Niemeyer, Hamburg, who also issued hundreds of arrangements for guitar alone and numerous compositions for the zither and a method for it in three parts with German, French and English text.

Becker, Julius Constantin, born February 3, 1811, at Freiburg, died March 1, 1879, at Oberlossnitz. He studied music when a youth in his native town under Anacker. Being naturally gifted he made remarkable progress which decided him to adopt a musical career. He commenced by teaching singing and the guitar in his native town. In 1835 he removed to Leipzig where he assisted Schumann in editing his music journal. He remained in this occupation until 1843, when he again took up his teaching profession in Dresden. He eventually returned to Freiburg, upon his retirement, where he died. His symphonies, operas and instrumental compositions were performed at the Gewandhaus, Leipzig. Among his various published compositions are several which include the guitar, the principal of which is *Serenade for violin and guitar,* Op. 36, published by Peters, Leipzig.

Beethoven, Ludwig van, born at Bonn, most probably December 16, 1770, and died in Vienna, March 26, 1827. Particulars of the life of this immortal musician are common knowledge, only his associations with the mandolin, guitar, and his compositions for these instruments will be noticed—facts which have received but little recognition from his many biographers. During the ten years from 1790-1800, when he was between twenty and thirty years of age, Beethoven was intimately associated and brought in daily contact with several mandolin players of ability and one of his sincerest and life-long friends was a mandolin virtuoso. In 1792 Beethoven visited Vienna for the second time, when one of his first patrons was Prince Lichnowsky, who granted him an annuity of six hundred florins to be paid during any period that Beethoven was out of constant employment. This Prince it was who took him in 1796 to Prague where he was introduced in the family of Count Clam Gallas, an enthusiastic amateur musician. During this period, the mandolin was held in esteem, enjoying universal favour, and particularly in Prague, this was the case—nine years previous, Mozart had produced in the city his opera, Don Giovanni—which had created a profound and lasting impression. The hero of the opera, Don Giovanni, accompanied one of his amorous serenades on the mandolin, Mozart having introduced the instrument with felicitous and masterly effect in the score. The mandolin was now the favourite instrument of the nobility and fashionable society, while the conductor of the Italian opera in Prague, Kucharz, was an esteemed mandolinist of renown when Beethoven visited Prague. Count Clam Gallas, in whose family Beethoven was introduced in the city, was an excellent pianist and did all in his power to further musical art by arranging and giving musical evenings; he it was who founded the Prague Conservatoire of Music. His wife, previous to marriage, Mlle. Clary, was also an amateur musician, a skilful performer on the mandolin, a pupil of Kucharz, and it is evident from the large collection of music—both printed and manuscript—for the mandolin and guitar, in the family possession, that the Countess must have taken more than ordinary interest in these two instruments. During one of their musical evenings, Beethoven dedicated to her the still popular concert aria, *Ah! perfido spergiura,* Op. 65, as the original manuscript in the master's hand testifies. On the first page is the inscription, " Une grande scene en musique par L. von Beethoven a Prague 1798," and on the third page, " Recitativa e aria composta e dedicata alla Signora Contessa di Clari di L. von Beethoven." Beethoven also wrote and dedicated compositions for the mandolin with cembalo (piano) accompaniment, to the Countess, during the same period, and several of these manuscripts in Beethoven's writing have been discovered in the library of Count Clam Gallas, by Dr. Chitz, of Dresden. Dr. Chitz said, " For my part I was fortunate to discover a series of compositions for mandolin and piano, the attribution of which is beyond doubt. They were slumbering in the library of Count Clam Gallas in Prague. One finds there the *Adagio,* published by Breitkopf & Härtel, and not on a scrap of paper, as the manuscript found by Mandyczewski, but in its complete, perfect form. Besides, and this is important, the autographed version of the collection carries the following dedication, " To the beautiful J. by L. v. B." The beautiful J. is the Countess Josephine Clary, who later became Countess Clam Gallas, mentioned previously. There are at least five compositions for mandolin and cembalo in this collection. Cranz, of Brussels, publish another edited by Ranieri, under the title of *Allegro.* One other of the manuscripts is *Andante with Variations,* which is also dedicated to Countess Clary.

During a part of the same ten years (1790-1800) Beethoven was living on the most intimate friendship with Wenzel Krumpholz, a Viennese mandolin virtuoso. Krumpholz was one of the first violins in the Court Opera orchestra in 1796 and has been immortalized by his friendship and intimacy with Beethoven. They were exceedingly fond of each other, Krumpholz being devoted to him, and Beethoven accustomed to addressing him, in play, as " mein Narr " (my fool). According to Ries, Krumpholz gave Beethoven some instruction on the violin, while in Vienna, and it is evident from Beethoven's compositions for the mandolin that he must have had instruction at some period, too, on this instrument also ; his compositions for the mandolin display an intimate and practical knowledge of the fingerboard and the technicalities peculiar to the instrument. What would be more probable than that his intimate friend Krumpholz, a recognised mandolin virtuoso, would at some time initiate him in the charming and subtle effects characteristic of this instrument, as he did with the violin? Krumpholz died very suddenly of apoplexy while walking on the Glacis, and Beethoven commemorated the event by composing his *Gesang der Mönche,* for three male voices, with the superscription, " In memory of the sudden and unexpected death of our Krumpholz on May 3, 1817." The mandolinist, Krumpholz, was one of the first to recognise Beethoven's genius, and he inspired others with his enthusiasm. Czerny mentions this in his autobiography, where he speaks of Krumpholz as an old man—he was but fifty—and Czerny also states that he it was who introduced Krumpholz to Beethoven. The two friends spent much time together in Vienna, and Thayer (vol. 2, p. 49) states that Beethoven wrote a composition for the mandolin and piano for his friend Krumpholz, which fact is also mentioned by Artaria in his Autographische Skizze. Beethoven himself possessed a mandolin, and a photograph of this instrument, suspended by a ribbon on the wall near the side of his last grand piano, was published in Bonn, his native city, by Emil Koch. By the courtesy of the late Richard Harrison, of Brighton, an illustration from this photograph is reproduced. The instrument is of the Milanese model and there is reason to believe it was the type of mandolin played by Beethoven and his friend and for which the compositions were written. The curator of the Beethoven museum in Bonn states there is now no mandolin in the museum, a result of the war and occupation. A unique place among Beethoven's early compositions is occupied by the two pieces for mandolin with piano accompaniment. Thayer, who knew of the sketches in the possession of the music publisher Artaria, seems not to have seen the composition recovered by Nottebohm, which is called *Sonatine.* He associated Beethoven's purpose with Krumpholz, who was a virtuoso on the mandolin; but a certain Mylich, Karl Amenda's student companion, also an able mandolinist, may have been in the composer's mind, for Amenda was a very intimate friend of Beethoven, of long standing, and much correspondence passed between them after Amenda left Vienna and was Provost at Talsen, Courland. In a note, now much mutilated, sent by Beethoven to Amenda, preserved in the Royal Imperial Court Library, he wrote "Tell the guitarist to come to me" and reference to another guitarist is also mentioned, both of whom are unknown. Whether the *Sonatine for mandolin and piano,* which is reproduced and which was composed by Beethoven in 1795, is the work referred to by Thayer and Artaria, cannot now be said; but it has been surmised. The original autograph of this composition is to be found in Beethoven's sketch book in the manuscript department of the British Museum, London (additional manuscripts No. 29801). This *Sonatine,* published by Breitkopf & Härtel, London, although entitled on the original manuscript *Sonatina per il mandolino composta da L. v. Beethoven* is in only one movement; it is interesting, however, to note that the phrase in C major, which commences the trio of this Sonatine is exactly the same as the composer afterwards used in the *Allegretto* of his Op. 14, No. 1.

Breitkopf & Härtel also published Beethoven's *Adagio for mandolin and piano* and it is evident that not one of his compositions for the mandolin was issued during his life. The *Adagio* which is reproduced is in the Berlin National Library. This composition provides conclusive proof that Beethoven was fully conversant with the technicalities and characteristics of the instrument and its fingering, for, to obtain the desired effects, it is certain that these staccato and arpeggio passages—the latter commencing at the fifty-first bar—could only have been written by one, not only thoroughly conversant with the fingerboard, but also with the mechanism of the plectrum and right hand. The

Sonatine

FOR THE MANDOLIN, COMPOSED BY

L. VAN BEETHOVEN IN 1795.

Allegro

FOR THE MANDOLIN, COMPOSED BY

L. VAN BEETHOVEN.

Adagio

FOR THE MANDOLIN, COMPOSED BY

L. VAN BEETHOVEN.

Ludwig van Beethoven.

mandolin was in common use in orchestras up to that of Stuttgart in 1755. Concertos for mandolin with orchestra, sonatas for mandolin and cello, etc., were the vogue of the eighteenth century. The compass of its fingerboard had been extended when Beethoven wrote for it; whereas a few years previous its highest note had been D, in the third position, his *Adagio* has a passage ascending to F, in the fifth position. It has been stated on good authority that there was the manuscript of a *Sonata for the mandolin,* Op. 33, which has disappeared. To professor Mandyczewski, renowned musicologist, of Vienna, is due the credit for bringing to light these hitherto unknown compositions, the *Sonatine* and the *Adagio.* He published both in 1888, in the supplementary volume of Beethoven's works issued by Breitkopf & Härtel. Of Beethoven's association with the guitar, little is recorded; there is the mutilated note in the Imperial Court Library, Berlin, evidence of his intimacy with guitarists, and the guitar virtuoso, Mauro Giuliani was a performing member, when Beethoven conducted the first performance of his Seventh Symphony. What instrument Giuliani played is not stated, Thayer says that he occupied a subordinate position; so did Meyerbeer and Hummel, who played the drums and Moscheles the cymbals. All were separately named and publicly thanked by Beethoven in a letter to the Vienna Zeitung, 1813. During the spring of the same year he wrote for the guitarist-composer Kuffner, a triumphal march for the latter's tragedy, *Tarpeia* or *Hersilia.* Michael Hamburger in Beethoven, Letters, Journals and Conversations reproduces a letter written by Beethoven, and dated from " Vienna, Spring, 1810 " to his friend Therese Malfatti, daughter of his physician Signore Fr. Mora de Malfatti; " Herewith, admirable Therese, you will receive what I promised you . . . Please be kind enough to give this song, transcribed for guitar, to your dear sister, Nanette. Time was too short, else the voice, too, would have been entered." Beethoven's biographer, Thayer, records an original composition for one or two violins and guitar. This is *Polonaise* Op. 8, *from his Serenade in D* and was advertised as one of his latest compositions on September 12, 1808 by the publishers The Chemical Printing Works, Vienna. This *Serenade* contained the foundation of his *Nocturne* Op. 42. Beethoven died during the evening of December 26, 1826, and his funeral, an imposing and impressive ceremony, was attended by a vast concourse. Hummel, Gansbacher and Schubert, all guitarists, took an active part in the last rites, the first of whom placed three laurel wreaths on the coffin before it was finally covered. He lies in the Wahringer cemetery and three paces away rest the remains of his devoted admirer, Schubert, with the amateur guitarist, Hardmuth, between them.

Bellenghi, Giuseppe, born Faenza, near Bologna, Italy, in 1847, died October 17, 1902, in Florence. A talented violoncellist and composer and a champion of the mandolin, was born in very humble circumstances, but richly endowed with an aptitude and love of music which asserted itself very early. He contrived to study the piano when a lad, but it was not long before he was attracted by the 'cello to which he devoted himself under several well-known masters, chief of whom were Teodulo and Jefte Sbolci. He removed to Florence, where for a period he was 'cellist in various theatres, and later appeared as soloist at important concerts in Florence and Bologna. He also taught the instrument and his pupils were numerous, the most talented was the Italian 'cellist, Elvira Paoli. Strange to relate, at this time he became enamoured of the mandolin and, neglecting his 'cello, devoted his artistic career and life to the popularisation of this instrument. At this time the mandolin was the favourite instrument of society, aristocracy and the nobility and he could forsee universal popularity for it and its music. Bellenghi's business acumen was as keen as his musical genius, and having made an exhaustive study of the mandolin and its music, commenced, about 1870 to teach the instrument. His time was now fully occupied with the mandolin alone ; his pupils were both numerous and wealthy, including members of the Royal family and titled nobility. He was mandolin soloist at the most important concerts and with the assistance of his pupils and celebrated musicians during 1880-1900 organised many concerts in Florence and Bologna, at which the celebrated mandolinists, Riccardo Rovinazzi, Silvestri and Caroline Grimaldi appeared. The scarcity of suitable music for the mandolin caused Bellenghi to write many light selections, which were published by Ricordi, Milan, and in 1882, realising a great demand for these publications, he commenced to publish his own works. In a short time he also published compositions of other mandolinists and thus laid the foundations of the well-known publishing house of Forlivesi & Co., Florence, which at the time of his decease had issued more than seven thousand musical compositions of various authors. Bellenghi's concert appearances, as mandolinist, were invariably patronised by Royalty and the elite of society and on several occasions he was invited to London by wealthy pupils to continue their study of the mandolin. The following notice appeared in the Musical Gazette, Milan, September, 1902 : " A note of mournful grief. At only fifty years of age, without warning, most suddenly, death has robbed us of the esteemed musician, Giuseppe Bellenghi. A Romagnolo by birth and instinct, he came to Florence when a young man, and from the moment he entered the city, he decided to make it his permanent abode. Unknown at first, by his natural genius, affability, and gentlemanly manner, he very rapidly won a good name. He was richly favoured with nature's artistic gifts, and moreover, endowed with prodigious industry and perseverance. He devoted his life and talents unreservedly to the violoncello and mandolin ; and wrote for these instruments, most worthy compositions, the best of their kind. A fruitful and spontaneous musical writer, he saw the success and popularity of his labours, traverse the whole world. The firm of Ricordi has published a great number of his arrangements for mandolin and guitar and they remain without fear of rivals. Bellenghi founded in 1882 the business of a musical instrument merchant and publisher in Florence, known as Forlivesi—

which was his wife's maiden name—and by his judicious management has flourished to its present importance . . ."—Count G. Gabardi. The business was continued by his son Renato. Bellenghi's compositions were very numerous and he published many under the name of G. B. Pirani. He is the author of *Comprehensive Method for the Mandolin, in three parts,* published in French, English, Italian and German. This was awarded the first prize at the International Music Exhibition and Contests, of Genoa, in 1892, held under the presidency of the violin virtuoso, Camillo Sivori. He also compiled a series of daily exercises for the mandolin entitled: *La ginnastica del mandolino,* with the object of strengthening the fourth finger, and a volume of *Ascending and descending major and minor scales in all positions for the mandolin; Six duos for two mandolins;* and *Theoretical treatise on the rudiments of music.* Bellenghi was the first to write and publish a method for the modern lute, and under the nom-de-plume of G. B. Pirani methods for the mandola and the guitar. The most popular of his compositions were the waltzes *Profumi Orientali* and *Renato,* both of which rapidly passed many editions. *Renato* was at the time of publication the most popular for mandolin bands. The former was arranged by Bellenghi as a song with French, Italian and English words. He wrote many light piano solos, piano duos, songs with piano or guitar accompaniments; works for two mandolins, 'cello and guitar; seventy arrangements and original compositions for mandolin band; about fifty for guitar solo, and a set of Variations for the mandolin, with accompaniment of piano or guitar, on Paganini's *Variations on the Carnival of Venice.* This work places Bellenghi in the foremost rank as a mandolin virtuoso. He also enlarged the scope and extended the musical possibilities of the mandolin, as nothing of so advanced a nature for the instrument had been published heretofore. These variations were dedicated to the memory of the blind mandolin virtuoso, Fridzeri. Forlivesi published many of the works of the esteemed mandolinist and composer Carlo Munier.

Beniezki, S. Ritter von, living during the first half of the nineteenth century was a skilful performer on the guitar, the inventor of the harpolyre, or harp-guitar and also of a double bass guitar, which he named the aclipolyra. He undertook a concert tour during the years 1842-43 with the object of drawing the attention of musicians and others to his new instruments. He gave concerts to demonstrate the possibilities of both, in Paris, Vienna, Munich and other cities, but only succeeded in arousing curiosity, for in a short time these, as so many others of a like nature passed into oblivion. The inventor was living as late as 1850.

Benzon, Siegfried, born in North Schleswig in 1793. He studied the violin and guitar and at the early age of twenty-four was Kapellmeister of the Stadttheatre, Mayence, remaining there until 1820. In that year he removed to Cassel, Hanover, where he was employed in a similar position ; but three years later sailed from Bremen to South Africa, after which nothing more was heard of him. He was a talented violinist and guitarist and the composer of solos for the guitar and the guitar in combination with strings and wood-wind. The best known of his compositions, which include the guitar are Op. 4, *Potpourri for flute and guitar,* published by Schott, London ; Op. 7, *Variations for guitar with accompaniment of string quartet,* Andre, Offenbach ; Op. 12, *Polonaise for flute and guitar,* also arranged by himself for flute and piano ; *Potpourri for flute and guitar,* Nagel, Hanover ; *Polonaise for solo voice with guitar and flute accompaniments ;* Polonaise, *Hört mich ihr Frauen an,* for voice with guitar and flute. Mendel and also the A.M.Z. mention other songs with the guitar, and other instrumental works which include it.

Berard, Jean Batiste, born at Lunel 1710 and died in Paris 1772 was a French vocalist and guitarist who commenced his public career as tenor in the Paris Opera in 1733, receiving his discharge, however at the conclusion of the season at Easter. During September he joined an Italian comedy, was very successful, won fame and remained with this company until 1736 when he was invited back to the Paris Opera. He was assigned a part in *Les Indes galantes,* by Rameau, but failed and the rôle given to another. Berard was, notwithstanding, a sound musician and later astonished the public by his skill on the guitar. After quitting the stage in 1736 he made a name in Paris as professor of the guitar and singing. In 1772 he was associated with Madam Pompadour and by her influence was awarded the decoration of the "Order of Christ." Berard was the author of compositions for the guitar and many of his manuscripts for voice and guitar are in the library of Paris Conservatoire of Music. A *Potpourri for violin and guitar* was issued by Richault, Paris.

Berger, Ludwig, born April 18, 1777 in Berlin and died there February 16, 1839. His musical talent was asserted at an early age by singing with his guitar. He attracted the notice of Clementi who undertook his tuition on the piano from 1804. So favourable an impression did he make on his teacher, that Berger travelled with him to London and Russia. He returned to Berlin in 1815, was a professor in the Conservatoire and resided in Berlin during the remainder of his life. Mendelssohn and his sister Fanny were his pupils. He left a large number of compositions for piano, songs, cantatas, etc., and was the first to set to music Muller's poems, " Mullerlieder," originally written for a play. During 1806 to 1814 he published many songs with guitar and in 1808 Andre, Offenbach, issued his Op. 8, *Sonata for flute, viola and guitar* and a musical curiosity for voice with guitar accompaniment entitled, *A sketch of my life.* The A.M.Z. and Riemann frequently mentioned his vocal compositions with the guitar. His memoirs were edited by Rellstab and published in 1846.

Berggreen, Andreas Peter, born at Copenhagen March 2, 1801, and died there November 9, 1880, was one of the most popular Danish song writers; his vocal compositions are of national repute. His first instrument was the guitar, which he studied and also harmony—before his fourteenth year, for at that age he began to compose. He was destined by his parents for the law but his strong love of music predominated and he continued the study of composition and the guitar after which his vocal works with guitar and for guitar alone, were published. All his early compositions were for the guitar and later for the piano. He now made use of the piano and organ, for in 1829 he composed the music to Ohenschlager's *Bridal Cantata.* His first opera, *The picture and the bust,* was performed on April 9, 1832, after which he wrote many other important works; it is by his songs, however, that he is remembered. Eleven volumes of national songs, thirteen volumes of school songs, church music and a collection of psalm tunes, appeared in 1853, the latter adopted universally by Danish churches. He was organist of Trinity Church, Copenhagen, in 1838, to which the success of his church compositions is attributable. In 1843 he was professor of singing in the Metropolitan School and inspector of singing in public schools in 1859. For a period he was editor of Music Tidings and wrote a biography of the Danish musician, Weyse, which appeared in 1875. His most famous pupil, Niels Gade, was also a guitarist. His guitar solos and collections of songs with guitar were all published in his native land and his memoirs appeared in 1896, edited by Skou.

Berlioz, Hector, born December 11, 1803, at La Cote Saint Andre, near Grenoble, and died in Paris, March 8, 1869, was one of the most original and remarkable of musicians, a master of the guitar, a keen admirer of its dreamy, melancholy tone and friend and associate of the famous guitarists of his time. The guitar was the only instrument on which he was practically proficient; it accompanied him on all his travels and for a period he earned a precarious existence in Paris by teaching the instrument. His father was a physician—beloved by all throughout the district of La Cote Saint Andre—whose principal desire was that his son should follow the same profession; but fate decreed otherwise. The boy's first associations with music are described in his autobiography from which the following is culled: "Rummaging one day in a drawer, I unearthed a flageolet on which I at once tried to pick out *Malbrook;* driven nearly mad by my squeaks, my father begged me to leave him in peace until he had time to teach me the proper fingering of the melodious instrument, and the right notes of the martial song I had pitched on. At the end of two days I was able to regale the family with my noble tune. My father next taught me to read music, explaining the signs thoroughly, and soon after he gave me a flute. At this time I worked so hard that in seven or eight months I could play quite fairly." During this period the lad received lessons on the flute and singing from a teacher named Imbert and "I improved fast, for I had two lessons a day, having also a pretty soprano voice I soon developed into a pleasant singer, and was able to play Drouet's most intricate flute concertos. Imbert's place was soon after taken by a man of far higher standing named Dorant. He played almost every instrument but he excelled on the clarinet, 'cello, violin and guitar. My elder sister, who had not a scrap of musical instinct, and could never read the simplest song, although she had a charming voice and was fond of music, learnt the guitar with Dorant, and of course, I must needs share her lessons. But ere long, our master, who was both honest and original, said bluntly to my father: 'Monsieur, I must stop your son's guitar lessons. Why? Is he rude to you or so lazy that you can do nothing with him? Certainly not, only it is simply absurd for me to pretend to teach anyone who knows as much as I do myself.' So behold me, past master of those three potent and perfect instruments, flageolet, flute and guitar. The flute, the guitar and the flageolet—these are the only instruments I play, but they seem to me by no means contemptible. I never was good at other instruments. My father would never let me learn the piano, if he had, no doubt I should have joined the noble army of piano thumpers, just like forty thousand others." Dorant came to their village to teach Hector Berlioz and his sister Nanci during July, 1819, and the lad must have practised the guitar assiduously during the two years that elapsed before he departed for Paris, since his teacher declared his inability to instruct him further. Wotton says: "In later years his powers of execution must have been considerable, if we accept Legouve's account of them. The occasion was in 1833 when Berlioz was discussing his approaching marriage with Eugene Sue and Legouve, at the latter's rooms. His host, having suggested some music, Berlioz picked up his instrument and commenced to sing. What? Boleros, dance airs, melodies? Nothing of the kind—the finale to the second act of *La Vestale,* the chief priest, the vestals, Julia—he sang everything, all the characters, all the parts! Unhappily he had no voice. (Barbier, however, says that Berlioz had a tenor voice and sang agreeably and was professionally engaged in the chorus of minor theatres); but that did not matter—he made one. Thanks to a system of singing with closed mouth, which he practised with extraordinary skill, thanks to the passion and musical genius that inspired him, he drew from his chest, his throat, and his guitar unknown sounds, penetrating lamentations which, mingled at times with cries of admiration and enthusiasm, even eloquent commentaries, united to produce an effect so extraordinary, so incredible a whirlwind of brilliancy and passion that no performance of the masterpiece, even at the Conservatoire, has moved me, transported me so much as this singer, without a voice and his guitar. After *La Vestale,* some fragments of the *Fantastic Symphony.*" When he was eighteen, Berlioz was sent to Paris to study for the medical profession, but he found it a loathsome and irritating occupation, though he strove to become reconciled to it in order to please his parents. His passion for music finally dominated, and he thereby lost the maintenance allowance from his father. Being now thrown upon his own resources, he taught and wrote for the guitar, his income was so precarious that he was compelled to live on the humblest and cheapest fare. "I was fortunate enough to get some pupils to whom I taught singing, the flute and the guitar," writes Newman of the date July, 1826, and it is most probable that this was the period when Aulagnier, Paris, published his studies and variations for the guitar. Quoting again from his autobiography he says: "Her (Maria Moke) interest in me was aroused by Hillier's account of my mental sufferings and—so fate willed—we were thrown much together at a boarding school where we both gave lessons, she on the piano—I on the guitar. I had been asked that summer by Mme. d'Aubre, the superintendent of a girls' school, to give guitar lessons to her pupils. I accepted the offer, and oddly enough my name still figures (1848) in the prospectus as a professor of that noble instrument." When Berlioz first made the acquaintance of Maria Moke, who later became Mme. Pleyel, is uncertain, as is also the date of their joining the staff of The Institut Orthopédique, the boarding school directed by Mme. d'Aubre. Hillier, writing of himself says: "My young compatriot had also made the acquaintance of Berlioz, who gave lessons on the guitar in a school where the former's 'bien aimee' was piano mistress. He had the naïvety to confide his love affairs to Berlioz and beg him act as love's messenger." Newman says: "When Hillier met Berlioz, the latter was earning his living by teaching the guitar and correcting proofs for the publishers." In 1830 Berlioz gained the Prix de Rome, at the Conservatoire of Music, to which was attached a government pension supporting the holder for three years in Rome. Here he associated with Mendelssohn and other music students; the evenings were spent with his musical companions in the garden portico, "where my poor guitar and worse voice were in great request, and where, sitting round the marble basin of a little fountain we sang *Freyschutz, Oberon, Iphigenia* or *Don Giovanni,* for to the credit of my fellow students, be it spoken, their musical taste was far from low. My usual remedy for spleen was a trip to Subiaco, which seemed to put new life into me. An old grey suit, a straw hat, a guitar, a gun and six piastres were all my stock-in-trade. Thus I wandered, shooting or singing, careless where I might pass the night. Sometimes a glorious landscape spread before me. I chanted, to the guitar accompaniment, long remembered verses of the Aeneid, the death of Pallas, the despair of Evander, the sad end of Amata and the death of Lavinia's noble lover, and worked myself up into an incredible pitch of excitement that ended in floods of tears." Speaking of a friendly villager, he writes: "I first won his affection by helping to serenade his mistress and by singing a duet with him to that untameable young person with the accompaniment of my French guitar," and he became known to the villagers of the district as the Frenchman who plays the guitar. Writing to his friend Hillier from Rome on September 17, 1831, he says: "Nothing pleases me so much as this vagabond life amid the woods and the rocks, in the evening dancing the saltarelle with the men and women. I make

Maria Luisa Anido

Maria Rita Brondi

Joseph Boehm

B. Bortolazzi

C. A. Bracco

them happy with my guitar ; before I came they danced only to the Basque tambour (tambourine) and they are in ecstasies over my more melodious instrument." Again: "Yesterday evening the children danced the saltarelle to the tambourine—I was looking on when the eldest girl, who is twelve, said with a coaxing air: 'Sir, oh, sir, play the French guitar'; I took my guitar and improvised saltarellas until my fingers burned." With companions he was returning on foot from Naples to Rome, and "in the evening at Capua we found a good supper, good beds and an improvisatore. After a brilliant prelude on his mandolin, he, the host, enquired of what country we were. I had heard his improvisations a month before," and Berlioz records the words and music "as he sang it, improvising his accompaniment without a moment's hesitation." Quoting again from his autobiography: "In Rome, often worn out and thoroughly out of sorts I would hunt him (Mendelssohn) out. With perfect good humour, seeing my pitiable state—he would lay aside his pen, and with his extraordinary facility in remembering intricate scores, would play whatever I chose to name —he properly and soberly seated at the piano, I curled up in a snappy bunch on his sofa. He liked me, with my wearied voice to murmur out my setting (with guitar) of Moore's melodies. He always had a certain amount of commendation for my little songs!" Leon Gastinel, who visited his lodging in Paris in 1840, described it as follows: "Berlioz lived in the rue de Londres and had installed his working room in a garret under the roof. A chair, a table on which lay his guitar, which served him in the composition of his works, were the only furniture." Berlioz and his guitar were inseparable, and when settled in Paris, and his daily journalistic occupation had proved exceptionally irksome, he was deeply dejected. "I strode up and down, my brain on fire; I gazed at the setting sun, the neighbouring gardens, the heights of Montmartre—my thoughts a thousand miles away—then as I turned I flew into the wildest rage. My unoffending guitar leant against the wall. I kicked it to bits; my pistols stared at me from the wall with big round eyes. I gazed back, then, tearing my hair, burst into burning tears. That soothed me somewhat; I turned those staring pistols face to the wall and picked up my poor guitar, which gave forth a plaintive wail." In his *Treatise on Instrumentation and Orchestration,* Berlioz devotes five pages to the guitar and mandolin. He states: "It is almost impossible to write well for the guitar without being a player on the instrument. It shall be our endeavour, notwithstanding, to point out the proper method of writing simple accompaniments for it; its melancholy and dreamy character might more frequently be made available; it has a real charm of its own, and there would be no impossibility in writing for it so that this should be made manifest. The guitar is suitable to carry out, even solely, more or less complicated many voiced pieces, whose charm principally consists when they are given, by real virtuosi. A number of virtuosi have cultivated the guitar, and cultivate it even today as a solo instrument, and know how to produce pleasing as well as original movements." In the chapter on the mandolin he deplores the fact that, "the instrument has almost fallen into disuetude (1856); for its quality of tone has something appealing and original about it." He draws attention to Mozart as having penned such a melodious accompaniment in the second act of *Don Giovanni,* and says: "Mozart quite well knew what he was about in choosing the mandolin for accompanying the amorous lay of his hero." After attending a concert by the guitar virtuoso Zani de Ferranti, Berlioz reported in the Journal des Debats: "Permit us to still speak to you with all sorts of praises, and even with true astonishment at seeing a true master of his art, lord of a spot in the musical domain. We have just heard Zani de Ferranti, the last but the first of guitarists. Truly it is impossible to imagine the effects which he produces on his instrument, so limited and so difficult. To Paganini's mechanism, Zani de Ferranti joins sensibility and an art to sing, which, so far as we know, was not possessed heretofore. Under his fingers the guitar dreams and cries. It would seem that nearing its end it implored life. The poor orphan of the lute and mandolin seems to say: 'Listen how I sing the beautiful melodies of *Oberon*—the king of genius; how I know the accent and deceit of timid love; how my voice can unite itself to the voice of mysterious tenderness; the lute is dead, do not let me in turn die also.' One could pass nights in listening to Zani de Ferranti—he rocks you, he magnetises you, and one experiences a kind of painful shock when the last chord of his poor protege strains itself, giving vent to its grief—a mosaic silence succeeds. We should also add that he writes excellent music for the guitar, and that the charm of his compositions contributes a good share to the prestige which it exerts upon its hearers." In his autobiography he records a discussion with Fetis and Zani de Ferranti and describes the latter as "an artist and remarkable writer." He was an intimate friend of Gatayes, the harpist and guitarist, and mentions him in terms of friendship in his autobiography. An illustration of the guitar which belonged to Berlioz, from a photograph taken for this volume, by courtesy of the Director of the National Conservatoire of Music, Paris, is reproduced. The instrument is in the Museum of this institution, of which Berlioz was for a time curator. The guitar is a full-sized typical French instrument of rosewood, made by Grobert, Mirecourt (1794-1869). The table is unvarnished and inlaid with rows of ebony and ivory purfling. It has a peg head and bears on its table the autographs of its two famous owners, Nicolo Paganini and Hector Berlioz. These signatures, inscribed on the bare wood in ink are parallel to each other at opposite ends of the bridge. The autograph of Paganini is now faded and partly obliterated—perhaps by an unsuccessful attempt to preserve it by chemical means, the wood underneath being a much darker colour; this is noticeable in the illustration, by the dark patch on the left. This historical instrument was loaned to Paganini by J. B. Vuillaume the violin maker, during the second visit to Paris of the illustrious violinist and when he returned it, Vuillaume presented it to Berlioz, whom he knew was an enthusiastic admirer, not only of the guitar, but also of the brilliant genius of its former player. Berlioz added his autograph and presented the guitar to the museum while he was curator. Newman says, "There exists in Cote St. Andre, his birthplace, a manuscript of romances with guitar accompaniment made by Berlioz. Another manuscript, presumably in the handwriting of Dorant (his guitar teacher), contains a copy of the celebrated romance, *Fleuve du Tage, accompagnement de guitare par Hector Berlioz.* Berlioz composed studies and variations for guitar alone, which were published by Aulagnier, Paris, and he scores for it in his operas *Benvenuto Cellini, Beatrice and Benedict,* and in the serenade of Mephistophles, from *Eight Scenes from Faust,* he writes in Act 2 an accompaniment for the guitar, tuned in E major. The latter, composed in 1829, was his original Op. 1. These *Eight Scenes,* a cantata composed in 1829 when he was twenty-six were used as a basis for one of his finest works, the opera, Op. 24, *The damnation of Faust.* Brown's Modern Tendencies says, "The influence of the guitar on Berlioz can be seen in his spacing of chords," and Wotton in "Hector Berlioz" says, "Possibly his harmony owed something to his practice of the guitar, the only instrument he ever learnt." Grove says, "Berlioz stands alone, a colossus with few friends and no direct followers; a marked individuality, original, puissant, bizarre, violently one-sided; whose influence has been, and will again be felt far and wide, for good and for bad, but cannot rear disciples, nor form a school. His startling originality as a musician, rests upon a physical and mental organisation, very different from, and in some respects superior to that of other eminent masters; a most ardent nervous temperament; a gorgeous imagination, incessantly active, heated at times to the verge of insanity; abnormally subtle and acute sense of hearing; the keenest intellect of a dissecting, analysing turn, the most violent will, manifesting itself in a spirit of enterprise and daring equalled only by its tenacity of purpose and indefatigable perseverance." For many years Berlioz was musical critic to the Journal des Debats, Paris. His contributions to this paper made for him a lasting name as one of the most brilliant French writers and he lives on, not only by his music, but by these newspaper articles and letters. His autobiography appeared in 1848 and various translations have been made, one issued by Macmillan, another by Dent and numerous of his letters and memoirs have been published by various authors.

Bertucci, Constantino, born March 12, 1841, at Rome, died there in 1931, was a celebrated mandolin virtuoso and composer. His father, a gardener who came of a poor but honourable family, was a skilled player on the mandolin and modern lute, and commenced to teach his son when five years of age. Three years later father and son were performing mandolin duos in public. At the age of twelve, Constantino made his debut as mandolin soloist at the Cafe Nuovo, Rome, at that time the resort of the most fashionable society. Bertucci was an amateur, engaged in other regular employment but practised assiduously and became known locally as a talented mandolinist under the nickname " Al ragazzino di Borgo." During this period he was receiving more advanced instruction, both theoretical and practical from Finestauri, a Roman, known as "Checco de nonna," who had learned his art from Cesare Galanti, one of the early players and a director of the Papal Chapel. Bertucci very early began to teach and in his public appearances was frequently accompanied on the calascione (a type of lute) by Paolo Curti. Bertucci related the following incident which he said was the turning point in his career, " On a certain fete, when playing at a garden party, there was present listening to us, a member of the band of the Papal Dragoons, a clarionetist and concert artist in the theatre. He requested me to play certain excerpts from operas, which I did, and in our conversation, I was compelled to acknowledge that I could not read music, for, like most young Italians of that period, I depended upon a good ear and memory. This musician, whose name was Baccani, proved a good friend to me ; he became my teacher, and to him I owe much, for by his teaching a new era dawned, and I made great progress." Bertucci also studied the guitar, and from 1860 he appeared at numerous concerts both in his native and other lands. He was commanded to play before the Royal Court, was presented by his pupil La Marquise Gavaggi and the recipient of several royal favours. In Rome, he gave instruction in mandolin playing to Gervais Salvayre, a young French musician, who, as the holder of the Prix de Rome, was studying in Italy. His pupil made remarkable progress and a life-long friendship ensued and when he returned to Paris, Salvayre composed for the mandolin and also employed it in his orchestrations. Bertucci organised a mandolin orchestra, which, in 1878 was engaged to perform in the Trocadero, Paris. This was very successful and the commencement of the popularity of the mandolin in France. Bertucci and his mandolin orchestra were one of the first, if not the first, to render instrumental music for transference by telephone, being relayed from the Trocadero to Versailles. Shortly after his return, Queen Margherita, who, when Princess Margherita, studied the mandolin with Belisario Matera, in 1873, commanded Bertucci's orchestra to play before the Court in the Royal Palace of Monza. Bertucci also conducted his mandolin orchestra in the Royal Gardens, on the occasion of the wedding of Prince Tommaso, in 1885. From 1881-1893 the mandolin enjoyed universal favour, one of the most celebrated mandolin orchestras was the "Royal Margherita," under the patronage of the Queen. This famous orchestra gave more than one hundred concerts during 1887-8 and performed before the Royal family, first in the Palace Pitti and also at the Royal reception in honour of the Queen of Serbia. Bertucci effected several improvements in the construction of the Roman mandolin, which was the model he favoured. His compositions for the instrument evince a purity in style and a classic tendency which cannot be too highly eulogised. Bertucci was the originator of unaccompanied solos for the mandolin—inspired no doubt by the unaccompanied violin solos of Bach. The most popular are Op. 19,

Fantasia on La Traviata and Op. 20, *Fantasia on Il Trovatore.* This style of composition, published in Italy about 1886 was an innovation adopted by mandolin composers elsewhere. He compiled a *Method for the mandolin* in three books; *Eighteen Studies for the mandolin,* dedicated to H.R.H. Princess Margherita; Fantasias in harmony for mandolin solo; mandolin solos with piano and compositions for mandolin band.

Bertioli, Alessandro, an Italian guitarist and teacher of his instrument living in London during the first part of the nineteenth century. He was the author of *Complete Method for the guitar,* described as Carulli's method simplified; *Forty-four progressive lessons for guitar,* published by Wybrow, London; *Select airs for guitar*; *New Tyrolese air for piano, and guitar,* with Italian words; *Six French romances with guitar;* and *Three Italian songs with guitar,* all of which were published by Chappell, London.

Bevilaqua, Matteo Paolo, born 1772 at Florence, died January 22, 1849, in Vienna. For a period in 1825 he was tenor vocalist and a member of Prince Esterhazy's Chapel, Vienna. He was also an excellent guitarist and flautist who published, during the first quarter of the nineteenth century, more than sixty compositions for the guitar and also a method for the guitar. The editor of the New Encyclopædia Musical, Stuttgart, writes in praise of Bevilaqua as an educated musician. He wrote for the guitar alone and in combination with various other instruments, and these enjoyed popular favour in their day. Op.11, *Variations for flute and guitar,* published by Diabelli, Vienna; Op. 14, *Variations for fortepiano and guitar,* published by Thaddeus Weigl, Vienna; Op. 18, *Quartet for violin, flute, 'cello and guitar,* Diabelli, Vienna; Op. 19, *Variations for flute and guitar,* Steiner & Co., Vienna; Op. 21, *Sonatine in C for two guitars,* Haslinger, successor to Steiner, 1826; Op. 24, *March and Andante for flute and guitar,* same publisher; Op. 33, *Five little pieces for guitar solo* and Op. 34, *Variations for guitar solo,* Steiner & Co.; Op. 35, *Sonata in G for two guitars;* Op. 62 and Op. 63, *Variations for flute or violin and guitar,* Mechetti, Vienna, and several like compositions including *Trio for two violins and guitar,* published in Rome. The original manuscript of Op. 33 is in the archives of the International League of Guitarists, Munich.

Bickford, Vahdah Olcott (Ethel Lucretia Olcott), contemporary, born Norwalk, U.S.A., resident in Hollywood, California, U.S.A. Her family removed to Los Angeles when she was a child and she displayed such passion and gift for music that her parents decided to give her a musical education. At the age of nine she commenced the study of the guitar under a local teacher and has continued one of its enthusiastic lovers ever since. She was one of the last pupils of Manuel Ferrer, residing in the master's house and receiving daily instruction and invaluable supervision of her studies. Vahdah Olcott, as she then was, returned to her home in Los Angeles when fifteen and began to teach the guitar. She became a member of the State Music Teachers' Association and appeared as soloist in concerts throughout California, under the direction of the renowned impressario Behymer. Her concert tours were in the eastern states during the autumn of 1914, when she met Zarh Myron Bickford and the following year they were married in New York City, after which they appeared at concerts together in New York and the eastern coast cities. During her residence in New York she was instructress in the most select schools and her private pupils included celebrities of the social and intellectual world of arts and letters. Her recitals in New York and Washington were artistic and financial triumphs as was also her performance in New York City Town Hall of the first performance in U.S.A. of *Giuliani's 3rd Concerto with string quartet.* As chamber music artist, she performed with the Zoellner Quartet in the *Boccherini quintets* and the *Paganini quartets.* She is the author of a *Guitar Method in two volumes,* Op. 25, with a sequel, an *Advanced Course,* Op. 116, all issued by America's oldest publishers, Oliver Ditson, and more than fifty original solos and transcriptions for guitar solo, published by Carl Fischer, New York.

In 1923 Mr. and Mrs. Bickford removed to Los Angeles, and in that year Mrs. Bickford was instrumental in founding the American Guitar Society, an international society for the welfare of the guitar and its literature and which has regularly issued numerous original compositions and transcriptions of the classic masters since its inception. It was through the intense enthusiasm, encouragement and practical assistance of Mrs. Bickford that the first edition of this volume was produced.

Bickford, Zarh Myron, contemporary, born December 11, 1876, at Whitingham, Vermont, U.S.A., living in Hollywood, California, U.S.A. His first musical instruction was given at a very early age by his mother and when twelve he earned one dollar each Sunday by officiating as church organist in Bernardstown, an incentive which led him to play other instruments. Under the best local musicians he became versatile, excelling on the violin, viola, mandolin and guitar after which he studied harmony and composition under Dr. Palmer in New York.

Bickford is a highly educated and capable musician who, in addition to many concert appearances with his talented wife, has played violin and viola in many important symphony orchestras ; has conducted both symphony and mandolin orchestras, and is on call in the film studios of Hollywood. His work as composer, arranger and literary contributor to musical journals, both in his own country and in England has been appreciated for many years. He is widely known as the author of *The Bickford Mandolin Method,* a work in four volumes, published by Carl Fischer, New York, and his *Concerto Romantic, for guitar and piano* is the first guitar concerto to be published in America. Bickford is a charter member; and has been twice President of the American Guild of B.M.G. ; is President of the American Guitar

Society, a member of the Board of Directors of the Musicians' Union of Hollywood and Los Angeles and chairman of the Board of Examiners. For a period he was coach of the Columbia University Mandolin Band and the Stevens Institute of Technology.

Birnbach, Henry August, was born at Breslau, 1782, and died in Berlin, December 31, 1840. His father, Karl Josef, was a violin virtuoso, the son of a German peasant, a clever performer on the guitar. Both Henry and his brother Josef were well grounded in the elements of music by their father, who also gave them instruction in violin and guitar playing. In 1795 the father obtained professional employment in Berlin, where he removed with his family. His son, Henry, possessed unusual ability and passion for music, and at the age of ten had obtained great proficiency on both instruments. In Berlin he studied the violoncello as autodidatic, for his parents had no means. He profited much by his studies on the violoncello in Berlin and in January, 1802, was engaged in the Theatre an der Wien, Vienna. Here he made the acquaintance of the celebrated violoncellist, Nicholas Kraft, who generously gave him advanced instruction in the art of violoncello playing, and upon the recommendation of Kraft he was appointed in 1804, 'cellist in the private band of Prince Lubomirski, at Fürsten in Galicia. He did not remain long in Galicia, for in 1806 he was appearing as guitar soloist and a member of the orchestra of the Royal Theatre, Vienna, and six years later was solo 'cellist in the opera, Pesth; but in 1815 retired to his native city, Breslau, where he was esteemed as a teacher. Birnbach was a virtuoso on both the 'cello and the guitar and also on another instrument—the arpeggione or guitar-violoncello, sometimes called the guitar d'amour or chitarra col'arco (guitar played with a bow). The arpeggione was invented in 1823 by Stauffer, a musical instrument maker of Vienna. As the name implies it partook of the construction of the guitar and the violoncello, being in shape similar to the guitar, but larger, about the size of a small violoncello. It was fitted with six strings, tuned identically the same as the guitar. The fingerboard, too, was fretted, but its higher portion, which on the guitar is attached to the table, was on the arpeggione raised above the table and the instrument was played with a bow in the position and manner of the violoncello.

The tone of the arpeggione resembled that of the obsolete viol d'amour, and when introduced, was received with popular favour (see Schubert). The guitar at this time was the fashionable instrument, and any instrument which bore a similarity to the popular favourite, was certain of being accorded recognition. Stauffer, the inventor, had received the patronage of the guitar virtuosi, the renowned Regondi having used his guitars; Legnani, too, played them, and moreover, supplied him with designs for the construction of a guitar which the maker labelled "Legnani Model". Stauffer was constantly seeking to improve and to give the musical world new ideas in instrument construction. He introduced the guitar with the detachable neck and fingerboard, the instrument being made so that the neck, with the attached fingerboard could be removed from the body, by loosening a screw bolt, inserted through the block of the neck, to the inner block which holds the table to the back. Stauffer claimed that a guitar so constructed would take less space, and therefore be more conveniently portable ; but the disadvantage occasioned by the necessity of having to adjust the neck to the body, more than counterbalanced the asserted advantage. In these guitars, as in the arpeggione, the fingerboard was not glued to the table, but was slightly raised as in the violin family. This style of guitar shared the fate of his other invention, and they are seldom seen. Among other musicians of repute who evinced enthusiasm for the arpeggione was Birnbach. He adopted it, studied it, performed upon it in public and also composed many works for it, which included a concerto with orchestral accompaniment, a favourite solo of Birnbach. He lived in Breslau until 1821, married in 1824 when he was 'cellist in Königstadter Theatre, Berlin, and the following year was 'cellist and virtuoso on the arpeggione, on which he was evidently the most able exponent, in the Royal Chapel, Berlin. Henry Birnbach and his brother Josef published many compositions for the guitar, also variations for the violoncello with guitar accompaniment and *Concerto for the guitar with orchestra*, Op. 6, *Three marches for guitar,* and *Six German waltzes for two guitars* were issued by Haslinger, Vienna. There was another Henry Birnbach, born in Breslau January 8, 1795, died August 24, 1879, Berlin, who has also written and published concertos, and other works for the piano, oboe and guitar.

Bizet, Georges, born in Paris, October 25, 1838, and died June 3, 1875, at Bougival, near Paris at the premature age of thirty-seven. He was the son of humble parents who at a very early age gave his first musical instruction and then placed him with Halevy, whose daughter he subsequently married. As a student at the Paris Conservatoire, he was awarded the Prix de Rome in 1857, when nineteen years of age. He was an enthusiastic admirer of the operas of Weber and Gounod, both of whom were guitarists and employed the guitar in their operas. Bizet's opera *La jolie fille de Perth* bears unmistakable signs of Weber's influence, particularly in the first chorus where the similarity of Act II of *Der Freischutz* is noticeable. This serenade which introduces the hitherto silent English horn is scored with a blend of richness and restraint, and when the guitar ceases to sound, plucked strings take the accompaniment. The influence of the guitar, introduced to Spain by the Moors, is always employed for their accompaniment of 'cante jondo'. This is very apparent in Bizet's popular opera *Carmen,* particularly in the 'chanson Boheme,' of Act II, where the guitarists and dancers appear on the stage and Carmen suddenly rises and sings " Ah, when the gay guitars ring out " to their accompaniment and that of castanets. The beautiful intermezzo between Acts III and IV has also been idealized by Bizet and made romantic and complete by his simple use of guitars and castanets. This Spanish gypsy opera with its piquant, delicate orchestration is universally admired except in Spain, where it is considered mere conventional French operatic music. Bizet employs the mandolin in his opera *Don Procopio* where Odoardi sings two stanzas, the second of which has an added counterpoint on the mandolin with an attractive cross rhythm, here reproduced:

Bjeloschein, P. A Russian guitar virtuoso who died in Moscow December, 1869. He studied the guitar under Wyssotzki and Sichra and was the composer of many fantasies, studies, dances and folk songs with guitar accompaniment which were published in his native land. Many of his unpublished manuscripts were in the possession of the editor of the Russian musical periodical, The Guitarist, of Leningrad.

Blangini, Giuseppe, born November 18, 1781, at Turin, died in Paris, 18 December, 1841. When a child he sang in the choir of Turin cathedral, studied music and became a very famous tenor and composer. In 1799 he visited Paris where he finished an opera left incomplete by the death of his compatriot, the mandolinist and composer, Della Maria. In 1809 he was musical director of King Jerome in Cassel; but returned to Paris in 1814 and shortly after was professor of singing in the Conservatoire. His compositions include more than thirty operas and nearly two hundred romances, nocturnes, etc., for one or two voices, many with guitar accompaniment. The A.M.Z. for the year 1807 mentions *Six Nocturnes for two voices with guitar accompaniment,* in two books and in 1812, his romance *Le fleuve d'Oubli, with guitar,* was published. His autobiography, entitled Souvenirs de Blangini, edited by Villemarest was published in 1834.

Blum, Carl Ludwig, surnamed Charles Blume, was born in Berlin in 1786, and died there July 2, 1844. He was of remarkable and varied talents and aptly described by a contemporary celebrated musical critic, as " a universal genius, uniting in one person the poet, the dramatist, composer, singer and performer. He writes verses to his own songs, music for his own operas, and, when necessary, he takes the role of the lover and serenades his lady on the guitar, of which instrument he is a consummate artist. He possesses a very fine voice and acts remarkably well." A pupil of Salieri, he was considered one of the most brilliant musicians of his day and enjoyed the friendship and esteem of Carl von Weber, Schubert, and other renowned musicians. He was the recipient of many marks of distinction, one of which was his appointment of composer to the Court of the King of Prussia.

Little is known of his childhood beyond that he studied the guitar and obtained proficiency upon it, for he appeared as guitar soloist at the Thalia Theatre, Berlin, in 1801, when fifteen years of age. He devoted himself entirely to the guitar and singing, and in 1805 joined a company of comedians under the direction of Quandt. In this troupe he was vocalist and guitarist and while travelling with them obtained a widespread reputation. His success induced him to relinquish his travels in order to study more thoroughly the theoretical side of his art, and when in Königsberg he terminated his engagement with Quandt and visited the local music director, F. Hillier, for harmony and composition. His teacher was the son of the Leipzig musician of that name. After a period of study he returned to Berlin, where in 1810, he was associated with C. von Weber, performing the role of Don Juan with immense success. In the same year he was appointed guitar instructor to the princesses and produced his first opera, *Claudine de Villa Bella.* This work, staged in Berlin, was received favourably by the German musical public, and from this commencement Blum composed innumerable vocal and instrumental works in addition to many operas. In 1817 he was in Vienna, where he found a teacher and friend in Salieri, with whom he studied for some time and with whose assistance he wrote another opera, *Das Rosen Hutchen* (The little hat of roses). This was accorded thirty-nine consecutive representations during Congress session in Vienna, and was followed by the ballet, *Aline,* in three acts, produced in 1820 at the Court Theatre. The success of this, his latest opera, was greater than his previous work and the violin virtuoso, Joseph Mayseder, who was at the time of its production, violinist in the Court orchestra, arranged the march from the ballet with *Seven variations and coda for violin solo with guitar accompaniment,* Op. 3, published by Artaria, Vienna. Lorenze also arranged it with *Variations for bassoon and guitar,* in fact, so popular was this march that it has been transcribed for nearly every instrument. Blum was a member of Ludlam's Cave, that group of the most brilliant musical personalities of Vienna, among whom were Weber, Schubert, Moscheles, etc., which met for musical friendship and joviality. In 1820, the King of Prussia appointed Blum composer to the Court and the year following, he was in Paris studying the styles of Boieldieu, Cherubini and Auber. Moscheles, in his diary, writes of the happy times they had together in the French capital. From Paris he visited London, returning to Berlin in 1822 where for four years he was director of the Royal Theatre. In January, 1827, he officiated in a similar capacity in Königsstadt Theatre and the same year undertook a journey to Italy; but after the second year at Königsstadt he retired, accepted no engagement of a similar nature, devoting himself entirely to composition. In 1827 the following appeared in an English musical journal: "A novelty has been performed in Berlin, a new magic opera, *Der Bramin,* the music by C. Blum. The story is taken from that inexhaustible mine, the *Arabian Nights,* and affords several highly dramatic situations, of which the composer has ably availed himself.

Mr. Blum is known to the public as an able song composer, and the present piece affords several good specimens of his talent in composition of that kind, as well as in several combined pieces of superior merit." The year 1829 saw the performance of another of his popular operas, *The orphan of Russia,* two of the airs and a duet from this receiving wild applause. He made several journeys through Italy Germany and England, and in February, 1830, was in Paris translating and arranging foreign dramatic works for the German stage and after his return to Berlin at the close of the year made a professional visit to Dantzic with the prima donna Henrietta Sontag. Blum was a very prolific composer and writer, and his compositions for the guitar are numerous and varied. To him is granted the distinction of being the first to introduce vaudevilles, or comic operas into Germany, and his translations of these were preferred before all others, for Germans recognised a vastly refined and superior merit in his style. In 1830 Schleslinger, Berlin, published a German translation by Blum of the first edition of Fetis' work, Music Placed within Reach of All. The most important of Blum's operas, in addition to those mentioned, are *Zoriade, or the peace of Granada,* in three acts, published by Schott, London; *Achilles; The pages of the Duke of Vendome; The ecclesiastical shoemaker; The somnambulist; Didone;* and *The Ship's Captain,* the last also *with accompaniment of flute, violin and guitar* by the composer, published by Bachmann, Hanover. He arranged the music of many operas, including *L'Ours et la pucha,* and *La marriage de douze ans.* The style of Blum's operatic music is very graceful and light. He was the author of numerous songs, romances and other pieces for voice, duets, and male voices with choruses, the majority of which were composed with guitar accompaniment, and in many he added obbligatos for flute, violin or clarinet. He was commissioned to contribute vocal compositions to *Orpheus,* a collection of part songs or vocal quartets by celebrated German composers with English words, published in parts and compressed score. This series commenced by Messrs. Ewer, London, about 1830, has been continued by their successors, Novello & Co. Among the lyric works of this worthy representative of the guitar, is a comic intermezzo for three male voices—tenor and two basses—Op. 21, with accompaniments for two guitars, entitled: *The three guitar players; The ballad singer, a musical curiosity for two voices with accompaniment of guitars and triangle;* Op. 127, *Soprano scena, with guitar accompaniment;* Op. 18, *Duo for soprano and baritone with guitar.* Blum was the author of a *Complete Grand Method for the guitar,* Op. 39—in two volumes, the first book treats of the theory and the second is practical. This is a compilation of some pretension, the work of a thorough master of the instrument, who recognised the possibilities of the guitar in its dual capacity as a solo instrument and one of accompaniment and he treated it accordingly. This was published by Schlesinger, Berlin; the original manuscript is in the library of the International League of Guitarists, Munich. Blum augmented his method by Op. 44, a series of studies for developing the fingers of both hands, with three other volumes of studies, viz. Op. 4, 8, and 9. In Blum's compositions for the guitar there is a style of writing far in advance of his time. Other composers for the instrument were content with either giving a melody supported by an accompaniment of the open bass strings, or, on the other hand, of writing their guitar works in continued full harmony of four or more parts. Blum's music introduced the sustained melody with a running accompaniment judiciously and skilfully interwoven, more in accordance with that manner of writing adopted and perfected by Zani de Ferranti and Mertz. The following are the principal of Blum's compositions for the guitar: Op 3, 5, 6, 7, 10, 12, 15, 18, 20, 21, 23, 24, 43, and 127 are *Vocal compositions with guitar.* Op. 16, 17, 25, 39, 100 are *Guitar Solos;* Op. 31, 64, and 122 are *Trios for flute, violin and guitar;* Op. 38, *Duo for guitar and piano,* published by Haslinger, Vienna. In addition there are numerous works without opus numbers which were issued by the publishers mentioned and by Schott, London, and Breitkopf & Härtel, Leipzig.

Blumenthal, Joseph, born November 1, 1782, at Brussels, died May 9, 1850, in Vienna. He studied under the Abbe Vogler in Prague and in 1803 was violinist in the Theatre an der Wien and conductor of the Piarist Church choir, Vienna. He composed several instrumental works which included the guitar, the best known are, *Three Serenades for violin, alto and guitar,* published by Steiner & Co., Vienna; *Variations for violin and guitar* and *Two Contredances for flute and guitar.*

Bobrowicz, J. N. de, was born at Cracow, Poland, May 12, 1805, and was living in Leipzig in 1857, after which nothing is known of his life. A pupil of Giuliani, he was the most skilful of Polish guitarists and composers for his instrument. His concert performances rivalled those of his compatriot, the renowned Felix Horetzky. The fame of Bobrowicz does not, however, rest alone on his musical genius, for he was a distinguished literateur and his translations and editions of the Polish classic writers form a lasting monument to his name, held in the highest esteem for this service to his nation's prestige. In his later years Bobrowicz was the director of the foreign department of a library in Leipzig. When a child he was placed in Vienna for education, remaining until he was fifteen, and during that time commenced the study of the guitar under the celebrated virtuoso, Giuliani, who was at the height of his fame and causing such a sensation in Viennese musical circles. Bobrowicz continued his guitar studies seriously and when his teacher left Vienna for Rome he also returned to his native Cracow. His musical progress had been phenomenal, and in 1821 when but sixteen commenced a professional career as guitarist and teacher. He very quickly acquired an enviable reputation, and the following year was elected a member of Cracow Musical Society. Being held in universal admiration and respect, his services as guitar soloist were in frequent demand and his name was to be seen on all the programmes of native and foreign musicians appearing in Cracow. He was honoured by the celebrated violin virtuoso, Lipinski, who engaged him to play the guitar score of one of Paganini's compositions, in which this famous violinist played the lead. His success added to his popularity and from 1821, the date of his first public appearance, until 1830, he had given over thirty guitar recitals. In 1826, he commenced to compose for his instrument, the first works being published in his native city by F. Piller. In 1829, Bobrowicz became Secretary of the Cracow Senate; but, by the unfortunate and memorable events of the succeeding year did not long occupy this important office. He was patriotic and enthusiastic in his endeavour for national freedom and played no insignificant part in the insurrection, enlisting immediately and serving throughout the entire struggle. For personal bravery and military ability, during the first campaign of 1831, he was promoted to a lieutenancy and placed in command of a regiment of horse artillery, and for valour during succeeding engagements was awarded the Cross of Virtue. After conclusion of hostilities in 1832, he removed to Leipzig, where he continued his musical life, appearing as guitar virtuoso in a series of concerts in the famous Gewandhaus, in the company of the most celebrated vocalists and instrumentalists of Europe. In 1833 he was guitarist at a concert given by Clara Wieck—later Madam Schumann—his items on this occasion were his transcriptions of four of Chopin's mazurkas. The press and critics reporting his playing, spoke of him as the Chopin of the guitar. His reputation as guitar virtuoso had now reached Germany and his compositions were issued by the most prominent publishers of Leipzig, Dresden, Vienna, Warsaw and London. He was not a voluminous composer—his opus numbers did not exceed fifty—but being popular, were issued simultaneously by various publishers, and consist of solos and duos for the guitar, with violin, 'cello, and other instruments. He was the author of a *Method for the guitar,* published by G. Sennevald, Warsaw, and also translated and appended, in the German and French languages, the original French edition of Carulli's Method. This was entitled: *Method for the guitar by Ferd. Carulli, new edition, revised and augmented by J. N. de Bobrowicz, pupil of Giuliani,* and published by Breitkopf & Härtel, Leipzig. After 1833, Bobrowicz was primarily engaged in literature and founded a magnificent establishment in Leipzig for the translation and publication of the classic literary works of the writers of his native land. From 1833 he published no less than three hundred and eighty volumes of the works of Polish authors. These included forty volumes—pocket edition—of the classics, ten volumes of A'Armorial of Niesieck, seventeen volumes—being the complete works of J. N. Niemcewicz, an edition of the Bible containing four hundred wood engravings, and the complete works of Adam Mickiewicz and numerous other Polish writers of renown. The following are his most popular instrumental compositions: *Themes with Variations for guitar solo,* Op. 6, 7, 10, 12, 13, 16, 18, 20 and 30 published by Breitkopf & Härtel, Leipzig; *Grand Potpourri for guitar,* Op. 21, Hofmeister, Leipzig;

Marches for guitar solo, Op. 19 and 25 and *Rondo Brilliant,* Op. 17, Breitkopf & Härtel, Leipzig; *Polonaises and Waltzes,* Op. 11 and 24, also for guitar and flute; *Souvenir de Pologne,* a Grand Potpourri for 'cello and guitar or piano, written in collaboration with J. B. Goss and *Four Mazurkas of Chopin,* for guitar solo with a few piano waltzes published by Breitkopf & Härtel, Leipzig.

Boccherini, Luigi, a highly gifted violoncellist and composer was born at Lucca, Italy, February 19, 1743, and died in Madrid May 28, 1805. Boccherini's name is associated with that of Haydn, his contemporary; both enlarged the sphere of the symphony and their compositions in this form bear striking resemblance. Boccherini was also a guitarist and a composer for the guitar. The first rudiments of music and the 'cello were taught Boccherini by his father and later by the Abbe Vannecci. The lad's ability was so marked that they were induced to send him to Rome, where he rapidly made himself famous, both as a performer and composer. He returned to Lucca and joined a violinist, Manfredi, a pupil of Tartini, and together they toured Italy into France, journeying as far north as Paris which they reached in 1768. Here they were accorded a brilliant reception and after their appearances at the Concerts Spirituels, Boccherini became the rage and publishers contended for his compositions. The Spanish ambassador in Paris, a skilful amateur musician, pressed them to visit Madrid, promising the warmest reception from the Prince of Asturias, afterwards Charles IV. Accordingly, towards the close of 1768, they started for Madrid, but their reception was extremely disappointing. They were, however, patronised by the Infanta Don Luis, brother of the King, and Boccherini was appointed composer and virtuoso to the Infanta and also to Friedrich Wilhelm II, King of Prussia, which latter appointment procured him an annual salary. When the death of Friedrich occurred in 1797, Boccherini's salary ceased, and he found himself practically unknown, except to a small circle of patrons. He obtained a friend in the Marquis of Benavente, in whose palace he was able to hear his music performed by his former associates of the Villa Arenas, whither his old protector, Don Luis, had retired after his mesalliance. Meantime, ill health compelled Boccherini to discontinue playing the 'cello, and he studied the guitar. This was attributable to the fact that his patron, the Marquis of Benavente, was a talented guitar player and Boccherini himself tells us that some of his music was inspired by hearing the celebrated Padre Basilio play fandangos on the guitar. The marquis commissioned Boccherini to write guitar parts to all his orchestral compositions and to other pieces for which the Marquis showed a preference. Special rehearsals were given, with Boccherini and his patron playing the guitar score, the average payment received for such guitar parts to each quartet, quintet or symphony being about four pounds sterling. Many other wealthy Spanish amateur guitarists followed the example of the Marquis of Benavente and commissioned Boccherini to write guitar solos and guitar accompaniments to songs and various instrumental pieces, and he was now constantly employed with the instrument, and experiencing a demand for guitar music, he wrote guitar parts for the majority of his symphonies and other orchestral compositions. In 1799 he wrote to the order of the Marquis of Benavente *Symphony concertante for guitar, violin, oboe, 'cello and bass,* a publication which is exceedingly scarce, and rarely mentioned ; but this composition possesses the same excellent qualities characteristic of his other works. There was advertised to be published, a series of twelve new quintets for two violins, two altos and 'cello, by the publishing firm Leduc of Bordeaux and Auguste Leduc of Paris. They were described by the publishers as posthumous compositions of Boccherini written for the Marquis of Benavente ; but although the work of Boccherini they are incorrectly titled. The popularity of Boccherini's music tempted unscrupulous persons to pass to an unsuspecting public an arrangement of his original works under a false title. As previously mentioned, Boccherini was commissioned by the Marquis of Benavente to write numerous instrumental pieces, and among such works were the *Twelve Quintets.* Now, these twelve quintets were originally composed for two violins, guitar, alto and 'cello, the manuscripts remaining in the possession of the Marquis. Some years after they were written, the Marquis was compelled by political troubles, to flee from Spain, and sought refuge in Bordeaux, France, and being in straitened circumstances, endeavoured to turn to pecuniary account every available asset. Fully aware of the popularity of Boccherini's music, he brought forth the manuscripts of the series of twelve quintets, as yet unpublished, and offered them to Leduc. The original instrumentation for two violins, guitar, alto and 'cello was not in accordance with the requirements of the majority of French instrumentalists, for the guitar was not so popular in France as in Spain. The publishers therefore made arrangements for the guitar parts of the series to be adapted for a second alto. This was entrusted to M. Garnault, a graduate of the Royal Conservatoire of Music, who was at the time a professor of music in La Rochelle. This able musician accomplished his task with care, and made similar arrangements for six out of the series of twelve, but three only were published out of the advertised twelve. Boccherini's Sixth quintet, Op. 30, which was published in 1780, is a nocturne, entitled *The Music of Madrid,* and nothing more original in design could possibly be conceived. In this work it was Boccherini's desire to illustrate the music that could be heard throughout the night, from sunset to sunrise, in the streets of the city. The solemn, plaintive strains of the ecclesiastical orders are intermingled with the dancing and merrymaking of the people, accompanied by the lively click of their castanets, their tambourines and guitars, the rasgado of the guitars being reproduced with realistic effect. All these novelties, portrayed with such realistic accuracy, lend an enchantment to this quintet of the most extraordinary interest and singularity. For the Marquis of Benavente and many other guitarists, Boccherini wrote numerous compositions of various classes. His

1

Drittes Quintett in E.

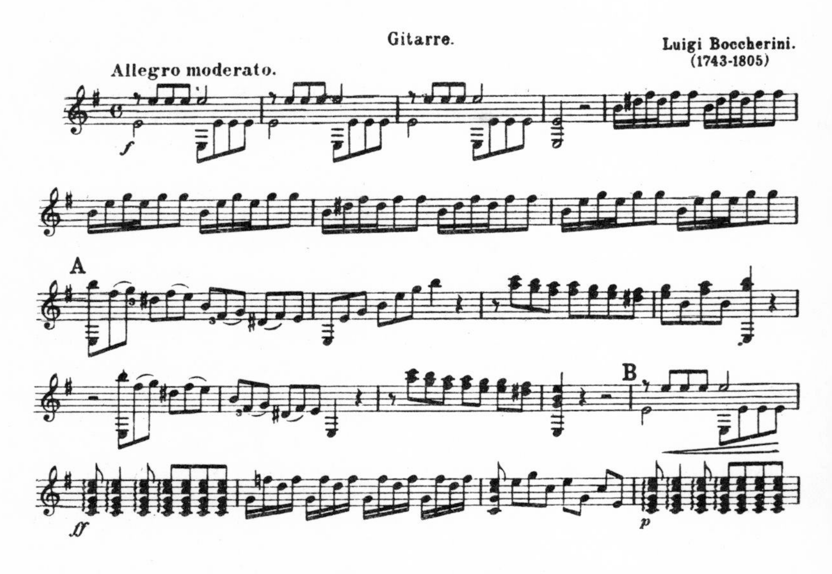

Zweites Quintett in C-dur.

3

Edward Bayer

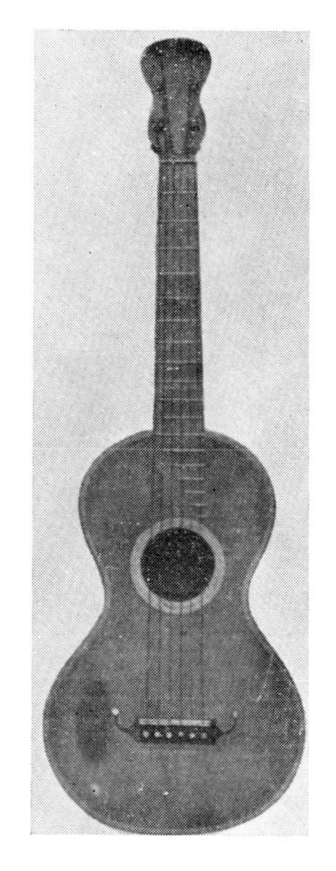

Berlioz' Guitar

Hector Berlioz

Ludwig van Beethoven

Beethoven's Mandolin

facility in composition was so great that he has been described as a fountain whose stream never ceased. His published compositions amount to about three hundred, and it is regretted that many of his pieces, particularly guitar works are in manuscript. Colonel Charmont, of Montezeville, near Verdun, France, brought back from Madrid, in 1812 a considerable number of original compositions and arrangements for the guitar by Boccherini; but after the death of the colonel, this priceless collection of guitar music unfortunately disappeared and although his relatives instituted searching inquiry they failed to recover, or even trace its whereabouts. Boccherini's *First, Fourth and Sixth Quintets for two violins alto, guitar and bass,* Op. 46 were published by Pleyel, Paris, and M. Cotelle, successor of Janet and Cotelle, music publishers, was in possession of the autograph scores. Boccherini also wrote for his patron, the Marquis of Benavente, in 1799, *Symphony concertante for grand orchestra of two first violins, two second, oboe, guitar, viola, horn, bassoon, 'cello and bass,* and in addition, nine other quintets for two violins, guitar, alto and bass. New editions of the following of Boccherini's quintets are published by J. H. Zimmermann, Leipzig—*First Quintet in D for two violins, alto, 'cello and guitar; Third Quintet, in E minor, for guitar, two violins, alto and 'cello,* Op. 50; *Second Quintet, in C, for guitar, two violins, alto and 'cello,* Op. 57. The original manuscripts of several of these quintets are in the library of the Paris Conservatoire and may be those referred to as being at one time in the possession of M. Cotelle, the music publisher. Towards the end of life, Boccherini was reduced to abject poverty, the unfortunate condition of Spain deprived him of patrons and he lingered till released by death, May 28, 1805. His memoirs were edited respectively by Picquot in 1851, Ceru, 1864, Schletterer 1882 and Malfatti in 1905.

Boccomini, Giuseppe, was born in Florence during the latter part of the eighteenth century and living in Rome in 1820. He was a guitarist, composer, the author of compositions for the guitar and also songs with guitar accompaniment. He was living in Rome in 1810 as a teacher of the guitar and two years later Piatti, Rome, published his method for the guitar entitled: *Grammatica per Chitarre Francesce ridotta ed accresciuta.* He is the author of *Six Waltzes for guitar solo,* published by Peters, Leipzig; an air from Rossini's *Tancredi,* arranged as a sonata for guitar solo and various vocal solos and duos with guitar accompaniment, published in 1820 by Ricordi, Milan. His compositions are mentioned by Mendel in his Dictionary.

Bocklin, de. There was a musician of this surname who was born in Strasburg in 1745 and died June 2, 1813 at Freiburg. It is presumed, but not confirmed, that he was the author of the following compositions which were recorded during the years 1807-8 in the Allgemeine Musikalische Zeitung. *Divertissement for piano with violin and guitar; Six Trios for guitar, flute and alto;* Op. 34, *Nocturne* *for violin, alto and guitar ;* Op. 35, *Amusements for violin, two guitars and violoncello.*

Bodstein, F. A., an Austrian guitarist and composer who published during the beginning of the nineteenth century, *Twelve Austrian national dances with coda. Two Grand Variations,* and a *Rondo Brilliant,* all for guitar solo. He was also the author of a *Method for the guitar* which was published by Hoffman, Prague.

Boehm, Joseph, born March 4, 1795, in Pesth and died in Vienna, March 28, 1876. He was a violinist of wide repute and a teacher of the violin who established a permanent position in the history of modern violin playing. He trained many pupils who became famous, among them Joachim, Ernst and Strauss. In 1819 he was violin professor in Vienna Conservatoire. He was leading violinist in a quartet and a trio at Schubert's concert, March 26, 1828, and on January 30 of the following year was violinist in a trio at another Schubert concert given to aid funds for the erection of a memorial to Schubert. The manuscript of Boehm's autobiography is in the library of Musikfreund, Vienna. In this interesting document, Boehm states that he played the guitar at the age of twelve and became so skilful on the instrument that he was fully occupied in teaching it. Later he gave many recitals, as guitar virtuoso, and he records that he was engaged by Schulz (also a guitar virtuoso and the father of the virtuoso Leonard Schulz) to perform on August 31, 1819, at the fashionable resort of Baden, near Vienna. This was recorded in the Allgemeine Musikalische Zeitung. Boehm was at the time a professor of the violin in Vienna Conservatoire. Manuscripts of his compositions for the guitar are preserved in the same library. His pupil, Ernst, also played and composed for the guitar and his pupil Joachim records that he also played the guitar and accompanied, with great proficiency the songs of his elder sister.

Bohr, Heinrich, was born March 5, 1884, at Vienna and educated at Krems Gymnasium. With the intention of entering the medical profession he commenced studies in Vienna University, which were neglected and later abandoned in order to teach the guitar and violin. He was very popular as a teacher in his native city and also as a composer. In 1924 Benjamin of Hamburg published eight of his solos for the guitar and a further eight were issued by Rondorf (Alfred). He was the author of an *Anthology* in two volumes ; a volume of *Twelve Studies for guitar alone* and an *Album of Ten Solos for guitar,* published by Goll, Vienna. Other of his compositions appeared in various music journals, and the Guitarrefreund, Munich, published several.

Bone, Philip James, contemporary, born 29 January, 1873 in Luton, England. The author of this work was educated and trained for the scholastic profession and became a schoolmaster under the Board of Education. When a lad he was attracted to the guitar and mandolin and played both instruments as pastime, with no serious intent. The interest in these instruments, however, soon developed into a passion, and his enthusiasm, which was contagious, spread to his fellow teachers, who requested instruction. Being self-taught, and conscious of his inability to do justice to the instruments and his pupils, he visited London to study under G. B. Marchisio, a professor of the mandolin and guitar at Trinity College of Music. His progress was rapid and he was chosen to give the first performance in England of two of Beethoven's compositions for the mandolin and piano—the *Sonatine* and the *Adagio*—at Trinity College, London. He was awarded the medal of the Royal Society of Arts, for mandolin playing, and, Dr. John Farmer, M.A., the principal examiner, suggested the instrument be made a life study. His love of music and the demand made on his leisure, teaching the instruments, caused him in 1903 to resign scholastic duties. He founded the Luton Mandolin Band, which, under his direction, obtained high honours in the International Contests, and performed in the Trocadero, Paris, before the French President. In Paris in 1909 he was awarded the gold medal as lute soloist, and received the personal congratulations of M. Guilmant, the renowned organist. For research in the first edition of this work, he was elected a Fellow of the Royal Society of Arts, and also a Member of the Royal Society of Teachers, and in 1951 elected President of the British Federation of B.M.G., on the twenty-second year of its foundation.

Boom, Jan van, born at Rotterdam in 1773, was a celebrated flute virtuoso and composer of works for flute and guitar. Little is known of his life previous to the year 1806, when he was a musician in the band of King Louis Bonaparte. At this time he was living in Utrecht as flautist of the Chapel Royal, which position he retained till the disunion of France and Holland. During the years 1809-10, he made several concert tours through Germany, where he received warm praise for his brilliant playing. Boom was a virtuoso in the highest degree and his playing of bravura pieces of his own compositions invariably excited the wildest enthusiasm. His compositions are accordingly, for the chief part, bravura; but among his fifty published works are several of artistic beauty, notably his duos for flute and guitar. These two instruments in combination were exceedingly popular during the end of the eighteenth century and stand unparalleled in their combination as duo instruments for chamber music. Boom's first publication was *Sonata for flute and piano*, issued by Plattner, Rotterdam, who also published Op. 2, 12, and 19, which were *Duos for flute and guitar* and Op. 5, *Theme with variations for guitar with quartet.* The same publisher issued many of his compositions of lesser importance for one or two flutes and guitar. *Twelve waltzes for two flutes and guitar,* were published by Schott, London, and for flute and orchestra. His son, Jan, born Utrecht, October 15, 1809, a pianist, after touring Denmark and Sweden became a professor in the Academy and Music School, Stockholm, in 1856 and in 1862 was commissioned by the government to visit the chief capitals of Europe to examine the various systems of musical education.

Bornhardt, Johann H. C., born at Brunswick, March 19, 1774, and died April 19, 1840, in the same city. He was a virtuoso on the guitar, a good pianist and musician of renown in north Germany, a prolific composer for flute and also a writer and composer of popular songs. He toured his native land as guitarist, receiving the praise of musicians, and he taught his instruments in the cities on route, residing alternately in Hamburg, Leipzig and Berlin. During his life, his songs with guitar, and his instrumental compositions were favoured with some success; they are now entirely forgotten. His songs and romances all with flute and guitar accompaniments, won for him a widespread reputation. He was the author of two methods for the guitar and one for the piano; the guitar methods passed many editions and were deemed worthy of translation and revision by several eminent guitarists. They were published—one edition revised by Chotek and issued by Haslinger, Vienna; another revised by Hoffman and published by Andre, Offenbach, and another published by Schott, Mayence. The most widely known of his instrumental compositions are: Op. 53, 130, 146, *Trios for guitar, flute and alto* published by Bachmann, Hanover; Op. 111, *Sixteen duets for flute and guitar;* Op. 51, *Three themes with variations for guitar solo; The Sentinelle, for flute, violin and guitar; Eight variations for guitar, violin and 'cello; The Concertmaster, a musical scherzo, for solo voice with violin, flute and guitar; Six Duos for two voices and two guitars;* many volumes of dances for guitar solo and flute and guitar and innumerable other light pieces for guitar published by Paez, Berlin; Breitkopf and Härtel, Leipzig; Rudolphus, Altona; and Bohme, Hamburg.

Bortolazzi, Bartolomeo. Dr. Zuth in Der Laute und Gitarre, Vienna, states there were two mandolinists of this name, father and son. The father was born at Venice in 1773 and the son, March 16, 1803. The son commenced to play the mandolin when eight years of age being instructed by his father. The father made concert tours through northern Italy, meeting with considerable success and in 1800 visited England where he was well received and stayed two years. This artist, by his extraordinary talent, produced the most wonderful and unheard-of nuances of tone and charms of expression, at the time considered impossible on so small an instrument. Instead of the nasal, monotonous tone which had hitherto been produced, he opened an enlarged sphere of capabilities for the instrument. It is to Bortolazzi that we are indebted for the revival of the mandolin as a popular instrument, a popularity which lasted for thirty years and caused the most celebrated musicians of the period to compose for it. In the beginning of 1801 Bortolazzi commenced the study of the guitar and the following year was teaching this instrument also, to the elite of London society. While in London he composed many light works for voices with guitar, and piano and guitar, one of the latter dedicated to his pupil, the Duchess of York, was published by Monzani & Hill, London. In 1803, he had quitted England and was touring Germany with his accustomed success. He appeared the same year in Dresden and Leipzig and the following year in Brunswick and Berlin, where critics and musicians were unanimous in praise of his playing. This was his final concert tour and in 1805 he settled in Vienna as teacher and composer. The most renowned musicians of the time esteemed it a privilege to appear at Bortolazzi's concerts, they acknowledged his amazing virtuosity and several composed works for the mandolin expressly for him. Hummel, the contemporary of Beethoven—and considered his equal—composed a concerto for mandolin and orchestra for him. The original autograph score entitled: *Concerto written by J. N. Hummel for Barthol. Bortolazi, maestro di mandolino, 1799,* is in the manuscript department of the British Museum, London. Bortolazzi's compositions are antiquated, and although of service in their day are of little use to present day players. He wrote a method for the guitar entitled: *New theoretical and practical guitar school,* Op. 21; and a method for the mandolin entitled: *School for the mandolin, violin system.* The guitar method was published in French and German by Haslinger, Vienna; it was a standard work in Austria during the early part of the nineteenth century and met with such success that it had passed eight editions up to 1833. The first eleven chapters are on theory and the twelfth concerns the instrument, after which follow scales, cadenzas, and studies in all keys, arranged progressively and thirty exercises on arpeggios, the work concluding with a fantasia for guitar solo of three pages. The mandolin method, published by Breitkopf & Härtel, Leipzig, in 1805 also passed many editions, the last revised by the violinist, concert director, Engelbert Rontgen, in 1893. The first lesson describes the various types of mandolins (Milanese, Cremona, Neapolitan), and is followed by various exercises for the management of the plectrum. Bortolazzi was the composer of many songs; Op. 5, *Six Italian songs with guitar;* Op. 8, *Variations for mandolin and guitar,* published in 1804 by Breitkopf & Härtel, Leipzig and Cappi, Vienna; Op. 9, *Sonata for mandolin and piano,* same publishers; Op. 10, *Six themes with variations,* in two books, for mandolin and guitar, published in 1809; Op. 11, *Six Italian songs with guitar,* Simrock, Bonn; Op. 13, *Six variations for guitar, with violin obbligato,* published in 1809; Op. 19, *Twelve variations concertante for guitar and piano,* Haslinger, Vienna; Op. 20, *Six French romances with guitar; Twelve airs for guitar solo; Rondo in A for guitar and piano,* Concha, Berlin; *Sonata for guitar and piano,* published in 1811 by Peters, Leipzig; *Six variations for violin and guitar,* Spehr, Brunswick; *Six dances and twelve books of guitar solos,* Haslinger, Vienna; *Six Venetian songs with guitar,* published 1802, by Chappell, London; *Today, a trio for three voices with piano,* dedicated to Count Waldestein, published by the author, London, 1801; *Cantate a L'occasion de la reception d'un frere,* London, 1801; *Maurer lied,* London, 1802, and numerous similar compositions published in England

and on the continent. The manuscripts of Op. 5 and Op. 11, songs with guitar and Op. 19 *Twelve concert variations for guitar and piano* and *Sonatas for mandolin and piano* are in the Musikfreund library, Vienna, and *Twelve variations for the guitar,* in manuscript, in Dresden. His portrait is reproduced from an engraving published by Breitkopf & Härtel, Leipzig.

Bosch, Jaime Felipe Jose, born 1826 at Barcelona, died March 30, 1895, at 23 rue de la Damas, Paris. He studied singing and the guitar when young and was later attracted to Paris where he became popular as a teacher of the guitar. On some of his compositions published there, in 1852, he is described "King of the guitar." Prat states that he was an intimate friend of Gounod who was so impressed by the playing of this Catalonian guitarist that he wrote a pasacaille for the guitar especially for him. In 1877 Bosch composed a four act lyric opera *Roger de Flor,* which with other of his manuscripts dedicated to his pupils, remain unpublished. He was the author of a *Method for the guitar,* which was published in 1890 by Girod, Paris. Collections of his Spanish songs with guitar accompaniment were published by Lemoine, Paris, who also issued about a hundred light compositions for guitar solo. Felipe Pedrell in the History of Spanish Music records Bosch as a worthy representative of his native land.

Bott, Jean Joseph, born March 9, 1826, at Cassel, Germany, died April 28, 1895, New York, U.S.A. His death was hastened by the theft of his valuable Stradivari violin. He is known as a violinist ; but he was equally talented as a guitarist and the author of compositions for the guitar. Bott was the son of Anton, a violinist, and his first instruction on the violin and piano was given by the father. So marked was his progress that he was appearing in public when eight years old and at this age he began to play the guitar. He continued the violin under Spohr until he was fourteen when he gave concerts in Frankfurt, Breslau, and other important German cities with success. After this tour he studied harmony with Hauptmann, and in 1849, when twenty-three was Court Concertmaster and three years later was Capellmeister to the King, in which position he acted conjointly with his erstwhile teacher Spohr, who mentions him in his autobiography. He was engaged in May, 1858, by the London Philharmonic Society to play David's Fourth Violin Concerto. He emigrated to U.S.A. where he was highly esteemed as the author of compositions for the violin and also for the guitar, the principal of the latter are Op. 19, *Five Waltzes and two ecossaises for guitar solo,* published by Schott, London, and Op. 25, *Six Waltzes for guitar solo*, published by Andre, Offenbach.

Boulley, du, Aubery Prudent Louis, was born December 9, 1796, at Verneuil, L'Eure, France, and died there February, 1870. His father, a talented amateur musician, gave his son instruction in the elements of music and the flute during the first few years. The father was an enthusiast on the flute and horn, and at the age of five the child commenced to play the former instrument. A year later he also commenced the horn and after two years on these instruments, he surprised the inhabitants of his birthplace by public performances of difficult concertos on both. He commenced the study of harmony under a local teacher and at the age of eleven wrote several marches and dances which were published; these compositions were popular in the district and were performed by all the bands and instrumentalists. He entered the Paris Conservatoire, in 1808, where he studied under Monsigny, Mehul and Cherubini for seven years. While in Paris he also studied the guitar under Ferdinand Carulli, evincing a marked predilection for it. During the interruption of the Conservatoire, in 1815, he visited London where he published some compositions—several guitar solos and songs with guitar accompaniment—but his stay was of short duration, for he returned the same year to Verneuil, his birthplace, where he married and settled. He was an enthusiastic musician and appeared as instrumental soloist, frequently guitarist, at concerts in Verneuil, and all neighbouring towns. At this time, and even as late as 1820, he was not wholly engaged in the musical profession, notwithstanding his training and love of the art. Between his numerous business occupations, he found time to compose, and in 1824 he brought out an opera entitled: *Les amants querelleurs* (The lovers' quarrel), produced at the Opera Comique, Paris. The success of this was short-lived, consequent on the author of the libretto refusing its performance in vaudeville. Boulley was now fully occupied with music, composed numerous instrumental works, principally guitar solos, duos, quartets, etc., which were readily accepted by Parisian publishers. In 1827 his health began to fail showing grave signs of tuberculosis, and upon medical advice he retired to the country village of Grosbois, where he occupied himself with agriculture, with the object of restoring his health. This new life and environment, could not nullify his love or interest in music and he wrote several theoretical treatises and methods of instruction, notably a *Dictionary of Music,* published in 1830 and a *Complete Method for the Guitar,* Op. 118. He had already published a Method for the same instrument, Op. 42, in the Spanish language, issued by Richault, Paris. While living in Grosbois, the French National Guard was formed, and the branch of the organisation in Verneuil presented him with the opportunity of forming a military band. He gathered together about forty players, whom he trained so efficiently that this band was the pride and envy of the district. Owing to the success and popularity of this combination of instrumentalists, Boulley became renowned as a conductor and was requested to organise and conduct many other military bands in the country. In the village of Grosbois, where he lived, he maintained an efficient band of twenty-three performers, two bugles, ten clarinets, four trombones, a horn, an alto ophicleides and three tympani. The musical compositions of Boulley are as numerous as varied; more than one hundred and fifty were published. During the first part of his life he was devoted enthusiastically to the guitar, but, as in the career of Kuffner, when military bands were introduced and became popular, he turned his attention to this branch of the art. Boulley's first compositions were sonatas, marches and dances for the pianoforte, and they were published by Joly, Paris. He was the author of several operas, orchestral symphonies and Op. 69, *Septet for violin, alto, 'cello, flute, horn, clarinet and guitar ;* Op. 76, *Quintet for guitar violin, flute, alto and piano ;* Op. 56. 66, 72, 74, 80 and 82, *Six quartets for guitar, piano, flute and violin*, all published by Richault, Paris ; Op. 32, 54, and 83, *Three trios for guitar, alto and piano ;* Op. 29, *Trio for guitar, violin and 'cello ;* Op. 31, 38, 46, 52, 67, 70, 78, 81 and 110, *Duos for guitar and piano ;* Op. 50, 75, and 115, *Duos for two guitars ;* Op. 60, 62, and 64, *Duos for violin and guitar ;* Op. 87, 88, and 94, *Duos for flute and guitar* ; Op. 68, *Five books of duos for piano and guitar ;* Op. 79, *Romance and Polonaise for guitar solo.* In addition there are several funeral marches and other compositions for military band, the guitar methods which were so popular during the commencement of the last century, numerous other guitar solos, collections of duos for violin and guitar and songs with the guitar, published by Richault, Meissonnier, and Janet, in Paris and George & Manby, London. His memoirs, edited by J. de l'Avre appeared in 1896.

Bracco, C. A., was born during the middle of the nineteenth century in northern Italy and died there in 1903. He was an Italian mandolinist, violinist and composer who held various appointments as musical conductor. He was an esteemed organiser of musical societies, was conductor of the Municipal Orchestra of Orvieto, the Philharmonic Society of Certosa, the Banda Operaia Genovese (Genoa) and the Club Musicale Genovese, a mandolin and guitar orchestra, for the members of which he wrote and dedicated in 1902, his most popular composition. This symphonic overture, *I mandolini a congresso, for two mandolins, mandola, lute, and guitar* was awarded the gold medal in the international musical competition organised by the proprietors of the musical periodical Il Mandolino of Turin. Its first publication was in the June number of this journal of the same year and was an immediate and pronounced success, being included in the repertoire of every European mandolin band of importance. It was the most classic and original composition for these instruments at the time of its publication. With its tuneful melodies, interesting changes of tempo, artistic and effective scoring for each individual instrument, it proclaimed an advance in the style and instrumentation of the mandolin orchestra. It maintains its unique position among original compositions for mandolin orchestras. At the International Concours for mandolin bands, held in Boulogne, France, in 1909, the number of contesting bands choosing this composition for the selection of their own choice, was so great as to cause unusual remarks from a member of the jury. Bracco was not a prolific composer, he was the author of several operettas, ballets and songs which were produced and published in his native land. His principal compositions are for mandolin, guitar, violin and piano. Op. 64, for mandolins and guitar and similar compositions were issued in Italy by Ricordi and others. His portrait is reproduced from an autographed photo taken a few years previous to his death.

Brand, Alexander. There were three German guitarists of the name of Brand who were famed, particularly in their native land. Alexander was living during the commencement of the nineteenth century. The A.M.Z of 1813 records his guitar playing with that of the guitarist, Scheidler, and the following year mentions his songs with guitar. His most important guitar compositions are, *Brilliant quartet for violin, alto, 'cello and guitar; Trio for violin, alto and guitar; Six waltzes for guitar solo; Six Brilliant waltzes for violin and guitar,* and other compositions for violin and piano, published by Schott, Mayence.

Brand, Frederick, born 1806, Regensburg, was the most celebrated of the guitarists of this name. He was living in Wurzburg, Germany, at an advanced age in 1880, where he had, for many years, officiated as conductor of the cathedral choir of the city. Dr. Zuth in "Laute und Gitarre" states that he died in 1874. He was one of the last of the guitar virtuosi and obtained fame as a player and composer principally in his native land. It was while living as a teacher of the guitar in Mannheim that he married, after which he removed to Frankfurt and later to Wurzburg. In the last city he became acquainted with the guitar virtuoso, Adam Darr, who, at the time, was private tutor in the family of an English gentleman resident in Wurzburg. It was not long before the two guitarists became known to each other and an acquaintance was formed which developed into close friendship. The two artists were in demand as guitar duettists and soloists at private and public concerts, and with such success in Wurzburg, that they planned an extensive tour together. They travelled through southern Germany and in numerous public and private engagements astonished their audiences by their artistic performances, in the role of guitar soloists, in duos for two guitars and in vocal items with guitar accompaniments. The flattering notices of praise and admiration that preceded the two artistes from town to town, combined with the enthusiastic receptions that greeted them in their concerts, gave the semblance of a series of triumphant marches. The A.M.Z. reported their concerts in Weimar. In addition to writing compositions for the guitar Brand composed light pieces for the piano. Op. 3, 7, 8, 10, are *Themes with variations for guitar solo;* Op. 18, *Eight simple duets for two guitars;* numerous dances, operatic airs, etc., and other light compositions, without opus numbers, for one and two guitars were published by Pacini, Paris, and Schott, Mayence; two books of operatic airs, arranged for flute and guitar and collections of German songs with guitar accompaniment, four volumes of which, in addition to the compositions previously mentioned, were issued by Schott, Mayence .A manuscript composition by Brand, for solo guitar with orchestral accompaniment—a fantasia on a theme from Bellini's *Romeo and Juliet*—was in the possession of

Otto Hammerer of Augsburg. A guitar Method by a guitarist of the name of Brand, was published by Breitkopf & Härtel ; the christian name is unknown.

Brand, J. P. de, was living in Germany during the latter part of the eighteenth century, and the author of *Sonata in C major, for guitar and violin,* published by Breitkopf & Härtel, Leipzig.

Branzoli, Giuseppe, born at Cento, near Bologna, Italy, died January 21, 1909, in Rome. When a youth he was gifted with exceptional musical talent making rapid progress on the violin which he studied in his native town and it was not long ere he commenced to teach the instrument in Cento, removing later to the more important city of Bologna. It was here that he became known as a composer and then first violinist in the orchestra of the Theatre Apollo, Rome. In 1870, after the death of his son Pietro—who was born in Cento—Branzoli suffered considerably from melancholy, and during these severe attacks of depression, neglected the art ; but he ultimately emerged victorious and was again occupied in its ministrations in the orchestra of the Theatre Massimo in Rome. With renewed energy and devotion he dedicated himself to music to stifle and conquer his grief. He was interested and instrumental in the founding of the Liceo Musicale di St. Cecilia in Rome and his name is sculptured in the masonry of the entrance hall. Branzoli was a professor of harmony in the new institution ; he had previously been the conductor of the Philharmonic Society and a professor of stringed instruments. While in Rome he commenced his career as musicologist with the co-operation of Professor Rodolfo Berwin who was also engaged in the library of the Royal Liceo Musicale di St. Cecilia, and of which Branzoli was librarian for some years. He was exceedingly desirous for the advancement of the mandolin and guitar, and, fired with this ambition, he founded and edited a music journal, which, devoted to the interests of these instruments, made its first appearance January 21, 1907. This periodical, Il Mandolini Romano, contained historical articles relative to these instruments, contributed by Branzoli, also music for mandolin and guitar by various composers. He continued the publication of this journal until his death, January 21, 1909, and the following number contained an appreciation and eulogistic sketch of his career with an elegy dedicated to his memory—a duo for mandolin and guitar—composed by Cav. Modesto Rasa. This journal was continued for two years after his demise and then ceased publication. Branzoli was the author of various compositions for the violin, mandolin, flute and violoncello in particular and some church music ; but his principal works are his methods of instruction. He left several unpublished manuscripts for mandolin, guitar, etc. and an *Elegy,* Op. 18, for orchestra, entitled ; *A tear over the tomb of Meyerbeer* in the possession of the publishers, Ricordi, Milan. His *Theoretical and practical method for the mandolin* was originally published in 1875 by Franchi and later acquired by

Venturini. This was in two books, with French, English and German text, the latter being issued by Universal Edition, Vienna. Each volume contained progressive studies in the form of sonatas and duets for two mandolins, and it was awarded the first prize in the International Music Exhibition of Bologna. In 1890 Branzoli revised and augmented it and the same year this new edition was awarded a similar honour at the Palace of Industry Exhibition, Paris. Branzoli also compiled a *Theoretical and practical method for the Milanese mandolin* with Italian and French text which was issued by the publishers of his *Scigolidita* (Studies of velocity) for the mandolin. Part 1 of these studies contains forty-eight exercises in the first position and Part 2, forty studies in all positions in addition to chords and arpeggios. His *Method for the guitar* was issued in 1899 by Carisch, Milan, with Italian and French text; the Guitar and Lute Methods both contain short descriptive history with illustrations of their respective instruments. About twenty of his compositions were conceived for mandolin band; they did not obtain the popularity of his Methods. His name is regarded in the highest esteem by mandolinists generally and a Roman mandolin band of wide repute, the "Mandolinistica Branzoli" was named after him. He was the author of two operas, *Torquato Tasso,* and *Sorrento* which were successfully produced in Rome. His musical research was made public in two volumes in 1899; *The lute and its story* and *Historical hand-book for violinists.* Written in an attractive, commendable style, and fully illustrated they display erudite knowledge of his subjects. In his *Historical and practical method for the lute,* dedicated to H.M. Queen Margherita, Branzoli is described as Honorary Professor of the Royal Academy of St. Cecilia Rome, and of other scientific societies. It is one of the most valuable treatises on the instrument, with diagrams of ancient lutes and an illustration of a lute made by Stradivari in 1700. The practical part treats of the ancient notation with numerous examples of lute music by ancient musicians, transcribed by Branzoli in modern notation. It was published in 1891 by Venturini, Florence.

Bream, Julian, contemporary, born July 15, 1933, at Battersea, London. His first instrument was the piano on which at the age of twelve he gained an exhibition award at the Royal College of Music, London. His real interest, however, was in the guitar, which, unfortunately is not included in this institution's curriculum. He received a little instruction on the guitar from Dr. Perott and later from Segovia. He has broadcast frequently and given many recitals in London and the provinces and was guitarist with the Bournemouth municipal orchestra in the *Rodrigo Guitar Concerto* on April 21, 1951. The Daily Telegraph said: "He established himself as a player and interpreter of the first rank and his guitar as an elegant and expressive instrument." He is unquestionably the principal British exponent of the instrument but has a strong predilection for the lute compositions of the old masters which he transcribes and uses as guitar music.

Brecneo, Luis, a Spaniard living in the seventeenth century who was an able guitarist and composer for the guitar and the author of a method for the instrument which is very scarce. It appeared under the title of *Metodo muy facillima para aprender a taner la guitarra a lo Espanol.* (Easy method for playing the Spanish guitar) and was published in 1626 by Pierre Ballard, Paris. Brecneo was a contemporary of Mersenne who, in his treatise on *Universal Harmony,* mentions in eulogistic terms the guitarist Brecneo.

Bremner, Robert, born in Scotland about 1720 and died at Kensington, London, May 12, 1798, was one of the earliest teachers of the guitar in Britain. He was also a teacher of singing who about 1740 established a music and musical instrument business in Edinburgh under the sign of the "Harp and Hoboy." He subsequently removed to London under the same sign and "opposite Somerset House in the Strand." Bremner wrote a Method for the guitar with the title of *Instructions for the guitar* and also published many collections of his national songs. The most widely known were *Twelve Scots songs for voice and guitar, with a thorough bass adapted for that instrument,* published in Edinburgh, 1760; Songs in *The gentle shepherd,* arranged with guitar accompaniment, Edinburgh, 1759; and others issued there and in London. He was the author of *Rudiments of music with Psalmody,* which passed several editions; but he will be remembered principally as the composer of the well-known hymn tune, *Dunfermline.*

Breton, Tomas, born at Salamanca, Spain, December 29, 1850, died December 2, 1923, in Madrid. He experienced great hardship during youth when a cafe violinist; but eventually rose to become conductor of the Royal Opera and of the Philharmonic Society of Madrid and through the influence of Albeniz was able to visit London as a conductor. Breton, like Albeniz, was a keen advocate of the National Spanish School (nationalism of Spanish music) and a prominent composer of Spanish zarzuelas (operas), oratorios, symphonies and chamber music which includes compositions for the guitar. In 1903 he was appointed Director of the National Conservatoire, Madrid. His most popular guitar solo is the jota *La Dolores.*

Broca, Jose, born September 12, 1805, in Reus, Tarragona, Spain, died February 23, 1882, in Barcelona. He was an excellent guitarist, composer, and the teacher of the renowned Spanish musicians, Pedrell and J. Ferrer, to both of whom he dedicated compositions. His principal guitar composition is Op. 19, *Fantasia and tone poem,* published by Vidal & Roger, Barcelona.

Brondi, Rita, born July 5, 1889, at Rimini, Italy, and died there in 1929. She received musical instruction from her father, when a child, continuing under the Italian guitarist, Mozzani, and finally with the Spanish master, Tarrega, in Barcelona. He wrote *Minuet* especially for her dedicated "to my favourite pupil, Senorita Marie Rita Brondi." When she returned to her native land she became a pupil for harmony and composition of Minozzi in Bologna and then commenced her career as concert guitarist. She appeared at the important concert halls of her native land and then visited Prague, Vienna, Paris and London where she lived for a time and studied singing under Tosti. She played in the Royal Palace, Rome, before the Royal family by command of Queen Margherita (a competent performer on the mandolin, and keenly interested in it and the guitar). Brondi is, however, more widely known by her historical musical research, made public in the book, *The lute and guitar,* issued in 1926, by Fratelli Bocca, Turin. A few of her studies and solos for guitar were published by Chiappino, Turin.

Broqua, Alfonso, born December 11, 1876, at Montevideo and died in Paris, November 24, 1947. He first studied music in his native city, then in Belgium and subsequently from 1900 in the Schola Cantorum, Paris, under d'Indy. His compositions founded principally on S. American folk-music, first appeared in 1910, and embrace operas, ballets, songs of his native land with guitar and items for one and two guitars and flute and guitar. *Evocations Criollas*, seven separate compositions for guitar solo were published by Schott. Broqua's most popular works for the instrument were published in Paris, where he was an honorary member of the Parisian Music Society, "Les amis de la Guitare."

Brunet, Pierre, a French musician living in Paris during the middle of the seventeenth century was a teacher of the mandola. He was the author of a Tablature de Mandore, published by Adrien le Roy, Paris, in 1578. Mandore is the name of an ancient instrument similar to the mandola—the tenor instrument of the mandolin family—the mandore or mandola being of earlier origin than the mandolin. The latter instrument derived its name from the former, and thus the mandolin is, as its name signified, a small mandola.

Burgmuller, Frederic, born in 1806 at Ratisbon, died at Beaulieu, France, February 13, 1874. From early infancy he studied music, and in 1829 removed to Cassel to study under Spohr. He made his first public appearance as pianist January 14, 1830, and received warm praise. In 1832 he was concertising in Paris and whilst there composed the music to the ballet, *La Peri.* He composed a great number of educational works for the piano, which are particularly valuable for their accuracy of expression and musical orthography. He is the author of three very beautiful nocturnes for violin, or 'cello, with guitar accompaniment, entitled, *Les murmurs de la Rhone,* they were written in *A minor, F* and *C* respectively. He has also composed several songs with guitar and piano accompaniment. An English edition of his *Three Duos for violin and guitar* was published by Wessell & Co., London. The original publishers were Schott, Mayence.

Busch, J. G., a German musician and guitarist living during the beginning of the nineteenth century who is known by his many simple, yet pleasing operatic arrangements for violin or flute and guitar which were published principally by Andre, Offenbach, about 1810.

Butignot, Alphonse, born August 15, 1780, at Lyons and died in Paris in 1814. He was a student in the Conservatoire of Music of his native city and made remarkable progress, obtaining the first prize for harmony in 1803. Butignot was a skilful musician and excellent guitarist whose brilliant career was terminated prematurely by tuberculosis, when fame and prosperity were about to dawn. He was the author of a *Method for the guitar,* published by Janet, Paris, and also songs and solos for the instrument issued by Boieldieu, Paris.

Buttinger, Charles Conrad, born at Mayence in 1788 was a talented performer on many instruments, principally the violin, flute, guitar and piano, and also an instrumental composer of some repute. He received a good musical education during his youth, and in 1819 was appointed Director of Music in Fribourg, Germany, a position which he held for eight years. In 1827, he removed to Breslau where he was in constant demand as a teacher and performer. He has composed much instrumental music, also a mass, a melodrama for choir and orchestra, several works for the bassoon, many songs with guitar and flute accompaniments, and guitar solos. A *Sonata for guitar solo,* many collections of *Original songs with guitar accompaniment,* and other transcriptions for guitar and flute were published by Schott, Mayence.

CALACE, Raffaele, and his brother Niccolo, were born at Naples—the home of the mandolin—sons of Antonio Calace, who had been established in the city as a stringed instrument maker since 1850. Raffaele, born December 29, 1863, died in his native city, November 14, 1934. Both lads received a sound musical education in Naples Conservatoire of Music, Raffaele obtaining the highest awards for composition. Their father died in 1880 and in 1889 Raffaele was associated in the business of a mandolin maker, named Rubino, who at the time was specialising in the manufacture of the mandolyre—a mandolin constructed in the shape of a lyre. Both brothers were acknowledged virtuosi on their respective instruments, Raffaele on the mandolin and Niccolo more especially on the modern lute (bass mandolin). They were versatile artists both as public performers and makers of instruments. The brothers commenced business in partnership, continuing their father's traditions and the superior workmanship of their instruments gained many Italian and foreign awards whereby the firm became the largest exporters of mandolins and guitars. They constructed numerous models of novel or ornate appearance. A short time later they commenced music publishing—first their own compositions—then the works of other composers. In 1898 Niccolo emigrated to

U.S.A., where he died in 1914, the business being continued by Raffaele until his death in 1934 and then by his son Giuseppe, who added the manufacture of violins and 'cellos. Raffaele made an extended tour of the far east as mandolin and lute virtuoso. He sailed from Naples in October, 1924, and performed in concerts in Tokyo, Osaka, Kyoto and Nagoya, made recordings, and after playing before the Emperor Hirochito and the royal family was the recipient of the insignia of the Order of the Rising Sun and several other honours. He returned to Italy during the summer of the following year, and was honoured by the title of Cav. The musical journal Il Plettro, of 1927 stated: "Raffaele Calace accompanied by his father-in-law, Dr. Colucci was received by the Duce in Rome, who expressed his appreciation of his musical compositions and the manufacture of musical instruments in Naples. At the conclusion of the interview Mussolini presented his autographed photograph, inscribed 'Il Maestro Calace en souvenir, Mussolini'." The musical compositions of the brothers Calace rank among the finest published for the instruments comprising works of simple execution to those of the most difficult and ambitious. Niccolo published about a hundred light compositions for mandolin and piano, a few solos and duos for the lute, and vocal items. Raffaele's contributions number about one hundred and seventy, which include two *Concertos for the mandolin,* one of which, Op. 113, is dedicated to the mandolin virtuoso Giuseppe Pettine; *Solos for mandolin with piano;* an excellent *Method,* a *Concerto for the lute* and a *Volume of Cadenzas and scales;* several *Lute solos with piano* and *Grand Duo for mandolin and piano,* dedicated to the mandolin virtuoso Fantauzzi. The classic traditions of the family are ably sustained and continued by Maria, the daughter of Raffaele, a pupil of her father and representative of his school. She featured as soloist in important concerts under his direction, and was a member of his classic quartet. Her first concert tour was in 1926 when she played in the Paganini Conservatoire of Music, Genoa, and later was mandolin soloist in the opera *Barber of Seville,* by Paisiello. She states that her father left many unpublished compositions.

Calegari, Francesco, an Italian guitarist born at Florence during the end of the eighteenth century, who spent a considerable part of his life in Germany, where he taught the guitar and published many compositions for this instrument. After his debut in his native city, Florence, he toured as guitar virtuoso, appearing in Milan and other cities of northern Italy. He then travelled through Germany, obtaining much success in Leipzig and Brunswick from whence he visited Paris, subsequently returning to Leipzig where he resided as teacher and composer. Calegari arranged numerous operatic selections for two guitars, for violin and guitar, and two albums, each containing eight operatic arrangements for solo guitar entitled: *Il dilettante di chitarra,* published by Ricordi, Milan. His other published compositions include a method for the guitar, fantasias, interludes, rondos and dances for guitar alone. Op. 2, 3, 4, 5, 6, 7, 8, 9, 10, 11 and 17 are guitar solos, published respectively by Hofmeister, Leipzig, and Ricordi, Milan, and other publishers of less repute in Florence and Brunswick. Op. 13 and 15 are duos for two guitars, and Op. 16 a Polonaise by Pleyel is arranged by Calegari for violin and guitar and published by Pleyel, Paris, and Hofmeister, Leipzig.

Calignoso or "The Furious," was the nom-de-plume of an unknown Italian guitarist, the author of an interesting method for the guitar entitled: *Il quarto libri della chitarra Spagnuola, nelli quali si contengono tutte le sonata ordinarie, semplice e passegiate, con una nuova inventione di passaoalli Spagnoli variati, ciacone, follie zarabande, aire diversi, toccate musicali balleti, correnti volte, gagliarde, alemande con alcune sonate pizzicate al modo del leuto con le sue regole per imparare a sonarle facilissimamente, Novamente composto e dotto in luce.* With the exception of the three pages which contain the rules for playing the Spanish guitar and which are preceded by a portrait of the author, this work, which forms one volume in quarto, is engraved entirely on copper, as is also the frontispiece, which has neither name of publisher, date or town. In the preface the author records that he had previously published three other works and that this was the fourth.

Call, Leonard von, was born in a village of southern Germany in 1779 and died while Private Chamber musician to the Court, February 19, 1815, at No. 556, Wieden, Vienna. He displayed unusual musical talent during infancy playing the flute, mandolin and guitar and in 1801 was established in Vienna as a virtuoso and teacher of these instruments. His first compositions and the majority were for the mandolin or violin, flute and guitar which were followed by part songs for male voices and choruses. These were appreciated and successful because of their originality, flowing melodies combined with ease of execution. Call's vocal compositions during the commencement of the nineteenth century, contributed in a large measure to the formation of the *manner gesangvereine* of Germany. In a short time his compositions were so popular that publishers were becoming wealthy; he was importuned for others and considerably more than a hundred and fifty instrumental works in addition to numerous others in albums and collections were issued. Publishers' catalogues contained about twenty different series of vocal items alone, each comprised about a hundred and forty for one or more voices. His instrumental compositions were principally solos for the guitar and duos, trios, quartets and quintets in which the guitar was an integral part, most frequently with violins, flute, 'cello and oboe. These he supplemented at intervals with vocal items for three and four male voices, several with guitar accompaniment which were exceedingly popular. He compiled a *Method for the Guitar* which was esteemed in its day but which has passed into oblivion. Call was one of the first to make popular this style of vocal, and instrumental music; but as frequently happens to

Giuseppe Bellenghi

Frederick Brand

Constantino Bertucci

Philip J. Bone

Vahdah Olcott Bickford

Vahdah Olcott Bickford

such composers, the demand waned in a short time and had he not died at the premature age of thirty-six he would have witnessed a forgetfulness of the popularity his compositions once enjoyed. He seldom appeared as a public performer, was of quiet, retiring disposition, a popular teacher, mourned by his wife, young children and intimate friends. Call's compositions are simple, yet interesting and although they do not warrant concert performance are admirably suited for hausmusic, for which purpose they were conceived. The parts are well balanced and he achieves variety and good musical effect. His form is usually in four or five movements and he prefers the minuet with which he is most successful. His principal instrumental compositions are Op. 8, 16, 21, 25, and 111, *Variations for mandolin or violin and guitar,* published by Haslinger, Vienna; Op. 108, *Grand Sonata Concertante in C for mandolin and guitar;* Op. 3, 9, 57, 117, 118, 121 and 130, *Quartets or Quintets for Guitar, violin, alto and 'cello; Trios or terzetts for Guitar, flute or violin, alto or 'cello,* about forty in all, of which the most important are Op. 60, 75, 85, 89, 93, 100, 106 and 134. These are interesting examples of chamber music in which the guitar is an integral part. In his *Duos for Violin and Guitar,* Call was again successful, with more than thirty for *Violin or 'cello and guitar;* more than twenty for *Two Guitars* and a like number for *Guitar and Piano,* which were issued in Vienna by Haslinger and also Mollo, and Simrock, Bonn. The most popular of the duos are Op. 74, *Sonata;* and the *Serenades* Op. 76, 105, 116, 143, 144, the last two for flute and guitar, published by Steiner, Vienna. Op. 26 is an *Easy Trio in C, for Three Guitars.* The majority of his vocal works were given guitar accompaniments. Op. 113 and 135 are two *Albums of songs with guitar;* Op. 136 *Terzett for soprano, tenor and bass with flute and guitar* and an interesting *Trio* for the same voices entitled *The Schoolmaster, with guitar.* Call contributed vocal compositions to "Orpheus" a series of collections of part songs and vocal quartets by celebrated German composers, with English words, issued by Ewer & Co., London, about 1840, and continued by their successors, Novello & Co. Call's guitar solos are of easy execution and not comparable to those of the celebrated guitar virtuosi. Several of his guitar manuscripts are in the library of Musikfreund, Vienna. Grove says he was: "a guitar player and composer of harmonious and pretty part songs which were greatly in fashion in Germany at the beginning of the century and contributed much to the formation of the 'Manner Gesangvereine' in that country. Some pleasing specimens will be found in 'Orpheus.' De Call is also known by his instruction book for the guitar."

Call, Thomas, an Englishman living in London during 1760, the author of "The Tunes and Hymns as they are used at the Magdalen Chapel, properly set for the Organ, Harpsichord and Guittar by Thomas Call at his Lodgings at Mr. Bennett's Stay Ware House, near Great Turn Stile, Holbourn and at the Magdalen House." An interesting caution to the "Publick" appears on the second page concerning any infringement of the copyright of Mr. Call's Tunes. It was published in 1760.

Camerloher, Placidus von, born in Bavaria 1720, died at Freising, Bavaria in 1776 was a renowned guitarist and violinist, a Canon of the Basilica of St. Andrew, Freising, and subsequently Councillor and Kapellmeister to the Prince. He was a prolific composer and has left many operas, including, *Melissa,* written for the Court of Munich and performed there in 1739. He was also the composer of the following: *Six Symphonies for Grand Orchestra; Twenty-four quartets for guitar with two Violins and 'Cello; Eighteen Trios; Concertos for Guitar with two Violins, Viola and Bass* in addition to masses, vespers, etc.

Campion, Francois, a French guitarist and lutist living during the close of the seventeenth and the commencement of the eighteenth centuries. In 1703 he was a member of the Paris Opera orchestra, retiring on a pension of £12 per annum in 1719. Among his published works is a treatise entitled, *Nouvelles decouvertes sur la Guitare, contenant plusiers suites des pieces sur huit manieres differentes d'accorder.* (New discoveries for the guitar containing several pieces in eight different methods of tuning). It was published in Paris in 1705 and his *Treatise on Harmony* in 1716 with an enlarged edition in 1739.

Cano, Antonio, born December 18, 1811, at Lorca, Murcia, Spain, and died October 21, 1897, in Madrid. He studied music in Madrid and during 1847 was associated professionally with the guitar virtuoso Aguado, who was then in the city. Cano compiled a *Grand method for the guitar* which was published in Madrid in 1852 followed by an album of *Twenty-four exercises.* A second edition of his Method, enlarged by a curious and interesting treatise on harmony as applied to the guitar, was issued from Madrid in 1868, in which year he was a professor of the guitar in the National Conservatoire, Madrid. More than fifty of his original compositions and arrangements for guitar solo were published by the Union Musical Espanol, Madrid, and about twenty others of his guitar compositions were issued posthumously by the same publishers some years later.

Carbonchi, Antonio, an Italian musician, born at Florence at the commencement of the seventeenth century. He was engaged in the wars with the Turks, and was created Knight of the Order of Tuscany for valour displayed during the conflict. Carbonchi, a musician and guitar virtuoso, was one of the pioneer guitarists and one of the first to write a variety of accompaniments to a melody. He was the author of a work containing a melody with twelve different accompaniments, each particularly suited to the guitar. It is entitled: *Le dodici chitarre spostate inventate dal Cavaliere Antonio Carbonchi,* and published in Florence in 1639. It was issued again in 1643, with a new frontispiece under the title of *Libro secondo di chitarra Spagnuola, con due alfabeti* *uno alla Francesce e l'altro allo Spagnuola ; dedicato alla illustriss Sig. Marchese Bartolomeo Corsini.*

Carcassi, Matteo, born at Florence during 1792, and died in Paris, January 16, 1853, was one of the most renowned of guitarists and composers for the guitar. Italy was pre-eminent for its virtuosi and composers for the guitar, having given to the world the majority of its most illustrious masters, chief of whom were, Giuliani, Carulli and Legnani. The name of Carcassi, however, is more familiar to students of the guitar than any other ; his compositions and also his exceedingly popular method for the guitar are the principal factors of his renown. Comparatively little is known concerning his early career, beyond the fact that he studied the guitar in his youth, and by his concentrated efforts and natural musical endowments, acquired at a very early age, most extraordinary skill upon the instrument. During his teens he had achieved an enviable reputation as a virtuoso in his native land, and at the age of twenty-eight was attracted to Paris, the goal of all musicians. He had just previously toured Germany where his playing aroused the attention of the musical public and he was importuned for compositions from leading music publishers. The first of his works was issued by Schott, Mayence, Op. 1, *Three sonatas for guitar solo in A and C major.* Op. 2, is dedicated to his friend and guitarist, Meissonnier who at a subsequent date established a music publishing business in Paris. It was while touring in Germany that he made the acquaintance of the French guitarist and they remained intimate friends, and when Meissonnier was established as a music publisher in Paris he issued the majority of Carcassi's compositions. In 1822 Carcassi made his first appearance before an English audience, in London, and received a warm welcome. He returned to Paris the same year but visited London for a period each succeeding year as guitar virtuoso and teacher. During the autumn of 1824 he made another concert tour through Germany where his playing was acclaimed with even greater enthusiasm than on his previous visits. He returned to London during the same concert season, playing at a concert given in June at the Royal Opera, when he was the only instrumentalist engaged, and on the 30 June, 1828, he was guitar soloist at the Argyle Rooms in company of Madame Stockhausen, the celebrated vocalist. At this period, Paris was the artistic centre of the musical world, and therefore the objective of all guitar virtuosi, and it was natural that Carcassi was drawn there in search of wider fame. His compatriot, Carulli, had obtained European celebrity by his concert performances, and through his compositions which were published there, and for many years had therefore drawn to himself the favour and patronage of wealthy Parisians. Carulli's compositions for the guitar, too, were readily purchased by the publishing houses, and he enjoyed a most enviable position. His perfect mastery of the guitar and the wonderful execution of his own compositions, invariably created a furore. Carulli's celebrated method for the instrument was at the time the universal favourite, in general use and, in addition, he had written and published more than three hundred compositions for the guitar, all of which were conducive to his reputation. But the celebrated founder of this school of guitar playing was growing old—his fingers no longer responded as they did in their suppleness of youth, and his magic touch had disappeared. He did not appear so frequently in public, and the Parisians were ready to transfer their allegiance to another guitar virtuoso. Carcassi was a younger man, in the prime of life, and he unfolded newer ideas and later methods in guitar playing. He introduced a different style of music, more modern, full of melody, brilliant, abounding in artistic and pleasing effects, and of but medium difficulty. Being fully master of all the varied resources of the guitar, he was able to execute his music with marvellous skill, and Carcassi very speedily excelled and outshone his celebrated and formidable rival, in the public esteem—a circumstance which naturally created some prejudice in the mind of Carulli, the acknowledged author of a once celebrated school of guitar playing. New ideas were evolved from Carcassi's research and imagination, and the musical world is indebted to him for numerous perfections in guitar playing. Publishers importuned him for his compositions, and the salons of all the artists and the nobility were open to him. In 1836 he returned for the first time to his native land, where his reputation had preceded him, and during his travels through Italy was the recipient of numerous public favours. Unlike Carulli, Carcassi spent a wandering, restless life, making numerous journeys between England and the continent ; but he eventually made a somewhat permanent residence in Paris, previous to his death, which occurred there January 16, 1853. Carcassi's concert guitar was an Italian instrument of most beautiful workmanship, constructed of satinwood with the then customary wood tuning pegs. The fingerboard, as was usual with Italian guitars, extended only as far as the body of the instrument, the remaining higher notes being obtained from frets inserted on the table of the guitar. The name of Carcassi, at the present day, is more familiar than that of any other composer for the guitar ; he maintains a prominent position among masters of the instrument for originality and individuality, which he indelibly impressed upon all his compositions and transcriptions. He perfected the method of fingering, introduced many novel effects, and carried the resources of the instrument to greater lengths than any guitarists before him. His *Complete Method for the guitar,* Op. 59, written for, and dedicated to his pupils, is a scholarly and useful volume, in fact, one of the best, if not the best compilation of its kind. It has been favoured with the widest and most universal circulation of any published guitar method, and it has enjoyed the distinction of being translated, revised, re-written, condensed, augumented, and mutilated by succeeding guitarists of every nationality. It is in three parts, and was originally issued by the publishers of his first compositions, Schott, Mayence, in German and French and subsequently in Spanish and English. The first authorised English edition was edited by F. Sacchi, a Cremonese mandolinist, guitarist and literateur, who was the teacher of the instruments in London to their Royal Highnesses the Princesses Victoria and Maud of Wales. It appeared in the English and French languages and the following preface was published in the original edition: "In composing this method it was not my intention to produce a scientific treatise; I have simply had in view to facilitate the study of the guitar by adopting a system, which in the most clear, simple and precise manner, might offer a thorough knowledge of all the resources of this instrument. The flattering reception, which, by artists and distinguished amateurs, has up to this day been granted to my works, has induced me to publish also the present one. A long experience, acquired in the course of my career as a teacher, having afforded me useful observations, I thought it advisable to collect them in writing, I took the greatest care to dispose on a progressive plan each lesson, in order that a pupil totally ignorant of this instrument might learn by degrees to play from the first to the last exercise without meeting any of those difficulties, which, through their avidity, are too often the cause of his getting discouraged. Independently of the fingering of the left hand, of which I have very extensively treated, the training of the right hand has always appeared to me one of the most essential points for succeeding in the acquisition of a steady and pleasing execution. I have fingered this hand all through as far as the chapter on positions in the second part; once arrived at that stage of practice, the pupil will have acquired sufficient knowledge to enable him unassisted to finger the passages. The third part serves only as a recreation, which, however, is not useless; it contains fifty pieces of various character arranged in progressive order. By the continual use I have made with my pupils of the rules on which this method is based, I can assert that any intelligent person who will attentively study this book from beginning to end, will acquire a perfect knowledge of the mechanism of the guitar. I shall always esteem myself amply rewarded for my labour, if I can obtain the certainty of having composed a useful work." After an introductory chapter on the rudiments of music, intervals, the construction of major and minor scales, a large diagram of the instrument and its fingerboard, and a brief list of the most common marks of style and tempo, the first chapter commences. This speaks of the construction of the guitar, and is illustrated by a diagram of the fingerboard and body. The position of holding the instrument, with explicit instructions on the manner of setting the strings in vibration by the right hand, numerous examples of arpeggios, preludes, and simple pieces arranged progressively and in such a manner as to facilitate their application, comprise the first thirty seven pages—the end of the first part. The second part is devoted to the performance of slurs, trills, vibrato, sons etouffés, and other effects, giving practical examples, with the positions, scales in thirds, sixths, octaves and tenths, and harmonics. The third part is a collection of fifty pieces for guitar solo in various styles, written expressly for the method and designed to improve the execution and musical taste of the guitar student. Carcassi supplemented this method, immediately after its publication, by a volume of *Twenty-five melodic and progressive etudes,* Op. 60, the object being to impart expression and facility in execution. The best of Carcassi's guitar solos are his fantasias and variations, classes of composition in which he especially excelled. Those fantasias upon melodies from the operas: *La muette de Portici, Le Comte Ory, La Fiancée, William Tell, Fra Diavolo, Le Dieu et la Bayadere, Zampa* and *Le Cheval de Bronze,* are not only artistically arranged and decidedly brilliant, but exhibit all the resources of the instrument without being too difficult for players of moderate ability. His arrangement of the overture of *Semiramis,* as a guitar solo, Op. 30; and Auber's *Gustave*, Op. 49, are also works of exceptional beauty. About eighty of Carcassi's compositions were published with opus numbers; they are distinguished by their refined style and originality, qualities which are by no means common, and his compositions are justly esteemed by all musicians. In addition to the pieces published under his opus number, there are a considerable number of works of less pretension, as rondos, waltzes and duos with piano. While in London he arranged guitar accompaniments to innumerable songs which were exceedingly popular both in England and on the continent.

Carrillo, Julian, born in 1875 at Ahualulco, Mexico, of Indian extraction. His first musical studies were in the National Conservatoire of Mexico City, where in 1899 he was awarded the prize which enabled him to continue his studies in Europe, at first in Leipzig Conservatoire and subsequently in Ghent. He returned to his native land in 1905 when he was appointed Director of the National Conservatoire of Mexico City. He later entered the U.S.A., making his abode in New York. He is the author of various treatises on harmony, fugue, counterpoint, instrumentation, etc., which appeared from 1913. As the composer of many ultra modern works for orchestra and piano his name is principally known. His *Preludio,* for soprano voice is accompanied by violin, flute, guitar, piccolo and harp; *Album Leaf,* a *Sextet for violin, flute, clarinet, guitar, piccolo and harp,* and *Concertino* for *violin, guitar, piccolo, 'cello, horn and harp.*

Carulli, Ferdinando, was born at Naples, February 10, 1770, and died in Paris, February 17, 1841. The son of a distinguished literator, secretary to the delegate of the Neapolitan Jurisdiction, he became one of the most famous of guitar virtuosi, composer and musical author. Like the famous Spanish guitarist Aguado, his first musical instruction was from a priest and his chosen instrument was the violoncello. He had attained proficiency when his attention was attracted by the guitar, and, abandoning his first instrument, he devoted his life and genius to the exclusive study and advancement of the more romantic instrument. During his youth there were few serious teachers and masters of the guitar; the instrument, however, was exceedingly popular in his native land but considered only capable as an accompanying instrument for the songs and serenades so common with Neapolitans. Carulli was a musical genius and in his youth commenced a series of studies and exercises for his personal advancement, as no teacher of the instrument was available, capable of guiding him to higher attainment, and so, like Giuliani, he was entirely self-taught. By degrees he realised the unlimited possibilities of the instrument in the hands of a skilled performer, he therefore studied persistently ; the success of his first efforts spurred him to further concentration in his study and the development of the hidden resources of the guitar. He was rewarded by the popular appreciation bestowed on him as performer and teacher in Naples, but had removed previous to 1797, for in that year he was established in Leghorn as virtuoso and teacher, and so successful were his concert performances that at the opening of the century he was touring Europe. The A.M.Z. records his concerts in Naples on June 20, 1805, with the guitarist Interlandi. In the spring of 1808, he was in Paris, achieving his accustomed success, so marked, that he made this city his permanent abode. He did not leave France for any considerable period, but resided as virtuoso, teacher and composer until his death at the age of seventy-one. It is recorded that the command he possessed over his instrument was so extraordinary, that never for an instant was he hesitant in the execution of the most difficult passages, of whatsoever nature they might be. He gave no indication of the slightest labour in executing with remarkable rapidity and perfect intonation, passages in double notes and chords extending full three octaves—the entire compass of the instrument. No sound, other than musical, ever issued from the guitar under his skilful command ; he measured the fingerboard with such geometrical precision and minuteness that there was never a suspicion of a foreign sound which is sometimes incident to rapid shifting of the left hand. He executed with marvellous power, rapidity, and absolute clearness of the tone, scales in single notes extending through the compass of the guitar, and, by means of harmonic notes to an octave higher than the extent of the fingerboard. His compositions, too, were novel in form and character, an innovation in the style of guitar music at that time, and these added considerably to his reputation. As artist, Carulli sought to improve the instrument, and spent much time with Lacote, the renowned guitar maker, who constructed several different models after his ideas, one of which was named the "Decacorde." This instrument made in 1828 from Carulli's designs was provided with four extra bass strings, ten in all, hence its name. Carulli lived in the friendship and society of the most celebrated musicians of the time, was regarded their equal, and among them were several who proved themselves artists of rare ability and made a name for posterity. Of these were the renowned organist and composer, Alexander Guilmant and the two guitarists, Victor Magnien and Filippo Gragnani and when Gragnani was receiving the applaudits of Parisians for his guitar recitals, Carulli dedicated to him his Op. 10, which was published by Nadermann, Paris. Guilmant evinced to his last days his interest in the guitar and mandolin, and spoke in admiration of his teacher, Carulli. Guilmant was President of the International Mandolin Concours at Boulogne in 1909, and his presidential address was an inspiration to all players and lovers of these instruments; the author of this volume recalls with gratitude the hearty congratulations of the venerable musician after the former's lute solos in this concours. During his last years, Carulli composed but little, and played but rarely in public; younger guitarists were appearing and the old school was losing its popularity. Notwithstanding, Carulli had the satisfaction of witnessing his own school supersede all others and of seeing the art of playing the guitar perfected. His musical compositions were full of originality, a spontaneous and prolific writer, his music added considerably to his reputation for they were the fashionable pieces of the day. He published an immense quantity of guitar music in the space of twelve years, more than four hundred compositions, many of extraordinary length. It is significant that during the same year, 1808, his compatriot, Giuliani, was receiving similar public favour in Vienna, for his guitar playing and composition. Carulli wrote concertos for guitar and orchestra, also quintets, quartets and trios, and solos, duos and trios for guitars. His schools for the guitar—methods, studies, etc.—the majority of which are very carefully compiled, the exercises admirably graded, display profound care and appreciation of the difficulties to be encountered by the beginner. In 1810 he wrote his exceedingly popular *Method for the Guitar,* Op. 241; dedicated to his son Gustave, a work of great merit, which was published by Carli, Paris. A very interesting preface states that the method was written for his son. It was the standard instruction book of the day, and its success so marked that it rapidly passed five editions. The sixth edition, much enlarged and containing an appendix, forty-four progressive pieces and six studies, appeared shortly after, issued by the successor of the original publisher, Launer. This edition contained a portrait of Carulli, a catalogue of his most popular compositions, and the author's notice respecting this revised and augmented edition. In the preface he states that since his first method was published in 1810, his experience had led him to make numerous alterations and additions to the exercises, with considerable advantage to those commencing the study of the guitar. This method gave to Carulli the distinction of being a founder of the modern system of guitar playing. A German translation of this work, edited by the guitarist Bobrowicz, was published by Breitkopf & Härtel, Leipzig, and an Italian translation by Pietro Casati was published in 1858 by Lucca, and subsequently issued by Ricordi, Milan. In 1825 Carulli wrote *Harmony applied to the guitar,* a skilful treatise on accompaniment, based on a regular system of harmony, arranged in a practical manner for the instrument, and no such work had been published previously; it was issued by Petit, Paris. Carulli's *Vocal Exercises,* or *Solfeges with guitar accompaniment,* Op. 195, preceded by the elements of music, met with the approval of masters and teachers of the vocal art. Carulli, in the preface to the first volume, states that this work should be included in the repertoire of the guitarist, for the guitar is without question, the most suitable and sympathetic accompaniment for the voice. He also claims that the principles of the volume are so very clear and concise, that by a careful study of the exercises of the two volumes, one may become a good musician, and also gain a fair knowledge of singing. Carulli was the author of a singing method published by Schott, Mayence, but this must not be confused with his *Solfeges,* which were written with the sole idea of giving instruction to guitarists in the art of accompanying vocal items on their instruments. His *Vocal Method,* for bass or baritone, Op. 316, was adopted by the Paris Conservatoire. He published a large number of studies and collections of simple and progressive lessons designed for the assistance of beginners, and one of special value to young players is Op. 114, entitled: *The useful and agreeable,* a volume of about ninety pages of studies, comprising some forty-eight preludes and twenty-four pieces accurately fingered, and ranging in difficulty from the simplest exercises in the easiest keys, to the most difficult melodies with intricate variations in the lesser used flat signatures. A similar work is Op. 276, *A little of everything,* about seventy pages of rondos, polonaises, etc., fingered and arranged progressively, and yet another, Op. 265, *Improvisations Musicales,* fifty-four brilliant preludes in various keys. Like other of his compositions, his Concertos are distinguished by the nature of their instrumentation, in which the guitar is the most important factor in their rendition, and also by a wealth and natural flow of melody and harmony, which could only emanate from an artist fertile in musical resource and conception, in conjunction with a profound knowledge of the science. Op. 140, *Little Concerto for guitar with accompaniments of violins, alto, bass, two oboes, two horns and double bass,* published by Carli, Paris ; Op. 207, *Two Concertos for guitar with violin, alto, bass or piano ;* Op. 8, *Concerto for guitar with orchestral accompaniment;* Op. 219, *Variations for guitar with orchestra, quartet or piano ; Concerto with two violins, 'cello and two horns,* Haslinger, Vienna ; *Fourth Concerto with orchestra or piano,* Petit, Paris ; Op. 208, *Two nocturnes for guitar with violins, alto and bass.* Carulli was the author of several trios for guitar, flute and violin, Op. 103, 119, 123, 149 and 255, all published by Carli, Paris ; and Op. 92, 131, 251 and 255, trios for three guitars, were issued by the same firm ; and he was a prolific writer for two guitars and guitar and piano, all in this branch of composition give evidence of his unique talent. These were issued by the most celebrated continental publishers: Simrock, Bonn ; Schott, Mayence ; Hofmeister and Breitkopf & Härtel, Leipzig ; Andre, Offenbach ; and in Paris by Carli, Richault, Launer, and Dufant & Dubois. The duets enumerated do not exhaust the number ; but all are characterised by richness of harmony, elegance of form, variety in the effects of instrumentation and individuality of style—features which distinguish them from the compositions of other eminent guitarists—and they are only surpassed by the guitar duos of Giuliani, which, however, are few in number compared with those of Carulli. The duos for guitar and violin, or guitar and flute, are characterised by the same rare qualities recognised in the guitar duets, and they differ from most compositions of this class, inasmuch as each instrument is equally dependent upon the other for the sustention of the whole. Under his guitar solos, are many descriptive pieces and sonatas, possessing exceptional degree of merit in which the ability and ingenuity of the author is manifested in displaying the characteristic subtleties of the instrument. Carulli, in his solos, was essentially a writer of programme or descriptive music, and these compositions enjoyed great popularity in their day. They are now old-fashioned—certainly there is the impress of age upon the majority and yet there are among them the choicest and rarest contributions to guitar literature. He wrote several piano solos and numerous songs with guitar or piano; *Bon Soir,* a nocturne for two voices with guitar, and *L'immortal Laurier,* for voice and guitar, were published by Schott, Mayence. Carulli's portrait was published many times and inserted

ORIGINAL MANUSCRIPT OF FERDINANDO CARULLI.

in the most important editions of his methods. His son Gustave, born in Leghorn, June 20, 1801, and died in Bologna in 1877, studied the guitar and singing under his father in Paris and continued his studies in Italy, where he lived for several years. Although a skilful guitarist he did not adopt the instrument professionally. While in Italy he wrote the farce *Le tre mariti,* which, published by Ricordi, was produced in La Scala Theatre, Milan, and he composed many works for voice and piano which appeared in Italy, France and Germany. He was a popular vocal teacher and a professor in the Paris Conservatoire where his *Vocal Method and Studies* were adopted. They were issued by Lemoine and also by Leduc, Paris, and Leduc published two volumes of his *Leçons Melodiques,* a continuation of his vocal method, in several languages. Several of his part songs attained popularity, one piece d'occasion, *Three airs varied* for violin to be played on the fourth string was accompanied by piano. Fetis asserts that this is the entire work of Gustave Carulli, while other authorities surmise that only the piano part is his work and that the solo was by Paganini. Carulli bequeathed his guitar to the National Conservatoire of Music, Paris, while a professor in that institution, and it is in the museum. This Italian guitar, with the dedication of the guitar method, was given by Ferdinand Carulli to his son in 1810. It was constructed to his design in figured rosewood with marquetry of ivory and ebony, the head and neck most skilfully executed and terminated in the shape of a bow of ribbon. The table—which is chastely inlaid with ivory and ebony bears the initials G.C. (Gustave Carulli) in carved ivory and form the terminations of the bridge. The sound-hole is partially covered by a delicate ivory cameo of a muse playing a lyre. By courtesy of Paris Conservatoire a photograph of this instrument is reproduced and also a fragment of Carulli's manuscript, written for his English pupil, whose name it bears and by whom it was presented to the author of this volume. The manuscript of *Twenty-three pieces for guitar* by Gustave Carulli is in the library of the International Guitar League of Munich.

Casella, Alfredo, was born at Turin in 1883, and after the completion of his musical studies in Paris Conservatoire under Faure, was very successful as a concert pianist and orchestral conductor in various countries. From 1912 he conducted concerts in the Trocadero, Paris, and was a professor in the Conservatoire and from 1916-21 was a professor in the Liceo St. Cecilia, Rome, where he was Secretary of the Societa di Musica Moderna. He is classed as an anti-romantic composer who has created guitar concertos especially for the guitar virtuoso Segovia. A sketch of his life by Perinello was published in 1904.

Castellacci, Luigi, born at Pisa, Italy, 1797, and living in Paris as late as 1845, was an Italian virtuoso on the mandolin and guitar, an instrumental composer, and the author of numerous French romances with guitar and piano accompaniments which enjoyed an amount of popularity. He was the son of musical parents and as soon as he was capable of holding a mandolin, his father placed one in his hands and gave him instruction on the instrument and in the theory of music. His progress was rapid, for while a child he appeared frequently as a musical prodigy in his native city. After having made a thorough study of the mandolin for some years, he extended his sphere of concert performances and obtained fame as a virtuoso throughout northern Italy, after which he turned his ability to the guitar, and devoting several years to this instrument, was then engaged in teaching both. About the year 1820 he left his native land on a professional concert tour as mandolin and guitar virtuoso, and as were his compatriots Carulli and Carcassi, he was attracted to Paris where he made a name in the musical world, particularly by his performances on the guitar and his vocal compositions with guitar accompaniment. He had arrived there previous to 1825, for at that date he was well established, appearing as guitarist in the most influential musical circles and recognised as a musician of the foremost rank. During his residence in Paris, his first compositions were published and several others were issued in other French cities where he appeared as guitar soloist. In 1825 he made a tour of Germany, and passing through Switzerland visited his native land. His talent was appreciated during this tour and when he arrived in Milan, gave several concerts and also in his native city of Pisa. During a brief stay he published several compositions for the mandolin and then returned to Paris, where he was popular as a teacher of his instruments. In 1834 he visited London and again during the season of the following year where he also published compositions for the guitar. He returned to Paris where he lived for some years and published over two hundred compositions, principally for the guitar and mandolin and romances with guitar. His music is of a light character, consisting for the greater part of dances, variations and fantasies for guitar. He is the author of two instruction books for the guitar, the principal, a *Complete and Progressive Method for the guitar,* published in 1845 by Lemoine, Paris, a work in two volumes and of some merit. It was issued simultaneously in Paris, Lyons and Milan and quickly passed several editions ; but outside France and Italy appears to have attracted very little attention and was not popular. The second method, a compilation of smaller pretensions, entitled: *Little Method for the guitar* was issued by Petit, Paris. Of his compositions, Op. 5, 6, 7, 16, 19, 27, 40 and 41 are for solo guitar ; Op. 9, 11 and 12, *Progressive Studies for guitar ;* Op. 13, 14, 15, 17 and 38, *Dances for guitar solo ;* Op. 43, *Three characteristic sketches for guitar ;* Op. 44, *Fantasia for guitar and piano ;* Op. 45, *Bolero for guitar and piano ;* Op. 33, *Twelve dances for two guitars ;* Op. 34, *Sixteen easy waltzes for two guitars ;* Op. 36, *Potpourri for two guitars ;* all these were published by Richault, Paris, who also issued a *Grand Fantasia for cornet, guitar and violoncello ;* Petit of Paris published a *Fantasia Dialogue for guitar, flute and horn ;* Op. 46, *Introduction and Bolero in harmonics for guitar* was published by Breitkopf & Härtel, Leipzig, during Castellacci's visit there. In 1835, Chappell, London, issued a collection of *Six Italian songs* and *Six nocturnes for voice with guitar and piano,* dedicated to his English pupil, Miss F. Swinfen. The most popular of Castellacci's romances appeared in Paris and were *Dell 'amor marinaro,* with guitar, in 1825, and *L'age de quinze ans,* with piano, dedicated to Mlle. Emilie Bourion, published in 1835.

Castelnuovo-Tedesco, Mario, contemporary, born April 3, 1895, at Florence. He studied music in the Cherubini Institute of his native city, continuing as a pupil of Pizzeti. At the age of fifteen he wrote *Cielo di Settembre* for the piano and in 1925 obtained a prize for his opera *La Mandragola,* creating a considerable impression as a musical composer in his native land, previous to the second world war. Emigrating to U.S.A. in 1939, he resided first in New York, eventually removing to Los Angeles. A successful composer of operas, overtures, choral works and songs, he has also composed for the guitar as solo instrument and with orchestra. His *Concerto for guitar and orchestra,* composed in 1939, dedicated to the guitar virtuoso Segovia, was performed at the Edinburgh festival of music and in London. It was also broadcast by the New London Symphony Orchestra with Segovia, again as soloist, from London, November 7, 1949, and November 4, 1950. Other of his guitar compositions are a *Quintet for guitar and strings ; Capriccio Diabolico* —composed in homage to Paganini—and *Sonatine,* both for solo guitar and dedicated to Segovia. The *Sonatine,* composed in homage to Boccherini—who, like Paganini, employed the guitar in his own compositions—was also dedicated to Segovia. This *Sonatine* is in four movements—*Allegro con Spirito, Andantino quasi canzone, Minuetto* and *Presto con brio. Tarantella* for solo guitar, dedicated to Segovia; *Preludio quasi un'improvisazione, Ballata Scozzese* and variations, etc., for guitar are published by Schott, London. A sketch of his life by Galli appeared in the Musical Times of 1921.

Castillo, David del, a Spanish guitarist and composer resident in Paris at the commencement of the twentieth century, who died there in 1922. He wrote many solos for the guitar, duos for guitar and 'cello, etc. On some of these he is described as Membre de la Societe des Compositeurs Espanols and Royal d'Isabel la Catolique. He was an adjudicator at the International Mandolin Concours, Boulogne, 1909, and other French competitions. His residence during 1912 in rue d'Anjou Asnieres, and later rue des Aubepines, Bois Colombes, was the resort of the musical intellegencia of Paris, famous poets, authors, guitarists and publishers. Castillo's biography and portrait was published in the Universal and Dramatic Directory, Paris, 1887-1911. His compositions, not difficult, were issued principally by Pisa, Paris, and Rowies, Paris. Several of his unpublished manuscripts are in the Library of the International Guitar League, Munich.

Cateura, Baldomero, born December 11, 1856, at Palamos, Gerona, Spain, died January 26, 1929, in Barcelona. His first musical studies were on the piano and singing; but these were discontinued when he became enamoured by the guitar, on which, under the tuition of Jose Pou—a popular guitarist and teacher in Barcelona—he made phenomenal progress. At the same time he played the bandurria (Spanish mandolin) and formed a quartet, subsequently a quintet of bandurrias, lutes and guitars which he so thoroughly trained that, under his direction, made successful tours of Europe. Prat states that he compiled *a Method for the bandurria* of one hundred and eighty-six pages, dedicated, *A la insigne escritore Baroness de Wilson, en prenda de admiracion y agradecimento,* which was published in 1896 by J. Ayne. Cateura, an intimate friend of Tarrega, is depicted in the reproduced photograph of Tarrega; he is the second from the right, his head being close to that of the master. Tarrega dedicated to him the guitar solo, *Maria.* The majority of Cateura's compositions are for guitar solo and for guitar in combination with mandolins; they were issued by Biblioteca Fortea, Madrid, and other lesser renowned publishers.

Charpentier, Gustave, born June 25, 1860, at Dienze, France, and living in 1951. At the age of fifteen he was compelled to commence work but studied music in his leisure and later in Lille Conservatoire. He manifested much precocity and made such rapid progress that the local municipal authority granted an allowance for the continuance of his studies at Paris Conservatoire ; his parents were not in a position to do so. He was a pupil of Massenet and obtained the Prix de Rome in 1887 and subsequently, in 1912, succeeded his teacher at the Conservatoire. He was an eminent composer of all classes of music and is known principally by his most successful opera *Louise*—the libretto, in addition to the music, being his own composition. Produced in Paris in 1900, it was an immediate success ; its eight hundredth performance was staged in Paris in 1931. It was broadcast from London, November, 1947, and again in June, 1950, the anniversary of his ninetieth birthday, when his recorded message was also broadcast. In the second act, Julian sings to his own guitar accompaniment an entrancing serenade to Louise.

Chavarri, Eduardo Lopez, born January 31, 1875, at Valencia, Spain, received his first musical instruction in his native city and it was continued under Felipe Pedrell in Barcelona Conservatoire. As a composer he is known by his orchestral, choral, piano and guitar works. He made concert tours with his wife—the Spanish singer Carmen Anduyar—and in June, 1930, they gave a series of broadcasts of Spanish songs and his compositions from London. He is the author of *History of Music,* published in Barcelona in 1914 and, in addition, various theoretical treatises on music. He has composed a number of guitar solos, of which the following are the most widely known: *Dansa lenta, Ritmo popular, Fiesta lejana en un jardin, Nocturne* (*Jardin le Granada*), *La mirada de Carmen, Lamento,* and *Gitana,* all published by Schott, London.

Chevesailles, was a French guitarist and violinist living in Paris during the middle of the nineteenth century. For a time he was violinist and guitarist in the Theatre Beaujolais, and subsequently founded a music and musical instrument business in the suburbs of the city where he was residing in 1835. He is the author of a *New Method for the guitar,* which, published by Mme. Joly, Paris, rapidly passed three editions. There were published under his name numerous waltzes and airs for guitar which were issued by Hentz Jouve, Paris.

Chrysander, William Christian Just, born December 9, 1718, at Goedekenroda, a village in the state of Halbertstadt, and died December 10, 1788. He was a protestant theologian and guitarist of repute in Germany, and for many years a professor of theology, philosophy, mathematics and oriental languages in the universities of Helmstadt, Rinteln and Kiel respectively. He wrote guitar accompaniments to the book of Psalms, which was in universal favour in the cities mentioned.

Ciebra, Jose Marie de, and his brother R. de, were born at Seville during the beginning of the nineteenth century, and Jose M. was living in London in 1858. Gracias a Soriano in his *History of Music* states on the authority of the Argentina amateur guitarist Dr. F. C. Cordero, a pupil of J. M. Ciebra, that the brothers studied the guitar in their native city under the maestro Juan Valler. Jose was the more popular and the Russian historian, Makaroff, in his Memoirs written in 1856, says: " A Spanish guitarist named Ciebra was born in Seville but had lived in London and Paris for the past twenty years. Abroad, he had written a large opera which had proved a failure when produced. As a composer he proved to be very mediocre. It was true his music had originality and was quite different from anything written by Giuliani or Mertz. It was also true that the pieces were very melodious and sweet, more so when he himself played them. Their main defect was an over all monotony in general and in details. The style was poor, and suitable only for dancing. The harmony was thin and pale, the tonality impossibly boring, the key never rising above two or three sharps. However, for the sake of a varied repertoire, which should include samples of different styles and manners, I learned two of his compositions. I enjoyed playing these; almost without exception, everyone, especially the ladies, liked them. I shall never forget the real furore they aroused when I played them on the boat during my trip abroad in 1875. Now I would like to say a few more words about Ciebra as a performer on the guitar. This was something which was most unusual and remarkable. As is the custom with almost all Spanish guitarists, he had grown very long nails on his right hand, which he held in an oblique position while playing, not perpendicularly, as guitarists usually do. Moreover, he did not actually strike the strings with the nail, but simply pressed it on the string, slipping off from the string on to the guitar. In this manner he was able somehow to draw remarkably tender, deep melodious sounds from the instrument, the equal of which I have never before heard from anyone—not even from the great Zani de Ferranti, who was known for the softness of his playing. The vibrato, when performed by Ciebra, was really divine—his guitar actually sobbed, wailed and sighed. Ciebra only showed these remarkable qualities in slow tempos as in largo, adagio or andante. The moment he had to play allegro or presto, the reverse side of the medal became evident. Then it became impossible to slip from the string to the guitar; instead it became necessary to strike the strings. This caused a disagreeable metallic sound, quite contrary to the velvety tones of his wonderful adagios. In a word Ciebra's performance could give his listeners the greatest delight for a few days, but not over any extended length of time since both his manner and his compositions became tiresome. When I returned home from Bruxelles, the news reached me that Ciebra had given a concert in one of Bruxelles' music halls but had not had much success, in spite of a large audience. I was sincerely sorry to hear that, since I consider him one of the most talented guitarists of his time." Ciebra was the author of a *Method for the guitar,* which was published in London but met with little approval and the published compositions of the brothers were insignificant. A *Grand Fantasia on an original theme* was issued by Lafont, Paris. The opera mentioned by Makaroff in his Memoirs was a Spanish lyric drama entitled, *La Maravilla,* libretto and music by Ciebra, and was produced at the Italian Theatre, Paris, on June 4, 1853. Several manuscript compositions are in the possession of their descendents, Maria Luisa Anido and Dr. Cordero of Buenos Aires ; a *Fantasia on a popular English air* and a duo for two guitars, the latter inscribed " 1st guitar Don J. de Ciebra, 2nd guitar Don R. Ciebra " are the principal. Dr. Cordero was a pupil of Ciebra during the temporary residence of the doctor in London, previous to his departure for Argentina, and the manuscript of the duo for two guitars was presented to this pupil inscribed " Souvenir d'amitie, Dr. Cordero, London, 1851."

Cifolelli, Giovanni, an Italian mandolin virtuoso and dramatic composer whose date and place of birth is unknown. In 1764 he made his appearance in Paris as a mandolin virtuoso and was highly esteemed, both as performer and teacher. While residing in Paris he published his *Method for the Mandolin* which was very popular in France and the most successful at the time throughout Europe. His more important works, however, were the operas *L'Italienne* and *Pierre et Lucette,* the former an opera bouffe in one act, the libretto by Framery. They were both commissioned by the Comedie Italienne, Paris, and were successfully produced at this theatre in 1770 and again in 1774. Several of the vocal items in *Pierre et Lucette,* songs and duets, were exceedingly popular in France and were republished in Paris in 1775 and again in 1780.

Cimadevilla, Gonzalez, born May 10, 1861, at Valladolid, Spain, and died August 19, 1931, in Madrid, was a well-known Flamenco performer and composer for the guitar. His *Method for the guitar* in two books was published by Luis Dotesio, Bilbao, and also by the Union Musical Espanola, Madrid. The latter publishers also issued nearly a hundred of his light dances for guitar solo, songs with guitar, duos for two guitars and mandolin with guitar.

Corbetti, Francisco, was born in Pavia, Italy, in 1630 and was living in Paris as late as 1689 ; after then nothing is known of his life. He was an Italian musician and guitarist celebrated during the middle of the seventeenth century who, as court musician, resided at the most important royal courts of Europe. He is known by two other names, Francesco Corbera and Francis Corbet, the Spanish and English versions of his name, and he is written and known accordingly. His parents desired he should engage in some other occupation than music, but his duties were continually neglected to play the guitar, and the persuasion and threat of his parents proving of no avail he became at a comparatively early age a most skilful and renowned performer on the guitar. After travelling through his native land as guitar virtuoso and vocalist, he visited Spain while still a young man and here he was known as Francesco Corbera. King Philip IV of Spain, who had

Raffaele Calace

Maria Calace

Niccolo Calace

Ferdinado Carulli

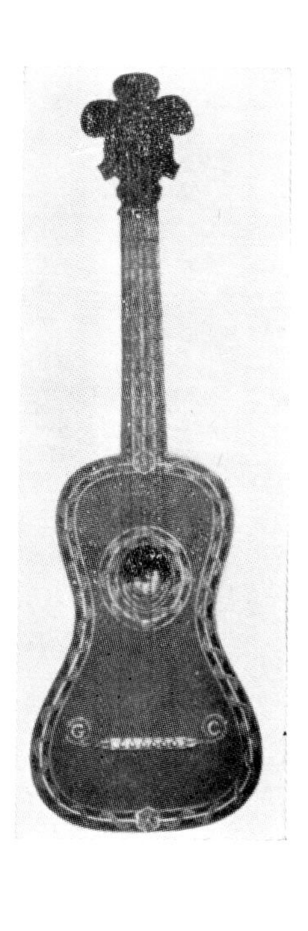

Carulli's Guitar

David del Castillo

heard him play, appointed him court musician, and while under his patronage in Madrid, Corbetti wrote and published his first work entitled: *Guitarra espanol y sus differencias de sonos.* After several years at the Court of Madrid, he made a tour through France and Germany, and during his travels performed before the Duke of Mantua who recognised his genius and engaged him chamber musician for a period of twelve months, and then recommended him to the favour of Louis XIV of France. It was by the influence of the Duke of Mantua that he was appointed court musician to Louis and he remained several years, his talent exciting the greatest admiration in Paris and Versailles. While court musician in France, Corbetti performed before Charles II of England and shortly after the latter's accession was invited and received an appointment in the Queen's household—an engagement which entailed a very liberal salary. The Court of England, during the reign of Charles II was described by a celebrated historian as " the disgrace of the country and the ridicule of foreigners—the King and his courtiers were entirely given up to gambling and love making." Corbetti, the court musician, was a great favourite with the King and his admirers, his playing and singing being a continual source of pleasure and amusement. His remarkable guitar playing so entranced the royal auditors, that to be able to play the guitar was considered the most fashionable accomplishment. Francisco Corbetti's introduction of the guitar into royal circles in England, and the extraordinary influence he exercised over society by his playing, is graphically described in the *Memoirs of the Cou.t of Grammont,* edited by Sir Walter Scott, and from which the following is an extract: " The court, as we have mentioned before, was an entire scene of gallantry and amusement, with all the politeness and magnificence which the inclinations of a prince naturally addicted to tenderness and pleasure could suggest ; the beauties were desirous of charming, and the men endeavoured to please ; all studied to set themselves off to the best advantage ; some distinguished themselves by dancing, others by show and magnificence ; some by their wit, many by their amours, but few by their constancy. There was a certain foreigner at court, famous for the guitar, he had a genius for music, and he was the only man who could make anything of the guitar ; his style of playing was so full of grace and tenderness that he could have given harmony to the most discordant instruments. The truth is, nothing was too difficult for this foreigner. The King's relish for his compositions had brought the instrument so much into vogue that every person played on it, well or ill ; and you were as sure to see a guitar on a lady's toilet as rouge or patches. The Duke of York played upon it tolerably well, and the Earl of Arran like Francisco himself. This Francisco had composed a saraband which either charmed or infatuated every person ; for the whole guitarery at court were trying at it, and God knows what a universal strumming there was. The Duke of York, pretending not to be perfect in it, desired Lord Arran to play it to him. Lady Chesterfield had the best guitar in England. The Earl of Arran, who was desirous of playing his best, conducted His Royal Highness to his sister's apartments; she was lodged at court at her father's, the Duke of Ormond, and this wonderful guitar was lodged there, too. Whether this visit had been preconcerted or not I do not pretend to say, but it is certain that they found both the lady and the guitar at home; they likewise there found Lord Chesterfield so much surprised at this unexpected visit, that it was a considerable time before he thought of rising from his seat to receive them with due respect. Jealousy, like a malignant vapour, now seized upon his brain; a thousand suspicions, blacker than ink, took possession of his imagination and were continually increasing; for, whilst the brother played upon the guitar to the Duke, the sister ogled and accompanied him with her eyes, as if the coast had been clear and there had been no enemy to observe them. This saraband was at least repeated twenty times; the Duke declared it was played to perfection; Lady Chesterfield found no fault with the composition, but her husband, who clearly perceived he was the person played upon, thought it a most detestable piece." Even to the last, King Charles manifested his partiality for Corbetti's guitar playing and singing, for he was entertained on the evening of Sunday, February 1, 1685, in Whitehall Palace, surrounded by his courtiers, a few days previous to his death. Corbetti remained in public favour in England till the revolution of 1688, when, compelled to flee, he found refuge in France, where he died some years later regretted by all who knew him. He was a skilful teacher of the guitar, and, in addition to instructing numerous members of the royal household and court, he taught De Vise, De Vabray, and Medard, the three most talented of his pupils. Medard was the author of the following curious French epitaph, and although the lines are in none good style, they clearly indicate the admiration with which Corbetti was esteemed by his contemporaries:

Ci-git l'Amphion de nos jours
Francisque, cet homme si rare,
Qui fit parler a la guitare
Le vrai language des amours.

A free translation is:

Here lies the Amphion of our days,
Francis Corbet, this man of rare quality,
Who made his guitar speak
The very language of love's jollity.

Cornet, Julius, born at Santa Candida in the Italian Tyrol in 1793, and died in Berlin, October 2, 1860, won a brilliant reputation in Germany as a dramatic vocalist and actor. Predestined by his parents for the legal profession, his love of music was so strong that he was allowed to study the art under Salieri, in Vienna, and afterwards continued his musical education in Italy. At the outset of his artistic career he created quite a furore as tenor vocalist with his guitar, and then jointly with Muhling undertook the management of the Hamburg Theatre, until the great fire of 1842. He made an artistic tour through

Sweden and Holland, and at one time was principal tenor in Auber's *Muette de Portici,* the libretto of which he skilfully translated into German, and he performed the role of Masaniello with conspicuous success. From 1854-8 he was director of the Hofoper Theatre, Vienna ; but his hasty temper could endure no interference from higher authorities, and he was forced to resign. Cornet was then appointed director of the Victoria Theatre, Berlin, but died before the building was completed. He was intimate with Schubert who mentions him in his correspondence ; he, with other of Salieri's pupils, took part on June 16, 1816, the fiftieth anniversary of their teacher's arrival in Vienna. Cornet was a guitarist of rare attainment. The A.M.Z. reported a concert given September 8, 1818, when Cornet was a great success and particular mention was made of one of his items, a *Romance,* by Th. Korner, with guitar accompaniment. He published several works for the instrument, *Lyre for Singing for Amateurs,* with guitar, and others issued by Christiani, Hamburg. Under his name there appeared in 1849 an excellent volume entitled: *The opera in Germany.*

Costa, Pasquale Mario, a nephew of Sir Michael Costa, was born at Taranto, Italy, July 24, 1858, and after musical education at Naples Conservatoire migrated to Paris. He wrote many songs but is known principally by his pantomime, in three acts *A pierrot's life.* It was while living in Paris in very precarious circumstances that this play was conceived and improvised during 1892-3. It proved an instantaneous success, in Paris, then Florence and ultimately at numerous theatres throughout the world. In 1896 it was produced at the Prince of Wales' Theatre, London, when the musical press recorded: "A most distinct attraction is Signor Costa's delightfully melodious, characteristic and exquisitely harmonised score—a worthy pendant to Wormser's *L'enfant prodigue,* music—higher praise it is impossible to give." One of the outstanding and most pleasing effects in the score, is the *Serenade* for mandolin with the orchestra which occurs in the first and third acts. From Paris Costa visited London where he was esteemed as tenor vocalist singing his own songs, and later retired to Rome. He wrote other operettas, pantomimes, songs and mandolin music, the most well known, a *Brilliant Fantasia for two mandolins and piano.* His compositions were published principally by Ricordi. Chappell, London, published a few of his light orchestral compositions and the serenade for mandolin solo from *A pierrot's life.* The *Serenade,* mandolin solo, was also issued by Rowies and P. Beuscher, both in Paris and the entire pantomime was transcribed for full mandolin orchestra by Gino Neri and performed October 3, 1926, in Theatre Verdi, Ferrara, by the Royal Circolo Margherita of sixty performers under their conductor, Christani. This Royal Mandolin Orchestra officiated at the funeral obsequies of their patron, Queen Margherita in Ferrara Cathedral. The *Death of Ase* and *Ave Maria,* were performed during the elevation with intense devotional feeling. Costa wrote a few other compositions for the mandolin, the most popular were a *Brilliant Fantasia* on *'Oje Caruli' for two mandolins and piano*, published by Ricordi, Milan, and *Fleurs d'amour for mandolin band*, published by Beuscher, Paris.

Coste, Napoleon, a French guitar virtuoso and composer was born June 28, 1806, in a village, department of Doubs, and died in Paris, February 17, 1883. The son of an officer in the imperial army, he displayed an inclination for military career so was placed with a methodical and strict tutor; but when he was eleven years was stricken with a very severe and protracted illness. His parents now realised the impossibility of a military career for his constitution was ruined. At the age of six he had commenced to play the guitar, an instrument of which his mother was exceedingly fond and on which she was a capable performer. The family removed to Valenciennes shortly after his convalescence and in this city, at the age of eighteen, Coste gave his first guitar instruction and appeared as guitar soloist at the concerts of the Philharmonic Society. In 1828 he performed in concerts with the guitar virtuoso Luigi Sagrini; together they played Giuliani's Op. 130, *Variations Concertantes for two guitars.* Two years later he removed to Paris to study under Sor and then essayed to make a name as guitarist. He took up residence in Faubourg St. Germain and in a short time obtained fame as soloist and teacher. His concert performances were warmly praised by the press and patronised by the elite of society. In Paris he came in contact with the most renowned masters of the instrument—Aguado, Sor, Carulli and Carcassi, and it was the personal and intimate friendship of these musicians which inspired him to concentrate more seriously than ever on the higher branches of his art and he gave the following ten years to the study of harmony and counterpoint. Up to this time he had not published any compositions, but now, in 1840, when he was master of harmony he began to issue his works. They did not, however, prove of pecuniary advantage, for the popularity of the guitar was on the wane, being superseded by the piano. In the International Music Competitions, sponsored by the Russian nobleman, M. Makaroff, then resident in Brussels, Coste submitted four compositions and was awarded the second prize from among thirty-one competitors; the first being awarded to J. K. Mertz, the renowned guitar virtuoso. Some few years after, when engaged at a concert, Coste had the misfortune to fall on the stairs and broke his right arm. His right hand now lost its suppleness and to his grief and disappointment was unable to again perform in public. Coste manifested the sincerest enthusiasm for his instrument and was one of the most renowned guitar virtuosi and composers for the guitar that France has produced and deserves a honourable place amongst her musical sons. His guitar was strung by him and bequeathed to the Museum of the National Conservatoire of Music, Paris. It is of extra large dimensions, is tuned a fifth lower than the ordinary guitar and the model and system of tuning are Coste's idea. It is a curious and unique instrument with a lengthy finger rest, elevated from the table; the fingerboard is luxuriously decorated with inlaid pearl designs and the edges of the body are inlaid with pearl and ebony. Coste published about sixty compositions which are characterised by original charm and vigour; the influence of his renowned teacher is noticeable in all his work. He submitted Op. 27, 28, 29 and 30 to the judges of the Makaroff competition held in Brussels in 1856, was awarded the second prize, and commissioned by the publishers of Sor's Method to compile a revised edition. This he did and augmented it with a notice of the additional, or seventh string, as used and advocated by Sor and Legnani and it was issued by Lemoine, Paris. Giuliani's Op. 36, *Concerto for guitar and orchestra* was a favourite concert item of Coste and he wrote a second guitar part in substitution of the orchestral score, thus converting it as a duo for two guitars. Coste was principally his own publisher, and he also published some of the works of Sor. His best known are Op. 12, *Concert Rondo*; Op. 27, *Twelve Waltzes*; Op. 28, *Fantasia*; Op. 29, *La Chasse*; Op. 30, *Grand Serenade*; Op. 31, *Dramatic Fantasia*; Op. 39, *Minuet*; Op. 45, *Diversion*; Op. 46, *Favourite Waltzes*; Op. 51, *Collection of solos*; Op. 52, *The Guitarists' Book of Gold*; Op. 53, *Album of Six solos,* the *Reverie* of this series is quite original; all the foregoing were composed for guitar alone and are of a certain degree of difficulty and several have been re-published by the International League of Guitarists of Munich.

Cottin. Two brothers and a sister of this name, all of whom were popular teachers and composers for the mandolin and guitar, were living in Paris during the latter part of the nineteenth century and were resident in Rue Bremontier in 1912.

Alfred, born December, 1863, at Paris, died there January 18, 1923, commenced his musical education by playing the violin, which he discarded for the mandolin and guitar. He was a pupil on the guitar of the master Tarrega, who dedicated to him his well-known tremolo study, *Recuerdos de la Alhambra.* He was the conductor of a well trained estudiantina (mandolin band) whose artistic performances were in constant demand, and the services of Cottin were in request as an adjudicator at numerous musical contests. For his public work in the service of music he was honoured by the government award of Officier de l'instruction Publique. He was the composer of many light compositions and transcriptions which were popular in their day and were published in Paris. The library of the Internationalen Gitarristen Verband, Munich, has an original manuscript of a *Trio for three guitars.*

Alfred Cottin

Jules, the brother, devoted himself entirely to the mandolin and compiled a *Method for the mandolin* in two books with French and English text; Various studies, exercises and arrangements of light compositions for mandolin alone, with piano, guitar or estudiantina were published by Lemoine, Paris, and Marcel Jumade, Paris.

Madeline, the sister, born December 18, 1876, was also the author of a *Method for the mandolin* which she dedicated to her brother Alfred, the guitarist. It was published in French, Spanish and Portuguese by Marcel Jumade, Paris, and a supplement containing duos for two mandolins and a *Method for the guitar* appeared later. These two methods were exceedingly popular, the publishers stated that one hundred thousand and fifty thousand copies respectively had been sold up to the year 1914. Madeline Cottin took an active part in the Tarrega centenary held in Paris, Nov. 1952.

Cowen, Sir Frederick Hymen, was born January 29, 1852, at Kingston, Jamacia, and died in London in 1935. He was brought to England when four years of age. He studied music in London and continued in Berlin, then Leipzig, under Hauptmann—a guitar player and composer for the guitar. Cowen has composed an opera, cantatas, symphonies, chamber music and songs. In his cantata *The Corsair,* composed for the Birmingham Festival of 1876 and also in that of *Harold,* he uses the guitar. Mme. Sidney Pratten was guitarist at the Birmingham Festival. Cowen wrote many songs, several of which attained national fame and a few were composed with guitar accompaniment. *In a chimney corner,* published by Chappell, London, was the most popular of these. Cowen was knighted in 1911 and a sketch of his life appeared in the Musical Times of November, 1898.

Craeijvanger, K. A., born Utrecht, Holland, 1817 and died there July 30, 1868, was a Dutch virtuoso on the guitar and violin, appeared with success in his native land. He was director of various important musical societies and in 1852 was conductor of the musical festival of Cleves and that of Utrecht the following year. Among his published compositions are *Fantasias, etc., for guitar solo, Quartets for strings,* which include the guitar and songs and choruses with guitar accompaniment; but his compositions are unknown beyond his native land.

Crescentini, Girolamo, born February 22, 1766, near Urbino, Italy, and died April 24, 1846, in Naples, was a male soprano and song composer whose fame was first acclaimed in 1783 in Florence. He came to London in 1785 where he lived until 1787, then visited Paris and Vienna. When he was appointed musical director in Naples, in 1825, he returned to his native land. He composed many vocal works with guitar and they are recorded by Eitner and also Riemann. *Twelve airettes with guitar accompaniment* were issued by Artaria, Vienna, and others similar by Simrock, Bonn.

Curschmann, Friedrich, born June 21, 1805, at Berlin and died August 24, 1841, in Danzig. He commenced his career as a law student, but his dominating inclination was musical, so in 1825, he became a pupil of Spohr and Hauptmann in Cassel, both of whom played and composed for the guitar. When he had completed his studies he removed to Berlin where he was esteemed as a singer, teacher, and composer. Spohr wrote: "Curschman possessed a pleasing baritone voice, sang songs to his guitar accompaniment, thus enlivening the culture of the art and becoming a favourite of their musical world." He is remembered by his songs, many of which composed with guitar accompaniment are fully enumerated in A.M.Z., and also recorded by Riemann. His memoirs edited by Meissner were published in 1899.

Czernuschka, Fritz, born July 26, 1883, at Brunn, was trained for the scholastic profession and was employed as a schoolmaster in his native town until 1905, when he devoted himself entirely to music. He has composed for the guitar alone and in combination with wind and stringed instruments. Several of his musical compositions were published in the music journal, Guitarrefreund, and he was a popular and frequent broadcaster from Brunn. His most widely known works are, *Studies for guitar,* No. 4 of which he dedicated to his brother Charles; *Moderato,* a ballad for the guitar; *Abenlied,* a trio for violin, alto and guitar and a *Gavotte* in A major, dedicated to the guitarist-composer Walter Huttl.

Cristofaro, Ferdinando de, born of respectable parents at Naples in 1846, died in Paris, April 18, 1890. He received his musical education in the Naples Conservatoire, the piano being his principal instrument and had his life been spared, his fame as a virtuoso on this instrument would have exceeded his achievements as a mandolinist. He was entirely self-taught on the mandolin and distinguished himself at an early age by his performances on this instrument. To the Neapolitans, Cristofaro introduced a new and completely advanced method of playing—accustomed as they were to seeing the instrument in the hands of strolling players and used chiefly for accompanying popular songs. The classical compositions, executed by Cristofaro, caused unbounded enthusiasm, astonishment and admiration and his accomplishment spread rapidly throughout his native land. He appeared in all the important cities and was then invited to Paris. He arrived in 1882, and was at once acknowledged the premier mandolinist of the day. He obtained a widespread and enviable reputation, and as teacher his services were in constant demand by French aristocracy and as mandolin soloist was the favourite artist in the salons of the intelligencia. Cristofaro was associated in his public performances with the most renowned musicians. M. Gounod acted as his accompanist upon several occasions. In 1888 he visited London and met with his usual success; he was appointed conductor of the Ladies' Guitar and Mandolin Band, also fully occupied teaching. He repeated his visit to London the following season, when he gave mandolin recitals in which Denza —the renowned song writer, a native of Naples also, and a composer for the mandolin—and other eminent musicians, took part. Cristofaro made arrangements to reside each season in London as conductor and teacher; but this visit was fated to be his last. He had concluded arrangements to resume lessons during Easter, but on April 18, 1890, died in Paris from ptomaine poisoning, after two days illness, caused by eating ices during the interval at a concert. It was stated that Cristofaro is interred in Pere-Lachaise cemetery, but exhaustive enquiries by the author, prove the assertion only partially correct; he was interred there and later exhumed and taken to his native land. As a mandolinist he takes high rank, as a gentleman and sound musician he was esteemed, and particularly for his sincere work in endeavouring to elevate the science and art of mandolin playing. He it was, who introduced the instrument to the English public and brought about its exceeding popularity. As an executant, he was in many respects unsurpassed, his tone was remarkable for its exquisite tenderness and delicacy —his expression and nuances were unapproachable—and his *tours de force* were models of artistic excellence. The higher mechanical attributes and other effects peculiar to the instrument, were by Cristofaro brought to that perfection, which classed him among the virtuosi of the time. As a soloist, or in part playing, or at the piano as accompanist, he well knew how to exhibit the mandolin to its best advantage. He had performed before the principal Courts of Europe and honoured by the appointment of mandolinist to the King of Italy. His favourite mandolin, constructed from his own specifications, of superb workmanship, was by that eminent maker Luigi Salsedo of Naples. In 1881 he had made a name in the musical world as a composer, and in that year several of his works were awarded high honours in Milan. The following is an extract from the Italian music journal, Revista Musicale: " Neapolitans will doubtless remember Signor Ferdinando Cristofaro, the greatest of mandolinists, and, in fact, the only artist who has been able to bring this instrument up to the high standard of importance that it today enjoys. Signor de Cristofaro was not only an elegant executant, but a composer of no mean order; and if confirmation were needed in support of this, his compositions would lend ready witness. Not contented with the well-merited success that he had obtained, Signor de Cristofaro felt that he must reach to higher fame. He conceived the idea of writing a melodramatic opera, the libretto of which was supplied by the renowned poet, de Lauzieres. The plot was laid in Venice in the time of the republic, and the title *Almina da Volterra.* At this composition he worked for two years, with a successful result, which was duly chronicled by the French journals. Signor de Cristofaro was an artist who, though absent from his native land, reflected the genius of his country, and honoured the city that gave him birth. He was none the less esteemed, and his talents appreciated by a people whose artistic mind is by some, considered not so fine as that of the land of the Sunny South, but who, living in a colder and sterner climate, could appreciate and honour a man for his worth and talents, such as are possessed in so marked a degree by the subject of this brief sketch." Cristofaro was the author of one of the most comprehensive and artistic methods ever published for the mandolin. It is in two volumes, and issued in five languages, English, French, Italian, Spanish and Portugese, treats of the instrument fully, and is illustrated by numerous diagrams. It commences with the elements of the theory of music, and all the exercises are melodious and arranged with a definite object, they are well graded and admirably suited for pupil and teacher, the majority written as duets for two mandolins. Several of these studies deserve notice for their beauty of melody and form, particularly the *Andante maestoso, Larghetto, Andante religioso,* in double stopping, and *Allegro giusto,* fugue style, all in the second volume. The method was published in November, 1884, by Lemoine, Paris, and it had reached the twelfth edition previous to the death of its author, in 1890. Cristofaro had compiled a method for the mandolin previously, when living in Naples, before he was thirty years of age which was published by Cottrau of that city in 1873. His compositions are written in the orthodox style, as for the violin, and not the modern unaccompanied, full harmony solo. They do not abound in great technical difficulties ; but require of the performer a firm control of both instrument and plectrum to produce the singing quality and full body of tone necessary for their interpretation. Without exception, all his compositions abound in pleasing, spontaneous melodies. His last composition, a *Serenade for solo voice and chorus, with accompaniment of mandolins and guitars,* is original, novel, and exceedingly effective ; the autograph manuscript was in the possession of the Ladies' Mandolin and Guitar Band, London. The following are among his principal published compositions: Op. 21, 22 and 23 are *Transcriptions for mandolin and piano,* published by Ricordi, Milan ; Op. 25 to 39 and about fifty others, Lemoine, Paris ; Op. 41, 44, 45 and 46 are *Divertisements and arrangements for mandolin and piano,* Ricordi, Milan. Op. 30 is dedicated to Queen Margherita, and *Bolero,* Op. 34 he dedicated to the mandolin virtuoso and composer Constantino Bertucci. His songs with guitar, Op. 35 and 48, and piano solos were issued by Ricordi.

DAMAS, Tomas, a concert guitarist, orchestral conductor and composer was born at Castilla la Vieja, Spain, during the middle of the nineteenth century. Cimadevilla states that he was a pupil of Tarrega. In 1885 he was orchestral conductor in Valladolid later removing to Madrid where he became known as a concert guitarist and composer. He was intimate with the guitar virtuoso Julian Arcas to whom he dedicated several compositions. About a hundred light compositions and transcriptions of national folk melodies for solo guitar were published in Madrid as were the following methods, *Method for the Guitar* issued in 1865 and described as a *New method* and a second method entitled *Complete and Progressive Method.* He also compiled a *Singing Method with guitar accompaniment* and a

Method for the Bandurria (Spanish mandolin). A few of his guitar solos have been reprinted by Schlesinger, Berlin.

Darr, Adam, an eminent guitar virtuoso, zitherist and composer, born at Schweinfurt, Germany, in 1811, and died October 2, 1866, at Augsburg. As a child he was endowed with precocious musical talents and mastered the flute and violin ; his extraordinary ability on these two instruments enabled him to appear as a prodigy with success. This early public training proved the commencement of a musical career which won him numerous triumphs in his prolonged travels, in after years, as a guitar virtuoso. It was not, however, until he was eighteen that he took up the study of the guitar ; but it became his favourite instrument, and by his natural musical aptitude and perseverance, he soon obtained such a command over the guitar that he was appearing as soloist in his native town. Meeting with encouragement he extended his sphere of operations and for sixteen years travelled as a guitar virtuoso and vocalist, during which period he performed before the royal courts of France, Belgium, Holland, Sweden and Russia, winning the applause of monarchs, the esteem and admiration of musicians, and eulogistic notices in the A.M.Z. Darr was the recipient of many valuable souvenirs and decorations conferred during his tours. For three years he resided in St. Petersburg as virtuoso and teacher of the guitar, and then, desirous of visiting his native land, he accepted a position as private tutor and music master in an English family, resident in Wurzburg. This occupation suited his inclinations admirably and he spoke of this as the happiest period of his life. But Wurzburg became still dearer to him by his associations with another guitar virtuoso, Kapellmeister Frederick Brand, both were highly trained musicians ; they were enthusiastic in their admiration of the guitar, and a close friendship existed, severed only by death. They performed together in Wurzburg, in public and private, and then toured central and southern Germany. In numerous public and private concerts they astonished audiences by their wonderful playing, in solos and duos for two guitars, and also in vocal solos and duos, with guitar accompaniment. The sincere admiration which preceded them from town to town and the enthusiastic receptions greeting their appearances, gave their tour the semblance of a series of triumphant marches. At the conclusion of their tour, Darr formed a friendship with the renowned zither player, Johann Petzmayer, Kammer-virtuoso to Duke Maximilian of Bavaria, and through Petzmayer's influence, Darr made a study of the zither. Petzmayer was also a guitarist who published many pieces for zither and guitar in Munich. In 1846 Darr settled in Munich where he was highly esteemed as a guitar and zither teacher, but ten years later removed to Augsburg where he was also occupied in teaching and compiling his celebrated and exhaustive method for the zither, which was published in 1866. This method, in three volumes, is still popular and esteemed because of its thoroughness, although published so long since. In addition to this method, Darr was a composer of solos, duos and trios for guitars; all his music is written with a true sense of the potentialities and limitations of the instrument, many were performed by Darr and his pupils in their numerous concerts. His superior education and profound knowledge of music gave him an exalted position in the musical and literary circles of his city, and it was a shock when it became known that through domestic trouble he had taken his life by drowning. The sad and unexpected event cast a deep gloom over his most intimate friends, some of whom, through the instrumentality of Otto Hammerer, an enthusiastic guitarist, erected a monument to his memory in the cemetery of Augsburg. Darr was a prolific composer, his works were published principally by Ed. Hoenes, Treves. His compositions abound in sentiment, permeated by a sad, pathetic strain, while his harmonies are rich and varied. He was the author of an operetta, *Robinson,* which was successful in Europe and America, several numbers from which he transcribed for guitar solo and others for voice and guitar. Many of his compositions remain in manuscript, a number were in the possession of his friend, Otto Hammerer of Augsburg, who gave permission to the International League of Guitarists of Munich to publish them. They are: *Le congé* a larghetto for guitar solo; duos for two guitars, *Adagio* and *Allegro moderato,* composed June, 1850—the solo was dedicated to his friend Hammerer; Duos, Nos. 1 and 2, for two guitars; *Duo concertante for guitar; Fantasia for violoncello and guitar; Four tonstücke for zither and guitar; Letze fantasia on German folk songs for guitar solo; Tyrolese ditto; Fantasia on 'Der Abschied v.d. Bergen,' Four Andantes for guitar; Study in C minor; Study in E minor; Two Rondolettos for guitar* and numerous vocal items with guitar. The International League, mentioned previously, own the original manuscript of *Tiroler Volkslied, guitar solo.*

Decker-Schenk, Johann, was born at Vienna in 1826 and died in St. Petersburg, October 19, 1899. He was the son of Friedrich Schenk, a guitar maker, who for some time was foreman in the workshops of the celebrated guitar maker, Staufer, Vienna, and who commenced his own business about the year 1849. Decker-Schenk was taught to play the guitar by his father and at the same time he also learned singing. He played before Duke Max of Bavaria and other royal courts at an early age and subsequently joined an itinerant operatic company and with his wife, a member of the troupe, they visited Russia. For some years he was a theatre director, but after the death of his wife, he abandoned the theatrical profession, and from 1861 resided in St. Petersburg as virtuoso and teacher of the guitar and mandolin and married a Russian. He was very popular and esteemed as a teacher and trained many pupils who became known in the musical world, chief of whom was Lebedeff. Decker-Schenk was a versatile composer, the author of several well-known Russian operettas which enjoyed continued popularity, particularly *Frena* and *The soldier and the girl.* He compiled a *Theoretical and Practical Guitar School* in two volumes, which was issued in Russia and also by Zimmerman, Leipzig ; music for one, two, and four guitars, and mandolin and piano. He was an artist beloved by all who knew him and played and composed for the Russian guitar of seven strings. One of his original manuscript compositions for solo guitar is in the library of the Internationalen Guitarristen Verband, Munich. In 1899 his many pupils erected a monument to his memory in the cemetery of St. Petersburg. His daughter Anette was also a concert guitarist.

De Filippis, Carlo, contemporary, born Ariano, Italy, during the early part of the twentieth century. He commenced to play the mandolin at the age of six and the guitar a few years later, after which he was engaged professionally in an orchestra. He emigrated to U.S.A. when fifteen and resumed his musical activities immediately. He has conducted several mandolin orchestras of note, namely, Newark, New York Plectrum Orchestra and Manhattan Mandolin Orchestra. He is a frequent broadcaster as mandolinist and was engaged to form the ensemble for *Neapolitan Nights* produced by the N.B.C. As a composer he has published several unaccompanied mandolin solos of which *Souvenir* was dedicated to the author of this volume. De Filippis is living in New Jersey, as a teacher of his instrument and esteemed as one of the foremost exponents of the mandolin in U.S.A.

Della Maria, Pierre Antoine Dominique, a mandolin virtuoso and dramatic composer, born at Marseilles in 1768, and died suddenly in the streets of Paris, March 9, 1800. He was the son of Italian parents, his father Domenico, a roving mandolin player, who, with his wife and friends formed an itinerant company of musicians—mandolinists, guitarists and vocalists. During their wanderings they visited Marseilles, where their playing and singing attracted unusual attention and approbation, and this success induced Della Maria and his wife to remain there, where they commenced to teach their instruments, and during this period the subject of this sketch was born. He was taught the mandolin when a child, and later received instruction on the violoncello, appearing as an infant prodigy on both instruments. When he was eighteen, Della Maria wrote his first opera, representations of which were given in the theatre of his native city, and caused great surprise among the musicians of Marseilles, for, apart from the inseparable inexperiences of a first production, it bore the indelible stamp of the creation of a genius. After this success, Della Maria travelled through Italy as mandolinist and violoncellist, but did not continue his musical education until he came under the influence of Paisiello in Naples, some years later, when Della Maria was violoncellist and mandolinist in the orchestra of the Royal Chapel, under the direction of Paisiello. Della Maria, conscious of his lack of knowledge, associated with the concert master, and realising his weakness, studied for a period under him ; the commencement of a lifelong friendship. Paisiello manifested more than ordinary interest in the mandolin virtuoso; he had proved his appreciation of the musical value of the mandolin by its inclusion in the score of *The barber of Seville,* written in St. Petersburg, a few years previously. During the last ten years of his residence in Italy, Della Maria wrote light works for numerous secondary theatres. Here he produced six operas, three of which were fairly successful, and one, *Il maestro di capella,* exceedingly so, bringing fame to its author. In 1796, Della Maria returned to Marseilles, arriving in Paris the same year, absolutely unknown; however, in a short time his reputation was such that he was the guest and friend of the most renowned literary and musical circles. Fate shortened and smoothed for him the rugged paths by which men ascend the heights of fame. The poet Duval wrote a complimentary article in the Decade Philosophique concerning the young artist, and later the two were intimate friends working in collaboration. Duval records that a personal friend, to whom Della Maria had been introduced suggested that he write some poem for the musician, and, acting upon this request made an appointment with Della Maria. The interview was the commencement of an intimate friendship, for, in Duval's words, the classical, soulful countenance of Della Maria, and his original and natural demeanour inspired a confidence that proved to be entirely justified. At this juncture, Duval had just completed *The prisoner,* commissioned by the Theatre Francais; but his ardent desire to gratify the request of Della Maria, decided him to write an opera, so, after alterations and additions the work was transformed to a lyric comedy. Within eight days of the receipt of the libretto, Della Maria had composed the music; the artists of the opera manifested enthusiasm and delight in the work and its success was assured. This was in 1798, it was published by Breitkopf & Härtel, Leipzig, and established the name of Della Maria as an operatic composer of renown and he immediately brought out six other operas—for his works were very popular with Parisians. The brilliant success of *The prisoner* was due to two primary causes, the first, the melodiousness and simplicity of the vocal parts, under a subservient and subdued skilful orchestration, and the second factor, his most fortunate choice of artists responsible for the principal characters. The actresses Mlle. St. Aubin and Mlle. Dugazon, found in the opera, parts analogous to their natural dispositions, and their names became popular throughout France by their interpretations. In this opera, Della Maria did not rise to extraordinary powerful conceptions; but his style was original which individuality is noticeable in all his compositions. Unfortunately, his style weakened in several of his later operas; the following were also successful, *The uncle valet,* one act; *The ancient castle,* three acts; but *Jacquot* (The school for mothers), three acts, the first representation in 1799, and *The house of Marais,* three acts were short lived. *La fausse Duegne* (The false wife), in three acts, was left unfinished by the sudden death of Della Maria, but in 1802 it was completed and staged by Blangini. All the above mentioned, with several others, were composed during four years and in this brief time Della Maria appears to have exhausted his natural resources. Being of a genial and sociable disposition, the young and brilliant artist made many friends. Duval the poet was one of the most sincere—they had just completed arrangements for retiring to the country together, intending to write a new opera, when Della Maria returning home, March 9, 1800, seized by a stroke, fell in the Rue St. Honore. He was assisted to an adjacent house by a passing stranger, where he expired a few hours later without regaining consciousness. As no trace of his identity was obtainable, police enquiries were instituted, and several days elapsed before his friends could be informed ; so at the premature age of thirty-two, the career of this brilliant artist ended. Della Maria was a mandolin virtuoso who wrote much for his instrument, as did his teacher, Paisiello, who made frequent use of it in his orchestral scores. Several of his church compositions were published by Costallat, Paris. He left many unpublished works, consisting of church and instrumental compositions and mandolin sonatas, which with his mandolin and violoncello, were preserved in Marseilles.

Denis or **Denies,** Pierre, born at Provence, France, during the early part of the eighteenth century, was a renowned mandolin virtuoso and teacher established in Paris. In 1780 he was music master in a ladies' seminary in Saint Cyr. Denis was an educated man, a sound musician, and the author of several music treatises. He compiled a *Method for the mandolin,* which was published in Paris in 1792 and also the author of the following which appeared in Paris: *Four Collections of Airs for the Mandolin ;* a *New System of Practical Music,* issued in 1747, and a *Treatise on Composition*, published by Boyer, Paris in 1773. Denis also made a French translation of Tartini, under the title of: *Traité des agrémens de la musique, composé par le célèbre Guizeppe Tartini à Padua, et traduit par le Sigr. P. Denis.* This was published by M. de la Chevardier, Paris. The Encyclopédie Larousse, Paris, states " A musician of the eighteenth century, Pierre Denis, born in Provence, and who was music master to the ladies of Saint Cyr, about 1780. He devoted himself to the popularization of the mandolin, of which instrument he was a consummate artist, and with this intent published a method for learning the instrument, and also Four Collections of little Airs for it."

Denza, Luigi, an Italian musician born at Castellamare, near Naples in 1846, who settled in London as a teacher of singing, and died there January 26, 1922. He was a pupil of Naples Conservatoire, came to London in 1879, won fame as a song writer and in 1899 was appointed a professor at the Royal Academy of Music, London, continuing as such for his last twenty-five years. He was an able mandolinist and guitarist and has published compositions for these instruments. He also used them in his opera *Wallenstein,* produced in 1876 and in some of the more than six hundred songs which he wrote. The most widely known of his songs in which he employs these instruments are: *Ricordo di Quisisana,* a serenata for solo voice and chorus, with accompaniments of 1st and 2nd mandolins, mandolas and guitars, dedicated to the Marchioness Laura di Noailles, published by Ricordi, Milan; *Fior del serenata* for voice with two mandolins and piano, and *Come to me,* valse for two mandolins, mandola and guitar, also published by Ricordi. A *Nocturne for mandolin and piano* was published by Ascherberg, London, and there were several other compositions for mandolin and piano published by Robert Cocks, London. Denza's song, *Funiculi-Funicula,* is popular throughout the world.

L. Denza

Derosiers, Nicolas. A French musician who resided in Holland during the end of the seventeenth century. In his later years he was chamber musician to the Electress Palatine at her palace in Mannheim. Very little is recorded of his life, but among his compositions are to be found several for the guitar: *Twelve overtures for guitar solo,* Op. 5, published in 1688 at The Hague, and a Method for learning the guitar, which was translated in French and published by Ballard in 1689 under the title of *Nouveaux principes de la guitare.* A suite of eight pieces for the guitar angelique with other instruments is recorded by Zuth, who also mentions other similar compositions.

Derwort, George Henry, a German musician and guitarist who came to England during the commencement of the nineteenth century, remained for many years, and enjoyed a reputation as guitar soloist and a popular teacher. He was living in London in 1824, and giving guitar recitals there in 1830. He made several visits to his native land where he appeared in concerts, but was teaching singing and his instrument again in London as late as 1835. He composed numerous simple pieces and arrangements for the guitar which enjoyed a certain amount of popularity at the time. The following were the most favoured of his compositions: Op. 7, 11, 12, 13, 16, 21, 22 and 27 *Themes with variations for guitar solo,* were published by Falter and also by Sidler, Munich; Paez, Berlin; and Paine and Hopkins, London. *Eighteen pieces for guitar solo,* entitled: *Dolce et utile,* were among others published by Wessell, London; *Progressive guitar accompaniments* to favourite Italian, French, German and Spanish songs, published by Paine and Hopkins, London, who also issued his *New Method for learning the Spanish Guitar.* Derwort also arranged many of the popular compositions of the day for guitar and piano, and many of the same class as trios for flute, violin and guitar. His songs with the guitar were published by Baumgartner, Leipzig, and Ewer and Johanning, London. During the years 1812 to 1815 the A.M.Z. records his various compositions for the guitar.

Diabelli, Anton, born September 6, 1781, at Mattsee, near Salzburg, and died in Vienna, April 7, 1858. He was an eminent pianist and guitarist and a very popular composer and publisher for both these instruments and also of church music. He received his first musical instruction as chorister in the Monastery of Michaelbeurn, and continued his studies some years later in the Cathedral of Salzburg. Being intended by his parents for the priesthood, he was sent to the Latin School of Munich, and in 1800, entered the Monastery of Reichenhaslach. Michael Haydn had superintended his first attempts at musical composition, and he had profited largely from his association and study with this master. Diabelli's talent for composition was manifested at a very early age, and he attracted considerable attention by his compositions for one or more voices, before he had reached his twentieth year. The guitar was his principal instrument, and these early vocal compositions were written with guitar accompaniment. When the monasteries of Bavaria were secularised in 1803, he abandoned his intention of taking holy orders, and decided to devote himself entirely to music and composition, for which purpose he visited Vienna, where he was already known by his vocal compositions, and was warmly received by Joseph Hadyn. In a comparatively short time, Diabelli had established a wide reputation as a popular and able teacher of the piano and guitar and soon acquired both wealth and fame. Grove says: " He soon became a popular teacher of the pianoforte and guitar, made money enough to become partner with Peter Cappi the music publisher in 1818 and in 1824 the firm became Diabelli & Co." He associated with the most celebrated musicians of Vienna, chief of whom was Joseph Haydn, brother of his teacher, Michael of Salzburg, who manifested a kindly interest in the young composer, and the advice received from this celebrated master was of inestimable advantage to him in after years. About 1807 Diabelli became acquainted with Mauro Giuliani, the guitar virtuoso, soon after the arrival of the latter in Vienna, and the two musicians, of about the same age, both intensely musical, and interested in the guitar became warm friends. Giuliani had distinguished himself in the musical world by his extraordinary guitar playing, his mastery of the instrument far exceeded that of Diabelli ; but the latter possessed a most thorough knowledge of music and was also an excellent performer on the pianoforte. They were soon engaged in writing compositions for guitar and piano, and appeared in public, playing their duets for these instruments. The guitar at the time was the instrument par excellence ; it was played in the royal courts, and by the musical populace, and all vocal compositions met with only limited success unless provided with a guitar accompaniment. At this time Giuliani introduced a new guitar to the public—the terz guitar. This was constructed upon the same principles and model as the ordinary guitar, but smaller ; by shortening the length of neck, the instrument was capable of being strung to a higher pitch—a minor third, hence its name " terz," the capo d'astro being used at the present time on the ordinary guitar to obtain the same effect. The length of string being

Matteo Carcassi

M: Carcassi

Mario Castelnuovo-Tedesco

Ferdinando de Cristofaro

Ferdinando de Cristofaro

Olga Coelho
Brazilian singer-guitarist

Adam Darr

Napoleon Coste

shorter, the tone was more brilliant and the labour of execution considerably lessened. Diabelli and Giuliani were the recipients of popular admiration for their combined talents on the piano and terz guitar and it was at the period of these public performances that Giuliani wrote his most beautiful and brilliant *Concertos for guitar and orchestra,* Op. 30, 36 and 37, which were published by Diabelli. These are among the choicest compositions ever written for the instrument. Arrangements of these were also published for guitar and piano, although originally conceived and performed by the author with orchestra, and they attracted considerable attention, not only in Vienna, but throughout Europe. The list of Diabelli's compositions is lengthy, he wrote a great quantity of music for the piano and more than two hundred compositions for the guitar, in addition to a *Method for the guitar* and albums or collections of pieces for it. His piano studies, which were written primarily for the use of his own pupils are still used by teachers and students ; they are graceful and capital study, while his original works and arrangements for piano display good taste. His twenty-nine solo sonatinas, and twenty-three charming duet sonatinas were popular, while his thirty six books of variations and four hundred and twenty-six books of potpourris, were also in demand. In fact, the merits of Diabelli, as an educational composer are unquestionable. His masses, and particularly the Landmessen, are performed in Austria, they are for the most part interesting and easy of execution, if not particularly solid. Diabelli wrote numerous songs and an operetta, *Adam in der Klemme.* His compositions for the guitar display the same qualities and characteristics as his piano works and are quite as numerous, many were published simultaneously in Vienna, Paris and London. These compositions are not the work of, nor for, the virtuoso ; but admirably suited for the amateur and student of the guitar. They lack the brilliancy of other celebrated guitar composers, but are well written, lie under the hand, and they proved a profitable source of income to their author. Diabelli was a keen business man, and in 1818, having acquired sufficient wealth by piano and guitar teaching and composing, he purchased an interest in the music publishing business of Peter Cappi, in Vienna, the firm being afterwards known as Cappi and Diabelli. In 1824, he bought out his partner and became sole owner and proprietor under the title of Diabelli & Co. Riemann states: " Diabelli was Schubert's principal publisher—he paid the composer badly, and in addition, reproached him for writing too much." He published the first compositions of Franz Schubert, when he was unknown, and these early compositions were songs with guitar accompaniment. Schubert was also a guitarist and wrote all his vocal works, in the first instance with the guitar. Some few years later, when the piano became more common, Schubert, at the request of his publisher, Diabelli, set pianoforte accompaniments to these songs. In 1852, Diabelli sold his copyrights and business to C. A. Spina ; he had up to this time printed over twenty-five thousand works, and it was one of the largest and most important music publishing businesses in existence.

Diabelli had published the majority of the compositions of Czerny, Strauss, and Schubert, and had purchased at various times the copyrights of the publications of other eminent firms in Vienna, those of Artaria, Leidesdorf and Mechetti in particular. During his later years, Diabelli was in daily contact with the most renowned musicians, his establishment was the rendezvous of all musicians visiting Vienna ; he enjoyed the friendship of Beethoven, and was in attendance during his last illness in 1826. Diabelli left the record of a successful musician and business man, qualities rarely found in combination. His quiet unassuming life made him many friends, some of whom erected a tablet to his memory in 1871, on the house at Mattsee in which he was born. Beethoven has immortalized him by using a waltz, composed by Diabelli, as a theme for his thirty-three variations. Diabelli's published compositions for the guitar alone, with other instruments, and with the voice, number hundreds. *Grand Serenades for violin, alto and guitar,* Op. 36, 65, 95 and 105 with *Six volumes of Grand Serenades* for the same instruments, all published by Haslinger, Vienna ; *Serenades and Nocturnes for guitar and flute,* Op. 67, 99 and 128 ; *Nocturne for two horns and guitar,* Op. 123 ; *Grand Trio for three guitars,* Op. 62 ; *Sonatas and other duos for guitar and piano,* Op. 64, 68, 69, 70, 71, 97, 102, 140 and 141 ; *Divertimento for guitar and piano,* Op. 56 (Diabelli dedicated the second volume to the publisher, Haslinger), issued by Ricordi, Milan ; *Thirty Light Studies for guitar,* Op. 39 ; *Preludes, Waltzes, Rondos and Variations for guitar solo,* Op. 103, 127 ; *Twelve Alpine Dances,* published by Joseph Aibl, Munich ; *Two Books, Nos. 5* and *6 Light and Agreeable Melodies for the guitar,* published in 1826 ; *Orpheus, a series of six albums of Duets for two guitars ; Six Waltzes and Twenty Duets Concertante for piano and guitar,* Johanning, London ; *Twelve Songs with guitar accompaniment,* George and Manby, London ; Philomele, a *Collection of songs with guitar,* Diabelli & Co., Vienna ; Op. 114 and 115, *Songs with guitar,* Bachmann, Hanover ; *Three Italian vocal duets with guitar*, Mechetti, Vienna ; Op. 98, *Songs with guitar and flute,* Simrock, Bonn ; *Rondo Militaire, for two mandolins, mandola and guitar,* and in addition there are more than fifty transcriptions of operatic melodies for guitar and piano ; several collections of pieces for guitar and violin and guitar and flute and nearly a hundred miscellaneous duos for two guitars. The original manuscript of Op. 103 is in the library of the International Guitarists' League, Munich.

Dickhut, Christian, a virtuoso on the 'cello, horn and guitar and an instrumental composer who was Court musician at Mannheim in 1812. He devoted much time experimenting with wind instruments, and in 1811 improved the horn by extending its tubes which produced a clearer and more sonorous tone. He was the composer of the following works which are of more than ordinary merit ; Op. 3, 4 and 6, were *Serenades for flute, horn or alto and guitar* which were published by Schott. The A.M.Z. mentions, *Two Serenades,* for the same instruments.

Doche, Joseph, Denis, born August 22, 1766, at Paris and died July 20, 1825, in Soissons, France. He was a dramatic composer, skilful guitarist, violinist and double bass player, celebrated as a writer of vaudeville. In 1785 he was capellmeister of Constance Cathedral and later removed to Paris. Grove states that the flowing and charming inspirations of Doche (father and son) were the most interesting from a literary, philosophical and musical point of view, during their period. Among Doche's compositions is Op. 4 a *Collection of Forty Melodies and Romances with guitar accompaniment.*

Doisy, Charles, or as sometimes erroneously named Doisy Lintant, was a French guitarist who died in Paris in 1807. He was a contemporary of C. Lintant, a guitarist and violinist of Grenoble and Paris. For many years Doisy enjoyed an enviable reputation as a professor of the guitar in Paris ; but during his later years he established a music and musical instrument business in which he was occupied at the time of his death. He had a sound education in harmony and composition, evidenced in his published works, and he wrote for the guitar in its capacity as a solo instrument, for accompaniment, and in combination with almost every other instrument. His published compositions number more than two hundred ; but during his early career, the guitar had only five strings, tuned as at present, but without the sixth or lowest E. Doisy's early compositions are therefore limited in range. It was not until the close of the eighteenth century that the sixth string was added, at the suggestion of Capellmeister Naumann of Dresden, and proving of great advantage was universally adopted by guitar makers. In his later Method and compositions Doisy used the additional string. He compiled several methods, one of which, entitled : *General rudiments of Music and Method for the guitar,* was published in 1801 by Naderman, Paris. Another of his Methods included original airs for violin and guitar and six romances with guitar. This was issued by Breitkopf and Härtel, Leipzig, and was an excellent method for the period and contained three diagrams displaying a guitar with but five strings. The A.M.Z. of 1820 reviews this method and his compositions for the guitar. Doisy was a voluminous composer, having to his name several *Concertos for the guitar with accompaniment of string quartet ; Serenades for guitar, violin and alto ; Grand Duos for guitar and violoncello ; Guitar and piano ; Guitar and oboe,* and in *Duos with the horn, bassoon, viola, flute and another guitar.* There also were published under his name, many collections of pieces for guitar alone and for violin and guitar and flute and guitar. *Les folies d'Espagne* consisted of no less than fifty variations by "Doisy, Professeur, Paris." Op. 15, with many other Duos for guitar and violin were issued by Simrock, Bonn.

Dorn, James, born January 7, 1809, at Lichtenau, Germany, was living in Carlsbad as late as 1853 when he gave instruction on the guitar to his nephew, Charles James Dorn. James Dorn was a virtuoso on the horn and an excellent guitarist who for some years was a member of the Royal Chapel of the Grand Duke of Baden. He received his first musical instruction when a boy under Schunke, and at sixteen joined a military regiment, continuing his musical education as a member of the band, playing the horn. In 1832 he toured England as horn virtuoso, won praise by his playing, and then returned to his native land, where he was Court musician in Carlsbad. Dorn published only a few compositions, among them are *Six Polkas for guitar solo,* issued by André, Offenbach, which were accorded much popularity and passed several editions. A volume of original manuscripts for the guitar by Dorn is in the library of the author of this work. It contains among other compositions a *Grand solo for guitar ; Introduction, Theme and Variations for solo guitar* and *Two Potpourris for guitar.* Dorn's brother, Valentine, also a French horn player, lived for a time in Boston, U.S.A., and was a member of various important orchestras. His son, Charles James, born in Boston, October 29, 1839, and died at Orange, Mass., U.S.A., November 30, 1909, returned with his parents to their native land when he was fourteen and in Carlsbad had instruction on the guitar from his uncle James, the Court musician, and afterwards returned to America where he was regarded one of the finest performers in the United States. During the last years, he rarely appeared in public as a guitar soloist, but devoted himself almost entirely to teaching and arranging music for the instrument. The music journals praised his sterling qualities as a gentleman and he was mourned by many pupils and a host of friends. Dorn was especially fond of the compositions of Giuliani and Mertz, and possessed an extensive library of guitar music. A music periodical said at the time of his decease: "In more than one branch of his chosen profession, Mr. Dorn attained an enviable reputation. As a composer of music for the guitar his name will long be perpetuated, for several of his best compositions are genuine classics, and can be found in the repertoire of many of our most celebrated guitarists. As an arranger, his work invariably bore silent testimony to his artistic ability, and that he possessed a thorough knowledge of the capabilities of his favourite instrument was in evidence on every page. As an instructor he was most conscientious. His earnestness in imparting his store of knowledge served as an inspiration to his pupils, while his many sterling qualities won their respect, and, in many instances, affectionate regard." The majority of his compositions were published by Oliver Ditson, Boston, U.S.A.

Donizetti, Gaetano, born at Bergamo, Italy, November 29, 1797, died there in 1848, was an operatic composer of universal renown who wrote for the guitar in his orchestral scores. He studied in the Conservatoire of Naples and his first opera, produced in Vienna in 1818 was speedily followed by others, sixty-five in all. Donizetti possessed considerable literary talent and he designed and wrote the libretto of the most successful of his works. In 1842 he was commissioned to write an opera for the Theatre Italienne, Paris ; it was *Don Pasquale,* an opera buffa in three acts, which was produced there January 4, 1843, and in London the following June. Notwithstanding the brilliant cast, Donizetti was not pleased with the rehearsals and requested the music publisher, Dormoy, to accompany him to his lodgings. Searching among numerous manuscripts he handed him one, a serenade, for Mario to sing to Norina in the garden scene. This proved to be the most celebrated air in the opera, the tenor love song, *Com' è gentil,* known in England as *Oh! summer night.* For this Donizetti wrote a guitar accompaniment and at the first performance, Mario was accompanied by Lablache, who played the guitar behind the stage. This serenade, in six-eight time, which occurs at the commencement of the third and last act, is admirably suited for the guitar, and the celebrated tenor, Mario, for whom it was composed, added to his own reputation and that of the composer by his realistic performances. In the descriptive catalogue of ancient instruments in the Paris Conservatoire, Berlioz, who was for a time curator of the museum, mentions the fact that Donizetti composed for the guitar in *Don Pasquale,* and that he also used the instrument in several of his lesser known works. His memoirs have been published by various authors from the year 1875-1907.

Dotzauer, Justus Johann F. Born at Haselrieth, near Hildburghausen, Germany, January 20, 1783, died in Dresden, March 9, 1860. His father, the pastor of Haselrieth was an enthusiastic amateur musician, a guitar player, and his son began his musical education at an early age under his supervision. The guitar was his first instrument, and under his father's tuition he obtained a practical knowledge of it. The ease with which he obtained a proficiency in guitar playing induced his father to continue his musical instruction, and he had regular training on the violin with Gleichmann, musical director of the adjacent Court of Hildburghausen. He still continued the practice of the guitar and the playing of this instrument in the company of musicians of lengthy experience, proved of benefit and inspired him with a desire to master other instruments. A few years later he commenced the study of the piano with Henschkel, and then the young enthusiast prevailed upon the local blacksmith to instruct him in the rudiments of the double bass. In addition to these instruments a Court trumpeter named Hessner, a pupil of the 'cellist, Arnold Schlick, instructed Dotzauer in the art of violoncello playing, for which he displayed exceptional interest. The violoncello was the instrument by which his name and fame as a musician is recorded, for Dotzauer was one of the foremost composers, players and teachers of that instrument. He manifested such decided preference for the violoncello that his father sent him in 1799, to Meningen, to continue under a virtuoso and teacher named Kriegk, 'cellist of the Royal Chapel. Dotzauer, now sixteen, had been grounded in the elements of music, and was able to perform with proficiency upon several instruments. He studied with Kriegk for two years and in 1801 received an appointment in the Royal Chapel of Meningen, as violoncellist, where he remained until 1805. His studies in composition were supervised by the organist Kittel, the last pupil of the great Bach, and in 1805 he visited Leipzig, where he became one of the founders of "The Quartet". The following year he visited Berlin, where he studied with the virtuoso, Bernard Romberg. In 1811, he entered the Court Orchestra of Dresden and in 1821 was solo violoncellist and remained in that position until his retirement in 1850; he had appeared with outstanding success as soloist in Vienna during 1834. The last ten years of his life were spent in composing, editing and teaching. His most outstanding pupils were Kummer, Schuberth, and his younger son, Karl Ludwig; the elder son obtained some renown as pianist. Dotzauer's compositions embrace the whole range of musical art, including an opera, *Graziosa,* performed at Dresden in 1841, masses, symphonies, several overtures, nine quartets, twelve concertos for 'cello and orchestra, sonatas, variations for 'cello, guitar solos, solos with guitar accompaniment and studies and exercises for the 'cello. The majority of his compositions, with the exception of the solos, tutor and studies for the 'cello, have passed into oblivion. The studies and method retain their value as the new editions prove. Many of his early works were composed with the guitar, only one such is now obtainable, a *Potpourri for violoncello and guitar,* Op. 21, published by Breitkopf & Härtel, London. It is in four movements, commencing with an Adagio in E minor, the second subject, an Andante, in lighter vein, and of somewhat greater length, terminates in arpeggio triplets. This is followed by a Larghetto in three-four time—a noble melody, introducing effective double stopping and harmonics, while the Finale, an Andante, reiterates the theme of the second movement, suddenly changes to presto—a two-four passage in triplets, where the bowing skill of the performer is called into requisition. The guitar is in one of the most resonant keys of the instrument, E minor, and while it supports the violoncello, it admirably displays the characteristics of the guitar and also the composer's practical knowledge of this instrument. This composition occupies a foremost position among duos for this combination of instruments.

Dragonetti, Domenico, born at Venice, 1763, died in London, April 16, 1846. Dragonetti, whose fame as a virtuoso on the ponderous double bass was unsurpassed, was also an extraordinary performer on the light guitar. He roused the monks of S. Giustina of Padua from their cells in the dead of night by his imitation of a thunderstorm, when testing his newly acquired Gasparo di Salo double bass, and he also attracted crowds in Venice by his guitar serenades. His father, Pietro, was also a guitar and double bass player accustomed to play the latter instrument by ear for dances, and when the son was nine he too adopted the guitar. He surreptitiously took his father's guitar to a remote part of the house to practise, and such was his ability that in a short time, and without his parents being aware of the circumstances, he made extraordinary progress and was a good player. It was part of his father's occupation to accompany on the guitar, the violinist Doretti, a composer of dance music. Doretti, upon one occasion, desired to try some new compositions, and took the manuscripts to Dragonetti. The son was in the room, and noticing that his father did not succeed, asked to be allowed to try the guitar; but Pietro, unaware of his son's ability, refused. Doretti, observing the assurance of the boy, persuaded the father to let him try, and he astonished both by reading the music fluently, accompanying Doretti's melody with chords as appropriate as a well-versed practitioner.

Dragonetti studied the guitar to obtain perfection, and, having made the acquaintance of a good violinist named Mestrino, associated with him as guitarist. Together they played for some time at the most brilliant public and private musical circles in Venice and when returning home delighted to amuse the citizens with their violin and guitar duets. Dragonetti's attention was given also to the double bass, and after only eleven lessons from Berini, and when but thirteen he was first double bass in the Comic Opera, Venice, and at fourteen held a similar post at the grand opera of the Theatre St. Benetto. At Vicenza he was a member of the opera orchestra, and while there discovered the marvellous bass from which he would never part. It had belonged to the convent of S. Pietro, and was his inseparable companion for sixty years. He bequeathed it to the vestry of the Church of St. Mark, Venice. In 1794 he was engaged at the King's Theatre, London, and was the constant companion of the violoncellist, Lindley, where for fifty years they played at the same desk in the Opera, Philharmonic, and other concerts, and their execution of Corelli's sonatas as duos for 'cello and double bass was an unfailing attraction. A few of his songs were published and others with piano and guitar remain in manuscript. He was a collector of pictures and musical instruments and possessed rare Italian guitars. He died in London, and was buried in the Catholic Chapel of Moorfields; his memoirs, edited by Caffi, appeared in 1846.

Dressler, Raphael, born 1784 at Gratz, died February 12, 1835, in Mayence. In 1809 he was flautist of the opera orchestra and in 1817 that of the Royal Chapel, Hanover. He came to England in 1820 and remained until 1834 when he returned to Mayence. He performed with the guitarist Pelzer, in the Concert Hall of the Opera, London, May 15, 1833, and received a hearty reception. He has written more than a hundred compositions for flute, with and without accompaniment, many with guitar. The principal is Op. 43, *Variations for flute and guitar,* "dedicated to my friend Theodore Gaude" another flute virtuoso, guitarist and composer. The majority of Dressler's compositions were published by Breitkopf & Härtel, Leipzig and Weinberger, Vienna.

Drexel, Friedrich, a German guitar virtuoso and composer living during the first half of the nineteenth century whom Mendel in his Lexicon describes as a talented composer of more than fifty songs with guitar and from the years 1821 to 1828 the A.M.Z. records his solos for guitar and songs with guitar. The following of his compositions were published by Breitkopf & Härtel, Leipzig. Op. 12, *Twelve Marches for guitar;* Op. 15, *Twelve light pieces in two books, for guitar;* Op. 16, *Six Songs with guitar;* Op. 18 and 19, *Three Polonaises in each, for guitar;* Op. 20, *Six Lieder with guitar;* Op. 28, *Six Cotillons for guitar and piano;* Op. 31, *Album of guitar solos;* Op. 32, *Volume of Twenty songs with guitar;* Op. 46 and 47 *Two books of guitar studies;* Op. 60, *Nine Rondos for guitar* and numerous similar compositions without opus number.

Drouet, Louis, F. P., was born in Amsterdam in 1792, and died in Berne, Switzerland, September 30, 1873. He was one of the most eminent of flute players, a talented guitarist, who had been a student at the Paris Conservatoire, and played there and at the Opera when seven years of age. His serious study of the flute commenced in 1807, after an extraordinary success which he achieved at a concert in Amsterdam with the violinist Rode; previous to this he had divided his attention between the flute and the guitar. From 1807-10 he was solo flautist and teacher of King Louis of Holland. In 1811 he was in a similar position at the Court of Napoleon 1, which he retained after the Restoration, being in 1814 first flautist in the Court orchestra of Louis XVII. He came to England in 1815 and commenced a business in London as a manufacturer of flutes but discontinued in 1819 and travelled as a virtuoso. This was a lengthy tour, embracing all Europe, in 1822 he was in Vienna, and towards its close, he resided for some time in Naples, and later at The Hague. Drouet's tour was very successful, his performances as solo flautist and with guitar accompaniment in his own compositions, elicited the highest praise. He was a wonderful executant, his dexterity most remarkable, although his tone was more delicate than powerful. In 1830 he was again in London and from 1836-1854 was Court Capellmeister in Coburg, afterwards he made a visit to U.S.A., residing for a short time in New York. He returned to Frankfurt and finally settled in Berne, Switzerland. Mendel states that he wrote a hundred and fifty compositions for the flute, a great number ot them with accompaniment for the guitar. The following are the most important, principally airs with variations for flute and guitar: *God save the King,* and Op. 123, 124, 132 and 137, all published by Cranz, Leipzig.

Dubez, Johann. An Italian born at Vienna in 1828 and died there October 27, 1891, was a virtuoso on the mandolin, guitar, harp and zither, and an instrumental composer. In 1846 he was violinist in the Josefstadt Theatre, Vienna, where he made the acquaintance of the guitar virtuoso, Giulio Regondi. Dubez, who was a member of the orchestra when Regondi was appearing in Vienna, was so fascinated that he adopted the guitar and studied it under Regondi and Mertz in this city. His progress was rapid, for, in 1847, he gave his first guitar recital in the old Vienna Academy of Music, playing Regondi's compositions and receiving great applause. He was a brilliant harpist also, and under Meyerbeer played the well known harp solo in the opera *Vielka.* Some years previous to his death he made a protracted concert tour, visiting Bucharest and Constantinople. In the former city he was commanded to perform before the Queen of Roumania, and in the latter before the Sultan and Court, receiving the decoration of the Medjidia Order. Dubez was the first president of the Vienna Zither Society founded in 1875, and also honorary member of the Prague Zither Society. His guitar compositions are similar to those of his teacher, Mertz, but the majority remain in manuscript. He composed several harp solos, which were published by Bösendorfer, Vienna, and Cranz, Hamburg, and his portrait was published in the Journal of the Vienna Zither Society in 1891. As guitarist, he ranks with Mertz and Regondi, and is one of the most celebrated Austrian guitarists. Among his published compositions are: *Fantasia on Hungarian Melodies for solo guitar,* published by Diabelli & Co., Vienna ; *Fantasia on airs from 'Lucia',* for guitar solo published by Spina, Vienna, on which he is described as " Harpist to the Countess Jeanne Esterhazy," and Op. 11, 33, 34, 35 and 37 harp solos which were published by Cranz, Hamburg.

Dunst, Etienne, an operatic singer and guitarist living in Vienna during the early part of the nineteenth century. He was engaged as one of the minstrels for the first performance of Schubert's opera, *The Magic Harp,* which was produced in the Theatre an der Wien, August 21, 1820. Gottfried Weber's Cecilia, reviews four of his compositions for the guitar. Op. 5, a *Caprice for guitar solo* was published by Schott, Mayence, and a few of his published and unpublished pieces for the guitar are in the library of the Munich Guitar Society.

EBERWEIN, Traugott Maximilian, born October 27, 1775, at Weimar, died December 2, 1831, while music director of Rudolstadt. At the age of seven he was a violinist in the Court Orchestra and in 1817, was the concert master. He rose to great eminence in the music world as one of the founders of the popular German music festivals. His works comprise eleven operas, masses, concertos, etc., and vocal compositions with guitar, the best known of the latter is a *Serenade,* Op. 93, for voice with guitar. The A.M.Z. of 1827 reviewed this composition. His brother Karl, born November 10, 1786, at Weimar and died there March 2, 1868, was Court violin virtuoso. Breitkopf & Härtel published in 1817, six of his part songs with guitar and one of his operas was produced in his native city, May, 1824.

Ehlers, William, born at Weimar in 1774 and died November 29, 1845, in Frankfurt, Germany. After studying music and literature he made his début in the theatre of his native place and by his singing and guitar playing received an instantaneous and hearty reception. He then commenced to teach singing, elocution and the guitar and was later the director of theatres in Mayence and Wiesbaden. In 1809 he made his first appearance in Vienna and was very successful. Five years later he was leading tenor in Breslau Theatre and remained in that position until 1824, recognised as one of the most popular operatic singers of Germany. He must have been in Vienna again, for in 1828 he was associating with Schubert and his companions, but the following year he established a music school in Frankfurt which was highly successful and two years later was musical director of the theatre. His songs with guitar accompaniment are enumerated in the A.M.Z. They were published by Cotta, Stuttgart; Boehme, and also Hofmeister, Leipzig, and in 1804 several volumes also with guitar were issued by Tubinger.

Eisenhofer, Franz Xaver, born November 29, 1783, at Ilmmunster, Upper Bavaria, died August 15, 1855, at Landshut. He was a theological student at Landshut and then of philosophy in Wurzburg. He became renowned in his native land for his many songs with guitar accompaniment. *Seven vocal duets with guitar* and others are enumerated in the A.M.Z. and in addition there are *Six songs with guitar,* without opus number; *German songs with guitar,* Op. 2; and *Two volumes of twelve songs with guitar,* Op. 5.

Ellis, Herbert J., born Dulwich, London, July 4, 1865, died at the premature age of thirty-eight, on October 13, 1903, in St. Thomas' Hospital, London, was unquestionably the most fertile English composer and arranger for the mandolin and guitar. The son of a licensed victualler, he received no musical instruction beyond that given by his mother, who had been a pupil of Sir Julius Benedict, and she taught him the piano and harmony. When a lad he became the delighted owner of a banjo, and he says: "Having the infatuation (for the banjo) I learnt several tunes out of my piano tutor, and then occurred to me the idea of writing my own music for it. Gradually growing ambitious, I did not rest until I had written an instruction book, which, in due course saw the light and without being egotistical, I think I can safely say that it was from the advent of my Thorough School that the banjo began to be popular." It was, in fact, due to the growing popularity of the banjo, from 1884 onwards, that his talents were developed, for he had no academic education in music; but an inborn aptitude for its study and diligent practice, marked Ellis for other than the commercial career originally intended by his parents. The publication of his banjo method established the position of Ellis, and the demand for his compositions and methods was decidedly marked, resulting in the issue of some thousands of pieces and books from his pen. About the year 1888 the mandolin and guitar were beginning to arrest popular attention, and Ellis adopted these instruments, too, and it was not long ere his Tutor for the Mandolin was issued by J. A. Turner, London. This was the first instruction book for the mandolin, printed in England, and to general surprise it ran through several editions and was the preliminary work that prepared the way for establishing the instrument in public favour throughout the country. The popularity of the mandolin brought with it a revival of the guitar, and here again, the skill and adaptability of Ellis was equal to the occasion, for yet another volume, his *Thorough School for the Guitar* was published and immediately found favour with teachers and players. In fact, his method for the guitar, in its unique and simple manner of arrangement, by its explicit diagrams and judicious sequence of studies is the simplest and best yet issued in England. There are other English guitar methods of perhaps greater scholarly and musicianly qualities; but to the beginner they are not so lucid or simple. During the period of his first publications, Ellis enjoyed the most enviable position as a teacher of these instruments in England—to few mortals, genius, and rare opportunity for success are lavishly bestowed in great profusion—but the hand that gives, sometimes witholds the power to retain these gifts, and so in the life of Ellis, he lacked the force of character and will to rise above his daily environments, and to these in a great measure are attributable the sad termination of so promising a career and his premature death. To him was given the faculty of expressing himself in the simplest and most attractive manner, and his total avoidance of technical difficulties made his compositions of particular attraction to beginners, and his name familiar to all English players of these instruments. Speaking generally, his compositions are characterised by simplicity of style, but on the other hand, his time was too fully occupied as a teacher and composer to allow for the deeper and more solid work, which would in all probability have followed, had his life been spared to more mature years. To Ellis and all English players, the higher branches of the mandolinistic art were unknown, and the majority of guitarists were satisfied with the limitations of an accompaniment; but since his advent, mandolin and guitar instruction books, and music have been published in profusion in this country. He also composed under assumed names. In 1892, Turner issued his *Thorough School for the Mandolin,* followed by *High School Studies for the Mandolin,* and this publisher's catalogue alone shows over one thousand works by Ellis, all of light character and in addition, a great number of the same style were also published by Dallas, London.

Elsner, Joseph Xaver, born June 1, 1769, at Grodgrau, Silesia, and died in Warsaw, 1854. He was the son of a carpenter whose chief hobby was the construction of stringed musical instruments. The lad played the violin and guitar, but had no regular instruction in music beyond a few lessons in harmony from Förster. In 1791 he was first violinist in Brunn theatre and eight years later was in charge of the National Theatre Orchestra, Warsaw. While employed in Warsaw he founded in 1815 the Musical Society which culminated in the National Conservatoire of Music; he was appointed the first director, a position he retained until the closure of the institution caused by the political troubles of 1830. His numerous and diverse compositions include nineteen operas, ballets, symphonies and church music, and during a visit to Paris, some of his compositions were performed in the Tuilleries. He was Chopin's teacher of composition in Warsaw, and was his trusted friend and adviser long after his pupil had departed from Warsaw. Elsner was familiar with the guitar, having played it from youth and in the volume Chopin, by Hedley, published by Dent, London, in Musician Series, we read: "When the stage coach, that was to take him (Chopin) to Vienna, reached the Warsaw suburb of Wola, a surprise was in store for Chopin. Joseph Elsner had arrived there before him with a male voice choir which now sang with guitar accompaniment, a short cantata especially composed by Elsner himself."

Esser, Heinrich, born July 15, 1818, at Mannheim, died June 3, 1872, at Salzburg. He was concertmaster in Mannheim, 1838, then musical director of the Court Theatre, Mannheim, and finally Capellmeister of the Opera, Vienna, from 1847, retiring on pension in 1869. Wagner entrusted him with the arrangement of the *Meistersingers,* for the piano. His compositions are numerous; but he excelled particularly in vocal works and his choruses for mens' voices were popular favourites. In 1843 Schott, Mayence, published many of his songs with their original guitar accompaniments, among which was his well-known *Drinking song.*

Eulenstein, Carl, born at Heilbron, Wurtemburg, Germany, in 1802, died in Styria, Austria, in 1890, at the advanced age of eighty-eight. His parents were very poor, his father was an amateur violinist of some ability whose services were in frequent demand at festive gatherings. While Carl was very young his father died and the widow with her young family were plunged in poverty. During his father's life the boy had manifested an extraordinary love of music and not being permitted to use his father's violin had constructed his own childish instrument. After the death of his father the lad was allowed the use of the violin, and although his mother was unable to pay for instruction, nothing deterred, he practised incessantly. His enthusiasm attracted the schoolmaster's attention, who, aware of the impecunious position of the family, generously taught him the violin and the rudiments of music and afterwards gave him instruction on the guitar and flute also. His progress was phenomenal, particularly on the guitar. At the age of fourteen, by persuasion of his uncle, he had reluctantly consented to be apprenticed to a magistrate's clerk; his ambition was to become a musician. He had begged and entreated his mother in vain; she was influenced by the uncle, who declared Carl was a lazy vagabond—as were all musicians. He was now placed with a bookbinder, and this occupation proving as irksome as the other, sterner measures were adopted and he was sent from home to a hardware merchant, with the request that he should be kept at work and away from music. The nearest approach to music that the lad now had, was in his employer's stock—jews-harps—and he was compelled to satisfy his musical inclinations with these. He would take several with him to bed and manipulate many at a time, the effect of which was extraordinary. His skill was made public, some years later, in London, when he performed before a learned audience at a lecture given by Sir Michael Faraday in the Royal Institute. Eulenstein practised these and a guitar in his bedroom each night, and it was not until he possessed an old French horn, that he was betrayed by his midnight music studies. The mournful sound of this instrument aroused his employer and Eulenstein was summarily dismissed. He was nineteen, turned out in the world, but released from irksome employment, decided to travel as a performer on the guitar and jews-harp. His sole possessions were his instruments and a few pence. He passed through Heidelberg, Frankfort, Hesse-Cassel and Hanover, walking with great difficulty more than six hundred miles, meeting with little encouragement and much adversity. At the theatre of Lurenburg, however, he performed with an amount of financial success, and at Stuttgart was patronised by nobility, and in 1825 commanded to appear before the Queen of Würtemberg. He then played in Tubingen, Freiburg and Basle, and from there walked through Switzerland, passing Zurich and Lausanne, entering France at Lyons. His plight was now pitiable in the extreme ; he received no support or encouragement, was shoeless, forced to sleep without shelter, and on the verge of starvation. In this dejected and forlorn condition he arrived in Paris, where his guitar playing fortunately attracted the notice of M. Stockhausen, a harpist of repute and husband of the celebrated soprano. He befriended him and through his kindly influence Eulenstein performed before Paer, the Duke of Orleans, Duchess de Berry and Charles X of France. It was at this time that he composed his Op. 1, which was published in Paris, and he left France in 1827, after a successful and protracted sojourn and came to London. He performed before the Princess Augusta, the Marchioness of Salisbury, and the Duke of Gordon, who manifested a kindly interest in his welfare. Eulenstein was commanded to perform before King William and played at many fashionable concerts and then returned to his native land ; but in 1828 he was again in London as a professor of the guitar. His patron the Duke of Gordon, hearing of his arrival invited him to his Scottish residence. It was in the depths of rigorous winter when Eulenstein journeyed there by coach and the Duke was waiting to greet him. He resided as private musician in the mansion of the Duke for some time, and made several professional tours through Scotland, receiving great praise in the adjacent city of Aberdeen, and also in Edinburgh. After these financial successes he toured England, visited Cheltenham and Bath, residing in the latter fashionable city as a teacher of the guitar and the German language. He lived here for some years, was held in the highest esteem, but returned to his native land and in 1879 was living at Gunzburg, near Ulm. In his advanced years he removed to Styria and died in a village there in 1890. Eulenstein was a man of prepossessing appearance, educated and polished in manners. His autobiography appeared under the title of: *A sketch of the life, etc.,* in 1833 and this 8vo volume contained his portrait; a second edition appeared in 1840. His portrait, which is reproduced, was published October 1, 1833 by a London music seller. Eulenstein was the author of several scholastic works on the German language issued in Bath and London. His compositions and arrangements for the guitar were among the most popular published in England, and his guitar accompaniments to favourite songs were to be found in all the albums and journals of the time. Although the greater number are exceedingly simple they display good taste, and were favourites among amateur guitarists. He is the author of string quartets, songs with guitar, duos for guitar and piano, guitar solos and duos, and a *Practical Method for the guitar.* This latter, published by Brewer & Co., London, met with an amount of favour and passed several editions. In the introduction Eulenstein says: " When Mr. Hummel was in Bath, the author of this work had a long conversation with him, and was much gratified to hear so eminent a pianist and composer express so high opinion in favour of the guitar, particularly of its effects in modulation." The following are his most popular compositions: Op. 1, *Twelve airs for guitar solo,* Richault, Paris ; Op. 9, *Introduction and Brilliant Rondo,* Johanning, London ; Op. 10, *Three Rondos,* Johanning ; Op. 11, *Two Rondos,* Ewer, London ; Op. 15, *Six Waltzes,* Ewer ; Op. 16, *Military Divertimento ; Variations for guitar tuned in E major,* dedicated to Her Grace the Duchess of Gordon ; *German Retreat in E major tuning ; Introduction and Variations* on Weber's *Last Waltz,* and a *Grand Waltz* of Beethoven ; *Souvenir de Bath* and *Tyrolese melodies with variations,* Leonard & Co., London ; *French melodies,* with symphonies and accompaniments by Eulenstein, published in 1828 ; Pleyel's *German hymn, for guitar solo,* D'Almaine, London ; *Reichstadt Waltz* and *Ritornella, duos for guitar and piano,* Chappell, London, and numerous other pieces of a similar nature. Speaking of his compositions for the guitar, The Harmonicon of 1831 said: " Mr. Eulenstein's rondos are remarkably delicate and pleasing and within the compass of ordinary players."

FAHRBACH, Josef, born August 25, 1804, at Vienna and died there June 7, 1883. In addition to being a well-known guitar virtuoso, he was a celebrated flautist and composer, the father of the renowned composer, Philip Fahrbach. For many years he was first flautist in Vienna Opera Orchestra and then toured with his own band. He was the composer of numerous instrumental works, principally for the guitar and flute. Op. 73 *Studies for the guitar* with twelve strings (six extra bass) and *Twenty-four harmonious Studies for solo guitar* were published by Cranz, Hamburg, who also issued his German and French editions of *Bathioli's guitar method.* This was augmented with cadenzas and studies from his pen and the same publishers also issued many of his studies and exercises and solos for flute. Fahrbach was the composer of numerous other pieces for guitar issued by Haslinger, Vienna, and other Viennese publishers of less note.

Falla, Manuel de, born Cadiz, November 14, 1876, died November 14, 1946. He was a student in Madrid Conservatoire under Felipe Pedrell from 1902-4 and won the national opera competition the following year with *La vida breve,* which established his reputation. In 1907 he migrated to Paris where for several years he obtained a precarious livelihood as music teacher. At the outbreak of the 1914 war he returned to his native land, residing in Granada. His popular opera *The Three cornered hat,* was his most successful work and in this he makes use of the guitar. Respecting this opera, Falla wrote, " My intention has been to evoke by means of the instrumentation in specific passages, certain guitaristic values," and they are also apparent in the orchestration of *La vida breve,* and *Nights in the gardens of Spain.* Regarding the guitar, he writes: " The instrument most complete and richest in its harmonic and polyphonic possibilities. The guitar as popularly used in Spain, represents two distinct musical effects ; that of rhythm, which is apparent and immediately perceptible, and that of harmony." From his home in Granada he contributed in 1930 an article on the musical value of the guitar, to the Austrian Guitar Review, Vienna, edited by Jacob Ortner, Professor of the guitar in the State Music Academy. Dr. W. Starkie, in his book, " Don Gypsy," relates a very interesting visit he made to the home of Angel Barrios in Granada where he also met Falla. Writing of his teacher, Falla says: " The keystone of the arch upon which Spanish music rests is the work of Felipe Pedrell." Pedrell, too, was a guitarist and composer for the instrument. Trend in Manuel de Falla and Spanish Music, frequently records the high opinion of Falla for the guitar and his association with the instrument and its players. It was soon after Trend's first meeting with Falla, in 1919, that he experienced the thrilling effect of a trio of two Spanish mandolins and a guitar. On page 38 he says: " I was able to make closer acquaintance with the guitar in a house just outside the Alhambra. The player, whose father's house it was, Don Angel Barrios, is a composer of distinction and one of the best guitarists of Spain. On hot summer nights Falla and he would sit on the patio, where by means of a towel the fountain had been muffled, but not altogether silenced and the guitar would be ingeniously transposed into a sharp key by a capotasto . . . and when Falla was confined to his bedroom with a cold, Barrios would come every evening with his guitar. Falla has always treated the guitar seriously and when the editor of the Revue Musicale invited him to send something ' pour le tombeau de Claude Debussy ' he composed the *Homenaje* for guitar solo and it was first tried over in his room at one of the meetings described." Further interesting particulars are to be found in A Picture of Modern Spain. Falla's most celebrated work for the guitar is this *Homage on the tomb of Debussy*, composed in 1920 and published by Chester, London. It is one of his most serious and profoundly emotional works and a fitting tribute to the memory of his friend, Debussy, who, though never in Spain, had shown his love of its native idiom in some songs and compositions. The influence of the guitar, the national instrument of Spain—which Falla regarded with the highest esteem—is most apparent in the instrumentation of the score of his ballet, *The Corregidor* and *The miller's wife* and he also includes the instrument in the score of *La vida breve.* The *Homenaje* for guitar solo dedicated to Dukas, first appeared in the Revue Musicale in 1933. Falla's music which has all the raciness of a guitar in the hands of an Andaluz was, like Albeniz and Granados, always conscious of the guitar and the vast debt owed to the guitar by modern Spanish music.

Fantauzzi, Laurent, was born at Marseilles of Neapolitan origin during the last quarter of the nineteenth century, and died 1941, during the German occupation. His father presented him with a mandolin when he was nine and his first knowledge of it was obtained without the aid of a teacher. At the age of eighteen he was sent to study music with an uncle, organist of the church of d'Ara Coeli, Rome. He studied diligently and a few years later gave mandolin recitals in Italy and received such encouragement that he was induced to visit Paris, where he gave recitals in the Salle Berlioz, one of his items was *Czardas* by Monti, the composer accompanying on the piano. His brilliant playing, combined with a liquid sonorous tone, elicited the praise of critics and in 1928 he extended his recitals to Berlin. After these tours he made his permanent abode in Marseilles, where, for many years he was professor of the mandolin in Marseilles Conservatoire of Music. He established a successful music and musical instrument business in the city and published his own and other musicians' compositions. His works are of a light popular style ; Op. 92, published in 1913, entitled *Crepscule* is an unaccompanied mandolin solo, dedicated to the poet-guitarist, Lucien Gelas, and is an interesting innovation of musical conception for mandolin alone. Fantauzzi was the author of a method for the mandolin, *L'Ecole du Mandoliniste Moderne.* In 1903, he founded and edited Le Plectre, a monthly journal, devoted to the mandolin and guitar, published until the second world war. As President of many music contests his services were in universal demand. In this capacity he officiated in France, Italy, Belgium, Monaco and Algeria ; his services to music were recognised by the French government by several awards of distinction. His portrait and biography appeared in The Music and Dramatic Directory (1887-1911), and also in La Vie Marseillaise, of June 24, 1925.

Ferandieri, Fernando, a famous Spanish guitarist and composer who flourished during the last half of the eighteenth and the beginning of the nineteenth centuries. He studied composition in Zamora University and in 1800 was guitarist and musician at the Court of Madrid. He was one of the first guitarists to adopt the sixth or bass E string (formerly the guitar had but five strings) and in 1799 his method entitled : *The art of playing the Spanish guitar by music* was published by subscription by Aznar, Madrid. A copy of this method was on view in the Spanish section of the Vienna Musical Exhibition of 1892. A

Herbert J. Ellis

Carl Eulenstein

Leopoldo Francia

Joseph E. Ferrer

Laurent Fantauzzi

L. FANTAUZZI O.I.

MANDOLINISTE

PROFESSEUR AU CONSERVATOIRE DE MARSEILL

Visiting Card of Fantauzzi

M. A. Zani de Ferranti

second edition appeared in 1816 revised by F. Pedrell, who, in his Biographical Dictionary of Spanish Musicians, records the life and works of its author. As a composer of national music, tonadillas, comedies, etc., more than two hundred by him were published between 1783-99, in Cadiz and Madrid. They comprised more than fifty guitar solos of fandangos, boleros, jotas and arias ; also a like number of duos for flute (or violin) and guitar ; four trios for guitar, violin and bass ; the same number of quartets for guitar, violin, viola and bass ; eighteen quintets and six concertos for guitar and orchestra. A few of his compositions have been republished by Schott, London.

Ferranti or **Zani,** Marc Aurelio de, a celebrated guitar virtuoso and man of letters, born at Bologna, July 6, 1802, and died in Pisa, November 28, 1878. He was descended from an ancient Venetian family believed to be the same as that of Ziani. At the age of seven he was sent to Lucca, with his preceptor, the Abbot Ronti, for education. He was gifted with very precocious intelligence, a prodigious memory, and poetic talent manifested itself from early childhood ; when twelve, he composed Latin poetry which was published. It was at this age that he heard Paganini, and so great an impression did it create, that music became his passion and he commenced the study of the violin under a teacher in Lucca named Gerli, junior. His progress was phenominal, and at sixteen his talent promised a violinist of the first order ; but he subsequently abandoned this instrument for the guitar, and it was by his extraordinary genius on the latter instrument that he is known to the musical world. In 1820 he visited Paris, where he was heard as an amateur ; but at the time he was pre-occupied with improved methods to be introduced in his playing, in fact, he possessed more ideas on this subject than he could as yet introduce in his performances, and his skill therefore could not achieve what he desired to perform. Consequently, at this time he received scant success ; but his perseverance did not waver, neither did lack of encouragement deter him from his purpose. Towards the end of the same year he travelled to St. Petersburg and was librarian to Senator Meitleff, later private secretary to Prince Varischkin, cousin of the Emperor, and he took advantage of the long periods of leisure these positions afforded, to meditate on the innovations he had entered upon, respecting improvements in the art of guitar playing. While in St. Petersburg he translated into Italian verse twelve of the poetic meditations of Lamartine. In 1824 he removed to Hamburg and the following year appeared as guitarist, although he had not yet perfected his system, nor had he acquired that remarkable talent which characterised his later performances. From 1825-27 he was concertising in Brussels, Paris and London, still intent upon his all-absorbing idea—the regeneration of the guitar—and seeking, sometimes in literature, sometimes in music, for the resources of his precarious existence. For the second time he visited Brussels in 1827, in a penniless condition ; but shortly after arrival, was appointed professor of Italian and the guitar in the Royal

Conservatoire. He was also employed in musical literary work, contributing articles to the leading music journals, and he was married this year. After continuous study he finally received his reward by discovering the secret of the art of singing, in sustained notes on the guitar. He had devoted several years to this discovery, obtaining all the extension of which it was susceptible, and then made his results public in two recitals which he gave in 1832, in Brussels and The Hague. Ferranti was most brilliantly successful, and from this time the talent of the virtuoso was augmented daily. The difficulties which he mastered with ease upon his instrument were inexecutable by other guitarists, and no one has been able to discover in what consisted his secret of prolonging and uniting his chords. His slurred chord passages, and melody with independent accompaniment on the same instrument, were marvellous and entrancing. After a third tour of Holland, he visited London, returning to The Hague, and was appointed guitarist to the King of the Belgians. With the violinist Sivori, he made a concert tour of America, remaining a year, and received praise for his guitar playing equal to that bestowed on his companion Sivori. Returning to Brussels in 1846, he continued his occupation as professor in the Royal Conservatoire till the end of 1854, when his restless spirit manifested itself again and he arranged an artistic tour through France, to his native land. Previous to his departure, he announced farewell concerts in Brussels and The Hague, and the Brussel's Echo remarked: " Very frequently we have to complain of the deluge of concerts showered upon us regularly in Brussels, from the beginning of Lent until after Easter. Fortunately, we have occasionally some sweet compensation. We could now cite several, but for today we will confine ourselves to the farewell concert of Zani de Ferranti, professor at the Royal Conservatoire and first guitarist to the King. We have heard this very distinguished artist many times, and upon every occasion his playing was so brilliant and so varied that he revealed to us some new wonder quite unexpected. What Paganini is on the violin, Thalberg on the piano, Servais on the 'cello, Godefried on the harp, Ferranti is on the guitar. He is a discoverer. He has done in excess beyond his celebrated rivals in vanquishing the difficulties, which a helpless instrument in the hands of others offers—but in his hands the guitar is no more the instrument you know—it becomes possessed of a voice and a soul. Ferranti has found new effects, harmonious traits of extraordinary wealth and power. Add to all the secrets of his technique, a clearness, a broadness and admirable equality of tone, add the rapidity, the vigour, the neatness of fingering, and far above all, the inspiration the rapture, the almost supernatural in the person, which evidences the true artist, and you will have but a faint idea of the talent of Ferranti. Before you heard him, you could not imagine that the guitar was capable of such effects—the vigour, and at the same time the subtle fineness, the sweetness in effects of mezzotint, in ethereal vaporous gradations of tone. The pieces which he composes are charming, and if Ferranti was not a virtuoso of the first rank he would shine among composers. Is it necessary for us to remark that the success of the artist has been immense?" In January, 1855, he arrived in Paris and was welcomed in the salons of the most eminent poets and musicians. Fetis lavished praise on him and wrote: "if the guitar has a Paganini it owes this glory to Ferranti." Berlioz enraptured by his performances, duly chronicled, in the Journal des Debats, the effects produced on him. Paganini, who, like Berlioz, was a fine guitarist, after one of Ferranti's recitals, wrote: "I heard you sir, with such emotion that I have scarcely enough reason left to tell you that you are the most miraculous guitarist that I have ever met in my life." Paganini had toured with the guitar virtuoso Legnani and together they had performed at numerous concerts. Pleyel extolled his fame to Alexander Dumas in January, and the following month Ferranti gave a recital at the poet's residence, and such a profound impression did his playing create, that when the last chords of his martial fantasia were vibrating, Dumas impulsively rose to his feet and exclaimed: "Sebastopol will be taken." The Parisian Chronicle, April 9, 1859, reporting a recital said: "Ferranti charmed for three whole hours the most select and aesthetical audience. He has made himself heard, the guitar alone has been the attraction of this charming soirée, but the genius of Ferranti is so supple, so extended, so varied that one did not have a suspicion of monotony. Again and again we applauded with real enthusiasm. The *Rondo of Fairies,* a work full of mysterious poetry and melancholic fantasy ; *O cara memoria* and *Walpurgis night,* a piece even more fantastic than the first, and of which the sparkling variations and finale were most miraculously executed. Do not scorn the guitar any more, gentlemen. When you have heard Ferranti you recognise the accuracy of the profound words of Fetis: 'An artist is always great when he opens new routes and draws the veil from the limits of his art.' The guitar only has limited resources ; but the soul which animated the instrument was vigorous, nothing stops it, it endues its power to the inert instrument. Between the hands of Ferranti the guitar becomes an orchestra, a military band ; if he plays the Marseillaise on the guitar, he makes a revolutionary of you ; if he sing a lovesong, there is a seduced woman ; if he sing a song of departure, we fly to the frontier." After a recital in Paris, November 11, 1860, Rossini wrote: "I cannot let you depart without telling you of the great pleasure your playing gave me. Your marvellous execution and sweet and harmonious compositions will assure a new era for the guitar. My sincere felicitations as admirer and friend, Giochino Rossini." From Paris, Ferranti travelled to Italy, and performed with his usual success in the important cities on his route. He arrived in Nice during March, and gave several recitals, the Gazette stated: "M. Zani de Ferranti had the honour to be heard last Saturday at H.I.H., the Grand Duchess of Baden, who had gathered the most brilliant assembly. The celebrated guitarist displayed as usual his astonishing ability, and obtained the high approbation of the elite audience." Ferranti passed on to Cannes, and in April gave many recitals in this fashionable resort, one journal remarked: "Not finding artists to assist him, the celebrated virtuoso bravely announced in his programme that he would execute five pieces of his composition alone, without the help of anyone, and he has charmed and enraptured his audience. I only know of one such instance similar, when Liszt did the same, and in justice, I must say that the Italian guitarist was rewarded with as great success as the Hungarian pianist." Makaroff, a Russian nobleman, and keen guitarist, who did much for the advancement of the instrument was residing in Brussels in 1856 and describes in his memoirs a visit to Ferranti. He writes: "When in Brussels I discovered the address of Zani de Ferranti and paid him a visit. I found him to be a very charming man of about fifty; very clever, intelligent and sociable. He told me that in the last years of the reign of the Emperor Alexander I, of Russia, he was in St. Petersburg and dedicated one of his guitar compositions to the Empress of Russia. He showed me his guitar, which was a very ordinary six stringed instrument made in Paris. Zani said that, owing to his being very busy with literary work, he had no time to play the guitar, but so persistent was I in my request for him to play to me that he could not refuse and thereupon played two pieces; one quite unknown to me, the other *Rose Waltz,* by Strauss. I was astounded by his exquisite playing and unlimited expression and technique. His singing tone (how he produced it, I do no know) was truly exceptional; wonderful, in fact, I have never since heard such remarkable playing. With great pride he showed me a framed sheet of paper on which was written in Italian: 'I certify by this that Zani de Ferranti is one of the greatest guitarists I have ever heard. His playing gave me the greatest pleasure and satisfaction. Signed, Nicolo Paganini.'" Ferranti resided in Bologna and there wrote: Di varie lezioni da sosituirsi alle invalse Nell Inferno di Dante Alighieri, published by Marsigli & Rocchi of that city. He gave concerts in other Italian towns for a time; but it was his wish to spend his last days in his native city. His desire was granted and he passed away amid his children and friends, November 28, 1878, at Pisa. Two hours previous he was in his usual health conversing with friends. Ferranti's published compositions do not exceed more than twenty, about fifteen of which were issued by Schott, London. Many remain in manuscript, among these are a *Method for the guitar, Concertos with orchestra,* and a variety of other pieces for the instrument. A catalogue and prospectus of his unpublished works was issued some years since, in Brussels, with the intent of publishing privately, but did not receive sufficient support to warrant the undertaking. Several of the manuscripts are in the library of the Internationalen Guitarristen Verband, Munich. Ferranti was the author of a poetical inspiration entitled: In Morte della Celebra Maria Malibran de Beriot, 8vo., published Brussels, 1836. This poem, which is as remarkable for the elegance and energy of the versification as for the beauty of ideas, was followed by Studies on Dante, and an edition of his poems, was published April, 1846, in London, Brusseis and Paris, as was also La comedia di Dante Alighiere, and other brochures. His published compositions for the guitar are: Op. 1 *Fantasia varie on a favourite air ;* Op. 2, *Rondo des fées ;* Op. 3, *Six Nocturnes ;* Op. 4, *Ma derniere fantasia ;* Op. 5, *Fantasia on the 'Carnival of Venice,'* for guitar tuned in E major, on which he is described as "Guitarist to the King of the Belgians" ; Op. 6, *Loin de toi ;* Op. 7, *Fantasia varie on a romance from 'Otello' ;* Op. 8, *Divertimento on three favourite English romances ;* Op. 9, *Nocturne sur la dernière pensée de Weber ;* Op. 10, *Fantasia on the favourite air, 'O cara memoria' ;* Op. 20, *Fantasia varie,* "dedicated to his pupil, Mrs. Emma Drummond, and played by the author at his concerts." This was published privately with others in Brussels and all the former were issued by Schott, London and Peters, Leipzig. There are also a few songs with piano.

Ferrari, Giacomo Gotifredo, born 1759 at Roveredo, died December 1842 in London. He was a versatile musician, proficient on many instruments, who accompanied Prince Lichenstein to Rome and Naples and was afterwards officiating at the Feydeau Theatre, Paris. He ultimately made his abode in London where he composed many operas and instrumental and vocal works. The A.M.Z. of 1802 enumerates these: *Different little pieces for guitar solo ; Italian Canzonettes with guitar accompaniments,* published 1807 ; *Favourite Canzonettas,* ditto, in 1809 and 1812 ; *Six duets,* English and German words ; *Six nocturnes,* German and Italian words, with two other volumes of songs, all with guitar, were published by Breitkopf & Härtel, Leipzig.

Ferrer, Esteve Joseph, born March 13, 1835, at Torroella de Montgri, province of Gerona, Spain, and died March 7, 1916, in Barcelona. He was the son of a lawyer who gave him his first musical instruction on the guitar. In 1860 he continued his studies under Jose Broca in Barcelona and commenced teaching and public playing a few years later. In 1878 he was guitarist at many concerts in Barcelona and obtained such success that he visited Paris and in 1882 was guitarist at the Comedie Francaise and professor in several institutions. He returned to Barcelona after appointment as professor of the guitar in the Conservatoire del Liceo, where he was occupied for three years and then visited Paris again, returning finally to his native land in 1905. Ferrer was a deeply religious musician whose compositions, numbering about a hundred, include sacred music, guitar solos, duos for two guitars, guitar and piano, guitar and flute, etc., which were published by Durand, Paris and also Pisa, Paris. He wrote a history of the guitar which appeared in Mundo Grafico, Madrid, and also a *Method for the guitar* which remains in manuscript. Ferrer's Op. 1, *Remembrances of Montgri* (his native town) dedicated to his teacher, Jose Broca, was published in 1873, and his last compositions were published in his native land by Union Musical Espanola, Madrid.

Ferrer, Manuel Y., born in Lower California about 1828, and died in San Francisco, California, June 1, 1904. He was an American guitarist and an arranger for the guitar, of pure Spanish parentage, who during childhood displayed musical tendency by strumming his parent's guitar and displayed his fondness for the instrument by fashioning a crude imitation. Later, he commenced the serious study of the instrument in earnest, and when about eighteen, left his native town, travelling by stage coach to Santa Barbara, and in the old mission there, met a priest, a clever guitarist, who gave him advanced instruction. Ferrer now laboured hard and enthusiastically at the instrument, and unconsciously built the enviable reputation in the musical world, which he afterwards so justly earned and deserved. Some few years later he removed to San Francisco, and here he taught his instrument for a period of fifty years. His public appearances as guitar soloist, and also as the guitarist of a quartet of instrumentalists were very frequent, in and around San Francisco. He was a born musician, who possessed a most intense, accurate musical memory, and a very acute and refined ear, which he used to advantage. Ferrer was a member of the famous Bohemian Club of San Francisco, to the members of which he dedicated his vivacious mazurka, *Alexandrina.* For several years he was conductor of the mandolin band, El Mandolinita, in the city ; the music performed by this orchestra was solely Ferrer's compositions and arrangements. He published numerous pieces for guitar solo, but many of his works remain in manuscript. One of his pupils, Miss E. L. Olcott (Mrs. Bickford) a distinguished guitarist, describes her master in the following passage: "In stature Ferrer was short, complexion dark, with small piercing black eyes, and when I knew him, his jet black hair was tinged with grey. He was kind and gentle to a degree and a man of very few words. In his teaching, however, he was very methodical and strict, though not unnecessarily harsh, invariably playing with the pupil, and though three or four years previous to his death he broke his arm, so that his hand was apparently stiff, he still possessed a wonderful execution. He did not retain the astonishing brilliancy and dazzling technique of his youth, as he was past his seventieth year then ; but to me there is a quality more beautiful and effective than dazzling brilliancy—the soulful quality—and Ferrer possessed this in a high degree with a sufficient amount of the former. When Ferrer touched the strings of the guitar, the sounds entered the heart, and his chords made music which lifted the soul to a higher plane. One of his favourite solos was his arrangement of a selection from Puccini's *La Boheme,* which remains in manuscript. His last original composition entitled: *Arbor villa,* mazurka, was written two years before his death, and is also unpublished, and I am proud to possess a copy written by his own hand. He taught the guitar up to the time of his death, which occurred very suddenly on June 1, 1904. He had gone from his home in Oakland to San Francisco to teach, and gave several lessons, when he was suddenly taken ill, and went to the home of his daughter. Later he was removed to hospital, where he died the same day, his third wife surviving him for several years." Though he lived to a ripe old age, his death was a great loss. Ferrer was one of the most distinguished of resident guitarists in America; he was also a versatile and prolific composer. Oliver Ditson of Boston, published a volume of his works, of about two hundred and thirty pages of guitar solos, songs with guitar and a few duos for two guitars. Just previous to his death he was engaged on a second volume, which was nearing completion. His later works are considered in advance of his early publications; but all are regarded with esteem, and Ferrer transcribed no compositions but those eminently suited and appropriate for the instrument, and these are so adapted that they appear as if originally conceived for the guitar; his method, too, is thorough and his fingering carefully studied and graceful. Though he travelled but little, his fame spread over other continents and his compositions find universal favour.

Fier, Jan B., a guitarist and composer living in Vienna during the beginning of the nineteenth century where his *Rondo for guitar solo,* Op. 8, was published by Weigl, Vienna. *Six Variations for guitar; Variations faciles,* Op. 11; *Cavatine with variations* and *Two Albums of Favourite Airs for guitar,* published by Wiener Allg. Mus., Vienna. Other variations were published by Trag and also Cappi, both of Vienna; *Variations for flute and guitar,* Op. 20, Maisch, Vienna. There were also eight books of operatic pieces for guitar which appeared in 1817 and several similar compositions which were published by Cappi, Vienna, and Simrock, Bonn. Several of his manuscripts for the guitar are in the library of the International Guitarists' League, Munich.

Fiorillo, Federigo, born at Brunswick, Germany, in 1753, and living in Paris as late as 1823. He is known principally by his classical studies for the violin, in particular his Thirty-six Caprices for the violin. Fiorillo's father, Ignazio, was a Neapolitan, a mandolin player who, at the commencement of the eighteenth century terminated his travels at Brunswick, when appointed conductor at the Court Opera House, and it was in this city that his son was born. His early musical education was superintended by his father, and he inherited his parent's love of the national instrument, the mandolin, and obtained complete mastery over it, displaying to advantage the delicate nuances of tone of which it is capable. As mandolinist he performed at most of the royal courts of Europe. The resources of the instrument at this period were limited as was also the demand for players, which compelled him to turn his attention to other stringed instruments, principally the violin and viola. In 1780 he journeyed to Poland, and in 1783 was conductor of the orchestra for two years in Riga. Two years later he was solo violinist at the Concerts Spirituels, Paris, and here some of his compositions were published and well received. In 1788 he made a visit to London, and played viola in Saloman's quartet; his last public appearance in London was at the Antient Concerts when he played a concerto for the viola. After leaving London he went to Amsterdam, and from there in 1823 he removed to Paris. Fiorillo's compositions include concertos, duos, trios, quartets, and quintets for stringed instruments. Grove says: "He appears to have been originally a player of the mandolin, and only afterwards to have taken up the violin."

Fischof, Josef, born at Butschowitz, Moravia, April 4, 1804, and died at Baden, near Vienna, June 28, 1857, was a skilful guitarist and pianist, who for a period was a professor of his instruments at the Vienna Conservatoire of Music. From birth he was of delicate constitution, but his mental capacity was by no means impaired, for it is stated that at the age of three he could read, and at seven he had a good knowledge of the piano and guitar. The child showed such extraordinary intelligence, combined with a marvellous aptitude for learning and retaining knowledge, that his father, a tradesman of Butschowitz, placed him in 1813 in a college of Brunn for the specific study of languages. He remained in this institution to 1819, and at the expiration of his term had obtained proficiency in his special subjects. He had received musical instruction from Jabelka and later continued under Rieger; but his parents were desirous he should adopt a professional career, with which intent he entered the University of Vienna as a student of philosophy and medicine in 1822. Nevertheless he studied music diligently as a pastime, taking lessons in composition from Seyfried. Fischof was naturally gifted for music, an acknowledged genius at improvisation, and, although still intent upon his university studies, he contrived while in Vienna to continue his musical education under Antoine Halm for piano and composition. In 1827 he sustained a sudden reverse in his fortunes by the death of his father, and was compelled to relinquish his medical studies and put to practical use his musical knowledge by giving instruction on the piano and guitar. By perseverance and systematic methods he built an enviable reputation as a teacher, and in 1833 was appointed professor at the Vienna Conservatoire. In 1851, he was commissioned by the Austrian Government to take charge of a deputation to the Great Exhibition of London; his special interest being the piano. After his return to Vienna, he published in 1853, a volume entitled: *Historical essay on the construction of the piano, with special regard to the Great Exhibition of 1851.* Fischof, a brilliant linguist and scholar, the author of several literary works on music was honorary member of many learned societies. He published several compositions for the guitar alone, and for guitar and flute, one of which, *Brilliant Variations on an original theme for guitar solo,* published by Pennauer and also Diabelli, Vienna, enjoyed an amount of popularity, as did also, *Paganini March for flute or violin and guitar,* published by Diabelli. He was the custodian and annotator of valuable material on the life of Beethoven.

Foden, William, born March 23, 1860, at St. Louis, U.S.A., died there April 9, 1947, at the advanced age of eighty-seven. When seven years of age he began the study of the violin and so rapid was his progress that at fifteen he was the conductor of a small orchestra. His attention was drawn to the guitar by the pianist of his orchestra who was also a guitarist, and Foden received his first instruction from him. So deeply was he interested in the instrument, that he put aside his violin to devote his leisure exclusively to its study. From Wm. O. Bateman, a lawyer in St. Louis, who was a skilful and enthusiastic guitarist, the youth received serious instruction and some time after made his first appearance as a guitar soloist in his native city. He followed this by concerts in Chicago, New York, and other important centres and thus established a reputation as the premier American-born guitarist. In 1911 he made an extended tour of the States with the mandolin virtuoso, Pettine, and the following year made his abode in New York City as a teacher. He was a regular contributor of articles, relative to the guitar, to various U.S.A. music journals until 1939, when he retired from public life and returned to his native city. Foden was held in the highest esteem by the fraternity; his most famous pupil was George C. Krick of Philadelphia. His published compositions amount to more than a hundred original works and arrangements and he left a similar number in manuscript. His *Grand Method for the guitar,* in two volumes, was published in 1921 by W. J. Smith, New York.

Fortea, Daniel, born April 28, 1878, at Benlloch, Castellon de la Plana, Spain, and died there March 5, 1953. He commenced the study of the guitar at an early age, on the methods of Aguado and Tarrega, and became a popular concert performer appearing in Madrid, Barcelona and other important cities of his native land. He compiled a *Method for the guitar* which was published in 1921 and a second edition in two books appeared in 1930. He was a prolific composer for the guitar, of light national airs and dances and instrumental works for guitar, bandurria (Spanish mandolin) and lute, in combination. The first of these he published himself and later added the compositions of other musicians and thus became the founder of the important music publishing firm of Biblioteca Fortea, Madrid, issuing over six hundred compositions for the guitar. The Spanish music press said of him: "Daniel Fortea's art as an interpreter is remarkably expressive and melodious, and his complete mastery of modern instrumental technique enables him to exhibit his exquisite gifts with the greatest ease. He possesses a charming personality which is evident in all his artistic and social activities and he is loved and enjoys a high prestige among musicians." His compositions reveal the atmosphere of Andalusian lyricism. His most famous composition, *Andaluza,* has been played by all eminent guitarists and other of his best known works are *Cuentos de Madrid, Madrigal, Estudios Poeticos* and *Elegia de Tarrega,* composed in memory of his master

Fossa, Francois de, a French amateur guitarist of note who was living in Paris during the first quarter of the nineteenth century. He was an intimate friend of Aguado, who, in the second edition of his method records that it was his friend Fossa who introduced the system for production of the artificial, or octave harmonics on the guitar, thereby enabling every note to be played harmonically throughout the entire compass of the instrument. Aguado also stated that Fossa had arranged the overture to 'Jeune Henri' as a *Duo for two guitars* to illustrate his innovation. Fossa translated into French the original Spanish edition of Aguado's *Complete Method* which was published by Richault, Paris, in 1827, and in gratitude Aguado dedicated Op. 2, *Three Brilliant Rondos* "to my dear friend De Fossa." Fossa was an officer in the French Army and not a prolific composer, his few works were issued by Richault, Paris; Schott, Mayence; and Simrock, Bonn. The A.M.Z. mentions operatic arrangements for guitar, Op. 1, *La Tyrolienne, variations; Divertisements for guitar* Op. 5 and 12, and *Divertisement* Op. 13, published by Simrock, Bonn. On the title page of his *Three Brilliant Rondos* he is described as "Chef de Bataillon au 23me. Regiment de Ligne." Several of his manuscripts are in the library of the Guitar Society of Berlin and two quartets with guitar are in the library of Mrs. Bickford, Los Angeles, California.

Fouchetti or **Fouquet,** an Italian mandolin virtuoso and teacher of European renown who was resident in Paris during the latter half of the eighteenth century. He was a popular teacher of his instrument up to 1788 after which nothing is heard of him. His pupils were members of the nobility with whom he was held in high esteem. He compiled a method for the mandolin which was published by Sieber, Paris, in 1770 under the title of *Method for learning to play easily the mandolin of four or six strings.* This treatise also included six serenades and six sonatas for the instrument.

Francia, Ferdinando, and his son Leopoldo, natives of Omeguo, Piedmont, Italy, were mandolinists and guitarists of European fame. The father, a very portly musician, died in Genoa June 13, 1904. His many published works include a *Method for the mandolin* in three volumes, a method for the guitar entitled, *Lo studio della Chitarra,* and light compositions for mandolin and guitar or piano, mandolin band and guitar solos. All were published in Italy principally by Ricordi, Milan, and Maurri, Florence. A few of his manuscripts are in the library of the International League of Guitarists, Munich.

Leopoldo, the son, received his first musical instruction from his father and continued at Milan Conservatoire. As mandolin soloist he was awarded the gold medal at the International Mandolin Contests held in Genoa, 1892, when the president of the judges was the famous violin virtuoso, Camillo Sivori. After this success Francia undertook a European concert tour which brought him to England. The Manchester Chronicle of October, 1908, wrote: "Francia, who is as handsome as he is clever, won the International Mandolin championship in Milan last year." For some years from 1900, he resided in England, making London his home: but made periodical visits to the continent. He toured Russia in 1909 and the musical press stated that he was acclaimed in his concerts, particularly in Moscow and St. Petersburg "where he is delighting crowded audiences nightly." The London Daily Telegraph said: "Signor Francia brought from his instrument a warmth of expression previously unknown on this beautifully shaped instrument, the mandolin." He was a versatile linguist of gentlemanly appearance and stage deportment who enjoyed widespread popularity in England and performed under the most celebrated conductors while his many concert and music hall appearances were universally successful. He toured with the most celebrated artists of the day including Mme. Melba. Just previous to the first world war he was on tour in the low countries and when war was declared, Francia was interned and died there on Armistice Day, November 11, 1918. He wrote a method for the mandolin entitled: The *Virtuoso School for the Mandolin* on which he is described as "Mandolinist to H.M. The Queen of Italy." *Italian studies for mandolin; Progressive studies on Velocity and Technique for mandolin* and more than three hundred light compositions for mandolin alone, with piano and in combination with other instruments. The majority of his works were published in London, principally by Dallas, Keith Prowse, Turner, and Paxton.

Franklin, Benjamin, born at Boston, U.S.A., 1706, and died Philadelphia, 1790. This famous American publicist made improvements in musical glasses, if he did not actually invent them, shortly before his death. A specimen of his glass harmonica is in London, South Kensington Museum. It is recorded that he was seriously interested in music, played the guitar well, and contributed articles on musical aesthetics which were published in 1765.

Fridzeri or **Frixer,** Alexandro Marie Antoine, are the names by which this musician was known. He was born January 16, 1741, at Verona, Italy, and died in Antwerp, 1819. Fridzeri was a man of unusual natural ability and artistic attainment and his skill as a musician was equally varied and wonderful. He was one of the most renowned of mandolin virtuosi, a clever violinist, organist, and a composer whose works met with popular favour. By an accident he lost his sight when a child; but it appears in no degree to have deterred his genius, it may be that the loss of this sense quickened and intensified others. From childhood he was very susceptible to musical impressions and was taught singing and the elements of music; apart from this he was self-taught in all the branches of the art, both practical and theoretical. When eleven he had learned to play the mandolin and to such a degree of proficiency that he was employed as singing boy to his mandolin accompaniment at the fashionable serenades customary and popular with Italian nobility. Gifted with a voice of sympathetic quality, the blind boy's romances, with his mandolin, were a great pleasure to these select assemblies. Fridzeri also studied other musical instruments and excelled in his performances on the flute, violin, viol d'amour and organ, and at the age of twenty was organist of the cathedral of the

Madonna del Monte Berico, Vicenza, removing there with his parents. For about three years he was organist and then commenced an exceedingly romantic career. At the age of twenty-four he left home with a companion and toured Europe as a blind mandolin virtuoso. His repertoire consisted of the concertos of Tartini, the principal works of Pugnani and Ferrari, and several of his own compositions. They travelled through northern Italy and central France and towards the close of the year, reached Paris. Wherever he performed, during his travels he had been highly successful ; but when he arrived in Paris, he was accorded but little encouragement. The mandolin was not so popular here as in his native land and he was compelled to turn to account his ability as violinist. He was violin soloist at the famous Concerts Spirituels, performing with brilliant success a concerto of Gaviniès and two of his own concertos, Op. 5. He lived in Paris for two years as a teacher of the violin and mandolin and then made a protracted concert tour through the north of France, Belgium and the Rhineland of Germany. In Strasburg, he was the recipient of much popular favour where he resided for twelve months and it was here that he wrote his first two operas, which were produced at the Comedie Italienne, Paris, when he returned to France. In the year 1771, he was again in Paris, now engaged in writing incidental music for the Parisian theatres and various string quartets and mandolin sonatas. Having been offered the appointment of private musician to the Count Chateaugiron, at the end of the year, he removed from Paris to take up his duties in Brittany and remained in the service of the Count for twelve years. During these years he applied his leisure to operatic composition, making periodical visits to Paris in order to superintend the production of his new stage works. Experiencing a demand for this class of composition he terminated his service with the Count and again lived in Paris ; but on the outbreak of the Revolution in 1789, he fled to Nantes, where he founded an academy of music and was once again occupied in teaching. For five years the blind musician was actively engaged in Nantes until the terrors of the civil war in Vendee and the wholesale massacres in the city in which he was living compelled him to fly for refuge to Paris. He was elected a member of the Lycee des Arts in 1794, and commenced a music printing establishment in Rue Saint Nicaise, near the Palaise Royal, which was doomed to early destruction: it was in this residence that he published his opera, *Les souliers mordóres.* Ill-fortune now pursued him, for in December, 1801, a bomb was hurled at the Palaise Royal and its explosion totally destroyed all Fridzeri's possessions. The unsettled state of the French government of this year compelled the blind musician, now sixty years of age, and reduced to poverty, to quit France finally and start again his wanderings. With his two daughters—both musicians, the elder a violinist and the younger a vocalist—they travelled through Belgium and arrived in Antwerp, where they settled, the daughters following the vocation of their father, and founded a music and musical instrument business, which was continued until the death of Fridzeri in 1819.

Fridzeri, totally blind, was an artist of undoubted genius, a man of remarkable character, severely tried under great adversity. His opera, *The two soldiers,* established his reputation as musician and writer of music which was at the same time melodious and brilliant, and his published works, though not numerous, embrace nearly every variety of musical composition. The following are the principal: Op. 1, *Six quartets for two violins, alto and bass,* published Paris, 1771 ; a *Second book of Six quartets,* ditto ; *Les deux miliciens* (The two soldiers) Op. 2, a comic opera in one act, produced successfully in Paris, 1772 ; Op. 3, *Six sonatas for the mandolin,* Paris, 1771 ; *Les souliers mordóres* (The brown shoes), Op. 4, a comic opera in two acts, produced in 1776 at Comedie Italienne, Paris ; *Two Concertos for the violin,* Op. 5, played by the author at the Concerts Spirituels, Paris ; *Six Romances* for voice with harp accompaniment, Op. 6 ; *Four duos* for two violins, Op. 7, Paris, 1795 ; *Lucette,* an opera produced in 1785 ; *Les Thermopyles,* Op. 8, a grand opera—this was transcribed by the author for piano solo ; Collections of songs with piano accompaniment, Op. 9 ; *Symphony concertante* for two violins, alto and grand orchestra, and other small compositions for the mandolin. Giuseppe Bellenghi, the esteemed mandolinist and composer of Florence, dedicated his most excellent variations for mandolin and piano, on the *Carnival of Venice,* " to the memory of Fridzeri, the blind mandolin player and composer."

Fürstenau, a family of German musicians, flautists and guitarists. Caspar, who was born at Münster, February 26, 1772, where his father was a member of the Bishop's band, was at an early age, left an orphan under the protection of the renowned violoncellist, Bernhard Romberg. This genius tried to force his protégé to learn the bassoon in addition to the oboe, on which instrument he had already received elementary instruction ; but his decided preference for the flute and guitar predominated, and while in his teens he became sufficiently proficient on the flute to assist in the support of the family by entering a military band, in addition to that of the Bishop of Münster. In 1792, his son, Anton Bernhard, named after the brothers Romberg, was born, and Fürstenau, with his wife and family, travelled through Germany during 1793-4, eventually settling at Oldenburg, where Fürstenau entered the Court orchestra and gave instruction to the Duke. In 1811 this band was discontinued and he again set out on his wanderings, this time with his son, now nineteen, an excellent flautist and guitarist. They performed duos for flute and guitar and flute duos, in all the important cities of Germany after which the father returned once more to Oldenburg, where he died, May 11, 1819. Caspar Fürstenau wrote much for the flute and guitar, and was the author also of several songs with guitar accompaniment. The most important of his compositions are: *Three Themes with variations for flute and guitar,* published by Schott, Mayence ; Op. 10, *Twelve pieces for two flutes and guitar,* Simrock, Bonn ; Op. 16, *Twelve pieces for flute and guitar,* in two books ; Simrock, Bonn ; Op. 29, *Variations for flute and guitar,* Andre, Offenbach ; Op. 34 and Op. 35, *Two Albums for flute and guitar,* Breitkopf & Härtel, Leipzig ; Op. 37, *Twelve pieces for flute and guitar,* and Op. 38, *Twelve pieces for flute and guitar,* Hofmeister, Leipzig ; *Six songs,* in two albums, with flute and guitar, Schott, Mayence ; *Six songs with accompaniment of guitar or piano,* Simrock, Bonn.

Fürstenau, Anton Bernhard, son of Caspar, born October 20, 1792, at Münster, was a more brilliant flautist than his father and occupied a very prominent position in the musical world ; he was named after the brothers Anton and Bernhard Romberg. He was taught the flute and guitar at a very early age by his father ; his progress was phenomenal, for at the age of seven, he was soloist at a court concert in Oldenburg. He remained with his father, and they made extended tours together ; but in 1817 he became a member of the municipal orchestra of Frankfort until 1820, when he removed to Dresden. Here he entered the opera orchestra as flautist and was in the service of the King of Saxony until his death, November 18, 1852. It was in Dresden that he first became acquainted with C. von Weber, the conductor of the Royal Opera, the two became intimate friends, and in 1826 he was invited by Weber to accompany him on his memorable visit to London. On February 5, Weber conducted *Der Freischütz* in Dresden for the last time and took leave of the members of the band, all except Fürstenau, the renowned flautist, who was to travel with him. They chose the route through Paris, and on March 5, arrived in London, where they were most hospitably entertained by Sir George Smart, organist of the Chapel Royal. This sad and indeed tragic story of Weber's visit to London, in response to the invitation of Charles Kemble, lessee of Covent Garden Opera House, is well-known to all lovers of music. Sick unto death—he was but thirty-nine—and throughout his stay, longing to return to the home, which only the prospect of making money for his family had induced him to leave. Weber's brief sojourn in England was one in which sunshine and gloom were strangely intermingled. Fürstenau, his devoted and affectionate companion, tended him with anxious care and made hasty preparations for their journey home, for Weber was filled with an inexpressible longing to see his family once more. On the night of June 4, Fürstenau assisted him to undress, but he sank under his sufferings, and died during the night. Fürstenau performed a flute concerto, May 1, of that year, at the Philharmonic Concerts ; he returned to Dresden, and remained in the opera orchestra till his death, November 18, 1852. He composed about two hundred works for various instruments, principally for flute and orchestra and with the guitar. He compiled two methods for the flute and the compositions by him and his father are mentioned in the A.M.Z. *Trio for two flutes or flute, violin and guitar,* published by Richault, Paris ; *Six Serenades for flute, bassoon, alto and guitar,* the second Op. 9, the third Op. 10, the fourth Op. 11, and the sixth Op. 18 were published by Hofmeister, Leipzig. His son, Moritz, also a flautist, made valuable contributions to musical history, and in 1852 was appointed custodian of the royal collection of music, and awarded the Royal Order of Saxony.

GADE, Niels Wilhelm, born February 22, 1817, at Copenhagen, died there December 21, 1890, was the most famous of Danish composers. He was the son of Sören Gade, a distinguished guitar maker of Copenhagen, and his brother, J. N. Gade, also followed the occupation of guitar maker. Two of the father's guitars are on display in Copenhagen museum. It was natural that Niels was taught the guitar by his parents; his early years were spent principally with the instrument and he attained a degree of proficiency far above the average. Grove says: "Gade learned a little about guitar, violin and pianoforte, without accomplishing much on either instrument"; but as this statement was supplied by the living author, his extreme modesty respecting his musical attainments can be appreciated. Riemann says: "He grew up half self-taught, without any real methodical instruction in the theory of music; but on the violin under Wexschall, he attained to a great proficiency, and also received regular instruction in the guitar and pianoforte." His early career did not receive systematic musical training until he entered the royal orchestra of Copenhagen as a violinist. He was the author of seven symphonies and several cantatas, and in 1876 visited England to conduct his *Crusaders* and *Zion* at the Birmingham Musical Festival. In addition he has composed many smaller instrumental works. His memoirs, largely autobiographic, edited by his daughter, Dagmar, appeared in 1894, and a second edition in 1912.

Gál, Hans, contemporary, born August 5, 1890, at Brunn, resident in Edinburgh. He displayed musical ability at an early age and studied in Vienna Conservatoire of Music, where he was a pupil of the erudite musicologist, Mandyczewski. He obtained his doctorate of music and philosophy in 1913 and the State Prize award of Vienna Conservatoire for composition. In 1918, he was appointed professor of music in his university and later removed to Mayence, where he was director of the Music Academy (1929-33). He is one of the most distinguished of the modern Viennese school of composers, a musicologist of wide repute and keenly interested in the mandolin and guitar. After the anchluss, he took refuge in Edinburgh, where in 1945, he was professor in the University. His various compositions free from traditional influence, with pleasing melodies, combine a modern tendency with harmonic eccentricities. He has composed operas, *Die heilige,* produced in 1923, orchestral and choral works, chamber music, songs and compositions for mandolin solo and for the mandolin band. Of his compositions for mandolin band the following are the principal. *Capriccio,* published by Osterreichischer Bundesverlag, Vienna, and composed in Edinburgh in 1948. *Kleine-Suite* in three movements (Morgenmusik, Melodie and Rondo) and *Intermezzo,* published by Musikverlag V. Hladky, Vienna. Of his unpublished compositions there are: Quartet for mandolin, violin, viola and liuto (or 'cello) entitled: Improvisation,

Variations and Finale on a theme of Mozart (the serenade ' Deh Vieni ' from Don Giovanni); Suite for three mandolins; Sonatina for two mandolins and a Suite for mandolin and piano in five movements, this suite is of some technical difficulty, beyond the ability of the average performer, and the composer, who is conversant with the difficulties to be encountered, informed the author that it was composed especially for a very skilful Viennese mandolinist. The Daily Telegraph critic wrote: "Hans Gál's compositions represent an individual style half-way between Reger and Hindemith. His music demands fairly advanced technique."

Gallenburg, Count Wenzel Robert, born December 28, 1783, at Vienna, died March 13, 1839, in Rome. He studied music with Albrechtsberger and in 1829 was director of the Karntnertor Theatre, Vienna. His wife, Giulietta Countess Guicciardi, was a pupil of Beethoven. His compositions include ballets, light piano music and Dr. Zuth records an original *March Triumphant for flute, violin and guitar.*

Gambara, Cavaliere Carlo Antonio, Knight of the Order of the Couronne de Fer, a celebrated mandolinist and instrumental composer. He was born of noble parentage, and educated in the college for sons of noblemen at Parma, where for eight years, he studied the violin and mandolin under Melegari, the violoncello under Ghiretti and counterpoint under Colla. After leaving the institution he was sent to Brescia to continue his musical education with Caunetti who was maestro di capella. His compositions which are principally instrumental, include *Four Symphonies for grand orchestra* and a *Quintet for mandolin, harp, violin, viola and violoncello.*

Gänsbacher, Johann Baptist, was born May 8, 1778, at Sterzing, in the Tyrol, and died July 13, 1844, in Vienna. At the age of six he was in the choir of the village church, where his father was the conductor. He learned to play the organ, piano, guitar and 'cello, at Innsbruck, Halle and Botzen, displaying unusual ability on all during his youth. In 1795 he entered the University of Innsbruck, but on the formation of the Landsturm the following year, he served as a volunteer, and was awarded the gold Tapferkeits-medaille. He removed to Vienna in 1801 where he was a teacher of music; but in 1803, after hearing the Abbe Vogler play, he became a pupil of this esteemed master. During the winter of 1803, the Abbe was celebrating the thirtieth anniversary of his ordination and an interesting circumstance connected with this anniversary was Gänsbacher's meeting Beethoven at the house of Sonnleithner in Vienna. By chance, Gänsbacher was present and heard both Beethoven and the Abbe Vogler extemporize on the piano in turn. Gänsbacher admired the playing of Beethoven, but was perfectly enraptured and enchanted with the Adagio and Fugue thrown off by Vogler. So excited was Gänsbacher after the performance that he could not retire to rest that night, but knocked up his friends at most

Daniel Fortea

William Foden

Guillermo Gomez

Carlo de Filippis

Hans Gál

unreasonable hours to describe what he had heard. It was this performance that decided Gänsbacher to continue musical study under the Abbe Vogler, and by his influence, Carl Maria von Weber also became a pupil. Gänsbacher reverenced his master and said: " Mere association with him was a kind of school," and needless to add, Gänsbacher was a favourite of the abbe and also of his fellow students, Weber and Meyerbeer. Gänsbacher and Weber were both enthusiastic guitar players, and they were frequently together in convivial meetings and serenades with other musical companions, accompanying their latest songs on their guitars. To play the guitar was a passport into jolly company and this was the instrument, which, slung over their shoulders, accompanied these young musicians on their excursions into the country, and many of their best songs were conceived and improvised with their guitars as they wandered amidst the enchanting scenery of upper Austria. Few scenes of artistic life are more charming than the picture of the details of Vogler's last Tonschule at Darmstadt. After the abbe had said mass, at which one of the above mentioned scholars played the organ, all met for a lesson in counterpoint. Then subjects for composition were given out, and finally each pupil brought up his piece to receive the criticism of his master and fellow pupils.

Gänsbacher says: " At first we took the exercises in the afternoon, but the abbe, who almost daily dined with the Grand Duke, used to go to sleep, pencil in hand. We therefore agreed to take our exercises to him henceforward in the morning." A work of some great composer was analyzed every day and sometimes the abbe would propound a theme for improvisation. Themes were distributed and a fugue or sacred cantata had to be written every day, while organ fugues were improvised in the cathedral on subjects contributed, in turn, by all. Not infrequently, the abbe would himself play, and upon these occasions, when in the empty church alone with his " three dear boys " his performances were the wonder and admiration of his pupils. From the mind of one of these " boys " the impression was never effaced, for Weber described them as a thing never to be forgotten. By way of varying the routine the master would take his scholars with him to organ recitals in neighbouring towns, and the pupils in their turn would diversify the common daily tasks by writing an ode to celebrate " papa's" birthday. In 1810 Weber wrote the words, Gänsbacher two solos, and Meyerbeer a terzett and chorus for this event. A happier household can hardly be imagined, and when their master died, his pupils grieved as if they had lost a father. In 1809, Gänsbacher spent some time in Dresden and Leipzig, revisiting his home in Vienna, and the following year lived for a time in Darmstadt to renew his studies under Vogler. Weber was an intimate friend of Gänsbacher, who retained a sincere affection for him, took him to Mannheim and Heidelberg where Gänsbacher assisted in his concerts, and it was Weber who advised him to compete for the vacant post of Court Capellmeister in Dresden. Meantime Gänsbacher lived alternately in Vienna—where he became acquainted with Beethoven—and Prague where he assisted Weber with his *Kampf und Sieg.* He also served in the war of 1813—as he had previously done in the campaign of 1796—as a courier. His unsettled life at length came to a satisfactory end, for at the time Weber was suggesting his living in Dresden, the Capellmeistership of the Cathedral in Vienna fell vacant in October, 1823; Gänsbacher applied, was appointed, and remained there for life. He died July 13, 1844, universally respected both as a man and musician. He was one of the eight musicians who bore the mortal remains of Beethoven to their resting place, and during Haydn's last years was a constant and intimate visitor in his house, and a source of comfort and pleasure to the aged musician during the infirmities of old age. He was a sincere friend of Meyerbeer in Darmstadt, and also showed interest in Schubert by performing his cantata on the subject of *Prometheus,* now lost, at Innsbruck in 1819 and at his death he composed and conducted a motet for Schubert's funeral. As a composer Gänsbacher belongs to the old school; his works are pleasing and betray by their solidity the pupil of Vogler and Albrechtsberger and they are recorded in the A.M.Z. Op. 3, *Six German songs with guitar accompaniments,* Peters, Leipzig; Op. 10, *Two Sonatas for guitar and violin,* Breitkopf & Härtel, Leipzig; Op. 12, *Serenade for guitar, flute, violin and alto,* Haslinger, Vienna; Op. 14, *Serenade for violin or flute and guitar,* Haas, Vienna; Op. 17, *Three Italian songs with guitar accompaniment,* Gombart, Augsburg; Op. 23, *Serenade for clarinet, violoncello and guitar,* Gombart, Augsburg; and Op. 28, *Second Serenade for clarinet, alto, violoncello and guitar,* Gombart, Augsburg.

Garat, Pierre Jean, born at Ustaritz, near Bayonne, April 25, 1764, and died in Paris, March 1, 1823, was guitarist and vocalist to the ill-fated Marie Antoinette and a celebrated singer with his guitar. The son of a lawyer he was destined for that profession, but developed a strong passion for music which he studied under Franz Beck, a composer and conductor in Bordeaux. Garat appears never to have gone deeply into the subject for he was a poor reader, and owed success to his natural gifts, combined with the opportunity of hearing Gluck's works and of comparing the artists of the French and Italian operas in Paris. He possessed a fine expressive voice of unusual compass including both baritone and tenor registers, an astonishing memory, a prodigious power of imitation, and when singing to his own accompaniment on the lyre-guitar the effect was both poetic and romantic. Garat may be said to have excelled in all styles but his predilection was for the music of Gluck. For a considerable time he enjoyed the patronage of Marie Antoinette, Garat being her guitar and vocal teacher, an especial favourite of the Queen, who upon more than one occasion relieved him from embarrassing financial difficulties. During the reign of terror he fled from Paris, and in 1792, with the violinist Rode, went to Hamburg, where the two gave very successful concerts. On his return to France he appeared at the Concerts Feydeau in 1795 and the Concert de la rue Cléry with such brilliant success, that he was appointed professor of singing at the Paris Conservatoire in 1799. Garat retained his voice until he was fifty, and when it failed, tried to attract popularity by eccentricities of dress and behaviour. He trained many pupils who attained celebrity in the musical world, and married a pupil, Mlle. Duchamp, when he was fifty-five. Garat was the author of romances with guitar accompaniment, which are unknown now ; they appear so uninteresting that it is evident it was Garat's style and appearance alone, that made them popular. Eitner records one in particular of his vocal romances, *Belisaire,* with lyre-guitar accompaniment. His lyre-shaped guitar, made in 1809 by Ignace Pleyel of Paris, is in the Museum of the National Conservatoire, Paris. It was especially constructed by order of a wealthy amateur who had been enamoured by Garat's playing and singing. It is of unique design, most delicately and richly inlaid, and the same museum also exhibits the guitar of his royal pupil, Queen Marie Antoinette.

Garcia, Fortea Severino, was born at Siete Aguas, Valencia, Spain, during the middle of the nineteenth century and died January 4, 1931, in Barcelona. He studied medicine in Barcelona University from 1880 and qualified as a doctor, was called to the colours and, as Infantry Captain, was the recipient of various military awards and decorations. During his university career he became acquainted with the maestro of the guitar, Magin Alegre, and studied the instrument as an amateur under his supervision and continued later under Arcas and also Cano. When he was given military notice of nineteen hours only, to embark for Cuba, his enthusiasm for the guitar was so intense that he utilised it to visit Tarrega to solicit the master's interpretation of certain of his studies. He was the author of about thirty arrangements for the guitar which were issued by Union Musical Espanola, Madrid.

Garcia, Manuel del Popolo-Vicente, a celebrated Spanish tenor vocalist, born at Seville, January 22, 1775, died in Paris, June 2, 1832, was the founder of a Spanish family of musicians, which has been characterised by Chorley as: "representative artists, whose power, genius, and originality, have impressed a permanent trace on the record of the methods of vocal execution and ornament." Being of Spanish nationality, it is natural they were all more or less able performers on the guitar, and have composed numerous vocal works with the accompaniment of this instrument. In youth Manuel Garcia was an eminent performer on the guitar, and is recorded as the teacher of the great Spanish guitar virtuosi, Dionisio Aguado and Huerta. He taught and played, then customary in Spain, with the finger nails, instead of the finger tips. Garcia commenced his musical career as chorister in Seville Cathedral at the age of six, and at seventeen was well known as composer, singer, actor, guitarist and conductor. By 1805 he had established an enviable reputation throughout his native land, and his compositions, principally short comic operas, were performed all over

Spain. In February, 1808, he made his first appearance in Paris in Paer's *Griselda,* and within a month was the principal singer in the theatre. He toured Italy until 1816 when he visited England for a short period, returning to Paris and was singing and playing in Catalani's troupe with his usual success. At the first performance of Rossini's opera, *The Barber of Seville,* on February 5, 1816, Garcia played the rôle of Almaviva. For an interesting account see Rossini. In the early months of 1823 he reappeared in London when he founded his famous school of singing. His salary had risen from £260 in 1823 to £1,250 in 1825, and he continued to gain still greater fame by teaching, than singing. The education of his illustrious daughter Marie, subsequently Mme. Malibran, was now completed—she had studied singing and the guitar under her father, and had also received guitar instruction from Ferdinand Pelzer, in London—and under her father's supervision made her début. Garcia now took an operatic company to the United States, and in 1827 they travelled to Mexico where he brought out eight operas. After eighteen months he set out to return with the proceeds of his labours, but the company was robbed of everything, including nearly £6,000 in gold, by brigands. Garcia eventually returned to Paris and continued teaching. He was a good musician and wrote with facility and effect nearly forty operas ; words and music seemed to flow naturally. He wrote many songs with guitar accompaniment, and always recommended the guitar as an accompanying instrument during vocal training, and he also made good use of the guitar in his operatic scores. In 1825 his vocal compositions appeared in London and Lemoine, Paris, published his transcription of Heller's *Six recreative studies for guitar solo.* Eitner mentions two volumes of his *Spanish songs with guitar accompaniment,* which were published by Beauce, Paris. It is because of his extraordinary and unprecedented success as a singer and vocal teacher, that his ability on the guitar and his associations with the instrument appear overshadowed. His son Manuel, equally conspicuous as a vocalist, was the inventor of the laryngoscope ; a professor of singing in the Paris Conservatoire, and afterwards at the Royal Academy of Music, London. To perform well on the guitar was a family attribute, for both his daughters were good guitarists.

Gardana, Enea, an Italian guitarist living during the last quarter of the nineteenth century. His published works, principally operatic transcriptions for guitar solo, were issued by Ricordi and also Lucca, Milan. Egmont Schroen in *The guitar and its History,* published in 1879 by A. Klemm, Leipzig, states that Gardana was one of the principal modern composers of that time. The English guitarist and composer Ernest Shand held an esteemed opinion of his compositions, evidenced by his manuscript notes on several of Gardana's operatic arrangements which are now in the possession of the author of this volume. Op. 3, 5, 10, 16, 18, 22, and 46 are for guitar solo, some of which were written for the guitar with nine strings (three extra basses). Op. 16 is an album of five transcriptions and one original composition.

Gassner, Ferdinand Simon, born January 6, 1798, at Vienna, and died February 25, 1851, at Darmstadt, where he was taken at an early age, his father being painter at the Court Theatre. Gassner was at first supernumerary in the Court Band, but in 1816 was violinist. He was later chorus master of the National Theatre, Mayence, and in 1818 musical director of Giessen University. In 1819 the title of doctor and the " facultas le gendi " for music was conferred on him ; but in 1826 he returned to the Court Band at Darmstadt, and was later chorus master and teacher of singing at the Court Theatre. He wrote many theoretical treatises, and during the years 1841-45 was editor of a Mayence music journal. In 1842 he made additions to the supplement of Schilling's Universal Lexicon der Tonkunst, and subsequently compiled a similar volume himself which appeared in Stuttgart in 1849. As composer he was active, and wrote operas, ballets, cantatas and guitar music. Schott publish four of his songs with guitar accompaniment. Hofmeister, Leipzig, issue *Variations for guitar and violin or flute,* and Andre, Offenbach *Variations for guitar solo,* Op. 8 and more songs with guitar.

Gatayes, Guillaume Pierre Antoine, born at Paris, December 20, 1774, died there October, 1846, was the illegitimate son of the Prince de Conti and the Marquise de Silly. In infancy he was placed in the theological seminary of the Abbot of Venicourt, where he received his education, including a knowledge of singing and the rudiments of music. While in the institution he obtained a guitar which he studied in secrecy, but was soon discovered. The Abbot, sympathising with the boy's perseverance and determination, allowed his instruction in guitar playing in addition to singing. At fourteen, life in the seminary became burdensome and he longed for liberty, so, in 1788, to free himself from all restraint he fled from the seminary taking his guitar with him. The troubles of the French revolution now intervened, and his parents, the Prince and Marquise, had been forced to flee. At fourteen, left to his own resources, he wandered through France, obtaining a precarious existence by singing to the accompaniment of his guitar. To prevent being discovered, he passed under an assumed name, that of Gatayes, and by chance lodged in a room adjoining that of the notorious revolutionary, Jean Paul Marat. This man would listen intently to the charming romances of his neighbour Gatayes, accompanied on his guitar, and was so impressed by the music that he assisted the struggling musician financially and they became close friends. At Marat's invitation Gatayes visited his benefactor daily and they passed many hours together playing and singing. Soon after this acquaintance, Gatayes received a serious injury to his knee which confined him to his room for a considerable time and this enforced seclusion he utilised by perfecting his mastery of the guitar and in the compilation of his first method for the instrument. On the morning of July 13, 1793, Gatayes had been playing to Marat as was his custom, and immediately after his departure, was startled to hear cries and great confusion from Marat's apartment. Gatayes hastened to the room and found Marat lying mortally wounded and his assassin, Charlotte Corday, standing by, calmly anticipating the infuriated mob which was assembling. At the end of this year, 1793, Gatayes commenced the study of the harp also, and became famous throughout his native land as a virtuoso on that instrument and two years later published a method for it. Gatayes' name, however, is more widely known by his numerous songs, which were exceedingly popular; his *Mondélire* was sung throughout the length and breadth of France. In 1790, when he was but seventeen, his *Method for the guitar* and *New Method for the guitar* were published by Petit, Paris, and these instruction books were the standard works of the time. He was a prolific composer, and his instrumental publications, which enjoyed as wide a popularity as his vocal, are chiefly guitar solos and duos, harp solos, and duos for guitar with flute or violin. His son, Josef Leon (1805-1877) also a harp virtuoso, guitarist, and composer, was intimate with Berlioz, who mentions him in his autobiography. Gatayes senior, is the author of many preludes, divertimentos, etc., for the guitar in addition to several Methods; *Collection of pieces for guitar solo,* Op. 27, Schott, Mayence; *Duos for two guitars or guitar and piano,* Op. 14, 25, 31, 32, 44, 47, 49, 57, 58, and 59; *Duos for guitar and violin or flute,* Op. 35, 39, 41, 42, 43, 48, 65, 68, 76, etc, Meissonnier; Sieber; and also Janet, Paris; *Trios for guitar, violin and flute,* Op. 55, 56, 69, 77, 80, 84, 85, 96 and 109, Janet Frère; Langlois; Richault; and Lemoine, Paris; *New Method for the Guitar,* Leduc and also Petite, Paris; *Duo for guitar and harp,* Op. 25, Meissonnier, Paris; *Little Method for the guitar,* Janet, Paris.

Gaude, Theodore, born Wesel-on-the-Rhine, June 3, 1782, a German guitarist and composer of some repute, was taught the flute and guitar by local players. He was taken to Paris during early life and continued to play the guitar under the best teachers, after which he commenced to give instruction. He made his début in Paris as guitar soloist and the success of his first public performance spurred him to increased concentrated study and in 1814 planned what he intended to be a protracted European concert tour, to terminate in St. Petersburg. Fate, however, decreed otherwise, for although the commencement of the tour was successful, he was stricken suddenly by a serious illness in Hamburg, where he was compelled to remain a considerable time to recover. The kindness manifested during his illness and convalescence, resulted in his abandoning the tour and he made Hamburg his permanent residence. He was held in the highest esteem as a guitar virtuoso and teacher. During the period from 1817 to 1833 the musical press, and A.M.Z. in particular, were lavish in his praise as musician and virtuoso, saying, " an artist who revealed undreamed of possibilities and beauties from his instrument." Gaude wrote about ninety compositions for his instrument, which were accorded a certain amount of popularity in Germany where they were published. The majority were for guitar alone and for the guitar with another instrument: *Studies and Exercises for guitar,* Op. 10, 21, 30; *Progressive studies for two guitars,* Op. 57 and 60; *Variations for solo guitar,* Op. 11, 18, 27, 29, 34, 44, 55, 56, 84, 85 and 86; *Duos, Sonatas, Serenades,* etc., for *flute and guitar,* Op. 1, 2, 5, 9, 22, 24, 25, 28, 35, 39, 40, 46, 54, 58 and 59; *Grand Duos concertante* and *Serenades for two guitars,* Op. 48, 50, 51 and 53; *Trio for guitar, violin and violoncello,* Op. 49; *Six original songs with guitar accompaniment,* Op. 19, and numerous arrangements for guitar, also vocal compositions with guitar, without opus numbers. The above were published by Cranz and also Boehm of Hamburg; Peters, Leipzig; Simrock, Bonn, and Andre, Offenbach. Many of Gaude's compositions are in the library of the International Guitar League of Munich.

Gelli, F. Vincenzo, a Slav guitarist and composer, living during the nineteenth century, of whom little is known. In the library of the Vienna Conservatoire of Music are the following of his compositions; Op. 6, *Variations* and Op. 7, *Guitar solos,* published by Cappi, Vienna; *Three Sonatine notturno for two guitars,* Hohenleithner, Vienna; *Serenade for violin and guitar,* Op. 10; *New Guitar Method with cadenzas and arpeggios,* Op. 3, with German and Italian text, published by Cappi, Vienna.

Geminiani, Francesco, born at Lucca, Italy, in 1680, and died at Dublin, September 17, 1762, was composer, celebrated violinist and guitarist. His renown in the musical world rests entirely upon his skill as a violinist, but he was also talented on the guitar. After preliminary instruction on the violin and guitar from a local teacher, he continued the study of the former instrument under Corelli, and was concert director in Naples. He came to England when thirty-four years of age where his reputation as violinist had preceded him. To the King's friend, Baron Kilmansegg, Geminiani dedicated twelve violin solos, and the Baron recommended him to the King's notice. He was acknowledged the greatest master of his instruments in England and enjoyed a good income from his well-remunerated teaching. In 1750, he went to Paris where he resided for five years, after which he visited England again. Geminiani was continually in want; he had a great passion for paintings, and instead of writing music, he painted, gave high prices for the pictures of others, and in this manner his earnings vanished. To retain his liberty, which his creditors were always seeking to restrain, he beseeched a pupil, the Earl of Essex, to take him as his servant, and it is recorded that the Earl claimed him when being taken to prison for debt. He is the author of much valuable music for violin and 'cello, and his *Art of playing the violin,* in twenty-three parts with twelve exercises, which appeared in London in 1740, was the first book of its kind to be published. About the same period Bremner of Edinburgh, issued his method for the guitar, entitled: *The Art of playing the Guitar, etc.* This work which is of no value at present, was published in no less than five languages, English, Italian, French, German and Dutch.

Georges, Alexander, born February 25, 1850, at Arras, France, an eminent French composer, principally of operatic and vocal music, many songs from his operas being well-known. He was educated musically at the Niedermeyer School, Paris, and was later a professor of theory in the same institution. He has written many operas—commencing 1890 with *Le Printemps*—symphonic poems, songs and compositions for mandolin bands. He manifested keen interest in the mandolin and other fretted instruments and officiated as President of the judges at the International Mandolin Concours held in Boulogne in 1909. His most widely known composition for mandolin band is *Fete a Florence,* a test piece familiar at many mandolin contests in France. He was Chevalier of the Legion d'Honneur, and was living in 1912 as a composer, in Rue du Rocher, Paris.

Gernlein, Rudolf, a German guitarist, song writer, author and composer was living in Berlin during the first half of the nineteenth century. Mendel in his Musical Lexicon describes him as a good guitarist and the composer of sentimental songs with the guitar. From 1831-5 more than seventy such songs with the guitar and also guitar solos were published in Berlin. For a period he was a music critic and journalist and in 1836 contributed to Gottfried Weber's journal Cecilia, issued by Schott, Mayence. He wrote a few guitar solos, but Op. 42, *Grand Fantasia* and *Variations, for solo guitar* has been reprinted and the theme only from this composition was reprinted a hundred years later, by Haslinger, Vienna.

Gervasio, Giovanni Battista, a Neapolitan mandolin virtuoso, who, with his wife, a vocalist, gave concerts in London in 1768 and the following year in Frankfurt and other German cities. Eitner states that Gervasio was the composer of duos for two mandolins and airs for mandolin with guitar, and in addition, pieces for the violin and flute which were published in Germany.

Giadrossi, Josef Dominik, born January 12, 1870, at Pola, Istria, died February, 4, 1920, in Gratz. He was the guitarist of Pietro Bianchi's famous quartet and afterwards resided in Gratz as a teacher of the guitar. While there he compiled his *Vollstandige Schule fur Gitarre*, of which a new and revised edition by E. Kubitz was published by Anton Goll, Vienna.

Giardini, Felice de, an eminent violinist and guitarist, born at Turin, 1716, and died in Moscow, December 17, 1796. He entered the choir of Milan Cathedral, became a pupil of Paladini for singing and composition, and also studied the guitar. He was a member of the opera orchestra, first in Rome and then in the San Carlo Theatre, Naples, and from there he commenced a tour through Germany, eventually arriving in London in 1750. His success as a violinist was immense and he became the favourite of the London musical world. Two years later he was leader of the Italian opera orchestra and appears to have infused new life in the band. In 1756 he was manager of the opera but suffered substantial pecuniary loss, and during the next eighteen years passed his time between the opera, organising and playing at concerts and teaching and composing. In 1784 he travelled under the patronage of Sir William Hamilton, the husband of the notorious Lady Hamilton, to Naples, where he resided for five years. He returned to London, and made an attempt to popularise comic opera at the Haymarket Theatre, but met with disastrous failure, after which he left England with his troupe to try his fortune in Russia. He failed in St. Petersburg and likewise in Moscow, and at length, weighed down by penury and distress, sank under dogged misfortune and died in the latter city. Giardini's portrait was painted by Sir Joshua Reynolds. He was described by Gardiner of Leicester as a "fine figured man, superbly dressed in green and gold ; the breadth of lace upon his coat, with the three large gold buttons on the sleeve, made a rich appearance, which still glitters on my imagination." Giardini wrote numerous chamber compositions, which included the guitar and the instrument was in use by his company on their tours. Eitner states that he composed *Six Trios for cetra (mandolin) violin and bass,* which were published in London in 1760. He bequeathed to Signor Testori, a soprano vocalist and guitarist of his troupe, who accompanied him to Russia, *Oeuvre de sonates d'alto with guitar accompaniment.* This and other of his compositions for the guitar remain in manuscript.

Gilles, Henri Noel, born at Paris, 1779, and died there in 1814. He was taught music by his parents and at seventeen entered the Paris Conservatoire of Music, studying the oboe under Sallentin. The following year he obtained the second prize with honours, and in 1798, succeeded in winning the first prize. He began the study of the guitar a year later, when he was second oboe in the Theatre Feydeau, Paris. In 1801, he was promoted to principal oboe which position he retained for about two years, when he entered the orchestra of the Italian Opera. His attachment to the cause of Napoleon, at the time of the restoration obliged him to quit France and he fled to New York, from here he removed to Philadelphia, subsequently returning to his native land. Gilles was the author of many compositions for the guitar, including solos and collections of songs with guitar accompaniment. The majority of these and his compositions for the oboe were published by Hanry, Paris.

Giuliani, Mauro, the most renowned of Italian guitarists and one of the most brilliant guitar virtuosi the world has known, was born at

Bologna, in 1780. In early life he was acquainted with the playing of the violin, flute and guitar ; but after a few years of indifferent instruction, and while still a youth the two first instruments were discarded and the guitar claimed his undivided attention. He was endowed with more than ordinary ability and aptitude for musical study, and while in his teens formed a style of playing totally different from that in vogue in Italy. His conceptions of the capabilities of the instrument and his determination in prosecuting these ideas to a practical issue, produced an unerring and brilliant technique, combined with a powerful, sonorous tone. Giuliani was, with the exception of his first rudimentary lessons, an entirely self-taught player, yet he takes a position pre-eminently above all previous guitar masters, both in his practical and theoretical knowledge of the instrument, and also as the founder of a distinct and refined school of guitar playing. His style of composition, too, far outshone the most brilliant of former writers for the instrument, and his compositions remain today a living monument to his genius. As a youth he attracted considerable attention by his playing in his native land, and before he was twenty had obtained the reputation as the first virtuoso in Italy. Having received such success and encouragement in his homeland, he undertook a continental tour, previous to the year 1800, and from that time his fame became widespread throughout Europe. He visited Paris at an early date, and while there Richault published his Op. 8, *Three Rondos for guitar*, an announcement on the title page stated that Giuliani was eighteen years of age. He travelled for some considerable time, and towards the close of 1807 was residing in Vienna as virtuoso, composer and teacher. During his residence here he gave instruction in the art of guitar playing to various royal and other notable persons. Among the most celebrated of his pupils were the two Polish virtuosi, J. N. Bobrowicz and F. Horetzky, the Archduchess of Austria—to whom Giuliani was appointed Chamber Musician—the Princess Hohenzollern, the Duke of Sermonetta and Count George of Waldstein. The German music journals from 1807-1821—periods of Giuliani's residence in Vienna—record his successful concerts and remarkable talent, in the most flattering terms, and all are unanimous in declaring him the supreme of guitar virtuosi. In Vienna, Giuliani associated with the most prominent musicians of the city, who held him in the highest esteem and admiration ; for many years he was intimately associated with Hummel, Moscheles, Diabelli, Mayseder and Hadyn, and he lived and moved in the society and intercourse of the most learned and influential. On February 26, 1818, he was guitar soloist at a concert in Vienna, and Molique, solo violinist, when the first public performance of a composition, an overture of Schubert was given, the composer himself being present. Giuliani's solos on this occasion were his own themes, with variations. His enthusiasm and devotion to the instrument was the means of bringing it to the notice of musical celebrities, who were not only entranced by the beautiful effects when in the hands of such a master, but who seriously studied it and individually composed and published music for it. Diabelli, Moscheles, Mayseder and Hummel were all near Giuliani's age and an intimate friendship existed, which proved very beneficial to Giuliani, for they had all been well-grounded in the traditional schools of music and were exceptionally proficient in their skill upon their respective instruments—were, in fact, virtuosi on the piano and Mayseder on the violin—and all were interested in and wrote for the guitar. With the assistance of Moscheles, Diabelli and Hummel, all pianists, Giuliani commenced to compose duets for guitar and piano, and these were performed publicly in the company of one or other of these artists, which increased his popularity in a marked degree. His own skill and powerful execution upon the guitar also brought the instrument favourably to the notice of Beethoven and Spohr, both of whom wrote for it, and Giuliani was regarded with distinguished favour by them. Giuliani was a member of the orchestra under Beethoven's baton, at the first performance of what was then advertised as "an entirely new symphony," the seventh, in A major, on December 8, 1813 and repeated on the 12th. Meyerbeer and Hummel played the drums, and Moscheles the cymbals, and Giuliani, with the other renowned musicians, was publicly thanked by Beethoven in a letter published in the Vienna Zeitung. What instrument Giuliani played is not stated, but his name was particularly mentioned in Beethoven's public letter of thanks. As an artist, he was continually striving to improve the instrument and its music, endeavouring also to produce new and original effects which might be introduced into his compositions and also in the art of playing the guitar. One result of his efforts in this direction was the introduction of the instrument known at the terz guitar, the size of the tenor guitar. This guitar, while of the same shape and construction, was much smaller than the ordinary guitar; its strings were considerably shorter and therefore capable of being raised to a higher pitch—a minor third—and the result obtained was an increase in the brilliancy of the tone. Giuliani, without much delay, introduced this terz guitar in his concerts, and composed many pieces for it which possess a very marked degree of excellence. He was associated in his concerts with Diabelli, and their duos for guitar and piano met with unbounded success, and so popular was the terz guitar or the guitar with the capo d'astro, after its introduction by Giuliani, that he was commissioned by the leading music publishers to write duets for this instrument with piano or guitar. He composed innumerable pieces for guitar solo, duets for guitar and terz guitar and for guitar and piano. These works attained a very extensive popularity, and nothing so good in the manner of duets for guitar and piano has since been published; they are particularly interesting on account of their remarkable originality and flowing melodies. All this style of music, and also his less ambitious publications, were eagerly sought by the musical public and Giuliani was importuned by publishing houses for new compositions so frequently, that before he departed from Vienna, more than a hundred of his compositions, opus numbers—not taking into consideration his smaller pieces—had been published.

In 1815, he was engaged with Mayseder, violinist, and Hummel, pianist, in giving a series of "Dukaten concerte" or subscription concerts. As guitar soloist, Giuliani played with immense success in the famous Augarten, and was also the guitarist in a series of six musical soireés given in the Royal Botanical Gardens of Schönbrun, in the presence of the royal family and nobility with Hummel, pianist, Mayseder, violinist, Merk, violoncellist and a flautist. For these concerts, Hummel composed his *Grand Serenades,* Op. 62, 63 and 66, *for piano, guitar, violin, flute and 'cello,* or in place of the two last instruments, clarinet and bassoon; also Op. 74, *The sentinel, for solo voice with accompaniments of piano, guitar, violin and violoncello.* These serenades, dedicated to Count Francois de Palffy were published by Artaria, Vienna, with an engraving on the title page depicting these musicians playing in the Royal Gardens. They are of exceeding difficulty, and only in the hands of players of exceptional skill could an interpretation be expected, as in addition to the great execution required for the performance of the work generally, each instrument was given a solo in variations of the most brilliant description, written expressly for each of the original performers, viz., Giuliani, Mayseder and Hummel. After the departure of Hummel from Vienna in 1816, Moscheles associated as pianist with Giuliani and Mayseder, and they appeared together in all the important cities of Germany. In 1821, Giuliani visited his native land, and performed in Rome with his accustomed success; but his stay in Italy was short, as previous arrangements had been made for a concert tour of Europe and in the winter of 1821, he was heard with admiration in Holland. He also toured again in Germany and from there travelled to Russia, meeting in St. Peterburg his erstwhile associate and friend, Hummel, who had journeyed some time previously to this city in the suite of the Grand Duchess Maria Paulowna. In St. Petersburg Giuliani received an enthusiastic reception, the cordiality of which was not exceeded and rarely equalled during his life and he resided there for several years; subsequently, in 1833, he made a first visit to London in the company of Hummel, and they performed at the most brilliant and fashionable concerts, their playing exciting much enthusiasm. It was in London that he met his most distinguished and only rival, Ferdinand Sor, who had visited London some years previously and established a reputation. Sor was a most remarkable guitarist, and in some respects he surpassed the degree of excellence attained by Giuliani; but the latter's playing was of a totally different style and his musical compositions, too, were more readily comprehended by amateurs than were those of Sor, as a consequence Giuliani soon found numerous adherents in England, and his compositions were immensely popular. So general was the public interest now taken in the instrument and its literature, that a monthly music journal, devoted solely to the interests of the guitar was published under the direction of the guitarist, Ferdinand Pelzer, the first number appearing in January, 1833. This periodical was entitled The Giulianiad, after the popular virtuoso Giuliani, and his and other eminent guitarists' compositions were published in each number. This magazine was issued regularly for about twelve months, after which its publication ceased. In June, 1836, Giuliani was again in London playing in the company of the pianist, Moscheles, and the violinist, Mayseder, and on the occasion of the first production in England of Beethoven's Seventh Symphony, Giuliani was again a member of the orchestra under Moscheles' baton, the instrument he played was again not mentioned. Giuliani's tone and expression in guitar playing were astonishing, and a competent critic wrote of him: "He vocalised his adagios to a degree impossible to be imagined by those who never heard him; his melody in slow movements was no longer like the short, unavoidable staccato of the piano, requiring a profusion of harmony to cover the deficient sustension of the notes, but it was invested with a character, not only sustained and penetrating, but of so earnest and pathetic a description as to make it appear the natural characteristic of the instrument. In a word he made the instrument sing." After leaving England he once more visited Vienna, the scene of his first artistic triumphs, and was living there as late as 1840. Speaking of his death, the English music press said: "In him the little world of guitar players lost their idol, but the compositions he has left behind are a rich legacy to which the present and future generations will, we have no doubt, pay every homage of respect and admiration." Giuliani's sister (Prat says daughter) Emilia Giuliani Gugliemi was also a talented guitarist winning fame by her concert performances. On June 26, 1807, she performed at an important concert in Vienna and was appearing there as late as 1841; the last heard of her was when concertising Europe in 1844. She was the authoress of several pieces and collections of melodies for guitar solo, including Op. 1, *Five Variations*; Op. 2, *Six books of operatic transcriptions for guitar solo*; Op. 3, 5, 9, *Variations*, and Op. 46, *Six Preludes for the guitar*, dedicated to Count Luigi Moretti, published by Artaria, Vienna, while all the former were issued by Ricordi, Milan. (Count Luigi Moretti was a talented amateur guitarist and composer whom Eitner cites as the author of about twenty compositions, Op. 9, 17 and 18 are *Duos for guitar and violin*; Op. 13 and 14 *Trios*, and Op. 16, *Quintet* published by Carli, Paris, and Ricordi, Milan). Gustav Schilling says of Giuliani: "History speaks about several musicians of this name. The most celebrated among them was Mauro Giuliani, a native of Bologna. He was a guitar virtuoso, a finely educated man who came to Vienna from Italy at the end of 1807. At that period he was at his best, though only a youth. Through his interesting talents in various ways, principally, however, by his perfect knowledge and partially by his own views about music, as well as his really wonderful playing on his instrument (which at that time in Germany rested only with him, and outside of him, excepting in Naples and a few other principal towns in lower and middle Italy, was considered a light, gallant plaything, though possibly as a pleasant accompaniment of small, easy songs), he drew all Vienna's attention to himself. Among those who would make up the so-called 'fine world,' he was made the musical hero of the day.

His compositions for the guitar, of which several appeared in Vienna and later on in Bonn and other important publishing centres, and which consist of variations, cavatinas, rondos, etc., with or without accompaniment of other instruments, rich in melody, show animus and taste. He uses his compositions, and this is characteristic of him, to make the guitar not only obligatory, but furthermore, an instrument on which can be presented a pleasing, flowing melody, with a full voiced, regularly conducted harmony. This necessitates a broad and full gripped manner of playing which is possessed by but few, as for example in his *Serenade,* Op. 3, and others." Schilling also wrote: "In 1808, Mr. Giuliani, on April 3, gave a concerto on the guitar in Vienna, composed by himself, being accompanied by the whole orchestra, which was extraordinarily pleasing on account of its rarity and because it was charming to the ear." According to Mendel's Musikalisches Conversations-Lexicon, Giuliani made several visits to his fatherland and died in Vienna in 1820, when but forty years of age. Prat states that he died in Vienna during June, 1840. When Giuliani departed from Vienna in 1821, just previous to his protracted tour through Germany and Holland to Russia, the continental critics and writers appear to have entirely lost sight of his whereabouts and concluded him dead. That they erred is proved by the fact of his appearances at concerts in London during 1833, and even as late as 1836 and also by the publication in England, by public subscription, of his *Third Concerto* and other of his compositions. It is possible that Mendel may have mistaken the death of Mauro Giuliani for that of another guitarist of this surname, for a Michele Giuliani was living in Vienna during the same period, the author of Op. 1, *Grand Variations for two guitars,* Weigl, Vienna; Op. 4, *Rondoletto for guitar, two violins, alto and 'cello,* Diabelli, Vienna; Op. 8, *Overture from 'Othello'* and Op. 9, *Variations for guitar solo.* A Giovanni Francesco Giuliani flourished in Vienna also at the same time, who was the author of *Four Quartets for mandolin, viola, 'cello and lute* and *Six Nocturnes for two sopranos with guitar or harp accompaniment;* the manuscripts of the quartets are in the Musikfreund Library, Vienna, and the nocturnes were published in Florence. Moscheles in his Diary, writing of the year 1814, says, "the youthful pranks and practical jokes devised with his artistic colleagues Merk and Giuliani;" and Umlauff, in the life of his father, Johann Karl, speaks of "the elder and younger Giuliani, Schubert, and other Viennese musicians meeting at the house of Frau v. Andre, weekly, making music till past midnight." The A.M.Z. also mentions Mauro Giuliani, the son, who was an excellent guitarist, singer and composer of Florence. Giuliani's portrait was published, and dedicated to him, by his friend and publisher Domenico Artaria, the proprietor of the renowned music publishing firm of Artaria & Co., Vienna; several other portraits of this artist were published during his life. Giuliani's published compositions can be grouped for convenience under three heads: I. Concertos for guitar; II. Compositions for guitar with orchestral instruments, duets for two guitars, and duets for guitar and piano; III. Guitar solos, guitar studies, and songs with guitar accompaniment. It is almost incredible to believe, that in addition to his numerous public appearances, his teaching, and his concert travels, Giuliani found time to write and publish nearly three hundred pieces, including a practical method for the instrument, several concertos, divers studies, numerous quartets and quintets, solos and songs. The *Grand Concertos for guitar, with accompaniment of full orchestra or instrumental quartet,* Op. 30, 36, 70 and 103 are compositions for the instrument without fear of rivals, they were published respectively by Artaria, and Diabelli, Vienna, and Johanning of London. *The Concerto,* Op. 36, *for terz guitar and orchestra,* published by Diabelli, Vienna, and Richault, Paris, has been transcribed for the piano by Hummel. *The Third Concerto,* Op. 70, *for terz guitar and quartet or piano,* dedicated to Baron de Ghill'any, was published by subscription in 1833 by Johanning, London, and Richault, Paris, and was highly praised by the editor of The Giulianiad, the same year, and this journal also mentions the eulogies bestowed on this concerto by Czerny and Hummel. Giuliani transcribed the polonaise from his *Third Concerto,* Op. 70, and also the rondo and polacca from the *First Concerto,* Op. 30, as duos for two guitars. Op. 103, is *Concerto for terz guitar with string quartet.* Dr. Zuth includes a *Concerto,* without opus number, *for guitar with flute, viola, violoncello and bass with two clarinets, two oboes, two bassoons and two horns.* On his first concerto Giuliani inscribes himself " Virtuoso di Camera di S. Maesta la Princessa Imperial Maria Luigia" (Archduchess of Austria), and on Op. 146 he also adds, " Chamber musician to the Duchess of Parma, Piacenza, etc." Giuliani composed in collaboration with Hummel, *National potpourri,* Op. 43, *Grand duo for guitar and piano,* and also a *Second duo,* Op. 93, both published by Artaria, and with Moscheles he composed *Grand duo concertante,* Op. 20, *for guitar and piano,* dedicated to H.I.H., Archduke Rodolphe of Austria, published by Richault, Paris. Giuliani composed numerous quartets, quintets and sextets for guitar and strings Op. 65, *Polonaise for piano, guitar, two violins, alto and bass,* Op. 101, 102 and 203, are the principal and also a *Serenade Concertante for guitar, violin and 'cello,* Op. 19, published by Artaria. Giuliani's duets for violin or flute and guitar are the choicest and rarest compositions ever published for these two instruments; they display to every possible advantage the characteristics, capabilities and beauties of both instruments. In these duets the guitar is not relegated to the background as an instrument merely for accent and beating time, the uses employed by many modern writers; but all his works are distinguished by conciseness and lucidity of thought and form, and by a dignified, aristocratic bearing, displaying in a striking manner the power to sing by both instruments: it is in these particulars that Giuliani's duos excel those of Carulli. The most widely known are Op. 25, 52, 76, 77, 81, 85, 126 and 127, although these do not exhaust the list. The duos for two guitars and guitar and piano met with astonishing popularity, and Op. 66, 116, 130 and 137 for two guitars, and Op. 68, 104 and 113 for guitar and piano, were published simultaneously by Ricordi, Milan; Simrock, Bonn; and Hofmeister, Leipzig. Giuliani's earliest compositions were published when he was a mere youth in his teens, and his guitar method was compiled when he was seventeen. He was but eighteen when he had made a name in Paris, and at this time he published his Op. 8. These first works are chiefly original themes with variations, and the first seventeen, with trifling exceptions, are among his easiest compositions; Op. 10 is dedicated to Princess Caroline de Kinsky. The *First Potpourri,* Op. 18, 20, and later compositions, require of the performer a more detailed and perfect knowledge of the entire fingerboard and demand greater technical ability. Of the more ambitious solos are the *Second Potpourri,* Op. 28, of eight pages, and *Grand Sonata Eroica,* also the *Third Potpourri,* Op. 31, of nine pages, well written to display the beauties of the guitar, a favourite of its composer and frequently performed by him at his principal concerts. It is designed in the arpeggio style, which, at a later period Regondi used, and it contains several effective cadenzas. The *Fourth Potpourri,* Op. 42, does not attain the standard of excellence of the former of its class, nor even of those compositions entitled, *Rossiniane,* Op. 119 and 120, dedicated to His Excellency the Duke of Sermonetta. Between these important compositions, Giuliani conceived numerous compositions of a lesser degree of difficulty, well adapted for the use of pupils and amateurs, which were appreciated by the class of players for whom they were intended; these were issued simultaneously by all the prominent European publishers. The most useful is the series entitled *Papillon,* Op. 30, three books, each containing about ten melodies of increasing difficulty. Op. 43, is a *Collection of easy solos,* suitable for students, as is also *Bouquet emblematique,* Op. 46, published by Clementi & Co., London. A work of merit is Op. 83, *Six Preludes for the guitar* wherein the art of modulation is exemplified with considerable skill and effect. Giuliani's *Practical Method for the guitar,* Op. 1, in four parts, was published by Ricordi, Milan, and Peters, Leipzig; the text was in three languages, French, Italian and German and a later edition in Swedish was also issued. This method was never popular, it contains very little text and explanatory notes—the chief characteristic of a successful instruction book—and in this respect is in distinct contrast from the method of his rival Sor, which contains more text than studies; it provides, however, a valuable addition to the studies of advanced students. About sixty original manuscripts including Op. 25 and 92 with Giuliani's autograph, are in the Musikfreund Library, Vienna. The original manuscript of a *Grand Sonata, for guitar,* and twenty others are in the library of the Internationalen Guitaristen Verband, Munich, and other autographed scores are in the Berlin State Library. Among his numerous compositions are several vocal items, invariably with guitar accompaniment, and in some, additional optional accompaniments have been provided by the composer, the piano, flute and violin appearing most frequently. *Six cavatinas,* Op. 39; *Three nocturnes,* duets for soprano and tenor, and *Le troubadour,* a collection

Alois J. Götz

Niels W. Gade

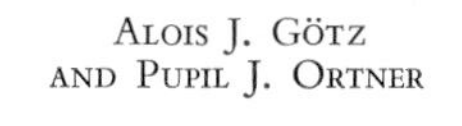

Alois J. Götz
and Pupil J. Ortner

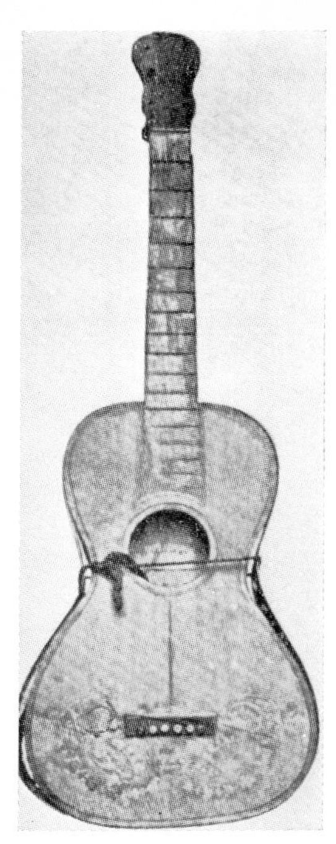

Charles Gounod and his Guitar

Mauro Giuliani

of French romances, were published by Simrock, Bonn ; *Three cavatinas with guitar,* Steiner, Vienna ; *Flattre kleiner Vogel* and *Der treue Tod,* Schott, Mayence ; *Près d'un volcan,* for contralto or baritone, Op. 151 ; *Ode of Anacreonte,* for soprano, Op. 151b ; *Three airettes,* for tenor, and *Pastorale for three voices with flute, guitar or piano,* Op. 149, Ricordi, Milan ; *Ad altro laccio ; The beauties of nature,* and others by Johanning, London, and *Der abschied der Troubadours,* a romance for voices with French and Italian words and accompaniments of guitar, piano and violin, composed in collaboration with Moscheles and Meyseder, published by Diabelli, Vienna.

Glaeser, Karl Gotthilf, born May 4, 1784, at Weissenfels, died in Barmen, April 16, 1829. He received his musical tuition in the famous St. Thomas' School, Leipzig, under Hillier, the violin with Campagnoli and also during this period had instruction in guitar playing from a fellow student. In 1808 he was living in Naumbourg, where he taught singing and founded an excellent choir for women. He was appointed musical director in Barmen, Westphalia, in 1817, where he also established a musical instrument business. He was the composer of numerous songs with guitar accompaniment, solos for the guitar, and piano compositions, which with theoretical treatises are mentioned by Riemann. Two volumes of dances for the guitar were published by Hofmeister, Leipzig.

Gollmick, Karl, born near Dessau, March 19, 1796, and died at Frankfurt, October 3, 1866, was the son of an operatic actor and tenor vocalist on the German stage. Karl Gollmick was a good guitarist and pianist and esteemed both as a skilful performer and teacher of his instruments. When but eleven, he composed a volume of six songs with guitar accompaniments, which found a publisher in Andre, Offenbach. He was educated first at Cologne, where Bernard Klein was his schoolfellow ; but the liking for his father's theatrical life manifested itself very early in young Gollmick, and his ordinary studies were somewhat interrupted thereby. He went to Strasburg to study theology and languages, which he neglected for music, and after a time returned home. In 1812, he visited Strasburg a second time and during his stay, studied harmony and composition with Capellmeister Spindler. Gollmick was an able pianist and in 1817 removed to Frankfurt where he taught the piano, guitar, and French language. Some few years later he was a member of the Stadttheatre orchestra under the direction of Spohr, where he was employed until pensioned in 1858 ; he entered the orchestra as drummer and previous to his departure was chorus master. After he had been in Frankfurt a few years he married and in after life made several short visits to London. He compiled a dictionary of music, the second part contains biographies of musicians, and it was published by Andre, Offenbach, in 1857. His principal work is the music dictionary, Critische Terminologie fur Musiker und Musikfreund, a treatise of merit, published in Frankfurt in 1833, a second edition was issued in 1839. In 1858, he retired and in 1866 his autobiography was published just previous to his death on October 3, of the same year. Gollmick is known principally as music critic and writer, whose numerous contributions, full of wit and satire, appeared in many journals. He wrote about a hundred and thirty musical compositions, guitar solos, songs with guitar and piano, and piano solos and duos. Richault, Paris, published *Six Waltzes for guitar solo,* in 1813 ; *Eight songs with guitar ; Six Waltzes for guitar,* Schott, Mayence ; *Russian melody for voice and guitar ; Six Romances with guitar,* published in 1822 and about a dozen others issued by Schott. His compositions with the guitar are mentioned in A.M.Z. His son, Carl, was also known as a guitarist.

Gomez, Guillermo, born August 5, 1880, at Malaga, Spain. His father, Jose, a distinguished professor of music, gave him his first musical instruction, and the lad played the guitar in the popular Flamenco style, with no serious intent. When the family removed to Seville, his parents became aware of his musical precocity and so they placed him with the musical director of Seville Cathedral for singing and harmony and he also studied the violin with Julis Dollega. He commenced his professional career as violinist in the opera orchestra. In 1897 Tarrega was playing in Seville, Gomez heard him, and was so enraptured by the master's guitar playing that he then determined to make the guitar his special study. As he had played the instrument in the Flamenco method he found it essential to recommence his study ; this he did and practised the method of Tarrega, his compositions and transcriptions, devoting all his energy to the object. In 1900, he emigrated to Mexico, where by his teaching and public performances, as guitar soloist, he raised the standard of playing on the Tarrega method. He organised musical quartets, quintets and sextets and performed successfully in all the principal theatres of Mexico and Central America. His pupil, Francisco Salinas, became professor of the guitar in the National Conservatoire of Music, Mexico City in 1935.

Gomez has written orchestral compositions, among which his *Suite Andaluza* in four movements, conceived as a guitar solo was arranged and performed by the New York Philharmonic Orchestra in 1929. This and his *Aires Andaluces,* composed in 1904, for guitar, was a decided success and both works have been arranged for orchestra, band, piano, etc. In addition there are more than twenty guitar solos with accompaniment of muted string orchestra, sonatas, etc., for guitar solo, and a *Method for the guitar* with English and Spanish text. Many of his compositions were published personally. Gomez is known internationally by his recordings and compositions.

Gomez, Vicente, contemporary, born at Madrid in 1911, living in U.S.A. When a child he became familiar with the gipsy guitar players who frequented his father's inn, the rendezvous for intellectuals, gentry and poor peasants, who had a taste for good music and good wine. Born in this atmosphere, Gomez acquired the Flamenco or gipsy style of playing and was an infant prodigy. He became a pupil of Quintin Esquembre, who was a pupil of Tarrega, but his serious classical training commenced when he entered Madrid Conservatoire. At the age of thirteen he made his first public appearance in the Teatro Espanol, Madrid, and then toured his native land. During 1932-3 he toured N. Africa and France, and in April, 1936, commenced a more extended tour of Russia and Poland, then to Cuba and ultimately to U.S.A. Gomez was guitar soloist in several films in Spain ; but during the civil war he fled to U.S.A., became an American citizen, and for three years served in the U.S.A. army. After his discharge, he toured all the Latin American States extensively and then made his début, April 24, 1938, in New York City, and was very successful. The following year he was in Hollywood in the popular film, " Blood and Sand," where his guitar playing was the prominent feature ; during this period he wrote and arranged various musical compositions. From Hollywood he flew to Milwaukee, where he was solo guitarist in the concerts of the Symphony orchestra, delighting his audiences with *El Albaicin*, his own composition, and *Nocturne Sevillano,* by Tucci. For other concerts, he flew across the states to New York, from Hollywood on to Chicago, returning to New York, May, 1942. He then visited his native land and made a concert tour of western Europe towards the close of 1948 when he was a frequent broadcaster. Vicente Gomez is said to be the only guitarist who has mastered the widely differing technique of classical and Flamenco music. He is an authority on the latter style, rich in tone effects and technique, so beloved by the Andalusian, and is a reputed composer of Spanish gipsy songs. The press wrote, " Gomez plays with freedom and abandon, has a very pleasing stage appearance and captivates his audience by his sincerity and individual style. Rarely one meets such spontaneity of delivery and technique." He has compiled a *Method.* His most popular solos are *Holy week in Seville, El Albaicin, Alegrida and Romance d'amour,* published by the American Academy of Music and the Mills Co., New York.

Gopfert, Carl, Andreas, born January 16, 1768, at Rimpar, near Wurzburg, died April 11, 1818, at Meiningen was a German instrumentalist and composer, who, at an early age was taught the piano, organ and guitar, after which he made a special study of the clarinet under the virtuoso Meisner. In 1788 he was first clarinet in the Royal Chapel, Meiningen, resigning after periods in similar positions in Vienna, Bonn, and Leipzig. He returned to Meiningen when appointed Hofmusikus of the Royal Chapel where he officiated until his death at the age of fifty. He was an able guitarist, a remarkable performer on the clarinet and the composer of many concertos for clarinet with orchestra, numerous duets for clarinet and guitar, guitar and flute, guitar and bassoon, and quartets and quintets in which the guitar is a member. He also wrote several compositions for grand orchestra, and some piano music. His biography appeared in the Leipzig Zeitung, and his compositions, published in Vienna, Bonn, Leipzig and Offenbach, are mentioned in the A.M.Z. for the year 1808. Op. 11, *Sonata for two guitars and flute ;* Op. 13, *Duo for guitar and bassoon ;* Op. 15, *Duo for guitar and flute ;* Op. 17, *Duo for two guitars ;* and Op. 18, *Duo for guitar and flute,* were published by Hofmeister, Leipzig ; Andre, Offenbach, published a *Sonata for bassoon and guitar.*

Götz, Alois Joseph, born February 13, 1823, at Ischl, near Salzburg, Austria, died July 9, 1905 at Innsbruck, Tyrol, was the son of Joseph Götz, a highly esteemed doctor of medicine, who, as the discoverer of the medicinal waters of Ischl made his own name and that of his town famous. His son's musical gifts were manifested at an early age, and he was given instruction in the theory of music and on the violin during his eighth year. When eighteen he was living with his elder brother, August, while studying for admission in the Forest Academy of Mariabrunner. August Götz was a guitarist whose playing of Giuliani's concertos made such an impression on his young brother that he neglected the violin to study the guitar, and his principal object in life became an obsession to regenerate the instrument. During his residence in the Academy he continued to receive guitar instruction and by his perseverance and determination obtained a good mastery over the instrument. Upon the termination of his studies he was stationed at Aussee, Styria, in 1844, where he commenced his duty of forester and it was here that he received the praise of Archduke John for his guitar playing with the violinist Hermann Roithner. Götz now began to compose for the guitar ; his first works were transcriptions of popular national folk songs for guitar solo. In Aussee he formed an acquaintance with the guitar virtuoso, L. Schulz, who had lived for some time in England (see Schulz) as a guitarist, and who was at the time in the district for health. The acquaintance proved beneficial to Götz, as he received instruction in the higher branches of guitar playing, which spurred the enthusiast to even greater efforts, and it was through this instruction that Götz decided to compile his method for the guitar. As a member of the civil service he was transferred to the Tyrol, in which romantic district he made his second home ; but this pastoral life was soon interrupted, for at the outbreak of war in 1848, Chief Forester G. Götz, with the Pustertaler Landesverteidiger was ordered to the neighbouring frontier. His guitar playing round the camp fires, made him many friends among whom were the poets, Adolf Pichler and Hermann Gilm. Götz was awarded the war medal of 1848 and decorated with the jubilee medal in 1873. During his residence in Reutte, he married in 1862, and for twenty years was Chief Forester of this district. He played before the Royal Court on several occasions, and received the warmest praise from King Ludwig II and the Dowager Queen for his solos and as guitar accompanist to vocalists. In 1880 he removed to Innsbruck and having retired from the civil service devoted himself with untiring energy to popularise the guitar ; during his late years he was afflicted with deafness and forced to retire from public life. His most renowned pupil was Jacob Ortner, who was a professor of the guitar in the Vienna State Academy of Music. Götz, honoured by his country with the title of Imperial Councillor, was preparing his autobiography for publication when death intervened, after a short illness at the age of eighty-three. He has published many compositions for guitar alone and in combination with zither, mandolin, violin, flute and 'cello, and three volumes of songs with guitar accompaniment remain in manuscript. He is the author of the *Reform Guitar School, in three parts,* published by Andre, Offenbach, who also issued several of his guitar solos, and others appeared in Vienna and Stuttgart. An autographed manuscript of a *Duo for two guitars* is in the library of the Internationalen Guitarristen Verband, Munich.

Gouglet, Pierre Marie, a French organist, guitarist and composer, was born at Chalons in 1726 and died in Paris, January 27, 1790. As a chorister, he received his first musical instruction in the cathedral and later studied the organ and guitar. For some years he was organist of St. Martin des Champs, and before he was eighteen, his *Escudiat* and a *Domine salvum* were performed in the Royal Palace, Versailles. He is the author of many French songs with guitar accompaniment which were published from about 1744 and also church compositions. His compositions are mentioned by Mendel and the library of the Paris Conservatoire contains his *Airs choisis avec acc. de guitarre.*

Gounod, Charles, born at Paris, June 17, 1818, died October 17, 1893, received his first musical education from his mother, a distinguished pianist, and having finished his classical studies at the Lyceé St. Louis, and taken his degree as Bachelier des lettres, in 1836, entered the Conservatoire, where he was in Halevy's class for counterpoint, and received instruction in composition from Paer and Lesueur. In 1839 he won the Grand Prix de Rome, by which he was enabled to continue his musical education in Italy. On his return from Italy he travelled through Austria and Germany, and became organist of the Missions Etrangeres, Paris. He had serious intentions of taking Holy Orders, and even went so far as to become an out-student of the Seminaire ; but, fortunately for music, he perceived his mistake in time. His first opera, *Sapho,* was produced at the French Academy in 1851, and the year following, he was appointed conductor of the Orpheon, Paris. His famous opera *Faust,* which was given its first performance in the Lyric Theatre, in March, 1859, placed him immediately in the front rank of modern operatic composers, and from this time his reputation increased rapidly. During the spring of 1862, Gounod was holiday-making in northern Italy, and on the evening of April 24, wandered alone by the shores of Lake Nemi. He was attracted by the sound of far-off music floating on the stilly air and, looking in the direction from whence it came, saw an Italian peasant passing, singing his native melodies to the accompaniment of his guitar. Gounod's attention was immediately arrested, and he was so enchanted by the musical performance, that he followed the peasant for some distance, and then ventured to speak to him. Said the immortal composer of Faust, to an intimate friend: "I was so enraptured that I regretted I could not purchase the musician and his instrument complete; but this being an impossibility, I did the next best thing, I bought his guitar and resolved to play it as perfectly as he did." So great an impression did this incident make on Gounod, that when he had returned to his hotel, he immediately inscribed on the guitar in ink, "Nemi, 24 Aprile, 1862," in memory of the happy occasion. The inscription may be seen in the photo of the instrument reproduced, being on the unvarnished table, just beneath the bridge. The guitar is of Italian workmanship and still bears intact and perfect the original label of its maker, Gaetano Vinaccia, Napoli, Rua Catalana, No. 46, 1834. It is constructed of native maple wood without figure, the back and sides varnished golden yellow. The edges of the table were originally inlaid, but this decoration is now missing. The ebony bridge has been, at some time, attached to the table, very roughly, by screws and the ends of the bridge terminated in delicately carved tracery in ebony, placed in relief over the lower part of the table. Its fingerboard shows signs of having been decorated also, and there remain but three of its ebony pegs. What a varied, chequered history this guitar—of all musical instruments the most poetic and romantic—divulges. Lovingly fashioned and delicately inlaid by a master of repute, in sunny Naples, sweetly responsive to the touch of its first owner, a peasant musician, and also of its last owner, an immortal musical genius, it suffered severe and rude shocks, bearing the marks of brutal kicks, its back torn from its body, its head, neck and finger board scorched, blistered and scarred by fire, and ruined by water, its delicate tracery and inlay now no more, it reposes in its rough wooden casket in a museum of Paris, to be contemplated and revered by future generations. When Gounod returned from his holiday in Italy, he took his recently purchased guitar with him to Paris where it was cherished in his residence in Montretout, a suburb near St. Cloud. "It was on this same guitar" said M. Malsherbes, the curator of the Paris Opera Museum, "that its vibrating strings gave the celebrated composer his first inspiration and conception of *Mirelle.*" During the Franco-Prussian war and the siege of Paris (1870-71) Montretout was sacked and pillaged and the guitar suffered kicks from the boot of a Prussian artillery officer, the fractures observable at the present day. The guitar in its forlorn condition was rescued from total destruction by a friend of the composer and placed in the Museum of Paris Opera. The author acknowledges the courtesy of the authorities of the Opera for photographs taken for reproduction in this volume. Prat states that Gounod was an intimate friend of the Spanish guitarist, Jaime Bosch, and that he composed especially for him a *Pasacaille* for guitar solo. Gounod was in England during the years 1870-5, where his choir, in which he employed guitars, was popular. The mandolin virtuoso, Cristofaro, associated with Gounod in many public appearances, the latter expressed delight in accompanying on the piano the original compositions of the mandolinist. In his critical study of Mozart's *Don Juan,* Gounod speaks in terms of great admiration of the serenade, with mandolin obbligato. He says: "This serenade is a pearl of transcendent beauty, an inspiration by its ravishing melody, elegant harmony and pulsating rhythm, which, under the subdued accompaniment of the orchestra, enhances the subtle charms of the mandolin." Gounod prepared a partial autobiography and memoirs have been edited by many authors, the first in 1890 by Rovet.

Graeffer, Anton, born at Vienna in 1780 and was living there as late as 1830, after which nothing is known of his life. He was a guitar virtuoso and composer who attained fame in Germany but whose renown did not extend to other lands. During his prime, Graeffer was appearing successfully at the same period as the most illustrious masters of the guitar, notably Diabelli and Giuliani. He enjoyed an honourable position as a teacher of the guitar and was the author of more than thirty compositions for the instrument, principally fantasias, variations, sonatas and dances. He compiled a method for the guitar entitled: *Systematic Guitar School,* which was published in 1811, by Strauss, Vienna, and a second edition appeared later issued by Schaumburg, Vienna. Graeffer was a highly educated man of literary ability, a member of the intellectual society of Vienna, and the author of an 8vo. book of seventy pages, entitled *Ueber Tonkunst, sprache und schrift.* (Fragments on music, etc.). This interesting literary compilation contains two folding pages of facsimile autographs, music, etc., of the greatest masters of music, deceased, or then living. It was one of the first publications of its kind to contain autographs of several of the most illustrious musicians and was published in 1830 by Sollinger, Vienna. The most important of Graeffer's compositions for the guitar were issued in Vienna, they are: *Variations for guitar solo,* Op. 3, published by Haslinger; *Variations,* Op. 5, Artaria; *Fantasia,* Op. 6, Weigl; *Grand rondo,* Op. 7, Haslinger; *Delassement,* Op. 9; *Variations,* Op. 11, 12 and 13, Mechetti; and *Grand Fantasia,* Op. 15, dedicated to Charles Troppauer, was published by Peters, Leipzig. *Ein Gedanke,* an excerpt from this last composition was republished by the Internationalen Guitaristen Verband, Munich in 1904. Graeffer also arranged for violin and guitar, the *Third Polonaise of Mayseder* and numerous smaller works.

Graener, Paul, born Berlin, January 11, 1872, can be recorded as a self-taught musician who spent a wandering life travelling all over Germany obtaining various conductor's positions. In 1896 he came to London as conductor of the Haymarket Theatre and was also a professor at the Royal Academy of Music for several years until appointed Principal of the Vienna Conservatoire. He resigned this position in 1920 to become a professor in the Leipzig Conservatoire, where he succeeded Max Reger. It is by his operas and songs that he is famed although his orchestral compositions are esteemed. In his opera *Don Juan's Abenteuer,* Op. 42, he uses the guitar with masterly effect.

Gragnani, Filippo, a very distinguished Italian guitarist and composer, born at Leghorn, in 1767, and living in Paris as late as 1812. He was a member of the renowned family of violin and guitar makers of this city and was placed with Luchesi for the study of harmony and counterpoint, intending to devote himself to church music. After remaining with Luchesi for some considerable time, Gragnani commenced to play the guitar, a circumstance which proved to be the turning point in a career which had been predestined otherwise by his parents. He had instruction on the instrument from a local player, studied it diligently for a period and eventually made a name in the first rank of Italian masters of the instrument. He undertook concert tours as guitar virtuoso in his native land, then through Germany, and at the commencement of the nineteenth century visited France, finally making his abode in Paris. Here his public performances invariably received the most lavish praise, but his fame rests mainly on his music which is characteristic of a man of scholarly musical training, and a master of his art, for his works are admirably suited for the instrument. His compositions were published principally in those towns he visited or where he resided as a professor of the guitar. Gragnani's first compositions were *Duos for two guitars,* Op. 1, 2, 3, 4, 6, 7 and 14, issued simultaneously by Carli, Meissonnier, and Richault all of Paris, and Gombart in Augsburg. Op. 5 a *Fantasia for guitar solo* was also issued by the same publishers. Gragnani wrote several quartets which met with more than usual favour, the first of these, Op. 8, *Quartet for two guitars, violin and clarinet,* was published by Carli and by Meissonnier, Paris, and they also issued Op. 9, *Sextet for two guitars, violin violoncello, flute and piano ;* Op. 12, *Trio for three guitars* and Op. 13, *Trio for guitar, violin and flute ;* Op. 10 ; *Theme with Variations for guitar solo ;* Op. 11, *Exercises for guitar ;* Op. 15, *Divertissements for guitar solo. Sinfonia for guitar solo,* and a *Sentimental sonata for guitar solo,* entitled : *La partenza,* published by Ricordi, Milan ; *Three Sonatas for guitar or lyre,* Monzino, Milan. In addition to the above, Gragnani composed many others which were published without opus numbers, principally duos for violin and guitar, piano and guitar, guitar solos and five books of guitar solos, entitled : *Guitarrenspieler,* published simultaneously by F. Dies, A. Werth and Heckel, Mannheim. New editions of his Op. 8 and 12, were published by Zimmerman, Leipzig, more than a century later. The original manuscript of his *Method for the guitar* is in the Milan Conservatoire Library. Fetis states that his published works for the guitar number about eighteen.

Grainger, Percy Aldridge, born July 8, 1882, Melbourne, Australia, contemporary. When eighteen, he came to London where he was popular as a pianist. He studied in Frankfurt and in 1915 visited America, became a bandsman in the U.S.A. army, an American citizen and eventually principal of the music section of New York University. After a successful tour of Australia in 1935 he founded a museum under his name in Melbourne University. Grainger was interested in British folk music, the melodies of which are the foundation of many of his popular orchestral compositions. He frequently scores for the guitar and mandolin and has evolved a new technique of writing for the guitar which he named "The Australian way," and he has also written guitar accompaniments, in the orthodox method, to various vocal compositions. He employs guitars in the score of *Willow willow* for voice 1st and 2nd violins, viola and two 'cellos—all the bow instruments are played muted. He writes: "I have written mostly for guitars to be played in what I call 'the Australian way.' This is done by tuning the guitars differently, usually a major chord, and striking the six strings

EXTRACT FROM

"Father and Daughter"

PERCY ALDRIDGE GRAINGER.

with the hand, thumb, or nails, backwards and forwards, after the Flamenco style. *Father and Daughter,* the Faroe Islands dancing ballad, is written for five men's voices, double chorus, strings, brass, percussion instruments and mandolin and guitar band. An extract from this is given; its first performance with an ensemble of forty mandolins and guitars was at a Balfour-Gardiner Symphony Concert and later by the London Choral Society. The guitars are divided into four sections, as will be seen from the extract, each with a different tuning from the usual method. Grainger has also composed a *Scotch Strathspey and Reel* for four voices and orchestra in which guitars are included. A sketch of his life, edited by Parker was published in 1918.

Granata, Giovanni Battista, born at Bologna, Italy, and living during the last half of the seventeenth century, was one of the earliest masters of the guitar and published *Soavi concenti di sonate musicali per la chitarra spagnuola,* Op. 4 (Sweet harmonies as musical sonatas for the Spanish guitar) in 1659; *Armoniosi Toni,* Op. 7, for *Guitar, two violins and bass,* 1664; *Novi capricci armonici for violin, viola and guitar,* 1674 and *Nuove sonate di chitarriglia Spagnuola pizzicate e battute.* The guitarist Corbetti mentions Granata in his work, *Guitare royale,* published in 1670.

Grétry, André Ernest Modeste, a famous operatic composer, born at Liege, Belgium, February 11, 1741, and died near Montmorency, France, September 24, 1813. His parents were of humble origin, his father a poor violinist placed him at the age of six in the choir of St. Denis; but displaying no musical ability he was dismissed when eleven as incapable. His next teacher, Leclerc, discovered the boy's latent talent, after which the organist, Renekin, taught him harmony; his taste for music developed rapidly, however, after hearing the operas of the great Italian composers, when performed by an itinerant Italian company under the direction of Resta. The impression these performances made on the youth caused him to try his hand at composition, and in 1758 he produced at Liege, six small symphonies and the following year, a mass for four voices, none of which was printed. In his memoirs he states that these compositions however, obtained for him the patronage of Canon du Harlez, who provided him with the means of studying in Rome, and that he commenced the journey on foot, March, 1759, with a smuggler for companion. He entered the College of Liege in Rome—which had been founded by a native of the Belgian city, for the benefit of his compatriots. Grétry remained in the institution for five years, although his teacher for composition and counterpoint had given him up as a failure in these subjects. During his residence in Rome he composed several small works, one of which, an operetta, was performed with success in the Aliberti Theatre, Rome. He was now intent on writing opera comique and ambitious of living in Paris, the centre of this art, so he departed from Rome on the first day of 1767, travelled through Switzerland and in Geneva made the acquaintance of Voltaire. Grétry remained in Geneva for twelve months as a teacher of singing, produced a one-act opera and then continued his way to Paris still fired with the ambition of producing operas. He showed his versatility by writing three, which were all staged in the year 1770. Many others followed, in rapid succession, until he had

While all are Sleeping

SERENADE IN " L'AMANT JALOUX "
WITH ACCOMPANIMENT FOR TWO MANDOLINS.
COMPOSED BY GRETRY IN 1778.

composed quite fifty ; many are now forgotten and only the following are heard ; *Le tableau parlant ; L'amant jaloux ; Richard ; Zemire et Azor* and *L'epreuve villageoise. Richard,* is still performed with approbation, *L'amant jaloux,* ranking next. This last composition, a grand opera in three acts, was written in 1778, and the second act contains the most exquisite serenade *While all are sleeping,* and to this serenade, sung by Florival, Grétry composed a delicate accompaniment for two mandolins, which is reproduced from the original score. Grétry's abode in Italy had no doubt been the means of bringing the mandolin favourably to his notice, and he uses the instrument upon various occasions with marked impression. He excelled in pastoral music, and of all his melodious compositions, this serenade is regarded one of the choicest ; by means of his vivid imagination and natural flow of melody, he created in his operas a realm of characters true to life. When the Paris Conservatoire of Music was founded, Grétry was appointed an inspector ; he retained this position only a year, for when the Institut was formed at the same time, one of the three directorships which were reserved for musicians, was given to him. Grétry was the author of several theoretical treatises on music, and during his last years was writing Reflections on the Art, which has not been published. He died September 24, 1813, and three days after was honoured by an imposing and impressive funeral in Paris. Memoirs by his nephew, A. J. Grétry, appeared in 1817 and others have been published up to 1920.

Gruber, Franz, born at Hochburg, a village of Upper Austria, near the river Inn, November 25, 1787, and died in Hällein, near Salzburg, June 7, 1863. The son of a linen weaver, he is immortalised as the composer of the German hymn, *Holy Night.* Gruber was musical from childhood, and officiated at the church organ of his native village when twelve years of age. In accordance with the custom of the period, his musical education included instruction on the guitar, in addition to a study of the organ and theory, on the latter instrument he was taught by the organist of Burghausen, a town not far distant. His youth was given to scholastic study and he became a qualified schoolmaster at the early age of seventeen and accepted a school in Arnsdorf, where he was also the church organist, remaining for twenty-two years. In 1833 he removed to a larger and more important sphere in Hallein, near Salzburg, where for thirty years he was organist of the principal church, occupying this position till his death at the age of seventy-six. When Gruber was living in Arnsdorf he was also organist of the church of the neighbouring village of Obendorf, and towards the close of the year 1818, this organ was out of repair and could not be used. On Christmas eve of that year the pastor of Oberndorf, Joseph Mohr, called on the schoolmaster, Gruber, with a Christmas hymn of seven verses he had just written, with the request that he set it to music, for two solo voices, tenor and bass, and chorus with guitar accompaniment. Gruber perused the poem, composed the vocal parts and accompaniment as desired and returned it the same evening to the parish minister. On Christmas night of the year 1818, in the insignificant parish church of St. Nicholas, Oberndorf, on the lonely mountain side, the devotional and inspiring hymn *Holy Night* was sung for the first time, Pastor Mohr, tenor, Gruber, bass, and the church choir with guitar accompaniment. This priceless treasure would in all probability have been lost but for a simple incident. In the spring of the following year, Karl Mauracher, of Fugen, organ builder, was commissioned to erect a new organ in Obendorf Church and while engaged chanced upon this Christmas hymn. The words and music impressed him so much that he requested a copy from the pastor and caused it to be sung in Fugen Church. From this humble introduction, the hymn entwined itself in every civilised land and is sung by persons of all Christian creeds. A stained glass window, portraying Gruber with his guitar and a few bars of the music has been placed in Obendorf Church. Gruber was a prolific composer whose works were not printed, only sufficient manuscript copies being made for local requirements. It is certain that other gems of song with guitar accompaniment, and pieces for guitar were amongst his compositions. Further details are recorded in *Still night, holy night* by Franz Peterlechner and *Die Geschichte eines,* by Dr. Karl Weinmann.

Guichard, Francis, born August 26, 1745, at Mans, died February 24, 1807, in Paris, was an abbot who for some time was music director of Notre Dame Cathedral, Paris. His parents removed to Paris shortly after his birth and he entered the cathedral choir when a boy. He continued as alto but the revolution of 1789 compelled him to resign his religious occupation and he obtained a livelihood by teaching the guitar and singing, and composing for the guitar. In 1795 certain of his compositions were very popular and he was the author of many fantasias for solo guitar which were enumerated by Eitner. The most celebrated entitled *Les plaisirs des soirées,* was published by Porro, Paris. He also compiled a *Method for the guitar,* issued by Frere, Paris, in addition to much church music.

Gyrowetz, Adalbert, born February 19, 1763, at Budweis, Bohemia, and died in Vienna, March 19, 1850. His father, a choir master, taught his son the rudiments of music and singing but with no serious intent, for the youth was a law student who afterwards became private secretary to Count Franz von Funfkirchen. He was, however, still keenly interested in music and for two years maintained himself in Naples by his compositions, among which were a number of solos for the lyre-shaped guitar, written for the King, with whom this was a favourite instrument. He visited Paris, but on the approach of the revolution, came to London during October of 1789, where he was held in the highest esteem and engaged in concerts with Haydn. He departed from London in 1804 upon his appointment as capellmeister and opera director in Vienna, remaining as such until 1831. He was a prolific and versatile composer of operas, ballets, symphonies, guitar solos and Italian songs with the guitar. The majority of the latter compositions were issued in Italy, others appeared with those of the most renowned musicians of the time in various collections. The A.M.Z. of 1802 records *Twelve Waltzes for guitar and violin* (the second album of the series) and in 1806 the same journal records *Italian airettes and other songs with guitar*. Another *Twelve Waltzes for violin and guitar* were published by Schott, Mayence, and a second edition was issued in 1806. In 1847, shortly before his death, his autobiography was published in Vienna, and a new edition, by Einstein, appeared in 1915.

HACKEL, Anton, born April 17, 1799 at Vienna, died there July 1, 1846, was a government accountancy official and a composer of sentimental songs with guitar and piano accompaniment. He studied singing and composition in his teens with Emanuel A. Forster. In 1825 his vocal compositions were published with those of Schubert and other celebrated musicians of the time, principally in album form. The Allgemeine Musikalische Zeitung records his collections of songs with guitar.

Halvorsen, Johan, was born at Drammen, near Oslo, Norway, in 1864, and died in Oslo in 1935. He studied the violin in Stockholm Conservatoire and at the age of twenty-three was concert-master in Bergen. After a period he visited Leipzig for further study under Brodsky and then accepted a position as leading violinist in Aberdeen. Realising need for continued study he was under Cæsar Thomson in Liege, then toured as violin virtuoso for a time until appointed conductor of Bergen symphony concerts. He was subsequently conductor of the National Theatre, Oslo. His music includes violin concertos, orchestral works, etc. All his compositions reveal the particular charm and romanticism of the far north and are reminiscent of the music of Grieg, whose niece he married. In his symphony *Bergensiana,* which is founded on Norwegian folk songs, he scores for and uses the mandolin with felicitous effect.

Handel, George Frederick, was born at Halle, Lower Saxony, on February 23, 1685, and died in London, April 14, 1759. His father, a surgeon, sixty-three years of age when the son was born, knew nothing of music, cared for it less, and regarded it as a degrading pursuit or an idle amusement. Consequently, he endeavoured to keep his son's mind from matters musical, and to stifle the genius which early displayed itself in the child ; but notwithstanding, someone contrived to convey into the attic of the house, a spinet, and he devoted much time learning to play it. When the boy was seven, his father made a visit to a son by his former marriage, in the service of the Duke of Saxe Weissenfels. The lad begged to accompany him to no avail, so resorted to strategy by following the carriage for such a distance that his father was compelled to take him in the coach. This visit resulted in the father changing his attitude to music, for upon arrival at Weissenfels the boy was soon making friends with the court musicians, and on one occasion, after service, he was lifted on to the organ stool and by his performance surprised everyone present. The Duke heard of the child's precocity, the whole facts of the case, and through his kindly intervention, the father gave consent for him to receive a musical education. He was placed with the organist of Halle Cathedral and received instruction in theoretical and practical music, the latter embracing the organ, violin, oboe and harpsichord. For the oboe Handel had a decided predilection, and showed it by a general and frequent use of the instrument in his compositions. After studying in Halle for three years, he was sent to Berlin to continue his musical education, and by his remarkable powers as organist was regarded in the city as a prodigy. Soon after his residence in Berlin his father died and he was compelled to find employment to support himself and his mother. He obtained an appointment as violinist in the opera orchestra, Hamburg, and was soon promoted to the harpsichord (conductor). In 1705 his first opera, *Almira,* was produced, and it was succeeded by *Nero,* the same year. In 1706 he undertook a journey to Italy, visiting Venice, Rome, Florence and Naples, and wrote many operas and much sacred music in these cities; his compositions being invariably received with favour. It was in Italy that Handel became acquainted with the mandolin, the tone of which at this period was very similar in timbre to that of the oboe, for previous to about 1850, the instrument was strung with gut strings, like the violin; it was also of smaller dimensions and compass, these conditions producing a nasal oboe-like tone. Berlioz writing of the mandolin about 1856, said: "Its quality of tone—thin and nasal though it be—has something appealing and original about it," this quality however has changed since the instrument has been enlarged in body, extended in compass, and strung with steel strings. For three years Handel lived in Italy and returned to his native land when offered the post of Capellmeister to the Elector of Hanover, afterwards George I of England. Receiving welcome invitations to visit England, he quitted Germany and arrived at the end of the year 1710, and in a few months his operas were being produced in London on a magnificent scale. They were received most enthusiastically and his fame was established in England. In 1726 he became a naturalised British subject and lived in London.

He wrote numerous operas, oratorios and instrumental music and in one at least of his oratorios he writes a part for the mandolin. It is quite probable that he employs the mandolin in other of his compositions. His manuscripts, preserved in the Music Library of Buckingham Palace, were presented by Smith, Handel's amanuensis, to the King as a token of gratitude for the pension granted him after Handel's death. It was in 1747 that he composed his oratorio, *Alexander Balus,* which was produced at Covent Garden Theatre, March 9, 1748, and to the aria, *Hark! Hark! Hark! he strikes the golden lyre*, which is Cleopatra's opening song, Handel scores an exquisite accompaniment of

Hark! hark! he strikes the golden lyre

FROM "ALEXANDER BALUS"
WITH MANDOLIN ACCOMPANIMENT.
COMPOSED BY HANDEL IN 1747.

André E. M. Grétry

Johann N. Hummel

Vincente Gomez

exotic orchestral colour, with the mandolin, flute and harp. It is regrettable that when the oratorio *Alexander Balus* was broadcast by the B.B.C., this aria which Handel composed for the dulcet tone of mandolin, flute and harp, was substituted by the strident blare of trumpets! The mandolin part is reproduced. It is as a choral composer that Handel predominates beyond other immortal musicians, and this beautiful aria with its appropriate and delicate accompaniment is evidence of his wonderful genius. His memoirs written by Mattheson were published in 1740.

Harder, August, born at Schoenerstadt near Leisnig, Saxony, July 17, 1775, and died in Leipzig, October 29, 1813, was the son of the village schoolmaster and attained to considerable fame in Germany as a guitar virtuoso, pianist and composer. His parents were desirous he should enter the church, and, educated with that object, was engaged in ecclesiastical duties and his education devoted principally to theology. As part of his daily curriculum he was instructed in piano and guitar playing and after having acquired a sound elementary education, entered Leipzig University to continue his theological studies; it was during residence that he renounced his university and ecclesiastical career, to devote himself to music. His practical knowledge of the piano and guitar made him a favourite with fellow students and solely for the love of the art he gave musical instruction to enquiring acquaintances. This instruction was given during leisure; but the interest displayed in his teaching, proved of such benefit to his pupils that ere long, he was importuned by many others for tuition. This was an incentive to further his own musical education, by the study of harmony and composition. Such was the demand made upon him in giving musical instruction, that in 1800, at the age of twenty-five, he had established a reputation in Leipzig as a foremost teacher of the piano and guitar. He was an able soloist and made several appearances also in Vienna, where he lived for a period and published many compositions. Mendel in his Lexicon, speaks in praise of his ability as a guitar soloist, placing him in a prominent position among German guitar virtuosi. For a time he was associate editor, with Kanne, of the influential and historical music journal, the A.M.Z., and his guitar compositions received frequent mention during the years 1803-1815. He published about fifty compositions for the guitar and his songs and romances are held in high esteem in his native land; his name is particularly associated with these songs, for which he is justly celebrated. He was living in Leipzig during the French invasion, and a few days previous to the battle was overcome by an attack of extreme nervousness, which developed to fever. His friends removed him from the city just before the battle, but the excessive commotion and uproar aggravated his malady to such a degree that he lay unconscious for several days, and succumbed on October 29, without regaining consciousness. He was mourned by many friends by whom he was esteemed as musician and respected as a man. Harder compiled a *New Practical and Theoretical Guitar School,* a work of more than ordinary pretensions and of considerable merit, with German and Italian text, the original manuscript is in the library of the International League of Guitarists, Munich. It was supplemented by a volume of advanced studies published by Haslinger, Vienna. Under his name are published forty-six collections of songs and romances with piano or guitar accompaniment, issued principally in Leipzig, Berlin and Bonn. *Six songs with guitar* and a *Sonata for guitar and piano* were issued in 1810 by Haslinger, Vienna. Op. 1, 8, 12, 15, 22, 42, 43, and 54, were songs with guitar published by Breitkopf & Härtel, Leipzig ; *Twelve Albums of pieces for guitar solo ; Brilliant Variations on an original theme for guitar, piano and flute,* Pennauer, Vienna ; *Progressive Variations for guitar solo,* Hoffman, Prague, and *Progressive pieces for guitar solo,* Haslinger, Vienna, who also issued eight other volumes of variations for guitar solo on original themes or well-known melodies.

Hardmuth, Louis, a Viennese amateur musician and guitarist living during the first part of the nineteenth century who is known more universally as founder of the world renowned lead pencil manufactory. The A.M.Z. for the year 1824 mentions his Op. 7, *Romance with guitar* and the Musikfreund Library, Vienna contains his Op. 3, *Six Variations on an original theme for guitar solo,* which was published by Sauer & Leidesdorf, Vienna, in 1824. He is interred between Beethoven and Schubert.

Harrison, Richard, and his brother Frank Mott, were musicians living in Brighton during the end of the nineteenth and the commencement of the twentieth centuries. Richard, the elder brother was a mandolinist, and Frank Mott, Bachelor of Music, and a Doctor of Philosophy, London, was a guitarist and composer for the guitar. For many years they were the proprietors of a successful music and musical instrument business in Brighton and both travelled extensively on the continent to obtain information and instruction on their respective instruments. Richard was a pupil of Cristofaro, the mandolin virtuoso, in Naples and was subsequently the author of a *Method for the mandolin,* published by Robert Cocks, London, the copyright of which was acquired later by Turner, London. The original publishers advertised it as " Harrison's Method of playing the Neapolitan Mandolin on true Italian principles," and a new and enlarged edition appeared shortly after. Frank Mott, the guitarist was a pupil of Mme. S. Pratten and in 1897 was a professor of the guitar, Trinity College, London. He was the author of *A guide to artistic guitar playing,* which was also published by Cocks. This volume contains nine original solos and six songs with guitar accompaniment. About twenty of his compositions for the guitar and songs with guitar were issued by Turner, London, and ten arrangements of *Norwegian airs for solo guitar* were published by Lucas, Weber & Co., London. He edited, condensed and revised Sor's *Method for the Guitar,* also published by Cocks, and wrote a

" Sketch of the life of Mme. S. Pratten " which was issued in book form in 1899 by Barnes & Mullins, Bournemouth. Frank Mott Harrison is more widely known, however, by his researches on the life of John Bunyan and is the recognised authority on the author of " The Pilgrim's Progress." From 1917 he was a member and afterwards an Alderman of Brighton town council. He died from pneumonia, January 25, 1945 and bequeathed his rare, priceless collection of Bunyan bibliotheca of nearly one thousand items to the town library of Bedford. Richard Harrison, the composer and arranger of a few other publications for the mandolin, *School of Scales* and *Thirty-Six Duets for two mandolins,* published by Turner, was a cultured and expert collector of rare musical instruments and books, particularly those relating to Dr. Johnson ; he died during the first world war. As the brothers moved in educated and influential circles they did much to elevate the status of the mandolin and guitar in public opinion.

Haslinger, Tobias, born March 1, 1787, at Zell, Austria, and died June 18, 1842, in Vienna. He is known as a prominent Viennese music publisher, a musician and composer who established one of the largest and most influential music publishing businesses, issuing more than ten thousand musical compositions. Haslinger was an intelligent, energetic personality on intimate terms with the most celebrated musicians ; Beethoven and he were in constant communication and the many letters to him from Beethoven prove the intimacy. Haslinger prepared a complete catalogue of Beethoven's compositions in full score, beautifully produced in manuscript by a single copyist. He was one of the thirty-six torch bearers who surrounded the bier of Beethoven, and it fell to him to hand the three laurel wreaths to Hummel, who placed them on the coffin before the closing of the grave. Among Haslinger's compositions are airs with variations and other light pieces for guitar solo and songs with guitar. He and his son Karl, who succeeded to the business, were intimate friends of all the prominent guitarists of the time and issued a comprehensive catalogue of their compositions.

Hasse, Johann Adolph, born March 25, 1699, in the village of Bergedorf near Hamburg, died at Venice at the age of 84 on December 16, 1783. His father was the village schoolmaster and organist and the son commenced his musical career as tenor vocalist and lived to be acknowledged one of the most popular dramatic composers of the period. He lived for periods in Dresden, Venice, and from the year 1724, Naples, where three years later he was a professor in the Naples Conservatoire. He came to London upon invitation to undertake the direction of opera, in rivalry to Handel ; but showing no liking for the object, or England, he did not remain long. His early studies had been with the masters of the Italian school in Naples, and his compositions are therefore representative of that tradition. He was a prolific composer of more than a hundred operas, symphonies, masses, etc., also a *Concerto in G major for solo mandolin, with two violins, 'cello, lute* *guitar and contrabass.* A new edition of this concerto edited by H. Neemann was published in 1938 by Vieweg, Berlin. It is probable that he makes use of the mandolin and guitar in other of his compositions; but owing to the destruction of his manuscripts during the siege of Dresden in 1760, they are exceedingly rare. His periods of residence in Italy and his student life in Naples, the home of the mandolin, was undoubtedly the means of bringing the instrument to his notice. His memoirs were first published in 1820 by Kandler.

Hauptmann, Moritz, born at Dresden, October 13, 1792, and died in Leipzig January 3, 1868. Sir George Smart records in his Journals that "he died loaded with decorations." His education was conducted with the intent of adopting his father's profession of architect. Being well grounded in the elements of music, but without serious intent, he also played the violin and guitar, the former under Scholz, and harmony and composition under various teachers. In 1811 he visited Gotha, where Spohr was concertmaster, and it was while there that he decided to make music his profession. After leaving Gotha, he was for a time violinist in Dresden Court Orchestra, but in 1815 went to Russia where he lived for four years. On his return he entered Spohr's band in Cassel as violinist, and it was here that he manifested his remarkable talent as a teacher of the theory of music. In a short time he became a most celebrated teacher, pupils flocked to him from all parts of Europe and even from America. Upon Mendelssohn's recommendation, he was appointed music director of the famous Thomas-Schule, Leipzig, in 1842, and also a professor in the Conservatoire. Among his pupils were Joachim, Burgmuller, Bott, Cowen and Sullivan. When a young man, Hauptmann studied and played the guitar, several of his early compositions were written for this instrument, and it is interesting to know that of his celebrated pupils all those named displayed more than a passing interest in the instrument. Gumprecht states that Joachim, the violin virtuoso, played the guitar and accompanied with great proficiency the songs of his elder sister before finally adopting the violin. Burgmuller composed and published three nocturnes for violin or violoncello with guitar entitled: *Les murmures de la Rhone,* and also songs with guitar. Bott published solos for the guitar, Op. 19 and Op. 25. Cowen uses the guitar in his cantata *Harold* and *The Corsair,* and his widely-known song *The chimney corner* has a guitar accompaniment, while "Sullivan's favourite guitar, made by Davis, London," was sold by order of his executors, May 22, 1901, at the auction rooms of Puttick & Simpson, London. It is probable that they all received their appreciation of the instrument from their esteemed teacher who is recorded as "endowed with an ear of unusual delicacy and a lover of the guitar." Hauptmann, a Doctor of Philosophy, published about sixty compositions, instrumental and vocal, and was the author of an opera, *Mathilder,* composed in early life and performed with success repeatedly in Cassel. Several of his early compositions were for the guitar, the most widely known was Op. 8, *Divertisements for violin and guitar.*

This was mentioned by the A.M.Z. and published by Schreiber, Vienna ; his memoirs were edited by Paul in 1862, and Krehl in 1918.

Hauschka or **Hauska,** Vincent, as his name sometimes appears, was born at Mies, Bohemia, January 21, 1766, and died in Vienna, 1840. He was a son of the schoolmaster of Mies, and at the age of eight his parents removed to Prague, where his father had been appointed to a school. Hauschka commenced the study of music with the mandolin, which was his first instrument ; he was a cathedral chorister and then received systematic musical instruction from Seeger, and Laube, the father of the violin virtuoso. He adopted the 'cello as his second instrument and made good progress on both and a few years later he continued the study of the 'cello under Christ, one of the most celebrated of Bohemian virtuosi. At sixteen he was a member of the orchestra of the Count of Thun, remaining in his service until the death of the Count, two years later, when the orchestra was disbanded. He then made a concert tour through Austria and Germany, visiting Carlsbad, Dresden and other important cities where his performances on his instruments were praised. Towards the end of 1792 he removed to Vienna where his public performances attracted considerable notice and won for him an enviable reputation. Some few years after his residence in Vienna he was appointed financial councillor in the Administration of Public Property and he then relinquished music professionally. He still took an active interest in the art and founded the Vienna Philharmonic Society, of which he was treasurer and conductor for the years 1826-8. He was also one of the founders of the Geselschaft der Musikfreund, Vienna, and the Concert Spirituel. He continued to write for the instruments, but his compositions remain in manuscript, chiefly nocturnes for mandolin, alto and violoncello ; quintets including these instruments ; concertos for 'cello and church compositions, which are in the Musikfreund Museum, Vienna.

Hayes, Elton, contemporary, born 1916, at Bletchley, Bucks., whose parents were theatrical actors. At the age of ten he commenced the study of the violin which he continued for some years ; in the meantime he had appeared as boy vocalist. His wish was to adopt the stage, so attended Fay Compton's Dramatic Academy where he won a scholarship. In 1929 a friend who was in debt for thirty shillings approached him for assistance and offered a guitar as security. Hayes advanced the amount, took possession of the guitar and was soon able to strum a few chords. Some time after, while walking in a London street carrying his guitar, he was accosted by a stranger who asked if he could play the guitar, saying he was the Musical Director of Wyndham's Theatre and required guitar music played behind the scenes. An audition was arranged ; he was engaged although only able to play the simplest accompaniments. In 1940, during the second world war, he joined as a gunner, took his guitar with him and within six weeks of army life was entertaining his companions at army concerts. He was promoted through the necessary stages to captain and when home from the far east appeared in the "In town tonight" broadcast. Previous to his army service he had taken part in the children's hour broadcast under the title of "He sings to a small guitar," and from now on, he was in constant demand on the air and films. He has done much to make the guitar widely known and popular as an accompaniment for the voice.

Held, Bruno, a Bavarian musician, who for some time lived in Munich, and in 1815 was residing in Mannheim. He was a flautist and guitarist, the author of several compositions for these instruments, which appeared principally in Mannheim and Augsburg. Schott, Mayence, published dances for orchestra and vocal compositions by him.

Held, John Theobald, an Austrian musician of no relation to the former. He was an amateur musician born in Prague in 1760 and practised as a doctor of medicine in his native city. He was an excellent musician, vocalist and guitarist, the author of a number of collections of songs with guitar and piano accompaniments, also solos for the guitar which are mentioned in A.M.Z. and which were published in Prague and Leipzig during 1796.

Henkel, Michael, born at Fulda, Germany, June 18, 1780, and died there March 4, 1851, as town cantor, episcopal court musician, and a professor of music at the gymnasium. He played the guitar, organ and piano, and for many years was the director of music and organist of Fulda Cathedral. He was a prolific composer for the organ, and the author of a highly esteemed method, in two volumes, for the instrument, which was published by Schott, Mayence. Henkel wrote many sacred, school, and choral works, and also compositions for guitar and piano, chiefly sonatas, variations, studies, etc., which were chronicled in A.M.Z. *Vienna Congress, waltzes for flute and guitar ;* Op. 4, *Sonata for guitar and piano ;* Op. 10, *Six German Lieder with guitar ;* Op. 24, *Sonata for flute and guitar ;* Op. 25, *Divertissement for guitar and piano ;* Op. 31, *Three Variations for flute and guitar ;* Op. 36, *Pieces Concertantes for flute and guitar ;* Op. 44, *Sonata for piano and guitar ; Six Duos for flute and guitar ;* and a scherzo entitled *The Cuckoo, for flute and guitar.* These were published by Hofmeister, Leipzig ; Simrock, Bonn ; Andre, Offenbach and Richault, Paris.

Himmel, Friedrich Heinrich, was born November 20, 1765, at Treuenbrietzen, Brandenburg, and died in Berlin, June 8, 1814. Being intended for the church his parents sent him to Halle to study theology ; but the excellence of his piano playing induced King Frederick William II, to educate him as a musician and he was with Capellmeister Naumann, in Dresden, for three years. Naumann was a guitarist who improved the stringing of the instrument (see Naumann) and Himmel studied harmony, composition, and the piano and guitar. The King appointed him chamber musician and sent him to Italy for two years where he produced several operas in Venice and Naples. Himmel returned to his native land and was appointed Court Capellmeister in Berlin. He made visits to Stockholm, St. Petersburg and Copenhagen and to Paris, where some of his small pieces for the guitar were published. From France he made a short visit to London, returning to Vienna and then to Berlin in 1802. His numerous operas were produced in Berlin and he wrote piano sonatas, masses and numerous songs, some with guitar accompaniment and pieces of a light nature for guitar alone, and for two guitars ; during his latter years Himmel devoted himself solely to vocal composition. The following are a few of his compositions which include the guitar and which are recorded in A.M.Z. from the year 1810. *Six Dances for two guitars,* Chanel, Paris ; *Six Songs with piano or guitar ; Six Songs of Goethe with piano or guitar ; Twelve old German Songs with guitar ;* a second volume of the same ; *Two French Romances with guitar ; Grosse im Angluck, with guitar ; Songs of Rousseau with guitar, flute, 'cello and piano,* published in 1797, and many others issued by Simrock, Bonn, and Schott, Mayence. His memoirs were edited by Arnold in 1810 and by Odendahl in 1917.

Hoffmann, Johann D., a German guitarist living during the first part of the nineteenth century, who revised Bornhardt's guitar method under the title of *New edition with a large collection of modern and popular melodies,* a copy of which is in the library of the Munich Guitar Society. Hoffmann is the composer of some songs with guitar accompaniment and Op. 2, *Variations for guitar solo,* published by Andre, Offenbach. He composed *Sonatas for two mandolas, mandolin and bass ; Concerto for mandolin with strings and wind instruments,* and *Divertimenti for mandolin, violin and bass ;* all the manuscripts are in the library of Musikfreund, Vienna.

Holland, Justin, born in 1819 at Norwalk, Virginia, U.S.A., and died March 24, 1887. His father, Exum Holland, was a farmer who noticed his son's talent for music when quite young ; but at the time the locality offered scanty opportunity for either hearing or learning music. In 1833 he went to Boston where he remained for only a short period, and then removed to Chelsea, a city near Boston, where he spent his early youth and manhood. It was in Boston that he met Senor Mariano Perez, a Spanish musician, and clever performer on the guitar, and young Holland commenced the study of this instrument under him. He also had for one of his first music teachers, Simon Knabel, a member of Ned Kendall's Brass Band, who enjoyed a wide reputation as an arranger of music. Subsequently, Holland studied with William Schubert, also a member of Kendall's Band, and a brilliant performer on the guitar. After making good progress on this instrument, Holland adopted the concert flute, receiving instruction from a Scotsman named Pollock. While studying music he was compelled to labour hard and deny himself, to meet the expenses of his musical education, and the time devoted to study was necessarily taken from that which should have been given to sleep. In 1841 he entered Oberlin College, an institution located in the northern part of the state of Ohio, and he remained here for two years, when he travelled to Mexico, for the sole purpose of becoming familiar with the Spanish language, to be able to read and study the methods of Sor, Aguado and other Spanish guitarists. Holland returned to Oberlin in 1845, married, and made his home in Cleveland. From that time he was engaged in teaching and arranging music for the guitar, in which occupation he obtained a widespread reputation through the United States. In his music one recognises a high degree of excellence and a correct understanding of harmony. In July, 1884, in connection with some of his advanced pupils, he organised the "Cleveland Guitar Club" which gave public recitals of guitar music from the following December and received generous praise from the press and musicians generally. Holland continued teaching until October, 1886, when his health failing, he travelled south in the hope that a change of climate might restore him. He did not recover, but died March 24, 1887, at the age of sixty-eight. Holland was practically unknown outside his own country; but a sketch of his life appeared February, 1877, in Der Freimaurer, a magazine published in Vienna. He possessed a high order of education, spoke five languages fluently, was a man of excellent social qualities and keen intellect, and held in high esteem and friendship by all the musical artists in his vicinity. Holland did not publish any original compositions, but arranged numerous works for his instrument. He is the author of *Comprehensive Method for the guitar,* published by Ditson, Boston, and also *Modern Method for the guitar,* published in 1874 by Brainard, Cleveland. His arrangements for the guitar were issued in collections, each containing about twenty selections, under the titles of: *Winter evenings; Gems for the guitar; Bouquet of melodies;* and *Flowers of melody.* He also wrote guitar accompaniments to numerous songs, one of his collections was entitled *Summer Evenings.* Holland also arranged about thirty duos for two guitars, the same number for guitar and violin, and was the author of a treatise of three hundred and twenty-four pages on certain subjects of moral reform. His son, Justin Minor Holland, was also a skilful guitarist, and, like his father, published many arrangements for the guitar. He was the teacher of Arling Shaeffer, who also compiled two Methods and a number of trifling pieces for the guitar. Justin Minor Holland possessed a rare library of guitar literature, collected by his father, and was living in New Orleans in 1888, in the Government service, and in that year his *Method for the guitar* was published by Oliver Ditson, and rapidly passed three editions.

Horetzky, Felix, a Polish guitarist, born at Prague in 1800 and died in Edinburgh in 1871. He is considered one of the best guitarists of Bohemia, and has been erroneously claimed as that nationality. When he was a child he played the guitar, but with no other intent than amusement. His family returned to their native land when he was in his teens, and made their abode in Warsaw. It was here that he took regular instruction in guitar playing and the theory of music, and from the time he was under a teacher, receiving systematic instruction, his interest in the instrument which had only amused him previously, developed into a passion. When fifteen he commenced a career as clerk in the Chamber of Accounts in Warsaw, but his disposition was too active to be reconciled to this monotonous life. Having become so absorbed in music and the guitar, and his employment proving irksome, he resigned and commenced to teach the guitar. He also continued his musical studies with increased vigour and a few years later visited Vienna. Here he studied the methods and compositions of the foremost Viennese masters, received higher instruction on his instrument from Giuliani, eventually performing in public with him and also with Diabelli. Such was his success and reputation, that he obtained the patronage of the Royal Court, and was appointed guitar instructor to the Archduchess, and several other members of the royal household, before he had been resident in Vienna a year. His restless nature still predominated and not content with his honourable position, undertook a protracted and roving tour of Europe, travelling through Germany, performing in Frankfurt and other important cities, and then Paris. Just previous to 1820, Horetzky visited London and met with his usual success, for his advent occurred at a very opportune time—when England had become familiar with the names of the guitar virtuosi who had created such sensations in Vienna, and Horetzky advertised the fact of his arrival from this famed city by announcing himself on his first compositions published in England as "F. Horetzky, from Vienna." He toured Great Britain and eventually made his abode in Edinburgh. In this city he met with a favourable reception, was recognised by the musical public and patronised by society as the foremost teacher of the guitar in Scotland ; his numerous pupils came from afar, and included the most influential and fashionable members of Edinburgh society. Horetzky made visits to London, where he was heard as guitar soloist, winning the praise of critics and the music press, and with the guitarist Leonard Schulz, appeared as guitar duettists. Schulz composed and dedicated to Horetzky a *Grand Fantasia, for guitar solo,* Op. 48, which was published by Johanning, London. Horetzky's most celebrated pupils in this country were Sczepanowski, a Pole, to whom he gave instruction in Edinburgh in 1833 (see Sczepanowski) and Dipple, whom he taught in London. The latter was a talented amateur guitarist and flautist, the author of small pieces for the guitar and songs with guitar accompaniment, published in London about 1840. Horetzky remained in Edinburgh until 1840, and afterwards lived for a time in London, previous to travelling to Paris on a visit to his home. From France he made a concert tour through Germany and his native land to Russia. Horetzky commenced to write for his instrument just before his departure from Vienna, about

1816, and his compositions appeared in those countries he visited, principally in Austria, England, Germany and Russia. His publications for guitar number considerably more than one hundred and fifty, and they were exceedingly popular with amateur guitarists of Great Britain, for they appealed to average performers by their simplicity and effectiveness: his celebrated *Maestoso* and *Adagio* are pearls of classic beauty. Horetzky's songs with guitar accompaniment, and solos and duos for guitar were to be found in all the popular albums and journals, and many collections of his smaller compositions were issued in series, under the titles of *Lyra, Aurora,* etc., each album contained about forty pieces. These collections were published by George & Manby, Wessell & Co. of London ; Richault, Paris, and Fischer, Frankfurt. The following are his best works: Op. 1, *Duos for guitar and terz guitar,* dedicated to his pupil Count Leopold de Lazanzky, Diabelli & Co., Vienna ; Op. 2 and Op. 9, *Brilliant Waltzes for guitar,* Chappell, London, and Schott, Mayence ; Op. 10, *Six Landler for two guitars,* Diabelli, Vienna ; Op. 11, *Rondo for guitar,* Chappell ; Op. 12, *Serenade and Variations for solo guitar,* Richault, Paris ; Op. 13, *Duos for two guitars,* Schott ; Op. 14, *Grand Fantasia,* Simrock, Bonn ; Op. 16, *Grand Variations* and Op. 17, *Divertimentos,* Johanning, London ; Op. 18, *Amusements for guitar,* Metzler, London and Fischer, Frankfurt; Op. 20 and 22, *Four Variations with introduction and finale,* Johanning, London ; Op. 30, *Almenrader,* dedicated to his pupil T. J. Dipple ; Op. 35, *Recollections of Vienna, for two guitars,* George & Manby, London, and *Sixty national hymns for guitar,* Chappell, London ; Horetzky was the author of various studies and exercises for the guitar and original songs with guitar and he wrote guitar accompaniments to numerous popular vocal compositions. Many of the latter were issued in Scotland and dedicated to his pupils and friends there. *Quande avvolte,* a vocal serenade with guitar, *The Spanish bride,* a vocal bolero with guitar ; *Lady awake ; The voice of the tempest ; Good night ; Spinnerlied,* and *Kennst du das land,* all with guitar were published by Wessell & Co., London.

Huber, Johann Nepomuk, born May 13, 1803 at Insel Richenau, a German student of theology, who was subsequently chaplain in Waltersweiler near Offenburg. He was the author of well-known theoretical and didatic treatises on music and his works and compositions were recorded in the A.M.Z. He published through Trag, Vienna, *Three Fantasias for guitar solo ;* Op. 6, *Waltzes for guitar* ; Op. 7 and Op. 8, *Variations ;* a *Sonata ; Twelve Landler,* also for guitar and vocal solos and duos with guitar accompaniment.

Hucke, George H., born in 1868, died in London, March 20, 1903. His father Heinrich, a German, was a pupil of Spohr, and for some years leading violinist under his baton in the Court Orchestra of Hesse-Cassel. George and his three brothers were destined for musical careers, and were taught the violin by their father. When he was eight, George came under the instruction of Dr. Hartmann, bandmaster to the Duke of Cambridge, continued with him for several years and gained practical experience in orchestral work. Ten years later he was musical amanuensis to Canon Harford, a reputed musical authority at Westminster Abbey, and Hucke remained with him until death at the early age of thirty-five. He was also connected with his brothers who had established a successful music teaching studio in Hammersmith, London, just at the period when the claims of the mandolin were awakening popular interest in the country. The violin had been his especial instrument, and it was natural that he should avail himself of the possibilities presented, so adopted the mandolin. Hucke made no pretensions as a public performer, but his first contributions to music for the mandolin were offered to Turner, London, at that time the only publisher of music for the mandolin in England. The favour with which these compositions were received, induced Hucke to continue; the period for his composing was limited, by fate, to ten years, but it was the time of a great demand for mandolin publications. In 1893, Turner published Op. 50, *Forty Progressive Studies for the Mandolin,* followed by forty-five original compositions and in addition, numerous arrangements, albums, organ music and a tutor for the guitar, which testify to his untiring energy.

Huerta, y Katurla Don A. F., born at Orihuela, Valencia, Spain, June 6, 1804, and died in Paris 1875. His parents were in a comfortable position and he was given a classic education; but an inclination which he could not resist drew him to the study of music. He was a student in the San Pablo College at Salamanca from the age of fourteen and made a special study of music. His aptitude for study, combined with his natural ability soon gained him distinction in his special subjects, singing and guitar playing and he continued his vocal training and the higher study of the guitar subsequently under the renowned Garcia. The unsettled state of the country at this period interrupted his studies—Spain was in the throes of the Peninsular war—and Huerta, pressed in the military service, in a regiment of cadets, contrived to make his escape after a few weeks, and fled to Madrid, then the patriotic focus of Spain. Here his sympathies were enlisted in the cause of General Riego, and Huerta served under him when the enemies of the constitution were defeated. Being now enthusiastic in his love of liberty and martial glory, Huerta threw himself heartily in this new vocation, and made the acquaintance of the poet-soldier, Colonel Evaristo de San Miguel, a Captain-General of the Halberdiers of St. Ildefonso, and from this friendship resulted the famous national hymn (the Marseillaise of Spain) The *March of Riego,* or *Riego's hymn.* Huerta composed the music to the poet-soldier's words; in less than a week the whole Spanish peninsula was singing it and eventually became known through Europe. It was originally published in Spain with guitar accompaniment and Ricordi of Milan also issued it with guitar. It is unnecessary to recall the ultimate defeat of Riego, how his supporters were forced to flee or share the fate of their leader; many took refuge in France and England, and their national instrument, the guitar, was brought more prominently before the people of these two countries. Huerta, with many compatriots fled to France and after his exciting experiences gave himself entirely to music, and as vocalist and guitarist his services were in frequent request by Parisian society. Young and full of ardour for his profession, he gave singing instruction with his former teacher, Garcia senior, Malibran, and Adolphe Nourrit, the celebrated, but unfortunate tenor, and as proof of the sincere friendship existing between Nourrit and himself, dedicated a composition to him. Huerta was a capricious artist and acted according to impulse without calculating the consequences. He had been engaged to perform in Havre and travelled from Paris to Rouen in the company of several business men about to sail for America. "What is the use of you giving a concert in Havre?" they said, "come with us to America, you will be worth your weight in gold there," and without further consideration he embarked with them when the people of Havre were assembling at the theatre. After a time of singing and guitar playing in the United States, he visited Martinique and Cuba with the renowned Garcia and his opera company. The wandering minstrel encountered a series of misadventures, however, as a vocalist and guitarist, he obtained his intense desire. He associated in his travels with an artist painter both of whom had gone to pursue their professions on this virgin soil, sharing everything in common, until Huerta discovered his erstwhile friend had absconded with all Huerta's life savings, about four hundred pounds. To add to his discomfiture, he lost his voice, a principal means of support, but undaunted he applied himself with increased energy to the guitar, shaving his head, his eyebrows and half his beard and remaining in his room until he had made himself incomparable on his guitar. After three month's concentrated study he appeared again in public and was acknowledged the foremost guitarist in America; the press stated that he had such mastery and control over the instrument that it responded like a miniature orchestra. When he returned to Europe he resided in London and associated in his concerts with the most distinguished musicians, La Pasta, Donizelli and Lablache. On May 18, 1827 he was soloist at a brilliant concert with Moscheles and Mori, and on the 22nd of the following month was soloist at a concert under the patronage of the Duchess of Gloucester with De Beriot, violinist, Moscheles pianist, Labarre, harpist and Mme. Pasta, vocalist. On the 29th of the same month he played sonatas on the guitar in the mansion of the Duke of St. Albans with Mmes. Pasta and Stockhausen and on June 6, 1828, was soloist at the Royal Argyle Rooms. Huerta resided in London until 1830, appearing in concerts which were successful artistically and financially and his services were freely bestowed on behalf of the Spanish refugees, in less fortunate circumstances. During his residence in London he married his pupil, Miss Angiolina Panormo, one of "the roguish dark-eyed daughters" of the celebrated guitar maker, Louis Panormo. Huerta visited Paris again and was the recipient of honourable welcome from men famous in politics, literature and art. Mme. Emile de Girardin dedicated some verses to him, Lamartine and Victor Hugo lavishly praised him, while Armand Marrast extolled his guitar recitals. Fetis praises his guitar playing in the Revue Musicale of 1830, saying: "the marvellous power and agility of his fingers is prodigious; he executes, with his left hand alone, themes with intricate variations, and he has raised the guitar to the sublime height that Paganini did the violin." From Paris Huerta visited his native land, in 1833, where he gave recitals, embarking from Valencia to tour the east, visiting Malta, Constantinople, Egypt and the Holy Land. A detailed account of Huerta's genius appears in Historia de la Musica Espanol, fourth volume, 1855-59 by Soriano Fuertes, who states that the chief characteristic of Huerta's playing was his ability to produce a sustained, singing tone, of exceptional duration and beauty. Huerta was guitarist to Isabel II of Spain and was offered a position at Court, which "the restless child of wild Spanish nature," as the contemporary guitarist, Mme. Sidney Pratten, described him, declined. He performed before most of the Sovereigns of Europe, was Knight of the Order of Gregory the Great and of the order of Carlos III; but above all his honours he valued the intimate friendship of Rossini. Huerta's favourite guitar was a concert, or full-sized instrument constructed by his father-in-law, Louis Panormo of London. He was not a prolific composer and his first compositions were issued in Paris. Op. 2, *Six Waltzes for the guitar,* Meissonnier, Paris; *Six Waltzes* dedicated to the Hon. Miss Fox, published in London in 1828; *Five Waltzes,* being the second set, dedicated to Miss Howley; *Three Divertimentos,* dedicated to Miss L. Hatton; *Overture to 'Semiramide,'* and a *Fantasia on 'Semiramide,'* Chappell, London; *Four Divertimentos,* composed for and dedicated to his pupil, Miss Angiolina Panormo and published by her father, L. Panormo; *Souvenir of Mairena fair,* a *Mazurka with variations for the guitar* and a *Spanish national cachucha,* originally composed for eight guitars, arranged for one, were published by Panormo, London. These last compositions are in the library of the Royal College of Music, London, also *Grand Waltz,* published by Willis & Co., London. His wife was the composer of several songs with guitar which appeared in London.

Hummel, Johann Nepomuk, was born at Pressburg, Austria, November 14, 1778 and died in Weimar, October 17, 1837. Hummel, a classic writer and player of the pianoforte was also a talented guitarist and one of the most renowned musicians who have composed works for the guitar and mandolin. The son of Joseph Hummel, a conductor of military music in Wartenburg, he received instruction from his father in the musical art during early childhood. It was about the year 1786 when his father was conducting the orchestra in the theatre of Schikaneder—Mozart's friend and the author of the libretto of *Die Zauberflote*—that the boy, who had made considerable progress in singing and piano playing, became the inmate of Mozart's house and for two years enjoyed the privilege of Mozart's instruction. When ten he had made such extraordinary strides in piano playing that his father took him on tour through Germany, Denmark and Holland, and he played in England for the first time in 1795. The brilliant piano playing of the youth won the universal praise of musicians throughout his concert tour, and at its termination in the end of 1795, he returned to Vienna and resumed his studies in counterpoint under Albrechtsberger, and composition under Hadyn and Salieri. In April, 1804, he was appointed capellmeister to Prince Nicholas Esterhazy—the position formerly held by Hadyn—and remained until May, 1811. Soon after this date and until 1816 he was a famous teacher associating with the guitar virtuoso Giuliani, when all Vienna was applauding their duos for guitar and piano until 1815. Hummel was of great assistance to Giuliani, as he had been established for some years in the city previous to the arrival of the guitarist. The two virtuosi were engaged in concert performances until Hummel departed to fill the position of conductor at Stuttgart, and in 1815 Hummel, Giuliani and the violinist, Mayseder, were engaged together in the series of " Dukaten Concerte " (Subscription concerts). They performed at a series of six musical soireés in the grounds of the Royal Botanical Gardens of Schönbrun, before members of the royal family and nobility ; upon these occasions they were augmented by the 'cellist Merk and a flautist of renown. For these concerts Hummel composed *Three grand serenades for piano, guitar, violin, flute and 'cello or piano, guitar, violin, clarinet and bassoon,* Op. 62, 63 and 66. The guitar part of the allegretto from his *Grand Serenade,* Op. 63, is reproduced, and it can be seen that the guitar is allotted an important position in the quintet and its importance is manifest in all his compositions which include the instrument. He wrote at the same time, *The Sentinel,* Op. 71, for solo voice with variations, and accompaniments of piano, guitar, violin and 'cello. These serenades were dedicated to Count Francois de Palffy, an admirer and patron of Hummel and published by Artaria, Vienna, with an engraving on the title page depicting the several musicians playing in the gardens. These compositions are of more than ordinary technical difficulty and only in the hands of artists could a correct interpretation be expected, for each instrument is requisitioned in its solo capacity with variations of a most florid description—written respectively by each of the original performers, viz., Hummel, Giuliani, Mayseder and Merk — and in addition, brilliant execution is required for the rendering of the compositions generally. In 1816, when Hummel removed to Stuttgart, his connection with these artists ceased and his part performed by Moscheles. Hummel remained in Stuttgart till 1820, when he transferred to Weimar, from where, in the suite of the Grand Duchess Maria Paulowna, he travelled to Russia, honoured by a most cordial reception. In 1825 he visited Paris, travelling through Belgium and Holland, returning to Vienna in 1827. From the years 1830 to 1833 he was in England conducting the Royal Opera, London, and during his stay in this country he made many provincial tours. While in Bath he became acquainted with the guitarist Eulenstein, who, in his autobiography records a conversation with him on the merits of the guitar, reiterating Hummel's high opinion of the instrument and particularly of its effects in modulation. Hummel departed from England in 1834, retiring to Weimar where he died three years later. Brought up in the house of Mozart and receiving direct instruction from the immortal genius, he was consequently deemed the main conservator of Mozartian traditions—an expert conductor, a good teacher, the leading and most brilliant German pianist, a very clever extempore player, and a prolific composer of all classes of music, including operas, symphonies, masses, guitar solos and mandolin sonatas. During the time he was living with Mozart, his master composed several songs and arias with mandolin accompaniment, a circumstance that would naturally impress him favourably. When twenty-one Hummel composed a concerto for the mandolin and orchestra, which he dedicated to the mandolin virtuoso Bortolazzi, a recognised genius who was five years his senior. The original autographed manuscript entitled *Concerto written by J. N. Hummel for Barthol Bortolazzi, maestro di mandolino, 1799.* is in the library of the British Museum, London. Hummel was living in Vienna at the time of writing this, receiving higher instruction in counterpoint and composition from Albrechtsberger, Haydn and Salieri. The former and the last of these masters composed for the mandolin (see Albrechtsberger and Salieri), and in his treatment of the viola in combination with the other strings, Hummel's instrumentation closely resembles that of his teacher Salieri. This Concerto for the mandolin, a lengthy, classic composition, is scored for " mandolino principale," with two violins, viola, 'cello, double-bass, two flutes and two horns in G. The introductory theme, *Allegro moderato e grazioso,* in G, two-four time is led by the orchestra for forty-five bars, after which the mandolin enters, reiterating the melody to the pizzicato of the strings. An *Andante con variazione,* in two-four time follows, with a rapid movement throughout for the mandolin which does not ascend above the third position. Variations in G minor proceed, succeeded by a *Rondo* in six-eight time, after which the mandolin has lengthy and rapid variations on this theme also, the final bars are taken by the full orchestra. This Concerto was first broadcast by the B.B.C. symphony orchestra with Hugo D'Alton, mandolinist, from London, March 15, 1953. A Grand Sonata for mandolin and piano by Hummel, published by Maisch, Vienna, was composed for and dedicated to Signore Fr. Mora de Malfatti, Beethoven's physician, whose family was held in the highest repute in Viennese musical circles and were skilful performers on the mandolin and guitar. Beethoven was intimate with the family, notably the daughters Therese and Nanette, for the latter of whom he wrote a guitar accompaniment (vide Beethoven). Hummel's composition is in three movements: Sonata, Andante Siciliano and Rondo. An extract is reproduced. Hummel's piano compositions are still esteemed but their popularity has vanished. These and his numerous compositions for the guitar are marked by strong poetical feeling, clear form, and much technical cleverness. Hummel evinced a predilection

EXTRACTS FROM

Concerto for Mandolin and Orchestra.

Composed for Bartolomeo Bortolazzi, By J. N. Hummel, in 1799.

MANDOLINO PRINCIPALE.

Allo. moderato e grazioso.

Tutti 45 Solo

Tutti Solo

Tutti 8

Rondo

Tutti 13 1

Tutti

Andante con Variatione

Tutti

Don A. F. Huerta

G. B. Marchisio

Johann Adolph Hasse

Richard Harrison

Burle Ives at the Festival Hall, London, 1953

Larghetto, from Grand Duo for Piano and Guitar, Op. 53.

J. N. HUMMEL.

for the guitar, second only to that of the piano, and associated himself in a practical manner with its players and votaries. Although he made no public appearances as a performer on the guitar, he was a capable exponent, thoroughly conversant with its resources, and lavish in praise

Allegretto, from Grand Serenade, Op. 63,
(Quintet for Piano, Guitar, Violin, Flute and 'Cello).

J. N. HUMMEL.

of its powers as an instrument of harmony and modulation. That he was seriously and constantly interested is evidenced by his compositions for it; they commence with Op. 7, and conclude with Op. 93. He was the author of many operas, the principal *Die Eselhaut* or *Die blaue*

Insel, a fairy play, produced in the Theatre an der Wien, Vienna, March 10, 1814, the original manuscript is in the British Museum Library. The *Adagio and Cantabile,* romance for tenor in the second act, has accompaniment for guitar, two violas, two 'cellos and double-bass. This is a unique and effective instrumentation heightened by the pizzicato of the 'cellos and double-bass against the arco of the violas. Hummel's operas are forgotten; but not so his masses. The most widely known of his compositions for the guitar are the following—additional pieces appeared principally in Vienna, Stuttgart and St. Petersburg, published during his visits there. *Six Dances for two guitars,* Richault, Paris; *Waltz for violin or flute and guitar,* Spehr, Brunswick; Op. 7 *Guitar with other instruments;* Op. 43, *National Potpourri, Grand Duo for piano and guitar,* composed in collaboration with Giuliani; Op. 53, *Grand Duo for piano and guitar,* Artaria, Vienna, from which the Larghetto is reproduced; Op. 62, *Grand Serenade in C major, for piano, guitar, clarinet and 'cello*; Op. 63 and 66, *Grand Serenades for piano, guitar, flute and 'cello;* published by Artaria, Vienna; Op. 91, *Six Waltzes and Trios for flute, or violin and guitar,* also arranged by Hummel as a *Duo for two guitars,* Haslinger, Vienna; Op. 79, *Grand Potpourri for guitar and piano,* in collaboration with Giuliani; Hummel wrote the orchestral score to Giuliani's *Third Concerto for guitar and orchestra.* Vocal compositions with guitar are Op. 71, *La Sentinelle, solo with variations and chorus in D with piano, guitar, violin and 'cello,* Haslinger, Vienna, and Peters, Leipzig; *Der Ausar Bohemisches, song with piano and guitar,* Cranz, Hamburg, and Eck & Co., Cologne; *Six Romances of Florian with guitar,* Gerstenberg, St. Petersburg; *Songs of Rosseau, with guitar, piano, flute and 'cello,* Vienna; and the Musikfreund Vienna

Grand Sonata

FOR MANDOLIN AND PIANO.

possesses the autograph manuscript of a *Sonata for mandolin and piano,* an extract from which is reproduced. The English music critic, Edward Holmes, visited Hummel when living in Weimar and records in A Musical Tour, "If there is anything in physiognomy, in the tone of voice, in hearty likings and as hearty dislikings, in honest sentiments and true delicacy of mind, this great musician is fifty times more to be loved for himself than to be admired for his genius," and Phillips in his Musical Recollections, writes: "Hummel was a man of remarkable gentleness of manner and address and did not give the least idea of a person of genius, but rather denoted a seeming unmindfulness of his genius and elegance." Hummel's memoirs edited by Montag were published in 1837.

Humperdinck, Engelbert, born Siegburg, Germany, September 1, 1854, died September 27, 1921. His first musical studies were under Hiller in Cologne Conservatoire where he won a bursary which enabled him to continue in the Royal Music School, Munich. Here he won the prize to study in Naples where he met Wagner who invited him to Beyreuth. In 1881, having obtained another prize he travelled in Italy, France and Spain. He resided in Barcelona for two years as a professor in the Conservatoire from 1885-1886. In this Spanish city he became acquainted with the guitar and its players and makes use of this instrument in the score of *Was ihr Wollt.* He is famed as the composer of the opera *Hansel and Gretel.*

Hunten, Franz, born December 26, 1793, at Coblentz, where his father, Daniel, was organist, and died there February 22, 1878. He came of a musical family, his two brothers, Peter and William were also musicians of repute. Franz was given his first musical instruction by his father on the piano and guitar; the latter instrument a favourite of the family. In 1819 he entered Paris Conservatoire of music where he studied the piano under Pradher and composition under Reicha and Cherubini. He lived by teaching and arranging music for the piano and the guitar and during his best period was an exceedingly fashionable teacher, his lessons and compositions commanded high prices, although his compositions, with the exception of a *Trio concertante for piano, violin and 'cello* are of little value. Hunten's *Methode nouvelle pour le piano,* had at one time a good reputation and was published in several languages by Schott, Mayence. He composed light pieces for the guitar, which were recorded in A.M.Z. *Variations for guitar solo,* dedicated to his brother, Wilhelm, published by Simrock, Bonn; *Three Waltzes for flute and guitar; Variations for solo guitar,* Schott, Mayence, and songs with guitar accompaniment, one of which entitled *Mathilde* was very popular. Grove speaks of him as "an educational composer of some merit, who wrote about two hundred pieces, easy and moderately difficult." Several of his pieces are widely known, and his studies for piano, Op. 158 are exceedingly useful and agreeable. Sir George Smart, in his Journals, says: "He lived by teaching and arranging music and his lessons and compositions commanded high prices."

Hunten, Peter Ernest, the youngest brother of the foregoing was born July 9, 1799, at Coblentz, and was living as late as 1878. Like his brothers, he was also a pianist, guitarist and composer, and settled in Duisburg as a teacher of his instruments. He was a prolific composer for the guitar and the best guitarist of the family. His chief published works for the guitar are: Op. 7, *Variations for solo guitar;* Op. 8, 21, 24, 25 and 26, *Serenades, Rondos and Variations for violin, or flute and guitar;* Op. 13, 14 and 48, *Brilliant Variations for two guitars;* Op. 18, 20, 22, 23, 27, 28, *Trios for violin, alto and guitar, or flute, violin and guitar;* and Op. 45, *Twenty-four waltzes and exercises for solo guitar.* The above were published by Schott, Mayence; Andre, Offenbach, and Arnold, Elberfeld. Hunten also published many works for the guitar without opus numbers, consisting of solos for guitar, duos for two guitars, and trios which included the guitar and are recorded in the A.M.Z.

IBERT, Jacques, contemporary, born at Paris, 1890, studied at the National Conservatoire and won the Prix de Rome in 1919. After the completion of his studies he was appointed Director of the French Academy in that city in 1937. He has composed a charming *Entr'acte for flute and guitar,* which was published in 1936 by United Music Publishers, London, and broadcast from London with Julian Bream, guitarist, December 10, 1951. Ibert's *Le Chevalier Errant,* a symphonic suite in four movements is founded on the theme of his ballet, *Don Quixote.* The third movement of the suite opens with a solo for the guitar and is continued with the strings of the orchestra. The first American performance was given by the Chicago Symphony Orchestra, November 27, 1952, and repeated the following day.

Ives, Burl, contemporary, born Jasper County, Hunt City Township, U.S.A., a son of Frank, farmer, and later bridge constructor. He commenced work as a labourer with his father and later entered Eastern Illinois State Teachers' College with the intention of a scholastic career. Study proving uncongenial he quitted the lecture room in a sudden impulse, took to the roads and led a wandering life singing to the accompaniment of his guitar. He obtained employment in a New York restaurant and was thus able to take lessons in singing. He became a popular broadcaster, singing folk songs with his guitar to the English speaking world. His visit to England in 1953 was an unprecedented success, notably in the Festival Hall, London, where, on several occasions he held his vast audiences spellbound. He was described by his contemporary, the singer-guitarist, poet and novelist, Carl Sandburg: "The greatest folk-ballad singer of them all." His autobiography under the title of "Wayfaring Stranger" is published by Boardman & Co., London.

JAGER, Franz, was born at Vienna, 1796. After education he commenced his career as assistant schoolmaster, studying singing and the guitar seriously at the same time. He had acquired such proficiency by the year 1817 that he relinquished his scholastic duties to become tenor in the Theatre an der Wien and in 1820 transferred his services to the Karntnertor Theatre in the same city. He removed to Berlin in 1824 and resided afterwards in Stuttgart, retiring from public life after service as singing master at the Court Opera, Würtemburg. He was at one time very intimate with Schubert who spoke and wrote well of him, and he was also an honorary member with Schubert of the Styrian Musical Society. Jager was the first to sing the songs of Schubert in public. He was the vocalist at a concert in Vienna, March 4, 1819, singing Schubert's *Shepherd's Complaint* when Giuliani was the guitar soloist. The musical press was loud in its praise of Giuliani's virtuosity and of the "beautiful composition, sung most feelingly in Herr Jager's enchanting voice." He was also a member of the male voice quartet at a concert on August 27, 1822, in the Theatre an der Wien when Schubert's *The little village,* with its original accompaniment for the guitar was rendered. The guitar accompaniment was played by a member of the quartet, most probably by Jager or Josef Schmidt, as both were capable guitarists. The A.M.Z. states that he published songs with guitar accompaniment. There was a C. Jager, the composer of songs with the guitar, Op. 11, 12, and 21 and two albums, the first of which appeared in 1814, entitled, *Journal for the guitar,* recorded in Whistling's Handbuch.

Janon, Charles de, a guitarist of repute who lived in America. He was born at Cartagena, Colombia, South America, in 1834, and died March, 1911, in New York. Charles de Janon was the youngest of a family of ten whose parents left South America in 1840 and settled in New York. When a child, he displayed exceptional musical tendency and at ten a local teacher gave him musical instruction. He commenced with the violin and piano and made good progress on both ; but when fate placed a guitar in his hands, these instruments were neglected and finally abandoned. The guitar appeared to exercise a powerful charm over the young man, for commencing its serious study in 1843, he continued assiduously throughout life. As a guitarist, De Janon was entirely self-taught ; the only available book of instruction was that of Ferdinand Lois, and when he adopted the instrument there were few guitar teachers in America. Compelled to rely upon his own resources, and by his natural musical ability, perseverance and enthusiasm, he obtained a mastery over the instrument and is ranked among its most accomplished American performers. De Janon was a versatile and musicianly arranger for the guitar and his transcriptions embrace nearly every variety of composition. They display a certain charm and taste and are familiar to all performers in America and to a lesser degree in Europe, being among the best and most popular of any publications for the guitar in America. De Janon strove continually to elevate the standard of guitar-playing and was highly respected in the musical world. He was the teacher of Arling Shaeffer, who published two methods for the guitar and also a number of trifles for it. De Janon was the composer of a few light guitar solos, the most successful were *Valse Poetique, Serenade,* a spirited *Polonaise* and various transcriptions of which these are worthy of notice: *Chopin nocturnes,* Op. 9, No. 2; The *Grand March* and *Evening Star,* from '*Tannhauser,*' and *Kathleen Mavourneen.* His revision of the Guitar Method of Carcassi is considered by American guitarists the best edition of that famous instruction book; it contains in addition to Carcassi's studies, many others by Carulli, Sor and Giuliani. His compositions to the number of nearly one hundred were published principally in New York and Boston; there were a few original works and transcriptions of popular and classic items, characterized by musicianly arrangement. His chief publishers were Oliver Ditson, Boston, and B. F. Harris and Frederick Blume, New York.

Jansa, Leopold, born Wildenschwert, Bohemia, March 23, 1795, died January 24, 1875, at Vienna. He is famous as a violinist and like Paganini was a guitarist. He played this instrument and the flute and violin but it was not his parents' intention that he should become a professional musician, for in 1817 he entered Vienna University to study law. He neglected his legal studies for music and after studying the violin, made his first public appearance as violinist in Vienna. In 1824 he was a member of the Royal Orchestra, and in 1834 was appointed musical director in his university. Five years later he visited London where he assisted at a concert in aid of Hungarian refugees and for this he was dismissed from the Royal Orchestra of Vienna. Jansa then settled in London where he was esteemed as a teacher, but some years later returned to his native land. His last public appearance was in Vienna, in 1871, at the age of seventy-seven. To him is due the credit of being the teacher of the foremost lady violinist, Mme. Neruda. His compositions are mainly for the violin, but several have guitar accompaniments and his early compositions were variations for flute and guitar. Op. 2, *Theme with variations for flute and guitar,* published by Mechetti, Vienna; Op. 25, *Three brilliant variations for flute and guitar*, Richault, Paris.

Janusch, Michael, a flautist and guitarist living in Prague at the beginning of the nineteenth century who later removed to Vienna. He was commissioned to contribute German dances to Terpischore, a collection of fifty compositions by the most celebrated musicians of the period, published by Mechetti, Vienna. He wrote much for the flute and guitar, his early works being published in Prague and recorded in the A.M.Z. Op. 1, a *Sonata for flute and guitar* was issued by Hoffman, Prague.

Jeckel or **Jeckl,** Joseph von, born in Vienna, 1766 and died at

Dobling, near Vienna, June 15, 1824. He was an apothecary, a cultured amateur musician, intimately associated with the Schubert family. For a long period it was the custom for Franz Schubert to meet at the apothecary's home for music practice with members of this family and friends. Schubert's father and mother writing to him when he was away from home at the end of June 1824, said: "Herr von Jeckel, the apothecary in Dobling, died suddenly of apoplexy on the 15th, aged 58; he said to his wife, half an hour before he died, 'I feel I shall die befor the day is out' and when she replied, 'Don't talk like that, and don't frighten me so,' he said, 'Well, well, I can't help it'." The apothecary took an active part in the Schubert's family circle and composed several works for and including the guitar, the principal are Op. 8, *Introduction and Grand Variations Concertante for guitar, two violins, viola and 'cello;* Op. 14, *Valses for guitar solo* and Op. 9, *Brilliant variations on a theme from 'Zelmira' for guitar.* These were published by Artaria, Vienna, and are recorded in Whistling's Handbuch.

Jelyotte, Pierre, born April 13, 1713, in Lasseube, Basses-Pyrenees, and died September 11, 1787 at Estos. He commenced a musical career as chorister in Toulouse Cathedral, studied a time for the priesthood then resigned and adopted music as his profession. As an instrumentalist he was very versatile, being an accomplished performer on the guitar, harpsichord and alto vocalist and composer. In 1733 he was singing to his guitar accompaniment in the Paris Opera and the following year at the Concerts Spirituel. He was Court guitarist, taught the King to play the guitar and composed the music for the comedy *Zelisca* which was performed at the court in 1776. His life and compositions are recorded by Riemann.

Jemnitz, Alexander, born August 9, 1890, Budapest. He studied music first in the National Conservatoire of his native city and continued at Leipzig under Max Reger. For a period he was conductor at Czernowitz Theatre, after which he removed to Berlin to continue his study under Arnold Schönberg. He returned to his native town where he was living in 1939 as composer. His knowledge of the characteristics and capabilities of various instruments is prodigious and he utilises this knowledge with remarkable effect. His compositions are in the modern style, they include works for full orchestra, choral and chamber music, the latter includes a *Sonata for Saxophone and Banjo* and a *Trio* of which the guitar is a member, and various other solos.

Joly, a French guitarist and violinist living in Paris during the latter half of the eighteenth century who also established a music publishing business there and died in 1819. In 1790 he was a member of the Theatre Montansier orchestra transferring to that of the Jeunes Artistes, Paris. He was the author of numerous pieces for guitar solo, sonatas, airs with variations, etc., and also violin and guitar duets, which are recorded by Fetis. Joly compiled two methods for the guitar, one entitled *Joly's Great Tutor for the Guitar,* appeared in 1793. The majority of his musical publications were issued in Paris from his own business. The most popular of his compositions were a *Sonata for guitar solo* and *Fleuve du Tage,* an air with variations for flute and guitar which were published by Richault, Paris.

Jusdorf, J. C., was a German flute virtuoso living in Gottingen during the commencement of the nineteenth century. The A.M.Z. of Leipzig published during the years 1803-1811 the titles of many of his songs with guitar and flute, the last of these was Op. 27, *Fourteen lieder with guitar.* Schott, Mayence, issued *Six Songs with guitar and* Eitner also records several with guitar and flute. He is known principally as the composer of duos for two flutes and concertos for flute and orchestra.

KALLIWODA, Johann W., born at Prague March 21, 1800, and died at Carlsruhe, December 3, 1866, was a violinist and popular composer, a pupil of Prague Conservatoire. It was during a visit to Munich that Prince Furstenburg appointed him conductor of his private orchestra which position he retained until 1853 when he retired on pension. He travelled but little, his fame resting entirely on his varied and comprehensive musical compositions. These include an opera, *Blanda,* composed in 1847, symphonies, overtures, concertos, solos and duos for violin, clarinet, piano and guitar. The author of this volume possesses the following autographed manuscript compositions of Kalliwoda, formerly in the library of the celebrated English guitarist and composer Ernest Shand.: *Serenade for guitar and two violins* (no opus number) ; Op. 20, *Concertante for two violins and grand orchestra and also for two violins and guitar ;* Op. 191, *Three Waltzes Brilliant, for two violins and grand orchestra, or for two violins and guitar ;* Op. 196, *Introduction and Grand Polka, for two violins and orchestra and for two violins and guitar ;* Op. 219, *Serenade for two violins and orchestra and for two violins and guitar ;* Op. 140, *Carulli's guitar Concerto for guitar and orchestra and for two violins and guitar ; Elegy* by Ernst, Op. 10, transcribed for two violins and guitar ; Alard's Op. 21, transcribed for two violins and guitar. On all these compositions he is described " Maitre de Chapelle de S.A.S. le Prince de Furstenburg." Kalliwoda's Memoirs appeared in 1909 in the Deutsche Arbeit.

Kanne, Friedrich August, born March 8, 1778, at Delitzsch, Saxony, died December 16, 1833, at Vienna. His youth was devoted to the study of theology and medicine ; but he became known as poet, musician and music critic. In early life as an amateur musician, he was interested in singing and the guitar, and when twenty-five, in 1803, Penig, Leipzig, and Dienemann & Co. published twenty of his original songs with guitar, in two books. The first and second volumes appeared under the title of *Journal pour la guitare.* The third and fourth books followed as Op. 13, and were published by A. Harder. In 1807 he was vocalist in the Opera, Vienna, and meeting with much success, he henceforth devoted himself entirely to music and resided in Vienna. From 1821-4 he was editor of the influential music journal A.M.Z. which was published by Steiner & Co. Kanne was considered one of the finest music critics of the time. Sir George Smart made his acquaintance in Vienna and describes him in his Journals as "a fast speaking author and composer of German operas, who was for five years editor of the Vienna Musical Review." Kanne was the first to publish detailed criticism of Schubert's songs and one of the fifty most celebrated musicians chosen to contribute a Variation on Diabelli's given theme, in 1824. The A.M.Z. for the year 1804 mentions his Op. 9, *Six songs in two albums, with guitar.*

Kapeller or **Capeller,** Johann Nepomuk, a German guitarist and flautist, known by his surviving compositions. In 1799 he was a member of the Munich Court Orchestra. He was the composer of *Twelve light pieces for flute, alto and guitar ; Quartet for two flutes, violin and guitar,* published by Schott, Mayence ; *Twelve Trios for flute, alto and guitar ; Quartet for two flutes, guitar and violoncello,* published by Breitkopf & Härtel, Leipzig in 1819. Kapeller was the inventor of a shake-key for the flute which has been universally adopted. The A.M.Z. for the year 1819 reveiwed his compositions and they are also recorded in Eitner's Lexicon.

Kargl, Anton, a German guitarist living during the commencement of the nineteenth century whose compositions were recorded in the A.M.Z. for the year 1811. Op. 2, *Trio in D, for guitar violin and viola* and Op. 3, *Trio in G, for guitar, violin and viola ;* both were issued by Breitkopf & Härtel, Leipzig.

Keller, Karl, born at Dessau, October 16, 1784, and died July 19, 1855 at Schaffhausen, Switzerland, was a flute and guitar virtuoso in the orchestra of the Royal Chapel, Berlin, until the year 1806. In 1814 he removed to Cassel, where he occupied a similar position for two years and then undertook a concert tour as flautist. He was appointed Court musician in 1817 at Donaueschingen where his wife (Wilhelmine Meierhofer) had been engaged as opera singer. Keller was subsequently promoted Capellmeister and was teacher of the guitar and singing to the Queen of Westphalia. The music journals from 1817-34, frequently praise his songs with guitar. The majority of his works are written for the flute ; but he compiled a *Method for the guitar* and several compositions which include the guitar. *Grand Variations,* Op. 14, for *flute and orchestra or flute, violin guitar and viola ;* Op. 30, *Serenade for violin, 'cello, viola and guitar,* both published by Andre, Offenbach. Several of his vocal compositions were exceedingly popular, particularly *Kennst du der Liebe Sehnen?* ; *Helft Leutchen mir vom Wagendoch ; Sehnsucht nach der Heimath ; Der Guck Kasten* and

Kommt Bruder, all published by Breitkopf & Härtel, and Schott. The former also issued Op. 38, *Eight songs with guitar* and another album of *Eight songs with guitar* and various other vocal items were published by Aibl, Vienna. Whistling's Handbuch records *Divertissements for flute and guitar.*

Kelley, Edgar Stillman, born April 14, 1857, at Sparta, Wisconsin, U.S.A., and died in New York, November 12, 1944, was a talented American composer, lecturer, writer and pedagogue whose music is scholarly and interesting. He was a professor in the universities of Yale, Cincinatti and Berlin. In his Musical Instruments, published by Ditson, he says: "The tone of the mandolin is fine and wiry; but singularly penetrating so that its presence in the orchestra, even in a forte passage, is quite obvious. In the *Feast of Lanterns,* from the *Aladdin Suite,* I have combined mandolin and harp. In spite of the spirit of levity usually associated with the instrument, I believe it capable of truly serious treatment. In the orchestra version of my setting of Poe's *Israfel,* I have employed the tremolando of the low strings, as I fancy they faintly resemble the wires of which the poet writes. The low register of the mandola possesses a rich warmth which might prove of value to the composer." Later he states that Rimsky Korsakoff also included the guitar and mandolin in his orchestrations. Kelley was the composer of symphonies, pantomimes, chamber music and songs; his music for the film, *Ben Hur,* travelled the world.

Kingsley, Victoria, contemporary, guitarist and soprano vocalist of wide renown, who has toured the world singing to the accompaniment of her guitar. Born in north-west England, her first education was in Scotland, and continued at Oxford University, where, having taken her degree, she decided to adopt the stage as her profession. With this intent she studied at the Royal Academy of Dramatic Art and became a member of Repertory touring companies previous to singing with her guitar. She was a pupil on the guitar of Pujol and also of his wife (Mathilde Cuervas) for the Flamenco style of playing. She is continuing the traditions of the troubadours, sings in sixteen languages; her recitals being more interesting by brief and interesting remarks before each item, presented with charm and humour. She possesses an unlimited and varied repertoire of all periods and classes and is a frequent broadcaster. Of her performance in Los Angeles on August 10, 1952, the press wrote: "In Victoria Kingsley's hands the guitar becomes an instrument of beauty and dignity, few could hold an audience for an entire programme without a moment's flagging of interest and never disappoint the listener. Miss Kingsley really lives in her songs." Her clear charming voice, enhanced by her refined guitar accompaniment, is most intriguing; her art is unique in British minstrelsy.

Ketelbey, Albert W., contemporary, born at Birmingham, about 1885. He studied the piano locally, continuing at Trinity College of

Music, London, where he won a scholarship for composition. Among his various compositions are a comic opera, a *Caprice* for piano and orchestra, *Concertstuck* for piano and orchestra, string quartets and quintets for piano with woodwind. He has conducted broadcast concerts of his own compositions in most European countries and also at Bournemouth, Harrogate, Margate and other musical festivals. His most popular compositions are *In a monastery garden, Sanctuary of the heart, In a Chinese temple garden, In the mystic land of Egypt, Royal Cavalcade* and *In a Persian market;* in this last composition he scores for mandolins with felicitous effect.

Klage, Charles, born, May 21, 1788, at Berlin, died there October, 1850, a German guitarist, pianist and composer who has published about fifty compositions which appeared in his native land. In 1838 he made a concert tour as pianist through Germany, terminating in Dresden where he published his Op. 36 and 37. He subsequently returned to Berlin where he was associated with the music publishing business of Kraft & Klage, later that of Trautwein. His compositions were principally for the piano, guitar and songs. Op. 2, *Variations for guitar solo* was published by Haslinger, Vienna, while many piano pieces were issued by the same publishers and many light pieces for the guitar, also songs with guitar, in album form, appeared elsewhere in Germany.

Klier, Josef, a brother of the better known church composer, Augustin Klier, was born April 24, 1760, at Stadt Kemnath. He and his brother André were taught the rudiments of music and the guitar by their father and the lads were placed in the Seminary of Amberg. In 1777, Josef entered the monastery of Weissenhoe, and after studying philosophy and theology in the University of Ingolstadt, was appointed a professor there. He returned to the monastery, was ordained June 24, 1783, and for many years was director of music in this institution. After the suppression of the monasteries, he lived at Neumark; but in the month of August, he was Abbott of Wondrech. Mendel in his Lexicon states that Klier was celebrated for the rich quality of his voice, a remarkable performer on the guitar and violin and the composer of trios for flute, violin and guitar which were published by Boehm, Augsburg.

Klingenberg, Friedrich Wilhelm, born June 6, 1809 at Sulau, Silesia, died April 2, 1888 at Gorlitz. He studied theology in Breslau and afterwards music, and in 1840 was cantor of St. Peter's, Leipzig. From 1844 he was a government musical director and an esteemed and popular conductor of choral societies. He formed many such organisations, which were very popular in Gorlitz. Riemann in his Music Lexicon mentions among his published compositions, *Twelve dances for guitar and flute.*

Klingenbrunner, Wilhelm, born October 21, 1765, at Vienna. He was a Treasury official who in youth played the flute and guitar as an amateur. In 1800 he collaborated with the well-known Viennese guitarist, Simon Molitor in the compilation of a Method for the Guitar entitled: *Complete instructions, combining all the works of previous guitarists, with a supplement on harmony,* which was published by Steiner & Co., Vienna. He was the author of numerous albums for flute and guitar and horn and guitar, the fifth and sixth of which were published in 1819 by Artaria, Vienna and Haslinger, Vienna. Klingenbrunner, a man of erudition, dramatist and musician also published compositions under the nom de plume of W. Blum and R. Kling. His manuscript autobiography, dated March 26, 1826, is in the library of the Musikfreund, Vienna.

Knab, Armin, born at Neu-Schleichach, Franconia, February 19, 1881. Intended for the legal profession, he devoted his leisure to music; he played the organ, piano and guitar and in 1934 was a professor at the High School for Church Music in Berlin. His compositions comprise dramatic works, song cycles and children's songs. He is a song writer and choral composer of distinction; the author of didatic treatises on music. Several of his songs from the well-known, *Des Knaben Wunderhorn* (Youth's Magic Horn) he composed with guitar accompaniment and presented the manuscripts to the Munich Society of Guitarists who published them in 1914.

Knize, Franz Max, born at Prague towards the close of the eighteenth century, was a Bohemian guitarist of repute and a prolific composer for the instrument in Prague, who taught the guitar and published works for it. He compiled two methods for the guitar, the first published in 1820 by Kronberger & Weber of Prague, the second in 1822 by Enders of the same city. This second instruction book was entitled *Complete Method in two parts,* on it he describes himself as "Composer and theoretical and practical teacher of the guitar." As a song writer, Knize was known in the musical world by a particularly pleasing ballad, *Bretislav a Jitka,* which became almost national in popularity. All his vocal compositions were written with guitar accompaniment and well received. His works for the guitar are chiefly divertissements, variations, national dances, etc. Op. 2, 3, 4, 5, 6, 7, 8, 10, 11, 15, 16, 19 and 20 were solos for the guitar issued by various publishers in Prague, principally Marco Berra, also Hoffmann, and Simrock, Bonn. Op. 12 is a collection of songs, poetry by Theodor Korner, and Op. 17, a similar collection by various authors. Op. 18 and 21 were songs in the Cheskian language, all of which were composed with guitar. Knize also published vocal operatic arrangements with guitar accompaniment.

Kohler, Gottlieb Henry, a German musician, born July 6, 1765, at Dresden and died in Liepzig January 29, 1833. His parents removed to Bautzen when he was a child and it was here he had his first musical instruction on the flute. After obtaining a certain proficiency he adopted the guitar and piano, and upon attaining manhood returned to his birthplace where he commenced his career as a teacher of these instruments. In 1794 he entered the Royal Orchestra as first flautist, but after four years in that service resigned to join the Leipzig Theatre orchestra, remaining until 1831, when he retired on pension. Kohler was a skilful performer on both the flute and guitar, appearing with success as soloist on both instruments. He published over two hundred compositions for the violin and piano, in addition to those of his chosen instruments, and also several collections of songs with guitar accompaniment. Op. 35, *Six songs with guitar,* published by Simrock, Bonn ; Op. 80, *Sonata for guitar and piano,* Hofmeister, Leipzig ; Op. 114, *Duo for flute and guitar,* Breitkopf & Härtel, Leipzig, and Op. 142 and 149, *Serenade for piano and guitar,* Schott, Mayence.

Kok, Joh. B., contemporary, born Amsterdam, March 1, 1889 received a sound musical education during youth when his instrument was the violin. He was a professional violinist until perceiving the musical possibilities of the mandolin and guitar gave them serious study. Sometime later he composed a few light pieces for mandolin band, which, published in album form by Seyfferdt, Amsterdam, were so successful that five more such albums were issued the following year. It was at this period the Gids voor Mandolin en Gitaar, a journal in the interests of the mandolin and guitar was founded, and Kok was commissioned by the editor to write a test piece for a competition, conditionally, if delivered the same day, so while travelling from Rotterdam to Arnhem he composed *Andante Grazioso.* His adjudication at this contest was the commencement of more than thirty years continuation and he adjudicated at the annual competitions, organised first by the Gids journal and those in co-operation with the Dutch Federation, and other European musical societies. Kok and his wife were teachers of wide repute and he was mandolinist under Mengelberg with the Amsterdam Concertgebouw Orchestra for the performances of Mahler's Eighth Symphony, *Song of the earth,* Ruyneman's *Hieroglyphen* for *Three flutes, two mandolins, guitar and piano* and other classic compositions. During the second world war, when all Dutch musical activities ceased, he compiled instruction books for the mandolin and guitar and many reprints have been published. In 1930, he founded the Radio Mandolin Orchestra and under his baton, more than one hundred and fifty broadcasts have been made from Hilversum, and his compositions—over two hundred—are known wherever the mandolin is played. In 1951, at the invitation of the Luton Mandolin Band, he visited Luton with the Excelsior Mandolin Band of Holland and endeared himself to all by his genius and unassuming, gentle disposition. When the Dutch Mandolin Band and Kok arrived they were received by the Mayor and civic officials and following the reception and lunch, a concert was given in the Town Hall, followed by other public concerts. For his Luton visit he composed and dedicated to Miss Irene Bone (musical director of the Luton Mandolin Band) a concert overture *Lutonia,* the original manuscript being presented by the composer at a public concert of the combined bands. Previous to his departure, he was requested to sign Luton's distinguished visitor's book. The following two years he was engaged to adjudicate at the competitions held annually in London under the auspices of the British Federation of Mandolinists and Guitarists.

Königs, Baron von, living in Vienna during the early part of the nineteenth century, an amateur musician who played the flute and 'cello and was a member of the Vienna Philharmonic Society. He was a member of that quartet which played to Schubert five days previous to the latter's death and the composer of Op. 1, *Serenade characteristique, for guitar, flute and alto with glockenspiel ad. lib.*, which is recorded in the A.M.Z for the year 1814.

Körner, Theodor, born at Dresden, September 23, 1791, and died August 26, 1813, a celebrated poet known in Germany as "freedom's poet and hero," the author of Lyre and Sword and many other exceedingly popular poems. He was a capable performer on the guitar and wrote songs, words and music, for it. In his youth he was delicate, could not attend a public school and was educated by his father, Dr. Körner, and private tutors. His home life was in itself a musical education; his mother played the guitar and on January 27, 1797, Dr. Körner wrote to the poet Schiller: "One more request to you from Minna (his wife). In Jena there is at the present time a certain instrument maker named Otto who makes Spanish cithers or guitars, and who for some time lived in Gotha. From him, my wife wishes to purchase a guitar at once. Be so kind as to buy or order one and have it packed by the maker." Schiller replied on February 7, "The instrument maker of whom you wrote, Otto, we could not find for a long time, as they would not allow him to settle in this town. At length he arrived here once again and asked Griesbach for the patronage and protection of the university. On this occasion I found him and ordered the guitar; but he does not make them for less than ten thalers (about thirty shillings). He said that he sent two guitars at the same price to Naumann and Brühl, and he promises to send yours in about a fortnight." Otto did not fulfil his promise, and the ensuing correspondence displays Dr. Körner's impatience at not receiving the guitar; but on April 28 he wrote: "The guitar has arrived and possesses a beautiful tone." From his father, Theodore had his first music lessons, and in a letter to Förster, dated September 5, 1803, when his son was twelve years of age, he writes: "Soon I shall have many musical treats in my house—my children possess good voices and I have placed them under a music teacher here." At a very early age Theodore showed a liking for his mother's guitar. In notes made by his father in 1814, we read: "In a high degree I perceived in him a decided gift for music. On the violin he promised to do well, when he developed a passion for the guitar, and his songs with the guitar rendered with great musical taste and feeling, give much pleasure." Theodor, his sister Emma, and Julie Kunze were all endowed musically, so the father formed a musical circle which met in his home weekly, under his direction, when musicians of renown took practical part in the gatherings, as for instance Capellmeister Paer, and even Mozart was a participant, for it is asserted that it was in Dr. Körner's house that he first made known his sketch of *Don Giovanni.* On January 27, 1805, Dr. Körner wrote to Schiller: "In our home we have much music and perform instrumental quartets with great enthusiasm. These practices we hold weekly and we may even have to obtain a larger hall." When sixteen, and on Easter, 1807, Theodor entered the School of Mines at Freiberg, Saxony, where the guitar was his constant companion. In his miner's dress with his guitar slung over his shoulder, Körner would roam the mountain sides, fancying himself back in the days of the troubadours, and all his life manifested this love for the instrument. His guitar was always by his side when in the social company of his friends, and one of these, Förster, states that Körner as a student possessed the gift to compose and sing poems and melodies to which his jolly companions joined in the chorus. In contrast to this quiet life at Freiberg, stands the wild students' life at Leipzig University, which he entered October, 1810; but owing to his participation in violent conflicts between the students, was forced to leave the following Easter. Even during these reckless months he did not neglect the guitar, for his friend Förster wrote: "I sat with him and other jolly companions in Auerbach's cellar, where by the side of the pearls from the Rhine and the blood from Burgundy, we became as happy as the celebrated five hundred, in the cell, out of which Faust rode away on a wine barrel. Under the oaks of Rosenthal, Theodor sung to me his gentle love songs, and I was by his side in the fateful scuffle when he was compelled to quit Leipzig, and he always had in me a sweetheart to whom he sung his poems accompanied by his guitar."

After various vicissitudes Körner arrived in Vienna during the autumn of 1811 and here he experienced a brief happiness and artistic activity. By his poetry and numerous recommendations the best circles of Vienna were open to him, and by his amiable nature won the affection of all, particularly the ladies. In Vienna his two plays, The Bride and The Green Domino were successful and he was appointed Royal poet. The height of his happiness was his engagement with the actress Antonia Adamberger; but it was of short duration, for during the French invasion in 1813, Körner enlisted in the celebrated volunteer corps of Major Lutzow, and the young poet was severely wounded in the battle of Kitzen. In a subsequent engagement he was mortally shot on the road between Gadebusch and Schwerin and buried under an oak tree; on its trunk, comrades carved his name. The last letters of the poet show his love of the guitar, on June 13, 1812, he writes: "The nights are now beautiful and so I always take my guitar and ramble through the neighbouring villages. A chestnut wood provides the necessary coolness, and my guitar which hangs on the nearest tree behind, occupies me in the moments I am resting." When he cele-

Charles de Janon

Theodor Körner

Theodor Körner.

Joseph Kuffner

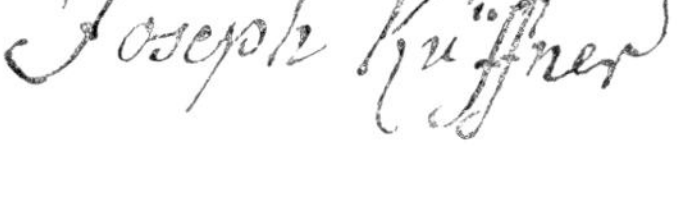

Joseph Küffner

Joh B. Kok

brated his twenty-first birthday, his last, on September 23, 1812, his father sent him a guitar and his sweetheart a fancifully worked guitar ribbon. The family guitar, the instrument that Otto made for his mother is among other relics of the poet in the Körner Museum, Dresden. The guitar given to Theodore by his father, was not the one taken to Freiberg, that remained the family instrument in Dresden, and after the death of his mother in 1843, came into the possession of her adopted son Captain Karl Ulbrich. This guitar is rather small, of very plain, neat construction, and the unvarnished table appears to be cedar wood. It bears inside the name of its maker, Otto, with the date 1797, and on the table below the bridge, very faded, is the signature "C. Th. Körner," in the poet's writing. The guitar which he played in Freiberg has not been traced, but the instrument used in Vienna, and which was sent to him as a birthday present by his father, is in the possession of the publisher Rudolf Brockhaus, Leipzig. Körner also possessed a Spanish lute which came to the family through W. von Humboldt, who purchased it during his travels. This lute, with his guitar is also in the Körner Museum, Dresden, with a few of his songs written for the guitar, and also a touching remembrance of his student days—a manuscript volume of songs with guitar, composed while at Freiberg and dedicated to Johanna Biedermann, a clergyman's daughter. Körner's excellent guitar playing is universally acknowledged and among his compositions are *Fifteen Variations for flute and guitar,* and original and other songs with guitar accompaniment, several published by the I.G.V., one from the Körner Museum, Dresden, entitled *Resignation,* is reproduced.

Korngold, Erich, Wolfgang, contemporary, born May 29, 1897, displayed precocious talent very early as a composer, for his pantomime *Der Schneemann* was produced in the Hopofer Theatre, Vienna, when he was eleven years of age. He is the composer of several operas which are widely known and in *Das Wunder der Heliana* he makes felicitous use of the guitar.

Krahmer, Johann Ernst, an oboist and guitarist born March 30, 1795, at Dresden and died in Vienna, January 16, 1837. He was a pupil of Kummer and Jackel and from 1815-22 was principal oboe in the Vienna Court Orchestra. His wife Karoline, a celebrated clarinet player, composed popular dance music which was published in Vienna during 1825. Krahmer wrote a method for the czakan (Bohemian flute) which appeared in 1830. The A.M.Z. and Whistling's Handbuch for the years 1830-5 record his published compositions, among them are *Valses with Trio and Coda for oboe and guitar,* Op. 21, *Military Rondo for one or two oboes and guitar,* Op. 36 ; *Variations and Rondo,* ditto, Op. 22 ; *Introduction and Variations,* Op. 32 and similar others. There was a Ph. Kramer living in Prague in 1830 the author of *Theme with Variations for the guitar with Spanish tuning,* Op. 2, and Whistling records his Op. 4, *Variations for guitar solo,* published by Hofmeister, Leipzig.

Kraus, Joseph Martin, born June 26, 1756, at Miltenberg, near Mayence and died in Stockholm, December 15, 1792. He studied law and philosophy in Mayence, Erfurt, and Gottingen and afterwards composition under the Abbe Vogler. He visited Stockholm with a friend, and remained there when appointed musical director in 1781. From 1782-87, by the aid of a grant from the King of Sweden, he travelled to Germany, France, Italy and England and when he returned was Royal Capellmeister. His compositions include operas, symphonies, overtures, etc. Riemann and also Eitner record his Op. 1, a *Sonata for guitar and piano.* His autobiography is in Berlin State Library.

Krebs, Franz Xaver, born at Eichstadt, Bavaria in 1765 was a vocalist, guitarist and composer of repute who made his debut as tenor vocalist in 1787 in the theatre of his native town and afterwards engaged in a similar capacity in the Hoftheatre, Stuttgart, during April, 1795. Moscheles in his Diary, records his association with Krebs and other musicians for musical discussion and beer, in the Birnbeck Kneipe. Krebs was the author of numerous vocal compositions with the accompaniment of one or two guitars. Op. 2 and Op. 10 to Op. 13 ; *Empfindungen beym, for solo voice and four part chorus with guitar,* published in 1812 ; *Six duets for two voices with two guitars ; Das Madchen, for soprano and tenor with two guitars,* all published by Peters, Leipzig ; *Berg u Thal, for voice and guitar* and *Lucas u Hannchen, for soprano and tenor with two guitars,* both issued by Schott,

Mayence ; Op. 3, *Six Waltzes and trios for guitar ;* Op. 8, *Three Waltzes and Polonaises for two guitars* and Op. 9, *Six Dances for two guitars.* Whistling records these compositions and there remains in manuscript a *Phantasy for soprano and guitar.*

Kreutzer, Conradin, born November 22, 1780, at Mösskirch in Baden, died, December 14, 1849, in Riga, Russia, was the son of a miller and when a lad was a chorister, first in his native town, then at the Abbey of Zwiefalten and after at Scheussenried. During this period, he played the guitar as a pastime and also when sent to Freiberg to study medicine, which, being irksome, he abandoned for music. The next five years were spent principally in Switzerland as vocalist, pianist and composer. Realising the necessity for further musical education, he visited Vienna in 1804, where he studied with Albrechtsberger in order to be able to write for the stage. His first opera, *Conradin von Schwaben,* produced at Stuttgart in 1812, gained him the position of Capellmeister to the King of Würtemburg ; however, in 1822 he returned to Vienna to produce his opera *Libussa.* Until 1840, he was officiating as conductor at various theatres, and it was during this period, in 1834, that he produced his two best operas in the Josephstadt Theatre, *Das Nachtlager in Granada,* and *Der Varschwender,* a fairy play. After these successes he was musical director in Cologne from where he visited Paris, returning to Vienna in 1846. He died in Riga, where he had accompanied his daughter, a vocalist, on a concert tour. Kreutzer composed thirty operas, in several of which he uses the guitar. Among his various published compositions are two duos for piano and guitar, one of which, *Polonaise,* Op. 10, was issued by Weigl, Vienna and various songs with guitar were issued by Schott, Mayence. His life was published in Musikal Charakterkopfe in 1879.

Kreutzer, Joseph, a German guitarist and instrumental composer, living during the early part of the nineteenth century. Prat states that he was brother of the celebrated violinist. Little is known of his career, beyond the fact that his compositions were recorded in continental music journals from 1822-28. His published works number more than fifty, the first half of which were issued by Simrock, Bonn. Op. 6, *Duos for two guitars ;* Op. 7, 11, 12, 13, 14 and 15, *Variations for guitar solo ;* Op. 17, *Twelve Dances for guitar ;* Op. 23, *Three Rondos for guitar ;* Op. 9, *Four Trios for flute, violin and guitar ;* Op. 16, *Grand Trio for guitar, flute and clarinet* (a new edition has appeared recently), Op. 12, *Six Variations on 'God save the King,'* published by Ewer & Co., London, which was popular in England, and many similar works, as trios, quartets and quintets without opus numbers. The original manuscript of a *Trio for flute, violin and guitar* by Kreutzer, dated 1842, is in the library of the International League of Guitarists, Munich.

Kruger, Emil, born March 27, 1845, at Gorlitz and died there,

December 18, 1907, was a member of the Royal Chapel Orchestra of Berlin and guitarist of the opera. For many years he was an esteemed teacher of the guitar and mandolin in his native city. He edited a new and revised edition of *Giuliani's Guitar Studies,* Op. 48, published by the International League of Guitarists.

Krumpholz, Wenzel, born at Zlonitz, near Prague in 1750 and died suddenly while out walking, May 3, 1817, was the son of a bandmaster in a French regiment and lived in Paris during childhood, where his father taught him music. His brother Johann Baptist, was a celebrated harpist and composer. Wenzel Krumpholz studied the mandolin and became one of its most brilliant exponents. He also was a skilful violinist and in 1796 was one of the first violins in the Court Opera orchestra, Vienna. His name is immortalised by his intimacy with Beethoven, who was exceedingly fond of him and accustomed to address him jokingly as " mein Narr," (my fool). According to Ries, Krumpholz gave Beethoven some instruction on the violin, when in Vienna, and it is more than probable that he also gave instruction on the mandolin. Krumpholz was one of the first to recognise Beethoven's genius, and inspired others with his own enthusiasm. Czerny mentions this in his autobiography, and states that he it was who introduced him to Beethoven. Krumpholz frequently played the mandolin to Beethoven, and Artaria in his *Autographische Skizze* states that he intended writing a sonata for mandolin and pianoforte for Krumpholz (see Beethoven). It is thought that this composition is the one sketched in Beethoven's note book, in the Manuscript Department of the British Museum, No. 29, 801, and first made public by Messrs. Breitkopf & Härtel, Leipzig. Beethoven was evidently moved by the death of his friend, for on the following day he composed the *Gesang der Mönche,* from Schiller's *William Tell,* for three men's voices—" in commemoration of the sudden and unexpected death of our Krumpholz." Only two of Krumpholz's compositions were printed, there remain in manuscript, compositions for the mandolin, including a *Sonata for mandolin and piano,* composed for and dedicated to Countess Josephine Clary, Prague.

Kucharz or **Kuchorz,** Johann Baptist, a Hungarian musician of repute, born at Chortecz, near Mlazowicz, Bohemia, March 5, 1751, and died in Prague, February 18, 1829. He obtained fame as organist, mandolinist and operatic conductor. Kucharz received his first musical instruction in the Jesuit Seminary of Koniggratz, Bohemia, and continued his musical studies in the Jesuit Seminary of Gitschin, and when he removed to Prague some years later pursued the study of the organ and composition under the well-known teacher Seegert. In September, 1790, upon the decease of Jean Wolf he was organist of St. Heinrichskirche, and engaged teaching the organ, mandolin and theory of music. During the same period he was organist also of the Monastery of Strahow. His reputation soon spread, for the following year he was conductor of the opera, Prague, where he officiated many years, during which several of his compositions were produced with success. It was while he was conductor of the Prague opera that he became associated with Mozart. He was intimate with him during the latter's residence in Prague, and at the first performance of *Don Giovanni,* October 29, 1787, Kucharz played the mandolin in the orchestra, accompanying the serenade *Deh Vieni,* Mozart conducting. Kucharz was a consummate artist on the mandolin and an esteemed teacher whose pupils numbered many of the most aristocratic members of society ; he remained conductor of the opera until 1800, when he resigned. Among his compositions are organ concertos, piano sonatas and sonatas and other works for the mandolin. Waldo Selden Pratt in The New Encyclopedia of Music, says : "He was an expert on the mandolin."

Kücken, Friedrich Wilhelm, born November 16, 1810, at Bleckede, Hanover, died April 3, 1882, at Schwerin. He studied the flute, violin and guitar and was a member of the Duke's orchestra. His first song compositions were so popular that he was appointed tutor to the Princesses in the Royal Palace. He was, however, not contented, so visited Berlin in 1832 to study with Birnbach and it was here that he composed the songs that made his name a household word. He continued his study with Sechter in Vienna in 1841 and two years later with Halévy in Paris. The music journals of 1837 praise his separate songs and also albums of songs with guitar accompaniment. From 1851 he was Kapellmeister at Stuttgart, resigning in 1861. He has composed operas, piano and violin music, in addition to his numerous and exceedingly popular songs, many of which were written with guitar ; Op. 17, 19, 20, 23, 24, 27, 31 and 32 are most widely known. Wessel & Co., London, possessed sole rights of publication in England. Other of his songs were arranged with guitar accompaniment by E. Salleneuve.

Küffner, Joseph, born at Wurzburg, March 31, 1776, and died there September 8, 1856, was the son of Wilhelm Küffner, a musician of repute, a native of Kalmunz, near Regensburg, whose family for three generations had been musicians. Wilhelm Küffner had made extensive tours as musician, visiting the important cities of western Europe, eventually settling in Wurzburg, where he was Royal Capellmeister. His son Joseph lost his mother at the age of eleven, and his father intending that he should pursue a scientific and literary career, placed him in a local school, where he accomplished his studies in a creditable manner after which he continued his education in philosophy and law at the university. During youth his father had instructed him in the rudiments of music and at an early period he had obtained a certain proficiency on the guitar and violin. In 1793 after leaving the university he was articled to a lawyer ; but in his leisure continued to play the guitar and also received instruction on the violin from the concert director, Ludwig Schmidt. When Küffner had completed his articles and duly qualified, he entered an office with the intent of making his début ; the death of his family intervened and his financial circumstances were materially affected. He was necessitated to give lessons in Latin and on the violin and guitar and the time left at his disposal was utilised to the greatest extent by perfecting himself on his two instruments. In 1798 he was offered a position by the Bishop, as supernumerary musician of the chapel, at an annual salary of one hundred and twenty-five gulden, with the Bishop's promise to secure for him a more lucrative position under the administration. The desire to write music now occupied his attention ; but he was unacquainted with the principles of harmony, his musical study up to the present had been solely to the practical side of the art. A musical friend offered him the loan of Knecht's treatise on harmony and composition, which he gladly accepted and studied with avidity. He then tried composing light pieces in four parts, and receiving encouragement from his musical associates, resolved to continue his education in this direction. He studied under Frölich, and it was not long before he commenced to make himself known by small compositions for the harpsichord, the flute, and guitar. When Wurzburg and its territory passed under the rule of Bavaria, all Küffner's prospects of a more lucrative position in the chapel, or under the administration vanished and he therefore accepted service as bandmaster in a Bavarian regiment ; his productive activity in this sphere was the means of his composing numerous pieces for military band. For several years he had no occupation but military duties as bandmaster, and he therefore employed himself by writing studies and music for the guitar, and other compositions for strings in combination with the guitar, in addition to military music. His success in this department brought his name prominently before the musical public, and when Wurzburg fell to the Archduke Ferdinand, this prince, a talented musician, appointed Küffner, in 1801, chamber and court musician with a salary of four hundred florins with the additional position of chief superintendent of military music and an increment ot three hundred florins. The financial position of Küffner was more satisfactory than it had ever been and in 1801 he married. From now fortune seemed to smile on him, his compositions were accepted by the principal music publishers, and day by day his reputation became enhanced. Küffner's first compositions, published under his opus number —serenades for the guitar, flute or violin and alto—were on the models and style of the then exceedingly popular compositions for this combination of instruments, by the guitarist Leonard de Call. In 1811 Andre, Offenbach, commenced to issue Küffner's serenades and during the year had published nine, in addition to many works for military band. These publications obtained for Küffner a brilliant reputation, and then Schott, Mayence, commenced the publication of his serenades for guitar, violin, and alto, with his Op. 10, and this firm alone issued nearly seven hundred of Küffner's musical works. They embrace nearly every form of musical composition, and were included in the repertoire of the majority of the musical societies of northern Europe. During this period Küffner was on terms of intimacy with Beethoven and in the spring of 1813 the latter wrote a Triumphal march for

Tarpeia or *Hersilia,* a tragedy by Küffner which was advertised as newly composed, March 26, 1813. Brilliant offers were now showered upon Küffner to induce him to settle in various cities, but he preferred to remain court musician and lead a quiet life among friends. In 1814 the grand duchy of Wurzburg was newly reunited to Bavaria and Küffner was placed on the pension list, as were all the musicians of the Royal Chapel ; but this circumstance, which formerly would have carried trouble by its existence, did not cause inconvenience, as Küffner's compositions were eagerly sought by publishers, which alone placed him in a position of independence. In 1825 he visited Paris and while there wrote several pieces for the guitar which were published by Leduc, and also Lemoine, and when he visited Belgium in 1829, the important musical societies honoured him with a public reception and demonstration, and he was the recipient of numerous honorary diplomas from musical institutions. He presided, in August, 1830, over a grand contest of twenty-nine musical societies organised in Brussels, and received an ovation. In 1833 the musical society of Wurzburg presented him with his portrait painted by Gustave Wappera, and an engraving from this portrait, by H. Schalck is reproduced. The year 1837 saw the publication of his first and second symphonies, Op. 75 and 76, issued by Schott, and very shortly after, the third appeared published by Andre, Offenbach. During this time, Küffner was soaring high in the musical world and his fertility was in no way diminished. He made arrangements of all the modern operas, for military band, for piano solo, for violin, flute, alto and guitar, guitar solo, and various other instruments, and also composed a multitude of original works of various character. Küffner's published compositions with opus numbers exceed three hundred and fifty, in addition there appeared a still greater quantity without numbers, and at his death he left more than sixty unpublished manuscripts. Küffner died in his native city of Wurzburg, September 8, 1856, at the advanced age of eighty years and several months. In reviewing his compositions it is necessary to note, although exceedingly popular in their day, the majority are now among the forgotten. Küffner wrote much for the guitar ; he was, in fact, a prolific composer for all instruments, but the guitar and violin were his first and favourites, and all his early compositions were written for these ; their success was phenomenal. Küffner appears to have published no method for the guitar, although he penned many valuable studies, scales, and exercises for the use of beginners and also wrote several lessons for beginners in the form of duets for two guitars. The former are Op. 80, *Twenty-five sonatas for beginners ;* Op. 87, *Twelve easy duos for two guitars,* and Op. 168, *Sixty easy duos for two guitars.* Küffner published more than thirty popular serenades for violin or flute, alto, and guitar, and it was these which gave him prominence in the musical world at the very commencement of his career. They are Op. 1, 7, 10, 12, 15, 21, 35, 39, 45, 60, 63, 61, 110, 117, 119, 144, 145, 151, 152, 186, 187, 198, 214, 246, 248 and 292 ; *Quartets for flute and strings with guitar,* Op. 11, 94, 135, 155 and 156. He also arranged for guitar solo more than a hundred operatic selections, principally moderately easy transcriptions, whose chief value is in their simple musicianly arrangement. At the time when musical societies were to be found in every city and town of Germany and more particularly in Belgium, Küffner's compositions were the works performed and upon which these institutions prospered and flourished. With these societies, Küffner's name eclipsed all others in the musical world, and his reputation was exceedingly great. His instrumental music was characterized by brilliancy and ease of execution, two of the most important factors essential to popularity. He made use of the guitar in numerous compositions as solo instrument, in duos with the piano, the violin, 'cello, clarinet and horn, and as vocal accompaniment, and also in trio, quartet, and quintet with the above and other instruments, and in all instances he displays the guitar to advantage, which can only be accomplished by a practical master of the instrument. The majority were published by Schott, Mayence, and Richault, Paris. About thirty of his original vocal works were published, in every instance the accompaniment was for the guitar, and many popular and favourite airs appeared in England. His publications also include methods of instruction for the oboe, clarinet, bassoon and cornet, and in collaboration with Schad he compiled several volumes of progressive exercises for the piano. Seven of his symphonies for grand orchestra were issued by Schott, and fifty methodical studies for the clarinet, with English, German, French and Spanish text, many overtures, entractes, etc., for orchestra and military band, by Andre, Offenbach. Küffner wrote several operas, chief of which were *Der Cornet, Jean of Wieselbourg, Sporn und Scharpe,* and *Tarpeia* or *Hersilia,* the tragedy for which Beethoven wrote a Triumphal march, all published by Schott. The above do not exhaust the list or variety of his musical productions, they are a host as diversified as numerous.

Kühnel, Frederic, born in Austria in 1820 and died in Russia, 1878. He was a guitar virtuoso of whose career little is known. He toured Europe as guitarist and during the years 1841 and 1842 was appearing in Prague and Vienna. The A.M.Z. and other musical press of this date were lavish in his praise. He afterwards toured Germany and Russia and eventually established himself as teacher and performer in the latter country where he resided till death. Few of his published compositions are known. Whistling records his Op. 3, *Grand Fantasia for guitar solo,* published by Bohmanns Erben, Prague ; *Variations for guitar solo,* Op. 2, Sokol & Wehner, Prague ; Waltzes and other light pieces were issued by Russian publishers.

Kummer, Gaspard, born December 10, 1795, at Erlau near Scheusingen, Hungary, and died May 21, 1870. He is known as a composer for the flute, guitar and orchestra. He was given instruction on the guitar and flute by a player in his native town, named Neumeister, and after having obtained a proficiency on both, continued his musical education under a vocalist named Staps, with whom he studied harmony and composition. In 1831 he was solo flautist in the Royal Chapel of Coburg and the following year promoted to the musical directorship. Kummer was particularly successful as a composer for wind instruments —the oboe, flute, clarinet and bassoon—and was commissioned to write compositions expressly for the trombone virtuoso Carl Queisser, which were frequently performed at the Gewandhaus Concerts of Leipzig. Grove states that the reports of his public appearances rarely mention him without some term of pride or endearment. Kümmer was held in high repute on the continent as a teacher also, for Friedrich Kiel was sent to Coburg, by the reigning prince to study under him. He was a prolific composer, more than one hundred and sixty of his works have been published, in addition to numerous collections and albums, principally flute concertos with orchestra, orchestral works, duos, quartets and quintets which include the guitar and a few songs. Op. 5, 10, 18, 28, 34, 38, 40, 55, 56, 63 and 70 are *Duos for flute and guitar ;* Op. 81, 83, 92, *Trios for guitar, flute and violin ;* Op. 75, *Grand quintet for guitar, two flutes, viola and violoncello.* These were very popular and he also arranged several with piano, although originally composed for guitar. They were published by Andre, Offenbach ; Simrock, Bonn ; and Schott, Mayence, and a new edition of the *Grand Quintet,* Op. 75 was issued by the Volpe Music Co., New York.

Kunze, Charles Henry, a musician who lived at Heilbronn, Germany, during the close of the eighteenth century. He was a composer of chamber music, music for wind instruments, duos for flute and guitar, guitar solos and songs with guitar accompaniment, which were published by Schott, Mayence ; Gombart, Augsburg and Andre, Offenbach.

LABARRE, Trille, a guitarist living in Paris at the close of the eighteenth century of whom little is known beyond his published works. He was the author of Op. 7, *a New Method for the guitar, for those wishing to learn without a master,* which appeared in 1793 ; Op. 2, *Sonatas for violin and guitar,* published in 1788 ; Op. 8, a *collection of thirty-one pieces for guitar ; Graduated studies for guitar,* published in 1794 and a *Collection of very pretty Romances for guitar,* published by Bailleux, Paris, in 1787. From the title pages of his publications it is evident that he was a professor of his instrument. Several were issued by H. Naderman, Paris, and two of the sonatas have been edited, revised and fingered by Prat and published by Jose B. Romero, Buenos Aires. There was a Theodore Labarre, a harpist, who published much for the harp and a few songs with guitar, which were issued by Schott, Mayence.

Lang, Alexander, born at Ratisbon, March 6, 1806, and died in Erlangen, February 18, 1837. His father, an official of position in the service of the Prince of Tour and Taxis, encouraged and cultivated his son's inclination for music by first teaching him the guitar and then the piano. When in his teens he entered Heidelburg University where he studied jurisprudence and music. In 1834 he was appointed professor in the University of Erlangen and the same year founded in that institution the Cæcilia Musical Society, which he conducted until his decease three years later. Among his published compositions are *Duos for two guitars,* and also for *guitar and piano.*

Lang, Eddie (whose parental name was Salvatore Massaro) was born 1904 in South Philadelphia and died in the U.S.A., March 26, 1933, from complications arising after a throat operation. His musical career commenced by studying the violin, which he played in various jazz bands of the Eastern States for eleven years, and then he put aside the violin and adopted the guitar upon which he became famous by performing with Paul Whiteman, Bing Crosby and Jack Benny. As guitarist in the jazz orchestras of Paul Whiteman, Venuti, etc., he was considered by many, unequalled technically, in this style of guitar playing. Innumerable of his solos were recorded as were also jazz duos for two guitars with other dance band guitarists. He played with a plectrum and all his compositions and recordings were for that method of playing. He visited London in 1924 and appeared in the films " The King of Jazz " and " The Big Broadcast ". Some of his recordings were factored under the pseudonym of " Blind Willie Dunn ". The music press of the day said: " He was probably the greatest figure in the whole history of swing music " and a short biography was issued by Parlophone Record Company.

Lanz, Joseph, born January 20, 1797, at Michaelnbach, Upper Austria. He was a son of the local schoolmaster and for a time was violinist in St. Peter's church, Salzburg, and a teacher of the piano and guitar. He removed to Vienna and in 1826 was commissioned with Schubert and other famous composers to contribute to Terpischore, published by Sauer & Leidesdorf, Vienna. On November 12, 1828, he and his friend Franz Schubert visited Sechter and made arrangements to commence the study of fugal composition but *homo proponit, Deus disponit,* for on November 19, just a week later, Schubert was dead. Among the published compositions of Lanz are: Op. 19, *Soiree Champetre,* a *Serenade for flute, violin and guitar; Serenade a la Rossini, for flute, viola and guitar*, both published by Diabelli, Vienna, and Op. 9, *Due Rondini, guitar solo,* issued by Leidesdorf, Vienna.

Laparra, Raoul Louis, born May 13, 1876, Bordeaux, and died in Paris, April 4, 1943. He studied in Paris Conservatoire under Massenet, won the Prize of Rome in 1903 and became famous after the production of his three act opera, *La Habanera* at the Opera Comique, Paris, in 1908. This opera was an instantaneous success and in it Laparra employs the guitar with felicitous effect. An ardent admirer of Spanish music and the guitar, he contributed " La musica y la danza popular en Espana " to the Encyclopaedia of Music, Paris, and he writes in the highest praise of the Spanish guitarist, Barrios, of Granada. The eminent guitarist Ida Presti was soloist during the three month's production of *La Habanera* at the Opera Comique in 1947. Of the guitar, Laparra wrote: " One may call the six strings of the guitar, six different souls within one harmonious body."

Laurentiis, Carmine de, an Italian mandolinist of repute in Naples during the first half of the nineteenth century. He is known as the first teacher who gave serious instruction to the youth Carlo Munier. He laid the foundations of a correct and intelligent system of technique, which developed by experience and inherent ability of the pupil, produced one of the most renowned exponents of the mandolin. Laurentiis was the author of a *Method for the mandolin,* published in 1869 by Ricordi, Milan. This is unique ; it is the earliest published method for the instrument and maintains its usefulness to the present day. Compiled on an excellent system, its studies are admirable in design and well graduated ; it is concluded with six original caprices for mandolin solo. This unpretentious book, the excellence of which is in its exercises and studies, rather than its didatics, passed many editions. An English version by F. Sacchi, a Cremonese mandolinist, guitarist and literateur—was issued by the same publishers. Sacchi was a contributor to various music journals, the composer of several light works for mandolin and guitar, issued by Schott, London, and teacher of the mandolin to their Royal Highnesses the Princesses Victoria and Maud of Wales.

Lebedeff, Vassilj Petrowitsch, born at Capiatovski, Saratov, in 1867, and died in St. Petersburg, February 8, 1907. His first musical instruction was on the guitar and for some years he was an amateur guitarist in his native town ; it was not until he came under the influence of the guitarist and composer Decker Schenk that he adopted the guitar professionally. In 1886 he removed to St. Petersburg where he made the acquaintance of the artist who shaped his musical career, and after some month's study with Schenk, a life-long friendship existed between master and pupil. When Lebedeff had completed his military training in 1890, he commenced a career as teacher of the guitar in St. Petersburg. The same year he undertook a professional tour, visiting Paris, where as guitar soloist the Figaro and other influential journals record his brilliant performances. Lebedeff returned to his native land in 1892, gave many recitals in St. Petersburg and other centres and enjoyed an enviable position, both as teacher and virtuoso. In 1898 he was appointed professor in the Royal Military Music Academy and after the death of his teacher, the following year, was the only guitarist of repute in St. Petersburg. Prat says he formed and conducted a large balalaika orchestra in 1890 and that he was also a good vocalist, singing to his own guitar accompaniment. Many of his compositions and his *Method for the Guitar* were published by J. H. Zimmerman, Leipzig, and several of his manuscript compositions for guitar solo are in the library of the I.G.V., Munich, presented by their author.

Lecuna, Juan, born 1898 at Valencia, Venezuela, and after preliminary musical studies in Caracas continued his education in U.S.A. His piano compositions are published in Paris and he has also written a piano concerto, string quartets and a *Suite Venezolana for Four Guitars.*

Ledhuy, Adolphe, a guitarist living in Paris during the beginning of the nineteenth century, the author of several music treatises and also compositions for the guitar. His two best known volumes were, Principles of Music, published in Paris, 1830 and Discourses on Music, published by Levrault, Strasburg, 1834 and other theoretical treatises on music. In 1833 he collaborated with the pianist Bertini in the publication of a music periodical, The Musical Encyclopédie, which circulated in Paris during 1833-5. Ledhuy was also the composer of guitar works, now rarely heard of, the most widely known are : *Brilliant Spanish nocturne for guitar solo,* Op. 26, for which the two lowest bass strings are lowered a tone ; *Twelve Studies for guitar,* Op. 18 ; *Etudes caracteristiques for guitar,* Op. 21 and a *Tablature for the guitar,* published by Lemoine, Paris. There was a guitarist and guitar maker of this name, living in Coucy-le-Chateau, France, in 1806 who constructed guitars of novel design, chiefly after the pattern of the lyre and it was from Ledhuy's model that Salomon obtained the idea for his harpolyre.

Leduc, Alphonse, born Nantes, March 9, 1804, died in Paris, June 17, 1868, was a French virtuoso on the guitar, bassoon and piano, and an instrumental composer. His father was a skilful violinist, a pupil of Gavinies and also a good guitarist, who for some time was director of the Concerts Spirituels, Paris. The son's musical education was at its commencement undertaken by his parents and he continued at the Paris Conservatoire, where Reicha was his teacher for harmony. In 1825 he obtained the second prize for the bassoon. He founded a music publishing business in Paris in 1841 which developed to considerable importance and was continued under the same name by his son. He was the author of about fifty published compositions for the guitar. There was a Pierre Leduc born in Paris in 1755 and died October, 1816, who with his elder brother, Simon, a violinist, succeeded to the music publishing business of La Chevardiere, in Paris. Eitner records his publication of an Essay on the improvement of the Guitar or Lyre.

Legnani, Luigi, born November 7, 1790 at Ferrara, Italy, died August 5, 1877, at the advanced age of eighty-seven, in the house named "Locatelli," 195 Girotti St., Ravenna. When eight years of age his parents removed to Ravenna, at which time he commenced his musical education, singing and the guitar and at the age of seventeen was taking a prominent part in opera at Ravenna Theatre. His first public appearance as guitar virtuoso was at Milan in 1819, when his playing aroused the enthusiasm of his audiences and the admiration and praise of musicians and the press. From now he was one of the most renowned of guitarists and in October 1822 commenced a concert tour of his native land, continued to Germany and visited Vienna, where he resided many months. From Vienna he travelled to Russia where he gave many concerts with his accustomed success and in 1825 returned to his native land making his abode in Genoa, where he was occupied in teaching. In 1827 he was concert touring again—Fetis states, with Paganini—first in Switzerland, where his principal solo was his arrangement of *Swiss national melodies, with brilliant variations,* which captivated his audiences—and then again to Vienna, the scene of previous artistic triumphs. He is next heard of in Paris in 1829 when an unforseen incident arose. His recital had been advertised; but just previous to the concert he fell from his carriage and bruised his arm, although not serious, he was unable to fulfil the engagement. The Spanish guitarists, Sor and Aguado, hearing of his misfortune, immediately came to the assistance of the Italian guitarist and the concert proceeded. Legnani was in Genoa during 1835 giving concerts again with Paganini, and at the commencement of the following year, when the first signs of the violinist's malady were made manifest, and also during the months of October and November 1836, Legnani was his companion and guest. The two musicians lived together in Villa Gajona, on Paganini's estate, in the environs of Parma. Paganini's health prohibited his public performances, so with the assistance of Legnani he was occupied in arranging his compositions for publication. Legnani accompanied on the guitar Paganini's violin solos and took a general interest in his musical arrangements. They planned and prepared a concert tour together, as violinist and guitarist, and made arrangements to commence the following year, their principal centres being Paris and London. By the summer of 1837 Paganini's health had improved sufficiently, so the two artists gave a concert, June 9, in the Theatre Corignano, Turin, in aid of charity, followed by others for their benefit. They were at this time intent on their project of visiting Paris, where Paganini was to fulfil an engagement at the opening ceremony of the " Casino Paganini " but these were destined to be Paganini's last public concerts (see Paganini). The projected tour was abandoned, Paganini's health again troubled him—it was irretrievably broken—he was fast losing his voice so he sought rest and change of air in the south of France, and Legnani returned to Italy. Legnani visited Spain during the spring of 1842 and appeared at concerts in Madrid and Barcelona. Mariano Soriano Fuertes, the well-known Spanish music historian, in the Iberia Musical, Madrid, reports his concerts given in the Teatro Principal, May 29, saying: " The Italian guitar virtuoso, Senor Luigi Legnani, played fantasias and brilliant variations with the full orchestra, and solos of his own composition. He displayed a most remarkable agility of execution and produced a tone of infinite depth and rare singing beauty, particularly in his cantabile on the bass strings. He was recalled again, and again, after he had already repeated his programme." When Legnani was in Vienna he visited the most renowned guitar makers; he furnished them with valuable information concerning the acoustic details of the construction of the instrument and also designed several new models and also one of a terz guitar. Those guitars, made according to Legnani's instructions by Ries and also by Staufer, both of Vienna, bear labels of which illustrations are reproduced. The labels of Ries are "Model designed by Luigi Legnani, made by Georg Ries in Vienna, at the sign of the lute and violin," and those of Staufer read: "Johann Anton Staufer, in Vienna, after the design of Luigi Legnani"; both these makers' labels bear the seal of Legnani. Staufer retired in 1848 and removed to Prague. An Italian guitar used by Legnani, his favourite instrument, was in the possession of Herr Zeigler of Munich and exhibited with other historical instruments during the annual convention of the I.G.V. in 1904. During 1850 Legnani terminated his roving life as guitar virtuoso, returned to his native town, Ravenna, and was occupied in the construction of guitars. Lutgendorff in Die Geigen und Lautenmacher, Vol. 2, says there was a maker of good guitars named Luigi Legnani living in Ravenna during the nineteenth century. Legnani was a voluminous composer for the guitar; his published works exceed two hundred and fifty, and like Sor he wrote for the guitar with two extra bass strings, the usual manner of stringing the guitar in Russia. He compiled a *Method,* Op. 250, which was published by Ricordi, Milan, and augmented later by *Six Caprices.* His first composition was issued by the same firm, Op. 1, *Terra moto con variazione,* and also by Cipriani, Florence; the majority of his compositions were, however, published in Vienna. It was while in Vienna that he became associated with the musician Leidesdorf who at a later date established a music publishing business in the city and issued many of Legnani's compositions. In collaboration with Leidesdorf he composed Op. 28, *Variations on a theme of Rossini for guitar, piano, two violins, alto and 'cello,* which was published by Diabelli, Vienna. These two artists frequently appeared in public in duos for two guitars and guitar and piano. Legnani's compositions are varied; Op. 23, a *Duo Concertant for flute and guitar;* Op. 3, *Grand Studies; Thirty-six Studies or Caprices for guitar,* published by Weinberger, Vienna. Op. 10, is unique, a *Scherzo with four variations to be played by the left hand only,* which, with many other of his works was issued by Artaria, Vienna. The original manuscript of Op. 10, is in the library of the Musikfreund, Vienna. No portrait of Legnani is known; but an interesting document has come to light—a passport granted to him when about to travel to Geneva: "Governo Pontifico. In the name of the Cardinal Legate for the district of Ravenna. Departure from this city where he has resided for thirty years. Sig. Luigi Legnani of Ferrara, for the city of Geneva. The accompanying passport testifies our knowledge of, under our seal, and requests all Civil and Military Authorities that they allow, not only free passage but also render all and every assistance in the hope that no harm will befall him and to our more perfect and mutual goodwill. Dated Ravenna, 30 October, 1829. The Cardinal Legate, signed, Macchi." This document describes his personal appearance as "38 years of age, medium height and build, regular nose, medium mouth, moderate forehead, chestnut colour hair, occupation: a professor of the guitar and singing: domicile, Ravenna." Legnani was honorary member of the Philharmonic Societies of Rome, Florence, Verona, Ferrara and Munich.

Leidesdorf, Max Josef, born at Vienna, 1780, and died at Florence, September 26, 1840. He studied the piano and guitar and commenced his professional career by teaching his instruments in Vienna. As a piano teacher he was held in high repute, members of the nobility and aristocracy were his pupils, and he enjoyed the friendship of the most renowned musicians. For a period he was associated with the guitarist Legnani ; they performed together in public and also wrote and published several compositions for the guitar, and guitar and piano, conjointly. Schubert and Beethoven were his intimate friends and as Leidesdorf was the publisher of Schubert's early compositions, before he had made a name in the musical world, it has been inferred that he did so from motives of friendship. Leidesdorf was one of the most renowned musicians of Vienna and one of the fifty commissioned by Diabelli & Co. to write a variation on a given theme, for their volume Vaterlandische Kunstlerverein ; the second volume was published during the last months of 1823 or early in 1824. In 1804 Leidesdorf was the proprietor of a music publishing business in Vienna which prospered and in 1827 he disposed of his copyrights and publications to Diabelli, retiring to Florence where he was a professor in the Conservatoire. As pianist and composer, Leidesdorf is regarded a forerunner of Czerny, and will be remembered to posterity by a little note of Beethoven's, apparently written in 1804, sending Ries for some easy duos for two pianos—" and better still, let him have them for nothing " —the note began with a pun on his name " Dorf des Leides " and ended, " Beethoven minimus." Leidesdorf was one of the Viennese musicians who signed the petition to Beethoven, on February, 1824, praying him to produce the *Ninth Symphony* and *Mass in D,* and to write a second opera. He composed a few works for the guitar, the most widely-known are: *Two divertissements for violin and guitar,* published by Schott, Mayence ; Op. 28, *A theme of Rossini with variations for guitar, piano, two violins, alto and violoncello,* written conjointly with Legnani, and a *Volume of divertissements for violin and guitar,* both published by Diabelli, Vienna.

Leite, Antonio de Silva, born May 23, 1759 at Oporto, died January 10, 1833, was a Portuguese guitarist, composer, theorist, director of the National Conservatoire of Music, Oporto, and capellmeister of Oporto Cathedral from 1787-1826. In 1787, he wrote and published *Resumo de todas as ragrase precitos de cantoria assim da musica metrica como da cantochao.* He was the author of other theoretical treatises and compositions for the guitar, only a small proportion of which were printed. His Method for the guitar, in two volumes, entitled: *Estudo de Guitarra em quo se expoe o moto mais facil para apprender este instrumento,* appeared in 1796 and was the standard work of its kind in Portugal. Other of his compositions, unheard of out of his native land, are: *Six Sonatas for guitar, violin, and two trumpets* (a most unusual combination) also a hymn written for the coronation of John VI of Portugal, and much church music.

Lemoine, Antoine Marcel, born November 3, 1763, at Paris and died there April, 1817, was the founder of the renowned music publishing business, a guitar virtuoso, and skilful performer on the violin and viola. His father a dramatic artist, gave him his first instruction on the guitar and violin; beyond this, Lemoine was self-taught. His natural ability and perseverance were the sole means by which his name was prominent in the musical world. Lemoine's father had led a wandering, restless life, and when the son was sixteen and a half years of age, he married and during the next few years followed the example of his parents, wandering with his wife, obtaining a livelihood by violin and guitar playing. In 1781, he was in Paris and obtained employment as violinist in the Theatre Montansier, Versailles, staying two years, when he resigned and commenced as a teacher of the violin and guitar. During 1789 he was viola player in the Theatre Monsieur, and also founded the music publishing business, which, continued after his death by his son Henry, flourished apace and became famous particularly by the number and excellence of the compositions issued for the mandolin and guitar. In 1790 Imbault, of Paris, published several of his compositions and theoretical works, including a *Method for the guitar* which rapidly passed several editions. Three years later, Lemoine was entirely occupied with publishing; but after the revolution placed his business under capable management and officiated, successively as conductor of the orchestras of the Theatre Moliere, Mareux, and of the Rue Culture and St. Catherine. Although Lemoine had received no instruction in harmony or counterpoint, he composed, arranged, and orchestrated all the music performed in these theatres. In 1795 he revised and augmented his method for the guitar, publishing this edition himself, and in addition to writing compositions for other publishers he issued about twenty-five of his own works, consisting of variations, potpourris, etc., for solo guitar and duos for guitar and violin. When the six-string guitar, constructed in the shape of a lyre and named the lyre-guitar, became very fashionable at the commencement of the nineteenth century, Lemoine compiled and published in 1805, a new elementary treatise for the instrument entitled, *Method for the guitar of six strings.* A few years later his compositions for the guitar were eclipsed by those of Carulli. Lemoine, however, was fully aware of the superiority of the works of the rising generation of guitar virtuosi, and was among the first to issue the compositions of Carulli, Sor, Sagrini, Aguado, Giuliani, Kuffner and Castellacci. Lemoine died in the prime of life deeply regretted by an intimate circle of the most renowned guitarists of his epoch.

Lenau, Nicolas (Nicolas Niembach Edler Strehlenau) a famous

B. Lebedeff

Miguel Llobet

label of Legnani Guitar

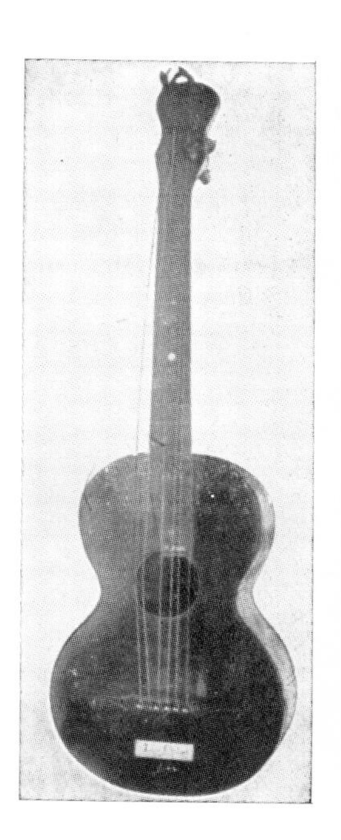

Lenau's Guitar

Joseph Mayseder

Edouardo Mezzacapo

V. Monti

A. Mascheroni

A Mascheroni

German poet, born August 13, 1802, at Csatad, a village in Hungary, near Temesvar, and died in Döbling, Vienna, August 22, 1850. Lenau's father was an officer of estates under the government, who died when his son was young. His irregular life had been the cause of serious troubles in the family, and after his death, his widow with her son removed to Buda, where he attended the middle school. When seventeen he entered the University of Vienna, taking a three year's course in philosophy, and then adopted the study of law and medicine. In 1829 he suffered a severe loss by the death of his mother, to whom he was attached by a most tender affection, and from whom he inherited his nobler qualities of character, his courage, keeness, and depth of emotion. Having all life been in delicate health, he derived much satisfaction and benefit from a legacy of about £850, bequeathed to him by his grandmother, and went to reside in Swabia, where he lived in most friendly intercourse with several of the Swabian poets. Those traits of Lenau's character—his tenderness, meekness, and sentiment—found great favour with these poets ; but Lenau did not remain long in this congenial atmosphere. For some time he had cherished a desire to visit North America, his vivid imagination had pictured realms of happiness among the virgin lands and forests of the new world, and in 1832 his dream's ambition was realized. With the remainder of his fortune, now about £500, he sailed the Atlantic, continuing his journey from Baltimore across the continent on horseback, as far west as Crawford county, where he bought four hundred acres of land, intending to make this his permanent abode. He passed a very lonely and sad winter in the then deserted country at Lisbon on the Ohio river ; he had no friends in this new home, and what was of greater consequence, his health was now even more delicate. Lenau could not endure the lonely life of a settler, so after a visit to Niagara Falls, returned to Europe the following year and when he reached his native land was received with triumph, for he had made a name among the great poets of his country. He lived alternately in Stuttgart and Vienna, in the latter city he resided with his brother-in-law, a clerk in the Imperial Palace. In 1844 he became engaged and was intent on improving his financial position so increased his energy for this purpose ; but his happiness was short lived and a few weeks after his engagement he suffered a stroke. On the eleventh of the following month he was admitted in a mental home, first in Stuttgart and after in Döbling, near Vienna, where he died. Lenau was one of the most celebrated poets of Germany, and his works, chiefly elegies, are of unsurpassed beauty. He was also a musician and played the violin, as the gypsy musicians, the genius of whom he has immortalized in so many of his poems. He was also a good guitarist, and accustomed to accompany all his songs on this instrument, and wherever he travelled took his guitar with him. The guitar—to which he wrote that poem, so full of tender thoughts and sad presentiment entitled: *To my Guitar*, is in the National German Museum of Nuremburg. This instrument, of which an illustration is reproduced, hangs forever mute in its glass shrine, devoid of interest to the uninitiated and casual observer; its strings which vibrated under its owner's sensitive touch are now broken and silent and its forlorn condition appeals to artistic temperaments only; but Lenau's poetry speaks to all. To those acquainted with the poet's career, this ordinary guitar of common shape and neglected appearance, will divulge what passions of a chequered life sleep within its mute form, waiting in vain, the touch of a master silenced by death. Kreissle von Hellborn in Life of Franz Schubert says: "the poet Lenau drew public attention to the treasures of Schubert."

Leonardi, Salvatore, born at Catania, Sicily, a contemporary mandolinist, guitarist, and composer for these instruments. He was taught the mandolin and guitar by an uncle living in Naples and studied the violin in Naples Conservatoire of Music. Having won several awards as solo mandolinist in International contests in Florence, Rome, and other cities, he toured extensively, became a versatile linguist, settled for a time as a teacher in Egypt, Malta, then London, and finally at the commencement of twentieth century made his permanent abode in rue d'Amsterdam, Paris. He was a teacher of high repute in the city, in universal request as an adjudicator at important music concours, and he took an active part at the dedication of a marble plaque on the grave of the guitarist Sor, in Paris, on the centenary of his death. Leonardi is depicted on the photograph taken during the ceremony on July 8, 1936. He composed several solos for the mandolin of exceptional merit and also superior orchestrations for mandolin band; the principal are: *Souvenir de Catane, Souvenir de Naples, Souvenir de Sicily* and *Angels and Demons,* all published in Paris. Dallas of London issued a few of his minor compositions. His biography and portrait appeared in the Music and Dramatic Directory, Paris (1887-1912).

Leone, a French musician living in Paris during the middle and latter part of the eighteenth century, was a violinist and mandolinist, the author of a volume which was published in Paris in 1770, entitled: *Analytical method for mastering the violin or the mandolin.*

Lfleche, a French guitarist, born during the latter part of the eighteenth century, who, in 1819 established a school of music in Lyons which was very popular and flourished for many years. He was the author of a few compositions for the guitar, and also published a Method for the instrument which contained chapters on the theory of music, lessons on harmony, and a chapter on accompaniment, in its special relation to the guitar.

L'Hoyer, Antoine, a celebrated French guitarist and composer who flourished during the early part of the eighteenth century. He played the guitar at an early age, joined a company of French comedians who toured their native land and subsequently entered the service of Prince Henry of Rheinsberg. Previous to the year 1800 he had resigned from this service, for he was touring Germany as guitar virtuoso and in that year settled in Hamburg as teacher of the guitar. He remained a few years and was esteemed as teacher and performer and in this city he published several compositions of a high order for the guitar, one of which was a concerto for the guitar with string quartet. The fame of L'Hoyer reached Paris and he was subsequently appearing with great success at the important concerts. He was a contemporary and friend of Carulli, who dedicated to L'Hoyer Op. 12, a *Grand Sonate for the guitar.* He lived in Paris some years where he published the majority of his compositions; his early works were issued in Germany. Op. 16, *Concerto for guitar with string quartet;* Op. 17, *Three Sonatas for guitar and violin;* and Op. 18, *Overture for guitar and violin,* were all published by Böhme, Hamburg; *Airs dialogues for four guitars,* published by Schoenenberger, Paris; Op. 28, *Two Sonatas for guitar;* Op. 31, 34, 35, 36, 37, *Duos for two guitars and* Op. 29, *Trio for three guitars* were published by Pleyel; Meissonnier; Simon Gaveaux and other Parisian music publishers. In addition L'Hoyer wrote many smaller pieces without opus numbers, principally studies, fantasias, duos, trios and solos.

Lickl, Aegidius Carl, born Vienna, September 1, 1803, died Trieste, July 22, 1864, was a guitar and piano virtuoso and composer. He was the younger brother of the more renowned pianist, Carl Lickl (1801-1877) and both sons received musical instruction from their father Carl George Lickl. In 1830, Aegidius removed to Trieste, where he lived as teacher and composer; Among his published works are oratorios, a symphony entitled: *Il trionfo del Cristianesimo,* performed in Trieste December 2, 1837, and several comic operas, produced originally in Trieste and afterwards in Vienna in 1848. Lickl also published much chamber music including numerous pieces for the guitar, recorded by Mendel.

Light, Edward, born in London during the opening of the nineteeth century, was a guitarist, guitar maker, and the inventor of a harp-lute or dital-harp. For many years he was organist of Trinity Chapel, St. George's, Hanover Square, London, and he devoted much time in attempts to improve the guitar. His efforts were futile for he evolved a different instrument. His was only one of the numerous efforts of the period to improve the guitar. Light's harp-lute had eighteen strings, and its tuning was a major sixth above the notation. In 1816 he obtained a patent for an improvement on this instrument, which he named the British harp-lute. His patent was for the application of certain pieces of mechanism called ditals, or thumb keys, in distinction from pedals, or foot keys. Each dital, by pressure, produced the lowering of a stop ring or eye, which drew the string upon a fret, and thus shortened its vibrating length, rendering the pitch more acute, somewhat after the mechanism of the harp. The most perfected instrument of this construction, Light named the dital-harp. In this instrument, each string had a dital to raise it a semitone at pleasure, and its sounding board was shaped somewhat like the lute, the back was also fashioned after that instrument, that is to say, without ribs or sides. Its tone was feeble, lacked resonance, and not equal to that of the guitar. Its most pleasing feature was its neat, artistic shape and elaborate gilt decoration, although a plainer model was made with a less number of strings, but neither was a success. Edward Light was the author of a guitar method published by Preston, London, in 1795, entitled: *The art of playing the guitar, to which is annexed a selection of the most familiar lessons, divertisements, songs, airs, etc.*, also, *Concise instructions for playing on the English lute,* and in 1819 he published *New and complete directory to the art of playing on the dital-harp, by the inventor.*

Lincke or **Linke,** Joseph, an eminent violoncellist, guitarist and composer, born June 8, 1783, at Trachenberg, Silesia, and died in Vienna, March 26, 1837. He received tuition on the violin from his father, a violinist in the service of Prince Hatzfeld, and was also taught the 'cello by Oswald, while still a child. A mismanaged sprain of his right ankle caused lameness for life, and it is in allusion to this deformity that Bernard wrote: "Lincke has only one fault—that he is crooked." At the age of ten he lost both parents and was obliged to support himself by copying music, continuing until the year 1800 when he obtained employment as violinist in the Dominican Convent of Breslau, after having served for some time as chorister. In this institution his education was supervised by Fleming, and he continued the study of the 'cello under Lose, and the organ, guitar and harmony under Hanisch. Lose was violoncellist in the opera orchestra conducted by C. M. von Weber and when Lose retired Lincke succeeded him as first 'cellist. He was now in contact with Weber, an enthusiastic guitarist, and during the period of service under his direction, Lincke continued the study of the guitar. In 1808 he went to Vienna, where Schuppanzigh engaged him for the famous quartet of Count Rasoumowsky, and in the service of this prince he lived in the company of Beethoven, whom he worshipped. Beethoven, too, was sincerely attached to Lincke who derived great advantage by playing the great composer's works under his personal supervision. Beethoven frequently mentions his name in terms of friendship in his correspondence, and in the Imperial Library of Berlin there is a comic canon in Beethoven's writing on the names of Branchle and Lincke. In 1818 he was first 'cellist in the Theatre an der Wien, and in 1831 was playing with the distinguished 'cellist Merk in the Royal Opera. Beethoven wrote violoncello works especially for him. His playing was remarkable for its humour, and he was particularly successful in expressing Beethoven's characteristic style, which may account in a degree his fondness for him. He has written concertos, variations, capriccios, etc., but only his first three compositions have been published, one of these, *The Troubadour, air with variations for the violoncello with guitar accompaniment,* was published by Mechetti, Vienna.

Lindpainter, Peter Joseph von, born December 9, 1791, at Coblenz, died August 21, 1856 in Nonnenhorn, Lake Constance. He studied the violin, piano and counterpoint in Augsburg and in 1812 was musical director of the Isarthor Theatre, Munich, until 1819, when appointed Kapellmeister of the Royal Orchestra, Stuttgart, which position he retained until his death. He was a conductor of international repute, and in 1853 accepted the invitation of the Philharmonic Society, London, to conduct several of his compositions. He has written many operas, oratorios, symphonies, and songs with piano, and also several with guitar. Dr. Zuth states on the authority of the A.M.Z. and Cäcilia that his Op. 111, *Ave Maria* and Op. 112, *Romance,* both of which were published in Stuttgart, and *The Vampyre* and other single and collections of songs were composed with guitar accompaniment.

Lintant. Charles, born at Grenoble, France in 1758 and died in his native city, March 17, 1830. When a child he showed extraordinary musical ability and was taught the violin and theory of music by a teacher of Grenoble. After two years' instruction the teacher advised his parents to send him to Paris to continue his musical education. In Paris he was under Bertheaume for the violin, and Benoit Pollet for the guitar and while in Paris he lived with his brother-in-law, a musician named Sageret, who was musical director of various Parisian Theatres. He derived great benefit and experience by his association with his brother-in-law, who placed Lintant, as principal violin in the Theatre Feydeau, under the conductorship of Lahoussaye and Blasius. He remained in this position for about twelve months, when, owing to the bankruptcy of his brother-in-law, Sageret, he was dismissed and then gained his livelihood by teaching the violin and guitar in Paris. As a teacher he was very successful and having obtained a competency, returned to Grenoble and was the lessee of several theatres. Lintant was not a voluminous composer ; he published quartets for strings and *Three duos for two guitars,* published by Nadermann, Paris ; *Three grand sonatas for violin and guitar,* Porro, Paris ; *Progressive sonatas for guitar and alto,* Frey, Paris ; *Ten airs with variations for guitar solo ; Little method for the guitar,* Lemoine, Paris ; *Collections of songs with guitar,* Janet, Paris ; *Theoretical treatise on accompaniment,* Gaveaux, Paris, and many other pieces for guitar, violin, etc. Lintant is very highly spoken of in the works of Tomas Brondi.

Litzius, C. Under this name many light compositions for the guitar were published at the commencement of the nineteenth century in Germany. There are bagatelles for guitar solo, a *Serenade for guitar, flute and alto ; Serenade for guitar and flute ; Trio for violin, viola and guitar ;* a *Practical method of general-bass* and a *Practical singing method, in three books,* all issued by Schott, Mayence, during 1813-44. These are recorded by Whistling and the A.M.Z.

Llobet, Miguel, born October 18, 1878, at Barcelona was killed May, 1937, in an air raid on Barcelona during the Spanish civil war. He was the son of a sculptor who intended he should study art, to become a painter; but the lad was so fascinated with a guitar given him by an uncle that his father's desires were unfulfilled; although later in life he was a skilful artist and made exquisite portrait sketches, that of his young pupil Maria Luisa Anido is of outstanding excellence. His first instruction on the instrument was from a local teacher, Magin Alegre, and his progress so encouraging that he entered the Barcelona Conservatoire of Music, where he was a pupil of Tarrega and Casals. After completion of study he made his public appearance in his native land, first in 1901, in the Conservatoire of Valencia, and the next year in that of Madrid. His concert appearances and recitals were so successful that in 1903 he played by command at Court before the Royal family. His fame as a guitar virtuoso had now reached France, and receiving many invitations for his services in this country, made his abode in Paris, from where he undertook artistic visits to Germany and England. His frequent recitals and concerts in Paris were the rendezvous of the most renowned musicians. On January 26, 1905, his playing at the Societe National de Trompette, was a brilliant success, and his recital, the same year at the Schola Cantorum, was equally successful, where he was the recipient of an ovation. Llobet was an adjudicator, under the presidency of Guilmant, at the International Mandolin and Guitar Concours, held in Boulogne in 1909 and during the following year, the writer and several French musicians—Monti, Feret, Goldberg, and others—experienced the thrill of an intimate and private seance with Llobet. He was guitarist at a concert given by the estudiantina (mandolin and guitar orchestra) conducted by Monti. The press said: "The star of the evening was the incomparable guitarist, Miguel Llobet. Words cannot express the admiration which he aroused. His triumph over that vast assembly of musicians was as great as it was deserved." In March of the following year, 1910, Llobet was appearing with his accustomed success in Buenos Aires and toured all the Latin States of South America previous to his entry in U.S.A. He returned to France and resided in the Rue Demours, Paris, occupied in teaching until 1913 when he visited Holland and Germany. His concluding recital was that given in Munich, which was organised by the I.G.V. immediately before the outbreak of the 1914 war. Llobet was in the Argentine and U.S.A. again during the war, his concerts and recitals in Buenos Aires during 1918 were as successful as his teaching; he was the teacher in this city of several talented pupils. Under the presidency of Mascagni he was a member of the artistic committee, in 1921, of the International Mandolin and Guitar Concours, held in Florence, after which he visited his native land, in 1925. He made continental concert tours during the next few years principally in Berlin and Vienna, and at his recitals in London on June 27 and 28, 1930, his soulful tone and brilliant technique evoked the sincerest enthusiasm from the intellectual audiences. The following day he broadcast from London, assisted in his programme by the Spanish vocalist, Carmen Anduyar, wife of Eduardo Chavarri, the composer. Llobet, essentially a virtuoso and concert performer, trained but few pupils, and they were principally in Argentina, the foremost was Jose Rey de la Torre. He edited Carcassi's Studies, made transcriptions for guitar solo of Catalonian songs and national dances; but wrote few original works. His *Romanza, El Mestre,* and *Six little popular songs of Catalonia*, are particularly pleasing and included by Segovia in his repertoire; they are published by Biblioteca Fortea, Madrid. Several of his compositions remain in manuscript in the library of P.S.G., one, an arrangement of *Le premier chagrin* (Schumann), for solo guitar was written September 7, 1903, for a German pupil. His portrait was published in the American Guitar Review of 1948. Llobet was honorary member of Malaga Philharmonic and other musical societies. The Irish authoress Mrs. Villiers-Wardell in "Spain and the Spanish" describes in eulogistic terms the guitar playing of Llobet whom she heard in Paris.

Lobe, Johann Christian, born May 30, 1797, at Weimar, and died July 27, 1881, in Leipzig, was solo flautist in Weimar Royal Orchestra from 1811 to 1842 when he removed to Leipzig, where, from 1846 to 1848 he was editor of the A.M.Z. His compositions are varied and include an opera in five acts, *Furstin von Granada,* quintets for strings, duos for flute and guitar, piano, and songs. Dr Zuth states that Lobe arranged selections of favourite airs from his opera for flute and guitar, which, with others for the same combination of instruments, were published by Schott, Mayence. The A.M.Z. also records other flute and guitar duos which were issued by Haser.

Lorenz, Friedrich August, born at Chemnitz, Saxony, February, 1796, was an instrumentalist of renown, excelling on the violin, guitar and bassoon. His first professional employment was as violinist in the churches of Prague and some years later chamber musician to the King of Saxony and a member of the Royal Court Orchestra, Dresden. He has written compositions for various instruments and among those published are *Variations for bassoon and guitar on the march from the opera 'D'Aline.'* This opera was the work of the composer-guitarist Blum and these variations were issued by Haslinger, Vienna.

Loreti, Alfred Heinrich, born March 22, 1870, at Rome, and studied music in the Royal Academy of St. Cæcilia of his native city. He removed to Zurich where he was an esteemed and popular teacher of the mandolin and guitar and a prolific composer for the instruments; about three hundred were published. The most noteworthy are Op. 263, *Segoviana,* a suite in four parts, published by Hug & Co., Zurich; Op. 167, *Filgrana;* Op. 241, *Bolero;* Op. 252, *Hoffnung,* all published by Hofmeister, Leipzig. Loreti, who was a scholarly musician, compiled a *Method for the guitar and lute* in four books, which was issued by Holzmann, Zurich. He presented the manuscript of an *Etude for the guitar* to the League of Guitarists, Munich, which was published in that society's journal of August, 1914.

Lully, Jean Baptiste, born near Florence, Italy, in 1633, died at Paris, March 22, 1687. Dubourg says: "The inclination towards music which he showed while yet a child induced a worthy monk, from no other consideration than the hope of his sometime becoming eminent in art, to undertake his tuition on the guitar, an instrument which in the sequel he was always fond of singing to." Grove also writes: "An old Franciscan monk gave the gifted but mischievous child some elementary instruction and taught him the guitar and the rudiments of music." The Chevalier de Guise, a French gentleman who had travelled in Italy, brought Lully to France as a present for his sister in 1646, when the boy was thirteen years of age, according to Dr. Burney—or, in the more qualified language of another writer—to serve as a page to Mlle. de Montpensier, a niece of Louis XIV, who had commissioned the Chevalier to find her some pretty little Italian boy for this purpose; it was customary for ladies of rank to maintain in their service an Italian boy who could sing to his guitar or mandolin accompaniment. In this instance, if such were the lady's instructions, the countenance of the youth did not fulfil the requirements; but his vivacity and ready wit, in addition to his skill on the guitar, determined the Chevalier to engage him. On his arrival and presentation, the lady was so dissatisfied with his looks that she changed her intentions and instead of page, he was made an under-scullion. Neither the disappointment he experienced, nor the employment to which he was placed, affected the spirits of the boy. In his leisure he still played his guitar, and a court official chancing one day to hear him, informed the princess of his extraordinary musical ability, and by his intervention Lully was placed under a teacher for instruction on the violin. Mademoiselle having discovered that he had composed the air of a satirical song at her expense, promptly dismissed him; but his ability was now sufficient to procure him a place in the King's Band. His promotion was very rapid, and he was soon chosen to compose the music for the court ballets. He wrote many operas, was successful as a church composer, and, as Surintendant de la Musique and Secretary to Louis XIV, he was in high favour at court and being extremely avaricious, used his opportunities to amass a large fortune. He wrote music for the guitar but few of his compositions were printed. Jose Parada and Barreto, in their Musical Directory of 1868, state, page 256, that Lully continued teaching and playing the guitar.

MAGNIEN, Victor, born Epinal, Vosges, November 19, 1804, died at Lille, June, 1885, was one of the most successful directors of the Imperial Conservatoire of Music, Lille, France, and, being baptised on November 22, St. Cæcilia's day, was a favourable omen for his future. He was a violinist, guitarist and composer of repute in France, who had studied the guitar with Ferdinand Carulli and the violin under Rudolphe Kreutzer. Previous to 1815 his father was an administrator of the province of Haute Marne, during which time the lad received preliminary musical instruction. When the allied armies invaded France his father, with other public officials, was dismissed. In 1817 he went to Paris to continue his music studies under Carulli and Kreutzer and two years later was acknowledged the most eminent amateur guitarist in Paris. In 1820 his family removed to Colmar, where his musical ability was soon recognised and requisitioned. His parents had not intended he should adopt music as his profession, so at the age of sixteen he commenced a career as clerk in the municipal offices; but a sudden reverse in the family fortunes arose which changed his career. Magnien, the father, had at this juncture espoused the cause of a Colonel Caron, and his political associations with this officer caused his dismissal by the authorities. The family was in financial embarrassment and the youth who had made music a pastime commenced teaching to assist the family. Young and inexperienced, he nevertheless applied himself to teaching the violin and guitar and was encouraged by members of the most distinguished families of Colmar. He was esteemed by the musical people of the district and offered a lucrative position in Mülhausen as a professor of music where he removed. Desirous of obtaining a more thorough knowledge of his art, he visited Paris for three months annually to continue his musical education. He took up again the violin and guitar, the first under Baillot and Lafont, the guitar under Carulli, and Fetis was his teacher for composition. Magnien now tried his hand at composition, his first efforts were duos for violin and guitar, which were published by Richault, Paris, as were many of his later works. Between the years 1827-31 this publisher issued more than thirty of his compositions. Acting on the advice of his teachers, he made several visits to Germany as a virtuoso, during the revolution of 1830. After his return he was appointed conductor of the Philharmonic Society of Beauvais, Director of singing in elementary schools, and a member of the examining committee of national elementary instruction. Magnien was esteemed highly during his sixteen years' residence in Beauvais and his success there attracted the notice of the musical authorities of Lille, where in 1846 he was appointed director of the Imperial Conservatoire of Music, a branch of the Paris Conservatoire. During his management, this institution flourished to a remarkable degree. Magnien excelled as a virtuoso and teacher of the violin and guitar, and was the author of concertos for the violin with orchestral accompaniment; duos for violin and guitar; duos, nocturnes, etc., for two guitars; rondos, fantasias, variations, etc., for guitar solo; studies for violin and guitar and masses, organ and piano works; some of the latter published in England. Op. 1 and 2, *Duos concertante for violin and guitar;* Op. 4, *Three books of duos for violin and guitar;* Op. 23, *Twelve favourite galops for guitar solo;* Op. 35, *Two duos for two guitars,* and many similar, issued in Paris. Richault, Paris, published more than fifty of his compositions. Magnien was the author of several theoretical treatises on music, one of which, *Theorie Musicale,* published in 1837, was popular in its day.

Mahler, Gustav, born July 7, 1860, at Kalischt, Bohemia, died May 19, 1911, Vienna, was educated at the Gymnasium of Iglau, Bohemia and Vienna University and from 1877 was a pupil of the Vienna Conservatoire. He officiated as conductor in various Austrian theatres from 1880 and three years later was appointed second capellmeister in Cassel and then succeeded Seidl as capellmeister in Prague in 1885. The greater part of his life was spent conducting in various continental cities and in 1892 he visited England as director of German opera at Covent Garden, London. From London he went to America, where for a period he officiated in a like capacity ; but through failing health returned to Europe a very ill man, and succumbed shortly after arrival. Mahler, the most eminent of symphonists makes use of guitars and mandolins frequently in his compositions. In his memoirs written by his wife and published in 1946 she says: "The Seventh Symphony was written in one burst, in the summer of 1905. The 'architect's drawings' as he called them, belong to midsummer 1904. As he wrote the serenade he was beset by Eichendorffish visions, murmuring springs and German romanticism." Is there any wonder that he employs three mandolins and three guitars? The first performance in England of this Symphony was in London, January 1913, under the conductorship of Sir Henry Wood, when such little regard was held for Mahler's instrumentation that banjos were substituted for guitars!

In Mahler's Eighth Symphony, composed in 1907, he employs two mandolins. His *Song of the Earth,* composed in 1908 is a symphony for tenor, contralto and full orchestra of four flutes, three oboes, five clarinets, three bassoons, four horns, three trumpets, three trombones, tuba, two harps, mandolin, celesta, strings and full percussion. Notwithstanding this massive instrumentation, Mahler's scoring is exceedingly clear and transparent and he produces novel and unusual effects from the various instruments and their combinations. His memoirs were written by his wife and sketches by various authors have appeared since.

Majo, Gian Francesco, born Naples about 1740, died in Rome, January 18, 1771, was a son of the music director of the King of Sicily. He was a pupil of Martini and in 1759 became known as an operatic composer, after his opera *Riccimero* was produced in Naples. This was followed by many others and much church music. In his opera *Astrea placata* which was produced in Naples in 1760 he employs the mandolin. He was maestro of the Royal Chapel from about 1760.

Makaroff, Nikolai Petrowitsch, was born during 1810 at Tschuchlom, Russia, and died in Tula, 1890. He was a wealthy amateur guitarist and enthusiast who commenced the study of the instrument under Sychra in St. Petersburg and used his wealth and life to promote the advancement and improvement of the guitar, its manufacture, its music and its players. He travelled very extensively, visiting all the important cities of Europe in order to interview all players of renown, to encourage and assist them financially. At his personal expense he financed and organised the European competition for music composed for the guitar, with the object of raising its standard. This was held in Brussels in 1856 and Makaroff was president of the judges, who were all professors in the Brussels Conservatoire of Music. He published, in Russia, a volume of his memoirs containing very interesting facts relative to guitar players, virtuosi, guitar makers. etc.

Malibran, Maria Felicita, born March 24, 1808 at Paris, where her father, Manuel Garcia had arrived only two months previously, and died September 23, 1836 in Manchester. She was one of the most distinguished of singers and a guitarist. When three, her parents visited Italy and at the age of five she played a child's part in Paer's *Agnese,* in Naples. She was so precocious that, after a few nights of this opera, she actually began to sing the part of Agnese in the duet of the second act, a piece of audacity, applauded by the audience. Two years later she studied singing in Naples with Panseron, the piano with Herold and the guitar with her father. In 1816 the family were in Paris and in autumn of the following year came to London where she lived for two and a half years and picked up a tolerable knowledge of English—she could already speak Spanish, Italian and French fluently, and shortly after she learned German with the same facility. When fifteen her father directed her musical education, and, in spite of the fear which his violent temper inspired, the individuality and originality of her genius soon displayed itself. Fetis states that it was through the sudden indisposition of Mme. Pasta that the first public appearance of Maria Garcia was unexpectedly made. Her debut took place June 7, 1825 ; the enthusiasm of the public knew no bounds, and she was engaged for the remainder of the season. In the midst of this popularity her father gave her in marriage, in spite of her repugnance, to M. Malibran, an elderly and seemingly wealthy French merchant ; but the unhappy marriage was dissolved within a year by Malibran's bankruptcy, and in September, 1827, she went to France. When she returned to England she had no rival, and continued to sing each season with increased éclat, both in Paris and London. She married the violinist, De Beriot, on March 26, 1836 and the following September was singing at the Manchester Festival, where her short, brilliant career came to an end. On Sunday, September 11, after a rapid journey from Paris she sang no less than fourteen times during the following evening. On Tuesday, though weak and ill, she insisted on singing both morning and evening, but on Wednesday her condition was more critical, yet she rendered *Sing ye to the Lord* with thrilling effect, the last sacred music in which she took part. She was rapturously applauded and the final movement of a duet with Cardaori Allan was encored ; Malibran accomplished the effort of repeating it—it was her last effort—for while the concert room rang with applause, she was fainting in the arms of friends and expired a few days after. Malibran composed ; many of her songs with guitar were published, and she used this instrument to accompany herself in some of her appearances. She was a pupil of her father and also of Pelzer, in London, and the latter became the owner of her favourite guitar, which, in 1913 was in the collection of his daughter, Mme. Pratten. Moscheles in his Diary (page 7) says: "We dined early and immediately afterwards, Malibran sat down to the piano and 'sang for the children' as she called it, *The Rataplan,* and some of her father's songs ; for want of her guitar accompaniment she used, whilst playing, every now and then, to mark the rhythm on the board at the back of the keys." Her principal songs with guitar are: *The Resignation, a romance,* published by Challier & Co., Berlin ; *The last thoughts of ;* and *Six Romances with guitar,* issued by D'Almaine, London. Schott, Mayence, also published this collection, which contains ten romances, and a separate song entitled *L'Ecossais.* Her memoirs have been published frequently from Pougin, in 1836, to those of Lanquine in 1911.

Manen, Juan, contemporary, born Barcelona, March 14, 1883, received his first musical instruction from his father, on the violin and guitar, and continued the former under Alard in Paris. He is a notable and prolific composer, a brilliant violinist, pianist, and conductor who has also expressed himself in compositions for the guitar. He toured and then resided in Berlin where he edited the works of Paganini. His published compositions include symphonies, operas, concertos for violin and orchestra, chamber music, and works for the guitar. Op. 22 is a *Fantasia-Sonata, for solo guitar,* of ten pages, composed for and dedicated to Segovia, who has fingered it. It is published by Schott.

Manjon, Antonio Giminez, born in 1866 at Villacarillo, Jaen, Spain, and died in Buenos Aires, January 3, 1919. He was a well-known concert guitarist, composer, and professor, whose early life was spent in Paris, with his colleague, Del Castillo, teaching the guitar. He toured his native land, Portugal, France and England and received warm praise for his performances and then settled in Paris again. He returned to his native land, gave recitals in 1889 in the El Dorado Theatre, Barcelona, and was a professor of the guitar in the Municipal Music School, Barcelona. In 1893 he toured South America giving recitals in Buenos Aires and all the important cities of the Latin American States. He made a return visit to Europe in 1912 appearing in all the important cities of France and Italy and then visited once again his native land where his recital during April, 1913 in Madrid Conservatoire of Music was a tremendous success. At the commencement of the first world war he returned ot Buenos Aires where he died.

Mara, Gertrude Elisabeth, born Cassel, February 23, 1749, and died at Reval, January 20, 1833, at the age of eighty-four, soon after she had been the recipient of a birthday poem from Goethe. She was a foremost singer of the last century and an able guitarist. Her mother died soon after the birth and her father, a poor musician named Schmeling, is said to have secured his infant daughter in an armchair, while attending to his affairs. She developed rickets and it was long ere she recovered, if indeed, she ever did. Schmeling increased his income by repairing musical instruments, and the child took every opportunity of playing any within her reach. Noticing her interest, he taught her the guitar and she was soon able to take part in violin and guitar duets; but even now, in her fifth year, she could not stand without support and was carried by her father to where they were to perform. They visited Frankfurt fair, where the child's playing excited surprise to such an extent that several kindly amateur musicians provided for her and her education. At nine years of age she was playing with her father in Vienna, when their concerts attracted the notice of the British ambassador, who advised Schmeling to take the child to England and provided him with letters of introduction. The Musical Magazine of 1835 said: "She was brought by her father to London when quite a child where she played the guitar . . . ; when ten years of age she played before the King." In England Schmeling was advised that she study singing. Under Paradisi, she made rapid progress and when they left England continued under Hillier for five years in Leipzig and became the first great singer that Germany had produced. She travelled Europe, appeared at all the Royal Courts, saved immense sums which were spent by her worthless lovers and in old age was forced to teach her art again. Her autobiography, edited by Riesemann, was published in 1875.

Marchisio, G. B., born at Turin in 1865, inherited musical talent from his father, a pianist of note; his aunts, Barbara and Carlotta Marchisio, were celebrated prima donnas who appeared as duettists at the London Philharmonic Concerts, June 30, 1862. He was familiar with the best ecclesiastical, classical, and operatic music at the Sala Marchisio, under his father's direction, and educated at Varazze, Riviera, under Padri Salesiani, and when eleven years of age composed a Kyrie which was publicly performed. He commenced a business career, to which he did not take kindly, but which afforded an opportunity of visiting London. Here he pursued musical study while earning his livelihood by teaching French, German and Italian. At this period the mandolin and guitar were becoming popular, so Marchisio made a special study of these to the neglect of the violin and piano. A demand for the music and literature of these instruments arose, which he filled, and from 1892 was occupied in these pursuits and as professor of these instruments in the Guildhall School of Music and Trinity College, London. At the latter institution, his historical-lecture recitals were an innovation and in 1898, the author of this volume, a pupil of Marchisio, gave the first performance in England of two of Beethoven's compositions for the mandolin, the *Sonatine* and the *Adagio*. Marchisio was the director of several bands, which played successfully at important concerts. The massed band of five hundred performers was under his baton in St. James' Hall in 1900, and also his band of sixty in Queen's Hall. More than two hundred studies and characteristic compositions for mandolin, a *Method,* Volume of *Melodious Studies* and a *Concerto for mandolin and piano,* were published in London by Schott, Ascherberg, Paxton, Essex & Cammeyer and others. A few of his compositions were published in Italy. For the massed band concerts, he composed two works, a *Vocal quartet with full mandolin orchestra* and *Barcarola for solo tenor voice with full mandolin orchestra.* Other compositions were a *Piccolo Sinfonia for plectrum quartet with piano, ad lib.* A *Method for the Guitar in sixty Lessons* remains in manuscript. In his Mandolin Method and teaching prospectus, Marchisio emphasised that the mandolinist must be seated, that only clowns, minstrels and itinerant performers stood.

Marin, Rafael, born in the Pedroso de la Sierra province of Seville, Spain, July 7, 1862 was a renowned Flamenco guitarist. He resided in Madrid for some years as soloist and teacher, but in 1900 was performing in the Paris Exhibition where he was so successful that he gave instruction in his style of playing to many members of the nobility, society, and high political personalities of France. Marin was the originator and founder of various artistic musical societies, whose object was the popularisation of the guitar. His fame rests principally on his *Guitar Method* which appeared in 1902, published by Autores Espanoles, Madrid. It is a unique compilation of more than two hundred pages, illustrated with photographic reproductions and explanatory text, to make clear the method of obtaining the effects necessary for Flamenco playing.

Marschner, Heinrich, born August 16, 1796 at Zittau, Saxony, died December 14, 1861, at Hanover, was a dramatic composer of the romantic school, ranking next to Weber. In early life he played the guitar, as did Weber, and when a young man was a skilful performer, and, again resembling Weber, was a most entertaining vocalist when singing to his guitar accompaniment. The guitar was his principal instrument from 1808-14 during when he composed several works for it. He commenced to write songs with guitar and even orchestral music, without tuition, other than a few hints from professional musicians of his acquaintance. He possessed a beautiful soprano voice, which with his guitar, brought him favourably to the notice of musicians of repute. When he grew to manhood he had systematic instruction in the theory of music from Schicht, Leipzig, where he had been studying law until 1816. His singing and guitar playing brought him many friends among whom was Rochlitz, and, acting on his advice Marschner renounced his legal career and adopted music as a profession. In 1817 he entered the service of Count Thaddaus von Amadee, a Hungarian, and went with him to Vienna where he made the acquaintance of Beethoven who advised him to continue the study of composition. While in Pressburg, he wrote two operas, one of which, *Henry IV*, was produced in Dresden by Weber with such success that Marschner in 1824 was appointed assistant conductor of German opera, under Weber. Weber had wished to obtain the position for his friend Gänsbacher, also a guitarist; he however recovered from his disappointment and a friendship ensued which was beneficial to Marschner. He was not a

EXTRACT FROM

Twelve Bagatelles for Guitar Solo, Op. 4.

H. MARSCHNER.

pupil of Weber, although intimately connected, and the striking similarity in their dispositions, the harmonious way in which they worked together, and the cordial affection displayed for each other are historical. When Weber died in 1826, Marschner resigned, travelled for a few months and in 1827 was appointed capellmeister of Leipzig, where he wrote and produced his most famous opera, *Der Vampyr,* which was an instantaneous success. It was staged at the Lyceum, London, in 1829 and its sixtieth performance was in the same year. He wrote other operas, the most popular, *Des Falkner's Braut,* was dedicated to William IV of England. In 1831 he was Court Capellmeister at Hanover, where two years later he produced his masterpiece, *Hans Heiling ;* its success was immediate and it maintains its popularity in Germany to the present. Marschner wrote many more operas, numerous songs for one or more voices, choruses for male voices and vocal items with the guitar ; his favourite subjects were ghosts and demons and he delineated these uncanny spirits with amazing power. He employs the guitar in his orchestral scores and his early compositions are mainly for this instrument. Op. 4, *Twelve Bagatelles for guitar solo ;* Op. 5, *Twelve songs with guitar accompaniment,* published in 1814 ; *Der Freibeuter,* and *Mailied*—poems by Goethe—songs with guitar, published by Schott, Mayence, and several collections of songs with guitar, without opus numbers, which were recorded in A.M.Z. during the years 1813-40, issued by Breitkopf & Härtel, Leipzig. An extract from his op. 4, *Twelve Bagatelles for guitar solo,* is reproduced. Marschner's memoirs, edited by Rodenberg in 1893 were followed by other editions.

Marucelli, Enrico, born 1877 at Florence and died there in 1907, was a talented mandolinist, guitarist, double bass player, and composer who came to England when a young man. He was a popular teacher of the mandolin in London for a few years and with Mezzacapo was conductor of the Ladies' Mandolin and Guitar Band—an ensemble of over sixty players, of rank and title. This band performed in the Royal Albert Hall in 1901 and a *Serenade* was composed for the occasion and conducted by Marucelli ; other items were *Reverie* and *Tolede,* composed and conducted by Mezzacapo. In 1900 Marucelli was conductor of the massed bands of five hundred performers in St. James' Hall, when his *Spagnola* was performed with great success. Marucelli returned to his native land at the close of 1901. He was a versatile musician and composer whose works for the mandolin, bravura compositions, are of world repute. He compiled two *Methods for the Mandolin* which were published respectively by Monzino, Milan, and Maurri, Florence, an edition in English was also published. His *Guitar Method,* published by the same firm, had passed its tenth edition in 1930. More than thirty compositions for two mandolins, mandola, guitar and piano, a *Vocal Method, in three parts* and light pieces for the guitar, were also issued by Maurri, Florence. Dallas of London issued several of his trifles for mandolin and Marucelli composed others issued under the name of E. M. Celli.

Carlo Munier

Wolfgang A. Mozart

Enrico Marucelli

Giuseppe Mazzini

Mazzini's Guitar

Mascheroni, Angelo, born at Bergamo, Italy in 1856, and died in 1905 was a popular song composer who wrote mandolin solos and obbligatos to several of his vocal works. He was educated at the Bergamo Conservatoire of Music, under Alessandro Nini, and made such progress that at the age of nineteen he was conductor of an operatic company which made the tour of Italy, France and Spain. He then spent some years in Greece and Russia after which he visited all the cities of importance in North and South America. Five years of his life had been spent in Paris perfecting himself in the vocal art at the Conservatoire, and a short time later he made a name in England. Mascheroni was gifted with a rare natural vein of melody, permeated as it were with the best traditions of the Italian school, and he enjoyed the inestimable advantage of having thrived in the musical atmosphere of the great artistic centres of Europe and America. In his compositions, there is beneath the beautiful melodic structure, a foundation of sound musicianship upon which the lighter graces and charms of lyric arts flourish. When Mascheroni arrived in London, unknown, he experienced the greatest difficulty in disposing of his song, *For all eternity;* when the copyright was sold by public auction, after the publishers had made a competence by it, it realised as many thousand guineas as the two guineas paid for it originally—a record price for a musical copyright. Other of his successful vocal compositions are: *Woodland serenade,* with mandolin obbligato, published in 1892 and *Ave Maria,* composed at Mme. Patti's Welsh castle. Mascheroni was the composer of several original works and also arrangements for mandolin and piano. The principal are: *On the banks of the Rhine,* a tarantella, composed in 1894, published by Augener, London; *Fantasia on 'Faust'* (Gounod); *Un Reve; Bolero; Melodie Sclav* and others of similar style which were issued by Turner, London. Mascheroni's son, who was taught the guitar and mandolin by his father appeared as guitar soloist in London in 1902.

Massenet, Jules Emile, born May 12, 1842 at Montaud, Loire, France, died in Paris August 13, 1912. He entered the Paris Conservatoire at the age of eleven and to meet the expense was drummer in a theatre orchestra. He was awarded the Prize of Rome in 1863 and was later a professor of composition in the same Conservatoire. His three act opera *Cherubin,* produced in Monte Carlo in 1904 was performed in Paris the following year. In the last act, Massenet employs the mandolin with felicitous effect, and also in other of his compositions. Writing to the editor of L'Estudiantina in 1909, a music journal issued in the interest of the guitar and mandolin, Massenet said: " It is with pleasure I accept the Presidency of your Society for I participate in your artistic musical attainments." His reminiscences were published in the Echo de Paris in 1911 and enlarged by Leroux, appeared in 1912 under the title of Souvenirs d'un Musicien.

Matiegka, Wenzeslaus Thomas, born July 6, 1773 at Chotzen,

Bohemia, died January 19, 1830, in Vienna. He was a chorister in the Seminary of Kremsier and studied law in Prague University, meanwhile continuing his musical education under the Abbe Gelinek. When he had concluded his University career he entered the service of Count Ferd. Kinsky in Chlumetz but resigning in 1800 he removed to Vienna where he was organist and choirmaster at the churches, first of St. Leopold and then St. Joseph. He was also a teacher of the piano and guitar on which instruments he had a wide reputation. He has left more than thirty compositions for, and including, the guitar. Wm. Klingenbrunner, a contemporary guitarist, in his autobiography, the manuscript of which is in the Musikfreund library, Vienna, records interesting notes on the life of Matiegka and the esteem in which he was regarded by contemporary musicians. All the musical directories of the period praise his works and life. On his Op. 1, 2 and 31, *Sonatas for the guitar,* he states that he is a professor of the guitar. Op. 5, 6, 7, 10, 15 and 27 are *Variations for guitar ;* Op. 19, *Duo for violin and guitar ;* Op. 18, *Trio for clarinet, horn and guitar ;* Op. 21, 26, *Trios for flute, alto and guitar ;* Op. 24, *Trio for flute, alto and guitar ;* Op. 20, four books, each containing *Six progressive guitar solos.* All the foregoing were published by Artaria, Vienna and a *Serenade* of Beethoven arranged for *violin, alto and guitar* and a *Grand Sonata for guitar* were issued by Andre, Offenbach.

Matini, Riccardo, an esteemed Italian mandolinist and composer, who, during the latter part of the nineteenth century wrote many pleasing compositions and operatic transcriptions for mandolins which were published in his native land. His *Method for the Mandolin,* in two volumes, with Italian, French and English text was published by Maurri, Florence, as were many of his mandolin compositions and a comic opera, *A telegram,* in three acts, also a one act lyric play *Stelle.* Matini is known to mandolinists by various melodious and unique nocturnes and serenatas which were very popular, especially *Ombre Notturne, Ore Liete* (dedicated to Federico Sacchi, a Cremonese teacher of the mandolin and guitar in London and instructor to members of the Royal family) and *Nebel,* a fantastic serenade. These were published by Bratti, Florence, and Ricordi, Milan, who also issued many other of his Serenatas, Notturnos, Minuets, etc., for mandolins, mandola, guitar and piano. Matini was the mandola player in the celebrated plectrum quartet under Munier in 1900. This quartet of first and second mandolins, mandola and lute obtained the highest award in the International Music Contests convened in Genoa in 1892 under the presidency of the violin virtuoso Camillo Sivori.

Mattera, Belisario, an Italian musician and eminent mandolin virtuoso was the first recorded mandolinist to give instruction on the instrument to members of the Royal family of Italy. During a period, at the commencement of the nineteenth century, the nobility and aristocracy emulated the Royal family and consequently the mandolin was very popular with the musical public.

Maurer, Bernard Joseph, born 1757 at Cologne, and died there April 26, 1841. From 1777-80 he was 'cellist in the Royal Chapel, Bonn. He removed to Cologne where he was a teacher of the 'cello and guitar and subsequently theatrical music director. In 1802 he published *Six Songs with Spanish guitar accompaniment* which were reviewed in A.M.Z of the same year ; *Six Progressive Sonatas for violin and guitar*, in two books, without opus number, published in 1805 and Op. 1, *Six Progressive Sonatines for violin and guitar,* issued by Simrock, Bonn.

Mayr, Johann Simon, born June 14, 1763 at Mendorf, Bavaria, died in Bergamo, Italy, December 2, 1845, was a son of the church organist and schoolmaster from whom he received musical instruction until he was ten, when he entered Ingolstadt seminary. At the commencement of his career he was a law student and by the assistance of a patron was able to realise his desire of a musical career by continuing his studies in Bergamo. He had already published a few compositions, songs with guitar, which were issued in Ratisbon. Mayr was capellmeister in Bergamo in 1802 and three years later a professor of composition in Bergamo Institute, where Donizetti was his pupil. In his last years he became blind ; his more than seventy operas, oratorios, etc., were popular before the advent of Rossini and the municipal authorities erected a monument to his memory in Bergamo in 1852. The A.M.Z. of 1807 records his *Twelve Canzonetti Venetian, with guitar,* and Whistling's Handbuch records a *Vocal duet with guitar* and an *Air with flute and guitar,* published by Bohme, Hamburg. His memoirs, edited by Alborghetti and Galli, appeared in 1875.

Mayseder, Joseph, the renowned violin virtuoso and composer, born at Vienna, October 26, 1789 and died there November 21, 1863, was associated for some years with famous guitarists in their public concerts, and he studied and composed for it. The son of a poor painter, he commenced to play the violin at eight years of age, first with Sucher and then with Wranitzky. When he had completed his studies, and still a youth, Schuppanzigh, cf Beethoven fame, took great interest in him, entrusting him with the second violin in his famous quartet. The Viennese school of violinists, called into being by Schuppanzigh and influenced by Spohr, which so encouraged the brilliant virtuoso style, found in Mayseder an excellent exponent. Hanslick says, that when Mayseder was eleven he gave his first concert in the famous Augarten, Vienna, July 24, 1800, and was brilliantly successful. He made his name rapidly, for in 1811 the municipality awarded him the large Salvator Gold Medal and in 1817 he was presented with the freedom of the city. Spohr, in 1812 declared him the foremost violinist in Vienna, and although barely twenty he was frequently invited in social circles to try his artistic strength against Spohr. In 1815 he became associated with the pianist Hummel and the guitarist Giuliani and they played together very frequently in Vienna. All the members of this trio were proficient guitarists and when Hummel departed from Vienna he was succeeded as pianist by Moscheles, also a guitarist. For their concerts Mayseder composed, in collaboration with Giuliani and Moscheles, the music to a romance by Blangini, entitled *Der abschied der Troubadours* (The departure of the Troubadours) published by Diabelli & Co., Vienna, for voices (German and Italian words) with *accompaniment of piano, guitar and violin.* During this time Mayseder evinced great interest in the guitar, gave time to its study and he and Giuliani publicly performed the duos concertante composed by Giuliani for violin and guitar. In 1816 Mayseder was a member of the Royal Opera orchestra, rising to solo violinist in 1820, and fifteen years later was chamber virtuoso to the Emperor, in which capacity he played at the Opera and in the Cathedral of St. Stephen. When the composer-guitarist Blum visited Vienna in 1817, Mayseder was violinist in the orchestra during the production of Blum's *Das Rosen Hutchen* and his ballet *Aline.* The latter, a tremendous success, was arranged, transcribed and adapted for every instrument alone and in various combinations, among them was one by Mayseder, Op. 3, *Violin solo, seven difficult variations and coda on the march from the ballet 'Aline' with accompaniment of guitar,* published by Artaria & Co., Vienna. In 1862 the Emperor bestowed on Mayseder the Order of Franz Joseph, and his numerous pupils spread his name far and wide. Carl von Weber, also a guitarist, has recorded his impressions of Mayseder's playing when he said: "A fine player, but he leaves one cold." The influence which the guitar virtuoso Giuliani exerted over Mayseder and other celebrated musicians of Vienna was considerable. Giuliani was an educated man, a remarkable genius on his instrument, who was welcomed in the highest artistic and social circles of Vienna, and by his playing placed the guitar in a most enviable position in the estimation of musicians of Vienna and the public generally. Mayseder and Giuliani were frequently performing together in public, and this fact, combined with the popular demand for the instrument and its music, induced Mayseder to study it. Mayseder's published compositions number about sixty. Op. 1, *Variations on 'Schone Minka' for violin and guitar,* published by Artaria, Vienna; Op. 4, *Variations on a Greek theme for violin and guitar,* Haslinger, Vienna; Op. 15, *Variations in D on 'Partant pour la syrie,' for violin and guitar,* Artaria, Vienna, also Richault, Paris; Op. 17, *Fourth Polonaise for violin and guitar,* Haslinger. The three following compositions were published respectively for violin and orchestra, violin and quartet, and violin and guitar, by their author. Op. 24, *Variations,* Carli, Paris; Op. 45, *Brilliant Variations in E on an original theme;* Op. 43, *Concert variations in D,* both published by Cranz, Hamburg. Giuliani transcribed for flute and guitar Mayseder's polonaises, Op. 10, 11, 12, originally conceived for two violins, alto and 'cello; they were issued by Richault, Paris.

Maza, Sainz de la, Regino, born September 7, 1897 at Burgos, Spain, a contemporary professor of the guitar in Madrid Conservatoire. His first musical instruction was on the piano, and when he was fourteen he commenced the study of the guitar under a local teacher. When his family removed to Madrid he gave more serious attention to its study by continuing in the Tarrega method under Daniel Fortea. Maza gave his first concert at the age of sixteen in Bilbao, subsequently touring Spain, giving recitals in the most important centres. One of the most notable was that in collaboration with Falla, in the Sociedad Nacinol de Musica, Madrid. During the years 1923-4 he again toured Spain and at the conclusion departed for Argentina. He was well received in Buenos Aires, where he lectured on the history of the viheula and its relation to the guitar, with musical examples and illustrations, in the National College of Buenos Aires University and was awarded the gold medal. Maza was guitar soloist in the first performance of Rodrigo's *Concerto de Aranjuez,* in Barcelona. His recitals in 1928, in London, then Paris, Berlin and Brussels were events of artistic value and highly praised by critics. He was commissioned by the Spanish government to lecture and give recitals in the universities of central Latin America and the music journals stated: " Sainz de la Maza is now on his way back from an extensive tour in South America where he gave more than a hundred concerts in Brazil, Uruguay, and Argentina, his art being everywhere accepted with the greatest enthusiasm." In 1948 he was again in Madrid. Reporting his recitals in New York during December 1953 the Times said: " Mr. de la Maza proved himself to be an instrumental artist in the great traditions established by Segovia. Like all good guitarists he can get a variety of timbre from his instrument—a variety almost equal to a harpsichord registration, he does not try for a very big tone and keeps his dynamics scaled down." Maza revised the *Method of Aguado,* published by Union Musical Espanola, Madrid, and is the composer of about twenty original guitar solos. Op. 1, *Andalusa* and fourteen arrangements for guitar were also issued by the same publishers, the most prominent are *Zamba, Alegria, Boceto Andaluz* and *Cantinela.*

Mazzini, Giuseppe, born at Genoa, June 22, 1805, died Pisa, March 10, 1872. The philosopher and patriot was an excellent guitarist and invoked the guitar as unique comfort for his moral suffering. He said: " I could live willingly all my life closed in a room if I only had with me my books and guitar." In his life, written by Bolton King, M.A., he says: " He played much on the guitar and sang well to it ; and his musical talents and clever reciting made him in demand among his middle class and patrician friends " (page 6). " His one relaxation—to sing to his guitar when left alone at night " (page 133). " He would when quite alone with the family sing to his guitar or finger out on it the score of some favourite opera " (page 146). Moscheles in his Diary (page 284) writes: " Let me tell you of my acquaintance with Mazzini. Felix (my son) is painting a portrait of him and so I have plenty of opportunity of meeting him. I had formed an utterly mistaken idea in my estimate of one whom I had always cried down as a conspirator ; he seems to me agreeable and unassuming ; his conversation, even on the subject of politics is mild and apparently inoffensive ; he is keenly interested in the subject of music. As a proof of this I may tell you that his guitar is his inseparable companion, even in his hiding places. He lives in rooms of the plainest description in Onslow Terrace and goes by the name of Ernesti." On the front of the house in which he lived in London, 183 Gower Street (Onslow Terrace) is a circular blue plaque inscribed, "London County Council. Giuseppe Mazzini, 1805-1872, Italian Patriot lived here." Mazzini's guitar with other mementos were presented by his daughter to the city museum of Pisa in 1922. He was interred in the Camposanto, Genoa, in close proximity to the last resting place of Paganini, both sons of that city. Further details of Mazzini's association with the guitar can be found in The Story of the Lute, by Maria Rita Brondi.

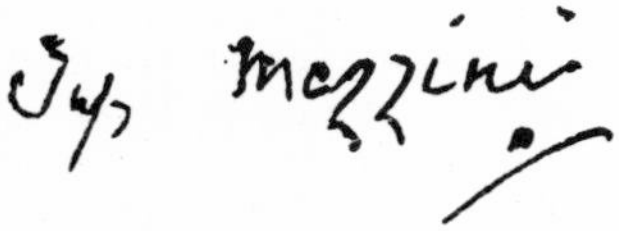

Meissonnier, Antoine and Joseph, were French brothers who obtained fame as guitarists and composers at the commencement of the last century, and both established music publishing businesses which prospered. The elder, Antoine, was born at Marseilles, December 8, 1783, and it was the intention of his parents that he should succeed them in their business, so he was trained and educated for a commercial life. When he was sixteen, business took him to Naples, and it was this journey that decided him to become a musician. In Naples he heard the guitar played by skilful performers and was thrilled, so studied it under a teacher named Vinterlandi. His progress was rapid and he continued by studying harmony and composition with the same teacher, residing in Naples several years and when sufficiently proficient, relinquished his business to commence as a teacher of the guitar. While in Naples he wrote a comic opera *La Donna Corretta,* produced there and later in Paris, then returned to his home in Marseilles. He was eventually attracted to Paris, journeying with his younger brother where both appeared as guitarists. Antoine was immediately popular as a guitar virtuoso ; he was patronised by the wealthy, and was on intimate terms with the most illustrious musicians who lived in or passed through Paris. He was an ardent admirer and close friend of Carcassi, who dedicated to him in felicitous terms, Op. 2, *Three Rondos for guitar solo,* published by Schott, London. In 1814 Antoine established a musical instrument and music-publishing business in Paris, which continued for about twenty years, and in addition to publishing numerous compositions of other celebrated guitarists, issued many of his own. His name was popularised by his songs and romances with guitar, and he was very prolific, for numerous volumes of these with guitar accompaniment were issued in octavo form with illustrated titles, by himself and other publishers of Paris. The A.M.Z. for the year 1809 records several of his canzonettas, evidently published during his residence in Naples. Other of his compositions are: *Grand sonata and rondo for guitar solo,* dedicated to M. Lepic, Colonel-Major of the Imperial Guards, originally published by Leduc, Paris, but in 1820 by the author; *Three grand trios for guitar, violin and alto,* and various fantasias and variations, etc., for the same combination of instruments; *Simplified Method for the guitar or lyre,* dedicated to his pupils, published by Sieber, Paris. The lyre or lyre-guitar was a modification of the ordinary guitar. Constructed on the model of the ancient lyre, it was tuned and played the same as the guitar; during Meissonnier's time it enjoyed a short-lived popularity. As music publisher, Meissonnier issued the choicest compositions for the guitar, among them were the *Three Duos for violin and guitar* by the distinguished violinist, Rolla, the teacher of Paganini.

Joseph Meissonnier, brother of Antoine is generally known as Meissonnier le Jeune, or younger. He too, was born at Marseilles, in 1790, seven years after his brother; the success of his brother's musical training induced him to play the same instrument. All musical instruction he received from his brother while living in Marseilles, and they visited Paris together where both were guitarists and teachers. In 1814 his brother commenced a music publishing business, and ten years later Joseph followed his brother's example and acquired the ancient music-publishing business of Corbaux, Paris. As he was also a guitarist and teacher he published many guitar compositions, the chief are: *Three duos for violin and guitar; Three rondos for guitar solo,* published by Hanry, Paris; Op. 2 and 4, *Collections of melodies for guitar,* Petit, Paris; Two Methods for the guitar and numerous collections of operatic melodies; variations and dances for guitar solo, published respectively by Hanry; Petit; and Dufant & Dubois. Joseph Meissonnier's son succeeded him as music publisher and after having amassed a considerable fortune, sold his copyrights in consequence of failing health and retired to Toulouse in 1855.

Merchi, Giacomo. There were two Italian guitarists and mandolinists of this name. Dr. Zuth states they were brothers, other writers that they were father and son. The most renowned was Giacomo who was born in Naples in 1730 and came with his relative to Paris in 1753 where they performed duos on the calascione, a species of mandolin with a long neck, greatly favoured at that period by Neapolitans. Gerber states they gave concerts in Frankfort in 1777 and Giacomo compiled a method for the guitar under the title of, a *Guide for scholars of the Guitar,* which appeared that year. They returned to Paris, where Giacomo was teaching his instruments as late as 1789. He made a visit to England, taught the mandolin and guitar for a time and published compositions for the guitar, fantasias, divertissements and variations, and also a number of French, Italian and English songs with guitar. Each year Merchi published collections of airs, preludes, and short pieces for guitar solo and songs with guitar. Twenty-six of these volumes had been printed up to the year 1788; and are recorded by Eitner. Op. 3, *Duets for two guitars;* Op. 7, *The scholar's guide for the guitar,* or, *Preludes as pleasing as useful, with airs and variations;* Op. 9, *Trio for two mandolins and violoncello;* Op. 21, *Twelve divertissements for two guitars, or violin and guitar,* dedicated to his pupil, Lady Ossory, published by Welcker, London; Op. 15, *Songs with guitar,* published in 1766; Op. 23, *Minuets and allemandes with variations;* Op. 26, *Sonata for guitar* and *Six Italian barcarolas with guitar,* published in Paris in 1755. Merchi composed in all about sixty works for the mandolin and guitar and a *Treatise on the harmony of music executed on the guitar, containing clear instructions and illustrative examples on the pincer, the doitger, the arpeggio, the batterie, the acct, the chute, the tirade, the martellement, the trill, the glissando, etc.* This volume in 8vo. was published in Paris in 1777.

Merk, Joseph, born at Vienna, January 18, 1795, some authorities say March 15, and died in Vienna, June 16, 1852. Merk was one of the greatest violoncellists of any period, excelling as a bravura player; he was also a fine guitarist and the greater part of his professional career was spent with guitarists. Grove states: "His first musical studies were directed to singing, the guitar, and especially to the violin, which last instrument he was obliged to abandon (according to Fetis) in consequence of an accident to his arm. He then took to the violoncello and under the tuition of an excellent master named Schindlocker speedily acquired great facility on the instrument." Schindlocker was first 'cellist of the Royal Opera, Vienna, and a guitarist and composer for the guitar. Diabelli of Vienna published in 1809 his *Serenade for violoncello and guitar.* Merk studied the guitar in addition to the violoncello with Philipp Schindlocker and soon displayed considerable ability on this instrument. In 1815 he was associated with the guitar virtuoso Giuliani and Mayseder and Hummel. He appeared in public on many occasions with Giuliani and frequently played the guitar at serenades and convivial meetings. Merk was a good vocalist, for singing had been his first musical study. In 1816, the year after the Royal Serenades with Giuliani and Hummel, Merk became first 'cellist in the Opera, Vienna; up to this time he had been occupied with desultory engagements as 'cellist and guitarist. He was a professor at the newly founded Conservatoire in 1823 and remained as such until 1848; during 1831 he was also in the Court Opera orchestra by the side of Lincke, the 'cellist and guitarist. He was chamber virtuoso to the Emperor from 1834 and made several concert tours to Prague, Dresden, Leipzig and Hamburg. His compositions for 'cello are numerous and there were several light pieces for the guitar which appeared in Vienna and Prague.

Merrick, Arnold, born during the end of the eighteenth century and died at Cirencester, Gloucestershire in 1845. He was an English organist and guitarist who had served in the Peninsular Wars where he became familiar with the guitar and the Spanish language. In 1826 he was organist of the parish church of Cirencester and a teacher of the organ and guitar; his most celebrated pupil was the organist, John Bishop. To Merrick is due the honour of being the first translator of Sor's guitar method from the original Spanish text. This English edition was published in 1827 by Robert Cocks, London. He also translated from the Spanish text, the earlier guitar method of Federico Moretti which had been published in 1792, 1799 and 1804 (see Moretti). Merrick translated into English many other standard musical treatises including those of Albrechtsberger and was himself the author of a treatise on harmony, figured bass and composition, published in two volumes by Robert Cocks, London.

Mertz, Johann Kaspar, born at Pressburg, Hungary, August 17, 1806, and died in Vienna, October 14, 1856, was a renowned guitar virtuoso and composer, the son of very poor parents. During childhood he played the flute and guitar on both of which he was entirely self-taught. The guitar, however, became his favourite and when twelve years of age was giving instruction on both. His youth was occupied in the uneventful occupation of teaching and music study to the year 1840, when, desirous of improving his financial position he transferred his services to Vienna. At the age of thirty-four he was established in this music centre, and on November 29 of the same year appeared as guitar soloist in the Court Theatre under the immediate patronage of the Empress Carolina Augusta. His success was instantaneous, he was applauded to the echo and shortly after appointed Court guitarist to the Empress. He then undertook an extended concert tour, travelling through Moravia and Poland where his concerts in Cracow and Warsaw were attended by musicians and the elite of society; his fame as virtuoso spread far and wide and he was invited to visit Russia. In the fortress of Modlin he was commanded by the Grand Duke Urusoff to play at the Court. He was next heard of in Stettin where he gave several concerts and in Breslau and Berlin playing in the Royal Theatres of both these cities. By 1842 he was in Dresden where he gave recitals in the Board of Trade building and met the young lady who became his wife. Miss Josephine Plantin, a professional pianist on tour had just arrived in Dresden and was engaged to perform at the same concert. This accidental meeting on the concert stage, commenced a friendship which resulted in a joint concert tour, accompanied by the sister of Mertz and on the journey to Chemnitz they became engaged. They were very disappointed upon arrival, for the city was deserted; being inadvisable to announce a concert they continued their journey to Altenburg and Leipzig. A concert in the Gewandhaus was advertised and two days after, Mertz was prostrated by illness so it was postponed for a fortnight. A second concert, however, was given in the Booksellers' Hall, November 13, 1842, when

Mertz played three of his own compositions, a *Fantasia on 'Montecchi,' Les Adieux* and the *Carnival of Venice.* The second item, a *Duo Concertante for guitar and piano* introduces passages in harmonics and accompanied by his fiancée, this concert was an artistic and financial success. They visited Dresden again, then Prague, and were married December 14, 1842, and in the spring of the following year made their abode in Vienna as teachers and concert artists. Fortune smiled on them, for they were occupied in giving tuition to members of the royal family and the elite of society. A pupil of Mertz at this period, who became famous in the musical world, was the virtuoso Johann Dubez, and another who would have become equally renowned, had she been placed in less affluent circumstances, was the Duchess Ledochofska. This lady, his pupil on the mandolin, by her rare musical ability brought her playing to a most artistic and brilliant perfection ; she was an acknowledged virtuoso and the composer of several original works for two mandolins, guitar, and piano. Mertz, in addition to his virtuosity on the guitar was a skilful performer on the flute, 'cello, mandolin and zither for all of which he composed. During the first month of residence in Vienna they appeared at a concert, sponsored by the Vienna Musical Society in the Musicians' Hall under the immediate patronage and presence of the Empress Carolina Augusta and a fashionable and critical audience. Mertz resided in Vienna until 1846 when his health caused anxiety. For a time he had suffered from neuralgia and was prescribed strychnine. Mertz and his wife had no knowledge of the drug, the prescription was dispensed by the apothecary to the wife, who thinking she had been given too little put all in one dose. Mertz was in terrible pain, an emetic was administered and physician called, but his life for some time was very precarious. For eighteen months skilful medical treatment and nursing brought him convalescent when he removed to the suburbs of the city. By the spring of 1848 he had regained his accustomed health and made his first appearance after his illness at a concert given February 6 in the Salon Schweighofer. Public sympathy was manifested by the enthusiasm displayed at this concert. The hall was filled to its utmost capacity and Herr Sernetz wrote that the crush to obtain admission was unprecedented, many being unable to be accommodated. Soon after this successful concert, insurrection in Austria and revolution in Hungary broke out, and all musical activities were at a standstill. His wife stated that all their prosperity vanished in a moment and it was on March 13, while in a melancholy, despondent mood that the set of waltzes, the original manuscript of which is in the library of the I.L.G., Munich, was composed. All business was at a standstill and to avoid being conscripted, Mertz with his wife, essayed to leave Vienna secretly. In great haste and fear they took what luggage they could lay their hands on and hurried to the station to find that the railway track was torn up and no train could run until late that night. Although there was ample time for them to return home for more of their belongings they feared to. At Brunn they essayed to give a concert but the turbulent state made it impossible and it was not until a month later that they dared return home. With finances exhausted, all pupils lost, and more in desperation than hope they strove unceasingly to regain their former prosperity. By 1851 they had recovered their former stability and this year they gave three concerts of special importance; that in the Concert Hall of the Musical Society, in the palace of the Grand Duke Esterhazy, and in the Salon Schweighofer. Recitals were given in Pressburg and in July of 1855 they were commanded to play before the Empress Carolina Augusta, King Ludwig I of Bavaria and the Grand Duke of Hesse Darmstadt, in the royal palace of Salzburg. King Ludwig was fascinated and at the conclusion took the guitar from Mertz, examined it thoroughly, and declared that he could not believe the wonderful music he had heard could come from such a simple instrument with but ten strings (Mertz played an ordinary guitar with four additional bass strings). They gave a recital in the mansion of President Ritter von Scharschmidt to a very distinguished and select company and a repeat concert for the Musical Society, previous to their departure for Reichenhall. This was destined to be his final concert tour. At the frontier town of Reichenhall he was accused by customs officials of trading in musical goods, notwithstanding his two guitars and supply of strings were necessary for an artist. While preparing to demonstrate, a terrific storm burst and he and his belongings were deluged in rain and he did not recover from the effects. They paid all charges, travelled to Gemunden where they gave a concert and played at a banquet given by the Duchess Julien and continued their tour to Hall by coach when other misfortune befell them; the horses fell lame and passengers were required to walk up the hills, which were many. It was very warm so Mertz carried his coat over his arm, to discover when he arrived at Hall, that he had lost the contents of his pocket. However, the concert was highly successful and his loss made good. His health, not robust, was severely tried during the winter, he became very weak and to recuperate spent several weeks of summer at Graein on the Danube. A slight temporary improvement induced him to give a concert in this town but it was with pain he completed the programme. They journeyed home by steam boat which ran aground near Tulu and were compelled to remain aboard all night, and the following morning were transferred to an open cattle boat. He was so ill that it was with the greatest difficulty he arrived home. A physician was called and the patient lingered for about a month until released by death October 14, 1856. No portrait of the artist was made but he is described by Makaroff in his Memoirs, who met him in Vienna in 1837. "He was a tall man, about fifty years of age, not stout or thin, very modest and with no pretence of greatness about him. His playing was marked by power, energy, feeling, clarity and expression." In 1856 this wealthy Russian, Nikolai P. Makaroff, at that time residing in Brussels, offered two prizes for the best compositions written for the guitar, with the purpose of stimulating and encouraging composers and players. Mertz was one of the thirty-one competitors, and his last effort was to submit his Op. 65, *Concerto for guitar solo,* consisting of three items, Fantasie Hongroise, Fantasie original and Le gondolier. The judges were professors of Brussels Conservatoire of Music—Leonard violinist—Servais and Demunck 'cellists—Blaes clarinetist—Kufferath composer, with Bender clarinetist and State Military Band conductor. Under the presidency of M. Makaroff sixty-four compositions were adjudicated on December 10, 1856, when the first prize of £40 was awarded to J. K. Mertz. He did not hear the news for he passed away just previous to the award. The second prize was awarded to the French guitarist Napoleon Coste, of Paris. As a composer and performer, Mertz takes rank with the most illustrious; his original compositions, transcriptions and operatic arrangements are gems. He was a musician of rare attainment, a guitarist of the first order and a poetic writer for his instrument. Whatever Mertz wrote was well deserving of being written, a vulgar melody or comonplace harmony seems impossible to his nature. The American guitarist George Krick wrote some years ago, "In remembering our artists of from one-half to a century ago, is it not as Shakespeare's Mark Antony remarked over the remains of all that was mortal of the great Cæsar, 'The evil that men do lives after them, the good is oft interred with their bones'? For it is true that the grand and sublime compositions of J. K. Mertz, Sor, Ferranti and others have lived to be monuments to their names, and if the public was appreciative of the guitar as of the violin and piano, monuments would bedeck many cities—erected to perpetuate the names of our famous composers for the guitar. While wandering through the streets of old historic Vienna, and seeing monuments that had been erected to Mozart, Beethoven and other grand old masters, I wondered if it were possible that such a city could have forgotten Mertz, who performed for their princes and nobility, and who dedicated many of his compositions and arrangements to their names. Could it be possible that the composer of hundreds of beautiful themes—though it be only for the guitar, that were neglected and laid on the shelf, covered with the dust of time—were like himself forgotten; but yet it was so, and even they who had published his music could only give an approximate guess as to the date of his death. His works live, however, in those who study the instrument to which he devoted his talents, and with all performers who study the guitar though it be in far distant America, across the water, J. K. Mertz's memory will never die." Mertz was a prolific composer, the majority of his works are transcriptions and arrangements of classical compositions for guitar solo, guitar duo, or guitar and piano, many were issued without opus numbers, and he was the author of a *Theoretical and Practical School for the guitar,* published by Haslinger, Vienna. This method is very brief, consisting of only twenty-nine pages of printed matter, the first ten treat of the theory of music while the last six are given to fifteen short studies. It cannot be compared with the more complete and detailed methods of Carulli and Sor, yet, like the compositions of Mertz, this method displays great originality, for from the very commencement he insists upon the alternate fingering of the right-hand—

a practice which must be obtained with great facility and delicacy by any guitarist desirous of rendering satisfactorily the compositions of Mertz. This method of alternate fingering for repetition of the same note was carried to a most marvellous perfection by the artist himself, and his solo playing resembled the sostenuto of the mandolin accompanied by a guitar. Mertz's first composition, a Hungarian original dance, dedicated to Anton von Josipovich, Duke of Turopolya, was published by Haslinger, Vienna, who also issued the five succeeding original compositions — melodies, polonaises and nocturnes for solo guitar. Op. 4, *Three nocturnes,* dedicated to Madame Aloyse Streibig, wife of the music publisher of Pressburg ; Op. 6, *The Carnival of Venice, variations for guitar solo,* a favourite of its composer. Under the title of *Opera Revue,* Op. 8, Mertz wrote thirty-three classic transcriptions from favourite operas for guitar, these arrangements are much superior to any published and were also issued by Haslinger, Vienna. *Six Waltzes,* Op. 9, dedicated to Josephine Haslinger, widow of the publisher, and Op. 13, *Barden-Klange,* thirteen original tone pictures, purest gems of melody, dedicated to his friend Charles Haslinger, son of the publisher, who succeeded to the business ; Op. 14 and 15, *Two Fantasias for guitar solo,* Hoffman, Prague ; Op. 16, 17, 21, 22, 24, 27, 28, 29, 30, 31, 34, 35, 62, 63, 85, 86, 87, 88 and 100 were operatic transcriptions for guitar published under the title of *The Guitarist's Portfolio,* Aibl, Leipzig, and Op. 33 and 50, also issued by the same publisher as was Op. 52, *Songs with guitar accompaniment.* Mertz wrote several duos for guitar with terz guitar, and guitar and piano, of which Op. 51, 89, 40 and 60 are the principal. These and others were published simultaneously by Aibl, Leipzig, and Ricordi, Milan ; Op. 32, *Trio for guitar, violin or flute and viola,* and three compositions for zither and violin, Aibl ; Op. 64, *Two books of Alpine songs for zither,* and Op. 65, *Three pieces for guitar solo,* previously mentioned, Haslinger, Vienna. Mertz made transcriptions for the guitar of the dances of Strauss and the songs of Schubert. Among his unpublished manuscripts are *Original Waltz for guitar and piano ; Fantasias on 'Montecchi,'* and *'Norma' ; Original fantasia in D minor ;* a *Mazurka ; Les Adieux,* a *Duo Concertante for guitar and piano with flageolet accompaniment ; Themes from 'Il Pirata,' 'Elisire d'amore,' 'Lucia di Lammermoor,'* and *Romance.* He was ably assisted in his concert performances and composition by his wife, who composed light pieces for the piano. Gloggl, Vienna, issued *Tarantella,* and Haslinger Op. 5, *Two Mazurkas for piano,* dedicated to the Baroness Julie de Schulzig. His wife survived him many years, to an advanced age, and in her last years was reduced to a lonely, destitute condition. At the death of her husband in 1856, she endeavoured to continue teaching but was forced by infirmity to relinquish and died in Vienna, August 5, 1903, at the age of eighty-four. In 1901 she loaned for exhibition several of her husband's manuscripts and at the third anniversary of the League of Guitarists, Munich, convened on November 3 of that year in Augsberg, under the presidency of Otto Hammerer, this society raised by subscription a sufficient sum to purchase from the widow his remaining manuscripts, which were placed in the library of the society in Munich.

Methfessel, Albert Gottlieb, born October 6, 1785, at Stadtilm, Thuringia, died March 23, 1869, at Heckenbeck, near Gandersheim. He and his elder brother Frederick were favourite song composers, and both have written many vocal works with accompaniment of guitar. In 1810, Albert Gottlieb was Court musician in Rudolstadt and two years later was musical director in Hamburg. He was the successor of Carl Weber in Prague, in 1816, and Court Capellmeister at Brunswick in 1832 where he remained ten years and then retired on pension. He composed in addition to vocal solos with guitar, part songs for male voices, many of which, as for instance *Krieger's Abschied, Rheinweinlied* and *Deutscher Ehrenpreis,* are still sung by German choral societies. His Op. 6, *Romances and Songs with guitar,* was published by Breitkopf & Härtel, Leipzig. He also wrote piano sonatas, etc., and was the composer of an oratorio *Das befreite Jerusalem,* and an opera, *The Prince of Basra.* Spohr in his autobiography mentions him frequently. On page 147, he writes: " Herr Methfessel, taking his guitar, would entertain the company with pleasing ballads and touching romances of his own composition; by way of a change he then sang a comic song or two and exhibited his liveliness of fancy, his richness of invention, wit and humour of expression, as well as his intimate knowledge of tone and harmony, and it was the singer Methfessel from Rudolstadt who more particularly kept the company in the merriest mood by his inexhaustible humour." Spohr had received a deputation of musicians—of whom Methfessel was one—to conduct a musical festival at Mannheim. Spohr accompanied them and they proceeded on foot to Heidelberg, carrying their luggage in knapsacks on their backs and having the appearance of an itinerant band. Spohr writes on page 59: " Methfessel who accompanied our four part songs with the guitar, carried his instrument slung by a band over his shoulders. Then followed our songs, and Methfessel again distinguished himself in particular by the execution of his humorous songs which he accompanied in a masterly manner on the guitar. These put the whole company in the merriest mood." Methfessel's elder brother, Frederick, born at Stadtilm, August 27, 1771, and died there May, 1807, was destined by his parents for the church, studying music only in his leisure as a pastime, the guitar, singing and piano. In 1796 he entered Leipzig University as a student of theology but continued his music for pleasure; he eventually accepted a position as preceptor, first in Alsbach, then at Ratzebourg in Mecklembourg, Coburg and other towns. However, his intense passion for music ultimately dominated his career, for, obtaining no satisfaction apart from this art, he returned to his native town where he commenced as a teacher of music and vocal composer. During his last year of life he was engaged in the composition of an opera, *Faust;* but already suffering from the illness which terminated fatally, his death occurred before the completion of the work. He wrote many collections of songs with guitar accompaniment, some of which with those of his brother, were issued by Breitkopf & Härtel, Leipzig, and Schott, Mayence. Op. 7, *Song for voice and guitar* and *Twelve songs for voice and guitar or piano;* Op. 12, *Songs with guitar,* were published by Simrock, Bonn ; Op. 23, *Three songs with guitar and flute ; Journal for the Guitar;* solos, in three books and *Twelve Italian songs with guitar.* His biography with a list of his compositions was published shortly after his death in the A.M.Z. and also under the title of Charakterkopfe by Riehl, in 1879.

Mezzacapo, Edouardo, an Italian mandolinist and composer who migrated to Paris towards the end of the nineteenth century where he was esteemed and popular as a teacher. He visited England periodically and in 1901 was in London, teaching the mandolin and conducting an elite musical society The Ladies' Mandolin and Guitar Band. During June of the same year this society performed with marked success two of Mezzacapo's compositions written for the occasion, *Reverie* and *Tolede,* under his baton in the Royal Albert Hall. He returned to Paris, residing at Avenue Wagram in 1912 as composer, professor of mandolin in the Academie International de Musique and conductor of the Lombard Estudiantina. His biography with portrait was published in Music and Dramatic Directory, 1887-1911. Mezzacapo was a prolific and popular composer for mandolin and mandolin band ; several of his compositions, written originally for the mandolin became concert solos of violinists of repute and passed many editions *Sympathy Waltz,* composed for the mandolin, has been arranged for orchestra and all instruments, and is of world-wide popularity. The majority of his works appeared in Paris ; Rowies issued more than sixty.

Miceli, Giorgio, born at Reggio, Calabria, Italy, October 21, 1835, and died in 1895. His family were of good position and at the age of seven he commenced the study of music with an uncle who taught him the rudiments of music and the mandolin. His father was condemned to the galleys for participating in the revolution of 1847, whereupon the child was sent to Naples where he was a pupil, first of Gallo and then of Lillo, in Naples Conservatoire. When sixteen, his operetta, *Zoe,* was produced successfully in the Theatre Nuovo. Forty consecutive performances of this operetta were staged and the year following he produced another which was equally successful. The Neapolitan authorities prohibited the performance of one of his stage plays, after seven representations, and Miceli was compelled to commence teaching. During 1864-5 he entered various musical competitions in Naples, Florence, etc., and a trio and a quartet of his compositions were awarded prizes. In 1870 he was commissioned to write a *Grand Serenade for mandolin band*, for the fetes of the Maritime Exhibition of Naples. This composition was such an outstanding success that it was reproduced for some years in numerous theatres of Italy. Miceli also composed songs with mandolin and guitar accompaniment, compositions for mandolins and guitars, and other instrumental music. Miceli was knighted in 1875. His son Giuseppe studied the mandolin, guitar, and composition, under his father, and also wrote for these instruments ; his principal publishers were Venturini, Florence, and Carisch & Janichen, Milan. His most popular compositions for these instruments are: *Danza Zingaresca* and *Serenata for mandolin and piano,* also an arrangement for mandolin and piano of his *Serenata,* originally composed for pizzicato strings. The last was issued by Ricordi, Milan.

Migot, Georges, contemporary, born February 27, 1891, at Paris. He was a pupil of Widor and d'Indy at the Paris Conservatoire of Music and awarded four prizes between 1918-20 for composition. He was severely wounded in the first world war and for some years was an invalid, but eventually partially recovered. Migot, the recipient of several decorations for his war service—among them the Legion d'honneur—was a musicologist of wide repute, the author of a history of music, aesthetic treatises on music, orchestral, choral, chamber and theatre music and in addition to these attainments he was a talented artist painter. He was a pupil of Tessarech for the guitar and displayed and continually maintained a serious interest in the guitar. In June 1926 he contributed the preface to The Evolution of the Guitar, by Tessarech and in November 1928 the preface also to the same author's La Guitare Polyphonique, both issued by Lemoine, Paris. His most widely known composition for the guitar is *Hommage à Claude Debussy,* recorded in the Musical Dictionary of Central Catalan Publications, Barcelona. Migot was a life long friend of his guitar teacher, Tessarech, and after his death was instrumental in the founding of the musical society, The Association Jacques Tessarech and became its first honorary president.

Miksch, Alexander, born about 1770 at Georgenthal, Bohemia, died in Dresden in 1813 was a younger brother of Johann Aloys Miksch (1765-1845) who, towards the close of 1819 was for some years chorus master under Weber in the Court Opera, Dresden. He had studied with his brother Johann, who was a first class teacher of singing, Alexander was a virtuoso on the waldhorn and guitar. He remained a member of the Court Orchestra under Carl Weber until his death. Riemann records that Alexander Miksch was the creator of the modern style of guitar playing. His compositions are enumerated in A.M.Z., and the Dresden National Library contains the manuscript of *Theme with Six Variations for guitar solo.*

Mirecki, Francois, born at Cracow in 1794 and died there in 1862, was a Polish dramatic and instrumental composer, principally for piano and guitar. As a son of musical parents he received musical instruction at an early age and it is recorded that at the age of six he made a public appearance as a painist, playing a concerto of Haydn. In 1814, while in Vienna, he commenced the study of the guitar and became associated

Alberto C. Obregon

Alberto C. Obregon

R. Sains de la Maza

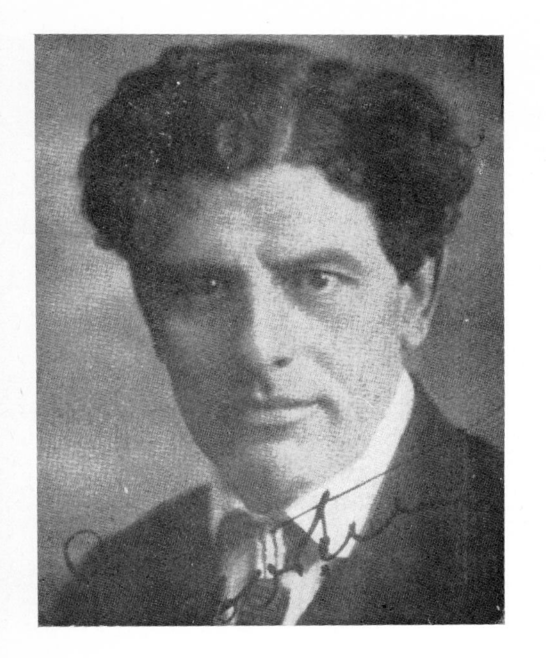

Jacob Ortner

Wm. Place, Jr.

Johann G. Naumann

J. M. Oyanguren

with the guitar virtuoso, Giuliani and the pianist Hummel, of whom he was a pupil and also of Moscheles and Beethoven. During 1817 he visited Paris where some of his lesser compositions were issued, piano pieces, Italian songs, instrumental quartets, etc. His opera in two acts, with Polish libretto *Notte negli Appennini,* was published by Ricordi, Milan, where he was living from 1822-26 and then removed to Geneva, returning to his native land and birthplace in 1838. He wrote divertissements for guitar and piano, arranged for the guitar an edition of a collection of vocal duets and trios, composed in 1720 by Clari, and compiled a Manual of Instrumentation, published in 1825. Mirecki is one of the national song writers of Poland. Many of his compositions for the guitar were published in 1823 by Carli, Paris, and other of his works for the guitar and also grand operas remain in manuscript.

Molino, Don Francois V., an Italian guitarist, violinist and composer was born at Florence in 1775 and died in Paris in 1847. He acquired the Spanish prefix to his name while living in Spain and several of his published compositions bear this title. He was taught the violin and guitar when a youth in Florence and made such extraordinary progress that he was enabled to devote himself entirely to the art of music by the assistance of friends. After completing his studies under Pugnani in Turin and winning great applause by his playing, he was for a time musical theatrical director in Turin. Tiring of this settled life he travelled as violinist and guitarist at the opening of the nineteenth century and continued a roving career for a period. He passed through Italy and Germany and in 1820 was in Paris, where he remained for a time as violin and guitar virtuoso and teacher. In Paris his playing was accorded great praise and he achieved much success and patronage, for he was a remarkable and brilliant performer on both instruments ; a popular and fashionable teacher, his compositions for the violin and guitar were sought by Parisian publishers. This settled, unromantic life did not satisfy the roving nature of Molino, for after some months' residence in Paris he journeyed as a virtuoso to Spain. He appeared before the Court of Madrid and was accorded marked favour, but in a very short time was serving as an officer in the Spanish army. For some years he was engaged with military duties ; but owing to a change in the government was compelled to leave Spain. At a subsequent date he visited London where for a season he was occupied in teaching the guitar to the most fashionable members of society, and after publishing several of his compositions in London he returned to Paris. Molino was welcomed in the first ranks of society in whichever country he visited, and he also enjoyed the patronage of royalty ; one of his appointments was that of Court Musician to the King of Sardinia. He was the author of numerous compositions for stringed instruments, published principally during the years 1800-20 and also of a *New and complete method for the Guitar*, issued in Italian and French. The first edition was published in Florence in 1795 and on the title page he is described as a professor of Violin and Guitar and Capellmeister to the

King of Sardinia. The French edition entitled *New and complete Method for the Guitar or lyre,* was dedicated to Mme. la Duchesse de Dalberg and translated by Nunez de Taboada. Published by Gambara, Paris, in Italian and French, it rapidly passed several editions and was such a success that a translation in the German and French languages was issued by Breitkopf & Härtel, Leipzig; this also ran through several issues although it did not achieve the degree of success accorded the original. A comprehensive volume of over seventy pages, issued in good class style, it contained numerous diagrams of the guitar, introductory chapters on the elements of music and concluded with original preludes, sonatas and rondos for the guitar with violin accompaniment. While in London, Molino compiled several collections of Spanish serenades with guitar and piano, these were described as: *Collections of the most beautiful airs characteristic of the national melodies of Spain.* The first volume of thirty-one pages folio, contained a list of subscribers, and the second volume, dedicated to Lady Antrobus, was issued by subscription by Clementi & Co., London. Molino's principal composition was Op. 56, *Grand Concerto for Guitar with full orchestral accompaniment of violins, clarinets, oboes, horns, altos and basses,* published by Lemoine, Paris. Op. 37 and 38 were *Nocturnes for violin and guitar with flute obbligato;* Op. 4 and 45, *Trios for violin or flute, viola and guitar,* the first dedicated to Count Durazzo, and both published by Breitkopf & Härtel; Op. 36, 44, and 46, *Duos for guitar and piano,* published by Lemoine, Paris and Andre, Offenbach; Op. 1, 6, 11, 13, 15, 21, 28 and 43, *Solos for guitar;* Op. 2, 3, 7, 10, 22 and 29, *Sonatas for violin and guitar,* published by Andre, Offenbach, Breitkopf & Härtel, Leipzig, and in Paris under the title of *The modern Lyre;* Op. 5, 12, 18, 31, 35 and 21, *Studies for the guitar,* the last issued by private subscription and dedicated to the guitarist Meissonnier; Op. 9, *Twelve Waltzes for guitar*, on the title page Molino is described as violinist in the chapel of the Court of the King of Sardinia. Numerous similar compositions of less pretensions were issued by George & Manby, London and continental publishers. His works are recorded by F. Pedrell, and an original manuscript, *Trio for violin, viola and guitar* by Molino is in the library of Milan Conservatoire of Music.

Molitor, Simon J., born November 3, 1766, at Neckarsulm, Wurtemburg and died February 21, 1848, in Vienna. He was taught the violin and guitar by his father, Johann Michael, continuing under the Abbe Vogler and became one of Vienna's most esteemed guitarist-musicians. From 1796-7 he was orchestral conductor in Venice and the year following was employed in the war office of Vienna and later promoted superintendent of the Italian and Dalmatian borders. He retired on pension in 1831, returned to Vienna and devoted himself entirely to music. From the age of nineteen he had essayed composition and also while a clerk in the war office, writing string quartets, songs with the guitar and violin and piano duos. In 1799 he collaborated with the guitarist, Klingenbrunner in the compilation of a *Guitar*

Method. Writing of the Lyre-guitar, in 1806—which was at the time a popular novelty—Molitor said: "The new Lyre, which a few years ago appeared in France—the ordinary guitar constructed in the form of the ancient lyre—is a welcome sight to lovers of the beautiful forms of antiquity. Its tone, though stronger than that of the guitar on account of a larger body, is nevertheless dull and as though held back within the instrument." Molitor's guitar method was published in French and Italian by the Chemical Printing Works, Vienna (the firm who issued Beethoven's Op. 8, the *Polonaise from the Serenade in D*, for violin and guitar). Molitor's published compositions, many and varied, are Concertos for violin, clarinet, string quartets, piano, guitar and vocal works. Op. 7, 10, 11, 12 and 15 are Guitar Solos; Op. 3 and 5, *Duos for violin and guitar*; Op. 6, *Trio for flute, alto and guitar.* Many of his compositions appeared without opus number, including a *Funeral March* composed on the death of his friend the guitarist F. Tandler also *Six Landler* and *Collections of solos for guitar.* Goll of Vienna issued new editions of his works and in 1919 published the treatise Simon Molitor and Viennese Guitarists, by the guitar writer, Dr. Zuth.

Montesardo, G. Girolamo, an Italian guitarist who flourished during the seventeenth century. Fetis states that he was born at Florence and was musical director of the Cathedral of Fano on the Adriatic. He was the author of a Method for the guitar, published in Florence in 1606 under the title of: *New Method for learning to play dances, etc., on the Spanish Guitar,* a copy of which is in the library of Vienna Conservatoire of Music. Eitner in his Dictionary records his songs with the guitar.

Monti, Vittorio, an eminent composer, mandolinist and conductor, was born at Naples, January 6, 1868, and died in Paris about 1925. He obtained fame in the musical world by his composition entitled *Czardas,* composed for the mandolin and exceedingly popular with violinists and other instrumentalists. He was an educated musician who migrated to Paris at the commencement of the twentieth century where he was a highly esteemed teacher of the mandolin and composer. He was subsequently conducting and teaching during the fashionable season at the Riviera resorts, returning to Paris at the conclusion. In 1910 he founded, in Paris, a society of professional, or semi-professional mandolinists, guitarists, etc.—an estudiantina or mandolin band—which he directed under the title of "The Monti Group." Among the members of this estudiantina were well-known mandolinists, guitarists and composers—Goldberg, Chas. Feret, his brother, and the poet-guitarist Gelas. The public performances of this estudiantina, at which world renowned mandolinists and guitarists appeared as soloists revealed the tonal beauty of these instruments and established new standards and ideals. It is not generally known that Monti was a mandolinist; his *Czardas* was composed expressly for this instrument also many other of his mandolin compositions were subsequently transcribed and published for violin, piano, and also set for songs. He was a versatile composer, employs the mandolin in the score of his opera, *Noel de Pierrot,* is the author of a *Method for the Mandolin,* with French and Italian text, published by Monzino, Milan, and a *Petite Mandolin Method,* Op. 245, English text, issued by Ricordi, Milan. Nearly one hundred of his compositions, salon music, with albums and collections were issued in Paris by French publishers, principally Pisa, Rowies, Beuscher, Besnard, Gregh, etc. Ricordi, Milan, and Breitkopf & Härtel, published numerous compositions for two mandolins and guitar or piano. Monti's compositions for estudiantina were orchestrated for two mandolins, mandola, lute, guitar, harp and flute. Some of his most popular mandolin compositions were set to Italian, French and English words as songs, the favourites were: *Cherubin, Ciao* and *Priere des Anges.* He provided guitar accompaniments to Tosti's songs and wrote French songs with guitar which were issued by Ricordi, Milan.

Moore, Thomas, born Dublin in 1779 and died in Devizes, 1852. The famous Irish poet came to England when a young man. He was an amateur musician and an able guitarist who became a social and literary success by playing his guitar and singing his way into the hearts of drawing room audiences, a modern troubadour. From 1807 onwards he wrote his Irish melodies—Irish folk tunes—the most impassioned and sincere poems are, The Harp that once, Last Rose of Summer, and The Minstrel Boy. He also set music to other lyrics and part songs. An interesting account of his guitar playing is recorded by Moscheles in his Diary where he states: "We saw at Sir Walter Scott's eldest daughter's, Thomas Moore, the poet, a lively sparkling Irishman, who, on the strength of his passion for music, immediately made acquaintance with me. He sang his own poems adapted to certain Irish melodies, harmonised and accompanied by himself on the guitar."

Moretti, Federico, a naturalised Spaniard of Neapolitan birth, born during the last decade of the eighteenth century and died at Madrid in 1838. He was 'cellist and guitarist at the Spanish Court. He had studied the guitar as an amateur in Naples and was the author of various methods for this instrument, which were published in Naples and Madrid, the earliest appearing in 1792. His most esteemed method was *The principles of playing the guitar of six strings,* which appeared in Madrid in 1799, dedicated to Reyna Nuestra Senora by Captain Federico Moretti of the Royal Walloon Guards. A third edition of this method, with Italian text was published in Naples in 1804. Moretti's treatise established the fundamental principles of modern guitar technique upon which subsequent methods were based. Sor said of Moretti: "I consider him the flambeau which was to serve to illuminate the wandering steps of guitarists," and Aguado in his Method praises him for his innovations. An enlarged edition followed and in 1821 he published a Musical Grammar, written in the manner of a dialogue; on the title page he is described "Brigadier and Associate of the Academico Filarmonica of Bologna," a second edition was published in Madrid in 1824. He composed variations, minuets and sonatas for guitar solo and Eitner in his Dictionary mentions a *Grand Duo for two lyres or guitars,* published in Paris. Moretti's guitar method was translated into English by Arnold Merrick (the Cirencester organist who translated Sor's method) and published by Cocks, London. Pedrell records the life and works of Moretti in his Spanish Dictionary, and the original manuscript of his *First Lessons on the Guitar* is in the library of Milan Conservatoire of Music. A Count Don Luigi Moretti, living during the first part of the nineteenth century was a talented amateur guitarist and the composer of more than twenty published pieces for the guitar. Op. 9, 17 and 18 are *Duos for violin and guitar;* Op. 13 and Op. 14 *Trios* and Op. 16 a *Quintet.* These compositions are also cited by Eitner and were published by Ricordi, Milan, and Carli, Paris. The same authority also mentions a number of his songs with guitar, Op. 24, which appeared in Madrid.

Moscheles, Ignaz, born at Prague, May 30, 1794 and died in Leipzig, March 10, 1870, was a renowned piano virtuoso and composer also a guitarist and composer for this instrument, which he greatly admired. For a considerable period he associated and was intimate with the most renowned guitar virtuosi, and appeared with them in their concert performances. His love for the guitar was undoubtedly inherited from his father, an amateur guitarist whose chief delight after business was to amuse himself and friends by playing his guitar and singing to its accompaniment. Ignaz had his first musical instruction, the rudiments of music and the elements of guitar playing from his father, and in his biography, published in 1872, he says: "My father, a cloth merchant by trade, found leisure with all his business to keep up his music, which he loved devotedly. He played the guitar and sang well." Moscheles' precocious aptitude for music aroused the interest of D. Weber, the director of Prague Conservatoire, and was admitted a student of the piano, remaining until just after his fourteenth year, when, by death of his father, he was obliged to rely on his own resources. He left his native city for Vienna, obtained pupils for the piano and guitar and gave his leisure to the study of composition, first with Albrechtsberger and after with Salieri. It was in 1815 that he commenced his career as piano virtuoso, and during the next ten years, with but little intermission, led the life of a travelling virtuoso. It was shortly after his arrival in Vienna that he became associated with the guitar virtuoso Giuliani, at that time the popular favourite of the Viennese musical world and the public association with the virtuoso pianist, Moscheles, considerably increased the reputation of both artists. They performed duos for piano and guitar at numerous fashionable concerts, their 'cheval de bataille' was Moscheles' Op. 20, a *Grand Duo Concertante for guitar and piano,* composed in 1813, with other duos for the same instrument by Giuliani. Moscheles in his Diary for the year 1814 writes of the "youthful pranks and practical jokes devised with his artistic colleagues, Merk and Giuliani." In 1816 Moscheles visited Germany and on October 6, was piano soloist at the celebrated Gewandhaus concerts in Leipzig when the programme included a cavatina for guitar solo. During this visit he made the acquaintance of Mendelssohn and the guitarist-composer, Carl Blum, and a lasting friendship commenced between these artists, terminated only by death. Moscheles returned to Vienna where he associated with several instrumentalists—a combination of recognised masters of their respective instruments. This party originally comprised Giuliani, guitarist; Hummel, pianist; Mayseder, violinist and Merk 'cellist; but when Hummel undertook a concert tour in 1818 he was succeeded by Moscheles as pianist, and this quartet of musicians, of such high repute, was in constant demand at royal functions and musical soirees; all were competent guitarists. Hummel, who had preceded Moscheles was no exception, and among their engagements was one worthy of record—a series of six serenades given by Prince Francois Pallfy in the Royal Botanical Gardens of Schonbrun. For this occasion Hummel composed Op. 71, a vocal solo with chorus and accompaniment for violin, 'cello, guitar and piano, entitled *La Sentinelle.* He had previously composed a series of grand serenades for these engagements which had been performed with immense success. Moscheles was a member of the quartet and took part in the celebrated Augarten and the Dukarten (subscription) concerts; but the year 1821 saw the dissolution of this excellent quartet of musicians, and for their final performance Moscheles composed a romance for voices, German and Italian text, with accompaniment of piano, guitar and violin. This composition aptly entitled *Der abschied der Troubadours* (the farewell of the Troubadours) was published by Diabelli, Vienna. Moscheles travelled to Holland and early the following year, in 1822, he played in Paris, subsequently in London, and in 1824 was in Berlin when he gave pianoforte lessons to Felix Mendelssohn, then a youth of fifteen. Moscheles visited London, January, 1825, in the company of the guitarist Schulz and his sons Leonard and Edward. Leonard and his father were guitarists; the brother played the physharmonica and later became a renowned pianist. Moscheles had performed in Vienna with these guitarists, and it was on his recommendation that the three were engaged at a Philharmonic concert in 1828 in London. On January 9, 1825, they had played by command at the Royal Palace when they performed Moscheles' *Grand Duo Concertante,* Op. 20, for guitar and piano, for this occasion arranged by the composer for guitars, physharmonica and piano. After his marriage, in 1826, Moscheles made London his permanent abode and from this time was pianist in all important concerts given by guitarists; his name was associated with the youthful guitarists Regondi and Pelzer, and when Giuliani arrived in England he received practical assistance from his former associate. At the first performance of Beethoven's *Seventh Symphony* which the composer conducted in Vienna, Moscheles,

Giuliani and Hummel played in the orchestra and were individually thanked, publicly, in a letter to the Vienna Zeitung; and when Moscheles conducted the first performance of the symphony in England at the Royal Philharmonic Concerts in London, his associate, Giuliani was again a member of the orchestra, the instrument he played is not stated.

In 1846 when Mendelssohn founded the Conservatoire of Music in Leipzig, he invited his teacher and friend, Moscheles to fill the position of first professor of the piano, and the prosperity of this famous institution was in a large measure due to his indefatigable zeal. Moscheles spent the summer of 1860 in Paris and an interesting conversation with Rossini is recorded in Moscheles' biography. The conversation, on musical matters in general, led to the growing tendency of the public to esteem noise and power in place of refinement and delicacy. He said to Moscheles, referring to many players, "They not only thump the piano, but the armchair and even the floor." Rossini spoke of the qualities of different instruments and then said that the guitarist Sor, and the mandolin player Vimercati, proved the possibility of obtaining great artistic results with slender means. "I (Moscheles) happened to have heard both these artists and could quite endorse his views. Rossini told me, that arriving late one evening at a small Italian town, he had already retired to rest when the mandolinist Vimercati (*quod vide*) the resident capellmeister, sent him an invitation to be present at a performance of one of his operas. In those days he was not yet as hard-hearted as he is now, when he persistently refuses to be present at a performance of his works; Rossini not only went to the theatre, but played the double-bass as substitute for the right man who was not forthcoming." In his diary Moscheles records: "We saw at Sir Walter Scott's eldest daughter's, Thomas Moore, the poet, a lively, sparkling Irishman, who, on the strength of his passion for music, immediately made acquaintance with me. He sang his own poems adapted to certain Irish melodies, harmonised and accompanied by himself on the guitar." Moscheles numbered among his most intimate friends, many celebrated guitarists, and the interest displayed in this instrument and its players was considerable. His published compositions for guitar are *Grand Duo Concertante for guitar and piano,* Op. 20, Artaria, Vienna; *The farewell of the Troubadours,* romance for voices with guitar, violin, piano and 'cello, issued by Diabelli, Vienna, and an arrangement of Hummel's Op. 53, *Duo for guitar and piano, for harp and piano.* His memoirs were published by his wife in two volumes in 1872 and fragments from his autobiography by his son in 1899.

Mosel, Ignaz, Franz (Edler von), born April 2, 1772, at Vienna, died there April 8, 1844, was Court Secretary, director of two Court Theatres and in 1829 custodian of the Court Library. He was a cultured musician and dramatic author who loaned his residence, The Melkerhof, in 1816 for the first concert of the Vienna Philharmonic Society. It was here that he made the acquaintance of Schubert who afterwards dedicated to him Op. 3. Mosel contributed variations to *Vaterlandischer Kunstler.* He also introduced Handel's music to Vienna and wrote additional accompaniments to the same. He edited a biography of Salieri and, like Schubert, was honorary member of the Styrian Musical Society. He was a torchbearer at Beethoven's funeral. Spohr mentions him in his autobiography and says that he was the composer of a lyric tragedy entitled *Salem.* His compositions include operas, overtures, church music and songs with guitar. Eitner and Whistling both record these songs which were issued by Diabelli & Co., Vienna, and Steiner & Co., Vienna. Memoirs of his life by Batka were published in 1911.

Mounsey, Elizabeth, born in London, October 8, 1819, and died there October 3, 1905, was one of two sisters, known in the musical world who were associated with Mendelssohn during his visits to London. Elizabeth, the younger, displayed unusual musical ability at a tender age. She studied the guitar under Pelzer and also the organ, and when fourteen was organist of St. Peter's, Cornhill, London, in 1834, retaining this position until 1882. The organ of this church, a fine instrument by Hill, was one on which Mendelssohn frequently played when visiting London. When quite a child, Miss Mounsey studied the guitar and appeared as a public performer in London during 1833, later she gave much time to the advanced technique of the instrument and her appearances as soloist elicited the warmest praise; in 1842 she was elected a member of the Royal Philharmonic Society. During his sixth visit, Mendelssohn conducted the Birmingham Music Festival and when he returned to London, September 30, 1839, he gave a recital, assisted by Miss Mounsey, at St. Peter's, and at the conclusion wrote several bars of music, a souvenir to this lady; this interesting manuscript now adorns the vestry of the church. Miss Mounsey was a contemporary of the guitar virtuoso Regondi, and on his advice she made a study of the English concertina for which instrument she wrote several compositions published by Wheatstone, London. Grove states that she has published many works for the guitar, organ and piano. Two of her solos for the guitar appeared in The Giulianiad, a music periodical devoted to the interests of the guitar and edited by the guitarist, Ferdinand Pelzer.

Mozart, Wolfgang Amadeus, born at Salzburg, January 27, 1756, died in Vienna, December 5, 1791, an immortal genius who has composed for the mandolin. His father, Leopold—an excellent violinist, who held an important musical position in Salzburg—was the author of a celebrated method for the violin, which, published in several languages, passed many editions. For a considerable period this was the only method for the violin, and it gives ample evidence that the author was a man of culture, far above the average. He immediately discerned the unusual musical gifts of his two children, Wolfgang and

Maria Anna, and devoted himself unreservedly to their musical education. Such rapid strides did the children make that he travelled with them as infant prodigies, when they performed before most of the European sovereigns. During 1770 they appeared in Italy, and for the next three years practically lived in that country. They travelled

Come, dearest mandolin, come.

SONG WITH MANDOLIN ACCOMPANIMENT
COMPOSED BY MOZART IN 1780.

"Come, dearest mandolin, come,
Thou shalt my only solace be,
Thy silver strings my soul will thrill
With joy and love and ecstasy."

[Zither, or Cither, mentioned in the text of the song, is the old German poetical name for mandolin, the strings of which were tuned in pairs and vibrated by a plectrum. It bears no resemblance whatever to the modern Zither.]

Contentment

SONG WITH MANDOLIN ACCOMPANIMENT
COMPOSED BY MOZART.
POETRY BY JOH. MARTIN MILLER.

as far south as Naples, and it was doubtless the periods of residence in this country that made him so familiar with the mandolin. When he was twenty-one, Mozart, with his mother, passed through Germany on their way to Paris. She had been in indifferent health, and while in the city became seriously ill, dying in her son's arms July 3, 1778, so the following September, with a heavy heart he left Paris for Salzburg, his home, mourning the loss of his mother, disappointed in his first love affair, and with all his cherished hopes frustrated he arrived in Salzburg, and during the years 1779-80, wrote much, and among the varied and

Deh vieni alla finestra.

(Come to the window, dearest).

SERENADE WITH MANDOLIN ACCOMPANIMENT FROM
" DON GIOVANNI."
OPERA COMPOSED BY MOZART IN 1787.

numerous compositions of this date is the song with mandolin accompaniment, *Come, dearest mandolin, come.* This was composed in 1780 and the poetry, viewed in the light of the sad circumstances of this period, convey a deeper and more intense meaning. It is not known when the song with mandolin accompaniment entitled *Contentment,* was composed, presumably at a later date when living in Prague, for the year following the writing of *Come, dearest mandolin, come,* he removed to Vienna, where his destiny was accomplished. After the success of his opera *Figaro,* in Vienna, he received an invitation from

Prague, with the commission to write an opera, so in September, 1787, Mozart and his wife arrived and took lodgings in the Kohlmarkt, the music publishing quarter. During their abode in Prague, the opera conductor Kucharz, a mandolin virtuoso, became an intimate friend of the Mozarts and the association of these two musicians is of interest to students of the mandolin and its literature. Mozart's favourite resort was the vineyard of Duschek at Koschirz in the suburbs of the city, and to this day are shown his room and the stone table at which he was accustomed to sit working at his score, often in the midst of skittle playing and conversation. The villa, now named "Bertramka," is on a slight eminence in the grounds, and a bust of Mozart by Seidan was unveiled by the owner of the property, June 3, 1876, and at the same time a hitherto unpublished letter of Mozart, dated from Prague, October 15, 1787, was printed. Mozart was most anxious concerning his new opera, although, as he assured his friend Kucharz, he had spared neither pains nor labour to produce something really good for Prague. On the evening before representation, the overture was still wanting and he worked at it far into the night, while his wife kept him supplied with punch and told him fairy stories to keep him awake! Sleep, however, overcame him and he was compelled to rest for a few hours; but at seven in the morning it was completed, the copyist received the score, and it was played at sight in the evening, and the first performance of *Don Giovanni* took place October 29, 1787. Upon the appearance of Mozart in the orchestra he was greeted with enthusiastic applause and a triple flourish of trumpets. The opera was received from beginning to end with rapturous marks of approval. Perhaps the most sublime of all operas, this has one manifest superiority; all the moods and situations are essentially musical, for there is scarcely a feeling known to humanity which is not expressed in some of the situations or characters. In the score Mozart writes a mandolin accompaniment for the entrancing serenade, *Deh vieni* (Come to the window dearest), a passionate love song sung by Don Giovanni, which breathes the very soul of tenderness, with its obbligato of delicate, staccato arpeggios for the mandolin, accompanied by the pianissimo, pizzicato of the strings of the orchestra. At its first performance in Prague, Mozart conducted and the opera conductor Kucharz, played the mandolin under the composer's direction. Berlioz, in his Treatise on Instrumentation, deplores the fact that the mandolin is not used more frequently in the orchestra, and says, "even at the opera (the last place in the world where such liberties should be taken) they venture to play the mandolin part of *Don Giovanni,* pizzicato on the violins, or on guitars. The quality of these instruments has not the keen delicacy of that for which they are substituted, and Mozart quite well knew what he was about in choosing the mandolin for accompanying the amorous lay of his hero." Grove writes, "The pizzicato of the violins is of a different colour of tone and offers but a poor substitute." Mozart had previously composed the canzonets with mandolin accompaniment; he was thoroughly aware of the charming arpeggios and staccato effects wherein the instrument excels, and this is manifested in all he has written for the mandolin, for they bear the same style and character. It is interesting to notice that Mozart's pupil, Hummel, also composed for the instrument. It has been asserted that the accompaniment to *Deh Vieni,* was written for the Spanish mandolin, and that this was the instrument Mozart had in view when writing his score, for the plot of the opera is laid in Spain, and the characters are Spanish. It is very doubtful whether Mozart understood the Spanish mandolin or bandurria, which is very rarely seen or played outside Spain ; he had lived for some years in Italy, the home of the mandolin, where it was in common use for serenades and would consequently be noticed. It is significant too, that the orchestral conductor, Kucharz was a mandolinist and Hummel, who was Mozart's pupil, composed a *Concerto for mandolin and orchestra* for the Italian virtuoso, Bortolazzi. The inclusion of the instrument in the score of this, the chef d'oeuvre of operas, and by an immortal genius —if it were the only such instance on record—is sufficient justification for its adoption as an integral member of the orchestra. Mozart died of malignant typhoid fever in Vienna, at the premature age of thirty-five and was buried the following day in a pauper's grave outside the city.

Munier, Carlo, born at Naples, the home of the mandolin, July 15, 1859, died in Florence, February 10, 1911. Munier stands in the front rank of composers, performers and writers for the mandolin, an inspired artist who towers among the mightiest, and who is justly recognised wherever the instrument is played or known. It would seem fate had predestined him to uplift the mandolin and had decreed and prepared his advent for several previous generations. Munier inherited his profound love of the mandolin from his ancestors, who were engaged in its construction and improvement for more than a century, and, figuratively speaking, he was born with a mandolin in his hands. He was grand nephew of the celebrated Pasquale Vinaccia of Naples, the perfector of the modern Italian mandolin. The name of Vinaccia is among the most celebrated of stringed instrument makers, for it was the inventive genius of this member of the family—born July 20, 1806, in Naples, and died there in 1882—that gave the instrument its steel strings and consequently machine head ; who extended the compass of its fingerboard and enlarged and improved the tonal capabilities and qualities of the instrument. Previous to this date, the mandolin was of smaller dimensions, its sound hole was circular, like that of the guitar, the bridge was a short narrow strip of ivory, and the body was rather smaller, being composed of from fifteen to twenty narrow fluted ribs. Its strings were of gut, similar to those of the violin ; they were tuned in pairs with pegs of ebony or ivory, and the compass of the instrument was very limited, the fingerboard having usually but twelve frets. The instruments of this period were decorated elaborately, their necks were veneered with tortoiseshell inlaid with strips of ivory, and a triangular design in tortoiseshell and pearl was inlaid in the table between the bridge and tailpins. The mandolin of today is the legacy of Pasquale Vinaccia, whose portrait is reproduced, and Munier was the grand nephew of the celebrated mandolin makers, the brothers Gennaro and Achille Vinaccia, honoured by the Royal appointment of mandolin makers to the Court of Italy. If heredity is to be considered, there is no surprise that Munier devoted his entire life to the uplifting and advancement of the mandolin, for it was an innate love of the instrument that led and shaped his whole career. His relatives were practical and theoretical artists on the instrument, and everything in his childhood's environment appertained to the mandolin—its manufacture, its performers, its study—and when with these circumstances we combine the rare natural musical genius of the man, it is easily understood how he became universally recognised the authority on the instrument. Young Munier commenced the serious study of the mandolin in his native city with Carmine de Laurentiis, a mandolinist and guitarist of good repute, and the author of a *Method for the mandolin,* which is founded upon an excellent system and which contains progressive studies most admirable in their conception (see Laurentiis). Carlo Munier made rapid progress under this master and after a time commenced the study of the guitar also with him and thus laid the foundation of a correct system of mechanism, and it was left to Munier's genius to strike out original paths in his advancement. At the age of fifteen he entered the Naples Conservatoire of Music, studying the piano under Galiero and Cesi, both of whom enjoyed enviable reputations, and with D'Arienzo he studied harmony and counterpoint. He was nineteen when he completed his studies at the Conservatoire of S'Pietro d'Maiella, having succeeded in obtaining the first prize for composition, and the second for harmony. During this period he appeared in many concerts in Naples and his first compositions, arrangements of '*La Traviata*' and '*Les Puritani*' *for two mandolins, mandola and piano* were published. These were the first compositions published for this combination of instruments, the second was dedicated to Her Majesty the Queen of Italy, who was an enthusiastic mandolinist in 1881. When twenty-two, Munier removed to Florence where he lived the greater part of his life, actively engaged as a composer and professor of the mandolin and guitar, in the most select musical institutions of Florence. He organised in 1890 the first plectrum quartet, with Luigi Bianchi and Guido Bizzari, first and second mandolins; Riccardo Matini, mandola, and himself, lute and director; this quartet, each member a talented composer and artist on his respective instrument, gave many performances throughout Italy, were received with acclamation, and did much to popularise this combination of instruments. In 1892 they obtained the first prize in the International Music Contests of Genoa, under the presidency of Sivori, the violinist, and Munier was awarded the gold medal as mandolinist and composer. From 1890 until his death, Munier was engaged with his quartet in concert work and he has left compositions of sterling merit written for this combination of instruments. He was a member of the Royal Circolo Mandolinisti

Regina Margherita in Florence, under the direction of the esteemed and venerable mandolinist Bertucci ; for a period Munier officiated as conductor of this royal mandolin society. On June 30, 1902, at a concert by this royal orchestra, Munier's quartet performed several of his compositions before a select audience of musicians and were accorded an ovation. He was ever striving for the advancement of the mandolin and on October 6, 1909, performed by royal command in the historic castle of Sommariva-Perno. Munier's solos were his *Prelude in D major* and his *First Mazurka de Concert*. Immediately after the recital, His Majesty Victor Emmanuel III, rose to greet him, shook him by the hand most cordially, warmly congratulated him upon his marvellous execution and dilated on the beautiful effects of which the mandolin was capable. Munier appeared frequently as mandolin virtuoso in his native land ; but did not extend his recitals to foreign lands. He contributed literary articles to the music journals, and was honoured many times by appointment as adjudicator in musical contests, both in Italy and other European countries. Held in the highest esteem by musicians of Florence, at his request, the Royal Conservatoire of Music generously placed their concert hall at the disposal of the Mandolin Band of Cremona for a recital to demonstrate the possibilities of the instruments. This concert, given in 1910 in the presence of musicians of repute, was an artistic success. In the spring of 1911 he made a visit to Antwerp and on his homeward journey spent a few days in Marseilles in the company of his compatriot the mandolinist Fantauzzi. Two months previously they were officiating as adjudicators in the Mandolin contests held in Cremona, and recalled with gratification the advancement made in the instrument and its music. Munier spoke of his plans for the future, of organising an imposing concert and recital in Florence ; but, *homo proponit, Deus disponit,* in a very few weeks he was suddenly called to the sphere from whence none return, for after a short illness in Florence, he died February 10, 1911, at the age of fifty-two. The following memoir is from an Italian music journal : "It is with profound regret that we record the death of the greatest mandolin artist and composer of our time, the renowned Carlo Munier. The mandolin world will miss him greatly and it can ill afford to lose its most sincere, devoted, and illustrious champion. Cut off in the prime of life, in the midst of his noble and successful work, we silently mourn our loss. Conscientiously and persistently he devoted himself to the serious and classic side of the welfare of the mandolin, and as a true artist, trickery in playing or composition was to him abomination, an enemy to the advancement of the mandolin. He has gone—but his work will live. His many compositions, known and admired by mandolinists throughout the world form a colossal monument that cannot perish ; they will delight future generations and bear testimony to his genius and noble inspirations. As I write I see before me his last letters, full of hope for the future concerning the success of the mandolin—his life's ambition, nay, his very life itself. Two of his latest overtures for mandolin band, I see also, works that emanate from serious musicians only. He leaves a widow, Armida, and two daughters, Elivra and Louise, with the whole world of mandolin players to mourn their loss." His world-wide admirers subscribed, through the medium of a Milanese music journal, and a bronze tablet suitably inscribed was erected to his memory. Munier, a man of education, attainment, and a versatile linguist, wrote concerning his early study of the mandolin: "At the beginning I confess I did not think the mandolin capable of such advancement, and I excluded from my repertoire a number of pieces that I believed impossible of execution ; but I thought, studied, and worked, then wrote my method, my studies, solos, duos, caprices, trios, quartets, etc., and I became so proficient that I could then execute what I had previously considered impossible. They became clear, easy of execution, and in fact trifling as compared with other difficulties." Munier was a prolific composer—he had published considerably over three hundred and fifty works previous to his death—many remained unpublished. With few exceptions, such as a *Trio for mandolin, violoncello and piano,* and several songs, his compositions are for the mandolin or guitar. His *Quartets for Two mandolins, mandola and lute,* written in the orthodox style of four movements, were the first of the kind published, they are Op. 76, 123 and 203. Op. 76, dedicated to Count Gabardi, was given its première with the composer as first mandolinist, in the Sala Philharmonica, Florence and published in 1903 by Forlivesi of that city. The most classic is the *Quartet in G,* the quasi adagio and minuetto are inspirations, and its fugue ingeniously worked out. *Lo Scioglidita*—four volumes of progressive studies and a volume of *Twenty studies* are among the most advanced exercises for the instrument, and of the same degree of excellence are the *Duos for two mandolins* of which there are several volumes, published by Carisch & Janichen, Milan and Maurri, Florence. Munier compiled an *Elementary Method for the Guitar,* Op. 284, published by Lapini, Florence. and *Duos for two guitars ;* all his compositions denote the cultured musician and abound with graceful melody, characteristic of the Italian school. In his *Love Song,* Op. 275, dedicated to Samuel Adelstein of San Francisco, Munier opened new possibilities and effects for the mandolin as an unaccompanied solo instrument. He was the author of a *Method for the Mandolin,* Op. 197, issued in 1909 in two volumes and numerous other studies, exercises and duos for two mandolins and a *School for Guitar,* Op. 137, in four books, published by Ricordi, Milan.

Mussini, Noel Niccolo, born Bergamo, Italy 1765, died Florence, 1837, was a virtuoso on the guitar and violin, a composer and dramatic singer of repute. He visited London in 1792 appearing with marked success as vocalist with guitar accompaniment and also as guitar soloist. Ten years later he was heard of in Cassel, in a like capacity, and was appointed Court Capellmeister, music director, and chamber musician to the dowager queen, in Berlin. In 1802 his daughter Giuliana married the celebrated musician Sarti, who died the same year in Berlin.

Nicolo Paganini

House in which Paganini died

Paganini's Guitar and Mandolin

Ferdinand Pelzer

(Mme. Sidney Pratten)
Catherina Josepha Pelzer

NAUMANN, Johann Gottlieb, born April 17, 1741 at Blasewitz, near Dresden and died October 23, 1801, in Dresden was a well-known composer in his day. The son of peasants, he studied music alone until becoming acquainted with a Swedish musician, Weestroem, who took the youth on a professional tour through Italy, where he was a pupil of Tartini. He lived for about five years in Padua, Naples, and Venice and when he returned to Dresden was Capellmeister to the Elector. Naumann studied the guitar in Italy and took home to Dresden several Italian guitars. The Duchess Amelia of Weimar, an ardent admirer of the guitar, commissioned the violin maker, Jacob Augustus Otto to make copies of her Italian guitars brought home by Naumann. Otto in his Treatise on the Structure and Preservation of the Violin, says: "The late Duchess Amelia of Weimar having introduced the guitar into Weimar in 1788, I was immediately obliged to make copies of this instrument for several of the nobility; and these soon becoming known in Leipzig, Dresden and Berlin, so great a demand arose for them, that, for the space of sixteen years I had more orders than I could execute. I must here take the opportunity to observe that originally the guitar had only five strings. The late Herr Naumann, capellmeister at Dresden, ordered the first guitar with the sixth or low E string, which I at once made for him. Since that time the instrument has always been made with six strings, for which improvement its admirers have to thank Herr Naumann. During the last ten years a great number of instrument makers, as well as joiners, have commenced making guitars; so that, since that time I have entirely relinquished the business, and now turn over any orders which I receive to my sons at Jena and Halle, who are much occupied in that way. The use of covered strings for the D and G is a small improvement of my own. In the guitar as brought from Naples, a thick violin string was used as only the A was covered." Naumann was a composer of church music, some of which is still in use. Hummel, also a guitarist, for a time studied with him. Further particulars are recorded under Körner. Naumann's memoirs were published in 1803 by Meissner and a second edition appeared in 1824.

Nava, Antonio Maria, born at Milan in 1775 and died there in 1828 was a vocalist and guitarist who resided principally in his native city and made a concert tour of Europe. He was highly esteemed in Milan and the cities of northern Italy from 1800-12 after which he visited Paris, then London, where he remained for a period, esteemed as a teacher of singing, and published several compositions for his instrument. He was the author of a *Method for the Guitar,* issued by Ricordi, Milan, in 1812. This was one of the most popular instruction books issued in Italy; it passed many editions, the last revised and augmented by Ponzio, who is described as "Maestro di Chitarra al R. Circolo Mandolinisti Margherita, Florence." Another edition was revised by F. Sacchi, described on the title page as "Instructor by special appointment to T.R.H. the Princesses Victoria and Maud of Wales."

This edition in two parts, with English text, was also issued by Ricordi. Nava's principal compositions are Op. 25, 41, 44, 51, 53 and 71, *Variations or Sonatines for guitar solo ;* Op. 52, *Duo for two guitars ;* Op. 54. *Variations for guitar and violin,* issued by Breitkopf and Härtel, Leipzig ; Op. 9, 26, 40, 58, 61, 63 and 69 *Duos for violin or flute and guitar,* Ricordi, Milan ; Op. 67, *Trio for flute, violin and guitar,* and more than seventy compositions for guitar solo, trios for flute, violin and guitar ; Duos for two guitars without opus numbers, and several volumes of songs with guitar, all of which were published by Ricordi, Milan. While living in London, he wrote several *Divertissements for guitar and flute,* published by Francis, London, and Eitner mentions another method entitled, *Complete Method for Guitar or Lyre.* His son Gaetano, born in Milan, May 16, 1802, and died there March 31, 1875, was taught by his father and then entered Milan Conservatoire. He became a renowned teacher of the vocal art, wrote a little for the guitar, was a professor in Milan Conservatoire in 1837 and teacher of the English vocalist Charles Santley.

Antonio Nava

Neuhauser, Leopold, born at Innsbruck, Tyrol, and living in Vienna at the commencement of the nineteenth century, a teacher of the guitar and mandolin, and recognised virtuoso of the first rank. His various compositions were instrumental and he was the author of a method for the guitar, published by Eder, Vienna, under the title of *The rudiments of the guitar, with many pleasing pieces.* Op. 2, *Six Variations for guitar and violin or clarinet,* and *Six Waltzes for two guitars*, published by Simrock, Bonn ; *Six variations for guitar and violin, or clarinet,* published in 1801 ; and several collections of *German songs with guitar.* Neuhauser left many unpublished manuscripts for the mandolin and guitar of which No. 2, of a series of instrumental nocturnes was composed for *Mandolin, violin, alto, two horns and violoncello.*

Neuland, Wilhelm, a German musician who lived during the first half of the nineteenth century, an excellent guitarist, pianist, organist and composer. He came to London about the year 1832, where he was highly esteemed as a teacher of the guitar, and after living here some time returned to his native land. He visited Paris where he taught the guitar and published many compositions for it, also church music and piano solos. From Paris he made another tour of his native land and then returned to London where he was living in 1840. His early compositions were published in England, and his later works appeared in Germany and France. The Giulianiad, a music journal devoted to the interests of the guitar, published in London, gives a very eulogistic report of the compositions of Neuland in its number for April, 1833. It also draws particular attention to the first eight bars of his Op. 5,

Fantasia for guitar solo, and states: "It is true that he (Neuland) has not been long in this country, but his genius is already acknowledged on every hand." Neuland was a contemporary of Regondi and Pelzer, the latter editor of The Giulianiad. This Op. 5 was published by Johanning, London; Op. 4, *Two albums of guitar solos;* Op. 6, *Six divertissements for two guitars,* Chappell, London; Op. 7, *Introduction and variations,* dedicated to his friend Ferdinand Pelzer, published by Duff, London; Op. 8, *Andantino and Rondo;* Op. 16, *Introduction and variations for guitar solo,* composed for and dedicated to Giulio Regondi, published by Schloss, Cologne; Op. 26, *Variations for two guitars or guitar and piano,* issued simultaneously by Chappell, London; Simrock, Bonn; and Richault, Paris; Op. 29, *Souvenir Germanique, for piano and guitar; Two volumes of divertissements for guitar solo and Eight duos for guitar and piano,* Simrock, Bonn; *Waltz for piano and guitar,* Petit, Paris; *Five favourite duos for guitar and piano,* Chappell, and many other guitar compositions, including operatic arrangements for flute, alto and guitar, which were published in England, France and Germany. *Two Grand Masses,* Op. 30 and 40, for four voices and chorus, with organ and full orchestral accompaniment; much vocal, church music and piano solos and duos were issued by Leduc, Paris; Simrock, Bonn, and Schott, Mayence.

Neuling, a German musician and mandolinist who lived in Vienna during the commencement of the nineteenth century. There appeared under his name a *Sonata for mandolin and piano in G,* published by Haslinger, Vienna, and Whistling also mentions compositions by this musician.

Niedzielski, Joseph, a Polish musician living during the commencement of the nineteenth century and died in Warsaw in 1852. He was a talented guitarist and violinist, who for some years was first violinist in the National Opera, Warsaw. He was esteemed as a teacher of his instruments, and the author of a *Method for the guitar,* which is of little renown.

Nuske, J. A., a German musician and guitarist who visited England during the early part of the nineteenth century where he resided as a teacher of the guitar. He composed many short, simple pieces for the guitar, which enjoyed popularity, several appeared in the Giulianiad for the year 1833. Nuske compiled an *Easy Method for the Guitar,* containing twenty-seven airs arranged for guitar solo which was published by Robert Cocks & Co., London. The following are among his principal works: *Fantasia for guitar solo,* Chappell, London; *Three Waltzes for guitar,* published in 1827 by Vernon, London; *Fantasia for guitar,* Boosey, London; *Venetian waltz,* George & Manby, London; *Three favourite melodies for guitar and piano,* and *Five operatic arrangements for guitar and piano,* Cocks, London, and numerous songs with guitar which were issued by various London publishers.

OBERLEITNER, Andrew, a mandolin and guitar virtuoso born at Angern, Lower Austria, September 17, 1786. His father was administrator of the lordship of Angern, and when a child the son received instruction from a private tutor in singing and violin. In 1804, when eighteen, his parents, desirous that he should enter the medical profession, placed him in a school of Vienna for the specific study of surgery. Oberleitner had as yet displayed no particular interest in music, he had studied the violin and played it as an amateur. In Vienna, however, he became acquainted with several fellow students who spent their leisure in playing the mandolin and guitar and whose serenades were the delight and good fellowship of society. Oberleitner was captivated by these instruments and had not been resident in Vienna many weeks ere he became a student of the mandolin and guitar. To such an extent the fascination of these instruments influenced him, that he neglected his medical studies, and after two years' musical application, acquired a most remarkable degree of proficiency, and won a reputation in Vienna as mandolin and guitar virtuoso. He had studied harmony and composition during the same period, and published about forty works for the guitar and others for the mandolin. These compositions were issued by various Viennese publishers and consisted of trios, quartets, variations, etc., for guitars and mandolins. On being appointed inspector of silver in the royal palace, his public appearance as a musician ceased, and his duties in this position were so multifarious that he also neglected composition ; but he continued the practical branch of his art by private recitals among friends. The following of his compositions were published by Artaria, Vienna. Op. 1, *Twelve Austrian Waltzes for guitar ;* Op. 4, *Twelve Allemandes of Vienna ;* Op. 5, *Twelve Waltzes of Salzburg ;* Op. 11, *Six Studies for two guitars ;* Op. 17, *Styrian dances for guitar ;* Op. 27, *Variations for guitar* and other similar works without opus numbers.

Obregon, Alberto, born at Santander, Castile, Spain, August 7, 1872, and died in London, 1922. His early education in France was continued in Dumfries, Scotland, where he played the euphonium in the school band. After the completion of his studies he returned to his home in Spain, entered his father's business and commenced to play the guitar for amusement and notwithstanding his father's protest that it was a waste of time, became enamoured by the instrument ; but with no intent of making music a profession. His elder brother was established at a branch of the family business in Australia and Alberto was sent to assist him. Having to embark from Barcelona he hurriedly purchased a guitar which he took on the voyage when his musical services were popular and in constant demand. On arrival in Melbourne he was solicited to teach the guitar and had a few pupils ; but when the crisis developed he quitted Australia for S. Africa. Landing at Durban he proceeded to Cape Town, where, under the immediate patronage of the Spanish and French consuls, he gave successful guitar recitals and then removed to Johannesburg where he lived as a teacher for three years.

Writing to a London music journal Obregon said: "When I returned to Spain after my travels in Australia and Africa I was staying in Barcelona and saw announced a guitar recital, the performer being Tarrega. Of course I was there punctually, and needless to say was astounded when I heard him play for I then discovered my shortcomings. Nevertheless it served me as a stimulus to try to follow in the footsteps of such a master and after ascertaining his address, the first thing I did the following day was to present myself at his house to ask him to give me lessons. At first he refused, saying he very seldom taught, but seeing my disappointment asked me to play to him. I played one of my own compositions and he then decided to become my master." Obregon came to London from Johannesburg, married an English lady and made his permanent abode in London. He was an esteemed performer and teacher, the conductor of a mandolin and guitar band and was commanded to perform on several occasions before their Majesties King Edward and Queen Alexandra, both of whom evinced sincere interest in the artist and his instrument. He composed a number of light pieces for the guitar, one of which *A ma mie* he dedicated to his teacher Tarrega. His works, about thirty, were published in London by Schott, Dallas, and Turner.

Ortner, Jacob, contemporary, born at Buchsenhausen, near Innsbruck, June 11, 1879, and living in Vienna; a retired professor, but still active in the interest of the guitar. Alois Gotz was his first music instructor on the guitar, and in 1919 he became a student in the Vienna State Academy of Music. He was appointed professor of the guitar in the same institution in 1924 and three years later was the founder and editor of the Austrian Guitar Review, a monthly journal devoted to the guitar. Haslinger, Vienna, issued seven volumes of his guitar compositions in 1925 under the title *Academic Edition.* His daughter, Hermine, is known as a vocalist with her guitar.

Oyanguren, Julio Martinez, contemporary, born July 3, 1905, at Duranzo, Uruguay, where he had instruction on the piano. In 1919 he removed to Montevideo and commenced the study of the guitar under Marichal. He served as lieutenant in the U.S. navy, after which he toured S. America professionally for five years and eventually made his domicile in U.S.A. During 1936-40 he gave regular Sunday broadcasts, many recitals in New York and other important cities. He played to President F. D. Roosevelt in the White House, who, delighted by his performance presented him with his autographed photo. The New York Post reporting his recitals said: "There are in the world very few virtuosi who can play the guitar as though it were a musical instrument, and a distinguished member of that group is Oyanguren." One of his most popular and original compositions, *Cancion del Alba,* was broadcast with full orchestral accompaniment. During the spring of 1941 he left New York for an extended tour of South America, commencing in his native land Uruguay. Oyanguren composes for the guitar in a refined, masterly manner, for although his works display no great difficulty of execution, he chooses his positions on the fingerboard to produce the most effective beauty of tone and does not sacrifice it for mere ease of execution. About twenty of his original compositions and transcriptions are published by Tatay & Co., New York, and the Victor Company issued his recordings.

PACE, Bernardo de, contemporary, born in 1886 at San Ferdinando di Puglia, Italy, and taken to Naples when two months of age. At five he played the mandolin and attracted the attention of Della Rosa, a well-known violinist of Naples who gave the boy free instruction on the violin, until he became aware that more time was being given to the mandolin than the violin. At the age of thirteen Pace won an International Mandolin competition, whereupon he toured as virtuoso, first in Italy then continued to Paris, Berlin and St. Petersburg. His first visit to England was when fourteen, being mandolinist with the Blackpool Winter Gardens' Orchestra where he remained three years. He then toured with his brother for seven years the Moss and Stoll Theatres in solos and duos with guitar. At the age of seventeen he played before the Sultan of Turkey and was engaged at the Court for seven months. Later he performed before the Kaiser, on board the Royal yacht and also Czar Nicholas of Russia. Pace was mandolin soloist with the symphony orchestra of ninety performers, under the conductor, Sir Landon Ronald. He is living in Brooklyn, U.S.A., the official mandolinist of the Metropolitan Opera, touring in vaudeville during off-seasons. Recordings of his mandolin accompaniments to songs of the famous Caruso were issued in U.S.A.

Padovetz, Johann, born at Warasdin, Hungary, and died in Vienna, November 5, 1873, was a teacher and composer for the guitar, held in repute, and resident in Vienna from 1829-38. For a period he lived in Prague and it was in these cities that the majority of his compositions were published. He played the guitar with four extra bass strings, the Russian style tuned A, B, C, D, the additional strings being on the left of the fingerboard and used only as open basses ; for this tuning he compiled a method. Little is known concerning his career. His Op. 5, *Introduction and Variations for guitar,* is dedicated to the more renowned musician Ignaz Kalliwoda, published by Diabelli, Vienna ; Op. 17, *Fantasia for guitar ;* Op. 18, *First Polonaise for two guitars,* dedicated to the musician Joseph Benedict, published by Richault, Paris ; Op. 21, *Fantasia on 'Robert the Devil,' solo guitar,* Richault, Paris ; Op. 51 and 52 *Operatic arrangements* and Op. 53, *Rondoletto in A,* Hoffman, Prague ; *Variations* Op. 2, 19, 25 and 26 ; *Operatic melodies,* Op. 20, 21, 22, 23 ; *Duos for two guitars,* Op. 5, 10, 18, 62 were published by Diabelli, Vienna.

Paganini, Nicolo, born at Genoa, Italy, October 27, 1782, and died in Nice, May 27, 1840. A commemorative tablet is affixed to the house of his birth in the Passo di Gatta Mora and another on the house in which he died in Nice with the inscription:

> "Nicolo Paganini died in this house on May 27, 1840.
> His magic notes still vibrate in the soft breeze of Nice."

The excitement produced throughout Europe by Paganini's marvellous performances on the violin remains unparalleled in musical history; yet although there exists a whole realm of literature on this artist, his mastery over the guitar and his great fondness for this instrument have received but meagre and scanty recognition. Little prominence has been given to his association with the mandolin and guitar, his familiarity and skill on these instruments, and the powerful influence his practical knowledge of them exerted over his violin playing, forming that individuality and peculiarity of style which placed him far in advance of all other violin virtuosi.

Paganini's parents were of very humble origin; but not quite so low as has been pretended in some suppositions that have been associated with the history of their marvellous son. His father, Antonio, it is recorded, was at one time a mercantile clerk, who owned a small store in close proximity to the harbour, and, although uneducated, was an amateur musician much devoted to the art. He was a skilful performer on the mandolin and exceedingly fond of the instrument, giving all his leisure to playing it, and he imparted his knowledge to his son. As he was musical, he desired his son to possess the same gift, and consequently perceived the first early indications in the infant. Riemann says that he began to instruct his son on the mandolin at a very tender age, for he states: "When he (Antonio) perceived his son's musical talent, he at first instructed him personally in the art of playing the mandolin and then handed him over to more skilful teachers."

It is important to notice that Paganini's early life was associated with the mandolin; it was the only instrument in the home and he was quite a child when he had obtained a practical knowledge of it. According to some authorities the musical discipline adopted by his parent appears to have been a shameful perversion. Antonio Paganini has been described as a man of extraordinarily avaricious character, inhuman and brutal, possessing but one redeeming feature—a love of music—and as soon as his son was able to hold a mandolin, he placed one in his hands and compelled him to practise from morning till night. A few months later the child was placed under Servetto for lessons on the violin, and for six months he also studied the instrument under Costa; one of the conditions imposed in accepting him as a pupil was that he should perform a new concerto each week, in church. Costa, the foremost violinist in Genoa, was maestro di cappella of the cathedral. Under his tuition young Paganini made rapid progress, and when he was but eight he performed three times weekly in the churches and also at various private musicales, and at this age, too, composed his first violin sonata, which unfortunately is lost. About 1795, when the boy was in his thirteenth year, his father took him to Parma and placed him under Alessandro Rolla, a famous violin virtuoso and skilful guitarist. For several months Paganini received instruction from Rolla, and it is difficult to explain why in later years he was unwilling to acknowledge this fact. Rolla was a good guitarist who published several instrumental compositions in combination with the guitar, and he frequently accompanied his young pupil on this instrument, a circumstance which would bring it prominently and favourably to his notice and be a strong recommendation for its study. It is quite probable that Paganini received from Rolla some instruction on the guitar in addition to the violin, for at a later period, when teaching, Paganini accompanied his own pupil Sivori on the guitar, and even composed duos for violin and guitar for this purpose. Paganini attended the musical festival of Lucca in November, 1798, under the protection of an elder brother ; up to this time he appears to have been wholly under the control of his father, who was exceedingly harsh, and this first experience of liberty resulted in his fleeing from home. Although only fifteen, he now led a wild, dissipated life in which gambling formed a prominent part ; but the year 1801 saw a complete change. Hitherto when touring Italy, he had been flattered to intoxication by his rapid successes and the unbounded enthusiasm which greeted his many public performances. Yet, notwithstanding his successful career as violinist, he now put aside entirely the instrument which had been the means of bringing him such fame, and for three years gave himself solely to the study of the guitar. During this period he was living at the chateau of a lady of rank, and the guitar was her favourite instrument.

Paganini gave himself up to the study of the guitar as eagerly and with the same amount of concentration as he had previously to the violin, and the mastery of the new instrument was as thorough and rapid as that of the former ; his performances at this period, 1801-4, were as celebrated as those of the guitar virtuoso Regondi.

Schilling says of him: "The celebrated Nicolo Paganini is such a great master on the guitar that even Lipinski (a famous Polish violin virtuoso, who had ventured to seek a public contest with Paganini at Placentia in 1818) could barely decide whether he was greater on the violin or guitar." Dubourg, in his notice of Paganini, says of this period of his life: "To those early days belongs also the fact of Paganini's transient passion for the guitar, or rather for a certain fair Tuscan lady, who incited him to the study of that feebler instrument, of which she was herself a votary. Applying his acute powers to the extension of its resources, he soon made the guitar an object of astonishment to his fair friend ; nor did he resume in earnest that peculiar symbol of his greatness, the violin, till after a lapse of nearly three years."

Riemann in his account of the artist says: "He played the guitar as an amateur, but with the skill of a virtuoso."

That Paganini's admiration of, and delight in the guitar, was no "transient passion" is proved in many ways, including the fact of his complete devotion to its sole study during the years mentioned. It certainly cannot be regarded a passing fancy for an artist of Paganini's attainments and genius to devote three whole years in the prime of a successful career to another instrument.

Paganini was intimate, and had performed in public, with the leading guitar virtuosi, and the guitar exercised an influence and fascination over his musical nature, as it has done in numerous other instances. During his whole career Paganini employed it as his accompanying instrument, with his pupils and musical friends, and the majority of his compositions published during his life, and most of his unpublished works, include a part for the guitar. His first compositions for this instrument were written between 1801 and 1804, his last in 1835, and it follows therefore that he gave his attention seriously and lastingly to the guitar. This was the instrument he fondled and caressed during those long periods of weakness when his strength was insufficient for him to resort to the more exacting position required by the violin ; and during the last year of his existence, when his malady had developed—when there was no hope of recovery and he was confined to his couch—it was the guitar which throbbed forth its plaintive harmonies under his reclining and lingering touch. In such a weakly condition it was the only musical instrument that he could muster sufficient strength to vibrate with effect. It is a significant fact, too, that with but one exception all his compositions that are authenticated and were published during his life contained parts for the guitar, the exception being Op. 1, *Twenty-four Caprices or Studies for Violin alone.* When an intimate friend enquired his reason for devoting so much attention to the guitar his reply was: "I love it for its harmony, it is my constant companion in all my travels."

Schottky, his friend and biographer, quotes Paganini: "I make use of it now and then to stimulate my fantasy for composition or to bring forth some harmony which I cannot do on the violin," and points out that the accompaniments of his concertos were always discovered on the guitar. Schottky also writes: "As I spent many a day near Paganini it chanced to be my pleasure to hear him improvise both on the violin and the guitar, which latter he likewise plays enchantingly."

Ferdinand Carulli, the guitar virtuoso, a contemporary of Paganini in Paris, says in his famous Guitar Method: "The fact may not be generally known that Paganini was a fine performer on the guitar and that he composed most of his airs on this instrument, arranging and amplifying them on the violin afterwards according to his fancy."

In 1805 Paganini again set out on his travels and accepted an engagement at Lucca, remaining there until 1808. The following years of his life were a complete series of brilliant triumphs. The author violinist, Dr. Phipson wrote: "Paganini had a natural gift for music, nearly as great as Shakespeare for blank verse ; he inherited it from his father, and perhaps from his mother. After it had been duly cultivated, it enabled him to astonish his contemporaries by his performances on the violin and guitar. When we remember that his father was a player on the mandolin, the latter accomplishment is less surprising. It was no doubt the twanging of his father's mandolin which originated the love of pizzicato passages so pronounced in his son's violin music and led to his proficiency as a guitar player."

There is no doubt but that Paganini's practical knowledge of the mandolin and guitar contributed in a large degree to the formation of that individuality of style for which his performances were so remarkable. "Most assuredly" said one Berlin music critic, "Paganini is a prodigy, and all that the most celebrated violinists have executed heretofore is mere child's play, compared with the inconceivable difficulties which he created in order to be the first to surmount them."

The same writer declared that Paganini executed an air quite sostenuto on one string, while at the same time a continued tremolo upon the next string was perfectly perceptible, as well as a lively pizzicato in guitar style upon the fourth string, thus producing upon one instrument a combination of violin, mandolin and guitar.

M. Guhr, an able violinist and intimate friend of Paganini, endeavoured to ascertain the chief differences of Paganini's playing over that of other celebrated violinists, and attempted to gain his information by interrogation ; but finding this method of no avail, he adopted a silent study or analysis of the means employed by the master. One of the chief points of difference enumerated in his volume on the subject is "his art of putting the violin into double employ, so as to make it combine with its own usual office the simultaneous effect of a mandolin, harp, or guitar, whereby you seem to hear two different performers."

Mr. Gardiner, of Leicester, attended one of Paganini's concerts in London, and the following is an extract from his report: "At the hazard of my ribs, I placed myself at the opera door, two hours and half before the concert began. Presently, the crowd of musicians and violinists filled the colonnade to suffocation, all anxious to get a front seat, because they had to pay for their places, Paganini not giving a single ticket away. The concert opened with Beethoven's Second Symphony, admirably performed by the Philharmonic Band, after which Lablache sang *Largo al factotum,* with much applause and was encored. A breathless silence then ensued, and every eye was watching the action of this extraordinary violinist ; and as he glided from the side scenes to the front of the stage an involuntary cheering broke from every part of the house, many rising from their seats to view the "spectre ;" during the thunder of this unprecedented cheering, his gaunt and extraordinary appearance, being more like that of a devotee about to suffer martyrdom, than one to delight you with his art. With the tip of his bow he set off the orchestra, in a grand military movement, with a force and vivacity as surprising as it was new. At the termination of this introduction he commenced with a soft dreamy note of celestial quality, and, with three or four whips of his bow elicited points of sound that mounted to the third heaven, and as bright as the stars. A scream of astonishment and delight burst from the audience at the novelty of this effect. Immediately an execution followed that was equally indescribable, in which were intermingled tones more than human, which seemed to be wrung from the deepest anguish of a broken heart. After this the audience were enraptured by a lively strain, in which you heard, commingled with the tones of the violin, those of the voice, with the pizzicato of the guitar, forming a compound of exquisite beauty."

Staccato runs, performed with the bow and concluding with a guitar note, were original with Paganini, and it is evident that his knowledge of the mandolin and guitar formed no unimportant part in his style of execution.

According to Pulver in Paganini and Toye in Rossini, Paganini was intimately associated with Rossini, in Rome, during the Carnival of February, 1822, when the two musicians dressed as blind street singers. Rossini wrote or improvised the music, and he and Paganini, disguised as women, played the accompaniments each on his guitar. Pulver asserts that Rossini composed a little ditty, the text of which he translates: "We are blind, And we were born so, We can live, By alms alone; Do not refuse the poor a gift, On this day of Carnival." They must have been an odd looking pair, for Paganini was very tall and cadaverous, while Rossini was very rotund. Their performances, which were given on Shrove Tuesday, both in public and private, were a huge success. L. Day in "Paganini" states that the two went to find Meyerbeer in his lodgings and the three of them took part in the Carnival, Meyerbeer passing the hat; onlookers remarking that these three beggars did not play badly.

Paganini was very closely associated with the guitar virtuoso Legnani, and they toured and performed together on many occasions. In the summer of 1834, after an absence of six years in concert travelling, Paganini revisited his native land, and, looking forward wistfully to a peaceful retirement, invested a portion of his accumulated wealth in the purchase of an agreeable country residence in the environs of Parma, named the Villa Gajona. It was here that he intended to prepare his remaining compositions for publication, and invited Legnani to share his abode. Legnani lived with Paganini for several months; they spent the time rehearsing Paganini's compositions, and in October, 1836, performed together at a concert in Parma, where Paganini was violinist and Legnani accompanied him on the guitar and was guitar soloist. The following month they were busy making final preparations for their projected concert tour to London and the two virtuosi played together at various concerts in northern Italy. On June 9 of the following year (1837) Paganini gave a concert, assisted by Legnani as guitar soloist, in Turin, the proceeds for the poor of the city. This was destined to be Paganini's last public appearance.

The two artists were at this time travelling to Paris on their way to London, for in the French capital Paganini was to fulfil an engagement in connection with the opening of the Paganini Casino. This structure, situated in the Rue Mont Blanc, was supposed to be a club for art and literature. It was an imposing building amid extensive pleasure grounds and provided with numerous indoor and open-air attractions with free public admission; but when the authorities refused to grant a licence for the building as a gaming house, the speculation proved an immediate failure. Paganini had, unfortunately, given his signature to this doubtful enterprise, and when it failed he suffered considerable legal worries and financial loss. Consequently, his prearranged plans to visit London with Legnani were frustrated, and in addition the worry arising from this unfortunate affair greatly increased his malady, phthisis of the larynx.

Early in 1839 the directors of the Casino instituted proceedings against Paganini for breach of contract, and, seeking relief from anxiety and illness he went to Marseilles, living for a few months with the notary Brun. Although almost a dying man, he found comfort in his violin and particularly his guitar. Sitwell in "Liszt" says that during Paganini's illness "He no longer practised his instrument, but would lie for hours stretched out upon a sofa on the days of his concerts; and perhaps there might be a mandolin on the table beside him." The following October he tried a change of air by sailing to his native land, and for a month or two resided in Genoa, the city of his birth; but on the approach of winter he removed to Nice. This was his last journey. His illness developed very rapidly, he lost his voice entirely, was troubled by an incessant cough and expired in Nice, May 27, 1840, at the age of fifty-eight. The five storey house in which he died, 23 Rue le Préfecture, bears a commemorative tablet. The street is narrow and gloomy and the once private houses are now shops.

As Paganini had not received the last Sacrament of the Church, the Bishop of Nice refused his burial in consecrated ground, and it was not until May, 1845, just five years later, that his embalmed remains were laid to rest in the cemetery of the Villa Gajona, by an order obtained by his son and friends from the Government. In 1926 they were transferred to the Camposanto in Genoa in close proximity to the tomb of the philosopher, patriot and guitarist Mazzini.

Paganini had been associated in his concert tours with the guitar virtuoso Legnani; he had also expressed his great delight of the guitar playing of Zani de Ferranti, in Paris; and Fetis, in his biography of Paganini, tells of him playing the guitar in the suburbs of Florence, when he attracted and enraptured an audience of passers-by. When in Paris he had occasion to visit the celebrated violin-maker Vuillaume, where he saw a guitar which took his fancy. This guitar, made by Grobert, Mirecourt, France (1794-1869), was loaned by Vuillaume to Paganini during his second visit to Paris, and, at the owner's suggestion, Paganini placed his autograph, in a bold hand near the left side of the bridge, on the unvarnished table. The guitar was returned to Vuillaume, who presented it at a later date to Berlioz, for Vuillaume was well aware of this composer's skill on the guitar and his esteem of the great violinist. Berlioz also added his autograph, on the opposite side of the bridge, and presented the instrument to the Museum of the National Conservatoire of Music, Paris, of which he was curator.

The illustrations of Paganini's own personal guitar and mandolin are reproduced by courtesy of Messrs. Schott, London, and Dr. Erich Kolmann, director of State Museums, Cologne. Both instruments were originally in the Heyer Museum, Cologne, but were transferred to Leipzig in 1925. They are of Italian origin. The mandolin is of Milanese type, but Paganini adapted it and strung it in the Neapolitan method, that is with eight strings in pairs, tuned the same as the violin. The London music journal, B.M.G., of June, 1904, stated: "The mandolin on which the great Paganini played his first concerto at Genoa and his small guitar have been presented to the town by his grandson." These were the instruments played in his youth for those mentioned previously are of full size ; and Messrs. Glendining, the London auctioneers, advertised and sold publicly on May 4, 1906 " an interesting guitar, formerly the property of the great Paganini." Another relic of Paganini in the Paris museum, is a plaster cast of his hand ; the long tapering fingers plainly denote his acute sensitiveness. The Opera Museum, Paris also contains a few minor relics.

During the period when Paganini was living in retirement, studying the guitar, he composed and published his Op. 2 and Op. 3, which were *Twelve Sonatas for Violin and Guitar,* in two sets of six each, issued by Ricordi, Milan, and Richault, Paris. The first set, Op. 2, is dedicated to Signor Dellepiane, and these and the others are each of two movements, the guitar playing arpeggios and chords, which are not difficult.

The series Op. 3, dedicated to " Alla ragazza Eleonora "—whom it is now impossible to identify—are in the same style as the previous set ; but in No. 5, the melody is divided alternately between the guitar and violin, while the guitar parts of the other sonatas are written with the usual arpeggios and chords. Op. 4 and Op. 5 each *Three Quartets for violin, viola, violoncello and guitar,* is inscribed " Composti e dedicati alle amatrice " (composed and dedicated to amateurs). The first quartet of this series introduces a beautiful canon for the violin, viola, and violoncello, the guitar being requisitioned in the trio, when it is allotted full sostenuto chords ; three variations follow, and the melody is then taken alternately by each instrument. The guitar in the second quartet is given full chords and arpeggios throughout. No. 3, is of more varied character, the guitar playing rapid arpeggios, at times the melody and finally an accompaniment of full chords and arpeggios.

The Variazione di Bravura for Violin and Guitar, an extract from which is reproduced, was published by Ricordi in 1835 and is founded on the theme of Op. 1. The variations are somewhat similar and the guitar part is simple.

Nine Quartets for Violin, Viola, Guitar and Violoncello were among the manuscripts preserved by his son Achille, but the first are most probably lost ; Nos. 10 to 15 inclusive were at one time in the possession of Alfred Burnett, London. Five of these quartets were dedicated by Paganini to his lawyer friend, Luigi Guglielmo Germi ; No. 14 was composed expressly for him. The first of these was written in the summer of 1829, and Nos. 11 to 13, while he was in Palermo. These manuscripts were purchased from the widow, Mme. Germi, and in November, 1910, six movements from these quartets were published for the first time, arranged for the violin and piano by Tolhurst and issued by Ascherberg, London. Quartet No. 11, requires the capo d'astro on the guitar, for the violin is written in B major and the guitar in A.

No. 13, in the key of F, contains a minuet, the guitar playing a counter melody to the violin and later in the larghetto, the guitar is given

Variations Bravura for Violin and Guitar.

COMPOSED BY NICOLO PAGANINI.

arpeggios of eight notes to the quaver beat. In No. 14, the capo d'astro is again required when the guitar is used for accompaniment only. The quartet No. 15, is unique, for the melody of the trio is given to the guitar, while the violin, viola and 'cello support it with a pizzicato accompaniment.

Variations Bravura for Violin and Guitar.

COMPOSED BY NICOLO PAGANINI.

GUITAR.

The Guitar plays alone from A to B after each variation.

Of Paganini's unpublished compositions, twenty-four were enumerated as forming the whole of his original manuscripts preserved by his son but only nine were found to be complete. There are title pages in his handwriting of compositions for the guitar in combination with other instruments, the contents of which are unfortunately missing; also the title pages of parts only of several duos and lesser works for violin and guitar which have disappeared. Prat states that the Italian guitar virtuoso, Luigi Mozzani possessed an original Paganini manuscript of a series of *Variations for Guitar Solo* which the owner treasured highly.

These were not the only manuscripts left by Paganini. Upon several occasions, during illness or convalescence, he availed himself of the hospitality offered by General Pino at his residence Villa Nuova, Lake Como. Paganini was there during the autumn of 1823 and told Schottky that they frequently played violin and guitar duets.

In 1910 Baron Achille II, Paganini's grandson offered his illustrious grandfather's musical possessions to the municipality of Genoa, his natal city, but they were declined on account of the price. They were then sold by public auction in Florence, February, 1910. Heyer of Cologne subsequently purchased one hundred and forty from the antiquary who had secured them at the auction. The Heyer collection of rare music and musical instruments was unquestionably the most comprehensive and finest in private ownership and when disposed by public auction in Berlin, during the early twenties, the items were so numerous that the auction continued for more than a week.

Codignola in "Paganini intimo" published in 1936 by the Genoa Municipality states that Op. 41 and Op. 47 are manuscript compositions for the guitar.

General Pino's collection contained also *Sonatas for Violin and guitar, Trios for guitar with two other stringed instruments* and the *Quartets* Nos. 7 to 15, in all of which the guitar plays a prominent part. *Sixty Variations on the popular Genoese melody 'Barucaba' for violin and guitar,* was published posthumously in Paris in 1851. The theme is very short and the variations difficult. These were composed in February, 1835, and dedicated to Paganini's lawyer and friend Luigi Germi of Genoa.

Twenty-six of the manuscript guitar solos were edited by Dr. Max Schulz and published in album form by Zimmerman, Leipzig, in 1925, and the guitar solo *Minuet* and the *Sonata,* Op. 25 were issued by Romero Fernandez, Buenos Aires. The Sonata has an accompaniment of violin, and free rein is allowed the guitar to rise to heights of technical achievement while the violin is relegated to the simplest of accompaniments.

The following manuscripts, enumerated by Dr. Julius Kapp were known to have been in the Heyer collection.

GUITAR SOLOS: *Grand Sonata* (Allegro risoluto, *Romance piu tosto, Largo, Andantino variato, Scherzando*); *Minuetto* (dedicated to Signora Dida); *Chitarra Marziale; Minuetto* (dedicated to Signora

BERNARDO DE PACE

JEAN PIETRAPERTOSA

Under the Direction of

ASHTON'S ROYAL AGENCY

38, OLD BOND STREET
LONDON, W.

STEINWAY HALL

Lower Seymour Street, W.

Under the distinguished Patronage of

MADAME LA DUCHESSE DE MANDAS, Ambassadrice of Spain.
HER GRACE THE DOWAGER DUCHESS OF NEWCASTLE.
THE ARCHDEACON OF LONDON.
HON. MRS. ANNIE MADOCKS.
MRS. FITZGERALD.
MRS. CH. ROME.
MISS E. VAN WART.

Signor JEAN

PIETRAPERTOSA

(*Solo Mandolinist, Grand Opera, Paris*)

WILL GIVE A

Mandoline Recital

ON

TUESDAY EVENING, 3rd DEC., 1901.

At 8.30 o'clock.

Assisted by . .

Miss GERTRUDE LONSDALE
Mr. FRANK BOOR
Mr. DENIS O'SULLIVAN

At the Piano ... ... Miss EDITH LADD
Mr. VICTOR MARMONT
Mr. MERVYN DENE

Tickets: STALLS (First 6 Rows), 10/6. STALLS (Reserved), 7/6.
STALLS (Unreserved), 3/- BALCONY (First 2 Rows), 3/-
BALCONY (Unreserved), 2/-

To be obtained from WHITEHEAD'S Ticket Office, St. James's Hall; CHAPPELL & CO., Ltd., 50, New Bond Street; LACON & OLLIER, 168a, Old Bond Street; WEBSTER & WADDINGTON, Ltd., 304, Regent Street; KEITH, PROWSE & CO., New Bond Street; ALFRED HAYS, 26, Old Bond Street; MITCHELL'S Royal Library, 33, Old Bond Street; GASTRELL'S, Sussex Place, Kensington; LOUIS A. BACK, 106, Piccadilly; MACKEY, Steinway Hall; Signor JEAN PIETRAPERTOSA, 50, York Street, Portman Square, W.; and of

ASHTON'S ROYAL AGENCY,
38, Old Bond Street, W.

J. MILES & CO., LTD., 68-70, WARDOUR STREET, W.

Emilo Pujol

Mme. Pujol (Mathilde Cuervas)

Emilia Ghiribizzi Grillen); *Sonata per Chitarra; Minuetto* (per la Signora Marina); *Minuetto* (alla Signora Dida); *Tre Minuetti e Waltz per Chitarra; Sinfonia Lodovisia per Chitarra;* and others without title.

DUETS for VIOLIN and GUITAR: *Six Duets; Sonata Concertante* (dedicated to Signora Emilia di Negro); *Canzonetta; Duetto Amoroso* (eleven movements); and *Centone di Sonate.*

Original Guitar Draft of Moto Perpetuo

OP. 11, NICOLO PAGANINI.

Duo for Violin and Guitar

NICOLO PAGANINI.

TRIOS for GUITAR and BOW INSTRUMENTS: *Two Minuetti for Chitarra, Viola and Violin; Trio for violin, 'cello and guitar* (in C major) dated London, August 4, 1833 (Allegrò con brio, Minuetto, Andante, Rondo); *Two Trios for two Violins and Guitar; Trio Concertante for Viola, Chitarra and 'Cello* (Allegro, Adagio, Waltz and Rondo); *Serenata for Viola, 'Cello and Guitar* ("dedicated to Mlle. Dominica Paganini by her brother Nicolo").

QUARTETS for GUITAR and BOW INSTRUMENTS, in which the guitar takes a prominent part: Quartets Nos. 9, 10, 11, 12, 13, 14, all dedicated to his lawyer friend Luigi Germi; Quartet No. 7, dedicated to Her Excellency Marchese Catterina Raggi; Quartet No. 8, dedicated to His Excellency Marchese Filippo Carega; Quartet No. 15, the guitar part only of Variations on 'God save the King,' all other parts are missing. There are title pages and parts of other compositions for and including the guitar.

A title page of a Violin and Guitar Duet, *Cantabile and Waltz,* which Paganini composed for, dedicated to, and played with his only pupil "the valiant lad Camillo Sivori" is reproduced, also the original draft of the well-known *Moto Perpetuo*, Op. 11, for Violin and Orchestra, which as usual, Paganini conceived on the guitar.

Paisiello, Giovanni, born May 9, 1741, at Taranto, died June 5, 1815, in Naples, an eminent composer of the Italian school in the pre-Rossinian period, was the son of a veterinary surgeon of Taranto. Being a native of that district of Italy, the home of the mandolin, it is to be expected that he was familiar with the instrument and natural that he employed it in his scores. At the age of five he entered the Jesuit school of Taranto where he attracted attention by his soprano voice. He was taught the rudiments of music by a priest and showed such talent, that his father, who had intended him for the legal profession, abandoned the idea and sent him to Naples to study music under Durante. During his five years' study he was engaged principally with church music; but towards the end of this time he indulged in the composition of a dramatic intermezzo, which, performed in the theatre of the Conservatoire revealed his particular talent. This composition was so successful that Paisiello was invited to Bologna to write two comic operas, which inaugurated a lengthy series of successes in all the principal Italian towns. Paisiello now made his abode in Naples, but in 1776, on the invitation of the Empress Catherine of Russia, who offered him a munificent salary, he removed to St. Petersburg. It was in St. Petersburg in 1780 that he wrote one of the best, if not the principal of his operas *The Barber of Seville,* and when he returned from Russia it was produced in Rome, and at first coldly received; but further representations made such a hold on the affections of the Roman public that later, when Rossini wrote a new *Barber of Seville,* it was considered almost sacrilege, nor would the audience at first allow it a hearing. In Paisiello's opera the mandolin plays a prominent part in accompanying a delicious serenade, in the first act. The mandolin part is reproduced from the score, and this cavatina, *Se il mio nome,* sung by Count Almaviva under the window of Rosina, has accompaniment for mandolin, two violins, viola, contra-bass, clarinet and horn. Rossini, in his *Barber of Seville,* in a similar scene, employs the guitar in combination with the other instruments. After eight years in St. Petersburg, Paisiello returned to Naples as capellmeister to

Mandolin with Orchestra from "The Barber of Seville"

COMPOSED BY PAISIELLO IN 1780.

MANDOLIN.

Ferdinand IV of Naples, and during the next thirteen years produced many operas which became widely known, chief of which was *La Molinara.* An air from this opera, *Nel cor piu,* long known in England as, *Hope told a flattering tale,* is destined to remain familiar, owing to the variations written on it by Beethoven. It was in Naples that Paisiello gave instruction in harmony and composition to his compatriot Della Maria, a mandolin virtuoso and violoncellist who at the time was playing in the orchestra under Paisiello's direction. Della Maria in after life obtained fame in Paris as an operatic composer. Paisiello, himself was summoned to Paris where Bonaparte treated him with a magnificence rivalling that of Catherine of Russia; but he returned to Naples two or three years later where he suffered severe reverses of fortune occasioned by the unsettled state of the government. Anxiety undermined his health in 1815; he experienced another blow by the loss of his wife and did not long survive her, for he died June 5 of the same year. His memoirs, edited by Arnold, were published in 1810 and by other writers since.

Panseron, Auguste, Mathieu, born Paris, April 26, 1796, and died there July 29, 1859. He studied at the Paris Conservatoire and in 1813 was awarded the Prix de Rome. He was accompanist at the Opera Comique and in 1826 was a professor of singing at the Conservatoire, and the author of vocal treatises, operas, masses and numerous songs, many of which were written with guitar. More than twenty of these were published by Schott, Mayence, and several had additional accompaniments of flute, horn or violoncello. Prat states that his songs with guitar were published by Boosey, London, under the title of *Le Troubadour du Jour.*

Payer, Hieronimus, born February 13, 1787, at Meidling, near Vienna, and died at Wieburg, near Vienna, September, 1845, was a musician of many and varied talents, an instrumental composer and also a distinguished writer of church music. He received musical instruction from his father on the piano and guitar, and was an infant prodigy on these instruments. He was organist of the church of his native town during his teens, and in 1816 removed to Vienna where he was a teacher of the piano and guitar. Payer was also a talented mandolinist but gave his attention principally to the piano and guitar which were the most popular instruments with all classes of society. His removal to Vienna was opportune for in a very brief time he won celebrity both as performer and composer and was capellmeister of the Theatre an-der-Wien. In 1818 he resigned his directorship of the Royal Theatre and toured as virtuoso. In his travels he passed through Germany and Holland, giving concerts in all the cities of importance, and where many of his compositions were published successfully. He eventually reached Amsterdam, where for a time he resided as teacher, virtuoso, and composer. In 1825 he removed to Paris, where for some years he lived in the esteem and admiration of the musical public; but his restless nature led him in 1832 to Vienna again, where he arrived in reduced circumstances. Ill-fortune seems now to have dogged him, his fame and prosperity were on the wane ; six years later affairs assumed a more serious aspect when he was paralysed after a stroke which completely cut off his means of subsistence. He lingered in the most abject and distressing condition the remainder of his life. Payer was a prolific writer and his works embrace every variety of musical composition, including operas, concertos, quintets, quartets, masses, and serenades concertante for mandolin and guitar and flute and guitar. He published about one hundred and sixty solos for piano, easy and moderately difficult educational works, variations, rondos, etc., which were very popular in their day. He was held in high esteem by musicians and was a contributor—with the greatest masters of the art—to the volume of variations published under the title of *Vaterländische Kunstlerverein* (Society of Artists of the Fatherland) a name famous through Beethoven's connection with it and his Op. 120. The guitar was a favourite of Payer, and during his life in Vienna, when some of the most famous virtuosi of the instrument were at the height of their fame, he made a name on the instrument. He wrote many compositions for the guitar and mandolin, but owing to his wandering life, they were widely scattered. The best known of his compositions for the guitar are two quintets which include this instrument: Op. 18, *Serenade and potpourri for piano, violin, flute, 'cello and guitar* and Op. 70, for *Piano, violin, flute, 'cello and guitar,* both of which were published by Mechetti, Vienna, as were his *Eight Waltzes for violin or flute and guitar.* Previous to 1831 his fame had reached England and in that year Wessel & Co., London, published many of his compositions.

Pedrell, Carlos, born at Minas, Uruguay, October 16, 1878, and died in Paris, 1941, was of Spanish descent and studied music, first in Montevideo and continued in Barcelona, Spain, under his uncle Felipe Pedrell, from 1898 to 1900. He was also a pupil of V. d'Indy at the Schola Cantorum, Paris, and in 1906 returned to S. America where he was resident in Buenos Aires and appointed national inspector of music and various other official musical positions. In 1915 he founded the influential Sociedad Nacional de Musica and later spent a part of his life in Paris. His operas were produced in the Teatro Colon, Buenos Aires, as was also a lyric drama, *La Guitarra.* He makes use of the guitar in these works and also composed for the guitar several solos, which were dedicated to Segovia, viz., *Lamento, Pagina Romantica, Guitarreo,* and others of less importance.

Pedrell, Felipe, born February 19, 1841, at Tortosa, Tarragona, Spain, died August 19, 1922, in Barcelona, was the uncle of the foregoing. He began his musical career as chorister in Barcelona Cathedral and was mainly self-taught, except on the guitar which he studied under Jose Broca. On this he made rapid progress, was regarded with the highest esteem by Spanish musicians and for thirty years was a professor in Madrid Conservatoire, which position he relinquished for a similar one in Barcelona. Pedrell was the originator of the Spanish National movement for musical compositions of his native land, a renowned musicologist, and the compiler of a standard music dictionary. He founded several periodicals devoted to the culture of Spanish music and was the author of a number of treatises on various aspects of the subject. His seventieth birthday, in 1911, was widely honoured, especially by ecclesiastical dignitaries and celebrated by a public holiday. His famous pupil, Falla, says: "The keystone of the arch upon which modern Spanish music rests is the work of the musicologist Felipe Pedrell. He was a master in the highest sense of the word, for both by precept and example he showed the Spanish musicians where their road lay and led them along it himself. I owe to the teaching of Pedrell and to the powerful stimulus exerted on me by his music, that artistic direction which is indispensable to every well intentioned apprentice" (Trend). Writing about the guitarist Tarrega, Pedrell said: "He gave the music of his instrument—so frail of body, but of spirit so sonorous and expressive—wonderful breadth and plentitude of compass, and the art stirred the spirit of the composer, opening up to his inspiration vast horizons. That is why the development of the classic style in modern composition gives to the works qualities which exalt and throw into relief the values of the instrument. Did not Debussy see in the art of Tarrega both orchestral effects and organ sequences?" Pedrell's compositions comprise operas, orchestral and church music, chamber music, songs and guitar works. Five of the latter, *Impromptu, Floriada, Dona Mencia, Betsabe* and *Al Atardecer en los jardines de Arlaja,* are published by Schott, London. His memoirs and bibliography edited by Reiff appeared in 1921.

Pelzer, Ferdinand, born at Treves in 1801 and died in London 1860, was a German guitarist who settled in England where he was a popular teacher of the instrument. He was the son of a schoolmaster and in youth studied the guitar. During the French invasion, General Le Graun was billeted at his father's house and Pelzer married the general's daughter at a very early age. In 1821 he was living in Mulheim, where his daughter Catherina Josepha, afterwards Mme. Sydney Pratten, was born. Pelzer toured Germany and France as guitarist and when his daughter was about seven she was also appearing in various continental cities as a prodigy on the guitar, playing solos and duos on the terz guitar with her father. About 1829 Pelzer was induced to visit London by a Captain Phillips; they became his guests and he obtained pupils for them, among whom were the daughters of the Duchess of Sutherland. Pelzer was a frequent guitar soloist in London and played duos for guitar and piano with Moscheles in Willis' Rooms. He made several trips to the continent, visiting his native land and returned to London where on May 15, 1833, was playing with the celebrated flautist Dressler in the Opera Concert Hall. Pelzer was a contemporary in London of Giuliani and Schulz, and the youthful Regondi performed duos with his daughter Catherina at fashionable musicales in the city. He published many short simple pieces and arrangements for the guitar alone and set guitar accompaniments to numerous songs which enjoyed popularity. He compiled two methods for the guitar, the first entitled: *Instructions for the Spanish guitar, written and dedicated to my friends, Captain G. H. Phillips and John Hodgson, Esq.;* published by Chappell, London. This contained very little original matter and the studies are extracted from the works of Sor, Carulli, Giuliani and Aguado. Pelzer's second method published by subscription, was entitled: *Instructions for the guitar tuned in E major, to which are also added twelve psalm and hymn tunes and the Gregorian tunes, respectfully dedicated to Mrs. George H. Harvey of Exeter.* This book contained a list of subscribers, among whom were Lady John Somerset, the guitarists Regondi, Sagrini, Miss Mounsey and Don Ciebra, the latter a Spanish virtuoso whose reputation at this time was pre-eminent in England. Pelzer's compositions, mainly trivial light dances and arrangements, were issued by various London publishers, chiefly Johanning; Metzler; Ewer; and Chappell.

Pettine, Giuseppe, contemporary, born February 12, 1876, at Isernia, Italy, and living in Providence, U.S.A. At the age of nine he was given instruction on the mandolin by an amateur, Camillo Mastropaolo, and three years later the family emigrated to U.S.A. Their destination was Providence, Rhode Island, and Pettine has resided there since. At the period when his family arrived in U.S.A. the mandolin was but little known and the lad was regarded a musical prodigy in the States. Although his English was very limited, elementary, and crude, he never-the less gave instruction on his instrument. There were no satisfactory instruction books or methods obtainable, so after studying musical theory and composition under the famous American bandmaster Reeves, he compiled and published one, which he afterwards revised and enlarged to six volumes. As mandolin virtuoso he toured the States from Maine to California, terminating in Boston, when he performed the most important works of modern European and American mandolin composers, including his own *Concerto* and also that of Ranieri. The music magazine Cadenza for September, 1908, said: "There is an indescribable something about his performance that awakens a responsive chord in the soul of a true musician and Pettine unwittingly revealed the secret of his power and why his playing arouses such universal admiration when he said, 'I love my instrument.' That this love was no passing fancy is proved by his life-long devotion to the instrument. No American mandolinist has accomplished as much." Pettine contributed more than any other individual to the popularisation of the mandolin in U.S.A. and through his instruction books, studies, public performances and teaching has raised the status of the instrument throughout the States. Homage has been conferred on Pettine by many musicians. Calace dedicated a *Mandolin Concerto,* Op. 113, to him. He is a versatile musician, an expert performer on the clarinet and saxophone, and during the early years of the century was saxophone soloist with various famous bands, and for a time conductor of a military band and orchestra. Among his pupils, Wm. Place, Jr., and Rose Helen Pizzitola, have established reputations as mandolinists of the first rank. Pettine's contributions to mandolin music include: *Modern system of the Plectrum's mechanism; Duo style studies; Concerto Patetico, with piano, in three movements,* (time of performance, 22 minutes); *Concert Overture for plectrum orchestra with oboe, flute, clarinet, bassoon, two horns and percussion;* and many pieces for unaccompanied mandolin. He has made recordings of more than twenty of his compositions, for mandolin and piano and unaccompanied mandolin solo. Pettine has been for many years the editor and publisher of a monthly music journal, Fretted Instrument News, an international magazine devoted to the culture and advancement of the mandolin.

Pettoletti, Pietro, an Italian guitarist of the nineteenth century who travelled through Europe, principally in France, Germany and Russia, and published various pieces for his instrument in the cities he visited. He is known by these compositions: Op. 1, *Six Waltzes for guitar,* published by Simrock, Bonn; *Variations for guitar,* Op. 11, 15 and 26, published by Schott, Mayence; Op. 15, a series of *Variations on the Russian national anthem;* Op. 11, *Divertissement for two guitars,* published by Lose, Copenhagen, and also Jurgenson, St. Petersburg; *Fantasias for guitar,* Op. 22 and 24, Lose, Copenhagen; Op. 28, *Fantasia for guitar and piano,* and Op. 32, *Fantasia on a Russian melody for guitar,* published by Schott, Mayence. His brother Joachim was violinist in the Italian opera for some years and the A.M.Z. for the year 1822 records his *Variations concertante for violin and guitar;* Op. 3, *Six instructive waltzes for guitar solo,* published the same year by Simrock, Bonn. There was a C. G. Pettoletti who issued through Breitkopf & Härtel, Leipzig, several *Duos for two violins* and *Concert Variations for guitar and violin.* Prat states that Pietro used the seven string guitar and died at the age of seventy-five in Russia.

Petzmayer, Johann, born at Vienna in 1803 and living in Munich in 1870, was a natural musician, the son of an innkeeper who obtained celebrity as a zither and guitar virtuoso and composer. When eighteen he possessed a common zither, taught himself as he did the guitar, and by his wonderful playing attracted numerous customers from far and near to his father's inn. Petzmayer's principal instrument was the zither and it was not long before his fame spread far and wide and he and his zither became popular in Vienna, so much so, that Strauss included it in his orchestral scores. It was due to Petzmayer that the zither, despite its simplicity, came into public favour, for he played his native landler—country dance music—in most of the continental theatres and concert halls, always with the greatest success. Petzmayer, a born musician, without education, by mere native genius, produced the greatest effects from the simplest source. In his hands the zither was invested with a charm to which few could be insensible, and it possessed that kind of attractiveness which was truly characteristic. In 1833 he made a successful tour through Germany and was commanded to perform before the Emperor of Austria upon several occasions, and four years later was appointed kammervirtuos to Duke Maximilian of Bavaria. About 1840 he became associated in Munich with Darr, the guitar virtuoso, and by his influence, Darr commenced the study of the zither, and the two artists were the sincerest of friends throughout life. Petzmeyer was the composer of various solos for the zither and the guitar and for the two instruments in combination ; they are light dances and appeared principally in Vienna and Munich.

Pfeifer, Franz, an Austrian guitarist living during the first part of the nineteenth century in Vienna, where in 1830 Artaria published his *Guitar solos* Op. 15, 19, 20, 27 and 28, and Cranz, Hamburg, published his Op. 16, 18, 20, 23 and 32. He was the author of a *Practical Guitar Method* and also arranged for guitar solo many of Schubert's songs, Op. 36, 38, 60 and 65. Pfeifer also wrote guitar accompaniments to many vocal works.

Pfitzner, Hans, born May 5, 1869, at Moscow, was the son of German parents, his father being a professional violinist. When seventeen he commenced his music studies in Frankfurt Conservatoire and after graduating accepted a teaching position in Coblentz and in 1903 was appointed Kapellmeister in Berlin. He became more widely known when Mahler produced Pfitzner's dramas in Vienna, and particularly the legend *Palestrina,* produced in Munich, June 12, 1917. The libretto is also by the composer and in three acts. In this opera and also in *Von deutscher Seele,* a romantic cantata for four solo voices, chorus and orchestra, he uses the guitar. It was produced in 1922.

Picchianti, Luigi, an Italian guitar virtuoso, music critic and composer, born at Florence, August 20, 1786, and died there October 19, 1864. Although contrary to the wishes of his parents, he neglected his business to study the guitar ; but his perseverance and persuasions at length overcame opposition, and he was able to adopt music as his profession when he entered the Academy of Fine Arts in Florence as a student in harmony and counterpoint under Disma Ugolini. Previous to becoming a student at the Academy he was known as a talented performer on the guitar and still continued its study. During the years 1821-5 he performed with success in Germany, France and England and then returned to his native land. When he had been resident some years in Florence he became editor of the journal The Gazetta Musicale and his influence and contributions were those of a scholarly musician. His talents were appreciated and acknowledged in Florence by his appointment as Professor of counterpoint in the music academy of his youth. Picchianti was intimate with the celebrated guitar virtuosi to whom he dedicated several compositions. In 1834, Ricordi of Florence, published a number of his theoretical treatises on music and second editions appeared the following year. He compiled a *Method for the Guitar,* numerous sonatas, studies, caprices and airs with variations for guitar solo, various church and orchestral items, and quartets and trios for strings and wind. Ricordi, Milan, published *Fantasia for guitar, flute and violin,* and Cipriani, Florence, issued numerous pieces, chief of which were *March for Two Guitars, Grand sonatas, Caprices,* etc. Many of Picchianti's guitar compositions were published out of his native land—in Vienna, Bologna, and Leipzig. *Le prime dodici lezioni,* etc., and more than fifty songs with accompaniment of guitar were published by Cipriani, Florence, and Breitkopf & Härtel issued *Trio for guitar, clarinet and bassoon.* He is recorded in the Musical Dictionary of Pedrell.

Pietrapertosa, Jean. There were two mandolinists of this name, father and son, living in Paris during the end of the nineteenth and commencement of the twentieth centuries. One made periodical visits to London where he was esteemed as concert performer and teacher. He was solo mandolinist of the Grand Opera, Opera Comique, Paris, and also of the Royal Opera, London. This musician gave several recitals in London, in particular that in Steinway Hall in 1901 was under very distinguished patronage. His portrait and biography were published in the Paris Music and Dramatic Directory (1887-1911). There are various mandolin methods ; a *Complete Method* and a volume of *Studies of agility,* Op. 228, issued by Ricordi, Milan, and other studies in one and two volumes published respectively by Beuscher, Paris, and Besnard, Paris. More than two hundred arrangements, transcriptions, and original light compositions were issued by Ricordi, Milan, and lesser known publishers, the work of these two mandolinists.

Place, William, Jr., contemporary, born at Providence, R.I., U.S.A., commenced the study of the mandolin under a local teacher and continued under Pettine. He attained great proficiency, a recognised virtuoso of rare attainment, and the chosen mandolin soloist at many of the American Guild Concerts. He was the first mandolinist to publicly perform the *Concerto* composed by his teacher, Pettine. In 1947 he retired from public life and was living with his wife, a talented harpist, at St. Martha's Vineyard, U.S.A. Place was the author of a *Mandolin Method,* in two books, published by Nicomede Music Co., Altoona, Pa., U.S.A.

Pleyel, Ignaz Joseph, born June 1, 1757, at Ruppersthal in Lower Austria and died in Paris, November 14, 1831, was a most fertile instrumental composer. He was the twenty-fourth child of the village schoolmaster and his musical talent displayed itself at a very early age. He studied the violin, piano and guitar, the two latter instruments under Wanhall in Vienna, and he attracted the notice of Count Erdody who placed him under Haydn, in 1774 to continue his musical education. In 1783 he was capellmeister of Strasburg Cathedral where he lived for eight years and then accepted an invitation to London to conduct the season's concerts. His first concert was on February 13, 1792. He returned to Paris where he lived as music publisher and musical instrument maker and was the first to publish the complete collection of Haydn's quartets, and in 1807 he added to his music publishing business the manufacture of pianos and guitars, a speciality was the lyre-guitar, which at the time was the favourite instrument of aristocracy. The instruments constructed under his personal supervision obtained celebrity. A very interesting guitar, made in his workshop was that played by Garat, the celebrated French singer. This instrument, a lyre-shaped guitar was made by Pleyel in 1809 and presented to Garat by a wealthy amateur, an enthusiastic admirer of his singing with guitar. This instrument is in the Museum of the National Conservatoire of Music, Paris. Another specimen of lyre-guitar made by Pleyel was in the musical instrument collection of Lutgendorff. Pleyel was an associate of the guitar virtuoso Sor who dedicated to him Op. 7, *Fantasia pour la Guitare, composee et dediee a son ami, Ignace Pleyel.* Pleyel was emphatically an instrumental composer whose early compositions were very highly spoken of by Mozart. While in Italy he wrote an opera which was produced in Naples ; but he is known by his instrumental compositions, twenty-nine symphonies, many concertos, quintets, quartets and small pieces for violin with the guitar. Whistling in his Handbuch records *Six Sonatines for guitar and violin,* published by Breitkopf & Härtel, Leipzig ; *Minuets and Rondos for violin and guitar,* Beauce, Paris ; *Six songs with guitar,* published in Brunswick and *Six lieder with guitar,* published by Cranz, Hamburg.

Pollet, a family of French musicians who flourished during the latter part of the eighteenth and the first part of the nineteenth centuries. They were all exceptional guitarists and harpists who did much to make these instruments and also the cittern, or flat back mandolin, popular, in their native land. The first to obtain renown was Charles Francois Alexandre, usually designated Pollet aine (elder) who was born in 1748 at Bethune, Artois, North France. He played the guitar and cittern, at first in his native town, later in Italy and in 1771, when twenty-three years of age had made a name as a performer and was induced to visit Paris. Here he won a brilliant reputation as a virtuoso on both instruments, was an exceedingly popular and fashionable teacher and during his first five years residence, published eighteen compositions—sonatas, variations, etc., for his instruments. He compiled a *Method for the Guitar,* published by Leduc, Paris, in 1786. He also wrote other compositions, some of which appeared periodically in albums, up to the time of the fateful revolution of 1793, when he retired to Evreux where he was living as late as 1811.

Pollet, Jean Joseph Benoit, a younger brother of the above was born at Bethune in 1753. He studied the same instruments as his brother, and also the mandolin under Wenzel Krumpholz, the mandolin virtuoso and friend of Beethoven. He was associated with his brother Charles in Paris, and assisted him as teacher and performer. On the advice of Krumpholz, the harpist, and his brother the mandolinist, he studied the harp also and is known as a virtuoso and composer for that instrument. Pollet is credited with being the first harpist to produce harmonics on the instrument—those liquid, ethereal tones. He died in Paris 1818. Jean was a more prolific composer than his brother and his published works embrace *Three concertos for harp and orchestra, Three Nocturnes for harp, guitar and flute,* published by Naderman, Paris ; *Four Rondos for violin and guitar ; Two Nocturnes for flute and guitar ; Sonatas and Variations for cittern* and a method and numerous compositions for the harp.

Pollet, L. M., a son of Jean Joseph, born at Paris in 1783 and died there in 1830, was taught the guitar and harp by his father and obtained celebrity as performer on both instruments and is known as a music publisher. He left a *Method* and a volume of *Studies for the guitar, Airs with variations for guitar solo,* published by himself ; *Waltzes for guitar solo* and *Rondos for guitar and violin,* issued by Richault, Paris. Joseph Pollet, son of the guitarist of this name was a musician and author of several theoretical treatises on music. During 1863 he was organist of Notre Dame Cathedral, Paris.

Ponce, Manuel, born December 8, 1886 at Fresnillo, Mexico, died April 24, 1948, in Mexico City. He was taught music by his sister and at the age of twelve was organist of Aquas Calientes Cathedral. Two years later he composed the *Gavotte* which was made popular by the celebrated dancer, Argentina. In 1901 he entered the National Conservatoire of Music of Mexico City and after three years continued his musical studies in Europe, at Bologna and Berlin. Returning to his native land in 1908, he was appointed a professor in the National Conservatoire and in 1947 honoured with the National Award of Arts and Science. Ponce introduced a new epoch in Mexican music, there had been previous attempts ; but it was he who created a real consciousness of the richness of Mexican folk music. He composed among other orchestral and guitar items *Concerto of the South, for guitar and full orchestra,* the first performance took place in Montevideo, October 4, 1941. The same year he made a tour of the South American republics, by air, to conduct his compositions in Argentina, Uruguay, Chile and Peru, with the virtuoso Segovia his guitarist. Ponce has composed symphonies, orchestral works and much for violin, piano, etc. ; first heard in his native land they spread to U.S.A. and Europe. Several of his compositions he dedicated to Segovia, the following were published by Schott, London. *Sonata Classica, in homage to the guitarist Sor ; Sonata Romantica, in homage to Schubert ; Mazurka, in homage to the guitarist, Tarrega ; Theme with variations, finale and fugue ;*

Three Canciones Mexicanas ; Eighteen Variations and Fugue on 'Folia de Espana' ; Twenty-four preludes in two books ; *Preludes faciles* and *Third Sonata,* dedicated to Segovia and *Variations on a favourite air,* Op. 57, *Duo for two guitars.* His last compositions for the guitar were written just previous to his death in 1948 for the Guitar Review, New York, and appeared in the Nos. 5 and 6 of that periodical. Among unpublished compositions there is an unfinished *Quartet for guitar and strings* also *Six Preludes Cortos,* for guitar, dedicated to Juanita Chavez, daughter of the Mexican composer and conductor, Carlos Chavez, for whom Ponce had always shown great tenderness from her birth.

Porro, Pierre Jean, born 1759 at Beziers, France, and died in Montmorency, 1831, was a guitarist and popular teacher of his instrument living in Paris from 1783. During the years 1787-1803 he published the following: *Journal de Guitare ; New Method of instruction for the guitar or lyre,* Op. 31 ; *Six Sonatas for violin and guitar,* Op. 11 ; *Collections of preludes, caprices and studies for guitar,* also works for guitar in combination with other instruments and a number of church compositions, many of which he published himself. His memoirs, edited by Donnadieu were published in 1897.

Prager, Heinrich Aloys, born at Amsterdam, December 23, 1783, and died in Magdeburg, August 7, 1854, was a virtuoso on the violin and guitar and a composer, who, for some years was the conductor of an itinerant musical company. He was later conductor in the Theatres of Leipzig (1818-28) Magdeburg, Hanover and Cologne. His principal instrument was the guitar for which he composed numerous pieces, also operas, instrumental quintets, capriccios, etc. The A.M.Z. for the years 1813-27 speaks highly of his compositions for the guitar. Op. 11, *Exercises for guitar ;* Op. 21, *Andante and theme with variations for guitar, flute and violin ;* Op. 26, *Theme with variations for violin and guitar,* all published by Breitkopf & Härtel, Leipzig, also Op. 29, *Collection of Songs with guitar.* His son Ferdinand, a talented pianist and guitarist, was living in London in 1834 esteemed as a teacher. It was by his influence that the Philharmonic Society of London invited Wagner to make his first visit to England to conduct their season's concerts of 1855. When Wagner arrived he resided in the house of his friend Prager, 31 Milton Street, Dorset Square. In collaboration with the guitarist Leonard Schulz, Prager composed *Three Duos Characteristiques for guitar and piano* which were issued by Mori, Lavenu & Co., London.

Prat, Marsal Domingo, born March 17, 1886, at Barcelona and died at Haedo, Buenos Aires, December, 1944. He studied in the Municipal Music School of his native city and was a pupil of Miguel Llobet for the guitar. For many years he resided in Argentina where he was esteemed as a teacher of the guitar. Prat was the first exponent of the Tarrega method in South America, and the author of Diccionario de

Guitarristas, a voluminous but unreliable tome published in 1934 by Romero & Fernandez, Buenos Aires.

Pratten, Mme. Sidney, née Catherina Josepha Pelzer, was born at Muhlheim, on the Rhine, Germany, in 1821 and died October 10, 1895, in London. She was the daughter of Ferdinand Pelzer and received instruction in the theory of music and guitar playing at a very early age from her father, and then studied harmony under Dr. Carnaby in London. When seven she was performing in public and creating a sensation as guitarist in concerts with Grisi, and also played with her father in various continental cities. About 1829 her parents came to London and the child-guitarist made her first appearance before an English audience in the King's Theatre, afterwards named Her Majesty's. She again played at concerts with Mme. Grisi and with Regondi—an infant prodigy on the guitar of about the same age—when they played duos for two guitars, Miss Pelzer playing terz guitar. The two diminutive performers were lost on the stage, and, to be seen by the audience were frequently seated upon a table or on the grand piano. The Musical Magazine for March, 1835 says: "On Tuesday last a morning concert took place at the Hanover Square Rooms, the first of the three announced by Miss Pelzer, the daughter of the guitarist, which were numerously and fashionably attended. Miss Pelzer herself contributed in a high degree to the gratification of the audience and was cordially and deservedly applauded for her performance. Kiallmark presided at the piano." In 1836, when fifteen she gave another series of three recitals in the Hanover Square Rooms, commencing February 24, and was assisted by the most eminent musicians in London. These concerts brought her fame as a performer and two years later she was established in Exeter as a teacher of the guitar; her pupils were the most fashionable members of society. It was in Exeter that Lady John Somerset took great interest in the young guitarist and persuaded her to reside in London. She was given apartments in her London residence, introduced to the nobility as an instructress, and was soon firmly established as a busy teacher. On September 24, 1854, she married Robert Sidney Pratten, the celebrated flautist; but their married life was of short duration for he died February 10, 1868. Prostrated by this severe blow she relinquished her profession for a time, but on May 17, 1871, gave a recital, performing Giuliani's *Third Concerto,* to the pianoforte accompaniment of a niece of Giuliani, the composer. In 1873 she gave a recital assisted by Gounod and his choir; her last public appearance was in November, 1893, when she performed in Steinway Hall, London. Mme. Pratten was the guitarist chosen to perform the guitar part in *The Corsair,* composed for the Birmingham Music Festival of 1876 by Sir F. Cowen. She was passionately fond of the guitar, knew its capabilities, was aware of its limitations, and to her it possessed the power of expressing feelings which no other medium could. She was the composer of about two hundred light pieces for the guitar, many of which she published herself and she compiled three methods for her instrument. The first in two parts published by Boosey & Co., London, was an exhaustive treatise; but it proved too complicated for amateurs, and so she issued her volume, *The Guitar Simplified,* which was the most popular of her methods, it had passed twelve editions at the time of her death. The third method was entitled: *Instructions for the guitar tuned in E major;* she also arranged guitar accompaniments to numerous songs. Her death occurred after a brief illness, October 10, 1895, and she was interred on the 18th, in Brompton cemetery, where a suitable memorial was erected to her memory by pupils and friends. A sketch of her life, by Dr. F. Mott Harrison, Mus. Bac., her pupil, was published in 1899 by Barnes & Mullins, Bournemouth.

Presti, Ida, contemporary guitarist, was born in the environs of Paris and when six years of age commenced to play the guitar. Her first teacher was Montagnon and she evinced such marked ability that when ten she appeared as soloist in the Salle Pleyel, Paris. Later she played at the Pasdeloup concerts and the concerts of the Conservatoire of Music, and made recordings at an early age. In 1948 her reputation was further enhanced by the performance of the *Aranjuez Concerto for guitar and orchestra* by Rodrigo which was broadcast from Paris and also from several continental stations. She has made concert appearances in Algiers, Strasburg, Luxemburg and on December 1, 1951, gave her first recital in London and later appeared as guitarist in films. She was heard again in London on March 16 of the following year and the next day broadcast from B.B.C. She appeared in television and gave various recitals in the provinces, and again broadcast from London, July, 1953. Reporting her London recital the Times said: "When Miss Ida Presti, a young French guitarist, made her English début, last autumn it was her prestidigitation that lingered in the memory. Her reappearance early in the week at Wigmore Hall confirmed this first impression of brilliance, but also gave further evidence of sterling musicianship."

Proch, Heinrich, born July 22, 1809, near Vienna, and died there, December 18, 1878. After completing his education in Vienna University, where he studied law, he gravitated to music, specialising particularly in singing and the violin and was a frequent public performer in Vienna, during 1833-4. He was a prominent and popular teacher of the vocal art and trained many pupils who became famous. In 1837 he was conductor of the Vienna Josephstadt Theatre and from 1840-70 was similarly engaged at the Court Opera after which he retired on pension. He made German translations of the popular Italian operas; but his fame rests on his lieder, many of which he composed especially with guitar accompaniment. The most popular are: Op. 1, 6, 10, 14, 18, *Das Alpenhorn*, and Op. 35, 36 and 38.

Prusik, Karl, born May 19, 1896, at Vienna, studied in Vienna University and graduated by his dissertation on the music of the lutenist

S. L. Weiss. Being disabled in the war he adopted the guitar and lived in Vienna as a teacher of this instrument, harmony, composition, and as composer. For some years he was associated with Dr. Zuth in the musical profession and was a frequent contributor to the Zeitschrift fur Gitarre, Vienna. He has published by Goll, Vienna, *Concerto in three movements for guitar solo ; Six songs with guitar,* words and music by Prusik ; *Der Spielmann, song cycle, with guitar ; Duos for violin and guitar ; Five landler for violin and guitar* and many folk songs with guitar.

Pugnani, Gaetano, born at Turin in 1727 and died there in 1805, a recognised violin virtuoso, one of the most celebrated and brilliant of the Piedmontese school ; he was also a talented guitarist for he played it during youth in addition to the violin and all his early compositions were written with guitar accompaniment. His musical education began at an early age, first under Somis, a pupil of Corelli, and continued under Tartini, thus combining the prominent qualities in style and technique of both masters. He was violinist to the King of Sardinia in 1752, but two years later began to travel. He achieved much success as a solo player at the Court of Sardinia and his reputation spread to the continent, so when he visited Paris, he was chosen to perform several times at the Concerts Spirituels, and received great applause. After playing in other cities of the continent he visited London, where for a time he was leader of the Opera orchestra. Here he composed an opera, orchestral music, symphonies, etc. In 1770 he was living in his native city where he founded a school of music for violinists and guitarists, as Corelli had previously done in Rome, and Tartini in Padua, and from this academy issued the most famous performers of the latter part of the eighteenth century, chief among whom were Viotti and Bruni on the violin and Molino and Sola on the guitar. Pugnani was a prolific composer whose early works were written with the guitar ; his Op. 2 and Op. 3, *Twelve Sonatas for violin and guitar* were published by Richault, Paris, and other compositions with the guitar appeared in Turin. His memoirs, edited by Fayolle, were published in 1810, and were also included by Carutti in his Miscellanea in 1895.

Pujol, Emilio, contemporary, born April 7, 1886, at Granadella, province of Lerida, Spain, and living in Barcelona. His first musical instruction was in singing and on the bandurria (Spanish mandolin) and he became a member of an estudiantina (band of mandolins and guitars) which appeared with phenomenal success during the Paris Exhibition of 1900. As bandurria soloist he attracted the notice of the French President, Loubet, who was profuse in praise of Pujol's artistry. Pujol had studied in the National Music School, Barcelona, and in 1900 when he became a pupil of Tarrega on the guitar he abandoned the bandurria to concentrate on the guitar. After seven years study he made a name in his native land as a guitar virtuoso and then undertook a tour of Argentina and Uruguay which was extended through the

Manuel Ponce

Ida Presti

Giuseppe Pettine

Giulio Regondi

Silvio Ranieri

United States. In 1912 and again in 1923 he was a member of the judges of the International Mandolin and Guitar Contests, organised by the municipality of Boulogne. His wife, under her maiden name, Mathilde Cuervas, appeared as guitar soloist, and as a Flamenco player was a brilliant success. Together they made an artistic tour of England during 1923 giving recitals and several broadcasts from London and other stations. During his visit to this country Pujol took the opportunity of visiting the Library of the British Museum for research and information respecting his forthcoming *Method for the Guitar,* particularly its historical association. From 1914, through the war period, he again visited South America residing in Buenos Aires until 1922 when he settled in Paris as virtuoso and teacher, making artistic visits to various continental cities. In 1924 he was guitar soloist in the Brussels Conservatoire of Music, assisted by the mandolin virtuoso Ranieri and this recital was followed by others in Berlin and Rotterdam. Pujol discovered in a Paris museum, an ancient vihuela—a very early type of lute-guitar, the predecessor of the modern guitar, which was popular ages ago in Spain. He had copies made of this instrument, then unearthed and made known the long forgotten compositions for it, and the technique required. Pujol was appointed professor of the guitar in the National Conservatoire of Music, Lisbon, in 1947, a position which he maintains with the high esteem of renowned musicians ; his lecture-recitals in this institution are particularly interesting and popular. As musicologist and musician, intensely devoted to his instrument, its history and future, he has contributed literary articles to music journals of several nationalities ; of special importance was his comprehensive survey of the guitar in the Encyclopedia de la Musique. He compiled in two books a *Rational Method for the Guitar* and a treatise : *The dilemma of timbre on the guitar,* Spanish and English text, both published by Romero & Fernandez, Buenos Aires in 1934. He has written a few studies and arrangements of the classics, issued by Schott, London, and Biblioteca Fortea, Madrid ; *Ten various studies* and *The New Technique* were published by Romero, Buenos Aires, and he contributed in 1948 guitar solos to the Guitar Review, New York. His wife, a celebrated guitarist of the Flamenco method known professionally under her maiden name, Mathilde Cuervas, was born April 1, 1887, in Seville, and undertook concert tours with her husband.

RADZIWILL, Anton Heinrich, Prince, Statthalter of Posen, born June 13, 1775, at Vilna and died April 7, 1833, in Berlin was an ardent admirer of good music, a fine player on the violoncello, the guitar, and a composer of no mean order. He married Princess Luise, sister of that distinguished musical amateur, Prince Louis Ferdinand of Prussia. Radziwill was an enthusiastic admirer of Beethoven, who invited him to subscribe to the publication of his *Mass in D,* the Prince having journeyed especially to hear this work. Radziwill was one of the seven who subscribed their names in answer to that appeal, and to him Beethoven dedicated his *Overture in C*, Op. 115, which was published in 1825. Further relations between Beethoven and the prince there must have been. He was best known by his music to Goethe's *Faust,* published in score and arrangements by Trautwein, Berlin, in 1835. As stated, he was a skilful performer on the guitar and violoncello and the author of various songs with guitar accompaniment. A series of *Four Lieder for one voice, with accompaniment of guitar and violoncello* was published by Breitkopf & Härtel, Leipzig, in 1815.

Ranieri, Silvio, born November 6, 1882, at Rome. A famous contemporary concert mandolinist of world repute living in Brussels. He studied the mandolin in his early youth and appeared in public as a concert performer when sixteen. In 1901 he migrated to Brussels where he was popular as a teacher of his instrument. He toured England and practically all European countries, then returned to Brussels where he was appointed conductor of the Royal Mandolin Band, a section controlled by the Brussels Conservatoire of Music. In April, 1913, he was giving recitals in Paris and in 1926 was designated to display the characteristics and attributes of his instrument in a recital in the National Conservatoire of Music of that city. On the twenty-fifth anniversary of his professorship at the Brussels Conservatoire, in 1926 he was presented with a bust of himself in bronze after a recital in which he was assisted by the guitar virtuoso Pujol. In 1921 he was a member of the artistic committee of the Grand Concorso International Mandolinistic organised by the city of Florence under the presidency of Mascagni. Ranieri compiled an exhaustive method in four volumes, published in four languages, English, French, German and Italian, by L. Oertel, Brussels, entitled *L'art de la Mandoline.* He has written a few compositions, all of which are of sterling merit; *Concerto in D major with orchestral and also piano accompaniment,* in three movements, *Allegro maestoso, Romanza,* and *Allegro giocoso,* published by Oertel, Brussels; A *Sextet for solo mandolin, Canto d'Estate; Souvenir de Varsovie for mandolin and piano;* edited three of Beethoven's original compositions for mandolin and piano; many transcriptions of ancient music and a few other original works. He also wrote a *Method for the Guitar* in two volumes in the same four languages as his Mandolin Method. The majority of his works appeared in Brussels, published by Oertel or Cranz.

Rebay, Ferdinand, contemporary, born June 11, 1880, at Vienna; his seventieth birthday was celebrated by musicians of that city in 1950. He was a student in the Vienna Conservatoire with Fuchs, Mandyczewski and Josef Hoffman. From 1916-20 he was conductor of the Schubert Society of Vienna, the Vienna Choral Society and the Vienna Male Voice Choir. In 1920 he was professor of the piano in the State Academy and ten years later a professor of the guitar in the same institution. He is an esteemed pedagogue whose published works comprise operas, oratorios, masses, etc. He makes use of the guitar in many of his compositions; *Spanish Dance for solo tenor and male voice* *chorus with guitar; Hirtenlied,* a Norwegian folk song, *for two female voices and male chorus with accompaniment of two oboes, horn and guitars; Sonata in E flat for oboe and guitar; Old Viennese waltz cycle for string quartet and guitar; Quartet in D flat for violin, viola, 'cello and guitar; Trio in D sharp for flute, bassoon and guitar; Three duos for clarinet and guitar* and *Four volumes of Duos for two guitars,* published by Hladky, Vienna. The majority of these compositions were first performed in 1930.

Regondi, Giulio, born at Lyons in 1822—some authorities state in 1824—and died in London, May 6, 1872. Among guitar virtuosi Regondi stands pre-eminent, and as a musician and composer he occupies a no less exalted position. Of his parentage and early years little is known. His father was an Italian, his mother a German, the father was for some time a teacher in the Gymnasium of Milan. Some writers assert that the man who assumed the name of father was no relation whatever, but seized the opportunity of making money by a precocious child, and there is no doubt that the harsh treatment by this man, during the early days of Regondi's career undermined his health and caused his painful illness and premature death. The child was an infant phenomenon on the guitar, and as such was forced in his musical studies and sacrificed by his supposed father, who took him as a guitar prodigy to every court of Europe, with the exception of Madrid, before he was nine years of age. In June 1831, they arrived in England, and after a provincial tour settled in London, where the boy performed at numerous concerts, creating quite a sensation in the musical world. The following extracts relative to his first appearance in this country, written by the editor of the Harmonicon, the most influential music journal in England, were published in 1831 in the June and July numbers of that periodical. In reading these notices it is very important that the musical events of the time should be taken into consideration—a period during which no greater sensation in the musical world has ever occurred, when the whole of Europe and the cities of Paris, Vienna, and London in particular were convulsed with wild excitement over the marvellous performances on the violin of Paganini. Strange to relate, Paganini and Regondi—the Paganini of the guitar—both left Paris and arrived in England during May, 1831, and both gave their first concerts in the following June. Previous to playing in Paris, Paganini had visited Vienna, where he had witnessed scenes of unequalled triumph, and had been the object of unparalleled sensations. Regondi was but a child of eight, and he too, had been winning the highest applause of the musical critics on the continent, and his fame as a guitarist had reached London sometime previous to his arrival there, and notwithstanding the unbounded enthusiasm and popularity which greeted Paganini, little Regondi's performances on his guitar attracted crowded and enthusiastic audiences, for his artistic achievements and results were in no degree less marvellous or successful than those of his immortal compeer. "Another prodigy! An infant

Paganini on the guitar! An evening paper states that a musical phenomenon has just arrived in London—a first-rate guitar player, although only eight years of age. His name is Jules Regondi. The Figaro, The Journal des Debats, The Journal de Paris and Galignani's Messenger, speak of him with rapture. They say that in addition to the mechanical precision, which generally is not to be acquired on the guitar under twenty years' practice, he evinces taste and feeling rarely witnessed in a performer on that instrument. Mercy on us! twenty years in learning to play on the guitar! For Heaven's sake let the instrument be hereafter put into the hands of none except those of Struldbrugs, the immortal inhabitants of Luggnagg, who must needs have a vast deal of spare time at command. The French journals, too, speak of Jules Regondi with rapture; and, doubtless we shall soon be elevated to the third heaven as saith Mr. Gardiner, by this miraculous child, who, in spite of his tender years, has discovered the means of applying high pressure to music and reduced the labour of twenty years to the space of about four. For we cannot suppose that he commenced his operations till well on his legs; unless, indeed he began while yet unborn—a thing not impossible to those who believe the story of the Holy Babe who sang a hymn, to His mother's surprise before His entrance into the world." The editor attended one of Regondi's fashionable concerts previous to the next issue of his journal and it is gratifying to read his second account of the youthful musician. "Among the many wonders of the day is Giulio Regondi, the child whose performances on the Spanish guitar are not only calculated to surprise, but please connoisseurs. This most interesting prodigy, for such he may be termed, who has only reached his eighth year, was born at Lyons; his mother being a native of Germany, but his father an Italian. To say that he plays with accuracy and neatness is only doing him scanty justice; to correctness in both time and tune he adds a power of expression and a depth of feeling which would be admired in an adult, in him they show a precocity at once amazing and alarming; for how commonly are such geniuses either cut off by the preternatural action of the mind, or mentally exhausted at an age when the intellects of ordinary persons are beginning to arrive at their full strength! The personal appearance of the almost infant Giulio at once excites a strong feeling in his favour. A well-proportioned, remarkably fair child, with an animated countenance, whose long flaxen locks curl gracefully over his neck and shoulders, and whose every attitude and action seem elegant by nature, not art, immediately interests the beholder; but when he touches the string and draws forth from it, tones that for beauty have hardly ever been exceeded; when his eye shows what his heart feels, it is then that our admiration is at the highest, and we confess the power of the youthful genius. This child is the most pleasing musical prodigy that our time has produced." Catherine Josepha Pelzer, afterwards Mme. Pratten was appearing at the same time as a prodigy on the guitar, and she and Regondi performed guitar duos in public. In July, 1836, Regondi was solo guitarist at concerts with Moscheles, Mme. De

Beriot, and Lablache—the most brilliant artistes of the day—and the press was eulogistic in praise of the guitarist; the following is a report of a concert where he played the guitar in the company of Moscheles, Sir George Smart and Sir M. Costa: "Giulio Regondi, too, performed to the delight and astonishment of all present; so much did this interesting child please, that he was a second time placed on the pianoforte, and again elicited the applause of the whole room." In 1841, when nineteen, Regondi made his first important concert tour with the 'cello virtuoso Joseph Lidel and they performed in all the important cities of Germany and Austria. Regondi's extraordinary guitar playing evoked enthusiastic praises from the correspondents of the A.M.Z in Prague and Vienna, for the very artistic and individual character of his performance and the sweetness of his cantabile. He appeared very frequently in Prague and Vienna, and under his hands the guitar quite filled the largest concert halls. In 1846 he made his second and last continental tour with Mme. Dulcken, celebrated pianist, teacher of Queen Victoria, and when he returned to England, toured the British Isles with Konrad Adam Stehling, also a guitarist; they performed as guitar duettists in various towns. It was at this juncture that Regondi gave attention to the English concertina, invented by Wheatstone in 1829, but left to the genius of Regondi to make known and popular. His companion Stehling, adopted the viola, and was principal viola in the Philharmonic and Crystal Palace orchestras to the time of his death, February 19, 1902. The charm of Stehling's guitar playing was said by critics to be indescribable, his execution was extraordinary and his taste and phrasing incomparable. Sor's *Method for the Guitar,* the German edition published by Simrock, Bonn, was "dedicated to my friend Stehling." Stehling possessed a comprehensive and unique collection of guitar music, which was disposed of by public auction in London, after his decease. The following extract from a Viennese music journal of 1841 is relative to Regondi's appearance in Austria. Regondi, then nineteen, was touring with the 'cellist Lidel, and this journal remarked among other eulogies that he took Vienna by surprise by his beautiful and marvellous playing, that he was by the grace of God, a great genius: "His name is Giulio Regondi, and he belongs to that classic land where Stradivarius and Amati lived—a land where a genius is no great variety; but an artist on the guitar, as Regondi is, is very seldom found. As a virtuoso he is more conspicuous in his mastership of the guitar than was Giuliani, Legnani, Gugliemi and others heard during the season. Regondi's mastership of the guitar is nearly incomprehensible and his playing is full of poetry and sweetness. It is the soul of melody, and he plays the guitar in its purity without any musical tricks. He is an artist whom all musical performers might copy, and even singers and actors, for his art is a natural one. Regondi is the very Paganini of the guitar, under his hand the guitar becomes quite another instrument than we have hitherto known it. He imitates by turn the violin, harp, mandolin, and even the piano so naturally, that you must look at him to convince yourself of the illusion, as you can hear the forte of the piano, the sweet pianissimo of the harp all combined in its six simple strings. He played in his four concerts, arrangements of 'Don Juan,' 'Les Huguenots'—after Thalberg's arrangement for the piano—and the overture to 'Semiramide.' All these were played with their full harmony as one might hear on the piano, but with inimitable tenderness." Richard Hoffman in his Recollections says: "While in London, I stayed with Giulio Regondi, a friend of my family, at that time a prominent figure in musical society. He played the guitar in a most remarkable manner, as well as the concertina, a small reed instrument invented by Wheatstone of telegraph fame. A most lovely quality of tone was produced by the mixture of different metals composing the reeds, and Regondi's genius developed all its possibilities. A criticism from one of the Manchester papers of that time describing his playing when he appeared there as a youth, gives a good idea of his unique style, which for the time being held his audience spell-bound, and I copy it verbatim from my father's scrap book: 'Giulio Regondi quite took the audience by surprise. That an instrument hitherto regarded as a mere toy—the invention, however, of a philosophical mind—should be capable of giving full expression to a brilliant violin concerto of De Beriot's, was more than even musicians who had not heard this talented youth would admit. The close of every movement was greeted with a round of applause in which many members of the orchestra joined. The performer has much of the "fanatico per la musica" in his appearance, and manifestly enthusiastic love for his art; he hangs over and hugs his little box of harmony as if it were a casket of jewels, or an only and dearly loved child. His trills and shakes seem to vibrate through the frame, and occasionally he rises on tip-toe, or flings up his instrument as he jerks out its highest notes, looking the while like one rapt and unconscious of all outward objects, in the absorbing enjoyment of the sweet sounds that flow from his magical instrument.' He played the most difficult music which he adapted to the powers or limitations of the little concertina. Among other things, a concerto of Spohr, which astonished everyone. My father knew him first, when, as a child in Manchester, he was travelling about with the man who called himself his father, but whose subsequent conduct belied any such claim. When the boy had made a large sum of money by his concerts, and seemed able to maintain himself by his talents, the so-called father deserted him, taking with him all the proceeds of the child's labours, and leaving poor Giulio to shift for himself. My father befriended him at this time, and his gentle winning disposition endeared him to all my family. Later in his life when a young man in London, he often took charge of me, and twice we went to Paris together where we enjoyed some of the choicest musical treats. I heard with him all the great singers and musicians of the day, Tamburini, Lablache, Grisi, Mario, Alboni, Persiani, and most of these before I was sixteen years old. Regondi's playing of the guitar always seemed to me his most remarkable achievement; he had added to the instrument two or three covered strings without frets which he used at will, and the wonderful expression he could impart to his melodies I have never heard excelled by any voice. I have heard him play Thalberg's 'Huguenots' and the 'Don Juan,' Op. 14, making the guitar respond to the most difficult variations with perfect ease."

Mrs. Felicia Hemans made him the subject of the poem entitled, "To Giulio Regondi—the boy Guitarist"; but her beneficial desires expressed for his welfare were not realised.

> Blessing and love be round thee still, fair boy!
> Never may suffering wake a deeper tone
> Than genius now, in its first fearless joy,
> Calls forth exulting from the chords which own
> Thy fairy touch. Oh, may'st thou ne'er be taught
> The power whose fountain is in troubled thought.
> For in the light of those confiding eyes,
> And on th' ingenuous calm of that clear brow,
> A dower, more precious e'en than genius lies,
> A pure mind's worth, a warm heart's vernal glow.
> God, who hath graced thee thus, O gentle child
> Keep midst the world thy brightness undefiled.

Hoffman continues: "His history was sad and full of mystery, which doubtless added further attraction to his talents, and many were the stories whispered as to his birth and parentage. He was much sought after in London, and a great favourite with the nobility of whom many were his pupils and devoted friends. He was the constant guest of two old ladies of the Bourbon aristocracy living in London, who treated him 'en prince' and always rose when he entered their salon. He never revealed to anyone his connection with these people, but I have always thought he belonged to them 'de race.' We were in constant correspondence until the time of his death which occurred in the early seventies. His lovely spirit passed away after many months of suffering from that most cruel of all diseases—cancer. I remember that a certain hope of reprieve from the dread sentence of death was instilled by his physicians and friends, by telling him that, if only he could obtain some of the American condurango plant, which at that time was supposed to be a cure for this malady he might at least be relieved. I sent him a quantity of the preparation, but it failed to help him, and so he died, alone in London lodgings, but not uncared for, nor yet unwept, unhonoured, or unsung! His fame was too closely allied to his personality to endure after him, save in the hearts of those that knew him best; but while he lived he showed himself a true and noble artist, full of the finest and most exalted love of music, a man whom to know was in itself a privilege not to be over-estimated." Regondi composed *Two concertos,* in D and E, for concertina and orchestra, and taught the instrument largely; his name was on important concert programmes both in London and the provinces. He was a friend of the violinist Molique who composed for him, Op. 46, *Concerto in G* for the concertina, which Regondi rendered with his usual success, April 24, 1864, at the concerts of the Musical Society, London. Molique also wrote a *Sonata,* Op. 57, and twelve other compositions for Regondi, and after hearing his remarkable playing, Sir Alexander Macfarren, Sir Julius Benedict, Sterndale Bennett, and Wallace—leading names among native musicians—all composed works for this instrument. Neuland, a contemporary organist and guitarist of repute, composed and dedicated to his friend Op. 16, *Introduction and variations for guitar solo.* Regondi was of rather delicate, slight build, a most attractive personality and a versatile linguist. His hands were rather small, so much so, that the strings of an ordinary guitar were too wide on the fingerboard, and previous to playing a strange guitar he adjusted the strings nearer to each other particularly the first to the second. A guitar made by Staufer, Vienna, and bearing in the place of the label, Regondi's autograph, was in the possession of Colonel Temple, London. Regondi had presented this guitar to a pupil and placed a note in the instrument to that effect. No one, since the time of Giuliani, created such an interest in the guitar as Regondi, and with him the last of the really great guitarists of the epoch departed ; but through him and his playing the instrument received an impetus, and his influence was great. His portrait was published on several occasions, that reproduced was issued by Wheatstone, London, in 1852, from a daguerreotype by Laroche ; another was published by Diabelli, Vienna, and a sketch of his life by L. Megarski, appeared in the Vienna Theatrical Journal of 1841. Regondi's published compositions for the guitar are few. He was primarily a concertist, a virtuoso, and his compositions require the skill of a virtuoso for their interpretation, for which reason they were not popular. They will, however entitle him to a foremost position as a refined musician, notwithstanding the exceptional powers of execution demanded by them. They are, Op. 19, *Reverie nocturne ;* Op. 20, *Fete villageoise ;* Op. 21, *First air varie ;* Op. 22, *Second air varie ;* Op. 23, *Introduction and Caprice,* all issued by Andre, Offenbach ; the International League of Guitarists, Munich, published his *Etude* No. 1. Ernest Shand, the English guitarist and composer, known more to the public as a popular comedian, possessed the following original manuscript guitar compositions and arrangements by Regondi : *Overture to Oberon ;* Stephen Heller's *Wanderstunden ;* an arrangement for guitar solo of Crouch's song *Kathleen Mavourneen,* and an original composition dedicated to a lady pupil. He wrote two concertos for the concertina, several methods, studies, etc., and more than two hundred original compositions and transcriptions for concertina solo, concertina with voice and with other instruments, and the exceedingly graceful piece *Les oiseaux,* Op. 12, was unquestionably a public favourite ; these concertina compositions were published by Ashdown, London ; Wheatstone, London and in Dublin. Regondi wrote a few songs : *Absence,* dedicated to Mme. Schuster, issued in 1854 ; *Tell me my heart why so desponding ; As slowly part the shades of night,* both published in 1855 and *L'aviso,* in 1860 by Wessell, London.

Reinhardt, Django, and his brother Joseph were French gypsies who learned to play the guitar by listening, while roaming in their caravan, to the records of Eddie Lang and like him they played the guitar with a plectrum. Django, the more brilliant and better known of the two, injured his left hand in an accident and had use of only two fingers, the others were paralysed. He was the guitarist of the Quintette du Hot Club de France and their star performer. This combination, formed in Paris in 1934, had spasmodic popularity in night clubs, concerts, and broadcasts, until disbanding in 1939. He visited London in 1937 where he made many records and broadcasts, and died at Fontainbleau, France, May, 1953, aged forty-three.

Respighi, Ottorino, born July 9, 1879, at Bologna is one of the most important Italian musicians of the day. His early musical studies were in the Liceo Musicale of his native city, later in St. Petersburg under Rimsky-Korsakov and Max Bruch in Berlin. In 1913 he was appointed professor at the Liceo di Cecilia in Rome and in 1924 succeeded Enrico Bossi as its principal. He is the composer of operas and orchestral music and in *Symphonic poem* introduces the mandolin in the third movement with a solo. This was performed in a series of symphony concerts given in La Scala Theatre, Milan, in the spring of 1939 when Mario Fiore was the mandolinist.

Riedl, J., a Hungarian musician who lived during the middle of the nineteenth century, the composer of Op. 3, *Trio for violin, alto and guitar,* published by Berra, Prague ; Op. 6, *Duo for guitar and piano,* published in 1844 by Hoffman, Prague, and *Six Waltzes for guitar solo,* published by Schott. These compositions were recorded in Whistling's Handbuch in 1844.

Rizzio, David, born at Turin, died Holyrood Palace, Edinburgh, March 9, 1564, was the son of a professional musician. He received his first instruction from his father and later obtained a position at the court of the Duke of Savoy. In 1561 he came with the ambassador to Scotland and with his brother Joseph, entered the service of Mary Queen of Scots, first as a vocalist with his guitar, until in 1561 he became her private secretary. He was stabbed to death, almost in the Queen's presence in Holyrood Palace on the evening of March 9, 1564. He exercised some influence on Scottish music and there is a strong tradition that he was the composer of several well-known Scottish airs. An illustration of his guitar, presented to him by Mary, Queen of Scots, is reproduced. Its extraordinary workmanship with intricate inlay of tortoiseshell, mother of pearl and ivory is suggestive of Moorish origin. The instrument is in the Museum of the Royal College of Music, London, presented by George Donaldson.

Roch, Pascual, born in 1860 in Valencia, Spain, and died in Havana in 1921. When a lad he was employed in a guitar factory and played the instrument as an amateur. Later he commenced business on his own account, manufacturing instruments principally for export. The label of the ordinary type was: "Fabrica de Guitarras, Bandurrias y Laudes, Pascual Roch, 146 San Vicente, Valencia." He also constructed a superior class which he labelled: "D. Francisco Tarrega, eminente guitarrista." Roch subsequently emigrated to Havana where he commenced teaching the guitar. He is known however by his admirable *Modern Method* for the guitar, which was published in 1924 by G. Schirmer, New York. This most excellent and comprehensive Method is of the school of Tarrega and published in three volumes with English French and Spanish text.

Rode, Jacques Pierre Joseph, was born at Bordeaux, February 26, 1774, and died there November 25, 1830. When eight years of age he commenced the study of the violin with Fauvel, a well-known violinist in Bordeaux, and remained under him six years. In 1788 he was sent to Paris where he was privileged in being a pupil of Viotti for two years, after which he made his first public appearance in the Theatre Monsieur, playing Viotti's *Thirteenth concerto,* with immense success. Although but sixteen, he was appointed leader of the second violins in the excellent orchestra of the unfortunate Theatre Feydeau and was frequently heard as soloist. In 1794, Rode began a series of concert tours with the famous guitarist and singer, Garat, visiting Holland and Germany. His success in Berlin and Hamburg was decided, and from the latter city he took passage for his native town; but the vessel was driven to England by adverse winds so he visited London. He appeared only once in public, at a charity concert, without creating much impression, and then returned to Paris where he was appointed principal violin professor at the newly founded Conservatoire. In 1799 he travelled to Spain to try his fortune on a concert tour and in Madrid met Boccherini, who is said to have written orchestral parts to Rode's early works. It was in Spain that he gave attention to the guitar which enjoyed great favour at court. Boccherini was himself a guitarist, Rode followed his example, and at this period wrote several of his lighter compositions with guitar accompaniment. When he returned to Paris, in 1800, he was solo violinist in the private band of Napoleon Bonaparte, and at this period drew the admiration of all Paris, and achieved his greatest success. Notwithstanding, in 1803, he went with Boieldieu to St. Petersburg, passing through north Germany on his way, for Spohr heard him when in Brunswick and was greatly impressed, so much so, that he aimed solely to imitate his style and manner. In St. Petersburg his playing aroused the greatest enthusiasm, and he was attached to the private service of the Emperor with a munificent salary. The five years of laborious service in Russia are declared to have had a deleterious influence over his playing, and from this time a decided decline of his powers set in. This was noticed when he returned to Paris in 1808. Rode composed much for the violin—concertos, caprices, quartets, and a *Polonaise for violin, or flute and guitar,* published by Berra and also by Hoffman, Prague; other compositions and several arrangements with the guitar were issued in 1820 by Simrock, Bonn; Haslinger, Vienna; and Janet, Paris. His memoirs edited by Pougin were published in 1874.

Rodrigo, Joaquin, contemporary, born 1902, at Sagunto, Valencia, Spain. He became blind at the age of three and made a special study of music with local teachers, subsequently becoming a pupil of Dukas in Paris after which he toured Europe extensively. He was awarded the National Prize of his native land in 1925, created a Commander of the Order of Alfonso X, the Wise, in 1945, and two years later appointed professor of Musical History in Madrid University. Among his various compositions is *Concerto de Aranjuez* for guitar and orchestra. This work in three movements, Allegro con spirito, Adagio, and Allegro gentile is of twenty minutes duration. Its first performance was given the following year in Barcelona when Sainz de la Maza was soloist and the conductor Mendoza. Numerous broadcasts of this concerto have been made by Ida Presti and Narciso Yepes from Paris. The Strad, an English music journal reported the latter's performance thus: "A concert with the Paris Conservatoire Orchestra, conducted by a young Spaniard, Ataulfo Argenta, included a splendidly restrained performance with Narciso Yepes of Joaquin Rodrigo's *Guitar Concerto.* This must surely be the only really successful concerto written for the instrument. The beautiful balance of ideas and harmonies, the sensitive atmosphere and orchestration are an ever fresh delight." Rodrigo's biography has been edited by Federico Sopena, Madrid.

Roemer, Matthaus, contemporary, born November 8, 1871, at Nordhalben, Germany, a doctor of philosophy who, after graduating at Munich University studied the guitar under the virtuoso Heinrich Albert and singing and composition with Krauss and Reinberger at the Musical Academy. He became a famous European oratorio singer and has composed more than sixty lieder with guitar, also *Holy Night,* for three part female choir, with accompaniment of organ and guitars; *Three lieder for soprano with violin, 'cello and guitar* and a *Quartet for guitars.*

Rolla, Alessandro, born April 6, 1757 at Pavia, Italy, and died at Milan, September 15, 1841. He was a violinist, guitarist, and composer who first studied the piano, but soon turned to the guitar and the violin, studying the latter instruments under Conti and Renzi. For some years he was leader of the orchestra in Parma, and it was here, in 1795, that Paganini was his pupil for several months. In 1802 he was appointed conductor of the opera at La Scala, Milan, and in this position won a widespread reputation, and was also a professor at the Milan Conservatoire for many years. Rolla had a strong predilection for the viola, and wrote concertos for this instrument, which he performed in public. His compositions comprise numerous violin duets, a few trios, quartets, and quintets for stringed instruments which include the guitar, and also concertos for the violin and the viola. *Three duos for violin and guitar* were published by Janet, Paris ; *Three duettini for guitar and violin,* Hug, Zurich ; *Three duos for violin and guitar,* Meissonnier, Paris, and *Five romances for voice with guitar,* Cons, Milan. Among his posthumous works are *Four Waltzes for flute, violin and guitar,* published by Ricordi, Milan. These compositions enjoyed considerable favour in his day.

Romberg, Bernhard, born November 11, 1767 at Dinklage, and died at Hamburg, August 13, 1841. He came of long musical stock, his father Anton, a bassoon player died in 1812. When only fourteen Bernhard attracted considerable attention in Paris during a visit there with his father. From 1790 to 1793 he was violoncellist in the band of the Elector of Cologne, in Bonn, at the same time as Ries and the two Beethovens. During the French invasion he made a concert tour through Italy, Spain and Portugal, was well received, especially in Madrid, where he played in duos for violin and violoncello with Ferdinand VII. His cousin Andreas travelled with him, and when they returned through Vienna gave a concert at which Beethoven took part.
He returned to Hamburg where he married and was a professor in the Paris Conservatoire from 1801-1803 and later a member of the Royal Orchestra, Berlin. In 1806 the French advanced again into Germany, so Romberg travelled through the south of Russia and remained there the following year ; but when the government was more settled he returned to Berlin and was Court Capellmeister until his retirement in 1817, when he removed to Hamburg, where he resided for the remainder of his life. Romberg was the earliest composer for the violoncello who retains his importance to the present. He struck out fresh paths in the technique of the instrument and combined true poetic feelings with sound musicianship. His celebrated concertos may be said to contain implicitly a complete theory of 'cello playing and there are few passages known to modern players, the type of which may not be found in his works. Romberg was the composer of several operas which were produced with varying success in Paris, and Berlin, and while in Vienna he composed Op. 46, *Duo for Violoncello and Guitar, a divertimento on Austrian airs,* which enjoyed popularity, and was published by Haslinger, Vienna. Romberg also composed songs with the guitar, published by Schott, Mayence, and Whistling enumerates *Terzetts* for voices with flute and guitar.

Romero, Luis T., was born at Madrid, Spain, in 1853 and died at South Boston, U.S.A., November 19, 1893. He played the guitar during youth in his native land and when in his teens the family emigrated to the Southern States of America, and in California he continued the study of the guitar under a compatriot, Miguel S. Arrevalo. It was in San Francisco that he made the acquaintance of his teacher and their mutual love of the guitar formed a life-long friendship. For a period Romero resided as a teacher in San Jose, but later, in order to enlarge his sphere, he removed to Boston where he remained until death. He was a popular teacher and concert artist; but his health, never robust, declined, and when the disease—pulmonary tuberculosis—became acute, he entered the Carney Hospital in South Boston on October 12, 1893 and died there on the nineteenth of the following month. It is stated on good authority that the pianist Paderewski had very little opinion of the guitar until he heard Romero play, and then was enthusiastic in its praise. Romero's compositions, light and pleasing, are principally arrangements and transcriptions for guitar solo and guitar duos. His publishers were Jean White and Walter Jacobs, Boston; Broder & Schlam, San Francisco, and Carl Fischer, New York.

Roser von Reiter, Franz de Paula, an Austrian operatic composer, was born at Naarn, Upper Austria in 1779 and died August 12, 1830, at Pesth. His life was spent in Vienna and Pesth as conductor of various theatres. He was capellmeister in Vienna from 1812-1821 and composed nearly one hundred operas, operettas, pantomimes, etc., in addition to instrumental compositions principally for strings and flute with guitar. No new compositions from him appeared after 1828. Op. 14, a *Theme* (by Hummel) *with Six variations for guitar and flute* was published by Breitkopf & Härtel, Leipzig, and the A.M.Z. of the year 1816 records others.

Rossini, Gioachino Antonio, born February 29, 1792 at Pesaro, Italy, died November 13, 1868 at Passy, Paris, was one of the brightest luminaries of the nineteenth century. The position of his parents was of the humblest, his father town trumpeter and inspector of slaughter houses and his mother a baker's daughter. For a period the boy was left in charge of a butcher of Bologna, where he received crude musical lessons from Prinetti, while his parents were touring with a theatrical company. At the age of thirteen he was playing the horn by his father's side in the theatre orchestra; however, in 1807 he entered the Liceo of Bologna where he studied under Mattei. At the end of the first year his cantata was awarded the prize, publicly performed the same year, and from then Rossini commenced dramatic composition completing in all about sixty operas, many oratorios, cantatas, and instrumental music. He had been engaged in Naples, and shortly before Christmas, 1815, left for Rome, where he was under contract to produce two operas. The first of these was coldly received, and the second, *Almaviva* (*The barber of Seville*), which made its first appearance at the Theatre Argentina, February 5, 1816, was immediately condemned. The reason was the predilection for Paisiello's opera of this name. Rossini, fully aware of this, with best of motives, previous to adopting the libretto, enquired of Paisiello if his so doing would cause annoyance—under the impression this would placate Paisiello's friends and admirers—it was not so, for at the outset a determined faction intended to wreck it. Paisiello uses a mandolin to accompany a serenade (see Paisiello), Rossini uses the guitar to accompany a serenade, and all

Rossini's innovations were not only foreign but distasteful to the Romans. From the commencement of the performance the audience manifested its hostility, and matters were intensified by an unfortunate circumstance. In the first act Rossini writes an accompaniment for the guitar to Almaviva's cavatina, *Ecco ridente il cielo,* which he sings with his guitar under the window of Rosina. It is in the delicious andante of this cavatina, with the guitar, that Rossini first employs the modulation to the minor third below, so common afterwards with Italian composers. Rossini borrowed the opening of the first chorus in his opera, *Aureliano* for this serenade. It is in the key of C, two-four time, accompanied by solo clarionet, violins pizzicato while the guitar ripples arpeggios in sextuplets, swelling towards the close with full chords. For the first performance Garcia, a skilful guitarist, played the role of Almaviva and accompanied himself with the guitar on the stage. An unfortunate omission put the unfriendly audience in hilarious mood, for when Garcia commenced, his guitar was not tuned! He realised the awkward situation, the orchestra waited for him to tune, adding to the amusement of the audience, who began to whistle and shout and during the turmoil Garcia broke a string. The whole house, now convulsed with laughter, showed no consideration for the young composer, Rossini, who, according to custom was conducting from the piano. The introduction was again played when Figaro (Zamboni) hurried on the stage with another guitar. Sutherland Edwards says: "When, however, Zamboni entered with another guitar, the anti-guitarists set up a loud laugh, and without waiting to see whether the baritone, unlike the tenor, had taken the trouble to tune this instrument, hissed and hooted so that not a note of *Largo al factotum* was heard." Wild derision and laughter took possession of the audience and the designs of Rossini's opponents materialised. Rossini in despair mounted the balcony, in vain, for the tumult continued. Though hissed on the first occasion, *Almaviva* was listened to with patience on the second, advancing in favour until it became one of the most popular comic operas, and ended in being known as *The Barber of Seville.* During the next eight years, Rossini wrote no less than twenty operas, and in others he uses the guitar. The English guitarist, A. F. Cramer, mentions a quintet for strings which included the guitar. Rossini had heard Zani de Ferranti and Paganini play, and he evinced a partiality for the guitar and mandolin. A conversation with Moscheles relative to these instruments is recorded in the latter's biography. Rossini died in Passy, France, November 15, 1868, honoured by an imposing funeral. His life and memoirs have been edited by more than twenty authors, the first by Carpani in 1824.

Roussel, Albert, born April 5, 1869, at Tourcoing, France, and died at Royan, August 23, 1937. When a youth he entered the French navy and commenced composing during the voyages. On the completion of his nautical service he continued his musical studies at the Schola Cantorum, Paris, where he was a pupil of d'Indy. He became a professor at this institute in 1902 and has composed symphonies, instrumental works, songs, etc. He served with the Red Cross during the first world war, and, broken in health, retired to Brittany. In 1929 a Roussel festival was celebrated in his honour in Paris and attracted world-wide attention. He wrote a composition for the guitar entitled *Segovia* which he dedicated to the virtuoso. This was Op. 29, published by Durand, Paris, in 1925, and Roussel later made a transcription for solo piano.

Rudersdorff, Joseph, born at Amsterdam in 1779 and died at Konigsberg, Germany, in 1866. He was a violinist and guitarist who displayed great musical genius at a very early age. His first instrument was the violin, and he obtained such marked proficiency that when eight years he appeared as soloist in his native town, playing a concerto of Pleyel. He then adopted the guitar and his mastery on this instrument was equal to that of the violin. At the commencement of the nineteenth century he migrated to Ireland and lived for more than twenty years in Dublin where he was esteemed as a musician. In 1822 he was professionally engaged in Ivanowsky, in the Ukraine, Russia, and from there he went to Hamburg in 1825 as concertmaster. He transferred to Berlin in a similar capacity in 1831 where many of his compositions were published. He was the composer of fantasias, polonaises, etc., for violin and guitar, piano works, and songs with piano and guitar. Op. 6, *Waltzes and Exercises;* Op. 7 and 8, *Variations* and Op. 11, *Five Pieces.* The foregoing, all for guitar solo, were published by Gombart, Augsburg, and Schott issued his songs with guitar. His daughter, Hermine, born in 1822, was a celebrated singer who possessed a powerful soprano voice. She appeared for several seasons at the Royal Italian Opera, London, also on the continent and in the United States with great success.

Rugeon Beauclair, Antoine Louis, a French musician and guitarist living in Paris during the commencement of the nineteenth century and employed in the postal service during the years 1808-1829, the latter year being the date of his death. Although not professionally engaged in music he was a talented amateur of some repute, and published a few compositions for his instrument, the principal were Op. 2, *Three grand duos for two guitars,* published by Momigny, Paris ; Op. 3, *Three trios concertante for two guitars and violin,* Naderman, Paris ; Op. 4, and Op. 8, *Sonatas for guitar solo,* Leduc and also Lemoine, Paris ; *Twelve waltzes for guitar solo,* Costallat, Paris ; and a number of themes with variations and similar compositions without opus numbers, all of which appeared in Paris.

Rung, Henrick, born March 3, 1807 at Copenhagen and died there December 13, 1871, was chorus master of the opera from 1842 and in 1851 conductor of the St. Cecilia Society for ancient church music and a composer of dramatic music and songs. He was an ardent admirer of the guitar and a performer who wrote for the instrument Op. 1, *Six Pieces;* Op. 2, *Polonaises;* Op. 3, *Short Lessons;* Op. 4, *Solo Album,* all of which were issued by Lose, Copenhagen. His son Frederick, born June 14, 1854 in Copenhagen and died there January 22, 1914 continued his father's work. In 1877 he was director of the St. Cecilia Society, from 1872 conductor of the Hoftheatre and later Kapellmeister. With operas, symphonies, dramatic and other works he composed two volumes of guitar solos, issued by Hansen, Copenhagen. Particulars ot his life and works were published by Thrane, in Cecilia in 1901.

SAINT-SAËNS, Charles Camille, born Paris, October 9, 1835, died Algiers, December 16, 1921. This eminent French composer, whose works comprise symphonies, operas, oratorios, organ music, ballet, operettas, etc., wrote in 1909 to the editor of L'Estudiantina—a Parisian music journal published in the interests of the mandolin and guitar, "Mandolines et Guitares ont des sons qui font aimer." (Mandolins and guitars give sounds which I love), at the same time accepting the presidency of their musical society. Saint-Saëns was a champion of instrumental music, who, with Berlioz and Gounod (both guitarists) stand pre-eminent as promoters of the revival of French music. An illustration of his guitar, in the Museum of Paris Conservatoire of Music, is reproduced by courtesy of the directors.

Sagrini, Luigi, born in 1809 at Monza, near Milan, Italy, and living in London as a guitar virtuoso and professor in 1840. He was an infant prodigy on the guitar and as such appeared with brilliant success at the most important courts of Europe, travelling for many years and eventually making his abode in Paris and London. From 1824-28 he was teaching and concertising in France where he was frequently performing guitar duos with the virtuoso Coste. The Harmonicon, an important English music journal, in its May, 1824 issue, stated: "The young Sagrini, thirteen years old, a professor of the guitar, gave a concert on March 15, 1824 in the hall of Mons Pfieffer, Paris. The extraordinary and precose talent of this young artist has been attended by the most brilliant success. At the court of Turin he astonished and charmed the most distinguished connoisseurs and the same effect was produced at Paris." At a concert in Valenciennes in 1828 Sagrini with Coste, performed guitar duos, their chef-d'oeuvre, Giuliani's *Duo for two guitars,* Op. 130. Sagrini was highly esteemed in London and associated in his concerts with the organist and guitarist Neuland, whom he had met in Paris. They appeared together in duos for two guitars and also piano and guitar, in London and Paris, and Sagrini's compositions were published under the title of, *A Guide to the guitar;* also *A set of preludes, exercises, etc.,* issued by Addison, London; Op. 4, *Variations for guitar solo,* Lemoine, Paris; Op. 5, *Five divertimentos for guitar tuned in E major;* Op. 11, 12, and 13, *Guitar solos,* Schott, Mayence. (Op. 13 was also issued by Johanning, London under the title of *Two books of favourite airs*); Op. 15, *Recreation for guitar solo;* Op. 16 and 17,

Joaquin Rodrigo

Ferdnand Rebay

Luis T. Romero

Exhibited in
Schubert Museum,
Vienna

Franz Schubert and his Guitars

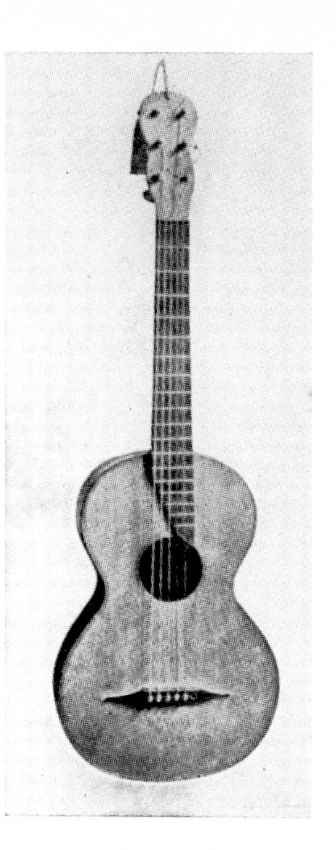

In the possession
of
Major Hans Umlauff

Duos for two guitars, Johanning, London ; Op. 27, *Fantasia on ' O cara memoria,'* dedicated to the Marquis of Bristol, Richault, Paris. In addition he composed numerous pieces which were published by Bochsa and also Holloway, London, and arranged guitar accompaniments to numerous songs. Although rather more difficult than usual they display the beauties of the guitar as an accompanying instrument.

Salazar, Adolfo, contemporary Spanish music critic, born Madrid, June 3, 1890 was a pupil of Falla at the National Conservatoire. From 1914-18 he was editor of the Revista Musical Hispano-Americano and music critic to El Sol in 1936. At the outbreak of civil war he emigrated to Buenos Aires and from 1939 lived in Mexico. His compositions include symphonies and other orchestral works, also piano, violin, and guitar solos, the most widely known of the latter is *Romacilla.*

Salieri, Antonio, born August 19, 1750, at Legnano, near Verona, Italy, died at Vienna May 7, 1825, was a very highly esteemed composer of whom Beethoven was proud to style himself " Salieri's pupil." He was a son of wealthy parents and learned music from his brother, a pupil of Tartini, and after the death of his parents removed to Venice, where he made the acquaintance of Gassmann, composer and late capellmeister to the Emperor. Gassmann became interested in the lad, gave him further instruction, took him to Vienna and brought him to the notice of Emperor Joseph, and at sixteen he was appointed director of opera in Vienna, remaining in this position for twenty-four years until 1790, when he resigned. Such was his phenomenal success that at the age of twenty-four he was court composer, and in 1778 received the additional appointment of court capellmeister. In that year he visited Italy, five of his operas were produced in Venice, Milan, and Rome, and spread his fame throughout the continent for he was commissioned to write an opera for Paris, which he personally superintended during April, 1784. Two years later he made another visit to Paris, where his opera *Les Horaces* had failed ; but his good fortune was amply retrieved by the most brilliant success of *Axur Re d'Ormus,* or *Tarare,* as it was originally named. This grand opera in five acts, produced in Paris, June 8, 1787, and the following year in Vienna, has remained his most important work. The fourth act contains that beautiful romance for tenor entitled: *I was born in the Roman country,* which is accompanied by mandolin, flute, and strings, the latter with the exception of the viola, played pizzicato ; an extract from the mandolin part of this orchestration is reproduced. Salieri composed many operas which he conducted in various continental cities ; but owing to the change of taste in dramatic music, he devoted his later years chiefly to church composition, choruses, and instrumental music. He enjoyed the most honoured position among contemporary musicians, for in 1816, when he celebrated his fiftieth anniversary of the commencement of his career in Vienna, he was publicly fêted, decorated by the Emperor, and compositions by each of his pupils, including Schubert, were performed. Salieri lost his only son in 1805, and his wife two years later, and in 1824, after fifty years' service at court, retired on full salary, but died shortly after. His memoirs edited by Mosel were published in 1827 and by von Herrmann in 1897.

Bin gebohren im Romischen Lande

(I was born in the Roman country).

ROMANCE FROM THE OPERA "AXUR, RE D'ORMUS,"

COMPOSED WITH MANDOLIN ACCOMPANIMENT BY SALIERI IN 1787.

MANDOLIN.

Salleneuve, Edward, born December 19, 1800 at Konigsberg but removed to Berlin in early youth where he studied music under Birnbach and Klien. Mendel states that he was one of the most renowned of German singers with the guitar, and also a celebrated teacher of singing and the guitar. The A.M.Z. of Leipzig from the years 1834-41 published titles of some of his songs with guitar and Whistling records the following of his published compositions. Op. 2, *Dances for guitar solo* ; Op. 9, *Variations for guitar* ; *Carlsbad galop for one or two guitars* and various arrangements for guitar.

Salmhofer, Franz, born January 22, 1900, at Vienna was a descendant on his mother's side of the Schubert family. When a boy he was a chorister in Admont Convent and entered Vienna Academy in 1914, studying composition under Schreker and the clarionet, until 1920, with Bartholomey. In 1926 he won the city of Vienna art prize and from 1929-1939 was conductor of the Burgtheatre. He has composed much incidental music, operas, ballets and chamber music in which he uses the guitar, notably in his *Slavic Rhapsody* and *Dance Suite for violin, viola and guitar.*

Salomon, M., born Besancon, Doubs, France in 1786, and died there February 19, 1831, was a guitar soloist, a professor of the guitar and composer for his instrument who is known as the inventor and patentee of two musical instruments which he named harp-lyre or harpolyre. It was constructed on the model of a large guitar, fitted with three necks, the centre one with a fretted fingerboard strung as the ordinary guitar, while the two side necks carried extra accompanying strings of which there were a total of twenty-one. It resembled the theorbo lute and was patented by Salomon in 1827. By its manner of stringing and tuning some novel and powerful effects were obtainable ; but it met with no success, so two years later, in 1829, he improved it and obtained a patent for another guitar, which was evidently on the pattern of a lyre-guitar by the maker Le Dhuy who flourished in Coucy-le-Chateau about 1806. Salomon also invented a tuning apparatus with steel rods, vibrated by a toothed wheel which was no more successful than the harpolyre. Two of these patent instruments are in the museum of the National Conservatoire of Music, Paris. Salomon wrote a method for his harpolyre and light pieces for it and the guitar. Op. 1, *Twelve Divertimentos for guitar solo* and Op. 2, *Valses for guitar,* were published by Launer, Paris.

Salvayre, Gervais Bernard, born Toulouse, France, June 24, 1847 and died May 16, 1916 at Saint-Ague, Toulouse. He began his musical education as chorister in the cathedral and continued in the conservatoire of his native city, previous to admission in the Paris Conservatoire. In this latter institution he studied the organ with Benoist and composition and fugue under Thomas and Bazin. He gained the Prix de Rome in 1872 and during his three years music study there acquired a special interest in the mandolin. Under the tuition of the mandolin virtuoso, Bertucci, he attained excellent proficiency and maintained interest in the instrument throughout life. His first published compositions were Italian songs issued by Ricordi, other notable compositions dating from this period were his opera *Le Bravo* and *The Last*

Judgment. When he returned to Paris in 1877 Salvayre was chorus master of the Opera Populaire, Theatre du Chatalet, and composed works for the stage. Later he was music critic to Gil Blas. In 1894 he was in charge of military music in Serbia and was awarded honours in that country and also in Russia. His ballet *Fandango,* produced November 26, 1877, was a decided success. Other important works are *Richard III,* an opera, produced in St. Petersburg in 1883, *Symphonic Overture, Stabat Mater,* other church music and operas, produced as late as 1913 in Paris, where he had been residing for some time in rue St. Florentin. He subsequently remodelled *The Last Judgment* which was eventually produced as *The Resurrection* and his opera *Le Bravo,* was transformed from an opera comique into a spectacular drama. whereupon it enjoyed immense success partly owing to the singing of the prima donna Heilbron and the tenor Bouhy. Salvayre composed for the guitar in this opera which has been produced in many lands. He is the composer of several light pieces for mandolin and piano, the most popular *Mattinata,* which with his songs with guitar were published by Lemoine, Paris. Salvayre was decorated with the Legion d'Honneur, July, 1880.

Salzmann, H., a German musician living during the first quarter of the nineteenth century, was the composer of the following which are recorded by Whistling and published by Hofmeister, Leipzig. Op. 1 and 2, *Variations for two guitars ;* Op. 3, 4, and 20, *Variations for guitar and flute* and Op. 9, *Guitar solo.*

Samazeuilh, Gustave, born June 2, 1877, at Bordeaux. His preliminary studies in music were with Chausson and continued at the Schola Cantorum, Paris, under d'Indy and Dukas. In 1912 he was living in rue de Prony, Paris, as music critic and composer. All his compositions—whether orchestral, violin, piano or songs—are characterised by elegance and personality. In 1925 he composed for, and dedicated to Segovia, a *Serenade for guitar solo* of which the composer made transcriptions later for the piano, violoncello and piano, and violin and piano. This composition demands of the performer the power to produce a sustained and singing tone ; its first performance was given in Buenos Aires by the virtuoso Segovia, July 23, 1928. Samazeuilh was the author of a life of his teacher Dukas, published in 1913.

Sancho, Jose, born in the province of Valencia during the latter part of the nineteenth century, was a noted guitarist and an original member of the Estudiantina Figaro, conducted by Domingo Granados and succeeded by Carlos Garcia Tolsa. With this world famous estudiantina he made an extensive tour of the U.S.A. and at its dissolution, Sancho in 1904 visited Buenos Aires where he was popular as guitarist and composer. In this city nearly fifty of his compositions for the guitar were published during the year he was there; but although eminently successful his natural roving disposition urged him to dispose of the copyrights of his publications, to the music publishing firm of Francisco Nunez of Buenos Aires and in March 1905 he migrated to North America. In 1906 many of his compositions appeared in Europe, they were published in Paris by the firms of Pisa, Gregh, and Beuscher, and also in Milan and Turin, Italy.

Sandi, Luis, born February 22, 1905 at Mexico City, studied in the National Conservatoire, became a choral conductor and subsequently chief of Public Instruction, Music Section. His music is original and permeated with Mexican folk lore. The most renowned of his compositions is *Norte,* a symphonic suite in three movements which was conducted by Chavez in 1941. Sandi makes use of the guitar in his compositions, one of which, *Les Guarecitas,* based on themes of the Yaqui Indians, is scored for guitars and chamber orchestra. *Fatima,* a *Suite galante para guitarra,* which comprises a *Prelude, Aire Tierno, Pascalle and Serenata,* is dedicated to the guitar virtuoso Jesus Silva and published by Ediciones Mexicanas, Mexico City. Copies of all Sandi's compositions are in the State Library, Philadelphia, U.S.A.

Sandrini, Paul, born at Gorizia, Italy in 1782 and died November 15, 1813 at Dresden. In 1805 he was oboist in the Royal Chapel Orchestra, Prague, and three years later was officiating in a similar capacity in Saxony. He was the author of the following compositions which are recorded by Mendel. Op. 12, *Duo for guitars;* Op. 13, *Six Cavatines for guitar;* Op. 14, *Six Italian melodies for guitar,* issued by Peters, Leipzig; Op. 15, *Sonata Concertante for guitar;* Op. 16, *Variations for flute and guitar,* Hofmeister, Leipzig; *Six Variations for guitar,* Simrock, Bonn, and *Twelve Landler* published by Haas, Prague.

Sanz, Gasper, born at Calanda, Aragon, Spain, and died at Madrid in 1710, studied for the priesthood in Salamanca University of which he was a Bachelor of Theology. In 1655 he was a pupil on the organ of Carisani, organist of the Royal Chapel, Naples, later a pupil in Rome of Colista on the guitar and he became the teacher of this instrument to Don Juan of Austria. Sanz compiled a very important Method for the guitar entitled: *Instruccion de musica sobre la Guitarra Espanola.* It was for the guitar of five strings as used at the period, the sixth, the lowest E had not yet been introduced. The opening chapters treat of the history of the instrument and its celebrated masters and concludes with songs and national dances. This treatise was first issued in 1674 from Saragossa and an edition in three volumes, published in 1697 was catalogued in 1949 by a London antiquary at £60.

Sarrablo y Clavero, Manuel, was born February 6, 1866 at Barbastro, Huesca, Spain, and died in Paris, December, 1947. At the age of fourteen he commenced a business career as clerk in Barcelona and it was not until he returned to his home at the age of twenty that he evinced any inclination for music, which occurred after hearing an estudiantina, when he became enamoured of the guitar and mandolin. With no assistance whatever, he learned to play these instruments so quickly, that by the end of that year he published an easy method, and this instruction book which was very clearly compiled, became exceedingly popular in Aragon. He taught a few friends and they planned a hiking holiday together, so taking their instruments for amusement they played and sang their way over the Pyrenees. So care-free and happy were they that they did not return home, but continued their travels through southern Europe, sometimes by train, but mostly on foot. They eventually arrived in Paris, where Sarrablo was so successful that he resided there as concert performer and teacher of the guitar and mandolin. Now he began the study of harmony and commenced to compose ; he also occupied his leisure in research, particularly in acoustics relative to the guitar and mandolin. He disposed of the rights of his discoveries to the instrument making firm of Thibouville Lamy of Paris and Mirecourt, who manufactured a class of mandolins and guitars which they branded "Sarrablo," but like so many other fancied improvements, are now forgotten. Sarrablo was the conductor of a famous dance estudiantina which was in popular demand. He was residing in Boulevard de Clichy, Paris in 1912, and was the composer of light musical comedies which were produced at the Moulin Rouge, Paris, and the Empire, London. More than four hundred arrangements for guitar, including compositions in the Flamenco style, with instructions, and works for estudiantina and mandolin were published by Jacques Pisa and other Paris publishers.

Scheidler, Christian Gottlieb, a German guitarist, lutenist and bassoonist who lived during 1752-1815. Dr. Zuth describes him as the last of the lutenists and first of German guitarists. He was a member of the Royal Orchestra, Mayence, retiring on pension to Frankfort where he was living as a teacher of the guitar in 1815. The manuscripts of several of his compositions are in Berlin National Library and the A.M.Z. for 1812 records his *Sonata No. 1,* and the following year *Sonata No. 2,* both for guitar ; Op. 1, *Romance for guitar* published by Schott ; *Five Pieces for the guitar ; Duo for violin and guitar* and Op. 21, *Sonata in D major* were also issued by Schott, Mayence. Dr. Zuth states that Scheidler played and composed for the guitar of seven strings.

Scheit, Karl, contemporary, born April 21, 1909, at Schonbrun. His father a military band conductor did not approve of him becoming a professional musician, although he studied the violin at an early age. It was not until he joined the youth movement when fifteen that he became acquainted with the guitar which was in general use for accompanying songs. Being entirely self taught he was unaware of the capabilities of the instrument until he chanced to acquire a trio for guitar, clarinet and flute by Kreutzer. With two friends he played this trio and his enthusiasm for the instrument was increased; he practised constantly, so much so, that his guitar playing caused an estrangement with his father, and the young man left home. He went to Vienna, attended lectures on the theory of music and the guitar, at Vienna Academy of Music and when Llobet played in Vienna, later followed by Segovia, he determined to make the guitar his life study. To perfect his playing of the music of Bach, he studied under the eminent Austrian composer N. David with the result that his teacher became interested in the instrument and composed several works for it, one of which a *Trio for flute, viola and guitar* he dedicated to his pupil. At the early age of twenty-four Scheit was appointed professor of the guitar in Vienna State Academy of Music. He compiled a *Method for the Guitar* in two volumes with German and English text, published in 1936 by Universal Edition, Vienna, also studies and exercises for the instrument. Scheit also plays the lute and transcribes the compositions of that instrument for the guitar.

Schindlocker, Philipp, was born October 25, 1753 at Mons, Belgium, and died April 16, 1827 at Vienna as Kaiserlicher Kammervirtuose. His parents removed to Vienna when he was a child and he received instruction on 'cello and guitar from Himmelbauer and eventually won wide renown on both instruments. After the completion of his studies he was occupied for some years as a teacher, but in 1795 he was solo violoncellist in the Royal Opera and St. Stephen's Cathedral. Three years later he toured and for a period was a member of the orchestra of St. Etienne Cathedral. He subsequently returned to Vienna where in 1806 he was solo violoncellist to the Emperor. Much of his music remains in manuscript, principally concertos for the violoncello with orchestra and guitar works. His only known published composition is *Serenade for violoncello and guitar* issued in 1809 by Diabelli Vienna. Schindlocker taught the violoncello and guitar to Joseph Merk, who attained to greater celebrity in the musical world, and who was associated with Giuliani, Mayseder and Moscheles—all guitarists—at concert performances in Vienna.

Schlick, Johann Conrad, born at Munster, Westphalia, in 1759 and died at Gotha, 1825, was a virtuoso on the violoncello and mandolin. He married in 1785 a musician of greater renown, Regina Strina Sacchi. She was a violin virtuoso and an excellent guitarist who had studied both instruments first in Venice, and after in Paris. From 1780 to 1783 she toured Italy winning universal admiration, by her playing, her attractive manners and good looks. In 1784 she was in Vienna and on March 29 and April 24 of that year gave two concerts in the National Court Theatre. She was acquainted with Mozart and requested him to compose something for her second concert, which he promised to do, and immediately wrote the violin part of the *Sonata in B;* the piano accompaniment he delayed writing. The day of the concert approached, and notwithstanding her importunity Mozart still postponed writing the accompaniment, and at the concert played from a few notes dotted on the manuscript. The Emperor Joseph from his box above noticing the blank sheets of music paper on his desk sent for Mozart. He completed the accompaniment at a later date with ink of a different shade, the difference being plainly discernable on the original, which was in the possession of Mr. F. G. Kurtz of Liverpool in 1899. Before his marriage Schlick was violoncellist in the Bishop's Chapel of Munster, his native city, and after concert tours with his wife, when they performed duos for violin and violoncello, and mandolin and guitar, they settled in Gotha, where he was violoncellist in the orchestra of the ducal chapel. Alfred Dörffel in his Leipzig Gewandhaus Concert programmes states, on August 30, 1803, Schlick and his wife performed a duo for 'cello and French guitar and a duo for mandolin and guitar was given by Bortolazzi and Grälius in October. His wife died in Gotha in 1823 and he survived her two years. Schlick composed much for the violoncello, concertos, solos, and in quartets with other instruments. He composed also *Sonatas for the mandolin, Two albums for the guitar,* published by Breitkopf & Härtel, Leipzig, in 1801, and Schilling and Fetis enumerate other compositions; many remain in manuscript, one of which, *Sonata for mandolin and piano* is in the National Library, Vienna.

Schnabel, Joseph Ignaz, born May 24, 1767 at Naumburg, Silesia, died June 16, 1831 at Breslau, was a violinist, guitarist, organist and composer of church and instrumental music. The son of a schoolmaster, he had early instruction from his father on the violin and guitar and at the age of eight had made remarkable progress on both instruments and then commenced to play the piano. He was placed in the Catholic Gymnasium of Breslau when twelve, to study theology, but through the intercession of his maternal uncle was able to return home to continue his musical education. The youth organised an amateur violin and guitar band of peasant lads of his own age but unfortunately his musical proclivities were interrupted for a time by deafness. However, he recovered later, and in 1797 went to Breslau where he was organist of St. Claire and first violinist in the Vincentinerstift. A few years later he was teaching the violin and guitar in the city and was also first violinist and deputy conductor of the Royal Theatre orchestra, and towards the close of 1804 was cathedral organist. Schnabel resigned from the orchestra when Weber was appointed, probably because of vexation for not being promoted capellmeister himself, or as a musician of thirty-seven years' experience, declining to serve under a lad of eighteen. When Weber took up his appointment in Breslau, he had to contend from the first, on account of his youth, with the prejudices of the managing committee and with strong opposition from the chief musical circles of the town. The leader of this opposition was Joseph

Schnabel, and the two continued on unfriendly terms, for some rudeness of which Weber was guilty towards Schnabel—who was an educated and highly respected man and musician—did not raise Weber in the estimation of the educated members of the public. Schnabel after his resignation, was in 1806 conductor of the Richter winter concerts, and in 1811 was summoned to Berlin by Zelter to investigate the methods and system of the Singakademie, with the object of establishing similar institutions in Breslau and all Silesia, which was the intention of the Prussian government. In 1812 he was musical director of the University and director of the Royal Institute for church music. Schnabel was the author of various published compositions, masses, offertories, hymns, songs, military marches and guitar music; a large number remain in manuscript. The most renowned of his published compositions which include the guitar is *Quintet for guitar, two violins, alto and 'cello,* a new edition of which is published by Zimmerman, Leipzig.

Schneider, Simon, born December 4, 1886, at Pasing, near Munich, Bavaria, was originally a zither player who after successful concerts in his native land, visited in 1903, Belgium, Holland, and Austria as a virtuoso. He later adopted the guitar, was a pupil of Albert on this instrument and composition, and commenced teaching and composing for both instruments, first in Munich and after in Hamburg. He emigrated to Buenos Aires, in 1921 where he continued the same musical activities. He gave a unique and highly successful recital in the concert hall of La Argentina, October 18, 1928, when he performed in the versatile role of guitar soloist, zither soloist and vocalist with his own guitar accompaniment; his programme being divided into three sections. Among his compositions are: *Twelve solos,* in album form, *for guitar; Three Albums,* each containing six solos and many songs with guitar, all published by Hofmeister, Leipzig; *Rondo and Three Minuets for three guitars* and a series entitled: *The classic masters, for guitar,* Bachman, Hanover; Op. 28, *Abendstanchen;* Op. 38, *March,* and *Melancholie* without opus number; Op. 90, and Op. 91, *Two albums of six songs each,* published by The Guitarfreund, Munich. His published compositions in Argentina were typical dances of that country, tangos, waltzes, etc.

Scholl, Carl, born January 8, 1778 at Quolkiev, Poland, a flautist and guitarist who at the age of twenty-one became a member of the Royal Chapel and opera orchestra, Vienna, remaining in those positions for forty years. He wrote much for the flute, including a method and various studies. For the flute with guitar, he composed Op. 19, *Introduction and brilliant variations, in A;* Op. 20, *Introduction and brilliant variations in G;* Op. 21, 22, 23, *Brilliant variations on Austrian melodies for flute and guitar,* all of which were published by Cranz, Hamburg.

Schönberg, Arnold, was born of poor parents at Vienna, September 13, 1874 and died after an illness of two years, July 13, 1951 at Los Angeles, U.S.A. He was a pupil in Vienna of Zemlinsky and in 1901 married the latter's sister who died in 1923. Regarded as the founder of the modern atonal school of music his early activities were interrupted by the first world war when he served in the Austrian army and after its conclusion continued teaching in Vienna. He trained pupils who followed his idiom, for Schönberg was the foremost leader of the neo-romantic school of composers. When Hitler came to power, Schönberg, being of Jewish descent, expatriated himself and in the winter of 1933 entered the U.S.A. and became an American citizen. When appointed, in 1936, Professor of Music at the University of California he made his abode in Los Angeles. He was an inspiring teacher and trained pupils of renown among whom was Alban Berg. There has never been another composer of such notoriety whose works have made so restricted an appeal; but Schönberg has an assured position in musical history. He has composed operas, other stage works, orchestral, chamber music, choruses and songs. A serenade entitled: *Resplendent night,* Op. 24, composed in 1923 is *for violin, viola, 'cello, clarinet, bass clarinet, mandolin, guitar and deep voice;* it was in this composition that Schönberg made first use of the twelve-tone technique in a consistent form.

Schrammel, Johann, born May 22, 1850, at Vienna and died there, June 17, 1897. His father, Kaspar, was a Viennese musician and his sons Johann and Josef who studied at the Vienna Conservatoire of Music became the founders of the novel quartet which bore their name. The two brothers, both violinists, with a clarinet player named Danzer, and a guitarist, Strohmayer, played folk music under the name of The old Viennese Chamber Quartet. This was their instrumentation employed up to 1877 and after that the accordion replaced the clarinet. Johann was the last of the old Viennese musicians and the composer of about one hundred and fifty songs with the accompaniment of two violins, guitar and accordion, and this combination became so exceedingly popular that all Viennese composers, and in particular, operatic composers, arranged their works with this instrumentation. The Schrammel guitar was much larger than ordinary and had seven strings.

Schreker, Franz, born at Monaco, March 23, 1878, and died at Berlin in 1934. His parents were in necessitous circumstances and his musical education at Vienna Conservatoire was made possible by the generosity of an anonymous lady. His principal subject was the violin and at the age of thirty he was conductor of the Popular Opera and the founder of the Vienna Philharmonic Choir. He was subsequently professor of composition at his Conservatoire, Director of the High School of Music, Berlin, and in 1932 professor of composition in the Prussian Academy of Arts; but the following year, under the Nazi rule, a suspicion of his Jewish ancestry arose and the shock of succeeding events was the cause of his sudden death by a stroke. A distinctly modern composer, his genius was to produce rich colouring with fascinating, sensuous combinations of tone which characterises his compositions. He uses the mandolin and guitar frequently and the latter instrument most effectively in the score of his opera, *Der Ferne Klang,* produced in Frankfort, August 18, 1912. Sketches of his life were published in 1919 by Bekker and in 1921 by Dr. Julius Kapp.

Schubert, Franz, Peter, born January 31, 1797, at Vienna and died there November 19, 1828, at the age of thirty-one. Over the door of the house in which he was born is a grey marble tablet with the simple words: "Franz Schubert's birth place," on the left of the inscription is a lyre crowned with a star, and on the right, a laurel wreath, encircling "31 January, 1797," the date of his birth.

His father, Franz, was assistant to his brother during 1784 at a school in the Leopoldstadt, and when about nineteen, married. There were numerous children, several of whom died in infancy, and in 1797 Franz was born. Franz Schubert, the most renowned and greatest of all song writers, and Carl Weber, his near rival in this respect, were both guitarists, and the majority of their songs were first conceived with guitar accompaniments. By a strange coincidence, both possessed light baritone voices, and both sang their own songs to their guitar accompaniment, without affectation, creating intense pleasure in the circles of their musical friends. Both recognised the extreme importance of a suitable accompaniment to the words. The guitar was Schubert's constant companion during his early career, before he possessed a piano, and all his vocal compositions were conceived and sketched out on this instrument.

Franz received a methodical and thorough education from his father, which included a solid grounding in the rudiments of music; he was taught the violin and guitar, and his brother Ignaz gave him lessons on the piano, and when the family had exhausted their musical knowledge, he was placed with the parish choirmaster Holzer, whom he soon outstripped. Before he was eleven Schubert was first soprano and solo violin in Lichtenthal Church, and in October, 1808, when eleven years eight months, he competed for admission in the Imperial School, where the choristers of the Court Chapel received their education.

Schubert was successful, and his homely grey suit was now exchanged for the gold laced uniform of the Imperial choir. In the school orchestra he played first violin. His playing soon attracted the attention of the leader, Spaun, nine years his senior, who took a fancy to the new pupil and remained his firm supporter through life. Schubert continued to play the guitar and used it to accompany his boyish songs, for at this early period he had already set several poems to music; his great difficulty was to obtain sufficient music paper on which to write them.

In 1813, when sixteen, he composed for his father's name-day, September 27, a *cantata, in two movements, for Three Male Voices with Guitar accompaniment.* The words and music were his own composition; this manuscript was in the possession of Dr. Schneider. The cantata contains one terzett for two tenors and a bass, and is inscribed: "In honour of my father's name-day festival, the words with guitar obligato accompaniment, composed by F. Schubert, on September 27, 1813."

The terzett, a simple tuneful melody commences with an andante in A Major, twelve-eight time, and concludes with a lively allegretto in six-eight. He had already composed many songs with the guitar and also string quartets, quintets, overtures for orchestra and church music. This cantata, written for and dedicated to his father, with its guitar accompaniment, was composed during his last months in the Imperial School. At this period he made the acquaintance of the poet-guitarist Körner who also composed and sang his own songs to his guitar accompaniment. Körner was in Vienna at the time Schubert was offered special inducements to remain a further term in the Imperial School, and he influenced him in his decision not to continue, but to devote himself entirely to art.

When Schubert was seventeen he returned to his father's house, and after a few months study at the Normal School, qualified as a schoolmaster and for three years was occupied in the uncongenial task of teaching the lowest classes; but he spent his leisure in the society and companionship of musical associates, and after a while was able, through the kindness of a friend, to live more after his own inclinations.

For some time Schubert's father had been dissatisfied with his son's half-hearted interest in teaching, and when Franz von Schober, a young man of good birth and some means, offered to allow him to share his lodgings and to keep house together, his father consented. Schober was four months his junior and had become acquainted with some of Schubert's songs while visiting a friend named Spaun, living in Linz. How Schubert managed to live during the year 1816 is not known; he commenced to give a few lessons but soon discontinued. His wants were few, but how they were supplied remains a mystery, as there was no sale for his compositions; it appears the household expenses must have been entirely met by Schober.

During this part of his career, and particularly when living with Schober, Schubert's songs were written with guitar accompaniments, in his poverty and humble lodgings he could not afford a piano. His guitar had grown very dear to him, for, by its assistance he had obtained favour in musical circles of friends, and when the instrument was not in use, it was always to be seen hanging over his bed. The poet Grillparzer, a confidant of Schubert, records in his diary that Schubert wrote him saying: "My piano is unluckily out of my possession and I therefore again play my guitar." Grove says: "The guitar was greatly in request in Schubert's time as a solo instrument and as an accompaniment also. Schubert wrote several part songs with guitar accompaniment."

Johann Karl Umlaff, an intimate friend, a tenor singer and guitarist, was one of the first to sing publicly Schubert's songs with guitar accompaniment. He rendered them also in French and Moldavian. Later he was appointed a judge and became the owner of one of Schubert's guitars, here illustrated. Umlauff records that he frequently visited Schubert in the mornings, before he was out of bed. He usually found him with a guitar in his hands and wrote: " He generally sang to me newly composed songs to his guitar." Carl Umlauff, in the life of his father speaks of the elder and the younger Giuliani (guitar virtuosi) with Schubert, and other Viennese musicians, meeting at the house of Frau v Andre regularly weekly and making music till past midnight.

Joseph von Henikstein was a wealthy member of the Vienna Philharmonic Society, he sang bass, played the mandolin and the 'cello and held open house for weekly concerts. Schubert was a member of this Society, and writing to his friend Jenger on November 7, 1827, said: " Dear friend, I am unable to appear for lunch at Henikstein's; but I shall come, without fail at 7.30 in the evening." Through his fellow lodger, Schober, Schubert made the acquaintance of the poets Grillparzer, Bauernfeld and Mayerhofer—the last an accomplished vocalist and guitarist, who for a period shared lodgings with Schubert—and also the artist painters, Schwind and Rugelweiser.

A contemporary drawing, made in 1820, and reproduced by Otto Deutsch in his Biography of Schubert, depicts Schubert sitting on the grass next to the guitar player, while the violinist is standing.

During the months of 1816, when keeping house with Schober, Schubert lived rent free; but the return of Schober's brother upset this arrangement and from that time he must have been indebted to Spaun, or some other friend in better circumstances for his lodging, existence, and visits to the theatre; for he earned nothing by teaching during 1817.

These poets and artists were accustomed to meet in the house of the four sisters Frolich, where musical evenings were spent and in the home of these talented sisters, the most celebrated musicians and authors of Vienna were daily visitors. Next to the poet Grillparzer, Schubert was their most intimate friend, and here in the circle of his musical adherents he played the piano and guitar, singing his songs to his own accompaniment, receiving the opinions and criticisms relative to his latest productions before putting the final touches to them. The majority of Schubert's accompaniments were conceived on the guitar, and only afterwards did he set them for the piano, and many of his early songs were originally published with guitar. Many of his accompaniments show clearly and indisputably the influence and character of this instrument; they are in truth guitar accompaniments. At a concert in Vienna, in 1827, Schubert was piano accompanist to songs of his composition and also of the mandolin solos of Baron Ransonnet. The programme of a concert given for the benefit of the dancer, Angioletta Mayer, in the Theatre-an-der Wien, on August 27, 1822, when Schubert was present, included one of his vocal quartets, with guitar accompaniment. This vocal quartet was *Das Dorfchen,* and Dr. Zuth states that the guitar accompanist on this occasion was Herr Schmidt. Also on September 24, 1822, at a concert in the Karntnertor Theatre, an item of the programme was a vocal quartet with guitar accompaniment by Schubert. Diabelli, Schubert's first publisher was a guitar player and composer for the guitar.

Krissle von Hellborn in his biography of Schubert, says: "His life was extremely simple, a few books, a guitar and a pipe made up his furniture. The guitar was greatly in request in Schubert's time as a solo instrument and as an accompaniment also. He wrote several part songs with guitar accompaniment, the vocal quartet, Op. 11, has an accompaniment for guitar and piano. His terzett, *Zum Namestag des baters,* composed in 1813 has a guitar accompaniment which is in manuscript."

Illustrations of two of Schubert's guitars are reproduced, one from the Museum of the Schubert Society, Vienna, and the other in the possession of Major Hans Umlauff. Both are the ordinary Viennese guitars of the period and the first was included in the Schubert Centenary Exhibition held in Vienna.

Schubert was a visitor to the workshop of the guitar maker, Staufer, Vienna, and when the latter invented the arpeggione, in 1823, Schubert adopted the new instrument. It was named the guitar-violoncello, or chitarra col arco, (guitar played with a bow) and as its name implies, its shape was that of the guitar, but its size that of a small violoncello. Its tone resembled that of the obsolete viol d'amour and for a time it received an amount of favour. Schubert who was enthusiastic in its praise, composed a *Sonata in A minor* with piano accompaniment for it. This was written during November, 1824 and dedicated to Vincent Schuster, a well-known guitarist who had adopted the new instrument, but was not published until some years later by Gotthardt, Vienna.

The following of Schubert's songs with guitar and piano, were published and advertised during his life, his recompense no more than the price of a frugal meal.

Op. 1, 2, 3, Various songs; Op. 7, Three songs published in 1821; Op. 11, Three Quartets for male voices, published in 1822 ; Op. 16. Two Quartets for male voices, words by Schober, composed May 13, 1816, published in 1823 by Cappi & Diabelli ; Op. 20 and 21, each three songs (a notice on these publications states that the guitar accompaniments are difficult), published in 1823 ; Op. 22, two songs published in 1823 and Op. 25, by Sauer & Leidesdorf ; Op. 31, composed in 1821 and previously set to music as Op. 14, with Op. 43, published by Pennauer in 1825 ; Op. 39, published by Cappi in 1826 ; Op. 97, *Faith, Hope and Charity,* published in 1828 by Diabelli.

Fifteen Original Dances, for flute or violin and guitar which he composed in 1819, when twenty-two years of age, was published by Diabelli and a new edition was issued in 1920 by Dr. Zuth, Vienna.

A *Quartet for flute, guitar, alto and 'cello,* discovered by Dr. Kinsky, curator of Cologne State Museum was published in Munich, 1926.

The entire manuscript in Schubert's handwriting, dated February 26, 1814, was discovered in 1925 and is in four complete movements, Moderato, Menuetto, Lento e patetico, Zingara and an unfinished set of

QUARTETT

für Flöte, Gitarre, Bratsche und Violoncell.

GITARRE.*)

I. Moderato.

Franz Schubert.
(26. Febr. 1814)

Variations on a theme from a Serenade by Fr. Fleischmann (1766-98). The guitar is frequently allotted the solo part, in the first and fifth movements particularly. Part of the guitar score of the Moderato is reproduced. It has been stated that this composition was originally a trio for flute, viola and guitar by W. Matiegka which Schubert arranged as a quartet by adding a 'cello part of some difficulty for his father, who played this instrument in their home circle. This has been disputed by equally eminent authorities who point to the fact that Schubert often employed foreign airs, as instanced by the well-known French melody in his Op. 10, dedicated to Beethoven and variations written in 1827 on a theme from Herold's opera *Marie,* Op. 82, etc. A weighty argument in proof of its genuineness is stated by some authorities to be the guitar part itself and its insertion into the whole quartet. The guitar part is so technically self-contained and musically perfect and the conception of all the parts is so uniform and well worked out, that it is difficult to imagine that the guitar part could have been subsequently composed and grafted upon the entire composition in place of a 'cello part.

Schubert's activity as a song writer extended over a period of seventeen years and no musician ever worked with less encouragement. It was not until 1819 that one of his songs was publicly performed and it was not until 1821 that any were printed. Through his brief career of stress, illness and poverty he was treated with unpardonable neglect and only a half-hearted and tardy recognition was evinced towards its close. He died of typhoid fever, November 19, 1828, and was interred on the following Friday, near the resting place of Beethoven, a last request to his brother Ferdinand. His friend, the poet Grillparzer wrote of him: "Fate has buried here a rich possession, but yet greater promise." His first memoir was published by Kreissle von Hellborn and numerous others have appeared since.

Schulz, Leonard, born Vienna in 1814 and died in London, April 27, 1860, after a long and painful illness. His father, Leonard, was a Hungarian guitarist who had settled in Vienna, and in 1818 was appearing in concerts at Baden, near Vienna, with the famous violinist and guitarist Joseph Böhm. The father was a popular teacher of the guitar in Vienna, where he and his two sons moved in the most renowned musical circles; several of his compositions were published by Artaria and also by Traeg of that city. Leonard stated that he commenced to play at the age of six and made his début at the age of eight on November 22, 1822 in the Romischen Kaiser concert hall, under the auspices of the Viennese Musical Society. The following year, on June 20, he, as guitarist, and his brother, pianist, gave a concert in the Landstandischen Hall, Vienna. Edward made the piano his principal study and when a child had the privilege of playing to Beethoven, in Vienna. The father and his two sons were in constant request as a trio of guitarists in the city and environs and during January, 1826 they came to London giving their first concert, April 24, in Kirkman's Rooms, when Edward played the physharmonica and the father and Leonard, guitars. They were commanded to perform before King George IV and at many important functions in the city. Moscheles in his Diary states that they played a terzetto for two guitars and physharmonica, January 9, 1826 at the Lord Lieutenant's Palace, Dublin, when he (Moscheles) also performed, after which Schulz and his sons returned to Vienna. Their playing in Vienna now attracted much attention; the following extract is from the correspondent of an English music journal relative to their concerts in Vienna during 1827. "Among the most interesting concerts, we would particularise that of the two youths Schulz and their father, who sometime since paid a visit to London and were honoured by the notice of your sovereign. The younger son, Leonard, performed with his father a brilliant rondo for two guitars the effect of which was delightful. But the greatest treat of the evening was *Der Abschied* (The farewell of the troubadours) a delightful fantasia for the aeolharmonica, (a new instrument discovered by Mr. Reinlein of Vienna) and two guitars. This composition is the joint production of Giuliani and Moscheles." Sir George Smart, conductor of the London Philharmonic Society, refers frequently to the Schulz family in his journals as his friends and neighbours in Gt. Portland St., London, and when he visited Beethoven in Vienna, Schulz provided letters of introduction to the most celebrated musicians. He called on Schulz's wife in Dembslov and wrote: "September 15, went to the village of Mödling, about one and a half hours drive on the road to Italy where I was very kindly received by Mme. Nina Schulz. A son who was there, a daughter, a little girl almost in arms together with the two boys and the father who are now in London make up the family," and on September 19, 1825, he writes, "I next called and took leave of Mme. Schulz at their house in Vienna." In 1828 when they visited England the second time, they performed at the concerts of the Philharmonic Society, on April 28,

Rizzio's Guitar

Sarrablo y Clavero

L. Spohr

L. Spohr

William Squire

Samuel Siegel

Camille Saint Saëns' Guitar

Andres Segovia

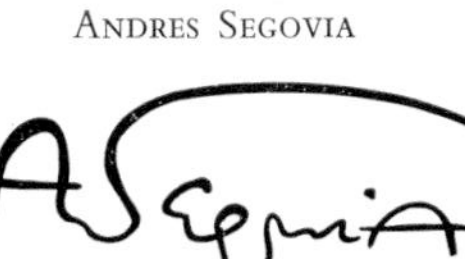

the father and two sons played a trio for two guitars and aeol-harmonica, or seraphine; this was doubtless the composition mentioned by the English music correspondent in Vienna. The sons remained in London as teachers and performers. Leonard was popular as a guitar teacher, concert artist and composer, but led a dissolute life. He was soloist, May 17, 1833 at the Hanover Square Rooms, when the principal solo was his Op. 10, *Fantasia for guitar in E major,* dedicated to Hart Sitwell. He made visits to Paris during 1833-1840 where he was praised for his excellent playing and the Paris music publisher, Meissonnier, issued several of his compositions. Schulz was described by a contemporary guitarist as "that wayward genius, Leonard Schulz." He was a genius of the first rank, but his disreputable life brought him to a premature death; for some time he lingered in the direst poverty, depending on fellow guitarists for the bare necessities of life and died in London, April 27, 1860. Friends erected a monument to the memory of his genius, over his grave in Brompton Cemetery, London. Makaroff during his European travels, undertaken for the purpose of interviewing famous guitarists, visited London, and Schulz, who at the time was a disreputable drunkard was eventually induced to play to him. Makaroff, in his Memoirs describes him as a brilliant virtuoso whose published compositions were poor. Schulz stated that publishers would not accept unless simplified, as otherwise they were unsaleable. He was the composer of about a hundred studies, exercises, arrangements and original works for guitar alone and with piano. The principal are Op. 9, *Variations for guitar solo;* Op. 11, 12, 13, 14, *Rondos for guitar* and Op. 15, *Modulations,* all issued by Johanning, London; Op. 21 to 32 various songs arranged for guitar solo published by the same firm; Op. 20, 33, two series of *Twelve arrangements for guitar tuned in E major,* Meissonnier, Paris, and Op. 40, *Twelve Studies for guitar,* published by Schott, London. In collaboration with Ferdinand Praeger, son of the guitarist, Schulz wrote *Three Duos Characteristiques for guitar and piano,* issued by Mori & Lavenue, London, and with the flautist Clinton he arranged *Eighteen Melodies for guitar and piano.* The publishers, Wessell & Co., said: "This collection has long been wanted; it forms the only work of its kind and is calculated to display the powers of advanced guitarists with considerable effect. The name of Schulz is a guarantee for the excellence of the arrangement." *Grand Fantasia, guitar solo,* Op. 48, was composed expressly for, and dedicated to, Mrs. Felix Horetzky, wife of the guitar virtuoso; Op. 101, *Divertissement,* was published by Johanning, London in 1845, and a number of his compositions were issued after his death by Mme. Pratten. His brother, Edward, also a guitarist, was a renowned pianist and for many years the most fashionable teacher of London society. He was the piano soloist, April 11, 1831 and a director of the Philharmonic Society, a gentleman of integrity whose distinguished manners endeared him to all. As a teacher he amassed a fortune, £1,000 of which he bequeathed to the Royal Society of Musicians. He published little for the guitar; the author of this volume possesses his manuscript, Op. 10,

Rondo a la chasse, for guitar. The Harmonicon of January, 1824, published accounts of his visits to Beethoven in Baden on September 25 of the previous year. The father, Leonard, wrote a few works, issued in Vienna and London. Op. 2, 3, *Variations ;* Op. 4, *Waltzes for flute violin and guitar,* Artaria, Vienna ; Op. 6. *Twelve Studies,* dedicated to Baron Gaspard d'Albertas, Diabelli, Vienna. While in England he composed variations and songs with guitar, one of which *The lady and her harp* was dedicated to Princess Esterhazy. Further particulars respecting Leonard, the son, are to be found in Makaroff's Memoirs.

Schumann, Frederic, a German guitarist living in London during the middle of the eighteenth century, the author of *A second set of lessons for one or two guitars,* Op. 11, consisting of twenty-one pieces, sonatas, etc., and from the title it appears he had composed a previous set. They were issued by John Johnson, violin maker and music seller, Cheapside, London, about 1770.

Schuster, Vincenz, an amateur guitarist, living in Vienna during the first part of the nineteenth century. He is known through his association with Schubert and the arpeggione, a new instrument introduced by Staufer, of Vienna, the maker of guitars. It was in shape and tuning similar to the guitar, but the size of a small violoncello and played with a bow. Schuster was a skilful performer and in 1824 Schubert composed for him the *Sonata in A, for arpeggione and piano.* The same year Schuster performed this sonata in the Romischen Kaiser Concert Hall in order to demonstrate the instrument. Schuster compiled a *Method for the Arpeggione* which was published by Diabelli, Vienna, and for the guitar *Fantasie,* Op. 7 ; *Variations* Op. 8 ; *Monferrine* Op. 13 ; *Potpourri for two guitars,* Op. 12 ; *Duo for guitar and piano,* Op. 14, and arrangements from Beethoven for one or two guitars, also published by Diabelli, Vienna.

Scivittaro, Maria (née Margherita Boccadoro), contemporary, born August 5, 1891 at Turin, Italy. Her father, an enthusiastic amateur mandolinist and guitarist gave her first instruction on the mandolin at the age of five and shortly after she continued under a musician Carosio. In 1898, at the age of seven she won the first prize for solo mandolin in the International Music Contests in Turin and then was soloist in the Salle Ristori of the city. Such an impression did she make that the artistic and influential members of society throughout Piedmont vied in their patronage and so her career commenced under most favourable auspices. At the age of nine she toured S. America as mandolin soloist, her first engagement on this continent being in the Casino, Rio de Janeiro. Her father contracted to tour the music halls ; but this proving too exacting and detrimental to her continued music study, was cancelled. She was still studying under her father, but by the death of her mother in 1904, her artistic career, which so far had been triumphantly successful was interrupted. The shock overwhelmed her father so much that all future plans were abandoned. At the age of sixteen she was touring Europe and in less than a year married J. Scivittaro, a violinist, the holder of the Grand Prize of Rome Conservatoire, and in 1911 made their abode in Paris. She made many recordings for the Pathe Co. and concert appearances until the war of 1914, when she devoted herself to hospital work and was a founder member of the "Foyer du Blessé." During August, 1930 she resumed her professional career when appointed solo mandolinist of Paris Opera and also broadcast recitals. It was at this time that Charpentier engaged her for recordings of his *Impressions d'Italie* and from 1945 she gave many recitals in Paris, Mullhouse, Strasburg and in Holland. The first performance in France of Vivaldi's *Concerto in C major, for solo mandolin with harp and cembalo,* was given by her in 1953, followed by broadcasts of this composition. For many years she has recorded for the Pathe Co. and is universally acknowledged a most brilliant mandolinist. Her portrait is reproduced by the courtesy of Ernest J. Tyrrell, London, to whom the author is greatly indebted.

Scott, Cyril Meir, contemporary, born September 27, 1879, at Oxton, Cheshire and living in London. He studied music in Frankfort and from 1900 resided in Liverpool. When he was twenty-one Richter conducted Scott's first symphony in Manchester and afterwards in Darmstadt. He is a pianist of marked ability and originality and his compositions embrace operatic, orchestral, choral, chamber music and seven books of poems. To the author of this volume he wrote that he had composed *Reverie for guitar solo* especially for, and dedicated to the guitar virtuoso Segovia. The manuscript, which was presented to Segovia, has not been published, but was performed by Segovia at his recital in Wigmore Hall, London, on May 11, 1918. His biography, edited by Hull, appeared in 1918.

Sczepanowski, Stanislaus, born in the Palatine of Cracow, Poland, in 1814, and living in 1852, was a Polish guitarist of rare ability. During childhood his parents taught him to play the violin and at the age of six he performed in public. In 1820 his family migrated to Scotland, made their abode in Edinburgh and became acquainted with the Polish guitarist Horetzky, who was exceedingly popular as teacher and soloist. He suggested the lad should play the guitar and taught him until he was nineteen. He made such remarkable progress that Horetzky recommended further study under Sor, the most famous of guitar virtuosi and teachers. Towards the close of 1833 he arrived in Paris, studied for some time with Sor and also gained knowledge of harmony and composition. In 1839, after the death of Sor, Sczepanowski returned to Edinburgh and proved himself a worthy successor of his first teacher. For a few years he lived in Scotland making concert tours in the provinces and London. Young and vigorous, with the impetus acquired by study under the most famous guitarist he rapidly won favour and in 1843 commenced a tour of Europe which terminated in his native land. He played the guitar in concerts with the violinist Lipinski in Dresden, and such was his success in Berlin that he was fêted by musicians ; in Posen he gave no less than fifteen recitals and also appeared many times in Cracow. He resided there for a time and then made a protracted tour through Europe, which concluded in Paris, where his playing won the admiration of Chopin, Kalkbrenner and Liszt. The French Press said of him : " Et de nos jours c'est M. Sczepanowski qui tient le sceptre de cest instrument." In 1847 he was again in London, prominent in teaching, and the following year commanded to perform before the Queen and Royal family, being also solo guitarist at musicales in the mansion of the Duchess of Sutherland. Several of his compositions were published at this period by Robert Cocks, London, when the musical press was unanimous in praise of his virtuosity : the Musical World, The Times, and Morning Post, all extolled his genius. At the close of 1848 he was invited to Warsaw where he was the recipient of honours worthy of his fame. He travelled to Russia, gave three recitals in St. Petersburg in the Theatre Michel where the success of his concerts excited the jealousy of certain Russian guitarists and then played in Wilna, where his rendering of his own compositions amazed musicians. Indefatigable in his concert travels he now entered on a protracted tour of eastern Europe, visiting Bucharest, Varna, Constantinople and Smyrna gaining a reputation in this part of the continent equal to that previously obtained in the north and west. After this tour he was again in London where he married an English lady, became a naturalised British subject and henceforth a teacher of the guitar and violoncello. Sczepanowski was a consummate master of the latter instrument and frequently played it in his concerts. His fame as a guitar virtuoso had spread to Spain for La Iberia Musical, Madrid, of February 20, 1842 records his virtuosity and states that he comes from Liverpool. The Illustrated London News, April, 1850 said : " M. Sczepanowski, the clever guitarist gave a matinee at the Beethoven Rooms, assisted by Mme. Macfarren, Misses Cole and other eminent artistes from Milan and St. Petersburg. Mme. Macfarren was pianist and Mr. W. Macfarren, conductor." His portrait with a sketch of his artistic career was published in the Illustrirte Zeitung, Germany, in 1852 and the same journal also contained one of his compositions, *A tear,* originally written for 'cello and piano, but transcribed by the author for piano solo. His most popular compositions for the guitar are : *Fantasia on English airs ; Introduction and Variations on a theme of Sor, for the left hand only ; La jota Aragonesa ; Les difficulties de la guitare,* an *Andante, Mazurka* and *Valse fantastique ; Souvenir of Warsaw ; Military potpourri ; Duo comic on the Carnival of Venice ; Four mazurkas ; Variations on a Polish air,* etc., published by R. Cocks, London.

Seegner, Franz G. An Austrian guitarist of repute and one of a family of renowned trombone players who lived during the first part of the nineteenth century in Vienna. The A.M.Z. during the years 1828-30 frequently records his concert performances and guitar compositions. He is described on his publications as Member of the Royal Chapel and Professor of the Guitar. He was the author of a *Theoretical and Practical Guitar School,* Op. 1, issued by Artaria, Vienna; Op. 14, *Bravour Sonata in D, for guitar and piano,* Wienberger, Vienna; Op. 15, *Caprices for guitar solo;* Op. 19 and 21 for *Guitar with string quartet;* Op. 30, *Variations Concertantes, for guitar with orchestra.* A new and revised edition of Seegner's guitar studies has been published by Schott, London.

Segovia, Andres, contemporary, born February 28, 1890, at Linares, Jaen, Spain. His parents removed to Granada when he was a child and shortly after he was placed with an uncle and aunt. His first interest in music was with the piano, violin and 'cello but with indifferent results and it was not until attracted to the guitar that his genius became manifest. With savings from his pocket-money he purchased a guitar from the maker Benito Ferrer, and because his family accused him of wasting his time and money on this instrument he considered it wise to practise secretly. Associating with Flamenco players he consequently adopted their style of playing, and later, after hearing the music of Arcas, Sor, and Tarrega decided to adopt their style so was obliged to re-learn. Many years after, he wrote: "As I had to fight the opposition of my family there was no question of a teacher, a school, or any other of the usual methods of instruction." With no encouragement from his family, or any external stimulus whatever, it was solely the love of the guitar that induced him to rent a small room where he lived alone and diligently studied and practised. His first concert was in Granada in 1909 and he extended his sphere with recitals in the Salle Erard, Paris, where his triumphant successes brought him in friendly acquaintance with many famed musicians, several of whom, amazed and surprised at his virtuosity, dedicated compositions to him. From France he travelled to Russia where in Moscow Conservatoire of Music, on March 2, 1926 his recital elicited high praise from the music press. In 1927 his recitals were acclaimed in bold headlines: "Segovia's fastidious artistry," his "Bewitching guitar," and "Amazing virtuosity." Reporting his London concerts the press said: "Praise is superfluous, his is, in its way, one of the most astonishing displays of musical and technical mastery at the present time. Despite the fact that he had learned of the death of his thirteen year old son, only a few hours before, Segovia insisted on giving his recital—the boy had been electrocuted when crossing an acqueduct near Geneva." For periods Segovia has been a professor of the guitar in Geneva Conservatoire of Music. In 1929 he was receiving applaudits in Japan and the same year flew with Manuel Ponce to the Latin American republics where Ponce conducted his orchestral works, one of which, *Concerto of the South,* a *Concerto for Guitar with full orchestra,* dedicated to Segovia, was given its first performance at Montevideo. This Concerto was performed in London, October 23, 1949 and the Daily Telegraph said: "Then came the greatest guitar performer of our time, Segovia, to give the first performance in England of a Concerto by Ponce . . . the happiest moments were those in which Segovia, whose performance was incomparable . . ." Segovia toured Canada in 1947, visited the low countries and England annually to 1953. He performed with the New London Orchestra a *Concerto for Guitar and orchestra* by Castelnuovo-Tedesco, repeated the following October, 1948 with the Halle Orchestra in Manchester, and followed by three recitals at the Edinburgh Music Festival, 1948. Of these recitals the press wrote: "The range of tone he accomplished was wonderful. No organ stops could have produced a greater scope" and "Segovia cast the accustomed spell of his astonishing technical skill and his poetic personality over everything he played." His annual appearance in London at the Festival Hall, November 12, 1952, when the first performance in England of the *Concerto for guitar and orchestra* of Villa-Lobos, under the baton of Sir John Barbirolli was a triumphant success, and on October 27, 1953, before an overflow audience under the same conductor in the Festival Hall, the *Concerto for Guitar and orchestra* of Castelnuovo-Tedesco and unaccompanied guitar solos received wild acclamations from the vast audience. The Times said: " . . . he was more welcome for the group of guitar solos which he gave after the interval, particularly for some modern Spanish pieces. Orchestra and conductor honoured him by assembling on the platform to hear him play and by applauding him to the echo, as indeed everyone did." Segovia is unquestionably the most artistic and classic exponent of the guitar since Tarrega and to him is due the exalted position the guitar holds in the world today. Numerous compositions have been dedicated to him by musicians of world repute and the poet Gabrielle d'Annunzio extolled his musical artistry in 1922 and again in 1932. Segovia proves conclusively that the guitar maintains its position as a solo concert instrument, and he achieves on it an intensity of tone and expression which reveals to the present generation the potentialities of an instrument that for decades has been in oblivion. Segovia's compositions are few; he has made arrangements and transcriptions from the classics and a "Segovia Edition" for the guitar is published by Schott, London. In 1947 his autobiography appeared, with five original solos entitled *Anecdotes,* in the Guitar Review, a journal devoted to the instrument, published in New York, which stated that he was compiling a Method for the guitar, supplemented by a set of gramophone records of his recording.

Sellner, Joseph, born March 13, 1787, at Landau, Bavaria, died at Vienna, May 17, 1843, was an excellent guitarist and distinguished oboist. His parents migrated to Austria while he was a child and he played the guitar and trumpet, and, as soon as of age, joined the band of an Austrian cavalry regiment as trumpeter and passed through the campaign of 1805. After the completion of military service, during which he had made a study of the oboe, he was for some years conductor of a private wind band in Hungary, and then principal oboe in the orchestra of Pesth theatre. He was a member of that orchestra in 1811 when Weber was opera conductor and Sellner played under his baton. During this time he was studying composition with Tomaczek and when he removed to Vienna in 1817 he entered the orchestra of the Court Opera and in 1822 was a member of the Royal Court orchestra. He was professor of the oboe and conductor of the pupils' concerts in the Vienna Conservatoire of Music in 1821 where he remained until 1838. Sellner wrote an excellent Method for the oboe which was published in both German and French languages and is one of the best methods for the instrument. He published some instrumental and orchestral compositions, an *Introduction and Polonaise for clarinet and orchestra; Sonata in D, for the guitar; Six Variations in A, on an original theme for guitar; Three Polonaises for flute and guitar* and other solos for guitar and duos for oboe and guitar, published by Berra and Hoffman, Prague.

Shand, Ernest, born January 31, 1868 at Hull, died November 29, 1924 at Moseley, Birmingham. His parents were named Watson and for professional purposes he took the name of Shand. For some time when a lad he played the violin; but when he became the possessor of a guitar he put aside the violin and by means of a cheap instruction book obtained an elementary knowledge of the guitar. No teacher of the instrument was available, nor was any music obtainable, but he chanced to find a secondhand copy of Aguado's Waltzes, and in his reminiscences published many years later, he stated that as he could obtain no other guitar music he was compelled to learn these difficult compositions. With determined application he made good progress and up to this time was entirely self taught; but realising the incompleteness of his technique wrote to Mme. Pratten requesting instruction. On one of her compositions, in a bound volume of guitar solos owned by Shand, she wrote in a large hand in red ink: "Of course I would teach you; but I cannot teach you anything, you are too great a genius." He later dedicated to her Op. 31, *1st Air varie guitar solo,* published by Boosey & Co. In 1896 he opened a studio in Bryanston Street, Portman Square, from where he made known that he was prepared to teach the guitar; but his venture met with no response whatever. If his own desires could have been fulfilled there is no doubt but that he would have devoted his whole life to the instrument; but the guitar world is small and his talents had perforce to seek their chief public expression upon a far larger and more popular stage. Shand was known to the British public as a variety artist—a comedian—who for many years headed the bills with the stars of variety, Lottie Collins, Gus Elen and Vesta Tilley, at the most popular music halls, and it was as a star comedian that he made in 1897 a successful tour of the Antipodes, and gave guitar recitals in Sydney. It must be emphasised that on no occasion did he use the guitar in the music hall or in any variety act, for he regarded the instrument seriously and always spoke of, and treated it with the deepest respect. He was a regular contributor to music journals particularly The Troubadour, wherein many of his articles and musical compositions appeared. His graphic and inimitable description in The Troubadour of his attempt to launch out as a teacher of the guitar with a studio in the west end of London, reveals the comedian in his most witty and amusing style. Among the cares of a life spent actively and with great success he made time to pour out a great mass of compositions for the guitar which will ever be a memorial to his genius.

Shand was the most prominent English guitarist and composer for the guitar, continually striving for its regeneration and advancement. He was the composer of more than two hundred works for the guitar alone, guitar with piano, songs with guitar and mandolin with piano. They include *Concerto for guitar with accompaniment of two violins, viola and 'cello or piano,* Op. 48, published by subscription and dedicated to his pupil, Lady Clayton. This concerto was given its first performance at Glasgow Arts Club ; it is in three movements, Largo, Adagio and Allegro ma non troppo, and displays Shand's command of the technique required of the guitar and also the composer's genius. His *Improved Method for the guitar,* Op. 100, published by Barnes & Mullins, contained ten original solos ; the work was not popular, being too difficult for the beginner. In the preface of the second edition Shand said : " After this method had been published it was shown to me by various professors and teachers of the guitar, that the preliminary exercises were too difficult for the average beginner. I have endeavoured to rectify this and have written *Twenty-three New Progressive Exercises* for that purpose. They will be found exceedingly easy and only very gradually increase in difficulty. I wish to take this opportunity to call attention to Mr. Froane's little book, The Guitar and How to Study It. It will be of great assistance to the earnest student of this Method." Shand dedicated Op. 66, *Tsigane* " to my friend Arthur Froane, Esq." At the death of Mme. Pratten in 1895 he composed and dedicated to her memory a *Funeral March,* Op. 89, which was published by Barnes & Mullins, Bournemouth. Several pieces for mandolin and piano were dedicated to the mandolinist Francia and were publicly performed with the composer at the piano. To his friend, the guitarist Cramer, Shand dedicated Op. 108, *Impromptu,* and *Les deux amis,* Op. 120 the last a duo for two guitars, and Op. 200, *Phyllis Gavotte,* named after his daughter, a talented actress, who was appearing in The Farmer's Wife, at the Court Theatre at the time of his decease. The principal publishers of his works are Barnes & Mullins, Schott, Bosworth, Boosey, Essex, Cammeyer and Weekes. Some of his compositions have also been issued in Argentina under the name of Sand. All his published compositions and unpublished manuscripts, his library of guitar music

Ernst Shand

and his favourite guitars, are in the possession of the author of this work .Chief among his unpublished manuscripts is *Grand Concert Duet for guitar and piano,* Op. 55, dated 1893, *Fantasia on Home sweet home,* and transcriptions of compositions of Mendelssohn, Grieg, etc.

Shelley's Guitar. The illustration reproduced is that of a guitar which has become celebrated in consequence of its associations. It was presented by the poet Shelley to a lady friend, and is now exhibited in the Bodleian Museum of Oxford. Although the life of the poet at the ancient seat of learning was brief, it is evident that he left a lasting impression in the University, not from his disgrace and expulsion, but by his extraordinary though perhaps ofttimes misapplied genius. The sublimity of his writings appeals to all artistic minds, and in spite of his philosophy and heterodox ideas, his poems are permeated with noble sentiment. Shelley's Oxford honours, however, came very late, and now there is no relic of the poet too poor for the University to do it reverence. In the mausoleum of University College—the society that expelled him—there is a most realistic representation, wrought in chaste marble of his drowned form, as it appeared when delivered up by the waves near Via Reggio, on the Italian coast. In the Bodleian, too, is treasured an incomparable collection of his manuscripts, also his watch and the copy of Byron's poems which he carried with him during his fatal trip. In another case are other interesting mementos, including a miniature of Shelley with a lock of his hair, but of paramount interest to guitarists is the guitar. This instrument was presented by the poet to Jane Williams, wife of Captain Ellerker Williams, who perished at sea with Shelley in a pleasure boat during a sudden squall off the coast of Leghorn. In January, 1822, while living in Pisa, Shelley wrote to his friend Horace Smith, in Paris, begging him to purchase a harp and some music, not too expensive, for Shelley to present to a friend. He urged haste, and an immediate advance from Smith's accustomed kindness "lest the grace of my compliment should be lost." For reasons best known to himself Shelley executed his own commission in Italy, and chose a guitar, and the music ordered was presumably, and with what gain to literature supplanted by that priceless song, *With a guitar.* It has been stated that Shelley was a guitar player; whether that be correct or not he was in the land of the guitar, and it is certain that he had been captivated and enamoured by its dulcet tones or he could not have expressed such appropriate sentiments in this poem, and also his ariette, entitled *To a lady singing to her accompaniment on the guitar.* Jane Williams was a pleasing singer who accompanied herself on the guitar, and impressed Shelley by her performances. In the poem '*With a guitar,*' Shelley has expressed such sentiments as only one intimate with the guitar could, and he has displayed his love for the instrument, which had the power to speak in the language he knew so well. When Shelley presented the guitar and the manuscript, he was living in Pisa, where the renowned guitar virtuoso and poet Zani de Ferranti was playing with extraordinary success, and it is more than probable that Shelley had been enchanted by his magic spell. It is no wonder that such a mind for romance, as possessed by Shelley should have been captivated by the delicate strains of the guitar ; his residence in Italy was the means of bringing the instrument prominently before him, and we can imagine the inspired bard revelling in the romantic sounds of the guitar in that sunny clime where he spent his short and sadly erratic life. The guitar was carefully preserved by the Williams' family, and was sought after by a devoted student of Shelley—Mr. Edward Silsbee, of Salem, Mass. The owner, Mr. Wheeler Williams would only consent to part with the guitar conditionally, upon its being presented to some public institution. Dr. Garnett, of the British Museum suggested the Bodleian Museum, Oxford, and Mr. Silsbee, having generously purchased the interesting relic, presented it accordingly. The guitar is of Italian origin, having been made by Ferdinando Bottari of Pisa in 1816, and it bears the original label. The table or soundboard is made in the orthodox Italian style of unvarnished pine, the lower portion being overlaid with rosewood decoration. Eleven rows of red, black, yellow and green purfling are inlaid round the table, along the fingerboard and around the sound-hole, and a broad black purfling is inlaid round the edges of the instrument. The bridge is oblong in shape, and is bordered with narrow edges of ivory, it has eighteen frets in all, patent pegs, and with the guitar is its original case, painted in imitation of fancy woods. The inscription placed near the instrument reads as follows: "The guitar, given by Shelley to Mrs. Jane Williams and forming the subject of one of his poems. Presented to the Bodleian on June 21, 1898, by Edward Augustus Silsbee, of Salem, Mass., an ardent admirer of Shelley's genius." There is exhibited also an illuminated copy of the poem *With a guitar,* the cover being tastefully embellished with a colourful sketch of the guitar. The poem is appended:

WITH A GUITAR

The artist who this idol wrought,
To echo all harmonious thought,
Felled a tree, while on the steep
The winds were in their winter sleep,
Rocked in that repose divine,
On the wind-swept Apennine ;
And dreaming some of Autumn past
And some of Spring approaching fast
And some of April buds and showers,
And some of songs in July bowers,
And all of love ; and so this tree—
O, that such our death may be!
Died in sleep, and felt no pain,
To live in happier form again ;
From which, beneath Heaven's fairest star
The artist wrought that loved guitar,
And taught it justly to reply
To all who question skilfully
In language gentle as its own,
Whispering in enamoured tone
Sweet oracles of woods and dells,

And summer winds in sylvan cells ;
For it had learned all harmonies
Of the plains and of the skies,
Of the forests and the mountains,
Of the many voiced fountains ;
The clearest echoes of the hills,
The softest notes of falling rills,
The melodies of birds and bees
The murmuring of summer seas,
And pattering rain and breathing dew
And airs of evening ; and it knew
That seldom-heard mysterious sound
Which, driven in its diurnal round
As it floats through boundless day,
Our world enkindles on its way—
All this it knows, but will not tell
To those who cannot question well
The spirit that inhabits it.
It talks according to the wit
Of its companions ; and no more
Is heard than has been felt before,
By those who tempt it to betray
Those secrets of an elder day ;
But sweetly as it answers, will
Flatter hands of perfect skill,
It keeps its highest, holiest tone
For our beloved friend alone.

Song with Guitar by Sibelius

„Heisa hopsa, bei Regen und Wind."
Aus Shakespeares „Was ihr wollt."

„Hallila. uti storm och i regn."
Ur Shakespeares' „Trettondagsafton."

"When that I was and a tiny little boy."
From Shakespeare's "Twelfth Night."

«Hallila, par la pluie et le vent.»
Poesie extraite de la piece de Shakespeare «Comme il vous plaira.»

Deutsche Nachdichtung – in Anlehnung an A. W. Schlegel – von Alfr. Jul. Boruttau.
The music having been composed to a Swedish translation the English words have been freely adapted from the Shakespearian text
Traduction française d'apres le texte anglais, par Amedee Boutarel.

Jean Sibelius, Op. 60 № 2.

Allegretto.

Gesang. / Säng. / Song. / Voix.

Und als ich ein win - zig Bübchen noch war,
Och när som jag var en li - ten smådräng,
O when that I was a — ti - ny boy,
Et lors que j'é - tais un — jeu - ne gar - çon,

Guitarre.

poco f ed energico

Sibelius, Jean, contemporary, born December 8, 1865, at Tavastehus, Finland. He was descended from lowly peasant stock, his father a doctor of medicine, played the guitar, of which he was very fond, as an amateur. The son evinced remarkable musical talent at an early age, was given a classical education and studied law; but his musical inclinations predominated and he devoted himself to music. He studied the art in Helsingfors, Berlin and Vienna and up to 1897 was a teacher in the National Conservatoire. He has contributed to almost every branch of music ranking among the foremost composers of the time. His father was a guitar player, the son has composed at least two songs, Op. 60, with guitar accompaniment No. 1, *Come away death,* No. 2, *When I was a little boy,* both from Shakespeare's *Twelfth Night.* These accompaniments are evident proof that Sibelius is thoroughly conversant and familiar with the guitar. They are published by Helsingfors Nya Musikhandel, Helsingfors, Finland, and also by Breitkopf & Härtel, London. Sketches of his life by Newmarch, appeared in 1905 and by Niemann in 1917.

Siegel, Samuel, born 1875 in U.S.A., and died January 14, 1948, in Los Angeles, California, U.S.A. He was one of the most celebrated of American mandolinists. He came to England where for some considerable time he was engaged at various concerts in London and the provinces and then toured France. He returned to America in 1934, after an absence of about ten years, gave recitals in the Universities of Chicago, Wisconsin and Cornell, organised an exceptionally large Music Correspondence School in Chicago which was very successful and then retired from public life. In 1934 he underwent a very serious operation and in the spring of 1940 was a guest of the mandolin and guitar artists Mr. and Mrs. Bickford in Hollywood, California, on his journey to reside with his son in San Diego. Siegel was the composer of many original solos and arrangements in the duo style, all of which were published in the U.S.A. Commenting on his European concert tour in 1923, the eminent music critic, Emile Grimshaw, wrote: "Never before have I heard a mandolin played with such a mellow and velvety quality of tone. As a matter of fact, tone has always been Siegel's principal object. He has a charming personality."

Sivori, Ernest Camillo, born June 7, 1817, at Genoa—the day after his mother had heard Paganini for the first time—died at Genoa, February 18, 1894, was an illustrious violinist; all authorities agree in giving him the premier place among modern Italian violinists since the days of his illustrious teacher, Paganini. Sivori commenced to play the violin when five under Restano, a violinist and guitarist of Genoa and the guitar a year or two later. He continued the violin under Costa until 1823 and when Paganini heard the boy he was so amazed at his remarkable talent that he gave him lessons, taught him all that it was possible to teach and even composed various instrumental works, which he wrote for and dedicated to him; among them are *Six Sonatas,*

Concertino and *Duo for Violin and Guitar,* which Paganini inscribed, " Cantabile and Waltz, to the valiant lad Camillo Sivori." These and other similar compositions were performed by master and pupil, Paganini and Sivori playing the guitar and violin alternately and were sufficient to launch the lad into Paganini's style. In 1827 he visited Paris and London, but returned to Genoa shortly after where he studied harmony under Serra for some time. Sivori spent a wandering life, travelling from the age of ten until death. He performed in all the European cities of importance and visited America in the company of the Italian guitar virtuoso Zani de Ferranti, about the year 1846. They performed together during this time, after which Zani de Ferranti returned to Brussels. Sivori extended his tour through Mexico to South America and in 1850 returned to Genoa. He then lost practically all his savings, which he had accumulated in the new world, by an imprudent speculation, and was compelled to travel again. In 1892, during the first Italian-American Exhibition of Genoa, the municipal authorities organised an International Music Contest for Mandolin Bands, solo mandolinists, guitarists, and quartets of the same instruments. Sivori was president of the judges and during these competitions manifested intense interest and expressed his great delight in the instruments. His memoirs edited by Pierrottet appeared in 1896.

Sodi or **Sody,** Carlo, a mandolin virtuoso of the early school, was born at Rome and died at Paris, after a lingering illness, September, 1788. He was living in Paris from 1749 where his younger brother, Pietro, had already made a reputation as a harpist in 1743 and was a member of the Comedie Italienne orchestra. At the suggestion of his brother, Carlo also visited Paris and the two brothers were in frequent request as mandolinist and harpist at select musicales. Carlo Sodi, by his public performances also won an enviable reputation as mandolin virtuoso and teacher of his instrument. In 1749 he too, was in the orchestra of the Comedie Italienne, remaining until 1765 when he was pensioned owing to the loss of sight of both eyes. Plunged in distress when old age was creeping on, his circumstances once so brilliant, suddenly declined ; he lingered until released by death when seventy-three, from an illness the result of penury and privation. A mandolinist of the name of Sodi was in England during the early years of the eighteenth century, for the mandolin was first heard in this country when a concert given for the benefit of Sodi took place in Hickford's Rooms, London on March 25, 1713. (Hickford's Rooms were demolished in 1937 to enlarge the Regent Palace Hotel). Sodi was advertised to play, " A Concerto on the Mandolin, being an instrument admired in Rome, but never Publick here." Sodi was the author of numerous operas and operettas, several of which enjoyed a brilliant but short-lived popularity. From 1753-60 his works were produced at the Comedie Italienne, Paris. The principal were: *Bajocco and Serpilla,* a parody, published in Paris in 1753 ; *Le Charlatan,* a comic opera ; *Les Troquers,* a comedy ; and *Cocagne,* published in 1760.

Sokolowski, Markus Danilowitsch, a Polish guitarist born in 1818, at Shitomir, Volhynia, Russia, and died at Moscow, December 25, 1883. In early childhood he manifested a profound love of music which his parents endeavoured to stifle considering it a waste of time, nevertheless he obtained some proficiency on the violin and violoncello ; but it was not until he heard the guitar played by a Polish artist, that his passion for music fully asserted itself. He studied the guitar in earnest, and receiving praise for his playing in his native town, gave recitals in Vilna and Kiev, after which he performed in St. Petersburg and Moscow. His recitals in Moscow during 1847 surprised musicians and he established an exalted reputation, for the Moscow Stadtblatt of March 1, 1847, said: "His recital was not proclaimed with the many voiced trumpet of Fama, and a concert given on an instrument of the times of the harpsichord, the lute and the cither, was a daring undertaking. Notwithstanding, the concert hall Rimski Korsakow was not large enough to accommodate all who desired admission. The recital of Sokolowski was one of the most remarkable given in Moscow. Do not speak of the guitar again as a feeble instrument! Every instrument is poor and feeble until placed in the hands of an artist. The guitar playing of Sokolowski is so easy and natural . . . now the tones fall as delicate as pearls, now they sparkle like diamonds, now sweetly ripple like silver bells . . . It was more than delight to listen, and the audience refused to be satisfied until the artist repeated part of his programme."

At this concert the young piano virtuoso Nicolas Rubinstein, then ten years of age, was also playing, and the two musicians afterwards toured together giving many concerts in Russia. Sokolowski played with his accustomed eclat in Moscow, St. Petersburg and Warsaw during the years 1864-68, and then visited Paris, Vienna, and other important continental cities. He made a brief visit to London where he met and formed a lasting friendship with the guitar virtuoso Regondi. Sokolowski's genius was recognised by the most eminent musicians whose names were associated on his programmes and he played before the principal European Royal Courts and on many occasions before the Empress Eugenie, the Princess Mathilde, Duke Robrinski, and other nobility. Sokolowski, a patriot, manifested deep interest in his unhappy nation's welfare, and the troubles of 1860-70 in Poland were a great trial to him ; but his life's ambition was to see the adoption of the guitar in the Moscow Conservatoire of Music of which institution his erstwhile friend and musical associate in his travels, Nicolas Rubinstein, was the director. For a considerable time he pleaded for its introduction, anticipating that it would be the regeneration of the instrument, and he took very sadly to heart the refusal of Rubinstein, and he could never mention the subject without deep emotion. His last public appearance was in the Chapel Royal, Moscow, in 1877, later he was afflicted with rheumatism so severely that playing was impossible. Sokolowski spent his last years in the family of a Moscow friend and was interred in Vilna by the side of the Polish poet

Kondratowitsch. A plain monument, surmounted by a bronze bust of the artist was erected with the inscription "Markus Sokolowski, celebrated European guitarist, died December 25, 1883, aged Sixty-five years." He was the author of many transcriptions and also original Polish and Russian melodies for the guitar—the favourite a fantasia, entitled *Polski*—which were published in his native land. His portrait and a brief career of his life appeared in a Russian Guitar Journal and later in the comprehensive guitar volume by Dr. Sajaitski of Moscow.

Sola, Charles Michel Alexis, born at Turin, Italy, June 6, 1786, living in London as late as 1829, was an Italian guitar and flute virtuoso and composer. He was taught music when a child, studying the violin in his native city under Pugnani and the guitar and flute with Pipino and Vondano, and for a year was flautist in the Theatre Royal, Turin. He served four years as flautist in the band of the 73rd Regiment of French Infantry ; but tiring of military life settled in Geneva, in 1809. Sola was twenty-three years of age, an excellent guitarist and flautist, and deciding to make music his profession studied harmony and composition in Geneva under Dominique Bideau, a compatriot who had been for some time violoncellist in the Comedie Italienne, Paris. Sola commenced composition and several of his works were published in Geneva, one in particular, the opera *Le Tribunal*, produced there in 1816 was the means of making him known to the musical world. About the end of 1810 he visited Paris where he published other compositions, and was popular as a performer and teacher of the guitar and flute. With his brother Alfreddo, a vocalist of some repute he toured Italy, as far south as Naples and in 1817 came to London where for about twelve years taught his instruments, principally the guitar, numbering among his pupils members of the royal family. The A.M.Z. of 1815 extols his guitar playing and guitar compositions. He compiled a Method for the guitar, published by Chappell, London, under the title of *Sola's instructions for the Spanish Guitar,* and in London he published many simple guitar solos, duos for guitar and piano, comic and sentimental songs and works for the flute, including concertos. All his compositions and arrangements, although simple, display taste and excellence in their guitar accompaniments which are remarkably effective. *Twelve Spanish songs, with guitar ; Gems of Harmony ; Sixteen duos for guitar and piano,* and more than twenty Italian songs published by Robert Cocks, London ; *Twentieth set of English songs, with guitar,* Willis, London, and many similar compositions were issued by Prowse and other London music publishers.

Sor, Fernando Jose Macario (his surname was Sors, which he changed to Sor), born at Barcelona, February 14, 1778, and died at Paris, July 8, 1839. He was one of the most renowned guitarists and composers for the guitar during the latter part of the eighteenth and the beginning of the nineteenth centuries, and the learned Fetis writes of him as " the Beethoven of the Guitar." His musical talent showed itself very early, for at the age of five he composed little airs which he played on his father's violin and guitar. The artists who heard and saw this child-musician recognised a genius, who, with the necessary training would develop into one of the greatest musicians of the age. The parents therefore decided to gratify the child's remarkable and intense passion, and he was found a teacher for instruction on the violin and 'cello. So marked was his progress that he was shortly after placed in a monastery of his native city to receive a sound general education, including instruction in harmony and composition. The youth now discarded the violin and 'cello, owing to his fascination for the guitar and this instrument he studied diligently. His determination to investigate every difficulty often led him in trouble with the monks, but it was admitted he was thorough in his studies and they found in their youthful pupil much which they themselves could learn. When at the age of sixteen he left the monastery, his teachers had every reason to be proud of him, for he astonished musicians by his proficiency in guitar playing and profound knowledge of harmony and counterpoint. He joined an itinerant Italian opera company in Barcelona, which afforded him an opportunity of becoming practically acquainted with the art of song and instrumentation, and the young musician now essayed to write opera. Having discovered, accidentally, in the library of the theatre in Barcelona, the score of an opera by Cipalli, named *Telemacco,* he adapted the words to new music and it was performed successfully when he was but seventeen. Its first performance was in Barcelona, then Venice in 1797, afterwards in London. Having thereby established a reputation he visited Madrid, where he found a powerful friend in the Duchess of Alba, who commissioned him to compose among other works the music of an opera bouffe ; but it was abandoned uncompleted because of the death of the Duchess shortly afterwards. The Duke of Medina was also greatly interested in the young artist, and at his suggestion Sor wrote several oratorios, which were followed by numerous symphonies, quartets for stringed instruments, church music and many Spanish songs. At this time Spain stood on the verge of revolution ; the return of Napoleon, followed by the fall of the Directory in France and the establishment of the Consulate, commenced a new epoch for Spain. The treaty of San Ildefonso in October, 1800, was followed by war with Portugal, and Sor, with many other artists of the time joined the Spanish army, serving for some time as captain. He remained in the army until compelled to take refuge in France with the adherents of King Joseph Bonaparte, and in the French capital associated with the most famous musicians, Cherubini, Mehul and Berton, who, charmed by his genius, prevailed upon him to devote himself to art again ; after a short sojourn in Paris Sor came to England in 1809. Prior to his appearance in this country the Spanish guitar was scarcely known, although it had been in general use on the continent for years. The precursor of the guitar in England was the cittern, an instrument smaller than the guitar, somewhat pear-shaped, with a flat back, strung with wire and played with a plectrum like a

Guitar made in 1680
by
ANTONIUS STRADIVARIUS

FERDINAND SOR

SHELLEY'S GUITAR

Aubrey Stauffer

Alex. Tansman

Rey de la Torre

mandolin. The modern Portuguese guitarra or as it is commonly named—flat-back mandolin—is constructed on the model of the ancient English cittern, but it is strung and tuned differently. The cittern had ten wire strings, the lowest two tuned singly, while the others were in pairs. Strung thus, it produced six open notes, C, E. G. C. E. G. the lowest being the same as that produced at the third fret of the fifth string of the guitar. The technique and the tone of this instrument was therefore quite dissimilar from that of the Spanish guitar. Sor was a performer of most extraordinary skill on the guitar, and his playing created a furore in London ; the elite of society greeted the new instrument with unbounded enthusiasm, its music presented a new phase in tonal art, such as had not been heard before, and its study afforded a pleasant relief to the tedium of fashionable life, while its outline—the outline of beauty—added further grace to feminine posture. Sor settled in London and was fully occupied in teaching and writing music for the guitar, it was owing to his remarkable success that numerous other continental professors of the guitar visited this country. While living in London he composed several works for the theatres and though he spent the most prosperous and successful part of his career in England, it appears his compositions were not of much pecuniary assistance ; but it is to this Spanish refugee that England owes its introduction to this charming instrument. Sor's mastership of the guitar must indeed have been truly great, for he is the only solo guitarist who has performed at the Royal Philharmonic Concerts, London. He was soloist at the Society's Concerts, March 24, 1817, in the Argyle Rooms, playing one of his own compositions, a *Concertante for the guitar, with violin, viola and 'cello,* and he electrified his audience by the wonderful command over his instrument. George Hogarth, in his Memoir of the Philharmonic Society, says: "He astonished the audience by his unrivalled execution." While Sor was popularising the guitar in England, Giuliani was engaged likewise in Russia, and when the latter subsequently came to England there was great rivalry between the partisans of the two masters. Giuliani had introduced in his concert the terz guitar, which being tuned higher, was more brilliant than the ordinary guitar, and his duets for piano and terz guitar, for guitar and terz guitar and concertos for terz guitar with accompaniment of orchestra, excited the greatest enthusiasm, and such was the popularity of one of these concertos that Hummel transcribed it for the piano. A music journal, devoted to the interests of the guitar was published, and named after Giuliani, The Giulianiad, which contained many of his compositions and also those of Sor and other renowned guitarists. Each of the celebrated masters had his followers, there were Sor clubs and Giuliani clubs, and when they departed from London, Giuliani travelled to Italy and Sor to Paris and Moscow, where he supervised representations of his ballet *Cendrillon.* The Paris journals wrote of him: "Early in December, 1822, he displayed his remarkable talents at the Salle des Menus Plaisirs, for the benefit of M. Guillou, first flute at the Grand Opera, where he charmed all Parisians by an instrument which might from its appearance have been taken for a guitar, but judging by its harmony must have been a complete orchestra enclosed in a small compass. He ought to be called 'Le Racine de la guitare'." While in Russia in 1825 he was commissioned to write a funeral march for the obsequies of Alexander 1, and composed the music of the ballet *Hercules and Omphale,* for the accession of Nicholas. On leaving Russia in 1828 he visited Paris once more, where he essayed in vain to obtain the representation of his dramatic works in the theatres of that city. Ill-health and consequent misfortune overtook him, and, pressed by want he returned to London in 1833, but remained only a short time. While in London he composed the music of the ballet *Le dormeur Eveille,* and later the fairy opera, *La belle Arsene.* In addition to these and several other stage works, Sor had up to this time written innumerable pieces for the guitar, with no success, for his music was not popular, his compositions were usually in four parts, after the style of Pleyel and Haydn, in fact they were too difficult for amateurs. Sor said: "When I arrived in France publishers said to me: 'Make us some easy tunes.' I was very willing to do so; but I discovered that easy meant incorrect, or at least incomplete. A very celebrated guitarist told me that he had been obliged to give up writing in my manner, because the publishers had openly told him: 'It is one thing to appreciate compositions as a connoisseur, and another as a music seller, it is necessary to write silly trifles for the public. I like your work, but it would not return me the expense of printing. What was to be done? An author must live." Sor appeared in public with the most celebrated musicians, with the violinist Lafont and the pianist Herz he performed Hummel's trio, *The Sentinelle.* The Harmonicon of February, 1831, stated: "M. Sor stands at a vast distance from all other guitarists, both as a performer and composer. He is an excellent musician, a man of taste, and his command over an instrument, which in other hands is so limited in its means, is not only astonishing, but what is more important—always pleasing;" and the same journal added, "Mr. Sor, who so long delighted and surprised the lovers of music in London by his performances on the Spanish guitar is now living in Paris." Sor returned to Paris, hoping that a change of climate would restore his health, but was disappointed, for after languishing in a condition bordering in want and misery, notwithstanding the universal esteem in which he was held, he died July 8, 1839, after a lingering and painful illness.

In contemplating Sor as an artist, one is amazed at his extraordinary genius and the rapid growth of his powers. At the early age of seventeen he stood before the public as the composer of an opera which had been received with great favour. His symphonies and other instrumental compositions showed a high order of talent and were very popular in Spain, as were also his songs. Sor considered the first requisites of a guitarist to be a graceful position, a quiet and steady hand, the power of making the instrument sing the melody, clearness and neatness of ornaments, and, of course, the necessary technique. Both as man and artist he was retiring and modest, and declared that as a guitarist he possessed no greater means than any other person. He had taken up the guitar believing it merely an instrument of accompaniment, as it was in Spain in the latter part of the eighteenth century; but he very early discovered the full capabilities of the instrument. The study of harmony, counterpoint, and composition for voices and orchestra, had familiarised him with the nature and progression of chords and their inversions, with the manner of placing the air in the bass or in one of the intermediate parts, of increasing the number of notes of one or two parts while the others continued their slower progressions. All these he demanded from the guitar, and found that it yielded them better than a continual jumble of semi-quavers or demisemiquavers in diatonic and chromatic scales. Sor had no patience with those persons who sought to conceal a lack of talent with the remark, "I only play to accompany." He reasoned that a good accompaniment requires a good bass, chords adapted to it, and movements approaching as much as possible to those of an orchestral score or pianoforte accompaniment. These ideas required a greater mastery of the instrument than the sonatas in vogue at that time, with long violin passages, without harmony or even bass, excepting such as could be produced on the open strings; hence Sor concluded, as already had Giuliani, Carulli, and Aguado, under similar circumstances, that there were no masters within his reach capable of properly teaching the instrument. He said: "At that time I had not heard of Frederick Moretti. I heard one of his accompaniments performed by a friend of his, and it gave me a high idea of his merit as a composer. I considered him as the flambeau which was to serve to illuminate the wandering steps of guitarists."

Sor's first experiments were in making accompaniments and he soon found himself in possession of various necessary positions. From his knowledge of harmony, understanding each chord and inversion, its derivation, in what part the fundamental bass was found, what should be the progression of each part for the resolution or transition about to be made, he was prepared to establish a complete system of harmony for the guitar. Nor did he confine his investigations to the theoretical part of guitar music, for he studied to improve the construction of the instrument, its position, fingering, and the best manner of setting the strings in vibration in order to produce the best quality of tone. The guitars of that period were made of thick wood, but Sor required instruments made for him to have the sounding-board, ribs and back, made of very light and thin wood, supported by bars inside to withstand the tension of the strings. He devised a new form of bridge which was applied to several guitars made in London and St. Petersburg and the rules formulated by him for the neck and fingerboard are today still used in the construction of the finest instruments. It was his precise nature that actuated his desire to perfect the art of guitar making. He associated with the two most eminent guitar makers of any period, Panormo and Lacote; the former was a violin maker in London at the time of Sor's visit and the theoretical ideas of the musician, worked out by the practical hands of this skilful luthier, brought into existence those magnificent instruments bearing his name. Sor also rectified the models of Lacote, the most eminent of French guitar makers, who constructed at his request instruments with seven strings—the extra string being added to the bass and used as an open note only. Sor approved of this innovation, for Giuliani and Legnani the two foremost guitarists of the Italian school, sometimes advocated an extra bass string. In his early days Sor had acquired perfection of technique and yet he always spoke of himself as only an amateur; he possessed great skill, certainty, power, and a remarkable full tone, and his playing was as much a revelation to great guitarists like Aguado and De Fossa as to amateurs. In fact after hearing Sor perform some of his own compositions, Aguado studied them, and even asked Sor to criticise his rendering of them. The two artists were intimate friends, resided in the same house in Paris and Aguado admitted that were he not too far advanced in life to overcome the inflexibility of his fingers and habits, he would adopt Sor's style of fingering and his method of striking the strings. The date of the publication of Sor's first compositions for the guitar is not known for certainty, but his Op. 1, *Six Divertissements,* appeared in London in 1819. In reviewing Sor's compositions his Method must be considered first, a most remarkable and philosophical treatise, the result of many years observation and reflection. It was originally published in Spain, the first English translation was by Arnold Merrick, printed by Fowler, Cirencester, and published by Robert Cocks, London. Sor prefaces his Method with, "I have supposed that he who buys a method means to learn it." Throughout the volume he never lost sight of the true meaning of the word "method," and he remarked that he could never conceive how a method could be made with a greater quantity of examples than of text. The first part is devoted to directions for constructing a guitar to produce the best results, but as these instructions concern chiefly the manufacturer reference to them is omitted, it is sufficient to add that he supplied the foremost guitar makers of the day with valuable suggestions regarding the interior construction of the instrument, and also the design and functions of the bridge. The chapters on "the position of the instrument," "the right hand," "the left hand," and "the manner of setting the strings in vibration," are full and exhaustive, and illustrated by numerous diagrams. His manner of holding the instrument was substantially the same as that of the other virtuosi of the period, but he sometimes used and advised his pupils to use the tripodion, as invented by Aguado. This was a small table placed in front of the performer, partly over the left leg and presenting one corner opposite the twelfth fret of the guitar, which was then rested on the corner of this table and on the right thigh. In illustrating the proper position of the right hand, Sor compares the fingers striking the guitar strings to the hammers striking the strings of the piano, and argues that the thumb, first and second fingers, like the hammers, should be placed in front of, and parallel to the plane of the strings of the guitar. He also established as rules of fingering for the right hand, to employ usually only the thumb, first and second fingers, and to use the third finger only when playing a chord in four parts, where the part nearest to the bass leaves an intermediate string. The Italian guitarists Carulli, Carcassi and Zani de Ferranti, all used the thumb more or less for fingering the sixth string, a practice which Sor severely condemned, on the ground that it contracts the shoulder, shortens the play of the fingers by one half, and places the wrist in an awkward and painful position. Sor's explanation of the proper manner of setting the strings in vibration is very explicit, and especial stress is placed on the importance of causing the vibrations of the strings to take place in a direction parallel to the plane of the sounding-board, to produce a pure tone. The chapters on " knowledge of the fingerboard," and " fingering on the length of the string," are based on the axiom that " the true knowledge of the scale is the key to all musical knowledge." Sor divides the scale into two halves of four notes each, viz., C.D.E.F. and G.A.B.C., wherein the order of the intervals is the same in each tetrachord. These tetrachords are separated by the interval of a tone and the last interval in each is a semitone. In a very ingenious manner he makes a rule for fingering the scale according to the tones and semitones involved, and it is obvious when the first note or tonic is determined, it is only necessary to observe the proportions of the intervals to obtain by a single operation what would require twelve different ones were the names and the modifications composing it to occupy the attention. The same principle is applied when fingering the scale on each of the strings, the author deeming it necessary, in order to obtain a perfect knowledge of the fingerboard, to acquire the habit of passing over each string for the whole length, considering the open string under different relations as tonic, dominant, etc. Every note is considered with respect to its place in the key and not therefore as an isolated sound. The same principle is applied in considering thirds and sixths, general formulae being established for fingering major and minor thirds and sixths on adjoining strings, in every key, according to their occurrence in the scale, without burdening the mind with a consideration of each note by name and whether it be natural, sharp or flat. After thirds and sixths, Sor says: " I have entered into all these details to prove to the reader the truth of my assertion, that the entire key to the mastery of the guitar (as an instrument of harmony) consists in the knowledge of thirds and sixths. Without this knowledge I believe that I should have succeeded in producing only a poor imitation of the violin, or rather of the mandolin. I say poor, because I should have been destitute of the great advantage of the former of these instruments, that of prolonging, increasing and diminishing the sounds; and of the brilliancy of the latter, which being, as well as the former, tuned an octave above the guitar, gives passages which the guitar can but very imperfectly imitate —at least in my hands." Sor's instructions applying to the harmonic sounds are quite complete; but though a mathematician, his theory respecting the vibration of a string is erroneous. He deduced from his investigations that the vibrations came solely from that part of a string between the left hand finger and the nut, while as a matter of fact the whole string vibrates, but in equal sections dependent on the distance from the nut, or bridge, where the vibrations may have been interrupted by the finger of the left hand. The article on harmonics is followed by chapters on " accompaniments " and " fingering with the ring finger " and the " conclusion " gives a resumé of his investigations and general maxims established for guitar playing. This Guitar Method of Sor is the most remarkable ever published, and, as stated before, contains much more text than music; it was undoubtedly intended to be used with the author's *Twenty-four lessons,* Op. 31. In his method and also in several of his compositions he sometimes advises lowering the bass E string to D. Carefully and conscientiously written, touching upon every point of guitar playing, it will remain a lasting monument to the remarkable talent and genius of one of the greatest guitarists the world has ever known. The compositions of Sor are numerous and varied, and during his periods of residence in London he wrote much for the theatre—ballets, pantomimes, etc., including *The fair of Smyra,* a comic opera; *Le seigneur genereux* (The generous lord), ballet; *Le Sicilien* or *L'amant paintre*, pantomime in one act, libretto by Anatole Petit; *Gil Blas,* and *Cendrillon. Le Sicilien* was staged June 11, 1827, it was not favourably received, but was amply compensated for by the brilliant success of *Gil Blas* and *Cendrillon,* both of which were produced at the Royal Opera, London, in 1822. *Cendrillon,* a ballet in three acts, libretto by Albert Decombe, was dedicated to the Marquis of Aylesbury and was successful also in Paris, where representations were given from the following March to 1830. This was without question Sor's most popular stage work; it is scored for full orchestra of thirty-nine instruments and the march from this ballet was a popular favourite and was arranged for solo guitar by the author. Both *Gil Blas* and *Cendrillon* were published in score by the Royal Harmonic Institution, London. He also composed many solos, duos and trios for voices, which appeared in sets of three, between the years 1810-22, piano solos and duos, and he compiled an exhaustive treatise on singing, French text, which has not been published, the manuscript was in the possession of Mme. Pratten.

Sor's compositions for the guitar are various lessons, studies, divertissements, easy pieces, fantasias, variations, with sonatas and duos for two guitars. Previous to publishing his Method, he issued the following lessons and studies: *Twelve Etudes,* Op. 6 and 29; *Twenty-four very easy exercises,* Op. 35; *Twenty-four pieces for lessons,* Op. 44. *The Progressive lessons,* Op. 31, were intended as an introduction to the study of the guitar, but because many amateurs complained of the greatly increased difficulty from one lesson to the next Sor composed the *Studies* Op. 35 and 44. Although well written and carefully fingered these were really more suitable for students of exceptional talent than for those of average ability. The author himself realised this, and among his last works wrote, *Introduction to the study of guitar, or*

Twenty-four progressive lessons, Op. 60, a set of exercises admirably adapted for the purpose indicated by the title. In general, his studies and lessons are not only carefully written, but each has a special object in the application of a rule, or in affording exercises on exceptions to general rules for fingering. The divertissements—which were invariably published in sets—and the fantasias are mostly on original themes; a few, however, are arrangements of favourite airs, Mozart's '*O cara memoria,*' Paisiello's '*Nel cor piu,*' '*Que ne suis-je la fougere,*' '*Gentil houssard,*' etc. They are all suited to the instrument, although somewhat difficult for those players unaccustomed to Sor's fingering. Of the sonatas, Op. 22 and 25 deserve especial mention, they are full of depth and earnestness with a vein of sadness running throughout. The *Fantasie elegiaque,* Op. 59, a work of particular merit, but great difficulty, dedicated to his friend Frederick Kalkbrenner, the celebrated pianist, was written to be played with the guitar held in position by the tripodion. Of this fantasia Sor says: "Without the excellent invention of my friend, Denis Aguado, I would never have imagined that the guitar could produce at the same time the different qualities of tone of the treble, of the bass, and harmonical complement required in a piece of this character, and without great difficulty, being within the scope of the instrument." In the execution of this piece, great clearness, taste, and the power of singing on the instrument is required. Sor's duets for two guitars, while well harmonised, lack the flowing melodies found in those of Carulli, and they are certainly less interesting; but it may be truly said of Sor that in the clearness and directness of his music, the spontaneity of his ideas, and in a certain charm pervading the whole, he was to the guitar what Mendelssohn was to the piano. Sor's music contains no mere bravura writing, but possesses grace, finish and charm. His compositions for the guitar, Op. 1 to Op. 35, inclusive, are all solos for the instrument with the exception of Op. 13, *Three valses and a galop for piano duet,* published by Simrock, Bonn. Op. 35 to 63 are published by Lemoine, Paris. *Fantasia,* Op. 30 and *Les deux amis* (the two friends) and Op. 41, *Duo for two guitars* were dedicated to his friend the guitarist Aguado.

Sotos, Andres de, a Spanish guitarist born in the province of Estremadura, Spain, in 1730 and was teaching his instrument in Madrid during the middle of the eighteenth century. Sotos was the author of a method for the guitar entitled, *Arte para aprender com facilidad y sin maestro a templar y taner rasgado la guitarra.* (Easy method for learning without a master, for tuning, playing arpeggios and chords with the thumb on the guitar with five strings and also those with four and six strings, and also the bandurria, and tiple). This volume of sixty-three pages was published in Madrid in 1764. His works are recorded in the Music Dictionary of Parada and Barreto, published in 1868.

Soussmann, Henry, born January 23, 1796, at Berlin, died 1848 at St. Petersburg, obtained renown as a flute virtuoso. He was the son of a musician of Berlin who gave him his first lessons in the theory of music and instruction on the violin and guitar. He commenced the study of the flute when six years of age with a teacher of some repute named Schroeck, and a year later the boy was playing in a regimental band of the infantry. When seventeen he served through the campaign of 1813-4 against France and at the declaration of peace he received his discharge, when he toured as a flute virtuoso in Russia. From 1822 he was first flautist in the opera, St. Petersburg, and in 1836 was promoted musical director of the Imperial Theatre. Soussmann composed much music for the flute which appeared principally in Russia. Op. 6, *Serenade for flute and guitar,* published in 1820 by Breitkopf and Härtel, Leipzig ; *Military song,* with French and German words, *with guitar accompaniment,* published by Schott, Mayence, and other similar compositions published by Andre, Offenbach.

Spina, Anton, an Italian guitarist, a pupil of Giuliani, who lived in Vienna during the commencement of the nineteenth century as a teacher and composer. In 1826 he was appearing with the virtuoso Stoll and is the author of a method for the guitar which was published in Italian and German by Artaria, Vienna, and also the following: *March for two guitars, from the opera, 'Cortez' ; Six waltzes for two guitars ; Rondo brilliant for violin and guitar ; Variations and operatic arrangements for solo guitar* and for *violin and guitar.* In 1852 he purchased the music publishing business of Diabelli, Vienna. There was a Frederich Spina, a relative of the former, a guitarist and composer whose works were published by the following firms, Artaria, Mechetti, Diabelli and Cappi, all of Vienna. Op. 4, 5, 13, 15, 17, 19, 21, 24 and 31 were dances for solo guitar. Op. 11, duo for two guitars. Op. 1, 2, 20, 23 for guitar and violin. Op. 27, 28 and 30 for guitar with string quartet.

Spinelli, Niccola, an Italian operatic composer, born at Turin, July 29, 1865, and died at Rome, October 17, 1906. He received his musical education in the Conservatoire of Naples and made a name in the musical world in 1889, when he obtained the second prize offered by the music publisher Sonzogno of Milan, for his one act opera *Labilia,* at the time Mascagni secured the first prize with *Cavalleria Rusticana.* Spinelli's opera at first actually took a higher place, the verdict of the judges being reversed by that of the public ; but his most popular and successful work was the three act lyric drama, *A basso porto*, the first representation of which was staged at Cologne in 1894. The plot of this opera centres around the slums of Naples, and Spinelli introduces mandolins and guitars in several scenes in his orchestral score. These instruments accompany the tenor song in the second act, where singing and mandolins and guitars are heard in the distance, and as a prelude to the third and last act, he has introduced a serious and charming Intermezzo for mandolins with the orchestra, where singing and mandolin playing in the distance give the signal to murder Cicillo. The opera is enhanced by this departure from the customary instrumentation, and the outburst of applause which greeted this intermezzo at the first production of the opera was extraordinary. The most striking features of this intermezzo are the parts scored for the two mandolins, and also the melody allotted to the violoncellos, for Spinelli makes good use of the mandolins, providing an elaborate cadenza in double stopping with rapid chromatic passages, all of which evidences a practical knowledge of the instrument ; but apart from these details this intermezzo possesses high attributes. The first performance in England was staged by the Carl Rosa Opera Co., during March, 1899 at Brighton ; and on October 11, 1900, this Intermezzo from the opera, *A basso porto* was performed by the Queen's Hall Orchestra under Sir Henry Wood, the solo mandolinists were Mlles. Florimond and Cesare Costers. It is published by Messrs. Ascherberg, London, for mandolins and orchestra and also for mandolins and piano.

Spohr, Louis, born April 25, 1784 at Brunswick, died October 22, 1859 at Cassel, was one of the most renowned of violinists and a celebrated composer. He was the son of a young physician ; both parents were musical, his father a flautist and his mother a pianist and vocalist. At five years of age he commenced the study of the violin, and when fourteen, undertook alone, his first artistic tour to Hamburg ; but returned home to Brunswick without obtaining a hearing and with finances exhausted. Struck by the lad's talent and bearing, the Duke of Brunswick gave him a position in his band and later paid the expenses of his continued musical education. Spohr travelled through Holland and Germany, and being offered the position of leader in the orchestra of the Theatre an-der-Wien, Vienna, resided there from 1812-15, and then made a tour through Italy. He returned to Germany in 1817, visited Holland and was appointed opera conductor at Frankfurt. It was here that he composed his opera *Faust* which produced in 1818 was quickly followed by *Zemire* and *Azor,* or *The magic rose,* in two acts, which gained greater popularity than its predecessor. The libretto on the well-known fairy tale, *Beauty and the beast*, was composed by Spohr in 1819, first performed March 24, 1822, and produced at Covent Garden Theatre, London, April 5, 1831. In this opera, Spohr writes a guitar accompaniment to the tenor aria of Ali, which is scored for guitar, first and second violins, viola, 'cello and bass ; the first violins are divided and the other strings are played pizzicato. Extracts from the guitar part are here reproduced from the original manuscript of the opera in the British Museum, London ; this extract is evidence of Spohr's familiarity and knowledge of the guitar. One song from this opera, *Rose softly blooming,* has remained a favourite to the present day. In 1820 he made his first visit to London when he played one of his violin concertos at the Philharmonic Concerts and he repeated his visits to conduct many of his own works. Spohr was a musician, second only to the most illustrious and as an executant and conductor takes rank among the greatest. His works comprise many operas,

Ali's song with accompaniment of guitar

IN THE OPERA

"ZEMIRE AND AZOR,"

COMPOSED BY SPOHR IN 1819.

oratorios, symphonies and compositions for strings and also his famous violin method. Several of his songs with guitar accompaniment were published by Schott, Mayence. In his autobiography Spohr records his associations with guitarists, particularly Methfessel. On page 147 he writes: "Fine voices joined and sang quartets and canons; Herr Methfessel taking his guitar, would entertain the company with pleasing ballads and touching romances of his own composition; by way of change, he then sang a comic song or two and exhibited his liveliness of fancy, his richness of invention, wit, and humour of expression, as well as his intimate knowledge of tone and harmony. Herr Hachmeister, the assessor of mines from Clausthal, taking then the guitar from him, in turn charmed the company with national songs in the Thuringian dialect, replete with such wit and humour as compelled the hearer despite himself, to laugh at the cares of life." Vol. II, page 59 " and Methfessel, who accompanied our four-part songs with the guitar, carried his instrument slung by a band over his shoulders." Vol. II, page 90, speaking of himself Spohr says: " The Duke of Sussex received me with great distinction . . . during a conversation we had upon the subject of English national songs, the Duke even sent for his guitar and sang to me some English and Irish national songs which afterwards suggested to me the idea of working up some of the most popular of these as a potpourri for my instrument and of introducing the same at my concert. This is Op. 59, the second of my works written in London." On page 124 he writes concerning his *Third Violin Concerto*: " The third part of this concerto is a Spanish Rondo, the melodies of which are not mine but genuine Spanish. I heard them from a Spanish soldier who was quartered in my house and who sang to the guitar. I noted down what pleased me and wove it into my Rondo. In order to give this a more Spanish character I copied the guitar accompaniments as I heard them from the Spaniard into the orchestral part." His autobiography, in two volumes is a remarkable record of his observations, and his memoirs by various editors, have appeared and a Spohr Museum established in Cassel.

Squire, William Henry, contemporary, was born in 1871 at Ross, Herefordshire. He won a scholarship at the Royal College of Music, London, and made a name as a popular 'cellist, song writer, a professor of the 'cello at the Royal College of Music, the Guildhall School of Music and an examiner at the Royal Academy. He was 'cellist in the Queen's Hall quartet under Arbos, and for many years leading 'cellist of the Promenade Concerts under Sir Henry Wood, who conducted Squire's orchestral compositions at these concerts during the years 1897-8-9. In My Musical Life, Sir Henry Wood states that Squire's tone and technique were superb. During the first world war Squire composed many sentimental ballads which were exceedingly popular and these and his light orchestral works were published by Boosey & Co., and Chappell, London. Eight of his light melodious compositions for mandolin and piano were issued by Turner, London. Squire records that when he was twenty-one, his first love played the mandolin and he became very interested in the instrument; these compositions were the result.

Stanford, Sir Charles Villiers, born September 30, 1852, at Dublin and died in London, 1924, commenced his studies in Cambridge, continuing in Berlin and Leipzig. When he returned to England he was appointed professor of music at his university and also the Royal College of Music, London, where he officiated for nearly forty years.

He composed operas, oratorios, orchestral and chamber music and in his opera, *Much ado about nothing,* published by Boosey, London, he employs mandolins and guitars in the second act to accompany Claudio's serenade. This was produced May 30, 1901, Covent Garden, London, and performed and staged magnificently. Stanford was knighted the following year and sketches of his life, edited by Streatfield appeared in 1913 and by Porter in 1921.

Starcke, Friedrich, born 1774 at Elsterwerde, Saxony, died December 18, 1835 at Dobling, Vienna, while a pensioned military bandmaster. He composed much, his works include the guitar and a pianoforte method entitled, *Wiener Pianoforteschule,* published early in 1821. This is famous because Beethoven contributed five Bagatelles in Part 3 and printed at the heading was " A contribution from the great composer to the publisher." Op. 5—49 are *Variations for flute and guitar ;* Op. 119 *Serenade Concertante for violin, alto and guitar,* issued in 1811, also many songs with guitar.

Stauffer, Aubrey, born July 14, 1876, at Denver, Colorado, U.S.A., and died August, 1952, at Laguna Beach, California, U.S.A. He was educated at the public schools of his native town and began the study of music under Arling Shaeffer at the age of fifteen, the mandolin and guitar being his chosen instruments. The following year he commenced the study of harmony and composition and then realised more fully the potentialities of the mandolin. During 1898-9 he was a member of the faculty of Denver Conservatory of Music, specialising in fretted instruments. In 1900, after the renewal of his acquaintance in Chicago with his teacher Shaeffer, he concentrated on mandolin compositions, particularly unaccompanied solos in duo, trio, and quartet form. His most popular numbers were *Ben Hur* and *Bandurria.* As mandolinist he visited France and England in 1903 and wrote two comic operas during his stay. Dallas, London, at this period published his compositions for the mandolin. When he returned to the States he conducted with success both choral and orchestral societies, in Chicago, Pittsburg and New York, for the next six years ; but when President of Stauffer Productions Inc., his career as concert performer terminated. He was now occupied in arranging and orchestrating for films, writing plays and revues. His operetta *The Waltz King,* based on the life of Strauss, ran over two years. His obituary, appeared October, 1952 in B.M.G., and his portrait is reproduced by courtesy of his esteemed and intimate friend Ernest J. Tyrrell, of London.

Stegmayer, Ferdinand, born at Vienna, August 25, 1803, died there May 6, 1863, was the son of the actor and poet of that name who received his first musical instruction from his father and Albrechtsberger. Later he studied the guitar under Triebensee in Vienna, the violin and piano under Riotte and Seyfried, and was a skilful performer on all three instruments. His early professional life was as a teacher of singing and the guitar in Vienna, and at the age of twenty-two was first chorus master in Vienna, and later musical director of the Konigstadt Theatre, Berlin. During 1829-30 he was capellmeister of Rockel's German Opera Company in Paris and afterwards in a like capacity at theatres of Leipzig, Bremen, Vienna and Prague. The English musician Sir George Smart visited him in 1825 and in his Journals writes of him as: "a clever young man from Vienna." From 1853-54 Stegmayer was a professor in Vienna Conservatoire of Music, teaching male students choral singing and the dramatic and vocal arts. He has published choral works, duos for horn and guitar and many songs with guitar which were issued in Vienna and by Schott, Mayence.

Steibelt, Daniel, was born October 22, 1765, at Berlin and died at St. Petersburg, October 2, 1823. His father was a pianoforte and harpsichord maker and little is known of his son's early career until his musical ability attracted the attention of the Crown Prince of Prussia, afterwards Frederick William II, who placed him with Kirnberger for lessons on the harpsichord and composition. In 1787 he was a solo pianist and his playing evoked the greatest praise, for he was essentially a performer of the new school. His success in Paris was phenomenal; he was regarded the reigning virtuoso and while there, wrote his first opera, *Romeo and Juliet,* in 1792. The success of this completely confirmed Steibelt's position and he was regarded the rival of Beethoven. His music for the piano, though considered difficult, was exceedingly popular, and he numbered amongst his pupils the most eminent personages of the time, including the future Queen of Holland. In 1796 he came to England by way of Holland, played in London during May of the following year and here he wrote his most famous piano solo, *The Storm;* its popularity was enormous and far exceeded that of any previous musical publication. During his residence in England, Steibelt wrote for the stage, also much instrumental music, and having married an English lady who was an expert performer on the tambourine, he introduced this in many of his piano compositions. He led a very unsettled life, touring the whole of Europe, receiving the greatest favour in Paris whither he returned after each tour. Steibelt was fond of descriptive pieces which are now all forgotten with the exception of *The Storm, Le Berger et son troupeau,* and his *Fifty Studies.* Steibelt composed several pieces for the guitar in combination with other instruments. *Favourite Rondos for Flute or Violin and Guitar in D,* were published respectively by Simrock, Bonn, and Hoffmann, Prague. *Rondos* for the same instruments were also published by Berra, Prague and Haslinger, Vienna. *Three duos for guitar and violin,* Op. 37, were published by Nadermann, Paris, and other Parisian music publishers issued similar pieces for the same instruments, which, like his other compositions were very popular in his day.

Steinfels, Adolf, a guitarist and musician living in Vienna during the commencement of the nineteenth century who published through Diabelli, Vienna, Op. 5, *Allemandes;* Op. 6 and 16, *Potpourri;* Op. 7, 9 and 17, *Variations;* Op. 8 and 14, *Landler;* Op. 11, *Fantasia;* Op. 12 and 13, *Rondos;* Op. 15, *Polonaise.* All were for solo guitar and Op. 18, *Monferines for one or two guitars.*

Sterkel, Johann Franz, born December 3, 1750, at Wurzburg and died there October 21, 1817. He was educated at Wurzburg University, took holy orders and in 1778 was chaplain to the Elector of Mayence. For a period he travelled and lived in Italy and in 1793 was music director to the Elector of Cologne and from 1805-13, capellmeister in Ratisbon. For an interesting account of his meeting with Beethoven in 1791, reference should be made to Grove. His more than one hundred published works include operas, symphonies and many songs with guitar accompaniment, which were issued by Schott, Mayence; Simrock, Bonn, and Diabelli, Vienna.

Stockmann, Julius M., born in 1839, at St. Petersburg and died December 4, 1905, at Staatstrat, Kursk. He was a student of oriental languages and archaeology, with the intention of entering the diplomatic service, but he eventually became a schoolmaster in Kursk, his native town. Anton Rubinstein, director of St. Petersburg Conservatoire appointed him professor of the guitar in the Kursk Music Academy in 1883 where he had many pupils. He has published through Jurgenson, St. Petersburg, compositions for guitar solo and duos and trios for two and three guitars. He bequeathed his rare and comprehensive collection of guitar music to the International Guitar Association and his autobiography was published in The Guitar and Guitarists, by the Russian guitarist and author Dr. Sajaitzky.

Stoessel, Nicolas, born May 17, 1793, at Hassfurt, Bavaria, and died at Ludwigsburg in 1844. He was the son of a poor weaver, an amateur musician, who taught him singing when he was five. The boy also commenced to play the piano and organ a few years later and having already obtained some practical knowledge of the flute, violin and guitar, assisted his father by playing these instruments at village dances. In the autumn of 1806 he was serving in the 13th regiment of infantry, and took part in the campaign in Austria and Prussia. After the cessation of hostilities he returned to his native town, and, with the intention of qualifying for a schoolmaster, entered the seminary of Wurzburg, where his music master, Froehlich, gave him instruction in harmony. When his studies were completed he was appointed assistant schoolmaster in Neustadt-on-Saale; but his passion for music predominated and he accepted the position as bandmaster of the 4th regiment of light cavalry then in garrison at Augsburg. While in this employ Stoessel wrote much music for military band until in 1826 he was appointed chamber musician to the King of Wurtemburg in Ludwigsburg where he remained until death. He wrote several operas, military music, and compositions for the guitar. Op. 5, *Third Serenade for guitar, violin and alto* and *Six German Dances for flute and guitar,* were published by Gombart, Augsburg; Op. 13, *Fourth Divertimento for piano guitar and flute;* Op. 9, *Die stille Welte,* and other songs with the guitar were published by Schott, Mayence.

Stoll, Franz Paul, born April 26, 1807, at Chateau Schoenbrunn, Vienna, and was living in Amsterdam as late as 1843. He was a guitar prodigy, having obtained remarkable skill on the instrument while a child. It was not however until his playing attracted the attention of Count Palffy that his parents decided he should adopt music as a career. It was the generosity of the Count that enabled the lad to continue his study of the guitar under L. Schulz and Giuliani, and harmony and composition with Förster, of whom Beethoven spoke so highly. He progressed rapidly and receiving much encouragement gave in 1825 a highly successful recital in the Landstandischen Hall, Vienna, and the following year appeared in concerts with the guitarist, Anton Spina, who later acquired the music publishing business of another guitarist, Anton Diabelli, Vienna. Stoll now commenced a protracted concert tour which embraced Russia, Germany, France, and Holland. He was guitar soloist in the Leipzig Gewandhaus Subscription Concerts of December 7, 1835. This series of concerts was under the management of Mendelssohn, who had been appointed director in the spring of that year. In 1836 he was again in Vienna where he gave a series of successful concerts and the same year was playing in Munich with the guitar virtuoso Legnani. From Germany Stoll visited Holland and Mendel states that he lived in Amsterdam as a teacher. Stoll's recital in the famous Gewandhaus Concerts is recorded in the A.M.Z. for the year 1835. He was successful, not only as a solo virtuoso, but also in his performances with other stringed instruments and with orchestra. He has composed a few works for his instrument. Op. 2, 3, 7, 8, 9, 19 and 25 are *Variations,* etc., *for solo guitar,* published by Pennauer, Vienna; *Dances for guitar,* Op. 4; *Potpourri for two guitars* Op. 16, and *Fantasia for solo guitar,* Op. 18.

Stradivarius A. Illustration of a guitar made by the illustrious violin maker which bears the inscription Ants. Stradivarivs Cremonens F. 1680 on the back of its head. This instrument was brought from Brescia in 1881 and purchased by Messrs. Hill and Sons of London. The beautiful arabesque rose covering its sound hole is of intricate and delicate design and the coat of arms on the fingerboard denote the noble family for whom it was constructed. Another example of a guitar by this maker is in the Paris Conservatoire of Music Museum.

Straube, Rudolph, a German musician who was born at Trebnitz-on-the-Elster, Saxony, about 1720 and died in 1780. He studied music in the famous St. Thomas' School, Leipzig, under the great John Sebastian Bach, and was esteemed as a virtuoso on the guitar, harpsichord, and lute. He settled in London in 1759 as a performer and teacher of these instruments where he composed and published several duets for guitar and harpsichord, also duets for guitar and violin. The manuscripts of *Three Sonatas for the guitar* are in the library of the British Museum, London.

Strauss, Franz, father of the great tone-poet and court conductor, Richard, was born in 1822 at Tirchenreuth, near Munich, and died in the latter city, June 2, 1905. He received his first musical instruction, on the guitar, from concert director, Walter. When he was six years of age he left home with his music teacher and had made such progress on the guitar by the time he was ten that he was appointed court guitarist to Duke Max of Bavaria. He then commenced the study of the French horn and became a consummate master on this instrument. In 1847 he was a member of the Royal Court Orchestra, continuing until 1889 during which period he had performed under Lachner, Bulow, and Wagner, all of whom spoke and recommended him highly. Strauss enjoyed an enviable reputation as a virtuoso on the French horn and the guitar. As composer and conductor of various musical societies he was held in high esteem. His compositions which remain in manuscript are in the library of King Ludwig II who recognised his genius and conferred on him the title of Professor, and the Medal of Art. Strauss was a veteran guitar player and the father of a remarkable musician. He was interred in Munich, and an imposing concourse of people attended to honour his memory and show respect for his son.

Stravinsky, Igor F., born June 17, 1882, at Oranienbaum, a suburb of St. Petersburg. His father, a bass opera singer, had his son trained for the legal profession ; but in his twenty-third year the son met Rimsky-Korsakof, became his pupil for composition, and hereafter devoted himself entirely to music. During the Russian revolution he lived in Switzerland, became a French citizen and since 1937, an American. His first lyric opera, *Le Rossignol,* with libretto from the tale of Hans Andersen, composed in 1908, in three acts, was given its first performance at the Paris Opera, May 26, 1914. In this opera, which was later converted by Stravinsky into a ballet, he writes a difficult part for the guitar and Prat records that at the opera's première, Stravinsky acquired the assistance of the Argentine guitarist, J. M. Aravena Rodriguez. The difficulty of this guitar part caused it to be

Francisco Tarrega

Tarrega playing to famous guitarists.
Cottin, Macciochi, Cateura.

Pasquale Vinaccia

New Argyll Rooms.

Mrs. SALMON

Has the honour to announce that her

CONCERT

WILL TAKE PLACE AT THE ABOVE ROOMS

On FRIDAY, JUNE 6th, 1823.

Principal Vocal Performers.

Madame CAMPORESE,
Mrs. SALMON,
AND
Madame RONZI DE BEGNIS.

Signor GARCIA,
Mr. SAPIO,
Signor BEGREZ, Signor PLACCI,
AND
Signor DE BEGNIS.

Mr. VAUGHAN, Mr. TERRAIL,
AND
Mr. BELLAMY.

Principal Instrumental Performers.

Signor VIMERCATI, - - Mandolin.
Mr. MORI, - - Violin.
Mr. NICHOLSON, - - Flute.
AND
Mr. BOCHSA, - - Harp.

Leader of the Band, - Mr. F. CRAMER.
Conductor, - - - Sir GEORGE SMART.

TICKETS, HALF-A-GUINEA EACH,

May be had at the Royal Harmonic Institution, Regent Street; Messrs. Birchall and Co.'s, and Messrs. Chappell and Co.'s, Music Warehouses, New Bond Street; Messrs. Clementi & Co.'s, Cheapside; Betts', Royal Exchange;
And of Mrs. Salmon, 14, New Norfolk Street, Park Lane.

Parties of Six or upwards may be accommodated with Boxes, by an early application to Mrs. Salmon.

[For Scheme, see the other Side.

Vimercati Concert Bill

Giovanni Vailati

subsequently omitted, and the war intervening, the opera was not resuscitated until 1920, again in Paris. Stravinsky also composed a *Tango for guitar and three saxophones.* As a musician his originality is manifest; but opinions differ as to the value of his later compositions. Sketches of his life have been published, edited by Van Vechten in 1915, Wise in 1916, and Montague Nathan in 1917.

Strobel, Valentin, a celebrated lute and mandolin player who lived at Strasburg during the middle of the seventeenth century. He composed songs with accompaniment of two violins and bass, which appeared in Strasburg in 1652 and Mendel in his Lexicon records him the composer of a *Second Symphony for three lutes and one mandolin,* and another *Symphony for four lutes,* published in 1654.

Suppus, C. a German guitarist and composer living at the commencement of the nineteenth century of whom little is known beyond the fact that Simrock, Bonn, published his Op. 8, *Serenade for violin, alto and guitar, in E. major;* Op. 9, *Serenade for violin, alto and guitar, in A. major;* Op. 10, *Third Serenade for Two guitars, in A. major;* Op. 11, *Fourth Serenade for two guitars in D. major* and Zimmerman, Leipzig, published Op. 14, *Potpourri for violin, alto and guitar.*

Sussmayer, Franz Xaver, born in 1766 at Steyer, Upper Austria, died September 17, 1803 at Vienna, was a composer of repute and the friend and amanuensis of Mozart. In Vienna he received instruction from Salieri and Mozart, and with the latter the closest attachment existed, for in 1791 he accompanied Mozart to Prague to assist in the production of his last opera *Clemenza di Tito,* September 6, and he was at the bedside the evening before Mozart's death, when the latter endeavoured to give him instructions for completing his *Requiem.* The following year Sussmayer's opera *Moses* was produced in Vienna, and from this time he wrote many others. In 1795 he was capellmeister of the Court Theatre, where many of his works were staged, and he was commissioned to write two for Prague. Grove says: "Though wanting in depth and originality, his works are melodious and have a certain popular character peculiar to himself. He might perhaps have risen to a higher flight had he not been overtaken by death after a long illness." There is in the Manuscript department of the British Museum—additional manuscripts No. 32181, ff, 14455—Sussmayer's autograph score of a *Quintet in C, for violin, guitar, oboe, horn and 'cello,* entitled *Serenata;* it comprises an allegro moderato, andante, minuet and rondo. He also composed for the violin and guitar and several of his songs with guitar accompaniment were published by Schott, Mayence.

Sychra, Andreas Ossipovich, born at Vilna and died at St. Petersburg, December 3, 1850, was the most celebrated of Russian guitarists. His ancestors were of Polish origin who migrated to west Russia during the seventeenth century where his father was musician in the service of various Russian nobles. The first instrument played by Andreas was the harp, on which he attained great proficiency and was a successful concert performer during his teens; but for some unknown reason he discarded this for the guitar and is recorded a most brilliant virtuoso. He made no appearances out of his native land and little is known of his life beyond the fact that he removed from Moscow in 1820 to St. Petersburg, where he was highly successful as teacher and virtuoso, numbering among his pupils members of the nobility and society. Several of his pupils obtained fame in the musical world, the most celebrated was Wyssotzki. Sychra composed for, and played the Russian guitar of seven strings and he contributed various compositions to the Journal for the Guitar, during the years 1822-7 and also for the St. Petersburg Guitar Journal, during 1828-9. His portrait and biography were published by Dr. Sajaitzki, and his *Guitar Method* and compositions, which are of some difficulty, were all published in Russia.

TANDLER, Franz, born January 17, 1782 at Gross Waltersdorf in Mahren, died at Vienna, February 1, 1807. He studied medicine in Vienna University, playing the guitar and piano as a pastime; but later when he made the acquaintance of the guitarists Molitor and Matiegka he gave serious attention to the guitar. On his death both these guitar virtuosi composed a funeral march to his memory. His published compositions include *Variations* Op. 1; *Petite pieces,* Op. 2; *Twelve Waltzes,* Op. 4; *Variations,* Op. 5, all for violin and guitar; Op. 3, *Variations for flute, viola and guitar* and *Six different pieces for guitar solo.*

Tansman, Alexander, born June 12, 1897, at Lodz, Poland. He studied music first in his native city and afterwards continued in Warsaw. In 1919 he won two prizes for composition and made his abode in Paris. He gave a concert in this city the following year which brought him fame and then toured extensively as piano virtuoso and conductor. His works include operas, symphonies, concertos for piano with orchestra and other instrumental music. For the guitar he has composed a *Concerto with orchestra,* but his most popular work for the instrument is a guitar solo entitled *Mazurka,* published by Schott, London. In 1952 a guitar solo of his composition *Cavatina* was awarded the prize in the International music competitions of Siena, Italy. This composition exploits the resources of the guitar to advantage and is of unusual interest. A critic wrote: " In him can be found a strong mixture of poetry, the heritage of his race and gracious tenderness which will recognise no exaggeration of frivolity and that slow sadness, with a strong sense of dynamic movement."

Tarrega, Francisco, born November 21, 1852, at Villareal, Castellon, Spain, died December 5, 1909 in Barcelona, was the most remarkable of modern guitarists. Of humble origin, ceaselessly engaged in struggles against adverse circumstances, and suffering from an incurable and exceedingly painful complaint of his eyes, he gave to the world the example of a genial personality, an ardent temperament and an extraordinary intelligence, all of which he devoted with fervent spirit to his instrument, with the noble idea of raising it to the highest category of art. His first teacher was a local player, Manuel Gonzalez, popularly known as "the blind sailor," and at eleven years of age it is recorded that he performed in his native town a concerto by the famous guitarist Julian Arcas. It has also been stated that he was for a time his pupil and according to the guitarist Cimadevilla he was also a pupil of Tomas Damas. In October 1874 he entered Madrid Conservatoire of Music as a student of piano and harmony and the following year was awarded the first prize for harmony and composition. He however, commenced his career as a teacher of the guitar. He made visits to important continental cities and was accorded universal praise for his remarkable playing, particularly in Paris. Later, Tarrega was a professor of the guitar at the Conservatoires of Madrid and Barcelona and honorary member of many important art institutions of his native land, and Spain is proud in having given to the world its most eminent modern guitarist. His genius was equalled only by his modesty, for even in the final stage of his studies he submitted his compositions to the judgment of his intellectual friends, whose approbation was to him the greatest stimulus for increased efforts, and an illustration of one of these musical seances is reproduced. He taught many pupils who acquired fame, among whom were Llobet, Pujol, Obregon, etc., and he founded a school or method which emphasises the vital importance of the position of the right hand and its fingers, in the manner of vibrating the strings. Previous to the advent of Sor and Tarrega, the guitar was considered by most musicians only capable of accompaniment. Tarrega's transcriptions of the classic masters displayed resources of the guitar and Albanez, after hearing his compositions interpreted by Tarrega said that they were superior to his own piano versions. Tarrega's playing aroused the deep interest of Falla, Manen, Ponce, Turina, Villa-Lobos, Broqua and Castelnuova Tedesco, all of whom have written original compositions for the guitar. His pupil Pujol describes the maestro's home life: "Tarrega's home was a modest sanctuary, where all was imbued with harmony. The rejuvenating rays of the morning sun penetrated into the little dining-room, which after meals became the study of the master, the school-room of his pupils, and often also, the lecture hall for his intimate friends, whenever it occurred to them to visit him. A rectangular table of white wood with two lateral flaps, which when in use at meal times gave it an oval form, covering it a table-cloth, which by long use and frequent washing had forfeited both design and colour, a sideboard of the simplest shape, on the walls, oil-paintings, water colours, caricatures and photographs with dedications expressing admiration for the great master. I can still see him vividly before me when in the early morning he entered the room. With tangled beard and hair, a grayish-yellow cloth loosely tied around his neck, with its ends hanging down over his chest, a dark-coloured jacket of a thin cotton material with a white handkerchief protruding from one of his side pockets, around his waist a grey sash after the manner of the peasantry, his feet in large and comfortable shoes—thus he appeared walking with a thoughtful but not a ponderous step. His face betrayed the pain which the bright light caused his poor, long-suffering eyes, but the rhythm of his movements expressed something of a resigned inward dignity, a weariness after unremitting struggles, inspired by hopes which found their victorious fulfilment in uncertainty." Tarrega's portrait was published in Italian and Spanish journals during his life. He died of apoplexy in Barcelona where he was interred and six years after was transferred to his native Castellon de la Plana. A monument was erected to his memory in the public park of this town in 1916 and on a house in the Plaza Pascual is the following inscription: "In this house was born 21 November, 1852, to the honour and glory of Villareal, the eminent guitarist D. Francisco Tarrega." Streets in Villareal, Castellon, and Barcelona have been named after him. His compositions comprise studies, preludes, scherzos, minuets and concert fantasias, all of rare technical and musical value, particularly the well-known *Capriccio Arabe* and *Le Reve.* Among the works transcribed for the guitar are those of the classics and various modern composers. About fifty of his solos for the guitar and several duos for mandolin and guitar were published by Rowies, Paris, and Schott, London.

Tasca, Pietro Antonio, known also under the pseudonym of D'Antony, was born April 1, 1864, at Noto, Sicily, and died in 1934. He was a distinguished composer whose well-known opera, *A Santa Lucia,* which was an immediate success at its first performance in Berlin in 1892, introduces the mandolin and guitar. In the prelude a melodious song of pathetic inspiration for tenor voice, entitled *Amore e muerto,* and also in the first act of this melodrama, following a sublime vocal duet, the mandolin with the full orchestra combine in a pleasing serenade. Tasca wrote other operas, symphonies, an elegy, and instrumental works.

Tessarech, Jacques, born September 4, 1862 at Ajaccio and died at Nice, March 29, 1929, was an eminent guitarist, composer and didatic. He was educated and trained for a civil engineer, which profession he followed until music and the guitar in particular, claimed his undivided attention. His profession took him to N. America, France and England and his first wife was an English lady. His principal abode, however, was in Paris, near Montparnasse station, where for thirty years he dedicated his life to the study of the technique of the guitar. He was commissioned by the French musician C. M. Widor to contribute Treatise on the Guitar and its Technique, to Widor's Modern Orchestra, published by Riemann in 1904. Tessarech's most important work was The Evolution of the Guitar, a volume of fifty pages of music issued in 1823 by Lemoine, Paris. This and also the second edition which appeared in 1926 was prefaced by the French composer Georges Migot, and followed by The Polyphonic Guitar, also prefaced by Migot ; this was really a continuation of his first work and contained songs, studies, sonatas, and transcriptions of sixty-seven pages. He is described by a pupil as a thin, bent, old man, with a moustache and goatee beard, *a la* Napoleon. He wore knickerbockers and a woollen waistcoat with a thick scarf round his neck. He had long fingers and fine bony hands. Unfortunately, embittered by life's disappointments, he had become almost an ascetic misanthrope. For a time he held important positions in France and America ; but he sacrificed this career for his love of the guitar—in order to found a new school. Late in life, through the influence of several eminent musicians, he was appointed professor of the guitar in Nice Conservatoire—a teaching position which had been his life's ambition ; but death intervened. On account of his extreme shyness and nervousness he was unable to perform publicly ; but all who were privileged to hear him in the intimacy of his home, retain an unforgettable impression of his virtuosity. His pupils and admirers founded a musical society in Paris, The Association Jacques Tessarech, the first honorary president was Georges Migot, and secretary, Francisco Agostini, both favourite pupils of this eminent guitarist. *Four Melopees Corses,* for guitar solo were issued by Lemoine, Paris, and other compositions in manuscript with an unpublished *Method for the Guitar* are in the library of the Association.

Thomas, Charles Louis Ambroise, born Metz, August 5, 1811, died at Paris, February 12, 1896. This eminent French composer was the son of a musician ; he studied in the Paris Conservatoire and in 1832 won the Prize of Rome and in 1871 succeeded Auber as Director of this Conservatoire. This appointment was made after the phenomenal success of his three-act opera, *Mignon,* which was produced November 17, 1866, and contains an interesting part for the guitar.

Thompson, Thomas Perronet, a British general, born at Hull in 1783 and died in London, September 6, 1869, a member of Queen's College, Cambridge, was the author of several theoretical treatises. One is entitled : *Instructions to my daughter for playing on the enharmonic guitar, being an attempt to effect the execution of correct harmony on principles analagous to those of the ancient enharmonic.* This volume published in 1829 by Goulding & D'Almaine, London, is a treatise of learning and importance, with reference to music generally, for it applies to the science—is a profound examination of the principles—and the guitar is the instrument chosen to illustrate the author's theories and opinions. "The following pages," says the author, "had their origin in a desire to abate the untuneableness of the common guitar ; which, though an instrument possessed of many agreeable qualities, has the defect of being out of tune to a greater extent than any other that is played by means of either strings or keys. For the other instruments, as the piano, harp and organ, are at all events capable of playing in some keys with something like an approach to harmony. While on the guitar, the errors, instead of being collected into some particular keys, are disseminated as widely as possible among all, in consequence of the octave being divided into twelve equal intervals; which is in fact necessary as long as the frets on the different strings are to form continued straight lines in order to cause the octaves and the representations of the same sound in different parts of the instrument to be in tune with each other." These instructions contain "a diagram to scale of a guitar as made and sold by Louis Panormo, Musical Instrument Maker, 46 High Street, Bloomsbury. Price in common wood, ten guineas." The first illustration is a delineation of the enharmonic guitar fingerboard, to serve as a model for construction, and there are chapters on harmonics, false strings, etc., and also a detailed description of the guitar. The volume concludes with algebraical and mathematical formulae and tables, and practical exercises for solo guitar, by Signor Verini. This treatise is alluded to by Eulenstein in his *Method for the guitar* and a very exhaustive and favourable criticism was published in The Harmonicon, 1830.

Toepfer, Karl, born December 26, 1791 at Vienna. He studied at the university, graduated doctor of philosophy and became renowned as a dramatic actor and eminent guitarist. He was engaged in Breslau in 1810 removing to Hamburg the following year where he was esteemed as dramatist and poet. The music press of 1816 and also of 1824 praise his guitar recitals in Vienna. His compositons were published in the cities in which he lived. Op. 1, *Variations;* Op. 2, *Quodlibet,* both for *solo guitar* and *Triangle Waltz, Duo for two guitars* were published by Paez, Berlin. *Five songs with guitar* Op. 3, were issued by Förster, Breslau.

Torroba-Moreno, Federico, contemporary, born at Madrid, March, 1891, received his musical education at the National Conservatoire of Madrid under Conrado del Campo. He has composed many popular zarzeulas, orchestral and choral items, all of typical national character. The following are his most important compositions for the guitar; *Sonatine,* in three movements (Allegretto, Andante, Allegro); *Nocturne; Suite Castellana* (Fandanguillo, Arada, Danza); *Burgalesa; Preludio; Serenata Burlesca; Concertino,* and two volumes of *Pieces Caracterisques,* all of which are published by Schott, London. He is considered one of the leading Spanish composers of the century and classed with Falla and Turina in his effective use of Spanish folk idiom in his compositions.

Triebensee, Joseph, born at Vienna, 1760 and living as late as 1830, was a virtuoso on the oboe and guitar. He received his first lessons on both instruments from his father and a few years later obtained instruction in harmony and counterpoint from Albrechtsberger. In 1796 he was capellmeister to Prince Lichenstein whom he accompanied on his travels, when not in residence at his castle of Feldburg. In 1811 he was capellmeister of Brunn Theatre, and from 1829-30 engaged in a like capacity in Prague. While in Vienna he gave instruction on the guitar to Stegmayer, who also acquired renown as a musician and became a professor in the Vienna Conservatoire of Music. Triebensee was the composer of a few published works, among them are *Six Variations for oboe, guitar and piano,* and *Variations on a Tyrolese air for piano, violin and guitar,* published by Traeg, Vienna.

Tuczek, Vincent Franz, born in 1755 at Prague and living in Pesth during 1820 was a Bohemian vocalist, guitarist, conductor and composer, and the director of various theatres. In 1797 he was in the service of the Duke of Courland at Sagan, as musical director. Three years later Tuczek was living in Breslau and in 1802 was director of the Leopoldstadter Theatre, Vienna. His published compositions include operas, oratorios, masses, cantatas and piano and guitar pieces. Op. 2, *Five Minuets;* Op. 4, 7, 8 and 10 are *Variations* all *for solo guitar.*

Turina, Joaquin, born December 9, 1882, at Seville and died January 15, 1949, at Madrid. His first musical instruction was from local teachers, continued in Madrid and completed in Paris under Vincent d'Indy at the Schola Cantorum, where he formed intimate associations with Ravel, Debussy, and other of the students. Turina was a follower of the traditional national Spanish school of Pedrell and Falla, a brilliant pianist, conductor, and prolific composer, who has written much stage, chamber, and orchestral music. His most widely known composition is *Procession from Recio,* and his *Music Encyclopaedia,* published in 1917, in two volumes, demonstrates his erudition. He was an ardent admirer of the guitar and has written several compositions for the instrument which he dedicated to Segovia. *Sonatina, Fandanguillo, Sevillana, Rafaga,* and *Hommage to Tarrega,* all for solo guitar are published by Schott, London.

VAILATI, Giovanni, an Italian mandolinist, born at Crema, near Milan, about 1813 and died in the poor house there, November 25, 1890. He was an entirely self-taught blind musician, a natural genius on the instrument, who, by his remarkable playing, became known throughout his native land as "Vailati, the blind, the Paganini of the mandolin." His marvellous and brilliant execution was the surprise of erudite musicians, and he spent the greater part of his life travelling through Europe as a blind virtuoso. By the treachery of his life long companion, the blind musician lost his entire savings, and in old age was forced to seek the shelter of his native poor house, where he passed the remainder of a desolate career. A simple monument was erected to his memory, after his death, in the cemetery of Crema which bears the following inscription: "To Giovanni Vailati, the blind professor of music, who honourably upheld the name of his country over all Europe. Crema is grateful." His portrait, which was published in various Italian music journals is reproduced.

Valverde, Joaquin, born February 27, 1846, died at Madrid, March 17, 1910. When a youth he was flautist in various theatre orchestras but in 1871 was appointed theatre conductor in Madrid and in 1879 a professor of the flute in the National Conservatoire. His compositions include sixty Zarzuelas (Spanish operettas) and in the one entitled *Los Cocineros* he scores for the mandolin and guitar in a brilliantly original polka. His son Joaquin also employs the guitar in his orchestrations.

Varlet, A. H., was a French guitarist and teacher during the nineteenth century who compiled a method for the guitar under the title of *Complete Method for the Guitar* which was published by Joly, Paris, also *Three themes with variations for solo guitar,* Op. 13, issued by Lemoine, Paris.

Verdi, Giuseppe, born at Roncole, Italy, October 9, 1813, died at Milan, January 27, 1901, was one of the most popular operatic composers of the nineteenth century. He was the son of an innkeeper of Roncole and passed his childhood among the poor and ignorant labourers of his uninteresting village. His parents combined a little shop with their inn, retailing a few dry goods, and once a week the father walked to the neighbouring town of Busseto, three miles distant, with two empty baskets to make his purchases. These were chiefly from a Mr. Barezzi, a prosperous and good natured man, destined to be of invaluable assistance to the young Verdi in his musical career. When Giuseppe was seven years of age, his parents bought a spinet, and on this instrument the boy made his first attempts at producing music. He manifested much interest in the instrument, and displaying ability, was placed under the local organist for instruction ; two years later he superseded his teacher as organist. He was then sent to a school in Busseto, where Mr. Barezzi received him in his house and manifested great interest in the lad. This tradesman was first flautist in the cathedral orchestra, and his house the meeting place of the Philharmonic Society, conducted by Provesi, the cathedral organist. Young Verdi was employed by Barezzi, became a member of the musical society and received further instruction from Provesi until he was sixteen, when he removed to Milan, the musical centre of Italy. Here he met with the many adverses common to human beings, but eventually emerged triumphant as an operatic composer. After a lapse of a few years his compositions were sought by publishers and impresarios, and he published in all about thirty operas. One of the latest, *Otello,* by Arrigo Boito on Shakespeare's play, was produced at La Scala, Milan, under the direction of Faccio, February 5, 1887. This opera his last but one, and perhaps best, is a monument of genius. Verdi has introduced the voices of mandolins and guitars under felicitous conditions, for in the second act, the orchestra is supplemented by six mandolins and mandolas with four guitars—a small mandolin band—and these instrumentalists appear on the stage, where after their prelude they accompany the vocal item, *Dove guardi—Whereso'er thy glances fall—*

the libretto admirably suited for the instrumentation, and in his opera *Il Trovatore* the troubadour accompanies with his lute (guitar) the song *Lonely on earth abiding,* and Verdi also uses the guitar in his opera *Falstaff.* Verdi evinced far greater interest in the welfare of the mandolin and guitar than composing for them ; he was honorary member of the Circolo Mandolinisti, Milano, (Mandolin Band, Milan) and manifested personal interest in this society and the advancement of their instruments. The most valued treasures of this musical organisation are the autograph letters from the maestro, with congratulations on their artistic achievements and stimulating them to increased efforts and success ; the last of these exhortations is dated February 19, 1888, Genoa. Verdi's biographers are many and a whole issue of the Rivista Musicale of 1901 was devoted to his life and compositions.

Verini, Filippo, an Italian guitarist and vocalist, who as a prisoner during the Napoleonic wars was transported to Spain, but established himself in England during the early years of the nineteenth century, living in London as late as 1846. During July 1836 he was appearing as guitar soloist and his playing and compositions elicited the praise of the music journals. As a teacher he was esteemed, and Dora, wife of the novelist Charles Dickens, was one of his pupils. Verini compiled a method for the guitar in two parts, dedicated to Ferdinand Sor, entitled: *First Rudiments of the Spanish Guitar.* It contained an engraved diagram of the instrument, with instruction on chords and modulation, folio size, but was not popular. The following are his best known compositions: *Fantasia on La Cachucha, for guitar solo,* published in 1825 by Galloway, London. *Divertimento for guitar,* dedicated to Mrs. Perronet Thompson, Chappell ; *The nosegay, a divertimento for guitar,* published in 1834 ; *Twelve Italian songs for one or two voices and guitar,* published by Dover & Co., 1827 ; *Twelve songs and duets,* Italian, French and English words with various other vocal items and guitar solos, issued in 1846 by Boosey and also Chappell. Verini contributed the exercises in the treatise, *Instructions to my daughter for playing on the enharmonic guitar,* by General Perronet Thompson.

Vidal, B., born in 1750, and died in Paris, February, 1800, was a French teacher and composer for the guitar who was living in Venice and Milan during 1792 and then returned to Paris. He published about forty compositions of varying styles and difficulty and also wrote a method for the guitar issued in 1778 by Gaveaux, Paris, under the title of *A new method for the guitar, written for the use of amateurs.* Vidal also composed several concertos for guitar with full orchestra or string quartet which were performed in Paris with success. Mendel mentions his compositions in his Musical Lexicon and the manuscript of *Duo in C, for Violin and French Guitar* is in the library of the Conservatoire of Music, Milan. The first of his *Guitar concertos, No. 1, in D, with two violins and bass* was issued by Janet, Paris, the others by

Imbault, Paris ; Op. 4, 7, 8, 12 and 25 are *Sonatas for Guitar and Violin,* and Op. 6, *Sonatas for Guitar and Violoncello* all published by Bailleux, Paris. Among his less pretentious compositions are six sonatas, several potpourris, variations and collections of operatic melodies, all for solo guitar, published by Leduc and also Gaveaux, Paris. Grove states that B. Vidal was the earliest musician of this name, a talented guitar player and teacher, during the last quarter of the eighteenth century and published sonatas, short pieces, and a method for his instrument.

Vidal, Paul Antonin, born at Toulouse, June 16, 1863, and living in the rue Ballu Paris in 1912. He studied at the Paris Conservatoire of Music, was awarded the Prize of Rome in 1883 and after the completion of three years study in Italy, commenced teaching singing in Rome. He subsequently returned to his native land and from 1893 was conductor of the opera and a professor at the Conservatoire. He wrote many operas and orchestral suites and in one of his most popular compositions, the lyric drama, *Guernica,* written in 1895, he employs guitars and mandolins. At a concert in the Paris Conservatoire, March 1924, given by the Estudiantina (mandolin band) of the 18th Arrondissement, Paris, conducted by Charles Feret, an aubade, *A toi* for mandolins and guitars by Vidal was performed with acclaim.

Villa-Lobos, Heitor, contemporary, born March 5, 1881, at Rio de Janeiro, Brazil. His father, an amateur musician, gave his son guitar instruction before the boy was nine, for at that age he improvised variations on Brazilian folk tunes on his guitar. He adopted the 'cello but still continued the study of the guitar while receiving instruction on the former instrument, at first from Agnello Franca and continued with Francisco Braga, after which he taught the guitar and was employed in local theatres and cinemas. His first published composition was a *Solo for the guitar* entitled *Panqueca* (pancake). At this period he was intent on collecting folk songs and travelled Brazil extensively for this object, meanwhile being employed in various occupations. It was during the period of study with Braga, in 1909 that he composed his *Country Airs* for small orchestra. In 1922 he visited Paris for further study and when he returned in 1927 was appointed State Director of Musical and Artistic Education by President Vargas. Villa-Lobos is the most distinguished and prolific of Brazilian composers and the author of a volume on Brazilian folk music. He is the composer of all classes of music, operas, oratorios, symphonies, and uses the guitar in these works. He has composed the following for guitar solo: *Twelve Studies ; Suite Populaire Bresilienne ; Tango original ; Two Preludes ; Choros No. 1* (a dance typical of this sunny country) ; *No 5 of Bachianas Brasileiras,* originally composed for soprano and eight 'cellos and transcribed by the composer for *Soprano with guitar,* and *Three New Studies for solo guitar,* dedicated to Segovia. He visited England in 1948 and on February 2, a broadcast recital of his songs was made from London, the first item being *The old guitarist,* and on the 7th of the same month he conducted a broadcast of his *Choros, No. 6,* orchestrated for *bombardine, guitar and native Brazilian percussion instruments.* The principal publisher of his compositions is A. Napoleao, Rio de Janeiro.

Vimercati, Pietro, born at Milan, 1779, and died at Genoa, July 27, 1850, was an eminent mandolin virtuoso, musical director, and teacher who lived in the esteem of the most illustrious musicians of the period. He was the son of a musician who instructed him at an early age in the elements of the art. For two generations his ancestors had been established in Milan as stringed musical instrument makers. The most celebrated member of the family, Gaspare, was renowned for his mandolins, guitars and lutes. Pietro, the mandolinist did not attract public notice until he was about twenty-eight, and his first appearance as mandolinist, outside his native city was in Florence in December, 1808. when his success was instantaneous and assured. Such brilliant execution on the mandolin had been seldom heard, his fame spread through northern Italy and the flattering reception accorded his performances induced him to undertake a six months' tour and after playing in the most important musical centres he returned to Milan. For a period he was mandolinist in the Theatre Re where he was mandolin soloist during the entr'act. His visited England in 1823 and appeared in many important concerts with the most eminent musicians, a facsimile of one such programme is reproduced. His repertoire included the important violin concertos of the time and the musical critics were unanimous in praise of his artistic and musicianly performances. In 1829 he was touring Germany, receiving similar euconiums and it is recorded that his concerts in Vienna were veritable triumphs. From Germany he appeared in France, on his way to Spain, and after successful concerts throughout the peninsula he was performing again in France, his second visit, when the French musical correspondent of the London Harmonicon despatched a flattering report under the heading of: " M. Vimercati, a remarkable phenomenon on the mandolin." He undertook another tour of Spain and in 1835 was receiving the applause of musicians in Holland, and the year following praise from the music critics of Berlin and Weimar. After an extended tour of Russia in 1837 he returned to Vienna in 1840 where he lived for a period ; but being desirous of spending his last days in his native land removed to Genoa, where, although an aged man still took an active interest in the musical affairs of the city. He died there, suddenly, July 27, 1850 after attending a concert the day previous. His wife, the prima donna, Bianchi, took the principal role in Rossini's operas in Mantua, Berlin, and Weimar, during 1834. Vimercati enjoyed the friendship and esteem of Rossini who heard him perform on many occasions and styled him " the Paganini of the mandolin," perhaps the first of the many mandolinists to be classed with the incomparable violinist. Moscheles, too, had been amazed at his virtuosity, and a conversation between him and Rossini respecting Vimercati, is recorded in the

Life of Moscheles and the music journals said: "He had already astonished Italy and Germany by the rapidity and grace with which he executed violin concertos on his instrument. The French connoisseurs who were led by curiosity to attend his concerts, found themselves irresistibly detained by admiration." and "In January 1831, the well-known virtuoso on the mandolin, Vimercati, gave a concert at the Theatre Argentine which was well attended. This artist is an example of what genius and perseverance may effect upon the less promising of instruments." . . ."Vimercati, the celebrated virtuoso on the mandolin and his wife, who is an excellent singer, have been performing at the Theatre Re, Milan, between the acts, with unbounded applause." Mendel records that his execution and performances were quite inconceivable to those not privileged to hear him. He left several compositions for his instrument which remain in manuscript. His name headed the bill—reproduced by courtesy of Ernest J. Tyrrell, Esq.—of a concert given by the renowned vocalist, Mrs. Salmon, in the New Argyle Rooms on Friday, June 6, 1823; the conductor was Sir George Smart. Vimercati performed Fantasias of his own composition and Garcia with other eminent vocalists and Boscha, the harpist, assisted.

Vivaldi, Antonio, born *circa* 1678, at Venice, and died there in 1741. Early in life he entered the priesthood and was subsequently an abbot. A pupil of his father he became an expert and virtuoso on various stringed instruments, excelling as a violinist. For a period he was violinist in the orchestra of St. Mark's, Venice, afterwards entering the Court orchestra of the Landgrave of Hesse Darmstadt, returning to his native city, Venice, when appointed music director of the Conservatorio della Pieta in 1713. Wright, in his Travels Through Italy from 1720-2, says: "It is very usual to see priests play in the orchestra. The famous Vivaldi, whom they call the Prete Rosa, was prominent among them." He was a prolific composer whose compositions are stated to have had considerable influence on those of J. S. Bach, who not only studied them but made transcriptions for the clavier. His compositions, the majority of which remain in manuscript, display original ideas of form and instrumentation. Among his numerous manuscripts in the Royal Biblioteca National, Turin, are several for the mandolin and there are others in which this instrument is requisitioned. Gian Francesco Malipiero has edited from the original manuscripts in the Biblioteca National, Turin, the following compositions which are published by Ricordi. *Concerto in G major for two mandolins, two violins, viola, 'cello, double bass and organ.* It is in three movements, Allegro, Andante, Allegro. The Andante which is the shortest movement is scored for *two mandolins, two violins and viola only;* the complete work is of twelve minutes duration. *Concerto in C major for mandolin, two violins, viola, 'cello, double bass and piano* in three movements, Allegro, Largo, Allegro. The second movement is of six bars only, repeated, and in the first movement the violins are to be played pizzicato. The time of duration is seven minutes. *Concerto in*

Durata: min. 12

CONCERTO in Sol maggiore

per 2 Mandolini, Archi e Organo

F. V n? 2

a cura di
Gian Francesco Malipiero

Antonio Vivaldi
(1675?-1741)

D major for two violins, liuto and piano. This is not the ancient lute, but a bass mandolin, a melody instrument as used in mandolin orchestras ; it must not be confused with the ancient lute. The concerto is in three movements and the liuto is allotted the most intricate and important rôle. It is of eleven minutes duration. Vivaldi dedicated this and the two following compositions to a certain Count whose surname is now undecipherable—a skilful performer on the mandolin.

Durata: min. 7

CONCERTO in Do maggiore

Trio for liuto, violin and cembalo (piano) *in G minor* is in three movements and from the twenty-first to the twenty-fifth bars inclusive, the liuto has chords of three notes, in minims. Its duration is eight minutes. *Trio in C major* for the same instruments, duration nine and half minutes.

The B.B.C. in its third programme of January 21, 1950, broadcast a Vivaldi composition written in 1720 for orchestra with mandolin obligato; the mandolinist was Hugo D'Alton and the orchestra the London Philodorian. During the same month Vivaldi's oratorio *Judith* was broadcast on the third programme, and in this composition Vivaldi makes use of the mandolin to accompany an aria with delightful effect. The mandolinist was Hugo D'Alton and the work was repeated on February 11 and 13, 1951. The above do not complete the list of Vivaldi's compositions which include the mandolin. There remain in manuscript in the Biblioteca Nazionale di Torino, Italy, others as yet unpublished. His *Concerto in C major for solo mandolin, harp and cembalo* was broadcast from Paris during 1953 by the eminent mandolinist, Maria Scivittaro.

Vinas, Jose, born September 27, 1823, at Barcelona and died there in 1888. His first musical instruction was under the direction of Farreras in the convent Mercedarios of his native city. He was a skilful performer on the piano, violin, and guitar early in life, and became known as a composer and conductor. At periods he was conductor of an estudiantina and an orchestral conductor in theatres of Madrid, Valencia, and the renowned Theatre de Santa Cruz, Barcelona. The guitar was the instrument of his choice and by which he became known in the musical world. When twenty-one he toured Europe and his remarkable performances on the guitar received the praise and esteem of musicians. Soriano Fuertes in his History of Spanish Music, published in 1859, speaks highly of him as virtuoso and composer. During the latter part of his career Vinas was principal tenor soloist in Barcelona Cathedral and his home was the rendezvous of the most eminent musicians, especially guitarists, of whom Broca, Arcas, and Tarrega were of the community. His published compositions for the guitar number thirty-five original works and consist of studies, dances, twenty-four of which were issued by the Union Musical Espanola, Madrid.

WAGNER, Wilhelm Richard, born May 22, 1813 at Leipzig, died February 13, 1883, at Venice and interred at Beyreuth. The immortal dramatic composer and poet displayed his interest in the guitar on several occasions and it is common knowledge that his preliminary inspirations were frequently worked out on the guitar. He wrote guitar accompaniments to the songs of Lucia and Helden, which frequently occur and are of considerable extent in his melodrama *Enzio;* they are authenticated by W. Tappert in Richard Wagner, his Life and Work, published in 1883 at Elberfeld. There is evidence also of his choice of instrument in his *Meistersinger* when Beckmesser appears on the stage with his lute, and the accompaniment, which is of special interest is written in E minor, for the guitar, not merely because of its peculiar tones that accompany the *Serenade* of the self-satisfied Beckmesser (which sometimes degenerates into burlesque) but the tuning of the instrument was elaborated by Wagner into one of the most remarkable fugues ever conceived. The technical term for this number is *Fugue with Chorale,* this serenade of Beckmesser being used line by line after Bach's manner in his choral fugues.

Walker, Luise, born September 6, 1910 at Vienna, a contemporary guitar virtuoso. When a child she displayed exceptional musical ability, first studying the guitar under Dr. Zuth, and continuing in Vienna Conservatoire under Jakob Ortner, professor of the guitar in this institution. At the age of fifteen she gave on November 3, 1925, her first recital in Vienna and when the guitar virtuoso Llobet visited Vienna she took advantage of the opportunity to increase her knowledge by studying under this master. As concert performer she was well received by the musical press of Berlin, Prague, and other German cities, but her appearances in London and U.S.A., where she gave two recitals in New York during February of 1933, aroused but little enthusiasm.

Wanczura, Joseph, a native of Bohemia who lived from the middle to the latter part of the nineteenth century. He was a professor of the guitar and piano and a composer for these instruments of high repute in his native land. When a young man, in 1840, he migrated to Vienna, where he was occupied, first in teaching the guitar, and at a later period the piano also. Wanczura has written and published about fifty compositions for guitar solo, and duos for guitar and piano—principally of a light nature—rondos, variations, various dances, transcriptions and arrangements of other instrumental compositions, the majority were issued between the years 1831-4, by Diabelli, Vienna. Op. 1, 3, 4, 5, 6, 7, 8, 9, 18, 19, 21, are *Solos for guitar;* Op. 2, *Twelve lessons* and Op. 16, *Duo for two guitars.*

Wanhall, John Baptist, or as printed on English editions of his works—Vanhall—was of Dutch extraction, born at Neu Nechanicz, Bohemia, May 12, 1739, and died August 26, 1813, at Vienna. He was a contemporary of Haydn and during his life was held in high esteem as an instrumental composer. The son of a peasant, he had for his first music teachers, two country players Erban and Kozak, who taught him the elements of the guitar, violin and organ. His childhood was spent in various insignificant towns of Bohemia, near the place of his birth, and his musical education was consequently of fitful moods; but in one of these towns he met a musician who strongly urged him to persevere with the violin and guitar, and to write for these instruments. This advice, emanating from a skilled performer, carried a great influence and he applied himself to the study of these instruments and the theory of music. His ability soon made itself manifest, for in 1760, his playing attracted the attention of the Countess Schaffgotsch, who generously undertook to bear the expense of his musical education and sent him to Vienna to continue his studies. He was under Dittersdorf, who manifested great interest in his apt pupil, and Wanhall perused all the

F. Torroba-Moreno

C. M. von Weber

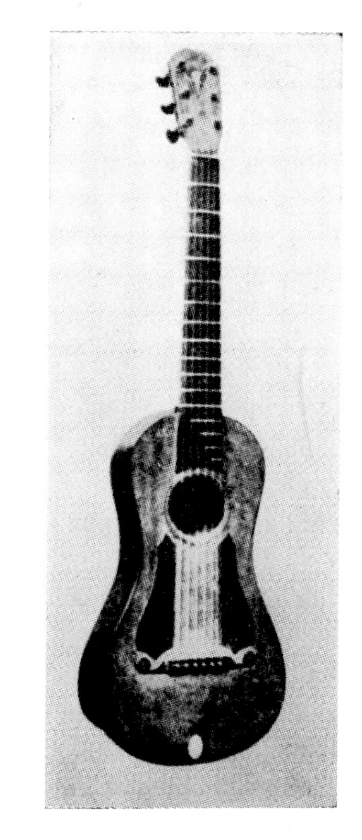

Weber's Guitar

August Zurfluh

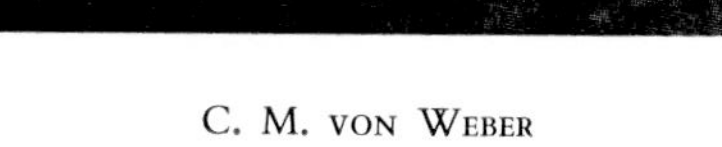

Charles Maria von Weber.
91. gr. Portland Street.

Weber's English Visiting Card

M. T. Wyssotzki

Maria Scivittaro

Luise Walker

Markus D. Sokolowski

works obtainable, played and studied diligently, and composed so abundantly that it was considered wasteful. In Vienna he continued the study of the guitar and published there many pieces for it and received the patronage of a nobleman, Freiherr Riesch, who paid the expense of an educational tour of Italy. When he returned to Vienna in 1772, he was afflicted with intense mental depression, and for a time bordered on insanity; he ultimately recovered. His life in Vienna was a continual round of incessant hard work, the monotony of which was relieved only by hurried visits to Hungary or Croatia, where he was hospitably received by Count Erdody. Wanhall was very popular until brighter musical stars—Haydn and Beethoven— appeared and eclipsed him. He was a very prolific composer, and the list of his works, enumerated by Dlabacz, is enormous. There are no less than a hundred symphonies, a like number of quartets, numerous masses and other church music, piano music, and many compositions for the guitar of which the following are the most prominent. Op. 42, *Six Variations for guitar and violin*, published by Peters, Leipzig; *Two books of dances for guitar and piano*, Cappi, Vienna; *Quartet for guitar, violin (or flute), alto and violoncello (or bassoon)*, Spehr, Brunswick; *Six duos for piano and guitar* in two books; *Theme (alla pastorella)*; *Variations for guitar, piano, violin (or flute)*, and *Six waltzes for guitar, piano, violin (or flute)*, all published by Simrock, Bonn. As several of Wanhall's compositions were published in Cambridge it is probable that he visited England, but no trace can be ascertained.

Wassermann, Heinrich Joseph, born April 3, 1791, at Schwarzbach, near Fulda, died, August, 1838 at Richen, near Basle, Switzerland, was a violinist and guitarist, a pupil of Spohr. After the completion of his musical education he was violinist at Hechingen, Zurich, and Donaueschingen respectively, and at a later period orchestral conductor in Geneva and Basle. Wassermann was the author of chamber compositions, comprising quartets and other works which include the guitar, and also orchestral suites, most of which are published in Switzerland. Op. 5, *Variations for solo guitar; Potpourri for violin and guitar* and *Waltzes for flute and guitar* were published by Fischer, Frankfurt.

Weber, Carl Maria von, born December 18, 1786, at Eutin, Holstein, and died in London, June 4, 1826, was the founder of German national opera and probably the most widely influential German composer of that century. He was a life-long ardent admirer of the guitar and as accomplished a performer on this instrument as on the piano. Baron Max von Weber, writing of his father, said, because of its subdued sympathetic tone, he made the guitar his constant companion. His most beautiful songs were written with guitar accompaniment, and these melodies, at first unknown, sung by him in a not powerful, yet pleasant voice with inimitable expression, and accompanied on the guitar with the highest degree of skill, were the most complete of anything ever accomplished in this manner. Weber was a musician in whose family music was long a hereditary gift; but the wandering, restless nature of his father did not act favourably on the gifted child's education. The family removed from Eutin in 1787 when the parent was leading a wandering life as director of a dramatic troupe, featured mainly by his grown up children. They visited all the German cities of importance, and, injudicious as this roving life appeared, young Weber grew up behind the scenes, so, from earliest infancy his home was in stage-land. In 1797, a new theatrical speculation took the family to Salzburg where Michael Haydn gave the boy gratuitous instruction in composition. When the family removed to Vienna, shortly after, Weber made the acquaintance of a young military officer, Gänsbacher, an amateur musician, excellent guitarist and a pupil of Vogler, the eminent music teacher of the city. This acquaintance developed into a life-long friendship and the two young men with other youthful musical companions formed a society where at their convivial meetings, sang their latest vocal compositions to guitar accompaniment and performed their newest compositions. Grove states that when he had removed to Breslau, "He had also acquired considerable skill on the guitar, on which he would accompany his own mellow voice in songs mostly of a humorous character, with inimitable effect. This talent was often of great use to him in society, and he composed many lieder with guitar accompaniment." Julius Benedict—later Sir Julius—Weber's pupil, life-long companion and his biographer writes: "Weber was

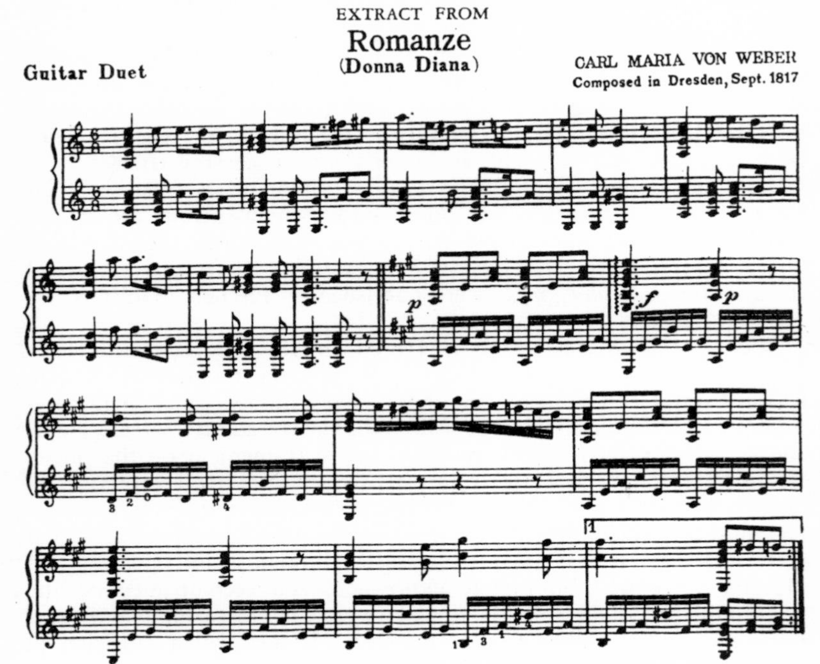

an admirable performer on the guitar and knew all the peculiarities of the instrument to perfection."

In Breslau, after his resignation at the theatre, he lived by teaching the piano and guitar, and when in 1810 he visited Mannheim he formed a life friendship with Gottfried Weber—also a guitar player, but of no relation—who arranged concerts for him. It was at one of these that he played for the first time his piano *Concerto in C.* A member of the audience was Princess Stephanie of Baden whose father, the Crown Prince Ludwig of Bavaria, had met Weber at Baden Baden a few months previous, and had been so delighted and enraptured by Weber's serenades with the guitar, that he walked about with him all the night. The Princess was therefore desirous of hearing him in this capacity, so after the concert he sang to her a number of his songs with guitar. Such an impression did he make that the Princess promised to procure for him the position of capellmeister of Mannheim, or grant him an allowance of one thousand guldens from her private purse. A message from the Princess was sent to Weber a few weeks later, however, saying that her promise had been made too hastily. For a period Weber lived in Darmstadt, where with Meyerbeer he studied under the Abbe Vogler and it was here in 1811 that he composed his one-act comic opera *Abu Hassan.* This was the first of his operas which retains its influence on the stage ; the second aria sung by Hassan in this work is accompanied by two guitars. Its first performance was on June 4, 1811, in Munich. The opera was broadcast on the Third programme of the B.B.C., London, March 25 and 27, 1949 when the guitarists of the orchestra were Julian Bream and Desmond Dupré.

During his residence in Darmstadt Weber composed many songs with the guitar. For Kotzbue's *Der arme Minnesinger,* he contributed four, and in a letter to his friend Gottfried Weber, dated May 16, 1811 he writes: "You will have received my guitar songs and noticed that I have set no accompaniment to the *Madchen.* How can you possibly think I should have been so silly?" This song *Madchen ach meide,* composed in 1802, is a canon, the last of the series of *Six Songs with guitar,* Op. 13, published by Gombart, Augsburg. The autographed manuscripts of these were contained in a volume, which, after being for some years in the possession of F. W. Jahns, disappeared mysteriously, fortunately the owner had carefully copied the contents. Grove says: "In February 1812 Weber visited Berlin and Professor Lichenstein, one of the foremost members of the Berlin Singakademie, was influential in introducing him to cultivated and musical families, where he soon became a favourite by his pleasing manners, his admirable pianoforte playing and extemporising, his inspiring way of leading concerted music, and above all his charming songs and his guitar." At Carlsbad, too, he took part in the musical evenings at Prince Eugene's, the principal attraction was his songs with guitar. Weber's roving life came to an end in 1813 when appointed capellmeister in Prague. He reorganised and conducted the opera until 1816 and while there composed on March 8, 1814 an *Andante for guitar and piano.* Apparently this composition was never published, for only the title page and a portion of the work prove evidence of its existence. Weber composed much for the guitar during residence in Prague, and with other compositions published in the city was an album of *Five songs with guitar accompaniment,* Op. 25. During the summer of 1816, on the anniversary of Waterloo, he visited Berlin to conduct his cantata, and when he resigned his position at Prague, in September, he spent the remainder of that year in Berlin, occupied in composition and to the month of December belongs the duo for guitar and piano Op. 38, *Divertimento assai facile per la chitarra ed il pianoforte, composta da Carlo Maria di Weber.* It comprises an Andante in C, Valse with two trios in A minor, Andante with five variations in G, and a Polacca in A. Extracts from the guitar parts of the Andante, the third variation and the Polacca are reproduced ; it was published by Schlesinger, Berlin. The following year Weber was appointed capellmeister of German opera in Dresden ; but this position from the outset was far from enviable, however, after a time matters improved and he was accustomed to pass the summertime at a small country farm house in Klein Hosterwitz, near Pillnitz. This house is still standing and bears a gilt bronze plaque commemorating the musician's stay there. It was there in August 1818 that he composed certain pieces for the guitar which were to be played in Max von Klinger's *Die Zwillingen* (The twins), Dr. A. Rublack's version of the tragedy. Weber's diary of August 15, 1818 says: "Composed the guitar pieces for *Zwillingen,* have sent them and written to Hellwig." Hellwig was director of the Royal Theatre, Dresden, and Weber's guitar compositions were performed for the first time in that city on August 18. The manuscripts of these works cannot now be found. Weber was living in Dresden during September 1821 and in that month composed the music to *Donna Diana,* libretto by Moreto, and in this comic opera he introduced a *Duo for two guitars.* This play had been set to music previously and performed in Dresden on October 2, 1817. The duo is reproduced from the original manuscript in the Royal Court Theatre Library, Dresden, and it was also in Dresden that he composed on January 10, 1821, the part song and chorus with guitar, *Tell me, where is fancy bred?*, for three female voices (two soprano and one alto) the original manuscript, also in the Dresden library. Weber's pupil and biographer, Sir Julius Benedict, writing of this period of the master's life says: "The dire disease which but too soon was to carry him off had made its mark on his noble features ; the projecting cheek bones, the general emaciation, told their tale ; but in his clear blue eyes, too often concealed by spectacles, in his mighty forehead, fringed by a few straggling locks, in the melodious voice, there was a magic power which attracted irresistibly all who approached him." In 1824 Weber received a commission to write an opera for Covent Garden Theatre, London ; he chose *Oberon,* and the sad, indeed tragic story of his visit to conduct this opera is well known. Sick unto death—he was but thirty-nine—and aware that his days were fully numbered, only the prospect of

EXTRACTS FROM

Duo for Guitar and Piano, Op. 38,

COMPOSED BY C. VON WEBER, IN 1816.

GUITAR.

making provision for his wife and family had induced him to undertake the work and roused him from the languor and depression that possessed him. On February 5, he conducted for the last time in Dresden, then took leave of all the members of the orchestra, except Fürstenau, the flautist and guitarist who was to travel with him. He arrived in England on March 5, 1826 and his brief visit was strangely intermingled with sunshine and gloom. For a time all passed smoothly, and when the opera was produced April 12, the enthusiasm was intense, and although his life was fast ebbing he took part in concerts until a week previous to his death, but sank under his sufferings June 4, in the house of his host, Sir George Smart. Although the last effort of a dying man, this opera shows no trace of mental exhaustion; it engraves Weber's name among the immortals. Constant in his love of the guitar, he displays the beauties of the instrument in his final work by setting it in an unparalleled atmosphere of charm and colour, the centre of a sublime situation, for the guitar is the instrument which accompanies in *Vision* No. 3, Rezia's song to Oberon, *Oh, why art thou sleeping?* The song with its accompaniment is a rare gem; its setting the impress of genius, for with his profound command of tone colour, Weber introduces the guitar in a remarkably effective manner. An introductory bar for the horns, succeeded by four bars of plaintive diminuendo for clarinets and bassoon, the guitar breaks forth in its most sonorous key (E major), and when the song and accompaniment fade, oboes, clarinets and bassoon, with a mysterious tenderness, which only Weber can divulge, continue the final six bars. Sir George Smart presented Weber's tuning fork in its original kid embroidered case to John Black; it passed to the author of this volume, who presented it to Luton Museum. Max Muller states that he heard the entire opera *Der Freischütz* emerge from Weber's guitar before it took the form as we now know it. Weber composed more than ninety songs with guitar accompaniment, and compositions for the guitar in combination with other instruments. Grove says: "His musical treatment too, of songs in dialect, especially those of a humorous rollicking character was excellent. The form of these songs is most simple and generally strophical; the accompaniment frequently for the guitar." A complete list is impossible; the following are the most widely known: Op. 13, *Six Songs with guitar,* composed in 1811; Op. 25, *Five songs with guitar,* published in Prague and Leipzig; Op. 29, *Three Canzonets with guitar;* Op. 38, *Duo for Guitar and Piano,* issued by Schlesinger, Berlin; Op. 42, *Six Songs with guitar*, Diabelli, Vienna; Op. 54 and 64 *Folk songs with guitar,* Schlesinger, Berlin; Op. 71, *Six Songs with guitar; Schummerlied,* a *part song for four male voices with guitar,* Diabelli, Vienna; *Four Songs with guitar for Kotzebue's Der Arme Minnesinger; Romance with guitar* for Costelli's *Diana von Poiters,* composed in 1816; *Song with guitar* for Kind's *Der Abend am Waldbrunner,* composed in 1818; The third scene of act 3, of Gaston's *Rundgesang* is accompanied by guitar, two clarinets, two bassoons, two trumpets and two kettle drums, and in the fifth scene of act 2, he writes *Minuet for flute, viola and guitar.* This delightful little composition has been frequently broadcast and recordings have been made with Luise Walker, guitarist. The originals of the majority of the foregoing are in Dresden State Library. Weber wrote innumerable similar works and it is certain that all such incidental compositions cannot now be brought to light. Boosey & Co. published an album of *Eighteen Songs*—English and German words—with their *original guitar accompaniments,* and many others were issued by Leuckart, Successors, Leipzig. In the Life of Carl von Weber by his son, Baron Max von Weber, interesting facts are recorded relative to his songs with guitar, for speaking of his father and his father's friend, Gottfried Weber, he says: "Most of their songs were composed for the guitar, an instrument so appropriate to these pieces, and one which misuse and tasteless treatment have alone brought out of fashion. A rich treasury of songs of this description has been left to the world by Carl Maria von Weber; and assuredly one day, when that world has been sufficiently surfeited with its present food for epileptic soul sufferers, and can find once again a taste for the solid, genuine, and true in art, will they again emerge into light, from the darkness of their temporary oblivion." He also writes: "Most of the songs composed by Carl and Gottfried Weber were written with guitar accompaniment; but the romantic music which succeeded, degenerated into guitar tinkling, and unrightfully brought discredit on the beautiful instrument, whose nature is so adapted for vocal accompaniment. There are many of the most beautiful song compositions that require just this style of accompaniment, and which not only reject the tone of the piano as antipathic, but when combined with it, entirely lose their character and fineness of feeling." It must be noted that several new editions of the collections of Carl Weber's Songs with guitar were published in Vienna during 1921—a century after their original publication. The following extracts are culled from the Life of C. von Weber, by his son, Baron Max Weber.

"In merry social meetings of artists and lovers of art, of which he himself, with his joyous songs and sparkling guitar, was always the life and centre."

"Referring to his life in Heidelberg and the students; he naturally won at the first start, all the hearts of the merry crew. He sang some of his sprightliest songs to them, tickled their fancies with his sparkling guitar."

"Often might they be seen, on such occasions, strolling by moonlight along the valley of the Neckar, whilst the sprightly notes of the guitar and the sound of sweetly murmured songs floated on the still night air."

"Often, too, on bright nights, the three sworn friends, after their quiet supper at the Three Kings, would wander through the hushed streets of Mannheim, with their guitars and by their newest songs, gently wake . . ."

"New ideas every now and then started and improvised upon piano or guitar."

"Most of their (Gottfried and Carl von Weber) lieder were composed for the guitar; an instrument so appropriate to their pieces, which misuse and tasteless treatment have alone brought out of fashion. A rich treasury of songs of this description has been left to the world by Carl Maria von Weber."

"The merry Carl Maria would jump upon some garden table of a pot house, with his guitar around his neck, and sing with his old glad joviality, his most roguish songs to the soldiers and their girls, until the welkin rang with the loud merriment."

"Their travelling carriage was packed with guitars, musical scores and bottles of wine."

"The Princess said that she heard so much from cousin Ludwig of Bavaria, of his beautiful singing to the guitar, that she would feel personally obliged if he would allow her also the chance of enjoying so great a pleasure. A guitar was fetched, and, standing in the midst of a small circle of the Court party, Carl Maria sang some of his sprightliest songs. The Princess, now with tears in her eyes, now with laughter on her lips, forgot all to linger on, and hear more, and yet still more."

Writing to his friend Gottfried, Carl said, "I have found no soul to which to cling like yours—no hours such as we have passed together—none of that exhuberance of heart's joy, which makes me take guitar in hand, and sing in spite of myself."

"Carl was scarcely allowed out of the Duke's sight and partook with him of every meal. Melodies had to be improvised on the piano or guitar to the Duke's poetry."

"He used to sing us his own songs which were not then generally known, with somewhat weak, but charmingly seductive voice with inimitable expression; his accompaniment on the guitar was the most perfect thing of the kind ever heard and won all hearts."

"At other times the music of seductive serenades arranged by the young Capellmeister (Weber) whose guitar moved his hearers, now to laughter, now to tears, floated over the waters of the Elbe."

"And when the young pair (Weber and his wife) sang some of Weber's liveliest comic songs together, to the accompaniment of piano and guitar, the concert became one of universal jubilee."

"Often might the lively, lovely girl (Wilhelmine Schroder, afterwards Mme. Schroder Devrient) on those bright summer days be seen lying in the garden at the feet of Caroline (Mrs. Weber) singing with her to her guitar."

Carl Maria von Weber and his Songs with the Guitar, was the title of a volume by K. L. Mayer published in Munich in 1921. His life written by his son Baron Max von Weber, was published in three volumes 1864-8 and also by his pupil, Sir Julius Benedict. His favourite guitar, a gift from his fiancée, Caroline Brandt, was presented by his granddaughter, Frau von Wildenbruch to the Institut fur Musikforschung, Berlin, and numbered 723 in the permanent collection. The curator, Dr. A. Berner informed the author of this work that it was totally destroyed during air raids of the second world war, and stated that it was made about the year 1800 of maple wood inlaid with pearl and ebony and the letters 'C.B.,' the initials of his bride to be, were inlaid on the table; the maker was not known. By kindness of Weber's great granddaughter, Fraulein Mathilde von Weber, an illustration of the guitar is reproduced, also his English autographed visiting card tendered to an ancestor of E. J. Tyrrell, Esq., and presented by him to Luton Public Museum.

Weber, Gottfried, a doctor of law and philosophy, musical composer, theorist and guitarist, was born at Freinsheim, near Mannheim, March 1, 1779 and died at Mayence, September 21, 1839. He studied law until he was twenty-three and then practised in Mannheim, where he also held a government appointment. It was in Mannheim that his namesake, Carl Weber, sought a refuge after his banishment from Würtemburg in 1810, and although of no relation, he and his aged father, Franz Anton, found a home with Gottfried Weber's parents. This was the commencement of a lasting friendship between Gottfried, then thirty-one and Carl, eight years his junior. A year previous to their meeting, Gottfried, who was proficient on the guitar, flute, piano and violoncello, and thoroughly versed in the scientific branches of musical knowledge, had formed from two existing musical societies, The Museum, a band and chorus of amateurs, who, under his enthusiastic and able direction, and with some professional assistance, did much excellent work. Under Gottfried's management, concerts were organised for Carl Weber, on March 9, and April 2, which were highly successful. Gottfried Weber's influence obtained a hearing for the young composer in Mannheim and other cities, and the members of this society, fired by the enthusiasm of their conductor, did much towards establishing Carl Weber's fame in Mannheim. They organised a concert in Heidelberg, where Carl Weber made the acquaintance of Gottfried's brother-in-law, Alexander von Dusch, a talented violoncellist, and during this period the guitar played a principal part in the musical affairs of "The Museum," for the two Webers were both accomplished guitarists, and many of their musical items included songs, duets, and choruses with guitars. A detailed and interesting account of the relations, both gay and sad, between these distinguished men—Gottfried and Carl—is recorded in Max von Weber's life of his father. This volume shows the influence of each on the other, their pleasant wanderings in the company of other young musicians, singing their latest songs to the accompaniment of their guitars; their founding of a so-called secret society, with high aims of composer-literati, in which Gottfried adopted the pseudonym of "Giusto"; Carl, "Melos";

and Gänsbacher, "Triole"; and of their merry meetings in the "Drei Konige," or at Gottfried's house. When circumstances had parted them, constant correspondence showed the strength and tenacity of their mutual sympathy. Some of Gottfried's best songs were inspired by this intercourse, and they were exquisitely interpreted by his second wife, née von Dusch, to his guitar accompaniment. Towards the close of 1810, Gottfried Weber, Carl Weber, von Dusch, and Meyerbeer, founded a society which they named the Harmonischer Verein, with the object of furthering the cause of art, particularly the branch of thorough and impartial criticism. The two Webers also considered the publication of a music periodical, and although the plan did not materialize jointly, Gottfried Weber was the editor of Caecilia—a music Journal, published by Schott, Mayence—from its commencement, in 1824, until his death in 1839. During the intervals of founding the Mannheim Conservatoire of Music, superintending the court musical services and occasional duty as conductor in Mayence, the genial lawyer-musician laid the basis of his reputation by a profound study of the theory of music, the result of which appeared in a volume published about 1815, in German, French, Danish and English. Weber was appointed principal of the Darmstadt Conservatoire of Music in 1827, and the same year in recognition of his services to music was decorated with the Grand Cross of the Order of Merit. His compositions include many part songs for male voices, whith choruses and guitar accompaniment, which were first performed by himself, Carl Weber, Gänsbacher and Meyerbeer, at their meetings and during their walks together. In addition to these songs, generally strophic in form, his works embrace masses and other sacred music, sonatas, and concerted pieces for various instruments, including the guitar. His first composition, *Variations for the guitar with accompaniment of flute, or violoncello,* dedicated to Miss Therese von Edel, Op. 1, an original theme with six variations, was published by Schott, Mayence, and passed several editions. As the title states, it is written for the guitar which frequently takes the solo. The violoncello and flute parts are dissimilar and in the second variation the guitar is given the solo to the pizzicato arpeggio accompaniment of the 'cello, and in the fifth variation it accompanies the guitar with rapid passages. Op. 2, *a second set of variations* for the same instruments was published by Richault, Paris, and another was published by Breitkopf & Härtel, Leipzig; *Twelve songs with guitar;* Op. 19, *Eight songs with guitar;* Op. 21, *Fourteen songs with guitar* (in four albums) Peters, Leipzig; Op. 25, *Lyre and sword, songs with guitar;* Op. 31, *Six part songs in three albums, with guitar,* Schott, Mayence; Op. 32 and Op. 34, *Songs with guitar,* Peters, Leipzig; Op. 36, *Song with guitar,* Schott; Op. 37, *Themes with variations for flute and guitar,* Simrock; Op. 38, *Venetian barcarola for flute and guitar;* Op. 39, *Study on a Norwegian air for flute and guitar,* Simrock; Op. 42, *Tafellieder, part song and chorus for male voices with guitar,* Schott; Op. 43, *Collection of songs for two voices with guitar and piano* and more than fifty others, including vocal solos and part songs with choruses for male voices with guitar, issued by the same publishers.

Webern, Anton von, born December 3, 1883, at Vienna, died September 15, 1945, at Mittersill, near Salzburg. He was a student in Vienna University and took his degree of Doctor of Philosophy in 1906 after which he became a pupil of Schönberg for composition. For a period he was conductor in various provincial theatres and ultimately in Prague. At the conclusion of the first world war he resided at Modling near Vienna, as teacher and composer, but shortly after emigrated to U.S.A. He returned to his native land and was accidentally killed by a stray shot. Among his various published compositions are Op. 10, *Five pieces for orchestra,* in which the mandolin plays a prominent part, commencing pianissimo and fading away. Op. 18, *Three songs with accompaniment of guitar and clarinet,* published by Universal Edition, and *Two songs for mixed choir, or solo quartet, with accompaniment of guitar, celesta, violin, clarinet and bass clarinet.*

White, Josh, born 1916 in U.S.A. a contemporary vocalist who sings to his guitar accompaniment, is the son of a poor American negro preacher who died in 1930 leaving his family in dire poverty. Being without education and employment, the lad was forced by circumstances to associate with blind negro beggars to obtain a bare existence. With these folk singers, in all their poverty and squalour, the lad wandered, learning innumerable songs and ballads from his blind employers. Spirituals he had learned from childhood in his father's church. The beggars would not teach him the guitar ; however, by constantly watching them he learned to play without their knowledge. It is most amazing that from such deplorable poverty, surroundings and hardship, such a fine moral character of sincerity and fine artistry should emerge and with a commanding personality, universally respected. During his visit to England in 1950 he captured British audiences and reduced music hall audiences from frivolity to hushed silence by his virtuosity. His guitar accompaniments were in keeping with the words and his mood. With his daughter they broadcast frequently from London.

Wilde, Josef, born in 1778 and died December 2, 1831, at Vienna. He was a popular church and dance composer and also a musical director living in Vienna who contributed with the most celebrated musicians of the day to the collections of new dances, published under the title of *Souvenir* in 1824 by Weigl, Vienna, and in 1825 by Sauer & Leidesdorf, Vienna. For the guitar he has composed ; *Twelve popular waltzes ; Twenty-four waltzes ; Alexander's favourite dances,* and *Redoute Paree for flute or violin and guitar.*

Wolf, Alois, born January 7, 1775, at Vienna and died at Jassy in 1819. He was the son of Joseph Wolf a government bank official, and became acquainted with a junior of his father's department who played the guitar. Alois was interested in the instrument and received tuition from his friend. Such was his progress that in a few years he was popular as a teacher and held in high repute as guitar soloist in Vienna. In 1802 he married the concert pianist, Anna Mrasek and they performed together in public, until her death, six years later. His last public performance was in 1810 after which he retired to Jassy. The manuscript of his autobiography, and several manuscript compositions for violin and guitar are in the Musikfreund Library, Vienna. His compositions include sonatas, variations and dances for guitar solo, and for the guitar with other instruments, published by Steiner, Vienna and Simrock, Bonn ; Four books of *Potpourris for guitar and piano ; Six Variations for guitar and violin ; Duo Concertante for violin and guitar ; Theme with six Variations* and also *Amusements for guitar solo.* His wife published in 1804, *Theme with variations for clavecin and guitar ; Six Italian songs with guitar,* which appeared in 1806 and many albums of operatic arrangements for guitar and piano duos.

Wolf-Ferrari, Ermanno, born January 12, 1876, at Venice, and died January 21, 1948, Venice, was the son of August Wolf, a celebrated German painter and an Italian mother, Emilia. He became an eminent composer who was at first self-taught, but later studied under Rheinberger in Munich. From 1902-9 he was the director of the Conservatoire Lucio Benedetto Marcello of Venice. He has written several operas, also cantatas, symphonies, etc., but all his dramatic works were first produced in Germany. In 1912 he visited America. His best known work is the opera, *The Jewels of the Madonna* which was produced in 1911. In the second act, a chorus of men's voices is heard in the distance, from the direction of the sea, with Rafaele singing to Maliella an appealing serenade to the accompaniment of the men's mandolins and guitars. This is the most interesting and appreciated music of the act. He also makes use of the guitar in the score of his opera *Le donne curiose.* A sketch of his life by Teibler was published in the Monographien moderner Musiker in 1906.

Wyssotzki, Michael Timofejewitsch, one of the most celebrated of Russian guitarists, was born in 1790, and died in Moscow, December 28, 1837. During youth he was a member of a society which met in the home of the poet Cherascoff, where he became acquainted with the guitarist Aksenov, also a member. This acquaintance was the commencement of an intimate and life-long friendship and resulted in Wyssotzki studying the guitar under his friend. A few years after the death of the poet, Wyssotzki removed to Moscow in 1813, where he continued his musical study under the famous virtuoso Sychra, on the seven stringed Russian guitar and obtained fame as a virtuoso and composer in his native land nearly equal to that of his celebrated teacher and he trained several pupils who made a name in the Russian musical world. He compiled a method entitled *Practical and Theoretical Method* *for the guitar* and his more than eighty compositions, principally variations, etc., on Russian melodies, all published in his native land, added considerably to his reputation. His solo for guitar entitled *Prayer* and his *Variations on Russian songs,* Op. 38 and 70 are of universal renown. The original manuscript of *Polonaise for the seven string guitar,* is in the library of the Internationalen Guitarristen Verband, Munich. His portrait is reproduced from a contemporary engraving published in Moscow, and his biography was published in 1901 by Russanov, Moscow.

ZUCCONI, Francesco de, an Italian guitarist and mandolinist who was living in Vienna during the end of the eighteenth and commencement of the nineteenth centuries. His songs were issued under the title of *Journal of Select songs,* with guitar accompaniment, by Cappi, Vienna, who also published *Twelve little pieces for guitar solo,* Op. 7 ; *Fantasia for guitar solo,* Op. 11 ; *Six Allemandes for two guitars* and *Six Variations for mandolin and guitar,* all of which appeared during 1801-3.

Zumsteeg, Johann Rudolf, born January 10, 1760 at Sachsenflur. in the Odenwald, died January 27, 1802, from an apoplectic seizure after conducting a concert in Stuttgart. He was the son of a valet to Duke Carl of Wurtemburg, and was educated with Schiller at the Carlschule, near Stuttgart. To the poet he was allied by the most intimate friendship, and set many of his lyrics to guitar accompaniment. Zumsteeg was originally intended by his parents for a sculptor, but played the guitar and 'cello as an amateur at the age of seventeen. The love of music proving the stronger he adopted the 'cello as his professional instrument and music his vocation. He was violoncellist in the Stuttgart Court orchestra and on the demise of his teacher Poli, in 1792, succeeded him as capellmeister and director of the opera. Zumsteeg is known as the pioneer of the Balladen—a fully developed story with musical accompaniment—most of which he set with the guitar. Op. 6, *Ballads with accompaniment of flute and guitar, and 'cello and guitar,* published in Brunswick, and others were published by Simrock, Bonn ; and Schott, Mayence. His daughter Emilie was also a song writer, and published several vocal compositions with guitar accompaniment through Simrock and Schott. His memoirs were published in the A.M.Z., Munich in 1906.

Zurfluh, Auguste, an able guitarist and harpist who was living in the Rue du Cherche, Paris, during the year 1912. He was a very popular teacher of his instruments and a frequent adjudicator at musical competitions, particularly those of estudiantinas or mandolin bands. He compiled a method for the guitar which was published in French, English and German, under the title of *L'Ecole de la Guitare,* by Jacques Pisa, Paris. Numerous of his light compositions for guitar, mandolin, and songs with guitar, were issued by the same publisher and also by

Beuscher, Paris, and one hundred and fifty of his songs with guitar and for mandolin and guitar band were issued by Gregh, Paris. His principal compositions were dedicated to celebrities in the mandolin and guitar sphere, Op. 103, to his pupil Lucien Gelas, poet-guitarist, and the inventor of a novel system of construction for mandolins and guitars, and Op. 134, to his pupil Grout, an able mandolinist and composer. A revised edition of his guitar method was edited by Constantin Schwarz.

Zuth, Josef, born November 24, 1879, at Fischern near Karlsbad, and died at Vienna, November 1932, was a well-known musicologist and guitarist who was educated first at Karlsbad then at Leitmeritz, after which he was employed as a government official in Vienna for some years. During his leisure, in 1908, he commenced the study of the guitar and mandolin under J. Krempl and in 1910 continued his musical education in Vienna University, under Dr. Richard Batka. From 1918 he was occupied as professor of the guitar in the Volkshochschule, Urania, Vienna, and was the first teacher of the well-known Austrian guitarist Luise Walker. In 1919 Zuth graduated Doctor of Philosophy, with his thesis Simon Molitor, Viennese Guitarist and Composer. This was published by Anton Goll, Vienna, the same year. From 1921 he was for some years editor of the Zeitschrift fur die Gitarre, a journal devoted to the interests of the guitar, also issued by Anton Goll. The following year Zuth commenced regular musical criticisms and contributions to the Tageszeitung and was also an appreciated critic for other of the principal Viennese daily press. During 1927 he edited the series of Musik im Haus, and very many historical studies on the guitar and its music including a Handbuch der Laute und Gitarre, biographies of famous lutenists and guitarists, which was issued by subscription in 1928 by Anton Goll, Vienna. His daughter Liesl was also an able guitarist.

Molbe, Heinrich, the pseudonym of a versatile German musician, Dr. Heinrich von Bach who lived from 1835-1915, the composer of about two hundred vocal items, much chamber music for wood-wind and interesting, original works for the mandolin in combination with various instruments. Op. 32, 33, 35, 36, 37, 38, 85, 86, 87, 88 and 90 are *Serenades for mandolin with string quartet*; Op. 74, *Duo for mandolin and clarinet with piano*; Op. 75, *Duo for mandolin and violin with piano*; Op. 122 and 123, *Serenades for mandolin, clarinet, harp and string quintet*; also *Two Sextets for two mandolins, two mandolas, guitar and violoncello,* all of which were published by Hofmeister, Leipzig.

TO MY GUITAR

When the cold world has frowned and turned away
And life's hard trials wrap this earthly clay,
Then, as twilight marks the close of day
Speak, softly speak.

When disappointment turns this heart to stone
And all life's energy and hope seem flown
Then, in the silent hour when I'm alone
That silence break.

When blinding greed has darkened all my soul
And worldly strife seeks but the gilded goal,
Then, ere the darkness holds me in control
Touch thou my heart.

And let thy strains in melody arise
To waken love, ere love for ever dies
And lift my soul to those ethereal skies
Of song and art.

JOSHUA ROBERTS.

INDEX